PENGUIN BOOKS

Elizabeth

'Guy is no ordinary historian . . . The weight
of evidence suggests that he understands Elizabeth
better than any historian has'
Gerald DeGroot, Book of the Week, *The Times*

'A beautifully rounded portrait of both the woman
and the queen . . . This is a masterful biography'
Amanda Foreman

'A wonderful book and a magisterial account
of the latter half of Elizabeth's reign that calmly
reassesses every claim and myth . . . Compelling'
Jerry Brotton, *Sunday Times*

'Persuades us that pretty much everything we
think we know about Elizabeth is wrong'
Andrew Roberts, *Wall Street Journal*

'One of the very best historians we have in the country.
Guy is in his element prising off the myths that are
barnacled to the queen. It is brilliant, vigorous history
and a triumph of storytelling and scholarship'
Jessie Childs, *Daily Telegraph*

'A fresh, thrilling portrait'
Stacy Schiff, *The New York Times*

'Significant, forensic and myth-busting'
Anna Whitelock, *Times Literary Supplement*

John Guy is a Fellow of Clare College, Cambridge, and a world-leading authority on Tudor history. He has published sixteen books, including *'My Heart is My Own': The Life of Mary Queen of Scots*, which won both the Marsh and Whitbread Biography Awards, *Thomas Becket*, *A Daughter's Love*, *The Tudors: A Very Short Introduction* and *Tudor England*, which has sold 250,000 copies worldwide. He appears regularly on BBC Radio 3 and Radio 4 and has presented numerous television documentaries for BBC2. He regularly contributes to the *Sunday Times*, the *Guardian* and *The Times Literary Supplement*, among others.

Books by the same author include

Henry VIII: The Quest for Fame

The Children of Henry VIII

The Tudors: A Very Short Introduction (2nd edition)

Thomas Becket: Warrior, Priest, Rebel, Victim.
A 900-Year-Old Story Retold

A Daughter's Love: Thomas and Margaret More

'My Heart is My Own': The Life of Mary Queen of Scots

The Tudor Monarchy

Tudor England

Contributor to

The Oxford History of Britain

The Oxford Illustrated History of Britain

The Short Oxford History of the British Isles:
The Sixteenth Century

The Oxford Illustrated History of Tudor and Stuart Britain

Elizabeth

The Forgotten Years

JOHN GUY

PENGUIN BOOKS

PENGUIN BOOKS

UK | USA | Canada | Ireland | Australia
India | New Zealand | South Africa

Penguin Books is part of the Penguin Random House group of companies
whose addresses can be found at global.penguinrandomhouse.com

First published by Viking 2016
Published in Penguin Books 2017

001

Set in 10.56/12.98 pt Bembo Book MT Std
Typeset by Palimpsest Book Production Limited, Falkirk, Stirlingshire
Printed in Great Britain by Clays Ltd, St Ives plc

A CIP catalogue record for this book is available from the British Library

ISBN: 978–0–241–96365–4

www.greenpenguin.co.uk

MIX
Paper from
responsible sources
FSC® C018179

Penguin Random House is committed to a
sustainable future for our business, our readers
and our planet. This book is made from Forest
Stewardship Council® certified paper.

Contents

Acknowledgements

The vast proliferation of source materials, and from across northern Europe, for Elizabeth's reign in comparison with what had gone before made writing this book something of a voyage of discovery. I am especially grateful to the staff of the Large Documents Room at the National Archives at Kew for their kind assistance and to the curators of the Richelieu branch of the Bibliothèque Nationale de France in central Paris for providing me with digital copies of several key volumes of diplomatic dispatches. In Brussels, the archivists of the Archives Générales du Royaume, located so wonderfully close to the Musées Royaux des Beaux-Arts, went beyond the call of duty by producing entire bundles of documents, one standing over two feet high, for me to rummage through at very short notice when I discovered that the traditional sub-numbers of the files, as recorded in the nineteenth-century inventories, did not always match those in the recently computerized document-ordering system. As ever, the staff of the British Library, Cambridge University Library, the Folger Shakespeare Library and the superlative London Library provided exceptional help. The genealogical tables and maps of northern France and the Netherlands and of Ireland were drawn and digitized by Richard Guy of Orang-utan Productions from my rough drafts. For undertaking picture research and helping me to clear reproduction rights, I am most grateful to Emma Brown and Isabelle Yates.

The availability of new electronic searching aids has given me something of an advantage over earlier biographers, although the documents themselves still have to be tracked down and carefully studied. Some of the most exciting finds in the book, many of them from the Elizabethan State Papers, Foreign, at Kew, or from the Cotton or Lansdowne Manuscripts in the British Library, were achieved by the more traditional technique of pure serendipity. I am eternally grateful to my students, past and present, at Clare College, Cambridge, for listening to and critiquing my views of what I've called Elizabeth's forgotten years and for putting up, during their weekly essay supervisions, with the discussion forever turning round to comparisons with the queen and her ministers. I owe a particular debt to Dr Gabriel Heaton of Sotheby's, the New Bond Street fine-art auctioneers in London, who allowed me to study in some detail the recently rediscovered, and quite remarkable, cache of letters connected with the final years of Mary Stuart, Queen of Scots, shortly before they were put up for sale.

I've nothing but thanks and admiration for Peter Robinson and Gráinne Fox, my agents in London and New York, for their constant encouragement and for giving advice on the manuscript. I owe an immense debt to Venetia Butterfield and Daniel Crewe, my editors in the London office of Viking Publishers, for the speed and sensitivity with which they made helpful suggestions when editing my first complete draft, while leaving my style and overall approach intact and never trying to make wholesale revisions. Sarah Day copy-edited the final text with skill and efficiency, while Keith Taylor was as always a tower of strength as the editorial manager for the book. I am most grateful to everyone.

Julia has lived through the last four years with Elizabeth, Burghley, Hatton, Ralegh, Essex, Robert Cecil and the rest of the gang as if their life stories were being played out in our house, reading innumerable rough drafts, discussing them over mugs of tea at two and three o'clock in the morning, and taking substantial chunks of time out of her own work to help with scouring works of reference and then organizing and structuring my research materials as my submission deadline drew ever closer. She came to tolerate, and perhaps also to admire Elizabeth (as I think I came to do), more than I expected either of us would when I began, not least given that I first approached this topic in a frame of mind shaped by my 2004 biography of Mary Stuart. For her help and constant support, I can never adequately thank Julia or repay her love. Those of my readers who continue to use the acknowledgements in my books to catch up on the news of our animals will be pleased to learn that Susie and Tippy continue in fine form, and have recently been joined by Misty, a black stray who arrived on our doorstep as a kitten, cold, hungry and anxiously mewing – with her suitcase ready to unpack – dumped by her previous owners.

London
10 November 2015

DESCENDANTS OF EDWARD III: YORKIST LINE

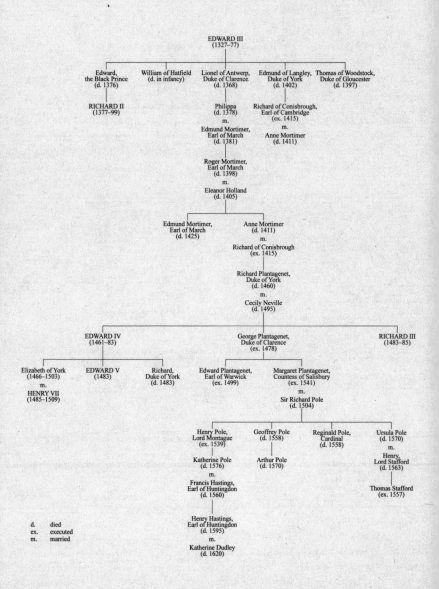

EDWARD III
(1327–77)

Edward, the Black Prince (d. 1376) — RICHARD II (1377–99)

William of Hatfield (d. in infancy)

Lionel of Antwerp, Duke of Clarence (d. 1368) — Philippa (d. 1378) m. Edmund Mortimer, Earl of March (d. 1381) — Roger Mortimer, Earl of March (d. 1398) m. Eleanor Holland (d. 1405)

Edmund of Langley, Duke of York (d. 1402) — Richard of Conisbrough, Earl of Cambridge (ex. 1415) m. Anne Mortimer (d. 1411)

Thomas of Woodstock, Duke of Gloucester (d. 1397)

Edmund Mortimer, Earl of March (d. 1425)

Anne Mortimer (d. 1411) m. Richard of Conisbrough (ex. 1415) — Richard Plantagenet, Duke of York (d. 1460) m. Cecily Neville (d. 1495)

EDWARD IV (1461–83)

George Plantagenet, Duke of Clarence (ex. 1478)

RICHARD III (1483–85)

Elizabeth of York (1466–1503) m. HENRY VII (1485–1509)

EDWARD V (1483)

Richard, Duke of York (d. 1483)

Edward Plantagenet, Earl of Warwick (ex. 1499)

Margaret Plantagenet, Countess of Salisbury (ex. 1541) m. Sir Richard Pole (d. 1504)

Henry Pole, Lord Montague (ex. 1539) — Katherine Pole (d. 1576) m. Francis Hastings, Earl of Huntingdon (d. 1560) — Henry Hastings, Earl of Huntingdon (d. 1595) m. Katherine Dudley (d. 1620)

Geoffrey Pole (d. 1558) — Arthur Pole (d. 1570)

Reginald Pole, Cardinal (d. 1558)

Ursula Pole (d. 1570) m. Henry, Lord Stafford (d. 1563) — Thomas Stafford (ex. 1557)

d.   died
ex. executed
m.   married

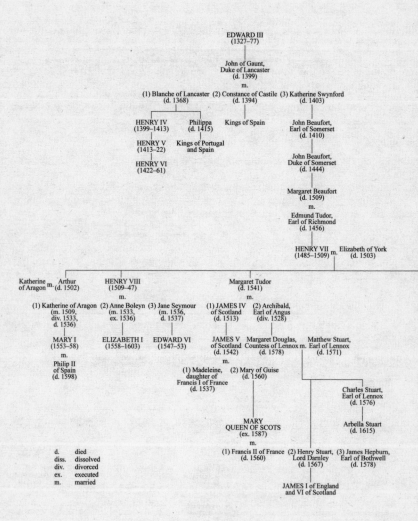

EDWARD III
(1327–77)

John of Gaunt,
Duke of Lancaster
(d. 1399)

m.

(1) Blanche of Lancaster   (2) Constance of Castile   (3) Katherine Swynford
(d. 1368)   (d. 1394)   (d. 1403)

HENRY IV   Philippa   Kings of Spain   John Beaufort,
(1399–1413)   (d. 1415)   Earl of Somerset
                                             (d. 1410)

HENRY V   Kings of Portugal
(1413–22)   and Spain

HENRY VI   John Beaufort,
(1422–61)   Duke of Somerset
                                  (d. 1444)

Margaret Beaufort
(d. 1509)

m.

Edmund Tudor,
Earl of Richmond
(d. 1456)

HENRY VII   m.   Elizabeth of York
(1485–1509)   (d. 1503)

Katherine   m.   Arthur   HENRY VIII   Margaret Tudor
of Aragon   (d. 1502)   (1509–47)

m.   m.

(1) Katherine of Aragon   (2) Anne Boleyn   (3) Jane Seymour   (1) JAMES IV   (2) Archibald,
(m. 1509,   (m. 1533,   (m. 1536,   of Scotland   Earl of Angus
div. 1533,   ex. 1536)   d. 1537)   (d. 1513)   (div. 1528)
d. 1536)

MARY I   ELIZABETH I   EDWARD VI   JAMES V   Margaret Douglas,   Matthew Stuart,
(1553–58)   (1558–1603)   (1547–53)   of Scotland   Countess of Lennox   m.   Earl of Lennox
                                               (d. 1542)   (d. 1578)   (d. 1571)

m.   m.

Philip II   (1) Madeleine,   (2) Mary of Guise
of Spain   daughter of   (d. 1560)
(d. 1598)   Francis I of France
                           (d. 1537)

                                                 Charles Stuart,
                                                 Earl of Lennox
                                                 (d. 1576)

                                                 Arbella Stuart
MARY   (d. 1615)
QUEEN OF SCOTS
(ex. 1587)

m.

(1) Francis II of France   (2) Henry Stuart,   (3) James Hepburn,
(d. 1560)   Lord Darnley   Earl of Bothwell
                      (d. 1567)   (d. 1578)

JAMES I of England
and VI of Scotland

d.   died
diss.   dissolved
div.   divorced
ex.   executed
m.   married

DESCENDANTS OF EDWARD III: LANCASTRIAN AND TUDOR LINES

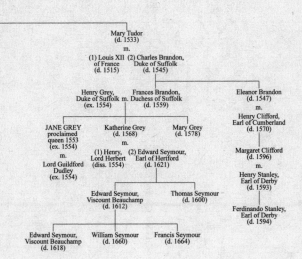

Mary Tudor
(d. 1533)

m.

(1) Louis XII   (2) Charles Brandon,
of France   Duke of Suffolk
(d. 1515)   (d. 1545)

Henry Grey,   Frances Brandon,
Duke of Suffolk m. Duchess of Suffolk
(ex. 1554)   (d. 1559)

Eleanor Brandon
(d. 1547)

m.

JANE GREY   Katherine Grey   Mary Grey
proclaimed   (d. 1568)   (d. 1578)
queen 1553
(ex. 1554)   m.

m.   (1) Henry,   (2) Edward Seymour,

Lord Guildford   Lord Herbert   Earl of Hertford
Dudley   (diss. 1554)   (d. 1621)
(ex. 1554)

Henry Clifford,
Earl of Cumberland
(d. 1570)

Margaret Clifford
(d. 1596)

m.

Henry Stanley,
Earl of Derby
(d. 1593)

Edward Seymour,   Thomas Seymour
Viscount Beauchamp   (d. 1600)
(d. 1612)

Ferdinando Stanley,
Earl of Derby
(d. 1594)

Edward Seymour,   William Seymour   Francis Seymour
Viscount Beauchamp   (d. 1660)   (d. 1664)
(d. 1618)

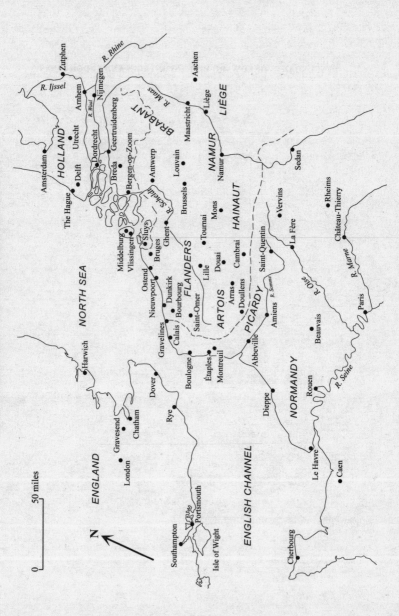

NORTHERN FRANCE AND THE NETHERLANDS

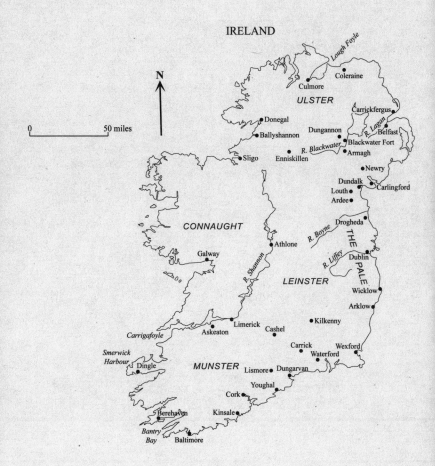

IRELAND

N

0   50 miles

Lough Foyle

Culmore
Coleraine

ULSTER

Carrickfergus

Donegal
Dungannon
R. Lagan
Belfast

Ballyshannon
R. Blackwater
Blackwater Fort

Sligo
Enniskillen
Armagh

Newry

Dundalk
Carlingford

Louth
Ardee

CONNAUGHT

Drogheda

R. Boyne

THE PALE

Athlone

R. Shannon

Galway

R. Liffey
Dublin

LEINSTER

Wicklow

Arklow

Kilkenny

Limerick
Cashel

Carrigafoyle
Askeaton

Carrick
Wexford

Waterford

Smerwick Harbour

MUNSTER
Lismore
Dungarvan

Dingle
Youghal

Cork

Berehaven
Kinsale

Bantry Bay
Baltimore

Author's Note

Dates are given throughout this book in the Old Style Julian Calendar in use in England during the sixteenth century, but the year is assumed to have begun on 1 January, not on Lady Day, or the Feast of the Annunciation (25 March), which then by custom was the first day of the calendar year. The New Style Gregorian Calendar, advancing the date by ten days, was issued in Rome in 1582 and adopted in Italy and by Philip II throughout Spain, Portugal and the New World in October that year. France followed in December, as did Brabant, Flanders, Holland and Zeeland in the Netherlands. The Catholic states of the Holy Roman Empire followed in 1583. England, Scotland, Ireland, Denmark and Sweden retained the old calendar until the 1700s, as did Friesland, Gelderland and Overijssel in the Netherlands. For obvious reasons of consistency, dates given in primary sources using the new Gregorian Calendar are converted to match the Julian Calendar used elsewhere.

Spelling and orthography of primary sources in quotations are for the most part given in modernized form. Modern punctuation and capitalization have also been provided where none exists in the original manuscript.

Units of currency appear in the pre-decimal form in use until 1971. There are twelve pence (12d.) in a shilling (modern 5 pence or US 8 cents), twenty shillings (20s.) in a pound (£1 or US $1.60), and so on. Modern purchasing equivalents for sixteenth-century figures are extremely difficult to calculate, as the effects of inflation and huge fluctuations in the relative values of land and commodities render them misleading, but rough estimates may be obtained by multiplying all numbers by a thousand.

Preface

Elizabeth was born at Greenwich Palace shortly after three o'clock on the afternoon of Sunday, 7 September 1533. The granddaughter of Henry VII, the Tudor dynasty's founder, and daughter of Henry VIII and Anne Boleyn, she was the last of her father's children to inherit the throne. After a run of chastening, sometimes terrifying experiences during her Catholic half-sister Mary Tudor's reign, she was proclaimed queen by the heralds on the early morning of Thursday, 17 November 1558. Anointed and crowned in Westminster Abbey at the age of twenty-five, she ruled for forty-four years, longer than any of her adult predecessors apart from Edward III, a considerable achievement in itself.

With so many years to cover, Elizabeth's biographers have tended to flag once she passed the age of fifty. Having established a pattern for the years of peace before the arrival of the Spanish Armada of 1588, they either skate over the years dominated by war or fall back on the convenient short cut of William Camden's monumental *Annales* (he wrote in Latin), completed in 1617 and published in two unequal instalments between 1615 and 1627. The book, now better known as *The History of Elizabeth*, is a mini-archive in itself. But it is a treacherous guide.

Despite Camden's claim to have written an unbiased history firmly rooted in the archives, a forensic comparison of his quotations with the original documents shows that he regularly doctored his sources to fit his theories. His account institutionalized a whole raft of hoary myths full of reverential nostalgia for the dead queen. To insulate her from criticism, he drew a veil over her vanity and her temper tantrums. Most conspicuously, he glided over topics that were still politically explosive when he was writing. Usually, this meant anything connected to the question of the succession and particularly to Mary Stuart, Queen of Scots, whom, sensationally, Elizabeth had executed. Anxious not to offend the new king of England, Mary's watchfully indolent son James I, whose re-interment of his mother in a spectacular marble tomb at Westminster Abbey was taking place even as the earliest draft of the *Annales* was approaching completion, Camden was also eager to protect the reputation of his former patron, Sir William Cecil, who had served Elizabeth faithfully (if in his own way) from the time she was barely sixteen.[1] Since Cecil, promoted in 1571 to be Baron of Burghley and the next year to Lord Treasurer, had been Mary's nemesis, Camden declined to pry into what – like the Roman historian Cornelius Tacitus before him – he called the *arcana imperii*, or 'mysteries of state'.[2]

Worse still, Camden's bestselling translator, the gunner and mathematician Robert Norton, barely an adult when Elizabeth died, cheerfully proceeded to bowdlerize the *Annales* while preparing the English version most commonly available today. Between 1630 and 1635, years during which Charles I's suitability to rule first began to be seriously challenged by critics of the monarchy, Norton inserted many spurious interpolations into his three English editions of Camden's text. With the barely cloaked intention of using Elizabeth as a stick with which to beat her Stuart successors, Norton spun fresh legends, chiefly concerning the (allegedly) spontaneous outpourings of love and devotion to 'Good Queen Bess': he has her devoted subjects 'running, flying, flocking to be blessed by the sight of her glorious countenance as oft as ever she came forth in public'.[3]

Deeply versed in such apocryphal material, the biographers writing after the accession of Queen Victoria in 1837 raised Elizabeth to dizzy heights of veneration. After personally nursing her divided people through a Protestant Religious Settlement in 1559 that commanded wide assent (or so these authors believed), the fiery, red-haired heroine who shaped England's destiny went on to stride boldly where her advisers feared to tread. A cultural icon who presided over the greatest flowering of literature and art that the country had ever seen, she was the woman who had chosen to live her life as a 'Virgin Queen', 'marrying her realm' (as her propagandists liked to say) and so dedicating herself to the welfare of the people she loved so dearly, despite the personal cost.

The Victorians were followed unashamedly down this path in the twentieth century by Sir John Neale. Consciously striving to make

Elizabethan history popular, Neale wrote his highly influential *Queen Elizabeth* (1934), a classic biography notching up sales of more than a million copies throughout the English-speaking world and enchanting generations of readers. In his hands, Elizabeth became an all-powerful, all-seeing, all-honourable monarch and an 'affable prince': the problems she faced as a woman in government were brushed aside. Thus emerged the Queen Elizabeth we think we know today from her 'Coronation Portrait' in the National Portrait Gallery. That tree-ring analysis proves this painting was not begun until after she was dead, and that there is evidence the image is based on a face pattern which is not really hers, are inconvenient facts readily ignored by biographers mostly content to recycle the old myths.

A flurry of adulatory films, among them *Fire over England* (1937), starring Flora Robson, and the 1970s television series *Elizabeth R*, starring Glenda Jackson, peddled the same story. In the years of peace, Elizabeth spared her people from the turmoil of the Wars of Religion, which were devastating large areas of France and then the Netherlands. In the face of war, when it finally arrived, she became a warrior queen, defiantly confronting the threats posed by her Catholic cousin Mary Queen of Scots,* King Philip II of Spain and the pope, and marshalling her forces to defend her country, the Church of England and herself. Brave, patriotic seafarers like Sir Francis Drake and Sir Walter Ralegh could dream of reinventing England as an overseas imperial power thanks only to Elizabeth, England's first truly visionary queen.

In revolt against such idealistic complacency, James Anthony Froude, the scourge of romantic sentimentality, had drawn a line in the sand. Writing in the 1860s and later shunned by Neale, he dared to argue that Elizabeth, almost from the moment she was crowned, was little short of a liability. Habitually vain, she was unable to control her temper and was mean, short-sighted and indecisive. Her relationship with her leading (male) advisers was consistently adversarial, and by refusing to marry and have children to continue the dynasty or otherwise name

---

* Strictly, Mary was Elizabeth's cousin once removed, but in their letters they addressed each other as 'cousin'.

her successor, she acted selfishly and irresponsibly, putting the nation and her father's Reformation in the greatest peril. In Froude's narrative, Burghley, Elizabeth's chief minister, was her redemption and the power behind the throne. He alone had the courage to save her from herself. It was his vigilance and, later, that of his younger colleague Sir Francis Walsingham, a man always clutching a pen and famous for his black skullcap, large white ruff and obsession with state security, which kept the country safe.

Froude's coruscating attack had some solid basis in fact but was itself misleading. A pioneer of the research methods the best historians still use today, Froude had toiled for years equally in the dusty archives of Simancas, Paris and London, where he soon came to realize that the unpublished state papers graphically illustrate how far the younger Elizabeth could find herself startlingly at odds with councillors who were confident that they knew much better than she did. In what amounted to a hatchet job on the queen, Froude was over-schematic. And yet he brilliantly captured the seismic fault line between Elizabeth's unflinchingly old-fashioned ideas about monarchy and religion and those of her more radical Protestant advisers.

Like so many others, Froude wrote only about the earlier years of Elizabeth's reign, the years of peace. He had nothing whatever to say about the later, forgotten years of war. At first he announced his absolute determination to consider them. But after spending more than a decade trawling through the vast piles of barely catalogued, often illegible material, much of it unseen since it was first filed away, he found himself so wearied and demoralized that in the end he omitted these last years, completing his encyclopaedic twelve-volume narrative history of the Tudors in 1588 with the coming of the Spanish Armada. As a result, very few people know that Philip II and his son sent not just one invasion fleet against Elizabeth, but five.

It was left to Lytton Strachey, a doyen of the Bloomsbury set, whose zest for popular biography was to inspire Neale, to pick up the baton in the bestselling *Elizabeth and Essex* (1928). For Strachey, the darkest, most intriguing aspects of Elizabeth's entire life story were not the threats posed by Mary Queen of Scots and the European Catholic powers but the tumultuous inner conflicts she endured as, inexorably, she began to age: 'As her charms grew less, her insistence on their presence grew greater.' There were no transitions: 'only opposites, juxtaposed. The extraordinary spirit was all steel one moment and all flutters the next.'

A masterpiece of cinematic life-writing, liberally spiced with hefty doses of Freudian psychology and sparkling wit, Strachey's biography was a glorious contradiction of the Victorian view that for an ageing spinster to survive as a war leader she was obliged to divest herself of all human emotions. Instead, Strachey turned Elizabeth into a woman with deep sexual urges. Tragedy, he argued, struck when a frustrated elderly virgin, a woman with a feverish, hopeless wish to be eternal and whose thickly applied layers of cosmetics were engaged in a losing battle to achieve that desire, became infatuated with the handsome young courtier Robert Devereux, 2nd Earl of Essex. Secretly harbouring unfulfilled novelistic ambitions, Strachey could speak of 'the spectral agony' of Elizabeth's last years and unleash his imagination by saying of her flirtations, 'Her heart melted with his flatteries, and, as she struck him lightly on the neck with her long fingers, her whole being was suffused with a lasciviousness that could hardly be defined.'[4]

Fresh from his critical successes with *Eminent Victorians* (1918) and *Queen Victoria* (1921), Strachey was never a biographer to be intimidated by royalty or reputation. But as Virginia Woolf pointed out in her classic essay 'The Art of Biography' (1938), *Elizabeth and Essex* was a triumph of dramatic art but a failure of history. Biography, in Strachey's hands, Woolf cuttingly remarked, never had a fairer chance of showing what it could do, but whereas in *Queen Victoria* every statement was verified, every fact authenticated and new facts brought to light, in *Elizabeth and Essex* 'facts' were nebulous or wrong, even sometimes invented, and fact and fiction obstinately refused to mix.[5]

The reverberations of Strachey's intervention still echoed as late as 1953, when the opening night of the world premiere of Benjamin Britten's *Gloriana*, specially commissioned by the Royal Opera House to mark Elizabeth II's coronation and staged in her presence, scandalized her courtiers as much as it reputedly bored the new queen. Yet for all his flaws, Strachey could always distinguish what really mattered from the inconsequential. He saw clearly what Camden and his successors had failed to see for almost four hundred years: that 'the reign of Elizabeth falls into two parts'. After some twenty-five years, 'the kaleidoscope shifted; the old ways, the old actors, were swept off with the wreckage of the Armada.'[6]

My aim is to strike out from where Strachey blazed a trail and get closer to the truth about the ageing Elizabeth. Just as with my 2004 biography of Mary Queen of Scots, the rationale relates closely to the method. I have chosen to tell this most fascinating story by returning to the original, handwritten letters and documents in the archives rather than by recycling familiar anecdotes culled from unreliable memoirs or from the well-worn printed abstracts in the dozens of weighty volumes of *Calendars of State Papers* begun by the Victorians which so often omitted large chunks of the material and were themselves compiled as much to perpetuate as to engage with the myths.[7] By turning only to the original, unexpurgated versions of Elizabeth's letters and those of her leading advisers, and by separating out those passages recording her verbatim words from those drafted or inserted by others, I have made it my aim to scythe through spin and legend and come closer to her 'authentic' voice. When this is done, vivid glimpses of the real Elizabeth, so often carefully screened from our gaze, at last emerge from the shadows.

It would have come as a momentous shock to Lytton Strachey – he complained volubly to Virginia Woolf and others about the dearth of original sources for the 1590s and worked entirely from a narrow, randomly selected collection of printed texts – to learn that, despite the ravages of time, fire, flood and hungry rodents, such documents survive in daunting quantities. This fact ought to be better known. As Froude discovered, there was an exponential increase in the volume of handwritten state papers after 1580, but only a small fraction of the source material from the official State Paper collections in what is now the National Archives at Kew has ever been printed for the post-Armada years, and next to nothing beyond selected domestic or Scottish and Irish correspondence after December 1596.[8] Vast tracts of handwritten state papers to do with England's relations with the wider European and Mediterranean powers have been left almost untouched. Overall, there are up to a quarter of a million manuscript pages to search, not counting large parchment rolls, chiefly Elizabeth's Chamber accounts, which I managed to photograph parchment by parchment in the spring of 2013. (The Chamber accounts are the only continuous source from which Elizabeth's day-to-day movements and those of her chief advisers can most fully be worked out.)[9]

A significant number of the sources used in this book have not been properly read and digested, or even adequately catalogued, since the archives were first imperfectly arranged in the 1850s and 1860s. Among them are some thirty of Elizabeth's unpublished letters – and drafts of many more – which offer new or hidden insights into both her methods of working and, often, her private thoughts. The policy documents illustrating Elizabeth's profile as a war leader are scarcely better explored, even though her involvement in a fast-moving, pan-European crisis is absolutely central to establishing the frame in which any real understanding of her character and qualities as a ruler must be set.

Some aspects of this book will seem strangely unfamiliar to readers of Camden, Froude, Neale or Strachey. For that I make no apology. The last thing I wanted to do was to perpetuate the false or incomplete images of Elizabeth coming from their well-thumbed classics. Instead, the woman who will emerge from the pages of this book is an Elizabeth rarely glimpsed before. She was never the unstoppable juggernaut whose orders could not be challenged simply because she was queen, but nor, as Froude imagined, were her decisions the result of a masterful exercise in political ventriloquism. She was neither a triumphant Gloriana, a Hollywood heroine who saved her country single-handedly from the might of Spain, nor was she Strachey's sexually frustrated spinster, governed by lust, jealousy, passion, vanity. Notably, she was not Neale's 'affable prince', the woman who intoxicated country and Court alike with her regal intimacy and the intensity and effervescence of her spirit.

Such simplistic, diametrically opposed views of the same woman turn her into a caricature. The reality is more complex.

Introduction: A Virgin Queen

Henry VIII divorced his first wife, Katherine of Aragon, in the 1530s and married Elizabeth's mother, Anne Boleyn, for love and for sons. Anne was the love of his life. He simply adored her. She was his 'darling', his 'own sweetheart'. To her, he penned soul-baring letters; for her, he sacrificed his chief minister Cardinal Wolsey. He then broke with the pope and sent Thomas More, the Lord Chancellor, and his close friend and ally Bishop John Fisher to shameful deaths – all because they believed that what he was doing was morally and profoundly wrong.[1] In return, he expected Anne to produce the legitimate male heir he craved. Instead, she gave birth to Elizabeth.

So utterly convinced was Henry that Anne would give him a boy, he chose Edward and Henry as the child's names and ordered dozens of letters to be written in advance, ready to dispatch to foreign rulers and the nobility, announcing the 'deliverance and bringing forth of a prince'. When the news came that the baby was a girl, these had to be altered one by one. There was a hurried, improvised attempt to change the word 'prince' into 'princess', but there was only enough room to squeeze in a single 's'.[2] Thus, even as she took her very first breath, the future Queen Elizabeth was considered to be second best.

Henry never attempted to conceal his views on female monarchy.[3] With his yearning for a son topping his agenda, he cautioned that if a woman 'shall chance to rule, she cannot continue long without a husband, which by God's law must then be her governor and head, and so finally shall direct the realm'.[4] To him, power was quintessentially masculine and a female ruler dangerously vulnerable. An unmarried woman would be unsuited to be a war leader, he believed, and when, later, he did finally concede that a female might succeed him, he sought to dictate precisely how she would be permitted to marry.[5]

He expected his only legitimate son, Edward, born in 1537 to his third wife, Jane Seymour, to live to a ripe old age. Just in case, however, he made provisions for the succession of his two daughters,

Mary and Elizabeth, in his last will. If Edward were to die without an heir, each might, in turn, succeed him, but each would lose her place if she chose a husband who lacked the 'assent and consent' of certain privy councillors.[6] If both were to be disqualified by virtue of an unsanctioned marriage or to die, then the throne would pass to the so-called 'Suffolk' line, the descendants of Henry's nieces Frances and Eleanor Brandon. Frances and Eleanor were the daughters of his younger and favourite sister, Mary, the widow of Louis XII of France, who had taken the much-married Charles Brandon, Duke of Suffolk, as her second husband.[7]

Edward VI was a thoroughly healthy child until, at the age of fourteen, his immune system was shattered by a severe attack of measles. The following spring he succumbed either to tuberculosis or, more likely, given the description of his symptoms, to a feverish cold, leading to bronchial pneumonia. Keen to spend as much of his time as possible on astronomy, hunting, archery and other martial sports, and on rebuilding the English navy, Edward was wary of women and even more determined than his father not to be succeeded by one. He convinced himself (or perhaps was convinced by others) that his half-sisters' illegitimacy – both had been bastardized by Act of Parliament – disqualified them.[8]

When Edward first began to jot down a template for his own succession settlement, he still envisaged that, before his death, Frances Brandon might have a son: only at the last moment did he decide to make her eldest daughter, Jane Grey, queen. In June 1553, when he knew he was dying, he put aside his scruples and 'devised' the Crown 'to the L[ady] Jane and her heirs male', followed by her sisters, Katherine and Mary, and their heirs male, and, finally, by the eldest son of their cousin Margaret Clifford, daughter of Eleanor Brandon.[9]

But for all Edward's efforts to make Jane Grey the lawful queen, she would never be crowned. Ruling for only nine days, from the moment her accession was proclaimed until her imprisonment in the Tower of London, she was easily toppled when Henry VIII's elder daughter, Mary, led a swift and effective counter-coup. Capturing the throne at the age of thirty-seven, Mary Tudor was England's first female monarch. The only other woman to come close to ruling in her own right had been King Henry I's daughter Matilda, to whom he had tried to bequeath the Crown in 1135, but she had been forced to flee from London on the eve of her coronation, when the citizens turned against her. She had lost the throne to her cousin Stephen, leading to a long and bitter civil war.

Passionately committed to reversing her father's break with the Catholic Church, Mary, who, as Katherine of Aragon's daughter, keenly felt her half-Spanish identity, quickly engineered a marriage to Philip, the son of her powerful cousin the Holy Roman Emperor Charles V. Already ruling as regent in Spain for his gout-stricken father, Philip would shortly succeed (as King Philip II) to the sovereignty of Spain, the Netherlands and the Spanish-Habsburg lands in Italy and the New World. By choosing a husband early in her reign, Mary hoped to deflect the attacks of those who opposed female rule on principle. But her choice badly backfired. According to the marriage treaties, Philip was supposed to be nothing more than a king consort. He was not to exercise independent rights of patronage or to interfere in defence or foreign policy, to make appointments or to spend the Crown's money. In practice, he was soon doing all of these things, despite living for much of the time in Brussels.[10]

Styled 'King Philip I of England', Mary's husband was to all intents and purposes co-ruler. In official portraits he was painted seated in the more powerful position, at his wife's right hand, under a floating crown.[11] Despite the marriage treaties, Mary repeatedly deferred to him, out of what she described as 'wifely duty'. Although this worked tolerably well in years of peace, once Mary's much-vaunted pregnancies proved false and Philip had dragged England into an unpopular war against France, which he directed from the Continent, her authority collapsed. When she died in November 1558, from a prolactinoma, a non-cancerous tumour of the pituitary gland which causes pseudo-pregnancies, migraines, depression and the onset of blindness, she was mourned only by her innermost circle.

Upon hearing that his wife's last hours had come, Philip sent his roving ambassador and Captain of the Spanish Guard, the Count of Feria, to England to sound out Elizabeth in an effort to salvage Spanish interests. After a relatively brief audience, the shrewd Feria judged the incoming queen to be 'a very vain and clever woman':

She must have been thoroughly schooled in the manner in which her father conducted his affairs, and I am very much afraid that she will not be well disposed in matters of religion, for I see her inclined to govern through men who are believed to be heretics and I am told that the women around her definitely are . . . She puts great store by the people and is very confident that they are all on her side – which is certainly true. She declares that it was the people who put her in her present position . . . She is determined to be governed by no one.[12]

Elizabeth meant to show her steel from the outset. The trouble was this was easier said than done. To assume that a woman ruler could exercise power simply by being crowned is a fundamental mistake. As the first unmarried queen of England, Elizabeth quickly found herself occupying the hinterland between a man's and a woman's world. Often it took a battle royal to impose her will on even her most loyal privy councillors.[13] When John Aylmer, once Jane Grey's tutor, published a defence of female monarchy in 1559, his main argument was that a queen was acceptable as a ruler despite her gender, chiefly because she *did not* call the shots. Aylmer prefaced his remarks with the general observation that women rulers were 'weak in nature, feeble in body, soft in courage, unskilful in practice, not terrible to the enemy'. He (or his printer), remembering Philip and Mary, then added a pithy one-liner: 'A woman may rule as a magistrate, and yet obey as a wife.'[14]

Those biographers who have tried to argue that Elizabeth was accorded the status of an honorary man by virtue of her royal rank, or that monarchy as an institution is androgynous, have ducked the issue. England in the sixteenth century was a highly patriarchal society in which women, including royal ones, were viewed as subordinate to men. None of Elizabeth's contemporaries, other than a few Italian intellectuals such as Torquato Tasso, believed that a woman's high rank could trump her gender. Deeply entrenched psychologically, such attitudes would find their most vehement expression in Elizabeth's military commanders, who would seek to ignore or deliberately misinterpret her orders.[15] At no time was a woman ruler's vulnerability more exposed, they maintained, echoing Henry VIII's starting point, than when she was beset by a hostile power or when national security or the succession were in doubt. On such matters, Elizabeth could not rely even on Burghley, her chief minister, to take her side: 'God send Our Mistress a husband and by him a son that we may hope our posterity shall have a masculine succession' was his nagging, infuriating refrain.[16]

One weapon Elizabeth did have was language. No ruler has ever better understood the relationship of words to power. From the moment her first Parliament was summoned, she would seek to insulate herself from criticism by invoking the rhetorical trope that she had the support of the people. As she had informed Feria, 'it was the people who put her in her present position' and she 'is very confident that they are all on her side'. Much of her self-belief and all of her presentational skills came from studying classical oratory as a teenager with brilliant wordsmiths such as the famous Roger Ascham, not from mingling with the real-life 'people', for whom she did not have much time and whose name she regularly took in vain.

And yet, for all her powers of persuasion, not even her kinsfolk trusted her to rule on her own when she first came to the throne. Sir Nicholas Throckmorton, a cousin of her stepmother, Katherine Parr, Henry VIII's sixth and last queen, had known Elizabeth since she was a teenager. 'You must', he cautioned her in 1559 or thereabouts, 'beware of womanish levity, for where the king [*sic*] governeth not in severity and prudence, there doth emulation and ambition sow their seeds.'[17]

Using honeyed words and skilful political chicanery, Elizabeth's advisers tried to convince her that she had to play the game by their rules, and of all the men who surrounded her and sought to bend her to their ways, there was no greater master than William Cecil, Lord Burghley – this in spite of his many protestations to foreign ambassadors that he was no more than the queen's 'humble servant'. Turning thirty-nine in her coronation year, he had a pink complexion and was short and wiry with a thin face, grey eyes, brown hair and a beard and moustache already flecked with grey. Three warts were visible on his right cheek. The son of one of Henry VIII's yeomen of the wardrobe, who had profited from favourable grants of ex-monastic lands and founded an ancestral estate near Stamford in Lincolnshire, Burghley was a Cambridge graduate with a small army of highly educated protégés at his disposal, all, like himself, steeped in classical learning and the teaching of the Protestant reformers. Marinated in the ways of the Court since Edward's reign, when he first was made a privy councillor, he had offered his services to Elizabeth as her back-stairs fixer and had become the surveyor of her estates. Once she was queen and she had made him her principal secretary, he coaxed the then highly inexperienced twenty-five-year-old into a decidedly more Protestant Religious Settlement than she would later have countenanced, doing so simply by packing the committee responsible for drafting it with his own nominees.[18] That same year, 1559, he got his way again by threatening to resign if she refused to send ships and troops to Scotland to help expel an occupying French garrison at the port of Leith and to assist a group of insurgent noblemen who, fired by the Calvinist ideologue John Knox, were seeking to bring about a full-blooded Protestant revolution in the country. He even had the cheek to tell her that 'to serve Your Majesty in anything *that myself cannot allow* must needs be an unprofitable service'. That phrase speaks volumes for his working methods. And Elizabeth had no real choice but to swallow her pride, because by then he was far too valuable to lose.[19]

The next year, Burghley would severely reprimand Robert Jones, Nicholas Throckmorton's secretary, for talking privately with Elizabeth about matters touching on religion. 'He wished I had not told the Queen's Majesty a matter of such weight,' Jones reported, 'being too much for a woman's knowledge.'[20] Although a Protestant in her private devotions since her early teenage years, a position that had put her life in danger when her half-sister Mary returned the king-dom to Catholicism, Elizabeth was not sufficiently zealous for Burghley. She loathed the pope and rejected the Catholic doctrine of the Mass. But she found just as abhorrent the Calvinists' claims – Burghley secretly admired them – that Catholics could or should be excluded from the throne as idolaters. Just as vehemently, she insisted that representative assemblies such as Parliaments should have no voice in such matters.[21]

While England had a Protestant queen for the moment, when Elizabeth suffered a near-fatal attack of smallpox in October 1562, a panic ensued. It was a watershed, reminding everyone that she was mortal. She survived, but the following year, and again in 1566, Burghley covertly masterminded a pressure group inside and outside the House of Commons in a thinly veiled attempt to force her into marriage or into naming an heir, so that the succession of a Protestant candidate would be assured. Determined to gain control on this critical question, Elizabeth's chief minister threatened to deny her the funds she needed in taxes if she refused. He even began making plans for Parliament to create a statutory mechanism by which, if she suddenly died, the throne would pass only to a Protestant, excluding all Catholics from consideration, however exalted their rank.[22]

Furious at his brazen attempt to overstep his authority, Elizabeth drafted a closing speech for use at the end of the 1566 session of Parliament, denouncing the 'wrangling subjects' who had tried to force her hand. Except, when it was time to deliver the speech, she lost her nerve and sent Burghley's brother-in-law, Sir Nicholas Bacon, to deliver it on her behalf, handing him a version that left out the word 'wrangling', as the final manuscript of her speech makes plain.[23]

The psychological difficulties Elizabeth faced as a ruling monarch are thrown into a sharper focus when the physical setting of her Court is understood. Both Henry VII and Henry VIII had greatly enlarged the monarch's personal living spaces. While still giving audiences and dining in state in the Presence Chamber, Henry VII had added a new series of rooms known collectively as the Privy Chamber to his principal palaces to create a more intimate and secure environment for himself. Henry VIII later expanded these spaces in a massive programme of building works financed by the confiscation of abbey lands, turning them into a labyrinthine sequence of rooms and galleries filled with art treasures.[24] Their respective wives lived in completely separate, self-contained 'sides' of the royal palaces staffed by their own officers.

As he steadily aged, Henry VIII had gradually retreated from the Privy Chamber into the still more intimate world of the inner Bedchamber, otherwise known as the 'secret lodgings'.[25] There, largely defying the tradition that he should dine in state, he ate his meals informally, followed events occurring at home and abroad intently, even during his last illness, and dictated and signed his letters. Policy was settled only after he had summoned and closely questioned his advisers on the underlying issues. On matters he cared most about, such as religious policy or foreign affairs, he would read the key documents himself thoroughly before making a final decision.[26]

When Elizabeth moved into Whitehall Palace shortly after Mary Tudor's death, she inherited her father's almost bewildering hierarchy of interconnecting rooms and galleries.[27] After the Great Hall, where plays and entertainments were staged in the late afternoons or early evenings on days of festival, the sequence continued with the ceremonial Presence Chamber, then the Privy Chamber, with its crystal fountain and stupendous dynastic mural frescoed by Hans Holbein the Younger, followed by the outer and inner Bedchamber.[28] Access was controlled by guards and ushers operating under the overall control of the Captain of the Guard, the Lord Chamberlain and the two chief gentlemen of the Privy Chamber. Superficially, little had changed since her father's time, except that, unless Elizabeth was holding audiences there, her Privy Chamber and Bedchamber were predominantly feminine spaces, the inner Bedchamber exclusively so.

Of the queen's senior women, three or four regularly served in the Bedchamber and six or seven in the Privy Chamber. Below them were three or four chamberers of the Privy Chamber, usually women in their twenties or thirties, and six maids of honour in the Bedchamber, teenagers working under the supervision of the 'mother of the maids', who was responsible for their welfare and discipline. All these women were handpicked by the queen and worked to a precise set of written instructions or 'Ordinances'.[29]

Beginning early in her reign, Elizabeth received petitioners and held formal audiences with her advisers or visiting ambassadors in the Privy Chamber, where she also spent much of her time reading or playing the virginals, at which she was notably accomplished. She greatly enjoyed card games, chiefly Primero, in which the players would be dealt four cards from a forty-card pack and would then bet on the combination of cards they were given. Arriving for an audience in 1563, the French ambassador Paul de Foix found Elizabeth deeply absorbed in a game of chess.[30] Sometimes she danced or listened to her favourite musicians, twenty or more of them Italian, including two female lutenists.[31] And in the long summer evenings she would sit up until late outdoors, reading or conversing while eating marzipan or sugar 'comfits' (candied fruits) and drinking 'hypocras' (sweet white wine flavoured with spices). She especially loved marzipan: in 1562, the New Year's gifts she received included a model of Old St Paul's Cathedral and a full-size chessboard, both made of 'marchpane', or marzipan.[32]

To entertain her at dull moments, troupes of dark-skinned Italian actors and dancers – friends of her musicians – performed impromptu for her. Once, she allowed a troupe of female acrobats to put on a show, leading to sharp criticism of 'the unchaste, shameless and unnatural tumbling of the Italian women'.[33] At other times, a female fool amused her. Early in the reign, this was a midget known as Ipolyta the Tartarian, to whom Elizabeth gave a pewter doll; later, it was Tomasin de Paris, described as a 'woman dwarf', to whom she gave some of her old clothes to sell. The most curious of Elizabeth's domestic indulgences was a black African page-boy. She dressed him in a coat of white taffeta, trimmed with gold-and-silver stripes, a matching doublet with fine silver buttons, a pair of knitted white stockings and a pair of white shoes and exhibited him to visitors as a conversation piece.[34]

The predominantly feminine environment of the Privy Chamber and Bedchamber put Elizabeth at a distinct political disadvantage. Unlike her father and grandfather, she could not easily gather her advisers around her or quiz them on affairs of state unless she summoned them formally first, whereas in the exclusively masculine environment of her father's reign, trusted servants could routinely enter the Privy Chamber and Bedchamber, or even sometimes the 'secret lodgings', at almost any time when the king was awake. For Elizabeth, it would be unthinkable for male advisers, other perhaps than her chief physician, to see her if she were wearing her nightgown, cap and velvet slippers, which she sometimes kept on during the day and into the evening if not going out, or if her women were applying her make-up or curling her wigs.[35]

Burghley began work at six o'clock in the morning. He was always on call, but Elizabeth was a late riser. On one notable occasion in her mid-forties, she told a suitor who had thought it safe to turn up at eleven to return the next day after dinner (then eaten shortly after midday), adding, 'You know I am no morning woman.'[36] Her late rising apart, it took her women upwards of two hours to dress her. Merely fixing her starched ruff in position and pinning the flounce or lining of her skirts around the edge of a drum-shaped farthingale could take over an hour. Behind her back, male courtiers joked that it was quicker to rig a royal navy ship than dress the queen.[37]

The reduced casual access Elizabeth was able to offer her privy councillors outside formal audiences meant that she had far fewer opportunities than her father to hold them strictly to account.[38] She met Burghley in daily audience, sometimes late at night, but how was she to know whether he told her all she needed to know? It was, after all, he who controlled access to the state papers, he who routinely briefed her ambassadors, he who negotiated with foreign embassies, he who supervised her correspondence and drafted royal proclamations. More alert to the attempts of her advisers to gang up on her as the years went by, Elizabeth began teaching herself how to seek independent sources of intelligence when she suspected subterfuge and to play off her privy councillors against one another.[39] On a memorable occasion in 1570, as Burghley was leaving the room at the end of an audience, she ostentatiously turned for a second opinion to Sir Thomas Heneage, a smooth-tongued gentleman of the Privy Chamber. Burghley later gave Heneage a ferocious dressing-down, said by its mauled recipient to be 'a blast'. In his defence, Heneage protested that it was the queen herself who had initiated the conversation. What else was he to do but answer her?[40] From her side, Elizabeth found this sort of showdown immensely satisfying, as it helped to disabuse Burghley of the notion that her dependence on him was absolute. Some said she had begun to 'smile' on Heneage in revenge for Burghley's underhand dealings to force her to marry and settle the succession in Parliament.

The bureaucratic system Elizabeth presided over was heavily weighted against a woman ruler. Her father in the 1540s had established a tightly knit Privy Council of between eleven and nineteen members who were to take charge of the bulk of routine administration, leaving him alone to decide the key questions of state. Despite his jealous protection of his prerogative, Henry did not attend any of the regular meetings of his privy councillors, waiting instead for his principal secretary to report to him afterwards. Since none of his councillors would dare to mislead him or keep him in the dark, he could be sure of getting accurate information. The challenge faced by a woman ruler was that, unless her male councillors chose to involve her fully in their business and keep her properly informed, she had no ready means of checking what they were up to other than by quizzing them individually then comparing what they said and how it related to what Burghley was telling her. Mary Tudor had encountered precisely this problem when several of her privy councillors preferred to report to her consort, King Philip, despite legislation that had declared her to be as much 'solely and sole queen' after her marriage as she had been before it.

Convening several mornings a week at nine o'clock and dominated by Burghley, Elizabeth's privy councillors organized their routine largely as they themselves wished. When weighty matters arose, the queen might specifically request that they be considered, but it was mostly left to Burghley to report on the councillors' deliberations at his daily audiences with her. For the more important of these, he would prepare memos or sheets of headings with summaries of the arguments for or against a particular course of action.[41] Occasionally, he would present her with a formal written document known as a 'Consultation', setting out the Council's agreed position.[42] Otherwise, he spoke from memory. The clerks of the Council kept minutes of the proceedings, but beyond recording attendances these tended to be cursory, since most of the Council's administrative work was done by letter. The full record of what was said and decided in the Privy Council was kept only in the memories of those present. And, all too frequently, Elizabeth's councillors confronted her with decisions already stitched up.

She did not even draft all her own letters, although most biographers conveniently assume that she did. Elizabeth usually wrote important letters to foreign princes in her own hand, as well as letters of condolence to loyal servants who had suffered bereavements. Her favourite godson, John Harington, records how on one occasion she contrived to handwrite one letter, dictate another and talk all at the same time.[43] And yet, time and time again, her letters or her instructions to her resident ambassadors abroad, full of those resonant phrases we might otherwise believe to have come from her own pen, turn out, when the provenance of the early drafts is checked, to have been ghostwritten by Burghley or another senior councillor and merely awaiting the queen's signature.[44]

How exactly this worked was explained in 1567 by Diego Guzmán de Silva, the resident Spanish ambassador in London, who witnessed the queen in action while waiting in the queue for an audience. A letter, he says, was to be sent to the queen's accredited representative in Scotland. 'I have seen it,' he added, 'although I could not read it.' One of Elizabeth's privy councillors, her long-standing favourite and Master of the Horse Robert Dudley, Earl of Leicester, had dictated it to a clerk before Guzmán's astonished eyes while in the same queue, 'and he took it to the queen for signature in my presence.'[45]

In a revealing note of 1565 to Matthew Parker, Elizabeth's first archbishop of Canterbury, Burghley fumed that she was likely to try and alter the draft of a letter he was preparing for her signature 'more than I shall allow'. This was almost exactly the phrase he had used earlier when threatening to resign, an indication that he felt himself to be very much in control.[46] Only once in her earlier years in a situation like this is Elizabeth known for certain to have put her foot down and bypassed completely her meddling advisers. In 1566, she scribbled a letter to her newly appointed Lord Deputy in Ireland that its anxious recipient was ordered to conceal:

> Let this memorial be only committed to Vulcan's base keeping. Without any longer abode than the leisure of the reading thereof, yea, and with no mention made thereof to any other wight. I charge you as I may command you. Seem not to have had but secretaries' letters from me.[47]

Unpicking who precisely wrote which of the fifteen thousand or so surviving letters or warrants sent out in Elizabeth's name during the forty-four years she reigned turns out to be a huge and laborious task. At a rough estimate, no more than 2,400 of them were handwritten by the queen or dictated by her.[48] Far too much paperwork was flying around her Court for her to vet all of it, and for the first twenty or so years her councillors, led by Burghley, drafted the most secret and important letters to individuals or ambassadors on her behalf after receiving purely verbal instructions. Sometimes they exploited this lack of scrutiny for their own ends. On a few scandalous occasions in the 1560s, chiefly where Mary Queen of Scots was concerned, instructions to ambassadors would be sent out only after lengthy exchanges between Elizabeth and Burghley, which the latter regularly won.[49] In a similar vein, her ambassadors abroad would write sanitized reports to her, sending fuller and more explicit briefings to Burghley by the same courier.

Of course, it was not just the young queen's inexperience or the sheer volume of paper circulating around the Court that encouraged this murky system. Such laxity could suit Elizabeth as much as it did Burghley and his friends, as it enabled her to disavow what she had herself done. In 1570, two years after she had taken shameless advantage of a gale in the Channel to seize for herself 155 chests of Genoese treasure being shipped to the Netherlands to pay Philip II's troops, she sent a message to Philip's fourth wife, Anne of Austria,* explaining, 'Although there hath of late time happened some show of unkindnesses . . . betwixt us and the king of Spain', this was to be attributed entirely to the 'mishap of evil conditioned ministers'.[50] She was determined to shift the blame for the deterioration in Anglo-Spanish relations on to the shoulders of others.

Elizabeth had first learned to keep her fingerprints off her most politically explosive choices while in her early twenties. Then, she had been the focus of at least two plots to unseat her Catholic sibling, Mary Tudor, the more threatening of which was the Protestant Sir Thomas Wyatt's rebellion in 1554. The day after Wyatt was convicted of high treason, a delegation of Mary's councillors came to arrest Elizabeth and charge her as an accessory to the revolt.[51] They wished to know why she had made preparations suddenly to move from Hertfordshire to her property at Donnington Castle in Berkshire, where the keeper was one of Wyatt's closest friends. But they could never prove she had personally endorsed Wyatt's conspiracy or

* The daughter of the Holy Roman Emperor Maximilian II and his wife, Maria of Spain.

ordered the proposed move: her communications with Wyatt had been at arm's length. She managed to blame her underlings, one of whom was Sir John Harington, father of her godson of the same name, for an excess of zeal on her behalf. Mary Tudor promptly sent him to the Tower.[52]

Understandably, Elizabeth took this lesson to heart. Her favourite classical tags for the rest of her life would be *Video et Taceo* ('I see and keep silent') and *Semper Eadem* ('Always one and the same'), which she made her motto.[53] In her hands, the art of queenship would not simply be the art of statesmanship. It would involve surreptitious convolutions geared towards increasing her power and decreasing her vulnerability.

Elizabeth's war years, for all the drama and colour of the 1588 Armada campaign, are the forgotten years. Generally neglected by her biographers, or else discussed in a more or less perfunctory way, with the most crucial explanations of the decision-making process culled from Camden's *Annales* rather than directly from the archives, they are years when an ageing spinster, engaged in mortal combat with time and death, sought to uphold her most cherished ideals. Relatively little has been written about them, certainly in comparison to the years of peace, when the queen's Religious Settlement and her dynastic duelling with Mary Queen of Scots and with her own privy councillors over her marriage negotiations were at the top of the agenda.[54]

The year 1584, when Prince William of Orange, the leader of the Dutch Calvinists in their heroic struggle against the Catholic Philip II of Spain, was assassinated, is a clear turning-point. It marked the onset of the great pan-European and Atlantic crisis that would threaten to bring the queen and her country to their knees. Elizabeth found herself propelled into a military and ideological collision with a global superpower, one with vast resources and a worldwide empire. She would not see peace again in her lifetime: the war would last longer than the First and Second World Wars combined. The year 1584 would also mark the moment when everyone finally, grudgingly, came to accept that she had passed the age of childbearing: grudgingly, because that recognition also meant that they had accepted she could never have a biological successor.

During the years of peace, Elizabeth's vulnerability had been much increased by the unrelenting pressure of her councillors and Parliaments to persuade her to marry. After 1584, by comparison, certainty about her biological inability to bear children liberated her, because no one could any longer dispute that she had an unchallenged right to exercise alone both the masculine and feminine responsibilities of the monarchy: there could be no point in marrying her off if she was barren. Although for her it was an uncomfortable reminder of the passage of time, it was also a moment of empowerment. Confronted by the worst national emergency the country had experienced since her father's break with Rome, she determined that from this point onwards she must rule as well as reign. In such perilous times, she must assert her authority more firmly and more consistently than before. This was her calling, her solemn duty, and she believed that God expected no less of her.

She would not always be successful: clashes were bound to arise between her, her privy councillors and her military and naval commanders over long-term strategy, short-term tactics and the ever-escalating costs of such a long war. Her much-vaunted relationships with her last two favourites – the mercurial, charismatic, daredevil Robert Devereux, Earl of Essex; and, to a lesser extent, the swashbuckling Sir Walter Ralegh – can be properly understood only within the wider frame of the rows between them over military and naval strategy. But Elizabeth would be far more interventionist and much harder to handle than before. At the same time, she was forced to face up to her own mortality, as her hair and good looks succumbed to the ravages of time. No wonder she cultivated the impression that she was ageless, timeless, perennially young.

To make it appear that she was not yet a post-menopausal woman, she allowed and then actively encouraged her courtiers to reinvent her as a Virgin Queen. Contrary to the firmly entrenched belief of the Victorians (based on a misread sentence in Camden's *Annales*), she had not until then spun herself as such. Only in the summer of 1578, when she had led her Court on a slow progress through East Anglia, had this enduring concept of her later years made its first brief and somewhat tentative appearance.[55] Like her father, she travelled with a reduced Court around the countryside of (mostly) southern England once a year, sometime between late May and mid-September, for leisure and recreation. And, as part of an evening's entertainment at Norwich, the soldier-poet Thomas Churchyard had scripted a series of masques and pageants at the request of the civic leaders, in one of which the central theme was that Elizabeth could earn immortality only through her sexual purity. If she stayed single, she could enjoy a special status as a 'Virgin Queen', who by resisting the temptations of the flesh would also prevent its decay.[56]

At the time, the masque made no real impression on the queen's iconography. But once it was plain that she had entered the menopause, the conceit snowballed, until portrait painters and scriptwriters were exploiting it on an industrial scale. In the 1590s, it would explode into the 'cult' of Gloriana, seen with all its pomp and pageantry during the queen's Accession Day tilts, reaching its zenith in the airbrushed, stylized images crammed with the eulogistic, distracting symbolism that we know so well and culminating in the celebrated 'Rainbow Portrait', now at Hatfield House in Hertfordshire.

These later years had a dark side. The war against the Catholic powers would engulf multiple theatres: the Netherlands, northern France, the Atlantic and, latterly, Ireland. And, all the while, the queen was ageing. Her grandfather Henry VII had died at the age of fifty-two, her father at fifty-five, her half-brother at fifteen and her half-sister at forty-two. Many of her advisers, too, were growing old, and as they fell sick and died, a new and less scrupulous breed of courtiers and bureaucrats would come to the fore.

As Elizabeth approached her late sixties, it seemed to her councillors and Parliaments as if the looming question of the succession, for which she consistently refused to make adequate provision, could be postponed no longer. For all that, she jealously refused to yield. The question would stir up destructive bouts of rivalry, ideological conflict and mutual suspicion among the members of her innermost circle. The border between loyalty and treachery would gradually start to blur, as men looked to what would happen after the queen's death and began their preparations.

With the years taking their inexorable toll, Elizabeth would find herself tormented by insomnia, arthritis, digestive ailments, bad dreams and what she claimed was the insolence and insubordination of her younger, prettier attendants. Outwardly, she would seek to bridge the mismatch between her queenly role and her appearance by a mixture of spin and cosmetics. Inwardly, she struggled to assert her will and retain her grip on power as her courtiers battled for place and position and her newly emboldened subjects called for the monarchy to be made accountable to Parliament.

Truly, this would be the beginning of something new.

1. A City in Fear

On Wednesday, 23 September 1584, Mr John Spencer, the sheriff of London, was savouring the prospect of the end of his term of office in just a few days. New sheriffs, both for London and the adjacent county of Middlesex, had already been elected and would be sworn in at the Guildhall by the mayor on Michaelmas Eve.[1] A wealthy merchant whose aggressive tactics had netted him an enviable fortune from importing raisins, spices, olive oil, iron and wine, Spencer found his civic responsibilities irksome and looked forward eagerly to returning to trade.[2] Wearing his violet gown and gold chain of office, he set out with his constables on what he sincerely hoped would be one final, uneventful inspection of the city streets.

Such random patrols had become depressingly frequent. In the years since the bloody slaughter in Paris and a dozen other French towns of some thirteen thousand Huguenots – the name given to French Protestants – in the fortnight after St Bartholomew's Day in August 1572, there had been recurrent large influxes of refugees fleeing from religious persecution to the safety of London. Immigrant communities, chiefly French and Flemish but also German and Italian, were by now firmly entrenched, creating severe tensions with the local population, especially those in the clothing trade, as immigrant workers routinely flouted the rules laid down by the craft guilds. This made the mayor and aldermen determined to curb vagrancy, crime and the black economy and to keep immigrants in check.[3]

Alongside street patrols, security crackdowns had become as much a part of civic life in recent years as clearing animal dung from the streets and queuing for bread at the baker's shop. Tension and fear were everywhere. The threat level had first been raised in 1570, after Pope Pius V published a decree excommunicating Elizabeth and declaring her to be deposed on the grounds that she was a heretic, a schismatic and a tyrant, the bastard offspring of Henry VIII's unlawful second marriage. Nailed to the front door of the bishop of London's Thames-side palace at Fulham just a few weeks after a dangerous insurrection in the north of England was brutally crushed, the decree made her a legitimate target for any Catholic assassin. Before the pope proclaimed his decree, Catholics who refused to conform to the queen's Protestant Religious Settlement had been largely left alone. Parliament had imposed fines of a shilling a week to the use of the poor on anyone refusing to attend their local parish church, but enforcement was patchy. All this changed after the papal decree, when the assumption was increasingly that Catholics were traitors if they failed to come to church and instead harboured Catholic priests in their houses or frequented illicit Masses.

The Northern Rising had shown just how fragile the fledgling Protestant state really was. Carrying the Cross and the banners of the Five Wounds of Christ, the six thousand or so rebels had set out from Durham Cathedral and marched through North Yorkshire to Wetherby and Selby, besieging Barnard Castle in Teesdale and celebrating the Mass wherever they went. They saw themselves as defenders of the commonwealth, claiming that they wanted to save Elizabeth from a 'lawless faction of Machiavellians'. By this, they meant that they aimed to purge Burghley – they called him 'King Cecil' – and his Protestant friends from the Privy Council and Parliament. They would replace them with good Catholic noblemen loyal to the queen.[4]

Aghast at the scale of this dissent, Elizabeth had been ruthless in her response. The revolt itself was brought under control without significant bloodshed, but the reprisals were vicious. Mistrustful of her military leaders lest they show undue mercy, she turned to someone closely bound to her by family ties. Her aunt Mary Boleyn had married William Carey, and it was their son Henry, Elizabeth's first cousin – she called him 'My Harry' and had raised him to the peerage as Lord Hunsdon within days of her accession – whom she chose.[5] Hunsdon sent six hundred or more rebels to the gallows, leaving their bodies rotting there 'for terror'. Sixty more, mostly the younger sons of wealthy gentry families, escaped over the frontier into Scotland before fleeing abroad, mainly to Paris or Rome. There they joined eight hundred or so English Catholic exiles and Jesuits, who at once began to scheme and plot how best to put the pope's decree into effect.

The earliest and most threatening of these plots, the memory of which was still fresh in Sheriff Spencer's mind as he patrolled London's streets in 1584, was to make the career of the man who would soon become Burghley's most driven and effective colleague in the Privy Council. Francis Walsingham, tall, thin, sallow-cheeked, with brown hair and moustache and a 'lean and hungry look', like Cassius in William Shakespeare's *Julius Caesar*, was about forty years old, twelve years younger than Burghley. An ardent Protestant converted, like Burghley, to the new faith as a student at Cambridge, Walsingham was appointed to be Elizabeth's resident ambassador to France in 1570. Two years earlier, in his first letter to Burghley, he had set out his political creed, warning the chief minister of 'the malice of this present time', before urging that 'there is less danger in fearing too much than too little and . . . there is nothing more dangerous than security,' by which of course he meant 'the *lack* of security'.[6]

In 1570, Walsingham suspected a slippery Florentine banker, Roberto Ridolfi, of conspiring to enforce the pope's decree with the Catholic exiles and with the notoriously hawkish Don Guerau de Spes, Guzmán de Silva's replacement as the Spanish ambassador in London. The conspiracy had many twists and turns, but its inspiration was an offer first made on the eve of the Northern Rising by the highest-ranking English nobleman, Thomas Howard, Duke of Norfolk, to marry the Catholic Mary Queen of Scots. Once the marriage had taken place, an invading Spanish army would kill Elizabeth and make Norfolk king and Mary queen of the whole of the British Isles.[7]

Ridolfi's trump card was that Mary was conveniently close at hand. The daughter of James V of Scotland and his second wife, Mary of Guise, she was the granddaughter of Henry VIII's elder sister, Margaret, and thus Elizabeth's first cousin once removed. Known for her charisma and for her talent for making anyone she spoke to believe they were the only person in the world that mattered to her, she had the virtue of being incontestably legitimate, whereas Elizabeth's parents' marriage when she had been conceived was clandestine and bigamous, if indeed they were married at all.[8] Mary had made a highly promising start when she returned from

Paris to Edinburgh in August 1561 as an eighteen-year-old widow, after the death of her first husband, Francis II of France. But her rule disintegrated in 1567 after her second husband, Henry, Lord Darnley, fell foul of her nobles and was assassinated in a gunpowder plot. In desperation, Mary took James Hepburn, Earl of Bothwell, as her protector. He exacted marriage as the price, and it turned out just as catastrophically. Taken prisoner and forced to abdicate or be tied up in a sack and drowned, Mary fled the following year across the Solway Firth to seek asylum in England.[9]

Since then, Mary had been a queen in exile, an unwelcome guest living as a cuckoo in Elizabeth's nest. Her household was supported largely at the English queen's expense, under conditions of stringent security. Held mainly at Chatsworth in Derbyshire and Sheffield in Yorkshire, well away from London or the coast, Mary was in the custody of the Earl of Shrewsbury, one of the few nobles apart from Hunsdon whom Elizabeth trusted unreservedly. Armed guards were always close at hand, most especially when Mary was allowed to ride out with a handful of her attendants for exercise. And yet, for all that, both Norfolk and Ridolfi had been able to convey messages to her secretly.[10]

There was no sterner, more assiduous defender of his political inheritance and the Catholic faith than Philip II, but after briefly flirting with Ridolfi he shied away from seriously backing the plot. The Spanish king had spent just over sixteen months living at Whitehall Palace and Hampton Court when he was married to Mary Tudor. He had personally inspected stocks of artillery and weapons during a visit to the Tower of London, and had been given regular briefings on the state of the kingdom's finances and defences as recently as 1557. He knew only too well how large a force of men and ships would be required to bring to fruition such a grandiose invasion plan as Ridolfi's.[11]

From the vantage point of Paris throughout the long, hot summer of 1571, Walsingham helped Burghley to uncover the full extent of the Ridolfi Plot, rendering it dead in the water. Confronted by a web of conspiracy that involved some of the country's leading Catholic noblemen, Elizabeth took her opportunity to revive her father's draconian, much-criticized treason laws, making it a capital offence merely to 'imagine', let alone 'invent, devise or intend' her over-throw, even by words alone. Pressed hard by Burghley, she then brought the Duke of Norfolk, England's premier peer, to trial for his part in the conspiracy, and he was found guilty of high treason.[12]

In a frenzy over the Ridolfi Plot, Parliament met in May 1572 to debate Elizabeth's 'safety'. When Norfolk was convicted and sen-tenced to death, Elizabeth wavered over his execution, on the grounds of his noble status, whereas Burghley and Walsingham wanted Mary as well as Norfolk dead. Burghley's overriding aim was to push through a bill of attainder by which Mary would be declared a traitor and executed by Act of Parliament, thus avoiding the trouble of a trial or of marshalling proof of her guilt. To advance his plan, he organized an underhand campaign to denounce her in print as a Catholic murderess and sorceress. For him, the only 'good' Mary was a dead one. Elizabeth's mistake, he privately told Walsingham, was her inveterate willingness to give her cousin the benefit of the doubt.[13]

But could Mary, an anointed queen and a foreigner (since Scotland was still an independent country) commit treason in England? Eliza-beth did not yet think so. Regicide was anathema to her. And so, to appease the terrified Protestants in the House of Commons, she sac-rificed Norfolk, yielding to Burghley's pleas that she execute him. It was still not enough. Burghley wrote a letter in his own hand com-plaining shrilly to Walsingham of how the 'highest person' in the realm (meaning Elizabeth) had failed to slay the serpent Mary, too, and so had brought shame on her councillors. He lambasted Eliza-beth towards the end of this letter for her 'errors' and 'follies' in dealing with Mary, 'and yet they must be suffered to be endured for saving of the honour of the highest'.[14]

Elizabeth was curiously ambivalent about her Catholic cousin, whom she called 'sister' and whom in 1562 she had excitedly planned to meet.[15] Where the succession was concerned, she kept religion and politics apart. She had first suggested as much in 1561, when she had confided to William Maitland of Lethington, Mary's principal secretary, that if she should die, then Mary would have a near-invin-cible claim as the rightful heir: 'I for my part know none better nor that myself would prefer to her or, to be plain with you, that case occurring that might debar her from it.'[16] Blood mattered more to Elizabeth than particular forms of worship.

Threateningly from Burghley's viewpoint, many middle-of-the-road Protestants, not just Catholics – there, he maintained, was the greatest danger – believed that Mary could offer them dynastic security, for unlike Elizabeth, she had produced a male heir, the young Prince James. Ever since she had married Darnley in 1565 and become pregnant, Burghley had been haunted by this fear, freely admitting to himself late at night in memo after memo that an alarmingly high number of Elizabeth's subjects favoured Mary despite her Catholic faith. The 'people of England', he had declared then, would begin to 'favour all devices and practices that should tend to the advancement of the Queen of Scots'. They would be 'alienated in their minds from their natural duties' to Elizabeth, giving Mary the opportunity to stage a *coup d'état* and re-establish Catholicism.[17]

Burghley and Walsingham were ideological Protestants possessed of an apocalyptic, almost messianic vision of Protestant England's role in history. Fearful of a hydra of conspiracy centred around King Philip, the pope, Mary, the Jesuits and the Catholic exiles in Paris, they were adamant that the succession should pass only to a Protestant, and if this meant proscribing or disqualifying Catholics by Act of Parliament, then so be it.

But if her leading councillors put Protestantism ahead of hereditary right, Elizabeth took the opposite approach. When, as it seemed, the queen's life – and thus England's security as a Protestant state – hung by a thread, as Sheriff Spencer knew it did in 1584, this really mattered. Both Burghley and Walsingham had lived through the dark days of Mary Tudor's reign, when Burghley had been forced to conform to what he regarded as popish idolatry and Walsingham had fled into exile. Rather than risk a martyr's death, Elizabeth had also conformed, but while Burghley and Walsingham were determined never to see a Catholic on the throne again, Elizabeth was unshaken in her belief in the primacy of dynasty over religion.[18]

By 1584, when Spencer set out with his constables on his last official tour of London's busy streets, a still more dangerous point of contention than Mary Stuart divided England and Spain. In the Netherlands, the Calvinists had been in open rebellion against their Spanish over-lords since the late 1560s. Spanish power in these rich trading territories was relatively new. The region had been largely self-governing even after 1516, the year that Philip's father, Charles, had left Brussels to assume the throne of a united Spain. The Netherlands, where Charles was born, had been very dear to his heart, but when he abdicated in favour of his son in 1555, the relationship between Spain and the Netherlands changed dramatically. Most of the seventeen provinces were Dutch-speaking, chiefly those in the north. French (or Walloon) was spoken only in the south. But all seventeen were handed over to Philip, who promptly absorbed them into the wider Spanish empire, to be ruled through a regent.

The commercial bonds linking England and the Netherlands had always been strong, and they strengthened further after Elizabeth's Religious Settlement, when Antwerp became the only European money market where she could readily borrow money. When the Dutch Calvinists burst into open revolt in 1566, Burghley and Walsingham closely monitored events across the North Sea. They watched with growing apprehension as Philip made the most far-reaching choices of his life. Coolly and deliberately, he decided to unleash the Catholic Inquisition against the Calvinist heretics, then sent his finest general, Fernando Álvarez de Toledo, Duke of Alba, over the Alps at the head of a newly recruited Spanish Army of Flanders,* with orders to fuse the seventeen provinces into a unitary state with Brussels as its capital.[19]

Elizabeth was hardly a natural ally of the Dutch rebels, whom she infuriated with lectures on their duties of obedience to lawful princes and on the dangers of insurgent republicanism. But she was seriously alarmed: if Philip imposed his will on the Netherlands by force, then a victorious Spanish army, the finest and best equipped in Europe,

---

* The name 'Army of Flanders' is something of a misnomer. These troops were recruited from Spain, Italy, Burgundy, Germany and the southern, Walloon-speaking areas of the Netherlands, then welded into an elite fighting force. Some Catholics from Scotland and Ireland even joined as volunteers. To reduce friction, these troops were kept as separate administrative units: only Spaniards could serve in or command Spanish contingents, and so on. See G. Parker, *The Army of Flanders and the Spanish Road, 1567–1659* (Cambridge, 1972), pp. 25–35.

would be just a short sea voyage away from London. She had met Philip face to face when he was married to her half-sister, Mary Tudor, and had personal experience of his methods. While he had helped to save her when Mary accused her of treason, he had treated her as no more than a diplomatic pawn, a dynastic asset to be exploited at will in the interests of Spain.[20] He had ridden roughshod over English interests by forcing his wife into an unpopular war against France, losing Calais, the country's bridgehead into Europe and last continental possession. Shortly before or just after Elizabeth had been crowned queen, he had floated the idea of marrying her, but he then ditched her without even waiting for her reply, choosing Elizabeth of Valois, a French princess, as his bride.[21]

For almost ten years, Elizabeth had watched helplessly as contingents of brave English volunteers had died fighting in the Netherlands in support of their fellow Protestants. And yet, when an embassy from the States of Holland and Zeeland arrived at Hampton Court in January 1576 with an offer to make her their sovereign, she declined. In these years, her aims were to reconcile the rebellious provinces to Philip's obedience, to persuade him to restore their ancient liberties and to keep the Netherlands free from an occupying foreign army – no more and no less. She felt no obligation to assist the Dutch simply because they were Protestants.[22]

Then, in November, came a watershed moment, when mutinous Spanish troops brought fire and slaughter to the economic and cultural hub of Antwerp. Like the infamous St Bartholomew's Day Massacre, when thousands of Protestants were murdered in Paris and nearly six hundred houses looted, the sack of Antwerp stirred Elizabeth into action. Keen to work through a third party in her search for a broad settlement, she turned to Francis, Duke of Anjou. The brother and heir of King Henry III of France, Anjou was a moderate Catholic and so largely acceptable to Spain and the pope.[23] In shaping this policy, Elizabeth bypassed Burghley and Walsingham, both of whom were frantically lobbying her, if in slightly different ways and at different speeds, to offer the Dutch immediate financial and military aid.[24]

Elizabeth sent Walsingham to Antwerp in June 1578 as a special envoy to help cobble together a role for the Duke as a 'Protector' of the Netherlands. Walsingham did his best, but he never believed it could work. Narcissistic and irresponsible, Anjou was on an ego trip, intent more on winning a principality for himself than on coming up with a compromise that might pave the way to peace. Elizabeth had more than once to stop him from embarking on a military annexation of the Netherlands.[25]

By 1579, the Dutch revolt had become too extreme for the southern provinces, which made peace with Spain. It was at this perilous moment that Elizabeth began courting Anjou as a potential husband. She blew hot and cold but took her suit up seemingly in earnest a year later, when King Philip claimed the throne of Portugal.[26] If Philip could now unify the crowns and resources of the Atlantic empires of Spain and Portugal, it would not be long before he could be expected to reconquer the Netherlands and perhaps, after that, invade England.

When she met Anjou in the flesh for the first time in 1579, Elizabeth found him to be physically repulsive. His diminutive height and badly scarred face, caused by a severe attack of smallpox, were scarcely reprieved in her eyes by his bandy legs and deep, gravelly voice. The twenty-one-year age gap between them was another major embarrassment. But she persisted, concealing her true emotions. Nicknaming him her 'Frog' – curiously, he never seemed to mind – she sought to mould him into her ally, wearing a golden flower brooch 'with a frog thereon' and holding out to him the offer of an English crown as bait to entice him into doing exactly what she wanted.[27]

Under the illusion that he would shortly be married, Anjou made a second visit to London in the winter of 1581–2, and Elizabeth played to perfection the part of a woman in love. Walking with him and the French ambassador, Michel de Castelnau, Sieur de la Mauvissière, in her privy gallery at Whitehall Palace, she suddenly turned to the Duke and kissed him on the mouth. She even drew a ring from her finger and gave it to him 'as a pledge'.[28] Afterwards, she announced her betrothal, saying, 'It's now a fact. I have a husband. As to the rest of you, look after yourselves if you will.' Or so it was gleefully reported in Paris.[29]

But with her privy councillors split over the proposed match, she quickly abandoned it. Pressure came not least from her most trusted women – those who shared her Bedchamber – for she suffered from insomnia and was frightened of the dark. Every night, she insisted that at least one of these women sleep close by her on a pallet bed (i.e. a straw bed, or mattress). Believing that she was serious about Anjou, they had wept and wailed, 'and did so terrify and vex her mind that she spent the night in doubts and cares without sleep'. A day or so later, she sent for Anjou and told him the wedding, for the moment, at least, was off.[30]

When the Portuguese Cortes next assembled, in April 1581, Philip took an oath to observe all the laws and customs of the realm and was recognized as the lawful king of Portugal. And with the budget for the Army of Flanders doubled, thanks to the massively increased revenues of the combined Portuguese and Spanish treasure fleets, Philip's new supremo in the Netherlands, his nephew Alexander Farnese, Duke of Parma, rapidly recovered lost ground.[31] Within weeks, towns in Flanders and Brabant were convulsed in flames and a fresh wave of Protestant refugees flooded into London. Feeling that she had no other option, Elizabeth bribed Anjou with £30,000 (£30 million in modern values) to accept the titular sovereignty of the Dutch provinces.[32] But the fickle, power-hungry Duke lusted for more than an empty title. In January 1583, he attempted to seize Antwerp in a military *coup d'état* that failed disastrously, forcing him into a humiliating retreat to France. Indignant at his ineptitude, Elizabeth bluntly rounded on him, accusing him of being feckless and squandering her money.[33]

With the pan-European crisis fast coming to a head, Mary Queen of Scots on English soil and the Catholic exiles in Paris scheming frantically with the Jesuits and Mary's agents to enforce the papal decree deposing Elizabeth, the Privy Council sounded the alarm. The threat level soared in October 1583, when a young Warwickshire Catholic, John Somerville – his father-in-law, Edward Arden, was Shakespeare's kinsman – left his home with the declared intention of killing Elizabeth with a pistol while she was out riding. He made no attempt to conceal his plans and was arrested in Oxfordshire. Tried for high treason at London's Guildhall, he and three alleged 'accomplices' (one of whom was his mother-in-law) were found guilty by a jury of horrified citizens in a packed courtroom. Shortly afterwards, the would-be assassin hanged himself in his cell in Newgate Prison.[34]

Less than a month after Somerville's arrest, Walsingham – by now, he had some twenty spies and agents on his payroll – pounced on Francis Throckmorton, nephew of the same Nicholas who had warned Elizabeth to 'beware of womanish levity'. Like so many Elizabethan families, the Throckmortons were bitterly divided by religion. Nicholas, who died of pneumonia in 1571 – a rumour that he suffered a seizure after eating a poisoned salad is almost certainly false – was a staunch Protestant, tried for treason during Mary Tudor's reign and acquitted by a London jury. But his nephew, young and headstrong, was so fervidly Catholic he had volunteered his services as a courier to the French and Spanish ambassadors in London. A search of his papers, seized at his house by Paul's Wharf on the Thames, enabled Walsingham to uncover a menacing conspiracy. Throckmorton was embroiled in a plot first devised in Rome by a Scottish Jesuit, Walter Crichton, and now masterminded from Paris by Henry, Duke of Guise, a first cousin of Mary Queen of Scots. Guise was the leader of the ultra-Catholic faction in the Wars of Religion in France and the richest, most powerful man in the country. He was the one person in Europe, besides King Philip, who had the will, the money, the ships and the men to pull off an invasion of England. After securing large sums from Parisian merchants to help raise troops, Guise had ordered his officers to make themselves ready and told his mother that he hoped 'there would be ere long, *beau jeu* in England'.[35]

Walsingham would become haunted by the knowledge that he had stumbled across the plot purely by accident. Only because he had been warned by a spy that Francis Throckmorton was making regular visits to the French embassy was the young Catholic put under surveillance.[36]

Throckmorton was tortured on the rack. He bravely kept silent at first, but eventually the pain was unbearable and he babbled almost everything he knew. What he revealed was to cause a decisive rupture in Elizabeth's relations with Spain. Like Ridolfi, the Duke of Guise had planned to put Mary Stuart on the throne when the heretic bastard

Elizabeth was deposed and killed. To help engineer this, Throckmorton had provided Don Bernardino de Mendoza, the Spanish ambassador in London since 1578, with maps marked with suitable landing sites on the south coast of England to forward to Guise, along with a list of the names of leading Catholic noblemen and gentlemen who would willingly join the plot.[37]

For Burghley and Walsingham, this was the stuff of nightmares, and they acted swiftly. On 19 January 1584, Walsingham's brother-in-law Robert Beale summoned Mendoza to a meeting at which Walsingham addressed the envoy in fluent Italian. He accused him of colluding with traitors and with Mary Queen of Scots, and gave him fifteen days to pack his bags and leave the country.[38]

Worse was to follow. In early June, a month before Throckmorton was dragged to the gallows, Elizabeth received ominous news from her ambassador in Paris: the Duke of Anjou had died unexpectedly at Château-Thierry, fifty miles north-east of Paris. He was just twenty-nine and was thought to have died of advanced syphilis.[39] Elizabeth wept copious tears and went into official mourning for six months. When, early in September, Castelnau, not only the French ambassador in London but also an enemy of the Duke of Guise, was invited to watch her hunt in the park from a newly built terrace high up on the walls at Windsor Castle in Berkshire, she greeted him wearing a black dress and a long, diaphanous veil hanging down as low as the hem of her skirt, as if she were Anjou's widow.[40]

Anjou's death would have terrifying repercussions, which Elizabeth and Castelnau discussed at Windsor. With all three of Henry III's brothers now dead, France found itself faced by the challenge of a king of ambiguous sexuality with no male children, whose succession was disputed between his second cousin, Henry of Navarre, and Navarre's uncle, Cardinal Charles of Bourbon, archbishop of Rouen. Most jurists were clear that the shrewd, athletic, plain-speaking, thirty-year-old Henry of Navarre had a much better claim to the throne than the sixty-year-old cardinal. But he was a Huguenot, despised by the Guises. The deadlock presented the Duke of Guise with a golden opportunity to make a bid for dynastic pre-eminence. Castelnau, a moderate, fully agreed with Elizabeth that this was a threat which somehow would have to be neutralized.[41]

On 6 July, the stakes were doubled again. A courier arrived in London with the appalling news that, five days earlier, a young cabinet-maker's apprentice, Balthasar Gérard, had assassinated William of Orange, the leader of the Dutch Calvinists, in the hallway of his house at Delft. Tempted by the huge bounty of 25,000 écus (worth around £8 million today) which King Philip had placed on William's head, Gérard had packed a heavy pistol with three bullets and a large quantity of gunpowder. One bullet lodged in the fifty-one-year-old William's abdomen as he turned to climb the stairs to his private chambers; the others tore diagonally through his lungs, afterwards smashing into the staircase wall and spattering blood and plaster everywhere. William died within minutes.[42]

His assassination left the Dutch rebels leaderless. And with the Duke of Parma preparing to lay siege to Brussels and Antwerp before marching north, it seemed it was only a matter of time before the last rebel towns of the Netherlands would fall to him like ninepins. The Duke of Guise was quick to see the possibilities. Before the year was out, he temporarily shelved his plan to invade England in favour of a secret treaty with Philip, who undertook to pay him the astronomical sum of 50,000 French crowns a month (£16 million in modern values) to form a Catholic League to exterminate the Huguenots and make France uniformly Catholic again. Were he to succeed, Elizabeth's position would be dire: Protestant England would be vulnerable to a Catholic invasion jointly led by the pope, France and Spain.

So it was that when, just twelve weeks after William of Orange's murder, Sheriff Spencer strolled at a leisurely pace along Aldgate High Street on the eastern perimeter of the City of London with his constables, he knew he had to be vigilant. At a moment when a single assassin's bullet could have had catastrophic consequences, the Privy Council had ordered close searches for spies and Jesuits, coupled with random raids on the houses of known Catholics and 'Mass-mongers' (a term of abuse applied to undercover Catholic priests by Protestants). The city watches were put on maximum alert. More than a hundred known Catholics, both priests and laymen, were rounded up, and those who were considered the most dangerous were interned at Wisbech Castle in the depths of the Cambridgeshire Fens. Others were forcibly deported, loaded on to ships at Tower Wharf, their wrists bound together with ropes, and 'banished [from] this realm for ever by virtue of a commission from Her Majesty'.[43]

As Spencer turned a corner, he encountered a huddle of dubious-looking foreigners glowering as a gang of civic labourers, sent out earlier with bricks and shovels by the mayor, sealed up an illegal alleyway leading to an immigrant enclave just inside the city walls. In the midst of this group he singled out two men who turned out to be brothers, 'a little black man' in leather boots and 'a tall black man'. Dark-haired and swarthy rather than actually black-skinned, they were second-generation *converso* Jews from Venice, born to parents who had hurriedly sought Christian baptism to escape the Catholic Inquisition.[44]

Hearing the loiterers muttering suspiciously to one another in a foreign tongue, Spencer was instantly on his guard. He had been taught to believe that Portuguese or Italian Jews could be shady characters who led a double life. Like Walsingham, he thought many of them were spies or agents of the hated Jesuits. Could they even be assassins?

Spencer questioned the two men testily and ordered them to go about their lawful business. The Venetians refused, saying, 'This is the Queen's ground and we will stand here.' When cautioned by the constables that, if he refused to move on, he would be sent to ward (i.e. taken into custody), the man in boots sneeringly said, 'Send us to ward? Thou wert as good kiss our arse.'[45]

A proud, truculent pillar of the establishment who would one day fall foul of the law for beating his daughter, Spencer was not to be trifled with.[46] He knew that he had more than sufficient reason to arrest these insolent foreigners. And he was further provoked by what he took to be an empty threat from the taller of the two brothers. 'Sheriff Spencer,' said this man tauntingly, 'we have as good friends in the Court as thou hast and better too.'

Spencer, who was nicknamed 'the Hardhead', ordered his constables to seize the men, arresting their younger brother, too, for good measure. They resisted violently, striking the constables with their fists and lashing out at Spencer. At this point, the lawyer William Fleetwood, the city's chief law officer, known as 'the Recorder', arrived to take charge, ordering the Venetians to Newgate Prison. Squaring up to him, the man in boots demanded scornfully, 'Who are you?' When told that he was Master Recorder, the man retorted, 'You were as good eat the sole of my boot as send us to Newgate.'

As they were frogmarched to the nearest prison, at the Poultry Counter beside the Stocks Market, where fish and meat were sold, the Venetians persisted in their defiance. When the warder entered their names into the ledger at the gatehouse before leading them to their cells, they smudged the wet ink with their fingers, saying, 'Master Recorder sent us to Newgate, and not to the Counter, and to Newgate we will go.'[47]

A week later, Spencer would have the shock of his life. A royal messenger knocked at the door of his fine mansion, Crosby Place in Bishopsgate, bringing a letter from Walsingham. Now Elizabeth's principal secretary in succession to Burghley, who as the queen's chief minister was learning to delegate a little in order to focus more intensively on crisis management, Walsingham severely rebuked Spencer for apprehending the Venetians. For it turned out that Spencer had arrested Arthur, Edward and Jeronimo Bassani, the stars of the queen's sackbut and wind consort, and she wanted them back.[48]

Elizabeth was visiting Oatlands, a pleasure palace near Weybridge in Surrey built by her father for his third wife, Jane Seymour, when she discovered that her favourite musicians were missing.[49] This was not long after Castelnau's visit to Windsor, and she was in the later stages of her summer progress. In a fit of pique, she ordered Walsingham to investigate. Her impatience when thwarted on even petty matters was well known: one night in April 1572, when she was unable to sleep, she had ordered one of the grooms of the Privy Chamber to ride 'with all speed' through the night from Greenwich to Whitehall, seven miles in each direction, simply to fetch a white satin bolster he had forgotten.[50]

In a grovelling reply, Spencer sought to justify himself, explaining that he had not known the Venetians' true identity until after they were imprisoned. Galvanized into action by the angry queen, the Privy Council freed and pardoned the musicians and summoned Spencer and Recorder Fleetwood to appear at Whitehall on 8 October with their underlings to account for the arrests.[51]

Just as the Bassani brothers had predicted, the tables were turned. The Privy Council sent the luckless constables to the Marshalsea, a prison in Southwark on the south bank of the Thames. Spencer would plead in vain with Walsingham that 'as I would in no respect nor in any wise by any means willingly do anything that might displease Her Majesty or Your Honour, so likewise in the service of Her Majesty and to the good acceptation of Your Honour I will gladly and willingly spend both my life and my goods.'[52] Forced by the Privy Council to make an abject apology, Spencer and Fleetwood were then made to pay the not insubstantial bills for food and wine which the Bassani brothers had run up in prison, and afterwards the civic authorities were sued, apparently successfully, by the landlord of the Aldgate site, Lord Thomas Howard, for the losses that their workmen had caused him through bricking up the contested alleyway.[53] This, too, was no coincidence. Just a few weeks before, Elizabeth had stood as godmother to Howard's son and had sent the child's nurse a purse of silver.[54]

Given the rupture with Spain and the intense fear and surveillance in the metropolis by 1584, it was hardly surprising that Spencer should have arrested the swarthy Bassani brothers for their suspicious behaviour. He had done so believing that he was following orders from above. Spencer may have had a noxious temper, but so, at times, it seemed, did the queen. What the luckless sheriff found truly shocking was Elizabeth's subversive disregard for her own security, and most of all her lack of consideration for his dignity as an elected city official. It was a side of her he had never imagined could exist. Hauled before the Privy Council to account for his actions, he discovered in a visceral way that England was ruled by a queen whose mind and purposes even those closest to her would find difficult to read.

2. Crisis and Betrayal

William of Orange's assassination presented Elizabeth with the starkest, most dangerous choice of her life, one which was to provoke a clash between her feelings as a woman and her instincts as a queen. The question was clear: should she intervene on the side of the Dutch Calvinists in their struggle with their Spanish overlord, King Philip, thereby provoking war, or should she leave the rebels to their fate? If she failed to intervene, the Duke of Parma's army would triumphantly reconquer the whole of the Netherlands. Then Philip would have the best-equipped forces in Europe standing idle within easy striking range of the British Isles and safe harbours for his fleets should he wish to take control of the English Channel.

After Orange's murder, the beleaguered Dutch had been desperate enough to invite King Henry III of France to be their new sovereign. Walsingham, who for many years had been among the keenest to assist the Dutch rebels on both religious and military grounds, received a full report of their offer from his agent in Delft in early October 1584.[1] Although a Catholic, Henry – unlike the Duke of Guise – was no friend to Philip, and at first it was believed that he might accept the sovereignty. At a Privy Council meeting on 10 October, it was decided to send 'some wise person' to Holland to see if Elizabeth could in some way become a co-signatory, or guarantor, of a Franco-Dutch entente. This was her preferred position. If, however, the French king refused to protect the Dutch States 'from Spanish tyranny', she had already decided that she would not make a counter-offer to be their sovereign but would do what she could to rescue them. 'Her Majesty', wrote Burghley, summarizing the Council's position in a series of confidential memos, 'would strain herself as far forth as with preservation of her own estate she might, to succour them at this time.' She would do this knowing full well that it would mean war with Spain.[2]

Shortly after the Council meeting, Elizabeth came down with a severe gastric disorder, partly caused by stress and partly by her choice of breakfast, 'a confection of barley, sodden with sugar and water, and made exceeding thick with bread'.[3] When she recovered, she sent William Davison, Walsingham's ablest assistant and a passionate supporter of the Dutch rebels, to Holland to gather news. And with the Duke of Guise poised to launch a war of succession in France, she would need highly placed sources there, too. She therefore sent Henry Stanley, Earl of Derby, a trusted kinsman by marriage and a man with astonishingly elegant handwriting – to boost his credentials, she would shortly make him a privy councillor – to ingratiate himself in Paris on the ingenious pretext that he was to invest King Henry with the Order of the Garter. In this way, Elizabeth would quickly discover how the French meant to respond to the Dutch offer.

On Friday, 5 March 1585, a muddy horseman riding post-haste from Paris clattered over the cobblestones into the courtyard at Greenwich Palace. His name was Charles Merbury and he was Derby's courier, bringing the news that Henry had declined the Dutch offer of sovereignty.[4] Burghley immediately summoned a second Council meeting.[5] Eleven councillors assembled first thing on Monday morning at Cecil House on the Strand, with its thick brick walls, turrets reaching up towards the sky, banqueting house, and pleasure gardens with exotic plants leading on to the open fields of Covent Garden.

By then, the mood in the capital was close to fever pitch. The previous Tuesday, Dr William Parry, a Welshman and one of Burghley's former spies, who had been suborned by papal agents in Venice and Rome and turned traitor, had been gruesomely hanged in Westminster Palace Yard. A self-indulgent social climber, Parry had converted to Catholicism and received communion at the Jesuit College in Paris to seal a vow to assassinate Elizabeth. Robert Dudley, Earl of Leicester, watched him die from the vantage point of a wooden stand built specially for the occasion. Cut down from the gallows on the queen's orders the moment the ladder was kicked away after just one swing of the rope, Parry had his heart and bowels ripped from his body with a meat cleaver by the executioner while he was still fully conscious.* As the blade plunged deep into his body, he gave what a stunned spectator described as 'a great groan'. Finally, the hangman severed head and limbs from the corpse, to be impaled on London Bridge and above the gates of the city as a warning to others of the terrible price of treason.[6]

In the Netherlands, meanwhile, the Duke of Parma's army was crushing the Calvinists so mercilessly and effectively that it seemed as if the Dutch revolt would soon be confined to little more than the three northernmost provinces, Holland, Zeeland and Utrecht. With Antwerp predicted to fall at any moment, the Privy Council strongly urged the queen at its Monday meeting to intervene to save the Dutch. Burghley delivered their advice to her in writing, and the very next day she sent Edward Burnham, another of Walsingham's trusted assistants, to inform the Dutch States that, 'seeing it [is] a matter of so great peril in case the King of Spain should come to the possession of those countries . . . she is fully resolved to take the protection of them.'[7] (Mistaken claims by previous biographers, relying on Camden's *Annales*, that Elizabeth had to bludgeon Burghley into compliance can be explained by confusion over the authorship of certain crucial memoranda.)[8]

Negotiations over the precise terms of the Anglo-Dutch treaty were still pending when Burghley gave orders that the fortifications at the key ports of Dover and Portsmouth should be reinforced and stocks of artillery made ready at the Tower. Fierce storms delayed the Channel crossing of the Dutch representatives sent to finalize the terms of the treaty: they landed at Margate on the Kent coast only on 24 June. They signed the main points of agreement, or 'heads', on 10 August at Nonsuch Palace in Surrey, another of Henry VIII's pleasure palaces, whose gardens and Italian-style stucco decorations had been modelled on Fontainebleau ('Nonsuch' meant 'second to none'). Elizabeth, it was agreed, would send 'a nobleman of rank and reputation' to assist the Dutch in their fight against Philip, at the head of a large and well-equipped expeditionary force.[9] No time was to be lost. The Spaniards were mobilizing for war. They had already placed

---

* Ordinarily, felons and traitors were allowed to lapse into unconsciousness before disembowelling began.

an embargo on English and Dutch shipping at anchor in Iberian ports, a worrying fact Walsingham learned from the captain of the London merchant vessel *Primrose*, which had made a plucky escape from Bilbao when Philip's agents had attempted to seize it.[10]

On both sides of the North Sea, the 'nobleman of rank and reputation' most widely canvassed for the command of the English expeditionary force was the Earl of Leicester. Acclaimed as 'that valiant and mild leader', Leicester had been an unrivalled champion of the Protestant cause in northern Europe for almost twenty years. Many now hoped that he would lead the Dutch out of captivity, just as Moses had led the children of Israel out of slavery in Egypt.[11] Leicester himself was desperate to secure the posting. The biggest obstacle in his path stemmed from the fact that he was Elizabeth's favourite, the only man she ever truly loved. He was not alone in fearing she would not be able to bring herself to let him leave her side to take on so risky a venture.

Lithe, athletic and relatively tall, with piercing bluish-grey eyes, soft, flowing auburn hair and a moustache heavily flecked with silver-grey, Leicester had the flashy good looks Elizabeth found irresistible in a man. Their relationship went back almost forty years, to the time when he was plain Robert Dudley and she was a young girl living in Hertfordshire in the charge of a governess.[12] When she was nine and Robert a year or so older, her father, a distant presence in her life but someone whom she always revered as a God-appointed monarch and fount of true wisdom, had made her household a satellite of her half-brother Edward's.[13] Sir William Sidney, whose teenage son, Henry, was one of the young prince's constant companions and shared in his education, was in overall charge. The Sidneys and Dudleys were always close: Elizabeth first met the young Robert Dudley when he came to visit as a boy. In 1551, Henry Sidney would marry Robert's sister Mary, a woman who very likely introduced Elizabeth to the trashy Italian novellas she enjoyed reading.[14] It was Mary Sidney who nursed the queen through a near-fatal attack of smallpox, at a harrowing cost to herself: so badly pocked was her face when she, too, caught the disease, it ruined her life. Elizabeth, whose face was only lightly marked, shabbily rejected her friend, distancing herself from her both emotionally and physically in her eagerness to deny her own minor scarring, which she concealed with the careful use of ointments.[15]

By July 1553, when the fifteen-year-old Edward had died in Henry Sidney's arms, Elizabeth had named the dashing twenty-one-year-old Robert to the post of Keeper of Somerset Place, her London mansion.[16] Within a month of her gaining the throne, King Philip's roving ambassador, the Count of Feria, had singled him out as second only to Burghley in her inner circle.[17] It was Elizabeth's habit to give pet nicknames to her closest intimates. She addressed Burghley as 'Sir Spirit' and Walsingham as 'Moor' but Robert, more affectionately, as 'Rob' or 'Sweet Robin' and as her 'Eyes'.

Elizabeth did so little to conceal her feelings for Robert Dudley that in 1560 Nicholas Throckmorton, then in France, bewailed to Burghley the scandalous – Robert was a married man – gossip circulating about the couple. Many felt Elizabeth had allowed him to presume too much, even to hope that she might one day consent to marry him. Feria, who let no opportunity slip to score points off the Protestant queen, was one of the chief sources of rumours of their alleged sexual trysts. (Elizabeth took her revenge by keeping Feria's wife standing for over two hours waiting for an audience while heavily pregnant.)[18] And yet, when the queen believed she was about to die from smallpox, she had made a declaration that 'although she loved and had always loved Lord Robert dearly, as God was her witness, nothing improper had ever passed between them.'[19] Few were convinced. What doubly fuelled the scandal were reports that Robert was simply waiting for his wife to die: then he would marry the queen. He had married his wife, Amy Robsart, the daughter of a wealthy Norfolk landowner, in 1550. They had separated around the time of Elizabeth's coronation in 1559, after which Robert visited Amy scarcely once a year, and, when he did go, he was reputedly under the queen's strict orders 'to do nothing with her' and to go dressed all in black.[20]

Shockingly, on the afternoon of Sunday, 8 September 1560, Amy was found mysteriously dead with a broken neck and two deep gashes in her skull after supposedly falling down a stone spiral staircase while lodged at Cumnor Place, near Oxford.[21] Immediately judged guilty of murder in the court of public opinion, Robert strained every nerve to uncover the true cause of his wife's death. Even though the coroner's jury returned a verdict of accidental death, loose ends remained. What troubled many was that the jury's foreman, Sir Richard Smith, had once been Elizabeth's servant; that Dudley knew another juror personally; and that Thomas Blount, his agent, had dined with two of the other jurors before they reached their verdict.

Robert still believed that he could marry Elizabeth – but her survival instinct kicked in. After brooding over the matter for several days, she decided that it was impossible if she hoped to keep her throne. She could not be thought to be an accessory to murder, however innocent Robert might actually be.

That, at least, is how the story traditionally goes. But the evidence of Elizabeth's own words invites scepticism. Although passionately in love with Robert before and shortly after her accession to the throne, three months later she was dropping broad hints of a firm intention to remain single. 'I happily chose this kind of life in which I yet live, which I assure you for mine own part hath hitherto best contented myself,' she told Parliament then.[22] In his *Annales*, Camden claimed she emphatically added, 'I have already joined myself in marriage to a husband, namely, the Kingdom of England,' but he made that bit up.[23] What she actually went on to say was: 'In the end, this shall be for me sufficient, that a marble stone shall declare that a queen, having reigned such a time, lived and died a virgin.'[24]

In 1576, she spoke further on this theme, saying, 'If I were a milk-maid with a pail on my arm . . . I would not forsake that single state to match myself with the greatest monarch of the world.' The most she would concede, under intense pressure from Parliament, was that she would marry if she met the right man and if conditions were suitable at the time – 'I can say no more except the party were present.' On one point she was adamant, or so she made it appear: 'I hope to have children, otherwise I would never marry.'[25] But even this seemingly uncomplicated remark collapses into ambiguity on closer reading.

Psychologically, Elizabeth appears to have had serious doubts about marriage. This is not perhaps altogether surprising, given that her father had her mother beheaded after accusing her of multiple adultery and incest, and in the light of the searing experiences Elizabeth had endured as a teenager while living with Katherine Parr, her stepmother. Within weeks of Henry VIII's death, Parr had married her true love, the seductively handsome, sexually predatory, recklessly ambitious Thomas Seymour. Much admired by women for his 'strong limbs and manly shape', he would visit Elizabeth in her bedchamber early in the mornings before she had risen or was dressed: 'And if she were up, he would bid her good morrow and ask how she did, and strike her upon the back or on the buttocks familiarly, and so go forth through his lodgings . . . And if she were in her bed, he would open the curtains and bid her good morrow, and make as though he would come at her. And she would go further in the bed, so that he could not come at her.' One morning he 'strove to have kissed her in her bed'.[26]

A notorious incident then took place in a garden when Parr and Seymour frolicked with Elizabeth and Seymour 'cut her gown in[to] a hundred pieces, being black cloth'.[27] Soon, rumours of a sex scandal spread far and wide. Elizabeth had survived but, after that, she was a changed woman. This was the moment she was thrust into adulthood. She was especially humiliated by the need to deny a report that she was pregnant by Seymour. Such 'shameful slanders', she insisted, be 'greatly both against my honour and honesty, which above all other things I esteem'.[28]

Over the first twenty or so years of Elizabeth's reign, some thirty suitors had offered themselves to her, among them Philip II, Eric XIV of Sweden and the Archduke Charles of Austria. The earliest negotiations for her hand had begun long before, in 1535, when she was just eighteen months old: her mother and her uncle George Boleyn had sought to betroth her to Charles, Duke of Angoulême, the third son of Francis I of France.[29] Her last suitor had been Francis, Duke of Anjou, the failed 'Protector' of the Netherlands. All of these marriage negotiations collapsed, for a variety of reasons, not least among them the fact that Elizabeth's councillors believed they had a duty to decide themselves who her husband should be.[30]

At the climax of her supposed romance with the Duke of Anjou in the winter of 1581–2, Elizabeth had been play-acting to protect her defensive entente with France. True, she had given Anjou a ring and announced their betrothal, but only after he had demanded that she give a straight yes or no to the marriage proposal and Castelnau had handed her a letter from Henry III declining to support her in a possible confrontation with Spain unless she first married his brother. It was the talk of London that, at the Duke's final departure, she had danced with glee around her Bedchamber 'for very joy of getting rid of him'.[31]

Fifteen years earlier, in 1566, during a rare exchange of confidences, Leicester – the man best in a position to know – had told Jacob de Vulcob, Sieur de Sassy, a visiting French diplomat, that 'she would never marry'. He went on to reveal that, both before and after she was old enough to marry, she had said 'she had never wished to do so.'[32] This was an opinion supported almost forty years later by John Harington, who said 'in mind she hath ever had an aversion . . . to the act of marriage.'[33]

Leicester, admittedly, had been at pains to qualify his remarks. 'If by chance she should change her mind,' he observed, 'he was practically assured that she would choose no one else but him, as she had done him the honour of telling him so quite openly on more than one occasion.'[34] Of course, it suited him to cultivate a belief among foreign diplomats that she might one day marry him. The idea that he could wield a degree of influence that other councillors lacked lay at the heart of his skill as a politician.[35] And there could be no doubt about Elizabeth's romantic feelings for him. She was several times seen kissing him, and when she had invested him as Earl of Leicester in 1564, the French and Scottish ambassadors had caught her tickling his chin.

In 1575, in anticipation of a visit from the queen, Leicester had commissioned and openly displayed at Kenilworth Castle, his cherished country estate five miles from Warwick, a full-length portrait of himself with a matching one of her.[36] To do so was decidedly audacious: it presumed that he was practically a surrogate husband. Elizabeth brushed the ensuing criticism aside by claiming their relationship was like that between brother and sister, but the gossip continued, and over the years disgruntled Catholics repeatedly told

Philip II and the pope that the queen went on her summer progresses only to have Leicester's babies. If, however, he was for all practical purposes the only man in her life, the reverse could not be said of him. In or around 1571, he had begun a lengthy affair with the widowed Douglas Howard, Lady Sheffield. Named after her godmother, Margaret Douglas, Countess of Lennox, Sheffield was Elizabeth's half-cousin.[37] Leicester had fathered a son, Robert, by her, and, long after their affair was over, Lady Sheffield attempted to establish his legitimacy by claiming that she had been clandestinely married to Leicester.[38]

Leicester had abruptly ended their relationship in September 1578, when, early one Sunday morning, he secretly married one of the acknowledged beauties of the Court, who was also Elizabeth's close kinswoman.[39] Her name was Lettice Knollys. The eldest daughter of Sir Francis Knollys and his wife, Katherine Carey, she was a great-niece of Anne Boleyn and the queen's first cousin once removed. A powerfully intelligent woman with strong opinions and a striking physical resemblance to Elizabeth, but ten years younger, Lettice combined chic and a taste for display with a quick, tart wit. She had been the wife of Walter Devereux, 1st Earl of Essex and Earl Marshal of Ireland, and had five children by him. Recently widowed, she had been involved in a passionate liaison with Leicester for some time.

The next year, very possibly with Leicester's connivance, Lady Sheffield cut her losses and also married, without plucking up the courage to tell Elizabeth. She chose Sir Edward Stafford, an up-and-coming diplomat who was then about to leave for Paris to conduct negotiations with King Henry III on the queen's behalf. Turning twenty-seven, Stafford had first been noticed when he had befriended the Duke of Anjou, who briefly stayed with him during his first visit to England. His mother, Dorothy, was Elizabeth's distant kinswoman and Bedchamber servant. She had first served her in Mary Tudor's reign before fleeing to Geneva, then returned to join the queen's Bedchamber women by 1562. For thirty years or more after that she was one of three or four whom the queen particularly wished to sleep close by her on a pallet bed.[40]

Lettice's secret marriage transformed her into the queen's arch-enemy almost overnight, although despite the waves of jealous passion and revulsion that engulfed Elizabeth when she first heard of it, she chose initially to turn a blind eye. She hated her 'Sweet Robin', her 'Eyes', for his callous act of betrayal with every fibre of her body, but for all that she still loved him. So long as he behaved with circumspection, so long as his wife lived quietly with her father in the country, well away from Court, she felt she could deny what had happened. There was in any case very little she could do about it besides mourn losing him to another woman.[41]

In November 1579, her attitude had changed dramatically when Jean de Simier, the Duke of Anjou's chamberlain, whom Elizabeth had nicknamed 'Monkey', came to London to discuss a possible Anglo-French marriage treaty.[42] Leicester had opposed Anjou's suit in the Privy Council, where he had sat alongside Burghley since 1562 and wielded considerable influence on the shaping of foreign policy, and Simier, keen to blacken his name, had drip-fed Elizabeth some of the more salacious details of his amours.[43] What most infuriated her was Simier's disclosure, based on rumours circulating in Paris, that Leicester had gone through some sort of marriage ceremony with Sheffield and so was a bigamist. In February 1580, she summoned Sir Edward Stafford to an urgent interview and grilled him pruriently about his wife's sexual history, falsely claiming to have firm proof that she had been secretly married to Leicester. Offering to bribe him when her bullying failed, she tried to persuade him to compel his wife to testify in court about her marital status. When this failed, she turned spitefully on Leicester and demanded early repayment of some of his loans and debts, forcing him to sell her valuable estates at knock-down prices and to mortgage others, notably Wanstead, his fairy-tale country retreat in Essex.[44]

The following year, Lettice was pregnant. The child, named Robert after his father, was to die at Wanstead shortly after his third birthday, but his arrival on the scene, coupled with Leicester's decision in the summer of 1583 to throw discretion aside and move his wife into Leicester House, his London town house by Temple Bar beside the Strand, meant that Elizabeth could no longer deny the truth of their marriage. He and Lettice lived together openly there: they even invited Castelnau to dinner. His Catholic enemies put it about that the queen had banned Lettice from coming within five miles of the Court.[45] She was said to be seething at a report that her favourite was thinking of engineering a marriage between Dorothy, the younger of his newly acquired stepdaughters, and the young and impressionable James VI of Scotland. (When told of his intention, she retorted that she would never allow James to marry 'the daughter of such a she-wolf'.)[46] For several weeks, Leicester was in deep disgrace; but the queen's mood softened again and before long it seemed he was back in her favour.[47] But the next year, she was as incensed as ever, prompting him to lament, 'God must only help it with Her Majesty.'[48]

In 1585, then, no one knew for certain whether Elizabeth would agree to send Leicester to the Netherlands to save the cause of the Dutch rebels. The uncertainty prevailed, since everyone remembered how she had refused to allow him to leave her side in the winter of 1562–3 when, against her better judgement, she had briefly succumbed to his and Burghley's pressure to send a force to occupy the French port of Le Havre to aid the Huguenots. On that occasion, she gave the command to Ambrose Dudley, Earl of Warwick, Robert's elder brother. Robert had been forced to write her a grovelling letter of apology to excuse his absence from Court merely to greet his badly wounded brother on his return.[49]

Once the main treaty with the Dutch representatives was signed in August, Leicester came to think that, this time, he would secure the command as the queen's Lieutenant-General. Supremely confident, he began mustering troops from among his own tenants in the West Midlands and North Wales, then decided to take Lettice on an extended summer holiday to Kenilworth. It was a foolish mistake. Not only was the castle a gift from Elizabeth, its restoration had been financed with her money and he had entertained her there several times, most awesomely in 1575, when he had put on marine pageants and a breathtaking firework display in her honour. From 1566 onwards, he had been the impresario of her large-scale summer progresses, and the two had regularly ridden out and hunted together. Elizabeth's memories of these happy days were vivid.[50] But in the summer of 1585, it was Lettice, the queen's rival, who was offered six weeks of pleasure and relaxation with the man she loved, while Elizabeth was forced to kick her heels at Wimbledon, and Beddington in Surrey. Walsingham had accepted an invitation to join Leicester and his wife at Kenilworth, but on second thoughts he wisely cancelled, giving as his excuse the bad weather.[51]

Burghley and Walsingham both backed Leicester's claim to the Lieutenancy, and each wrote to ask him that summer if he was still willing to serve. Then, shortly before his commission was sealed, the queen revoked it. In dismay, Leicester appealed to Walsingham. Writing in bed after injuring his leg in a riding accident, he complained that 'she doth take every occasion by my marriage to withdraw any good from me.' 'I pray God,' he scrawled almost illegibly at the side of this letter after running out of paper, 'Her Majesty be resolute to help the States.'[52]

Elizabeth yielded in late September and named him Lieutenant, but then backtracked again. She loved him and might never see him again; she despised him for betraying her so utterly and wanted to deny him the one thing he wanted. Her inner turmoil triggered a run of migraine headaches. Leicester cautioned Walsingham in a scribbled note that the 'often disease' from which she had suffered so badly as a teenager had returned, 'and this last night worst of all'. She was 'very desirous to stay me', he confided. 'She used very pitiful words to me of her fear she shall not live and would not have me from her.' This time Leicester was smart enough to keep his mouth shut, not knowing which way she would jump if he were to say anything. 'And therefore,' he reported back to Walsingham, 'I would not say much for any matter but did comfort her as much as I could. Only I did let her know how far I had gone in preparation. I do think for all this, if she be well tonight, she will let me go, for she would not have me speak of it to the contrary to anybody.' No one doubted that the decision would be hers alone.[53]

At last, Leicester's commission was published and he embarked for Vlissingen in Zeeland to take up his command. He left Harwich on 9 December. The weather was fair and by the next morning he was within sight of Ostend. Sailing north, he disembarked at Vlissingen, the gateway to Holland, at around two o'clock in the afternoon.

On top of a personal staff of seventy-five and their hundred or so servants, he had raised at his own expense some four hundred infantry and six hundred and fifty cavalry as the nucleus of his forces. Despite allowing him to go, Elizabeth could never bring herself to provide him with troops or funds in excess of those she had agreed contractually with the Dutch. She had promised to supply some 1,000 cavalry and 6,400 infantry and an annual sum of £125,800 to maintain them. But at the height of his campaign, Leicester had some eleven to twelve thousand men at his disposal, including volunteers and those in Dutch service. He raised hefty loans to pay for all of these extra soldiers, the largest of which, from a consortium of City of London merchants, was secured by a crippling mortgage on lands in North Wales that were already mortgaged to the queen. These funds were quickly exhausted as Leicester unwisely undertook what was tantamount to a royal progress, travelling in great splendour as he made his way towards Holland. He established a rival 'Court' at The Hague and later at Utrecht, complete with feasting, dancing and entertainments of regal magnificence. To pay for this, he was obliged to lay out £1,000 a month from his own purse.[54]

On 14 January 1586, the new Lieutenant-General made a fatal miscalculation. Boxed into a corner by the Dutch Council of State and worried about the disarray into which much of the government of the northern provinces had fallen since William of Orange's assassination, he decided to accept the Governor-Generalship, the supreme executive power, and a position which clearly implied that Elizabeth had agreed to become sovereign of the Netherlands. He took this step with full knowledge that she had expressly forbidden it both in writing and in person. He felt he had no choice if he hoped to hold the States together, sending William Davison to London from Holland to explain his reasons. Davison was delayed by adverse winds, but he was in any case too closely linked to the cause of the Dutch Calvinists for his advocacy to carry much weight.[55]

Elizabeth's reaction was savage. Jealous, still hurt by his marriage and with her pride deeply wounded, she was determined to be frustrated no longer by the unwillingness of her advisers to obey her. She would be a monarch first and a woman second. Reasons of state would triumph over personal loyalties. On 10 February, she sent Sir Thomas Heneage, the smooth-tongued gentleman of the Privy

Chamber who had so annoyed Burghley when he had once presumed
to offer Elizabeth his advice, to present her defiant favourite with a
cuttingly worded rebuke.[56] 'How contemptuously we conceive our-
self to have been used by you', her letter began, 'you shall by this
bearer understand.'

> We could never have imagined (had we not seen it fall out in experi-
> ence) that a man raised up by ourself and extraordinarily favoured by
> us, above any other subject of this land, would have in so contempt-
> ible a sort broken our commandment in a cause that so greatly
> toucheth us in honour ... And therefore, our express pleasure and
> commandment is that – all delays and excuses laid apart – you do
> presently, upon the duty of your allegiance, obey and fulfil whatso-
> ever the bearer hereof shall direct you to do in our name, as you will
> answer the contrary at your uttermost peril.[57]

The tone and even the words of this last sentence were exactly the
same as those Elizabeth used to address the lowest and most unde-
serving of offenders. Leicester found the letter hugely insulting.
Worse, Heneage was armed with written instructions ordering him
to renounce the Governorship. Heneage was, said the queen, to
inform Leicester 'how highly upon just cause we are offended with
his last late acceptation of the government of those provinces ...
which we do repute to be a very great and strange contempt least
looked for at his hands, being as he is a creature of our own'.[58]

Part of the explanation for Elizabeth's volcanic reaction may lie in
rumours swirling around in London and later proved to be false that
Lettice was planning to join her husband 'with such a train of ladies
and gentlewomen, and such rich coaches ... that there should be
such a court of ladies as would far surpass Her Majesty's Court here'.
Elizabeth was said to have uttered a barrage of 'great oaths' – her
favourite expletives were 'God's death!' and 'God alive!' – insisting
that 'she would have no more courts under her obeisance but her
own.'[59] Later, she acknowledged her mistake, grudgingly conceding
that Leicester had meant well. But still she was furious about the
Governorship.[60]

Months of fighting followed, during which Leicester was repeatedly let down by his Dutch allies. Fearing an English takeover, the

already quarrelsome Dutch leaders were particularly upset when Leicester ordered restrictions on their trade and imposed martial law.[61] His clashes with his own generals were a further distraction, depleting the morale of his troops. His character scarcely helped: prone to outbursts of self-pity, he suffered from the classic vice of Elizabethan politicians – a tendency to personalize disputes. His enemies both in the Netherlands and in London made capital out of these failings, fatally undermining his position with the queen.

In the spring of 1586, Elizabeth offered an olive branch to Parma behind Leicester's back, using a variety of intermediaries.[62] Andreas de Loo, a wealthy Flemish merchant based in London and a passionate art collector who owned several important paintings by Hans Holbein the Younger, shuttled between London and Antwerp, putting out peace feelers. Meanwhile, an Italian silk merchant, Agostino Grafiña, travelled to Parma's camp and talked his way in by presenting the Duke with two fine geldings and two greyhounds. Parma was unimpressed: Elizabeth's proposal that he persuade Philip to put the clock back largely to where it had been before the Dutch revolt began was utterly unrealistic. So was her demand that Spain should indemnify the English merchants who had suffered losses through Philip's trade embargo.[63]

When reports of her overtures to Parma leaked out over the summer months, Elizabeth issued a strong denial. All was due, she said disingenuously, to 'a great error' made 'in our name, without our knowledge'. Keen to safeguard her reputation as the saviour of the Dutch Protestants even as she tried to wriggle out of the role, she declared that she was obliged to assist them 'for no better reason than the defence of our own State, which is inexorably linked with the security of our ancient neighbours in the Low Countries'.[64] The denial was dictated in fluent Italian, which, along with French, Latin and some rudimentary Greek, she had first learned in childhood and adolescence. She had always had a special love of Italian: her very first surviving autograph letter is one written in Italian to her stepmother, Katherine Parr, when she was ten.[65]

Leicester struggled to know what to make of these overtures to Parma. One thing was clear: his relationship with Elizabeth did not function well at a distance. Even Heneage took pity on him, reassuring him that the queen would never make a treaty with Spain without the consent of the Dutch States. By saying this, Heneage was exceeding his brief and Elizabeth soon rounded on him, too. 'Jesus,' she expostulated when word was reported back to her, 'what availeth wit when it fails the owner at greatest need?' 'Do that you are bidden', she snarled, 'and leave your considerations for your own affairs . . . Think you I will be bound by your speech to make no peace for mine own matters without your consent? . . . I am utterly at squares with this childish dealing.'[66]

And then, as failure and bankruptcy stared Leicester in the face and he hardly knew which way to turn, Elizabeth's love for him seemed to rekindle and she wrote him the most intensely personal letter of her whole life. Tearing off the mask of royalty, calling him 'Rob' and addressing him in the first person singular rather than the royal 'we', she spoke of 'a midsummer moon' taking possession of her:

> Rob, I am afraid you will suppose by my wandering writings that a midsummer moon hath taken large possession of my brains this month, but you must needs take things as they come in my head though order be left behind me. When I remember your request to have a discreet and honest man that may carry my mind and see how all goes there, I have chosen this bearer, whom you know and have made good trial of. I have fraught him full of my conceits of those country matters, and imparted what way I mind to take and what is fit for you to use. I am sure you can credit him and so I will be short with these few notes.

She even came close to an apology for her stinginess: 'It frets me not a little that the poor soldier that hourly ventures life should want their due, that well deserve rather reward.' For all its colloquialisms and apparent warmth, however, the letter was starkly non-committal. It was also relatively brief:

> Now will I end that do imagine I talk still with you, and therefore loathly say farewell ôô [i.e. 'Eyes' – his nickname], though ever I pray God bless you from all harm and save you from all foes, with my million and legion of thanks for all your pains and cares.[67]

On reading her letter, Leicester came to think that, despite his debts and tribulations, all yet might end well. He was too weak to offer open battle to Parma but believed he could liberate some of the newly fortified Spanish garrison towns and so free up the river traffic along the Scheldt towards the Rhine. He was roundly disabused of this notion after laying siege to Zutphen, one of Spain's most important military garrisons in Gelderland. The move forced Parma to march north to relieve it. Tipped off by a Spanish defector that the Duke would send in a supply convoy early on Thursday, 22 September, Leicester planned to ambush it at dawn. The morning was dull, with a thick autumn fog. When the English attacked, Leicester's stepson, the young Robert Devereux, Lettice's son by her first marriage, won his spurs in a triumphant light-cavalry charge. But then things went disastrously awry. As the mist suddenly cleared, some three hundred English infantry found themselves yards away from three thousand of Parma's crack troops. They were hopelessly outnumbered and, for all Leicester's bravado, his forces failed to prevent the convoy from relieving the town. Casualties were lighter than might have been expected, but towards the end of the fighting, Leicester suffered a personal blow when his favourite nephew, the renowned poet and courtier Philip Sidney, was hit by a musket shot. The bullet entered the left thigh 'three fingers above the knee' after one horse died beneath him and he was mounting another. Carried in Leicester's own barge along the River Ijssel to Arnhem, Sidney appeared to be convalescing well, but the bullet lay too deep to be removed. He developed gangrene and died a month after the battle.[68]

Back in London, Walsingham had uncovered what he declared to be a fresh and profoundly menacing plot to assassinate Elizabeth. This involved the supporters of Mary Queen of Scots and, on the fringes, Bernardino de Mendoza, now the Spanish ambassador in Paris, where he had made his home a safe-house for some of the most dangerous men in Europe. Walsingham claimed to have secured firm proof that those behind this latest plot were acting with Mary's explicit knowledge and consent.* Fearful that Elizabeth would not act decisively

* See Chapter 4.

against her royal cousin without added pressure from Leicester, despite the existence of this proof, both Burghley and Walsingham urged his recall on the flimsy pretext that he was needed to attend an imminent session of Parliament.

On 24 November 1586, Leicester finally returned to England. He was replaced in his command by Peregrine Bertie, Lord Willoughby, one of his ablest subordinates, who had led the cavalry charge at the Battle of Zutphen, unhorsing the enemy general and taking him prisoner. With his soldiers by now close to mutiny and his creditors in England and Holland alike demanding repayment and refusing to reschedule his loans, Leicester was happy to come home. He hoped to use the opportunity to lobby Elizabeth for greater support for the Dutch rebels in the future, for neither he nor they were satisfied with what they had achieved so far. They complained that he had wasted their money, imposed new levies on them and hired foreign troops without their consent. For his part, he had found them prickly, to say the least, and the overall effect of Elizabeth's insistence that he fight a defensive war had been to concede the strategic initiative to Parma.[69]

On arrival at Court, Leicester was questioned intently for several days by the queen and Burghley about his use of Crown funds. 'I thought myself very hardly handled', he protested to Burghley, since it was 'no way possible for me to give Her Majesty such a particular reckoning of the expenses as she looked for, and yet it might have pleased you . . . to have rather sought to make Her Majesty understand how impossible . . . it was to my place to answer or give account of particular auditors' books.'[70]

Leicester did not see how Elizabeth could reasonably expect him to account for the specific disbursements of his subordinates, when he had given them only general instructions. He felt the investigation smacked of a witch-hunt. But Burghley understood how vehemently Elizabeth believed that vast amounts of her treasure had been wasted in the Netherlands, and he was determined to keep his own job, even if that meant piling the pressure on a colleague.

Under different circumstances, this clash between the two titans on the Privy Council might have had explosive consequences, but the latest assassination plot meant that they would have to set aside all other concerns. Leicester was forced to swallow his pride and accept that the queen would never reimburse him the money he had spent from his own pocket in the Netherlands, a crushing humiliation for a man who had once imagined himself to be a serious contender for her hand. As the Court prepared to move from Richmond to Greenwich in readiness for the Christmas festivities, Burghley, Leicester and Walsingham found themselves confronting their biggest challenge since the beginning of Elizabeth's reign. For better or worse, they would have to close ranks.

3.   Brave New World

Just as the great debate over the crisis in the Netherlands was about to begin in the Privy Council in October 1584, a dashing thirty-year-old Sir Walter Ralegh had stepped on to the scene. Six feet tall and speaking with a thick West Country accent, he was a Devonshire man and a commoner. Blessed with an ivory complexion and shiny, curly black hair, he was the epitome of masculinity: arrogant, ambitious, a swashbuckling swordsman, mesmerizingly handsome, nattily dressed, learned, even something of a poet. Larger than life, one of the first men in England to keep an African manservant, he had already begun to challenge Leicester as Elizabeth's favourite.[1] King Philip, curious to know exactly who he was, was asking questions about him. Warned in a dispatch from London that Elizabeth 'continues to make much of the new favourite very openly', he scribbled in the margin, 'I do not know who this is.' That would not be the case for long.[2]

Lupold von Wedel, a star-struck Pomeranian nobleman whom Elizabeth invited as a Christmas guest to Greenwich Palace in 1584, noted that it was Ralegh with whom she chiefly conversed, even when Leicester was around. Wearing a wig of snaky golden curls to disguise the bald crown of her head, and a gown of black velvet sumptuously embroidered with silver and pearls in ostentatious mourning for William of Orange, Elizabeth had seemed enthralled by him as he knelt beside her chair during the dancing after dinner. Von Wedel gasped when she poked her finger in Ralegh's face, teasing him by remarking on a speck of dirt and offering to wipe it away. 'It was said', continued von Wedel, that 'she loved this gentleman now in preference to all others; and that may be well believed.'[3]

Leicester had encountered a rival before, but he had fended him off. Sir Christopher Hatton had first begun to attract Elizabeth's attention in the 1560s, and in 1572 she made him a gentleman of her Privy Chamber, showering him with gifts. Almost as tall and attractive as Ralegh and also in his early thirties when he first caught the queen's eye, Hatton was the consummate courtier. An unctuous flatterer who sported a feather in his hat as his personal trademark, he declared himself to be Elizabeth's 'everlasting bondman', seemingly without a hint of hypocrisy. 'No death, no, not hell, no fear of death shall ever win of me my consent so far to wrong myself again as to be absent from you one day,' he had effusively protested in 1573. 'Passion overcometh me. I can write no more. Love me; for I love you.'[4]

Hatton avoided entanglements with other women and, unlike Leicester, he never married. As a sign of her affection, Elizabeth nicknamed him 'Lids' or 'Lyddes' ('Eyelids'). Sometimes he called himself her 'Slave' or her 'Sheep', as when he wrote to her from his sickbed, again, probably, in 1573, quipping, 'Your Mutton is black; scarcely will you know your own, so much hath this disease dashed me.'

Once made a privy councillor in 1577, however, Hatton shifted his focus from seduction towards building his reputation as a statesman. He learned to work with Leicester on such issues as the Anjou marriage and the plight of the Dutch, and the two men ended up as genuine friends. When Leicester incurred Elizabeth's wrath by accepting the position of Governor-General of the Netherlands, he turned to Hatton for help more often than to Burghley. And Hatton reciprocated, making strenuous efforts on his behalf and colluding with Walsingham to doctor a report Leicester had written for the queen, blotting out passages they knew would infuriate her and altering others before reading the document out to her.[5]

Ralegh, by contrast, was never likely to assimilate fully to the prevailing Court establishment. An incorrigible maverick, a man of 'light and sudden humours', he would be denounced by the Jesuits as an atheist* for allegedly denying the immortality of the soul.[6] He chose as his motto *Amore et Virtute* ('By love and virtue')

---

* Ralegh befriended the playwright Christopher Marlowe and would almost certainly have agreed with a remark Marlowe puts into the mouth of the character Machevill (or Machiavelli) at the beginning of *The Jew of Malta*: 'I count religion but a childish toy/And hold there is no sin but ignorance.' By 'religion', Marlowe almost certainly meant '*forms of* religion', just as by the remark 'there is nothing more dangerous than security,' Walsingham meant '*lack* of security'. Such a remark did not in itself deny the existence of God, and neither Ralegh nor Marlowe was an atheist.

and some claimed he distinguished himself more in the first realm than in the second. Rumours of his sexual conquests were legendary: he had fathered an illegitimate daughter in Ireland and was said to have pleasured one of Elizabeth's lovesick maids against a tree-trunk. He was fond of grand gestures, but the oft-repeated account of how he first became a courtier after spreading his new plush cloak over a 'plashy place' for the queen to walk over is almost certainly apocryphal.

Ralegh's glittering career owed less in its earliest stages to his cloak than to two of his Devonshire connections. He was a nephew of the formidable Katherine (or Kat) Ashley,* whom in 1559 Elizabeth had chosen as her first chief gentlewoman of the Privy Chamber. Kat and Elizabeth went back further even than that. Kat, the daughter of Sir Philip Champernowne of Modbury in Devon, had entered Elizabeth's service as a teenager when the future queen was no more than five.[7] She would rise to become her governess and in or about 1545 she married John Ashley, Elizabeth's second cousin,† whom the queen would make a gentleman of the Privy Chamber and the Master of the Jewel House. Around the time Thomas Seymour made his early-morning advances to Elizabeth while she was living with Katherine Parr, he had joked about Kat with his servant and illegitimate half-brother, John Seymour, asking him to enquire 'whether her great buttocks were grown any less or no'.[8] Although Kat died of an unknown illness before Ralegh was twelve, he had merely to mention her name to catch Elizabeth's attention when he first appeared on the fringes of the Court in 1577.

Ralegh's other invaluable link to the Court was through his elder half-brother, Sir Humphrey Gilbert. A flamboyant, violent, inflammatory character and a brazen risk-taker, Gilbert was proud of his motto *Mutare vel Timere Sperno* ('I scorn to change or to fear'). Along with his kinsmen and circle of friends, many of them second sons or prodigals born out of wedlock, he stood for the values of raw monarchical power and personal glory as won by valour. Such men boasted that they looked forward to 'troubling Burghley's fine head' and to

---

* Otherwise known as 'Astley'.

† Ashley's aunt, Lady Elizabeth Boleyn (née Wood), was also Anne Boleyn's aunt.

stopping Elizabeth's 'frisking and dancing' by showing her how foolish it was 'to displace a soldier' in favour of a fawning bureaucrat 'with a pen and ink-horn at his girdle'.[9]

In 1580, Gilbert had secured for Ralegh a captain's commission in the army being sent to suppress a bloody revolt in Ireland. Ralegh was present at the siege of Smerwick in County Kerry, where a force of papal and Spanish adventurers had joined the rebel garrison. After a three-day bombardment, the garrison surrendered. The survivors were disarmed and, under Ralegh's supervision, all but thirty were massacred. A few weeks later, Ralegh boasted of his half-brother's macabre reputation in Ireland, writing to Walsingham that he had 'never heard nor read of any man more feared than he is among the Irish nation'.[10] This referred to Gilbert's role as a colonel during an earlier revolt in 1569, when he had not been shy to put the values he preached into practice, capturing twenty-five castles, imposing martial law wherever he went, slaughtering all who resisted him and humiliating those who surrendered by insisting that they first approached him in his tent by crawling on all fours along a corridor marked by the decapitated heads of their relatives.[11]

Within a year of the massacre at Smerwick, Ralegh had made his first major breakthrough with the queen. As his senior commanding officer's confidential courier, he was responsible for giving her private briefings on Irish affairs. During these audiences, he was never afraid to undermine his superiors by criticizing their failings. Elizabeth, for her part, relished what, in those years, was a decidedly rare opportunity to contest the advice offered by her military experts, since, for once, it gave her the ammunition she needed to force Burghley and Walsingham to approach matters of policy on her terms rather than theirs.[12]

Hatton would soon grumble that Ralegh was rising too fast and too high in the queen's esteem. He was especially vexed that she had nicknamed him 'Water'. Impetuously, Hatton sent Elizabeth three 'tokens' early one morning as she was on her way to hunt a doe. One was a diminutive bucket, which elicited the reply that he need not fear 'drowning'. She sent him back a gift of a dove: the bird, she said, which 'together with the rainbow brought the good tidings and the covenant that there should be no more destruction by water'.[13]

Despite his courtly talents, Ralegh retained many of Gilbert's muscular and insolent attitudes. Over the years, he would several times be disciplined by the Privy Council for brawling or duelling, at one point twice in a month.[14]

It was clear by 1584 that Ralegh's career would be shaped most fully by Gilbert's ardent belief in the promises offered up by the New World. For all the efforts of earlier brave English merchants and seamen in searching for new lands and the trade and prosperity they might bring, the Crown had been reluctant to invest in exploration and colonization. The chief obstacle was the five decrees issued by Pope Alexander VI in 1493 by which he conceded to Spain the right to occupy a region vaguely defined as 'such islands and lands . . . as you have discovered or are about to discover'. As modified by the Treaty of Tordesillas in 1494, the effect of the pope's decrees was to grant Spain and Portugal a duopoly over exploration and colonization of the non-European world.

Bristol seamen had made at least two voyages of Atlantic exploration, in 1480 and 1481, and Henry VII granted privileges to the famous Genoese navigators John and Sebastian Cabot in 1496 to sail across the Atlantic in search of a fabled north-west passage through the Arctic ice to the Pacific Ocean and the East Indies.[15] (This passage was believed to lie between Labrador and Greenland at a latitude of between 66 and 67 degrees north.) They failed to find it, but in 1497 Henry gave John Cabot a payment of £10 (equivalent to one year's wages) on his return as a reward 'to him that found the New Isle', referring to present-day Newfoundland, followed by a pension of £20 a year.[16]

When Henry VIII broke with the pope, English adventurers found fresh opportunities to challenge the Iberian duopoly of the New World, but Henry himself did little to promote colonization, despite his passion for all things naval. The French were well ahead of the English on that score, because they had more fully absorbed the discoveries made by Spanish and Portuguese cartographers.

A step forward was taken in Edward VI's reign. In 1553, prompted by a sudden dip in English trade, a syndicate of wealthy London merchants backed by the Privy Council made a concerted effort to discover a north-eastern passage to Asia through the Arctic Ocean and on into the Bering Sea. Three ships sailed from Tilbury in Essex. The expedition carried with it a letter signed by Edward, addressed to 'all Kings, Princes, Rulers, Judges and Governors of the earth, and all other having any excellent dignity on the same, in all places under the universal heaven'.[17] Two of these ships foundered when their crews became disorientated by the intense cold off the coast of northern Lapland. A year later, some Russian fishermen discovered the men frozen to death, some still seated in the act of writing their wills, pens in hand and paper before them.[18] The third ship, captained by Richard Chancellor, made it safely into the White Sea but got no further than the Russian port of St Nicholas. The expedition's one resounding success was that Chancellor finally reached Moscow, where he was able to negotiate an agreement with the tsar, Ivan the Terrible, for the syndicate's members to trade with his subjects. The result was the formation in London of the Muscovy Company, to which Mary Tudor granted a royal charter in 1555.[19]

In 1578, Gilbert aimed to follow in the Cabots' footsteps by discovering a navigable route from the Atlantic to the Pacific Ocean. But, more immediately, he secured a monopoly grant from Elizabeth, valid for six years, to 'discover, find, search out and view such remote, heathen and barbarous lands, countries and territories not actually possessed of any Christian prince'. His intention was to annex large tracts of Newfoundland for the queen, over which he and his heirs would enjoy freehold rights in perpetuity. When he revealed his plans to his half-brother, Ralegh instantly joined the venture.

The purpose and intended destination of their expedition were kept a closely guarded secret, but the plan involved a raid on Spanish assets in the Caribbean to raise capital, followed by the establishment of a North American settlement. Unfortunately, bad weather and a serious quarrel with his second-in-command forced Gilbert to turn back just beyond the west coast of Ireland. Ralegh was scarcely more successful. He braved the winter Atlantic storms as far as the Cape Verde islands, but at that point his supplies ran low and he, too, returned.[20]

Determined to succeed where he had so far failed, Gilbert organized a second expedition in 1583. This began more auspiciously. Landing at St John's in Newfoundland, Gilbert took possession of the harbour, displacing the Breton cod fishermen who plied their trade there and laying claim in the queen's name to the surrounding territory within a distance of six hundred miles.[21] He nailed a heraldic banner of the royal arms, cast in lead, to a wooden post, establishing the first English possession in the New World since John Cabot's voyage of 1497. Next, he began to search for mineral ore, excavating samples with the help of a German metallurgist he had recruited.[22] For many years he had mingled with alchemists, lured by the promise of riches. Like his more famous friend the astrologer and magus Dr John Dee, Gilbert believed that if he could only find the right minerals he could turn base metals into copper or perhaps even gold.[23]

It was not long, however, before a sickness struck down Gilbert's men. When Gilbert finally set out with the rump of his crew to reconnoitre and 'make plats [maps]' of the North American Atlantic coastline, an overloaded ship carrying his mineral samples and the bulk of the expedition's rations ran aground and sank in a gale. His men begged him to turn back before they all perished – and perish many of them did. Gilbert's own vessel was overwhelmed by mountainous waves in a hurricane off the Azores, and he was last seen standing on deck with a Bible in his hand, shouting, 'We are as near to heaven by sea as by land.' Only a single ship made it back to Falmouth.[24]

Ralegh had not joined this second expedition. He had invested in it, however, and encouraged Elizabeth to view it favourably. As soon as he learned of his half-brother's death, he petitioned the queen to grant him exclusive rights of exploration and settlement similar to those Gilbert had enjoyed. He was confident that she would not refuse him.[25] Already, the new favourite seemed to think of himself as untouchable, arrogantly addressing correspondents as if he were the queen's preferred mouthpiece and talking down to Burghley.[26]

In March 1584, Elizabeth assented to Ralegh's petition and granted him everything she had previously allowed to Gilbert. (The documents survive and show that Ralegh's and Gilbert's grants were identical.)[27] She had already allowed Ralegh to move into the prestigious higher floors of Durham House on the Strand, a large, rambling property overlooking the Thames.[28] These were state apartments once reserved for the use of visiting foreign diplomats; closer to Whitehall, they were, if anything, even more imposing than Leicester House. And to help Ralegh fund his new lifestyle, the queen had granted him rights to some valuable leases and given him a lucrative monopoly grant for wine and the licensing of vintners. From now on, everyone selling wine or keeping a tavern would first have to purchase a licence from him or be prepared to pay him a fine. This munificent gift, worth around £1,100 a year and reminiscent in its scale of an earlier grant Elizabeth had given to Leicester of the lease of the farm of the customs* on sweet (Mediterranean) wines, would underwrite Ralegh's credit for years to come.

Walsingham's fascination with cartography and exploration went back to the late 1560s, when he had first become a stockholder in the Muscovy Company.[29] As ambassador to Paris in the early 1570s, he had built up a network of important international contacts. He became close to Gaspard de Coligny, the Huguenot leader and Admiral of France, who had access to the astonishing maps and charts compiled by noted cartographers and hydrographers such as Jacques Cartier and Jean Rotz. A secret patron of colonial ventures in Brazil in 1555 and Terra Florida (now north-east Florida and southern South Carolina) in 1562, which were intended to create safe refuges for exiled Huguenots, Coligny was considering a proposal for an expedition to map the uncharted Pacific in August 1572 when he was assassinated in his bed by the Duke of Guise and his followers. His corpse was thrown from the window of his house into the street below, where it was mutilated by a mob of fanatical Catholics, the event that triggered the St Bartholomew's Day Massacre.

Throughout that terrifying fortnight, Walsingham's house on the left bank of the Seine had become a sanctuary for English Protestants seeking shelter. Chief among them was the teenage Philip Sidney,

---

* Leicester was allowed to 'farm' (i.e. rent out to investors) the right to collect the customs and excise duties payable on imported sweet wines. These investors paid him a fixed annual sum and kept the profits made from collecting duties at the ports for themselves.

who had escaped safely from the Louvre, where he had been staying. Sidney, whose face was badly scarred by smallpox at the same time as his mother lost her looks nursing Elizabeth, would go on to make his name as a diplomat and an imaginative writer of the highest order, only to be fatally wounded at the Battle of Zutphen. His curiosity about the New World was sparked in his first year at Oxford, when he read Thomas Hacket's translation of André Thevet's graphic account of Coligny's colony in Brazil.[30] Thevet, one of Walsingham's favourite authors, was the first explorer known to have imported significant quantities of tobacco into Europe from the Americas for medicinal use. Ralegh, ever a trendsetter, was in turn the first European to make smoking dried tobacco leaves in a long-stemmed clay pipe fashionable.

For all Walsingham's extreme caution where matters of state security were concerned, he was never that type of risk-averse investor anxious to keep his capital safe and accumulate modest profits slowly. Like so many of his generation, he was happy to serve both God and Mammon. In 1582, he put together a consortium, including Sidney, to promote a highly novel colonization venture. The project aimed to tempt English Catholics who were fearful that their property might be confiscated by Parliament for their refusal to conform to Elizabeth's Religious Settlement to seek a new home on the other side of the Atlantic on land that the consortium would provide.[31] But Elizabeth emphatically vetoed the scheme after Spain handed in a strongly worded protest.[32] And once she had assented to Ralegh's petition to enjoy the same exclusive rights of exploration and settlement as Gilbert had before him, the lie of the land was clear: if Walsingham wished to promote colonization and continue the search begun by the Muscovy Company in the 1550s for navigable routes through the Arctic ice to the Pacific Ocean, he would need to work with Ralegh, since otherwise it would be impossible to attract investors. Conversely, Ralegh would need to work with him if he hoped to persuade the queen to back the visionary grand strategy upon which he now decided to embark.[33]

Just a few days after William of Orange's assassination in July 1584, Ralegh began building a team of experts skilled in cosmography, astronomy, geometry, cartography and arithmetic. He was intent on merging his plans for colonization and conquest in the New World with a daringly global solution to the problem of King Philip and the Netherlands. He meant to appeal directly to Elizabeth, knowing from their earlier discussions of Irish affairs that she would consent to hear him out. So ambitious were his proposals, he set out to attach Walsingham to his cause to give them far greater credibility.

Ralegh recruited the highly regarded Thomas Harriot to lead his team of experts. An Oxford mathematician who left the ivory tower at about the age of twenty-three to make his fortune in London, Harriot had revolutionized algebra and the art of navigation by pioneering complex mathematical approaches to map theory and astronomy. Ralegh offered him 'a most liberal salary' and lodged him at Durham House, where he gave impromptu lectures to his new patron's circle of friends. Like Ralegh, Harriot smoked a pipe, a habit that would give him the less desirable distinction of being the first Englishman on record to die of cancer from tobacco-induced causes.[34]

Next to be recruited was Richard Hakluyt, another brilliant Oxford graduate, who, at thirty-two, was Walsingham's most knowledgeable adviser on anything to do with oceanic exploration.[35] A leading editor, translator and compiler of geographical and exploration literature, Hakluyt had already been given access to some of Walsingham's most confidential state papers. Then employed as a secretary by Sir Edward Stafford, Elizabeth's ambassador in Paris since 1583, he was approached by one of Ralegh's contacts and asked to return to London to write up a dossier for presentation to Elizabeth setting out Ralegh's plans for a global solution to the Spanish problem.[36]

Hakluyt was ideally suited to the role. Well acquainted with the leading French experts on the Americas, he knew Thevet, from whom he had borrowed a manuscript.[37] Encouraged by Walsingham, he had mingled in Paris with the many Portuguese exiles who fled there after King Philip claimed the throne of Portugal in 1580. Several had shown him secret maps and charts of the New World.[38]

On 5 October 1584, less than a week before the first of the two crucial Privy Council meetings to debate the crisis in the Netherlands, Hakluyt personally presented Elizabeth with a thick dossier setting out Ralegh's grand strategy.[39] He found her at Oatlands, with a reduced Court, having just returned from entertaining Castelnau at Windsor and preparing to move on the next day to Hampton Court. The timing was not coincidental: Leicester, whom Ralegh feared would oppose his strategy strenuously on the grounds that he had set his heart on leading an expeditionary force to the Netherlands, had left Oatlands a day or so earlier to return to London.[40]

The genius of the dossier on which Hakluyt had worked continuously for three months was its ability to explain fully and persuasively, in non-technical language, the New World's potential to redress the imbalances of the Old.[41] Its advocacy on Ralegh's behalf was not limited to short-term expedients, such as Gilbert's when he had scoured Newfoundland for precious metals or Walsingham's when he had planned to resettle intractable Catholics. The central premise, worked out in astonishing depth, was that nurturing a colonial empire in North America would create fresh markets for English labour and goods, thus compensating for the catastrophic drop in international trade that was likely to be triggered by war with Spain. In parallel, the threat of Spanish dominance in Europe could be averted – perhaps for ever – and the balance of power shifted in England's favour by using North America as a permanent naval and military base.[42]

Hakluyt divided his dossier into twenty-one chapters and began with a series of moral arguments. Colonization, preferably in the (as yet) unsettled lands between present-day North Carolina and Virginia, where the climate was less harsh than in Newfoundland, would be 'greatly for the enlargement of the Gospel of Christ whereunto the princes of the reformed religion are chiefly bound amongst whom Her Majesty is principal'. Since the indigenous people of North America worshipped idols and Elizabeth enjoyed the title Defender of the Faith, it would be both a godly and charitable thing to convert the infidels. As Hakluyt had sharply reminded Sidney in 1582, the first aim of overseas discovery was always 'God's glory'.[43]

Colonization would in addition liberate the native populations of the Americas from the unjust yoke of Spanish tyranny. Like the Spanish Dominican friar Bartolomé de Las Casas, from whose *Brief Relation of the Destruction of the Indians* he quoted extensively, Hakluyt argued that repeated Spanish atrocities had turned fully rational if, as yet, economically undeveloped peoples into mutinous slaves. Although still culturally immature, these indigenous tribes were far from barbarous: if treated with consideration, as human beings rather than as disposable commodities, they could be turned into powerful allies and trading partners.[44] An English translation of Las Casas's classic work had appeared in 1583 under the title *The Spanish Colonie*, possibly at Walsingham's behest, and it was from this edition that Hakluyt quoted.[45]

Having established a moral basis for colonization, Hakluyt turned, point by point, to the practical arguments which Ralegh saw as central to his case. An aggressive Atlantic policy, he explained, would do much to insulate English merchants from the risks of trading in Europe, as the New World would supply them with the exotic commodities which so far had to be imported from Asia and Africa and could at present be purchased only in Antwerp, Seville, Lisbon and Venice. New employment would be created throughout England for cloth workers and others in the finishing and manufacturing trades, who would find fresh purchasers to buy their goods in North America. As transatlantic trade increased, the queen's revenues from customs and excise duties would rise correspondingly. So would the fortunes of the shipbuilding industry, as shipwrights rediscovered the confidence to invest. Since royal navy ships were vastly outnumbered in wartime by armed merchantmen hastily requisitioned by the Crown, such investments would greatly strengthen national defences. Besides, a thriving colony in North America would be a convenient place to send the unemployed, criminals and bankrupts, who might otherwise be idle or in prison but would now be able to lead productive lives.[46]

Turning to geopolitical considerations, Hakluyt argued that the presence of vibrant English colonies in North America would thwart Spanish claims to universal monarchy. Sailing from their fortified transatlantic anchorages as well as from home, English seamen could 'be a great bridle' to Philip. Much of the 'mischief' in the world, Hakluyt continued, sprang from the prodigious wealth accruing to Spain from its annual influx of precious metals. By intercepting these convoys and denying Philip gold and silver from the New World, Elizabeth could strip him of the revenues that paid his European armies.[47]

Finally, Hakluyt set out Ralegh's belief that North American colonies would be the best possible stepping stones to China and the East Indies by way of a navigable channel through the north-western Arctic waters or, conceivably, a land route across Newfoundland to the Pacific Ocean. In common with Walsingham, Hakluyt believed that the chances of identifying a viable route to Asia by heading west were now more likely than finding a path through the north-eastern zone into the Bering Sea.[48]

If she were still in doubt, Hakluyt invited Elizabeth to consult 'an old excellent globe' standing in her own privy gallery at Whitehall, given to her father by 'Master John Verasanus'. She would, he claimed, win everlasting fame if she could bring to fruition the work her father had begun.[49] Psychologically, this seemed on the face of it to be a winning argument: Henry VIII had been an intrepid collector of maps and scientific equipment and had been especially impressed by a navigational instrument known as a 'differential quadrant' (a combined magnetic compass and universal dial which enabled a ship's pilot to attempt to determine longitude) presented to him by Jean Rotz. Persuading Elizabeth that her father, had he still lived, would have backed Ralegh was, however, a little misleading, as Henry had been decidedly reticent when petitioned by the London merchant community to become a sponsor of their early exploration ventures. His interests in navigation and cartography were geared towards military applications in his wars with France.

Elizabeth received Hakluyt's dossier graciously. After conversing with him briefly, she rewarded him with a grant of the first canonry or other church preferment to fall vacant at Bristol Cathedral.[50] On cue and in grand theatrical style, Ralegh then made his entrance, accompanied by two native Algonquians named Manteo and Wanchese, whom he paraded before the queen dressed in their traditional costumes. They were still on display when a puzzled Lupold von Wedel visited Hampton Court a few days later. 'Their faces as well as their whole bodies', he observed, 'were very similar to those of the white Moors at home. They wear no shirts, only a piece of fur to cover their genitals and the skins of wild animals to cover their shoulders.' To keep warm, they swaddled themselves in brown taffeta.[51]

In the spring of 1584, Ralegh had sent Philip Amadas and Arthur Barlowe, two experienced sea captains, on a short reconnaissance expedition to the Outer Banks of present-day North Carolina, an area that he was already naming Virginia in Elizabeth's honour. They had surveyed the many barrier islands lying off the mainland, notably the island of Roanoke, which they found to be densely wooded and abundantly supplied with fresh water, game and fish. After exchanging gifts with the local tribes and negotiating with their leaders, they had returned to Devon with the two Algonquians, making landfall in mid-September. Manteo and Wanchese were taken to Durham House, where Thomas Harriot quickly set about teaching them English. He also recorded their dialect and common idioms, intent on inventing a phonetic alphabet and handy phrasebook for the use of the first batch of Ralegh's colonists.[52]

Determined to persuade Elizabeth to approve a full-scale colonizing expedition, Ralegh set about making lists of the kinds of equipment and specialist manpower that would be required to support a North American settlement. In addition to military and naval personnel and construction workers, his lists included engineers, surveyors, shipwrights, agriculturalists, surgeons, physicians and apothecaries, who would provide the services the colonists would need.[53]

So persuaded by the force of his own gilded rhetoric had Ralegh become, he was confident Elizabeth would back his global strategy unreservedly. This may explain why he made no attempt to circulate Hakluyt's dossier more widely. Leicester asked for a copy several times but was refused. Walsingham alone received one, although his copy has since disappeared.[54] (Walsingham's papers are known to have survived intact for ten or so years after his death, but then much material, especially papers of a more personal nature, was weeded out and lost.)

Ralegh was still awaiting Elizabeth's answer on 7 October, when she gave Hakluyt leave to return to his duties at the Paris embassy.[55] Finally, she moved towards a decision, one that shaped much of the flow of energy for the rest of her reign. A month or so before Christmas, she told Ralegh he could indeed call his new colony Virginia and granted him the right to make a seal of his arms with the legend (in Latin) 'Walter Ralegh, Knight, Lord and Governor of Virginia'.

Then, on Twelfth Night (6 January 1585), when the Court was at Greenwich and she was eagerly looking forward to the evening's entertainment, she knighted him and offered him some assistance towards a second expedition to Roanoke.[56]

Well informed in Paris about these events by his spies, Bernardino de Mendoza fantasized that she would finance Ralegh's venture in full as long as her handsome new favourite did not sail with it and so leave her side.[57] In reality, Elizabeth's aid would be minimal. She gave Ralegh one of her own royal navy ships: the *Tiger*, a vessel rated at 160 tons, with a crew of eighty mariners, twelve gunners and eight soldiers. She also provided him with an inordinately large quantity of gunpowder. But she refused to back his global strategy or pay his men and made it plain she would never change her mind. 'The planting of those parts', she protested, 'is a thing that can be done only with the aid of the Prince's power and purse.' In her eyes, these were monstrously open-ended commitments, requiring almost unlimited resources. She saw colonial expansion as a dream to damnation.[58]

Ralegh received another crushing blow when his Roanoke expedition failed. On 9 April 1585, five ships, including the *Tiger* and two pinnaces, sailed out from Plymouth via the West Indies, carrying six hundred men under the command of Sir Richard Grenville, Ralegh's friend and an investor in his half-brother's earlier voyages. But calamity struck almost as soon as they arrived in North America: the *Tiger* ran aground and much of the food intended to support the colony during its first year was ruined by salt water.

Only a hundred or so of those, mainly soldiers, who landed on Roanoke Island would stay there for more than a few weeks. While Grenville and the rest sailed for home, these would-be settlers built a fort and some cottages and explored the surrounding territory as far north as Chesapeake Bay. Left in command was Grenville's deputy, Ralph Lane, a fortifications expert whose release from service in Ireland Ralegh had secured as a favour from Elizabeth.[59]

By June 1586, conditions were unexpectedly severe. Skirmishes with local tribes and a threat of famine meant that when Sir Francis Drake, Ralegh's fellow Devonian and England's most daringly versatile, if also most temperamental, seaman, sailed along the coast of 'Virginia' on his way home from death-defying raids on the Spanish settlements at Santo Domingo and Cartagena in the Caribbean, the settlers jumped at the chance of a safe passage home. Weeks later, Grenville, unaware of the evacuation, would return with a small relief expedition, but when he found the settlement deserted, he sailed away, leaving behind fifteen men, literally, to hold the fort, with enough provisions for two years.

No Englishman ever saw them again. The following year, Ralegh sent out yet another expedition, but the venture was no more successful. After that, Elizabeth was embroiled in the Armada crisis and forbade the dispatch of further expeditions, putting an end to Ralegh's plans to colonize 'Virginia' while she was on the throne.[60]

4. Armada of the Soul

In October 1584, a bare two weeks after Hakluyt had presented his dossier and nine days after the first of the crucial Privy Council meetings on the crisis in the Netherlands, Elizabeth faced yet another dilemma. It all started when Burghley and his fellow councillors put their signatures and seals to a revolutionary document called 'The Instrument of an Association for the Preservation of Her Majesty's Royal Person', otherwise known as the Bond of Association. The signatories solemnly swore to take 'the uttermost revenge' on all persons, including royalty, who were found to have conspired or colluded in an attempt (successful or otherwise) on the queen's life, and 'to prosecute such person or persons to the death'. Retribution was to be exacted on the spot. No 'pretended successor by whom *or for whom* [my emphasis] any such detestable act shall be attempted or committed' was to be spared. This clause was at once far reaching and arbitrary, as it promised to extend the long arm of retribution to all living heirs and successors of the intended beneficiary. Thus, if anyone were to threaten Elizabeth's life in the interests of the Stuart succession, both Mary and James VI could now be executed, whether privy to the attempt or not.[1]

From the outset, Burghley's aim was to bypass existing chains of command. And that included Elizabeth. The Bond was unusual because those who signed it declared themselves to be autonomous agents of the state, empowered to act on its behalf.[2] They protested their loyalty to the queen, but also asserted their loyalty to one another and to the Protestant cause. They had, in effect, bound themselves to do whatever they could to ensure that England's next ruler would be a Protestant, and not the Catholic Mary Queen of Scots.

All this was as abhorrent to Elizabeth as it would have been to her father. As she saw it, not only was it lynch law, it struck at the very heart of the principle of God-appointed monarchy, which she held dear and was determined to uphold. When Parliament met in November, a battle of wills ensued. Burghley was already drafting radical constitutional provisions with a view to empowering a 'Council of State' or a 'Great' or 'Grand Council' to choose Elizabeth's successor in conjunction with Parliament should she suddenly die or be assassinated, with the Council acting in the name of the Protestant religion so as to exclude the possibility of a future Catholic monarch.[3]

Elizabeth was determined to thwart him. The Act for the Queen's Surety, in the form in which she assented to it in Parliament in March 1585, blunted the effects of the Bond by providing that any claimant or pretender to the throne (meaning Mary) who stood to benefit from a plot to assassinate Elizabeth, or anyone colluding in an invasion, rebellion or attempt on her life, would be tried by a special commission of at least twenty-four privy councillors and members of the House of Lords, appointed by the queen and assisted by judges of her choosing. These commissioners were empowered to judge whether this claimant or pretender should be barred from the succession, but they were not to publish a guilty verdict. If such a verdict were to be reached, nothing could be done until due 'declaration' of the decision had been 'made and published by Her Majesty's proclamation under the Great Seal of England'. Only then, 'by virtue of this Act and Her Majesty's direction in that behalf', might revenge be exacted in keeping with the terms of the Bond.

The queen believed she had turned the tables on Burghley, limiting the potential for lynch law and recovering sufficient control to neutralize the most subversive effects of the Bond. But was she right?[4]

A month or so before the Bond, Mary Queen of Scots had been moved from the Earl of Shrewsbury's custody at Chatsworth and Sheffield, where she had largely been held for the past fifteen years, and transferred to that of the veteran Sir Ralph Sadler, who as a young ambassador to Edinburgh in the early 1540s had dandled the infant Mary on his knees. This was an unenviable duty: for the next five months, Sadler and his son-in-law John Somers would come under intense scrutiny, trapped between Elizabeth, who challenged every expense they incurred, however unavoidable, and Mary, who complained incessantly about her living conditions. Sadler held Mary temporarily at Wingfield Manor in Derbyshire before taking her to the more secure Tutbury Castle, a dilapidated motte-and-bailey fortress in nearby Staffordshire, notorious for its damp and draughty rooms and stinking drains. 'Use but old trust and new diligence' was the blunt warning that Elizabeth gave him on informing him that Mary's household was to occupy Tutbury.[5]

In a newly discovered and quite remarkable letter dictated shortly after the Bond was signed, Elizabeth opened her mind, if not her heart, to the woman who, in the 1560s, she had considered to have the best possible claim to succeed her by hereditary right.[6] Mary's flight across the Solway Firth to England in 1568 had presented the English queen with a stark choice. Should she protect her Catholic cousin or treat her as a threat? By October 1584, the answer was clear: Mary had become a dangerous threat, as Burghley had always said she would, chiefly through the actions of her Guise relatives.

For some reason, Elizabeth's letter and some forty other documents concerning this period of Mary's captivity were removed from the main body of the Sadler family papers in 1762 and then locked away in private hands until 2010, when they unexpectedly reappeared in a London saleroom.[7] When examined prior to the auction, some pieces of sewing thread could still be seen attached to them, indicating where they had been ripped out of an earlier bound volume. The cache included eight letters from Burghley and nineteen from Walsingham. Many vividly illustrate Walsingham's obsession with security: Sadler was given strict instructions about the restraint to be placed on his charge. She was, for example, 'not permitted to ride far abroad but only suffered [to go] on foot or in a coach to take the air and use some such exercise near the house where she shall lie'.

The most important letter, which Elizabeth signed with her customary flourish, is extraordinary for the insight it gives into the state of the complex relationship between the two queens at the time. Curiously, it was addressed to Sadler, who was to read all of it aloud to Mary. This indirect method of communication was made necessary, Elizabeth explained, 'through a vow heretofore made not to write unto her with our own hand until we might receive better satisfaction by effect from her to our contentment than heretofore we have done'.

Speaking her mind with rare candour and barely pausing for breath, let alone grammar or punctuation, Elizabeth levelled sharp criticism against Mary, who had pleaded that their mutual 'jealousy and mislike' should be set aside. Ever since Burghley had cancelled a rendezvous between the 'sister' queens planned for August or September 1562, following the massacre of a congregation of Huguenots in a barn at Wassy, near Joinville, in the heart of Guise territory, Mary had maintained that the two 'British' queens would be able to settle their differences woman to woman – if only they could meet. To such a plea, Elizabeth wished Sadler to give this reply:

> We wish she had been as careful for the time past to have avoided the cause and ground by her given of the just jealousy by us conceived as she now sheweth to mislike of the effects that the same hath (by due desert) bred towards her. For she herself knoweth (wherein we appeal unto her own conscience) how great contentment and liking we had for a time of her friendship, which as we then esteemed as a singular and extraordinary blessing of God to have one so nearly tied unto us in blood and neighbourhood, so greatly affected towards us as we then conceived, so are we now as much grieved to behold the alteration and interruption thereof, taking no pleasure to look back on the causes that have bred so unpleasant effects which we wish that either they had never been, or at the least we could never remember, and that she were as innocent therein as she laboureth greatly to bear both us and the world in hand that she is.[8]

Following these cutting remarks with an assurance that her goodwill was not wholly extinguished, despite Mary's 'sundry hard and dangerous courses held towards us', Elizabeth indicated that, should Mary seek a last-minute settlement, she might send one of her secretaries to attend her at Court. The reality is that she was genuinely torn: outwardly aloof but inwardly longing as much as her Scottish cousin for reconciliation so that normal queenly relations could resume between them. Should Mary wish to extend an olive branch, she confided to Sadler, she would consider any proposals she might have. And they would be welcomed.

A fresh start, however, would be difficult. After Mary's enemies in Scotland had forced her to abdicate in 1567, they appointed a regent to rule in the name of her young son, and her repeated proposals that Elizabeth should restore her to her throne by whatever means, perhaps jointly with James, had been strenuously blocked by Burghley. That Mary continued to insist on a personal interview as the precondition of reconciliation did not help. And yet there was more than a hint of hypocrisy in Elizabeth's stance, for she was denying her Scottish cousin what she had once asked for herself in uncomfortably similar circumstances. In 1554, facing arrest on suspicion of colluding in Wyatt's rebellion, she had appealed for a face-to-face meeting with her half-sister Mary Tudor before she was led away to the Tower. Beseeching her to 'take some better way with me than to make me condemned in all men's sight afore my desert known', Elizabeth had begged to be granted an interview so that she might 'answer afore yourself and not suffer me to trust your councillors – yea, and that afore I go to the Tower (if it be possible), if not afore I be further condemned'.[9]

In April 1585, Sadler was summarily relieved of his duties. He had allowed Mary to ride out hawking with insufficient supervision and had even (as the newly discovered documents reveal) given her permission during a rainstorm to make an unauthorized stop in the town of Derby at a widow's house, where she had spoken animatedly to several inhabitants.[10] Closely questioned by Burghley, Sadler gave his own account of the incident:

> Her entertainment to the women of Derby was in this sort. In the hall of the widow's house was the good wife with 3 or 4 at the most of her neighbours, whom she saluted with a beck [nod] with her head and kissed her hostess and none other, saying that she was come thither to trouble her and that she was a widow too, and so trusted they should agree well enough together having no husband to trouble them.[11]

Elizabeth was not amused, so instead Mary was put in the custody of Sir Amyas Paulet, a zealous Calvinist who had no time for what he called 'foolish pity', and taken to Chartley in Staffordshire, a manor house more comfortable than Tutbury but considerably more secure. Severe and uncompromising, Paulet was Walsingham's trusted ally. As another former ambassador in Paris, he had come into contact with several of Mary's agents, about whose malice he had never entertained the slightest doubts. A fervent supporter of the Huguenots and the Dutch rebels, Paulet was yoked to Walsingham in a concerted effort to bring Mary down.

They had little over a year to wait. In July 1586, four months before Leicester was summoned home from the Netherlands, Walsingham began unravelling the threads of what at first seemed to be one of the most menacing plots so far to assassinate the queen. Under the notional leadership of a rich, gullible, young Catholic dilettante named Anthony Babington, the conspirators aimed to send a troop of cavalry to Chartley to liberate Mary while she was out riding with her guards to take the air. At the same time, six gentlemen – 'all my private friends', as Babington helpfully explained in a highly compromising letter to Mary – would set out for the Court to kill Elizabeth.[12]

A dangerous plot existed, but the conspirators fell into a trap when, at a very early stage in their planning, they made the fateful mistake of welcoming as their postman a dubious seminary drop-out who was one of Walsingham's agents. The result was that all their and Mary's correspondence was delivered straight to Walsingham's assistant, the expert cryptographer Thomas Phelippes. When Babington got cold feet and threatened to pull out, Walsingham used his *agents provocateurs* to revive the plot, so as to secure the evidence he needed to put Mary on trial according to the Act for the Queen's Surety. In other words, rather than arresting Babington and his associates so as to nip the plot in the bud as soon as he learned of it, Walsingham secretly nurtured the conspiracy, almost to its fatal conclusion, in an extraordinary piece of puppetry.

Mary sealed her fate when she dictated to her two faithful secretaries, Claude Nau and Gilbert Curle, a ciphered reply to Babington in the course of which she asked him, 'By what means do the six gentlemen deliberate to proceed?' This was taken to mean that she had specifically endorsed the part of the conspiracy which sought to kill Elizabeth. She was entirely unaware that her letter would immediately be intercepted and passed to Thomas Phelippes.

A euphoric Phelippes nicknamed this the 'bloody letter', but instead of arresting Babington even at this advanced stage of the plot,

Walsingham and Phelippes decided to doctor the letter and send it on to Babington in the hope of securing more incriminating evidence. The main text was left alone, but Phelippes added a postscript, using an identical cipher: a blatant and audacious forgery of which he cheekily left his draft in the archives.[13] It was a clumsy subterfuge: an attempt to entice Babington to disclose the 'names and qualities' of the 'six gentlemen' and their accomplices. And it conspicuously failed, as Babington's suspicions were aroused: he burned the letter and fled. Ten days later, he was caught hiding in a barn with his hair cropped short and his face grimed to make him look like a farm worker.[14]

When Walsingham handed Elizabeth his file on the plot, she stalled. Along with Burghley, she was concerned that – with the original of the 'bloody letter' destroyed for ever – the evidence would be incomplete. Walsingham's ingenious solution was to arrest Mary's secretaries. Detaining them at his house in Seething Lane in London, he laid before them a brilliant forgery: an accurately ciphered reconstruction by Phelippes of the missing 'bloody letter' without the postscript. Pressed to the limit of their physical and mental endurance by Burghley during a series of long interrogations, Nau and Curle confessed that this was indeed the letter to Babington which Mary had dictated to them. Next, Walsingham either put a transcript of the 'bloody letter' in front of Babington or asked him to confirm from memory what it said. Without further ado, Babington authenticated the text, although his version, embarrassingly, included the forged postscript.[15]

Babington was hanged in a glare of publicity in September 1586, after which Elizabeth gave all of his now-confiscated lands to Ralegh, to help him pay his debts after the failure of his Roanoke expedition.[16] She knew it would be only a matter of time before Burghley pressed her to name the commissioners who would hear the evidence against Mary. By giving her assent in Parliament to the Act for the Queen's Surety she had boxed herself in: the law would have to take its course. Weighing strongly on her mind when at last she agreed to name commissioners was her belief that, even if they were to come up with a 'guilty' verdict, she could refuse to proclaim their sentence in keeping with the terms of the Act.

She knew that one regicide by its very nature encourages another, and that a regicide authorized by a law made by Parliament would alter the future of the monarchy in the British Isles for ever. It would tend to make the ruler accountable to Parliament, creating the impression that kings could be proclaimed or deposed by the people's elected representatives, and so diminishing for ever what Shakespeare's Hamlet called the 'divinity [that] doth hedge a king'.[17]

Mary was put on trial in the Great Hall at Fotheringhay Castle in Northamptonshire between 12 and 15 October 1586, watched by the local gentry. She took part only under voluble protest and was visibly shaken as, piece by piece, the case against her took shape. When she realized that all of her secret correspondence had been intercepted, she could no longer contain her emotions. She burst into tears and left the hall on the final day before the hearings were over. But despite her distress, she kept her wits about her, taxing Walsingham for the uncanny perfection of his proofs. 'It was an easy matter', she said, 'to counterfeit the ciphers and characters of others.' She was not fooled by Walsingham's methods, even if she did not know precisely what he had done in the business of the forged postscript.[18]

The commissioners were asked to reconvene on the 25th at Westminster, in the Star Chamber, where the evidence was reviewed again in full. Mary was found guilty in her absence. But when Burghley called upon Elizabeth to proclaim the verdict under the Great Seal in keeping with the terms of the Act for the Queen's Surety, she was numbed at the prospect of attenuating the ideal of monarchy by killing Mary, and refused. In her eyes, a queen, even one deposed by her own subjects or Parliament, was still a queen. Once she had been anointed and crowned, nothing could take that inviolable status from her.

On 4 December, under intense pressure from Burghley, Elizabeth grudgingly allowed the guilty sentence to be sealed and proclaimed. Now, she struggled to escape a fresh dilemma she had herself largely created. By insisting in Parliament on the clause of the Act that governed how revenge might be exacted against a guilty party ('by virtue of this Act *and Her Majesty's direction in that behalf*'), she had made a rod for her own back. Had she fulfilled all of her obligations under the

Act by appointing commissioners and then sealing and proclaiming their sentence, after which anyone who had subscribed to the Bond might lawfully kill Mary? Or would she physically have to sign her cousin's death warrant, the thing she most dreaded? After the appalling revelations of the Babington Plot, she finally wished Mary dead, but she wanted her to be quietly smothered by a private citizen, thereby relieving her of the responsibility of having her killed.

Elizabeth gave Walsingham brutally short shrift for informing her that she would now need to sign Mary's death warrant. Twelve days after the guilty sentence was sealed and proclaimed, he left London in dismay, telling Burghley: 'Her Majesty's unkind dealing towards me hath so wounded me as I would take no comfort to stay there.'[19] Things were no better after Christmas, when he reported himself sick. 'The grief of my mind', he declared, 'hath thrown me into a dangerous disease.' Dr Bailey – one of Elizabeth's personal physicians, who ordered her monthly supply of unguents and medicines from her apothecaries – would confirm this.[20]

Walsingham's illness was real. Ever since his time as ambassador to Paris in the early 1570s, he had suffered under stress from extremely painful, recurring urinary infections. Without the benefit of modern antibiotics, he had no alternative but, literally, to sweat it out.

William Davison, now back from the Netherlands and sworn in as Elizabeth's secretary and a privy councillor, advised Burghley that the queen would never sign Mary's death warrant 'lest extreme fear compel her'.[21] Resorting to a method he had used earlier in her reign when Elizabeth had failed to come around to his point of view, Burghley now fostered a false rumour that Spanish troops had landed in Wales, and briefed the queen accordingly. He and Walsingham then called on the newly appointed French ambassador, Guillaume de l'Aubespine, Baron de Châteauneuf, at his house in Bishopsgate Street, in the company of Leicester and Hatton. They effectively blackmailed him into conspiring with them to 'discover' a fresh assassination plot which was, in reality, two years old and had amounted to very little.[22] Centring on a shady character named Michael Moody, a servant of Sir Edward Stafford, the conspirators had allegedly talked of planting barrels of gunpowder in the room beneath Elizabeth's Bedchamber to blow her up, or of poisoning her stirrup or shoe. A beleaguered Châteauneuf was forced to connive in this deceit, as Henry III was by this time so threatened by the forces of the Duke of Guise encircling him in Paris that he felt he could not afford to jeopardize his accord with England.[23]

Told by Burghley to double the number of her bodyguards, Elizabeth momentarily caved in. On Wednesday, 1 February 1587, while at Greenwich Palace, she sent for Davison and asked him to bring with him the copy of Mary's death warrant Burghley had carefully drafted some weeks before, in which he called for speedy justice against a woman who was an 'undoubted danger' to Elizabeth and the 'public state of this realm, as well for the cause of the Gospel and the true religion of Christ'.[24] When he arrived, she called for pen and ink, and signed. She then ordered Davison not to let the document out of his possession or to show it to anyone before he had it sealed by the Lord Chancellor. Next, she made a joke. Walsingham was still recovering in bed in Seething Lane and she wryly told Davison he should call on him and tell him she had at last signed the death warrant – 'because the "grief" thereof would grow near to kill him outright'.[25]

Elizabeth and Walsingham shared a strong line in sardonic humour. The idea that he would die of grief at Mary's death was grimly ironic. Except that Elizabeth did not jest in vain. She had a far more lethal intent. For next she instructed Davison to order Walsingham to write a letter in his own name to Mary's custodian, Amyas Paulet, demanding that he do away with his prisoner. It was a desperate move. Paulet was to act as a private citizen, 'prosecuting' the Scottish queen 'to the death' without a warrant and taking the 'uttermost revenge' in his capacity as a signatory to the Bond of Association – this with all the risk of reprisal, not least after the event from Elizabeth herself.[26] Wisely, Paulet refused, calling the plan 'dishonourable and dangerous' and rightly foreseeing that Elizabeth would soon be looking for scapegoats.

Soon after visiting Walsingham, Davison made what he later realized was a catastrophic mistake. Although Elizabeth had ordered him not to allow the signed death warrant out of his possession or to show it to anyone, he let Burghley and Leicester see it. Immediately grasping its momentous significance, they ordered him to have it sealed that very afternoon.

Shortly after ten o'clock the next morning, however, Elizabeth sent Davison a message. If, she said, the warrant had not yet been sealed, he should delay the process. Deeply uneasy, he hurried to the Privy Chamber to warn her that it had been sealed already. She muttered something barely audible about his 'unseemly haste', and then (according to Davison) said she wished to be 'no more troubled with the matter'.

Davison was too experienced not to see the danger signals. He had the sealed warrant in his possession, but what was he to do with it? He quickly shared his doubts with Hatton, who in turn consulted Burghley. Acting on his own initiative, the queen's chief minister questioned Davison intently, then convened a clandestine meeting of ten privy councillors in his private lodgings for the next day. Before parting with Davison, Burghley ordered him to hand over the sealed warrant for safekeeping. He did.

With the death warrant signed and sealed and now safely in his possession, Burghley complacently believed that he could still mould or manipulate Elizabeth as he had done so often in the earlier years of their relationship. When his colleagues assembled on 3 February, he read the warrant aloud, then coaxed his fellow councillors into agreeing that Robert Beale, one of the clerks of the Privy Council and Walsingham's brother-in-law, should carry it to Fotheringhay as quickly as possible, 'without troubling Her Majesty further in that behalf'. She was to hear nothing more about Mary's execution 'until it were done'. Drafts of covering letters, prepared overnight by Burghley for Amyas Paulet and the commissioners chosen to preside on the day of the execution in the Great Hall at Fotheringhay, were read and approved and it was ordered that they be written out in fair copy. Burghley then swore everyone to strict secrecy. He asked all those attending to sign a record of the meeting, after which he sent Robert Beale to Seething Lane to secure Walsingham's signature from his sickbed. The proceedings were justified in the record as for Elizabeth's 'special service tending to the safety of her royal person and universal quietness of her whole realm'.[27]

★ ★ ★

That night, Elizabeth woke in fear, complaining that she had dreamed of Mary's death. Her loyal kinswoman and long-standing friend in the inner Bedchamber, Dorothy Stafford, whose turn it had been to sleep beside her on a pallet bed, reported a simultaneous nightmare.[28]

At daybreak, the queen sent again for Davison and told him of this strange 'augury'. In keeping with his oath, given to Burghley at the clandestine Council meeting, Davison answered evasively, skirting any mention of the sending of the warrant. Later, he would profess somewhat weakly that he felt there had been no need to say more: he had, he said, 'naturally' assumed that Elizabeth had already been told what had been done by more senior privy councillors.

For Elizabeth, this was not just a dream but a real-life nightmare. Faced with the conundrum of how to bring about Mary's death without sacrificing her most cherished ideals and fatally compromising the sanctity of God-appointed monarchy, she found herself emotionally paralysed. Then, her survival instinct kicked in, just as it had in 1560 when the news of the suspicious death of Leicester's first wife, Amy Robsart, had reached her. To protect her reputation and self-esteem, she decided to play poker with her councillors, for the highest possible stakes.

Determined not to let Burghley outwit her and knowing his working methods all too well, she began to prepare herself mentally for what she would do if, as she suspected, he had gone behind her back and sent the signed death warrant to Fotheringhay. Davison alone stood in the way of her ability to disavow knowledge of all that she and they had done. She could claim she was the victim of a Court conspiracy. Had she not recalled Davison the very day after she had signed the warrant and told him to delay in having it sealed? And had she not told him that on no account was he to allow the warrant to leave his possession? She conveniently chose to forget that she had also told him she wished to be 'no more troubled with the matter'. And if, as she hoped, her cousin were to be killed under the terms of the Bond of Association, she could blame Paulet and disclaim all responsibility for what she still regarded as a terrifying act of regicide.

On account of riding out for the day with a Portuguese diplomat, Elizabeth was almost the last person at Court to hear of Mary's death. The execution took place shortly after nine o'clock on the morning of Wednesday, 8 February. So fearful of what he was about to do to an anointed queen, the executioner bungled the task. His first strike of the axe was misaligned, missing the neck and hacking into the back of Mary's head. A second strike severed her neck, but not completely, and he had to slice through the remaining sinews, using the axe as a cleaver, with blood gushing everywhere. Mary died in agonizing pain. A shocked eyewitness wrote that 'her lips stirred up and down a quarter of an hour after her head was cut off'.[29]

The news travelled fast. Burghley and Hatton both knew before dawn the next day. Châteauneuf had heard by midday, and at around three o'clock in the afternoon all the bells of London rang out and bonfires were lit in the streets. When Burghley finally came clean in the evening and told Elizabeth that her cousin was dead, she gave 'a great sigh' but otherwise feigned indifference.[30]

Or at least she did for a time. On Friday the 10th, the sleeping dragon stirred. Refusing to speak to Burghley and using Hatton as her intermediary, she inveighed angrily against those who had attended the clandestine Council meeting, 'casting the burden generally upon them all but chiefly upon my shoulders', as Davison related, 'because (as she protesteth) I had in suffering it [the warrant] to go out of my hands abused the trust she reposed in me'.

That evening or the next, Elizabeth summoned her privy councillors – all but Leicester, who had conveniently absented himself – to attend her in her withdrawing chamber. There, she berated them all for their treachery. Burghley and Davison were singled out and attacked with venom for their part in dispatching the death warrant, 'for she protests she gave express commandment to the contrary, and therefore had taken order for the committing of Mr Davison to the Tower'. The councillors fell on their knees, pleading for forgiveness, to no avail.[31]

Within a week, Davison was dragged off to the Tower in a cart, despite being ill. According to Robert Beale, Burghley escaped a similar fate only because Elizabeth 'thought that to commit him to the Tower would kill him'. Not yet fully appreciating the danger he was in, Burghley began experimenting with drafts of two petitions on behalf of himself and his colleagues.[32] By the time he had perfected the second, a metamorphosis had taken place. When beginning the first he had used language that made it plain the blame was shared, but by the end of the second draft all of it was squarely transferred on to the shoulders of the unfortunate Davison. Burghley also systematically purged the archives. Documents he is known to have drafted or corrected himself, notably his drafts of the instructions sent to the commissioners at Fotheringhay and to Amyas Paulet, he recovered and burned.[33] If Elizabeth had an instinct for self-preservation, so did he.

Davison was lucky not to be hanged. Elizabeth consulted a panel of judges to see whether she could order this summarily by the royal prerogative and, in fear, some said she could. His life was spared only after a valiant intervention on his behalf by Lord Buckhurst. Another of the queen's kinsfolk, he was her second cousin. A zealous Protestant and Burghley's close ally, lately made a privy councillor for his loyal service to Elizabeth, Buckhurst had played no part in Mary's trial or in the sending down of the death warrant. Taking his courage in both hands, he told the queen to her face that she should consider the damage that would be done to her reputation if it ever became known that she had hanged her unfortunate secretary when, all along, the warrant he had allowed out of his possession had 'both your hand and seal' upon it. Were she to persist in seeking Davison's blood, Buckhurst dared to say, she would end up looking like a murderer.[34]

Elizabeth relented. But having been reminded that she had indeed signed the warrant, and wondering what had become of it, she did her own bit of archival sleuthing, after which the original of the signed death warrant that Robert Beale had fatefully delivered to Fotheringhay mysteriously disappeared. Since Beale records that he carefully preserved it among the records of the Privy Council for ratification in Parliament, we must assume that its disappearance was no accident. Today, it is known only from two hastily written copies made by Beale himself shortly before he left for Fotheringhay.

Who had won? Was it Burghley, who had achieved his long-held ambition to exclude the Catholic Mary from the throne and in the process spectacularly vindicated the right of a woman ruler's (male) privy councillors to bypass her if she wavered? Or was it Elizabeth, who had humbled her advisers and achieved what, in the end, she knew had to be done, but in a way that allowed her, in her own mind at least, to believe she had safeguarded the highest ideals of God-appointed monarchy?

To all practical effects, Elizabeth won. Davison was put on trial in the Star Chamber, the most feared tribunal in the land, since the basis of its jurisdiction was the royal prerogative. As his case turned on his word against the queen's and boiled down to a matter of interpreting her mind, he could not really mount a credible defence. Seeing that his salvation lay in keeping his mouth shut, he told his judges that he 'desired not to be urged to utter the private speeches that passed between the queen and him'. He suppressed all mention of Elizabeth's demand to Paulet that Mary should be assassinated. And he never disclosed publicly that those who had met in Burghley's lodgings had sworn an oath not to reveal their action to the queen.[35]

To save his own skin, Burghley was forced not just to lie but to commit perjury in court. On the eve of the trial, he and his colleagues filed a legal affidavit in the Star Chamber in which they blamed Davison for summoning the clandestine Privy Council meeting, for reading the death warrant aloud, for writing the letters and instructions sent to Fotheringhay and, especially, for reassuring everyone that Elizabeth meant the warrant to be dispatched. Or, at least, all but one of the ten councillors who had been present perjured themselves: Walsingham, honourably, refused to sign the affidavit, throwing his career briefly into jeopardy.[36]

After a draining ordeal lasting four hours, Davison was fined 10,000 marks (more than £6 million in modern values) and sentenced to imprisonment at the queen's pleasure. He could not possibly pay such a huge sum, but his fine was never collected and he was quietly released from the Tower after a year. His salary continued to be paid, but he was suspended from office permanently.[37]

Burghley, too, was far from unscathed. Elizabeth banished him from her presence. He was allowed to speak briefly to her in March, but as late as 1 June she was still freezing him out, denouncing him as a 'traitor, false dissembler and wicked wretch'. She partially relented later in the month, consenting to pay a visit to his magnificent country house at Theobalds in Hertfordshire, where she had stayed at least three times in the 1570s, before continuing on to Oatlands and Richmond palaces.[38] But their relationship would never be the same again. She had abjectly humiliated him, teaching him a lesson he would never forget: she was no longer the novice he had manipulated in the past, she was his absolute sovereign – certainly not a 'mere' woman whose will could be disregarded. Everything rested on her favour, which, as he now understood, could not be taken for granted.[39]

With Davison's conviction in the Star Chamber, Elizabeth considered herself sufficiently exculpated in the eyes of Europe from a charge of regicide. Writing to James VI, Mary's son, who would shortly be twenty-one and had declared his minority to be at an end, she feigned innocence and simply brazened it out. The whole affair, she professed, had been a 'miserable accident'.[40] Since the details were 'too irksome for my pen to tell you', she sent Robert Carey, the youngest of 'Harry' Lord Hunsdon's nine sons, whom she affectionately called 'Robin', to report them verbally. Carey, who had first met James while accompanying Walsingham on a mission to Scotland in 1583, had already made a favourable impression on the young king, but on this occasion James forbade him to cross the frontier for his own safety and forced him to deliver the queen's excuses to two of his councillors.[41]

Elizabeth harped on her innocence to James. 'I am not so base minded that fear of any living creature or prince should make me afraid to do that [which] were just or, done, to deny the same,' she protested. 'I am not of so base a lineage nor carry so vile a mind. But as not to disguise fits most a king, so will I never dissemble my actions, but cause them [to] show even as I meant them.' If indeed she had intended to have his mother executed at Fotheringhay, she informed James, lying through her teeth, 'I would never lay it on others' shoulders.'[42]

By the time she wrote this letter, Elizabeth had already decided to be her own woman and never again to be inveigled or bounced by her councillors into anything she strongly disagreed with, if she could prevent it. On this occasion, the results were bittersweet, but by sacrificing Davison she had subordinated Burghley and his coterie to her authority in ways they had never experienced before. Her victory had come at a high price. Whatever she chose to tell herself or others about it, an anointed queen had been killed at Fotheringhay. Elizabeth had to live with her conscience, but now she also had to move on. She would find it to be no easy task. For the searing events surrounding her cousin's execution struck to the core of her psychology. This, truly, was Elizabeth's Armada of the soul.

5.   No Warrior Queen

With Mary dead, Philip II was quick to claim the kingdom of England for Spain. Since May 1585, when he first placed an embargo on English and Dutch shipping, he had been contemplating more drastic retaliation for Elizabeth's decision to send the Earl of Leicester with an expeditionary force to intervene in the Netherlands. In January 1586, he asked one of his leading commanders, the Marquis of Santa Cruz, a veteran of the spectacular Spanish naval victory against the Ottoman Turks at the Battle of Lepanto in 1571, when the entire western Mediterranean was made safe from Islam, for a secret report outlining what would be needed for a full-scale invasion.

Had Philip joined with the pope and the Jesuits in an effort to overthrow Elizabeth at that moment, he would merely have reinforced the right of Mary and her Guise relatives to rule over the whole of the British Isles, which was hardly in his interests. Everything changed shortly before the regicide at Fotheringhay, when Mary revised her will. Naming Philip as her dynastic heir, she abruptly disinherited her son, James: that is, if James remained true to the Protestant faith in which her hated enemies in Scotland had brought him up.[1] This he seemed likely to do as, shortly before Leicester had embarked on his command in 1585, Elizabeth had decided to 'procure' – in other words 'bribe' – the susceptible James 'to depend' on her and not on Spain.[2]

James had signed a league with Elizabeth, ratified in July 1586, and since then he had been in English pay, receiving a generous annual pension of £5,000 (some £5 million today).[3] On top of this, Elizabeth, for the very first time, was prepared to recognize him as the rightful king of Scots. She wrote him emollient letters in her own hand addressed to *Mon bon frère, le Roy d'Écosse.* She even dangled before him the prospect of what she had thus far always refused to concede: the possibility of a future claim by dynastic right to the throne of England – providing that he stayed Protestant and behaved himself.[4]

In Rome the new pope, Sixtus V – famous for his mistrust of Spain and tendency to throw crockery about when crossed – urged Philip to 'prove' himself by performing some glorious deed in defence of God's church and of papal authority. Among the pope's suggestions was a plan to overthrow Elizabeth by converting James to Catholicism and installing him in her place. Much irked, Philip ordered his ambassador to the Vatican, Count Olivares, to make it clear to Pope Sixtus that he would gladly join him in deposing Elizabeth, but never to benefit James. He would rather, he said, put on the English throne his eldest (and only surviving) daughter, the Infanta Isabella Clara Eugenia.[5]

Confident that France would not interfere, as the struggle over the disputed succession there was so violent that Henry III no longer felt secure in Paris, Philip began assembling at Seville, Lisbon and Cádiz the individual components of what would soon become his great fleet, or *Gran Armada*. At that point, his information on Elizabeth's plans was sketchy and out of date, but by the spring of 1587 Bernardino de Mendoza, Spain's ambassador in Paris, had recruited a new spy, who was to operate under the code name of Giulio, or 'Julio'.[6]

For four hundred and fifty years, the role of 'Julio' and the industrial scale of his espionage during the Armada crisis – as revealed in Mendoza's secret dispatches – lay undiscovered.[7] In fact, 'Julio' was none other than Sir Edward Stafford, Elizabeth's ambassador to France. Since 1899, his name has been on a long list of potential suspects, but only modern electronic searching has had the power to cross-correlate several hundred references and so confirm his true identity. To suborn Stafford was a spectacular coup, bringing sweet revenge to Mendoza for his expulsion from England after the Throckmorton Plot. Over the next eighteen months or so, Stafford was to pass on a mass of highly secret intelligence about Elizabeth's diplomatic and military plans, receiving regular payments of between 500 and 2,500 gold escudos (£187,000 and £937,000 today), which helped to pay off his gambling debts.

Stafford may have been motivated by more than money. His resentment at Elizabeth's bullying tactics after he married Douglas Sheffield still rankled. Beyond that, he hoped to secure a prominent role for himself in a post-Elizabethan order should a Spanish invasion plan succeed. Walsingham suspected his treachery. For several months, he had been intercepting Stafford's correspondence, even opening and resealing his letters to his mother, Dorothy, undeterred by her proximity to the queen. But Stafford was crafty. He took careful steps to cover his tracks, providing Mendoza with the occasional piece of false information. And, without hard evidence, it was impossible for Walsingham to arrest the queen's ambassador, the son of one of her most trusted confidantes.

In March 1587, Sir Francis Drake, the English naval prodigy whom King Philip feared most, persuaded a reluctant Elizabeth to lend him four royal navy ships and two pinnaces to reinforce some twenty armed merchantmen he had assembled. He offered to do whatever he could to disable Philip's naval power and, for the moment, she agreed. Specifically, his plan was to blockade the Iberian coast and to pillage ships arriving from the East or West Indies.

Walsingham, eager to prevent 'Julio' from leaking this classified information, delayed informing Stafford of Drake's mission for almost three weeks.[8] By then, a dramatic turnaround had taken place. Drake's flotilla had barely left Plymouth when Elizabeth issued fresh instructions countermanding those she had given earlier. After brooding intently on the prospect of outright war with Philip, she had decided to pull back and sue the Duke of Parma for peace. Drake, meanwhile, was strictly 'to forbear' to enter any of Philip's ports, or to pillage his towns or harbours or attempt 'any hostility' whatsoever upon his lands. All he might still do was to intercept and attack on the high seas Philip's shipping to or from Asia and the New World.[9]

Elizabeth's revised commission never reached Drake. Sent to Plymouth on 9 April, it arrived a week too late. By then, her peace overtures to Parma had been favourably, if cautiously, received.[10] In consequence, Drake's daring attack on Cádiz on 19 April profoundly annoyed rather than pleased her. In a masterly assault later dubbed 'the Singeing of the King of Spain's Beard', Drake penetrated the port's inner harbour under the camouflage of French (or Dutch) flags. He sank or burned over thirty Spanish ships, then cheekily replenished his own fast-diminishing supplies from Philip's well-stocked warehouses. Sailing off to the Azores, the customary rendezvous of the Spanish king's New World and East Indian fleets, before making a final, perilous dash into home waters, he captured a hugely valuable prize, the *San Felipe*, a very large and rich Portuguese carrack laden with a cargo of porcelain, silks and velvet, pepper and spices, a small quantity of jewels and some slaves.

Elizabeth was deeply embarrassed by Drake's success. What she wanted at this moment was not war but peace. Newly discovered documents in the archives in Brussels recording Parma's side of the negotiations make it crystal clear that – subtle and seductive as the idea may have appeared to the Victorians – she was never a warrior queen.[11] For her, fighting Spanish soldiers in the Netherlands, even attacking enemy shipping on the high seas, was just about acceptable, especially when it came in direct retaliation for Philip's aggression. What she could not bear to contemplate – and what now seemed all too imminent – was the idea of the whole of northern Europe convulsed in battle and a Spanish army landing on English soil. Cheered on by the prognostications of Dr John Dee, who like Burghley and Leicester she had called upon several times before to cast horoscopes, she believed peace was attainable.[12] Even if the price was high, it was the only sure way to quench a firestorm that could topple entire kingdoms and governments. In almost complete denial of the fact that Philip had already decided to invade her country, come what may, she convinced herself that, deep down, peace was really what he wanted, too.[13]

Burghley and Walsingham thought otherwise. Both anxiously urged Elizabeth to prepare for war rather than waste precious time on diplomacy. But she dug in her heels. She sparred tetchily with them both, still barely on speaking terms with them after the events at Fotheringhay. She resolutely refused to order the musters and naval exercises they advised, because she did not want to lay herself open to a charge of bad faith in suing for peace. Once Drake had returned, he was ordered to mothball his ships.

Confined to bed for a fortnight with a debilitating attack of gout (from which he would increasingly suffer as the years went by), Burghley knew that Parma would profit from Elizabeth's inaction. The Duke, he warned, would use the peace talks to lull her into a false sense of security, while continuing to mobilize for war. As Lord Treasurer, Burghley was concerned that the Exchequer's cash reserves were spent, but Elizabeth rejected any attempt to replenish them. When he sent her a written protest, she slapped him down, berating him as 'old and doting'.[14]

As 'Julio' drily informed Mendoza, Burghley was forced to concede that there were matters she alone could decide, 'like the beheading of the Queen of Scotland'. After almost thirty years as queen, she had finally taught her chief minister that a woman ruler was capable of taking her own decisions, right or wrong, and that they were not to be challenged. Walsingham was less compliant. He bitterly complained that Elizabeth 'would only follow her own will, which would bring about her ruin and that of all her councillors'.[15]

Elizabeth proposed that a peace conference be held at Emden, in Lower Saxony.[16] She suggested that King Frederick II of Denmark and Norway mediate between her and King Philip, and she used Andreas de Loo, whom she had employed before, to broker the preliminary negotiations in Brussels. When she was an adolescent, one of her Latin and Greek tutors had been Danish, and she felt a bond with the country as a result.[17] Parma, however, rejected these proposals, not least as Frederick was a Lutheran. The remaining months of 1587 were wasted in fruitless haggling, much of it over the proposed venue for the talks.[18]

Deeply pessimistic as to the outcome, Burghley grumbled to de Loo that 'the only foundation which Her Majesty maketh to proceed in this treaty' was Parma's reputation as a man of honour.[19] For his part, Leicester, remembering his bruising experiences in dealing both with the Duke and with the Dutch, was horrified at what he saw as the queen's gullibility. 'What a treaty is this for peace', he fulminated, 'that we must treat altogether disarmed and weakened and the king [of Spain] having made his forces stronger than ever.'[20]

Fearful of a looming catastrophe, Leicester took his courage in both hands. On or about 7 November, he confronted Elizabeth face to face and urged her to prepare for a military confrontation with Spain. He begged her to unshackle Drake and let him build up a strong reserve of ships. They quarrelled furiously; so much so that the embers were still smouldering over Christmas. At eleven o'clock at night on Boxing Day, Elizabeth could contain herself no longer. Suddenly losing her temper, she berated her favourite, lashing out at him with her arms and fists and telling him that 'it behoved her at any cost to be friendly with Spain.' When Leicester reminded her of the damage Drake had successfully inflicted on Philip's ships with a relatively small force, she countered, realistically perhaps, that for all his prowess as a mariner, Drake had never engaged in an open battle at sea. 'I do not see', she snapped, 'that he has done much damage to the enemy, except to scandalize him at considerable loss to me.'[21]

On the evening of 2 February 1588, Candlemas Day, shortly before seating herself in her Presence Chamber at Greenwich Palace to watch a comedy by the dramatist John Lyly about the Man in the Moon, Elizabeth ordered a messenger to ride post-haste to her allies in Holland.[22] He was to deliver a letter she had dictated earlier, strongly denying rumours of a secret accord with Parma. She was, the letter somewhat disingenuously declared, greatly wronged 'that such false and malicious bruits should be given out'.[23]

She protested too much. Scarcely a month later, to the dismay of the Dutch, she formally opened peace talks with Parma. Representing her were five commissioners, led by the Earl of Derby. Beginning at Ostend and then moving to nearby Bourbourg, Derby sat down with Parma's representatives to discuss her proposals.

Elizabeth was determined to retain control so refused to let Burghley make more than a handful of minor amendments to her instructions. Derby's orders were to secure a general truce with Spain covering the whole of the British Isles. Nothing, however humiliating or dishonourable, was to stand in the way of such a truce. Belatedly, after intense pressure from the States General, she asked for religious toleration for the Dutch for ten (later reduced to two) years and demanded that Spanish troops withdraw from the Netherlands. But, with Philip denying that he had ever authorized Parma to begin this diplomacy, all the Duke could do was offer to suspend Spain's attacks on the queen's auxiliary forces in the Netherlands for a brief interval. Even then, his spokesman warned ominously, 'It should be lawful in the mean time for the Queen of England to invade Spain and for the Spaniard to invade England out of Spain and the Low Countries.'[24]

The peace talks foundered. They were bound to: what Elizabeth never knew was that 'Julio' was revealing in advance to Mendoza, and thus to Parma, every diplomatic move she intended to make, and also reporting Walsingham's alarm at the poor state of English war preparations.[25] Still she refused to change course. Even when Parma admitted that Philip would never agree to a general truce, she ordered Derby to resume the talks without preconditions. The new documents in Brussels confirm that she was still suing abjectly for peace as late as 20 June, a month after the combined forces of the Spanish Armada, numbering some 140 ships, finally sailed out of the port of Lisbon into open waters, presumed to be heading north towards the English Channel.[26]

Philip had appointed the same man he had commissioned to plan his *Gran Armada*, the Marquis of Santa Cruz, to lead it, but in January 1588 a typhus epidemic in Lisbon carried away the Marquis and hundreds of his men. To replace him, Philip chose the Duke of Medina Sidonia. For all his efforts to excuse himself on grounds of ill health, inexperience and poverty, Medina Sidonia was in fact very well qualified. A practical, strong-willed general who had been involved in the planning from the outset, he had a good theoretical knowledge of navigation, handed down from his father. It was true that he lacked combat experience but, according to the Venetian ambassador, he was the only one of Philip's men to have kept his head when Drake attacked Cádiz. His main drawback was an extreme vulnerability to seasickness.[27]

Elizabeth believed she had exposed Philip's duplicity when he ordered his fleet to set sail before the peace talks were over. In reality, she had stood little chance of avoiding war. Parma, as Burghley suspected all along, had been keen to string out the diplomacy, but only to give himself more time to prepare for his critical role in the invasion plan.

The Spanish strategy aimed at a land campaign, not a naval war. It required Parma to ferry a pioneering task force of twenty-six thousand crack troops from the Army of Flanders across the Channel in a flotilla of some three hundred flat-bottomed barges. At the heart of the plan was an order from Philip that the ships of the Armada should not attempt to make an independent landing on the south coast of England: their role was to patrol the waters between the Flemish coast and the Isle of Thanet, off the coast of Kent, to provide cover for Parma's barges. On board the main Armada fleet were 18,500 troops, mostly raw recruits, ferried from Spain. But they were Philip's reserve force: only after Parma's troops had landed in England were they to disembark. The combined armies were then to march at breakneck speed through Kent towards London. Success depended on the precise coordination of these events.

After Christmas 1587, Parma warned Philip repeatedly that this plan was too complicated and that, although work on the barges was well advanced and he was mustering troops at Dunkirk and Nieuwpoort, the king's timetable was too inflexible. The Army of Flanders, Parma explained, was far from ready to spearhead an invasion. Besides, it would be risky for his men to attempt to board their barges before Spanish troops had captured a large enough port on the Dutch coast. The sandbanks were treacherous, the tides perilous and the Dutch were experts at harrying enemy ships in shallow coastal waters from the relative safety of their flyboats.

Elizabeth was less dogmatic. While she stubbornly refused to muster a land army until she at last received confirmation that the Armada had been sighted, she had begun to make naval preparations earlier. On 20 December, even as her quarrel with Leicester was festering, she decided to gather her fleet for possible defensive action along the south coast. Uncertain whether Philip's target would be England, Scotland or Ireland and so ill-equipped to prioritize the threats she faced, she instructed the Lord Admiral, Charles, Lord Howard of Effingham, to make plans to thwart all of them.[28] A gentleman of the Privy Chamber since 1558 and the son of her first Lord Chamberlain, Howard had found his fortunes transformed in 1563 when he married Katherine Carey (better known as Kate), Lord Hunsdon's eldest daughter.* In Mary's reign, Kate had been one of Elizabeth's maids, and in 1560 she was made a gentlewoman of the Privy Chamber when she was barely fifteen. A year later, as a prank, the queen famously disguised herself as Kate's maid so that she could sneak out

---

* Hence Kate was the queen's first cousin once removed.

to watch Robert Dudley shoot at Windsor. The disappearance of the Howard of Effingham papers makes Kate's life impossible to reconstruct but, like other favoured gentlewomen of the Privy Chamber, she had custody of some of the queen's jewels, and in 1579 Bernardino de Mendoza had seen her presiding over the table of the ladies of the Privy Chamber.[29]

Elizabeth instructed Howard to 'ply up and down' the North Sea, 'sometimes toward the North and sometimes toward the South', to guard against an attack by Parma's forces on the east coast of England or Scotland. 'Our servant Drake', meanwhile, was to take the rest of the fleet to the West Country, where he would 'ply up and down between the realm of Ireland and the west part of this our realm'. If Parma's army should attempt to cross the Channel, Howard should do whatever he could to intercept and repulse it. But if the Armada were to arrive first, then he should at once send reinforcements to assist Drake.[30] 'Julio' informed Mendoza (with a number of unavoidable inaccuracies, since his own information was incorrect) that Howard and Drake had assembled a force of 160 ships (the correct number was 105) at Plymouth by 30 May (the correct date was the 23rd). Of these, twenty were royal navy ships, the rest auxiliaries, meaning armed merchantmen hastily requisitioned.[31]

Unlike Philip, a control freak who invariably required his instructions to be followed to the letter, Elizabeth was flexible enough to allow her commanders some degree of initiative. Another compelling difference between the two rulers is that she chose only military leaders she knew fairly well and she often liked to brief them in person. Philip, by contrast, barely knew his commanders, to whom he would send couriers riding through the night with written orders dictated to his team of some twenty secretaries.

Compared to Elizabeth's palaces, the Spanish Court was a cold, forbidding, austere world. Philip's Catholic piety was becoming so intense that by now he operated almost entirely from the confines of a cell-like study-cum-bedchamber at the heart of his recently finished palace-monastery of San Lorenzo de El Escorial, outside Madrid. Designed to resemble Solomon's Temple, this vast site, complete with large gardens containing 'sun passageways' meant for convalescing monks, had a cloister and a massive basilica next to the royal apartments where Mass was regularly sung. On either side of the high altar were places already earmarked for the gilded bronze tombs of the members of Philip's family. So close was Philip's bedroom to this part of the basilica, he practically slept above the place appointed for his tomb. The king's bedroom, itself filled on two sides with small images of saints, directly overlooked the high altar: an interior window allowed Philip to hear and watch the services without being observed. The walls of the small study off the bedroom, where he spent long hours on his paperwork at a tiny desk, were hung with images of the Virgin. In the private marbled and jasper-lined oratory leading off the bedroom, he prayed by candlelight before Titian's deeply moving scene of the Passion, *Christ and the Cyrenian*. Fray José de Sigüenza, librarian, historian and prior of the Escorial, who worked there for many years and had seen its foundations laid, said that 'by night, the pious king Don Philip spent long periods of time there contemplating how much he owed to the Lord who carried such a heavy cross on his shoulders for the sins of man and for his sins.'[32]

On Howard's advice, Elizabeth transferred the command of the squadron sent to patrol the eastern coastline to Lord Henry Seymour, who was assigned fourteen royal ships and twenty-six auxiliaries. This was because Drake, correctly, guessed that Philip had all along aimed at a land invasion and that his strategy would be to save the Armada ships primarily for use as a shield for Parma's troops so that they could cross the Channel. For that reason, Drake argued, it would be safer and more effective if his and Howard's ships combined to guard the Channel's western, and therefore windward, approaches, to confront the Spanish warships there.[33]

One of Howard's chance remarks makes it plain how far Elizabeth, rather than her advisers, was in overall control. He received his final orders from the queen at an audience on 13 April at Hackney, to the east of London. Afterwards, he wrote uneasily to Burghley, 'I would have been very glad to have seen your Lordship myself, but I could not obtain leave of Her Majesty, and yet it were fit that I should make your Lordship acquainted with Her Majesty's resolution touching the service on the seas, which, God willing, I will do before I depart, if no sudden alarm come, which I fear hourly.'[34] Elizabeth was not simply taking charge, she was still freezing out Burghley from the highest level of decision-making, even though more than a year had passed since the sending of Mary's death warrant to Fotheringhay.

No one in England knew for certain when, where or even whether the Armada would reach its intended destination. Late spring gales and the slow pace of his supply ships forced Medina Sidonia to make first for the safety of the port of Coruña on the Atlantic coast of northern Spain. Unfortunately for him, a violent storm dispersed much of his fleet before he could enter port and it took him weeks to regroup. Progress across the Bay of Biscay and along the French coast was painfully slow. In these days of anxious waiting, false alarms — several raised by teenage pranksters — led to some premature firing of the warning beacons placed along the south coast of England. Terrified families fleeing from the coastal villages to stay with relatives living inland in the mistaken belief that the Armada had landed would only compound this confusion.

Elizabeth could do no more than watch and wait. Her fate and that of her country lay in the hands of her commanders, chiefly Howard and Drake. Burghley, meanwhile, drew up a gloomy statement of the kingdom's desperate shortage of money. 'A man would wish,' he wrote phlegmatically, 'if peace cannot be had, that the enemy would no longer delay, but prove, as I trust, his evil fortune.'[35]

His wish would soon be granted. At about four o'clock on the afternoon of Friday, 19 July, the first Spanish vessels were sighted off the Lizard in Cornwall. As luck would have it, Howard and Drake were briefly off their guard, making essential repairs to their ships in Plymouth. Possibly, Drake may have been playing bowls on Plymouth Hoe, but he certainly would not have finished the game when the news of the sighting arrived, as legend claims.

The queen's plan for mustering her land forces, drawn up largely by Burghley and Leicester in June, came instantly into effect. First, the regular county militias, on standby since May, were assembled at agreed rendezvous points, with orders to 'impeach the enemy upon his first descent'. Next, some eight thousand troops from the counties closest to London were put under the command of Leicester, as the queen's Lieutenant-General, and ordered to gather at Tilbury. Reinforced by three hundred gunners and pioneers, they were given orders to attack if any of Parma's barges attempted to sail up the Thames estuary and land there. To fortify the estuary, Leicester stretched out a boom built from chains, ship's cables and old ship's masts across the river where it began to narrow.[36] Forts, mainly earthworks but complete with gun platforms and landing wharfs built of brick, were hastily thrown up at Tilbury and Gravesend so as to face each other on the opposite banks of the river – not just to attack enemy vessels but also to make it easier for Leicester's army to be ferried across in safety to the Kentish side if Parma landed soldiers there. Then, as the Armada neared the Isle of Wight, 26,750 more troops were ordered to march to London under the command of Lord Hunsdon, ready to defend the queen and the Court if the Spanish ships landed. (In the event, Hunsdon's force scarcely came into being, since events in the Channel intervened.)[37]

'Julio' betrayed the full extent of these preparations to Mendoza but, by the time his information reached Philip, the Armada had been defeated.[38] On the evening of Friday the 19th, the English emerged gingerly from port, sailing against the wind, and the next morning they pushed forward out of Plymouth Sound.[39] Around three o'clock that afternoon they caught sight of the Spanish fleet some distance ahead. By Sunday morning, the Spaniards were within range of the English gunners. In the ensuing battle, Howard and Drake – whose ships were smaller and faster – outsailed and outgunned their opponents, falling on the Spanish rearguard without permitting them to close, pounding them for three hours with superior artillery. In a decision much criticized in Spain, Medina Sidonia chose to abandon one of the largest of his front-line ships, the *Nuestra Señora del Rosario*, commanded by Don Pedro de Valdéz, after it was involved in a collision and dismasted.[40]

As 'Julio' informed Mendoza, the citizens of London were petrified, imagining that Spanish soldiers would be marching in at any moment. The shops were closed, heavy iron chains were hung across the streets and Elizabeth left Richmond Palace to seek refuge in the much more compact St James's Palace, across the park from Whitehall, which had an escape tunnel and was easier to defend. Spanish prisoners captured by Drake on Sunday, among them Don Pedro de

Valdéz, were rushed up to London on carts and paraded through the streets in an attempt to allay the Londoners' fears.[41]

Tuesday morning saw another sharp engagement off Portland Bill, and there was a third off the Isle of Wight on Thursday, during which the *Santa Ana*, the flagship of the Spanish second-in-command, Juan Martínez de Recalde, was set upon by smaller English ships and so badly damaged that it ran ashore near Le Havre. Dispatching an ensign in a longboat to warn the Duke of Parma to be ready to embark his men and munitions near Dunkirk, Medina Sidonia continued to press on past the Solent, one of the few places on the south coast of England where a large fleet could anchor in relative safety. It was a fateful decision: no secure port lay beyond that point, and none of his pilots was familiar with the hazardous waters of the Flemish coast.[42]

On the evening of Saturday, 27 July, the Armada anchored off Calais to await news from Parma, shadowed by the English. When at last it came, it was disastrous: Parma was delayed and his troops could not be assembled and embarked for another week. More seriously, his flat-bottomed barges, originally designed for river use, were found to be quite unsuitable for heavy seas. If that were not sufficient, the Dutch were blockading the Flemish coast with their much nimbler flyboats. And yet it hardly made much difference. Medina Sidonia now had to face up to a critical defect in Philip's plans. Even if the Spanish fleet could somehow control the deep water between the Kent coast and Flanders, that still left ten miles of shoal water where the larger Spanish vessels could not go but through which the English could move with relative ease. Philip's inflexible orders that he should cover Parma's troops but make no independent landing until the flat-bottomed barges had been escorted safely across the Channel condemned the Spanish plan of attack to certain failure.[43]

Sunday was quiet until shortly before midnight, when the English directed eight improvised fire-ships towards the enemy fleet, their skeleton crews jumping to safety straight after lighting the fuses. In the men's haste to flee, many of the Spanish ships lost their hawsers and anchors. Medina Sidonia was driven north-east along the coast towards Dunkirk, abandoning his largest, most heavily armed galleass, the flagship *San Lorenzo*, which ran aground off Calais, where it was quickly looted.[44]

Philip's strategy was doomed: with a freshening wind and the tide driving the Spanish ships northwards and with the English close behind them, the Armada could never return to Calais; and, once the Spanish ships entered the North Sea, they could never link up with Parma's forces. The decisive battle, lasting a whole day, took place on Monday, 29 July, off Gravelines. Seymour's ships reinforced those of Howard and Drake, so that for the first time the entirety of the rival fleets became locked in deadly combat. Despite intense bombardments from both sides, the Spaniards did not manage to board or inflict significant harm on a single English vessel. Stocks of ammunition were running dangerously low, but the English were nonetheless able to sink at least three Spanish ships and drive several others ashore. Casualties on the Spanish side were heavy. Despite these losses, Medina Sidonia at first believed he had lived to fight another day, but a fierce gale blew his ships perilously close to the Flemish sandbanks. On Tuesday, confronted by even stronger winds and heavier seas, he made the decision to attempt what one of his critics called a 'voyage of Magellan': he meant to bring the main body of his fleet back to Spain by sailing it up the North Sea and around the coasts of northern Scotland and western Ireland, leaving the slower ships behind to fend for themselves.[45]

Partly to boost the flagging morale of his soldiers in the long, anxious days before news arrived from the fleet, partly with an eye on Elizabeth's place in history, the Earl of Leicester asked her to inspect his troops in the camp at Tilbury. In his invitation, issued on the day the Armada lay at anchor off Calais, he warned her to keep well away from the coast but assured her that 'by coming, you shall comfort not only these thousands but many more that shall hear of it.'[46] His plan was genuinely inspired: a lover of stage plays and a notable patron of the theatre with his very own company of actors, he meant from the outset to choreograph Elizabeth's visit so as to reinvent her for ever as the Warrior Queen she had never really been. Little did he know how successful he would be.

It took just over a week to make the arrangements. On Monday, 5

August, he wrote to her again, rejoicing that she had consented to come and declaring that suitable lodgings – 'a proper sweet cleanly house' – had been found for her within easy riding distance, where she would be just as safe as at St James's.[47]

Arriving at Tilbury by barge with her bodyguards on Thursday the 8th, Elizabeth landed about noon at the wharf beside the fort. Whether she was then led on horseback to view the camp, which was pitched on the summit of a nearby hill, as Burghley afterwards claimed, or rode immediately to dinner at her lodgings at Ardern Hall in Horndon-on-the-Hill, four miles away, is impossible to say. Either way, Ardern Hall had been turned into a temporary 'palace' over the past four days: the yeomen and ushers of the Privy Chamber had been busy supervising the cleaning of the house and the moving of furniture, bedding and kitchen utensils.[48]

Next morning, Elizabeth returned on horseback to the camp to inspect her troops. Leicester rode out to greet her. Possibly, she was mounted on a white stallion: there is a portrait of what purports to be this very same horse, now at Hatfield House, commissioned by Burghley and handed down to Robert, his younger son. Nothing is known about what she wore, despite a proliferation of legends depicting her as a latter-day Boudicca, or as Britomart from Edmund Spenser's *Faerie Queene*. A later report that she wore a cuirass and carried a silver truncheon while dressed in a white gown and sporting ostrich feathers in her hair is pure invention.

Possibly she watched a military march-past; more likely, she rode around the camp with Leicester at her side to view the soldiers arrayed in their different companies. According to Burghley, who made a special trip to Tilbury to bring Elizabeth news of the interrogation of the captured Don Pedro de Valdéz, Thomas Butler, Earl of Ormond, carried the sword of state before her. If so, Leicester would have had to bite his tongue, since the tall, dark, handsome Ormond had once tried to unseat him: in 1566, when Leicester was briefly in disgrace, Ormond had even taken the favourite's place beside the queen's chair. For some unknown reason, she nicknamed him 'Tom Duff' or 'Old Lucas'.[49]

With her review of the troops completed, Elizabeth now addressed them. What she said has been hotly contested ever since. There are at least six different versions of this famous speech, all claiming authenticity, and several of them based only on second- or third-hand reports. 'Julio' is no help here. As soon as word arrived in Paris that Parma had failed to link up with the Armada as he was supposed to do, the treacherous Stafford changed sides again and began feeding so much false intelligence to Mendoza that his pay was cut.[50]

It is impossible to say now whether Elizabeth spoke off the cuff or merely created the impression that she did so. Her habit when delivering important speeches to Parliament was to prepare a draft in advance to shape her thoughts, master it, then put it away.[51] Much ink has been spilt over her exact words. The most authentic version of the speech is the handwritten one now in the British Library, copied down either at the time or shortly afterwards by Dr Lionel Sharpe, Leicester's chaplain. Sharpe was ordered to transcribe the speech verbatim as the queen was delivering it, so that he could repeat it the next day to those who had been unable to hear it. (This was an age without microphones or amplification.)[52]

'My loving people,' Sharpe's handwritten version of the speech begins, 'I have been persuaded by some that are careful of my safety to take heed how I committed myself to armed multitudes for fear of treachery: but I tell you that I would not desire to live to distrust my faithful and loving people.'

> Let Tyrants fear: I have so behaved myself that under God I have placed my chiefest strength and safeguard in the loyal hearts and good will of my subjects. Wherefore I am come among you at this time but for my recreation and pleasure, being resolved in the midst and heat of the battle to live and die amongst you all, to lay down for my God, and for my kingdom and for my people, my Honour and my blood even in the dust.

Elizabeth then delivered her punchline: 'I know I have the body but of a weak and feeble woman, but I have the heart and stomach of a King, and of a King of England too, and take foul scorn that Parma, or any Prince of Europe, should dare to invade the borders of my realm.'

She concluded with promises of tangible rewards to her troops for their loyalty and affection. 'To the which,' she said, 'rather than any dishonour shall grow by me, I myself will venture my royal blood. I myself will be your general, judge and rewarder of your virtue in the field.'

> I know that already for your forwardness, you have deserved rewards and crowns, and I assure you in the word of a Prince, you shall not fail of them. In the mean time my Lieutenant-General shall be in my stead, than whom never Prince commanded a more noble or worthy subject. Not doubting but by your concord in the camp and valour in the field and your obedience to myself and my general we shall shortly have a famous victory over these enemies of my God and of my kingdom.[53]

Sharpe, a Fellow of King's College, Cambridge, and an accomplished rhetorician in his own right, may conceivably have edited or rewritten what he heard of the speech on the day it was delivered to give it greater impact. Suspicions of this nature have been much encouraged by his observation that, besides repeating the speech next day, he was also required 'to send it *gathered* to the Queen herself', meaning he was asked to supply her with a fair transcript, conceivably for publication.[54]

Almost certainly, however, Sharpe's version of the speech comes closest to the one Elizabeth delivered on the day. Its preference for the first person singular instead of the royal 'we' and its gendered metaphors are typical of the style she adopted in her most intensely passionate moments. Just as telling is the emphasis she placed on 'the word of a Prince' as a guarantee of her good faith. As a young woman, she had read with her tutors the first and third *Orations of Isocrates to Nicocles*, the young king of Cyprus. She often said that a crucial passage on the duties of rulers from the first oration was permanently etched on her consciousness: 'Throughout all your life', it read, 'show that you value truth so highly that a king's word is more to be trusted than other men's oaths.'[55] Most persuasive of all is the stress the queen placed on the trust of her 'faithful and loving people' as her greatest 'strength and safeguard', a direct echo of the rhetorical trope she had first played on thirty years before while giving an audience to Philip II's ambassador, the Count of Feria.[56]

According to Burghley, the serried ranks of soldiers spontaneously acclaimed the queen's speech with a chorus of cheers, shouts and 'all tokens of love and obedience'.[57] With these sounds ringing in her ears, Elizabeth rode with her women to dinner in Leicester's tent. It seemed to all those present that the speech had become her apotheosis and Tilbury the setting for her greatest triumph.

And there was more, for barely had the queen begun to eat her meal than a breathless George Clifford, Earl of Cumberland, a handsome courtier and naval officer who had fought courageously in the sea battle off Gravelines and who Elizabeth had nicknamed 'Rogue', galloped into the camp bearing news.[58] Lord Admiral Howard, he said, had pursued the fleeing Spaniards north until they had passed Harwich, where he had turned back, his supplies and ammunition exhausted.[59] Drake, who had joined in and continued the pursuit beyond the border with Scotland as far as the Firth of Forth, later confirmed that the Armada had been scattered by the storms.[60]

Elizabeth's victory seemed complete. Yet it would not be long before the very same soldiers who had cheered the queen and laid down their weapons as she passed by would be cursing her. Her oratory may have been superb, but her moral victory would be hollow. She was about to make choices, and condone others taken by her councillors, that would create a stain on her reputation that could never be erased. Her triumph over Philip's *Gran Armada* of 1588 was undoubted. But it would be all too brief.

6.   A Funeral and a Wedding

Elizabeth's speech at Tilbury was a glorious moment, but after bidding Leicester farewell and returning to London by barge, she bunkered down once more at St James's Palace, just in case reports of the Armada's dispersal turned out to be false. There she stayed until early October, by which time a flurry of news bulletins graphically describing the wrecks of many Spanish vessels on the north and west coasts of Ireland gave her the reassurance she needed to move back to her more spacious apartments at Whitehall and Greenwich.[1]

For almost twenty years, the anniversary of the queen's Accession Day, Sunday, 17 November, had been one of the more spectacular fixtures on the courtly calendar. Its high point was a great tournament of ritualized jousting in the tiltyard at Whitehall at which the participants wore fancy dress. This year it took on a new dimension. The bells of the parish churches pealed out as far north as Northumberland for the very first time, and Thomas Cooper, bishop of Winchester, who had done more than anyone else to promote the idea of a 'gaudy day' in the queen's honour, preached a thanksgiving sermon at Paul's Cross, a large outdoor pulpit in the churchyard of St Paul's Cathedral. The queen announced her intention to attend, then abruptly changed her mind.

She had a very good reason. In the opening days of September, the Earl of Leicester had suddenly become gravely ill. Our information comes from a report sent to Philip II by a Genoese spy. After the camp at Tilbury had been disbanded in mid-August, Leicester set out for his estate at Kenilworth with the intention of travelling on to the spa at Buxton in Derbyshire to take the waters. He broke his journey at Rycote, near Thame in Oxfordshire.[2] From there, before moving on to nearby Cornbury House in the royal forest of Wychwood, he hastily scribbled Elizabeth a brief note that she would forever afterwards carry around with her.[3]

In the tense weeks and months immediately before the Armada's arrival, their relations had considerably softened. Their clashes over his marriage to Lettice, his unsanctioned actions while in the Netherlands and his opposition to her peace negotiations with the Duke of Parma had largely been forgotten, and he regularly dined alone with her again. In another remarkably intimate letter, this time written from the camp at Tilbury on 3 August, two weeks before it was broken up, he addressed her as 'my most dear lady'. This letter, once in private ownership, was recently rediscovered after it was sold to a library in Washington DC:

> I am loath my most dear lady to trouble you without some just cause, when at this time, God be thanked, there is none touching your army here, but all things as well as quiet and as forwardly bent to your service as any soldiers or subjects in the world can be, but yet I may not forget upon my knees to give to your most sweet Majesty all humble and dutiful thanks for your great comfort I receive from your own sweet self. I am sorry that I can write your Majesty no news, yet most glad that I may hold up my hands to God for the merciful dealings he useth towards you, for by the news now here he fighteth for you and the enemies fall before you. Let all honour, praise and glory be given him therefore.

He ended his letter, 'God ever more preserve my most dear lady that she may to the comfort of his people and church end in peace as she hath begun.' Twice, he inserted little eyebrows over the letter 'o' in the word 'most', rendering it as 'môôst', on both these occasions to remind her of his pet nickname, and he drew the 'eyes' symbol again immediately before his signature.[4]

His other letter, written from Rycote on 29 August, was equally affectionate. Calling himself 'your poor old servant', he asked her pardon for his 'boldness' in 'sending to know how my gracious lady doth and what ease of her late pains she finds, being the chiefest thing in this world I do pray for, and for her to have good health and long life'. Under the stress of waiting for news of the Armada, her migraines had resumed again, and when he had himself complained of vomiting she had given him some physic prepared by her apothecaries. 'For mine own poor case', he said, 'I continue still your medicine and find it amended much better than with any other thing that hath been given me. Thus hoping to find perfect cure at the bath with the continuance of my wonted prayer for Your Majesty's most happy preservation, I humbly kiss your foot.'[5] These are the last words he ever wrote. He died at Cornbury House six days later, with Lettice at his bedside. The room in which he is believed to have died still bears his name. The cause was said to be a 'tertian fever', meaning a fever now known to be malarial in type, triggering paroxysms on alternate days. He was just fifty-five.

Leicester had asked to be buried in the Beauchamp Chapel at St Mary's Church in Warwick, 'where sundry mine ancestors do lie'. As a younger man, dressed all in white with velvet shoes and silk stockings, he had proudly celebrated his admission to the French Order of St Michael there. Roger, Lord North, a close friend and witness at his secret marriage to Lettice, wrote an obituary. The Earl's death, he said, 'is a great and general loss to the whole land'.[6] For Elizabeth, the loss was immeasurable. It was also a searing reminder of her own mortality.

Following royal protocol, the queen did not attend the funeral. Pride of place went to Leicester's stepson, the twenty-three-year-old Robert Devereux, Earl of Essex, Lettice's son by her first marriage. He would head the solemn cortège of over a hundred mourners, all dressed in black, as it wound its way in state from Kenilworth to Warwick. Lettice could not bring herself to attend, but sent an epitaph in which she described Leicester as 'the best and dearest of husbands'.[7] Elizabeth's letters of condolence were normally generous and supportive, showing she was capable of genuine human sympathy, but she did not extend any to her arch-enemy. Never reconciled to the rival who looked so like herself and whom she believed to have betrayed her by stealing away her beloved 'Rob', she pettily took revenge by refusing to release Lettice from the nightmare of her husband's vast debts.

To Lettice's dismay, first Kenilworth and then all of her husband's other lands in Warwickshire were legally sequestered by the queen's bailiffs, including lands intended to provide her with an income during her widowhood.[8] Next, Leicester House, with its magnificent gardens overlooking the Thames, was seized and its contents and artworks auctioned off: these included the matching portraits of

Leicester and the queen, and many more of classical heroes, notably Julius Caesar.[9] Finally, the fairy-tale manor of Wanstead in Essex, already heavily mortgaged, was taken.[10]

Leicester's debts, mainly the loans and mortgages he had taken out to fund his expedition to the Netherlands, amounted to some £50,000, double the rental income from the Crown lands and more than the annual cost of financing the entire royal household. They left Lettice with a run of legal battles with the queen's officers lasting for many years. In a desperate attempt to protect herself, she quickly married again, doing what other aristocratic women in her dire situation had done earlier in the century to help avoid their creditors, as one of the peculiarities of English law was that it was much more difficult to sue a married woman for debt than a widow. She chose a commoner, Sir Christopher Blount, Leicester's gentleman of the horse, as her new husband. At the time, her son Robert described the match as 'an unhappy choice', since Blount was so far beneath Lettice socially. Later, however, he would find that he could count on Blount as one of his staunchest allies.[11]

Her heart weighed down with grief after Leicester's death, Elizabeth withdrew to her inner Bedchamber and locked the doors. Now bitterly regretting her harsh treatment of him after his return from the Netherlands, she refused to come out. Burghley and his fellow councillors had to order the doors to be broken down. Early in November 1588, she was said to be 'much aged and spent, and is very melancholy'.[12] Walsingham confirmed that she 'will not suffer anybody to have access unto her, being very much grieved'.[13] Vigorous efforts would later be made by her women to persuade her to join in the traditional Christmas festivities, but even when players and tumblers were summoned to distract and entertain her, they brought her little consolation.[14]

Without Leicester by her side, Elizabeth felt intensely vulnerable. She had lost the love of her life, her escort on state occasions, a respected confidant, the man who had stood by her chair at Court festivals. She had even sometimes allowed him to take up residence overnight in the vacant consort's apartments at Whitehall Palace, last occupied by King Philip while married to Mary Tudor. For all the attention she had lavished on younger men like Ralegh, no one could ever compensate for the loss of her own dear 'Rob', and she reacted as she often did when overcome by bouts of black depression. She surrounded herself with flowers, boughs and sweet-smelling herbs: her florist's bill for these months came to £13 6s. 8d. (some £13,000 today).

To brighten up her apartments, she had her Serjeant Painter, George Gower, cover some of the untreated wall surfaces with a special wash made of 'blue bice' (a brilliant shade of blue obtained from smalt) mixed with rose-water perfume. And she ordered extensive improvements to the orchards and gardens in the palaces where she most loved to walk, setting a small army of 'women weeders' to work at Greenwich and Hampton Court. She had always loved gardens, especially those with Italian-style alleyways, terraces, sunken groves, fountains, and arcades lined with statuary. She would walk, either in company or unobserved, depending on her mood, along paths shaded from the heat by tall shrubs and trees, or sit on raised cushions in an arbour or gazebo.[15]

The climax of the festivities to celebrate the defeat of the Armada was originally planned to follow directly on from Accession Day and Cooper's sermon at Paul's Cross but had been postponed at the very last moment to the following Sunday. Elizabeth attended, persuaded by Burghley not to put off the event for a second time. Spectacularly dressed in silver and white, she emerged from her Bedchamber and was driven in a canopied chariot pulled by two white horses from Somerset House on the Strand to St Paul's Cathedral. In front of her rode the royal trumpeters, followed by the gentlemen of the Privy Chamber and their footmen, bearing their poleaxes aloft. Directly behind her came the young Earl of Essex. Only the previous year, Elizabeth had granted him his stepfather Leicester's old place as Master of the Horse. Now, he was in daily attendance, riding behind her carriage wherever she went.[16]

When, around noon, the queen's chariot arrived at the great west door of St Paul's, Elizabeth was greeted by the clergy in rich silver copes, and a service of thanksgiving for the victory over King Philip was held. After the prayers, the queen took her seat in a side chapel

built out from the north wall of the church, open to the air and facing Paul's Cross, where she heard a sermon. The banners taken from
the captured Armada ships were on display for all to see.[17]

To his deep chagrin, Ralegh, who had played only a minor part in
the victory over the Spanish fleet, had been relegated to a place much
further back in the procession than he was used to. He was forced to
accept this demotion, because the queen's new Master of the Horse
was already superseding him in influence. Not long after Essex had
returned from the Netherlands as a war hero after leading his light-
cavalry charge at the Battle of Zutphen, Elizabeth had begun inviting
him into the Privy Chamber to play cards with her in the evenings.
'Nobody [is] near [the queen] but my lord of Essex,' boasted one of
his servants, with pardonable hyperbole. 'At night my lord is at cards
or one game or another with her that he cometh not to his own lodging till the birds sing in the morning.' During the Armada campaign
while his stepfather had been absent, she had even urged him to move
temporarily into Leicester's rooms at St James's so as to be nearer to
her.[18]

Some three or four months on from Leicester's death, Elizabeth
resumed her card games with Essex, looking for some form of cathar-
tic release. She was more than thirty years older than the dazzling
Earl, old enough to be his mother. She knew she should not allow
him to pay her this amount of attention or stay up with her so late,
but she could not help herself. Even before Leicester's death, a psychological bond had been developing between the two of them. She
may perhaps have regarded him as the son she never had; at the very
least, he would be a constant reminder of his stepfather. She was not
in love; that could never be. Her 'Sweet Robin', her 'Eyes', had always
been the only man for her. In any case, Essex had to tread carefully.
When he dared to berate the queen for taking Ralegh's side in a quarrel and stormed out of the room, she raged viciously against him and
against his mother for stealing away her beloved 'Eyes' from her.[19]

Around this time, Essex had himself painted by Nicholas Hilliard,
the finest and most celebrated of the Elizabethan miniaturists. In this
delightful image, he posed as 'The Young Man among the Roses'. Tall,
lissom, supremely poised, with fair skin, brown eyes and a mop of
curly, dark brown hair brushed away from his forehead, he certainly

looked the part. He had persuaded Hilliard to paint him outdoors, leaning nonchalantly with his legs crossed against a tree-trunk entwined with eglantine (a sweet-smelling, white briar rose with five petals, and the queen's favourite flower). A blue-blooded aristocrat who could trace his ancestry back to the Plantagenet kings and beyond, Essex always knew that his high birth gave him an advantage over Ralegh, a mere commoner. Where blood was concerned, Elizabeth was known to be a fierce defender of the social hierarchy.[20] For instance, her greatest objection to married bishops had nothing at all to do with theology but was because their wives, generally of low social origin, expected to be treated as if they were the wives of noblemen.

To commemorate Spain's defeat, silver coins and medals were struck in London and Holland, depicting the Spanish ships fleeing or the English fire-ships driving them off, and with such aphoristic inscriptions (bowdlerized from Julius Caesar and the Old Testament) as *Venit, vidit, fugit* ('It came, it saw, it fled') and *Flavit Jehovah et dissipati sunt* ('God blew and they were scattered').[21] And of the more vividly enduring attempts to immortalize Elizabeth, several courtiers, Drake among them, commissioned versions of a so-called 'Armada' portrait in which, for the first time, all semblance of realism was abandoned. In this celebrated image, sometimes attributed to George Gower and his studio, Elizabeth stands unashamedly resplendent before her chair of state. She wears a black velvet gown thickly trimmed with lustrous gold and rainbow silks and bedecked with pearls and pink-and-blue ribbons. Embroidered on her sleeves and skirt is a delicate design of suns-in-splendour, embellished with square, pointed diamonds and stylized flowers with pearl centres. She sports an elaborate collar with pendant pearls, partly concealed by an enormous ruff, and her right hand rests on a globe. Beside her elbow stands the imperial crown, and to the left and right of her head are scenes of Drake's fire-ships sailing out to meet the Armada at anchor off Calais and of the destruction of the enemy forces off a rocky coastline.[22]

What immediately challenges the viewer, however, is that the sitter is not Elizabeth. Her face bears only a passing resemblance to the very few known portraits for which she sat personally. The long, angular features for which the real Elizabeth was renowned are at strange variance with Gower's image. In real life, the queen's nose was famously elongated, with a slight hook at the end, whereas the face in the portrait is rounder and fuller, its eyes larger and less piercing.[23] The face belongs instead to a different, much younger woman: most likely one of the queen's Bedchamber women who posed for the artist wearing Elizabeth's clothes and jewels.

Biographers conventionally assume that Elizabeth sat regularly for her portrait. In reality, according to Burghley, who had attempted in vain to grapple with this difficulty in 1563, she found the whole business irksome. 'She hath been always of her own will and disposition very unwilling,' he commented then.[24] Despite the hundreds of images painted during her lifetime, she is only known for certain to have sat for an artist five times.[25] One of the great paradoxes of Elizabeth is that she surrounded herself with men who were fascinated by the visual arts, whereas she herself was profoundly diffident about her own image. Notoriously touchy over her appearance, she was highly mistrustful of artists. The exception was Hilliard, her favourite artist, for whom she most famously sat outdoors in 1572, when (as he remembered) she had quizzed him as to why the Italians, '[who] had the name to be cunningest and to draw best, shadowed not'. To this, Hilliard replied that shadow was used only by painters whose pictures possessed a 'grosser line'. 'Here Her Majesty conceived the reason, and therefore chose her place to sit in for that purpose in the open alley of a goodly garden, where no tree was near, nor any shadow at all.'[26]

Far from the market being flooded with official images of her, it was Elizabeth's courtiers, not Elizabeth herself, who commissioned the overwhelming majority of her most famous portraits, usually to display to her when she stayed at their houses on her summer progresses as a pledge of their loyalty. And many of the most widely reproduced images were not of a particularly high standard. When the 'Armada' portraits were painted, consumer demand for the royal likeness vastly outstripped the number of official types that could be produced, creating the quite different problem of the manufacture of debased images. In 1563, when he had attempted to draft a proclamation regulating artists, Burghley had made a concerted effort to persuade Elizabeth to commission an official facial image of herself that could be used as a pattern by artists unable to work from life but, for some reason, Elizabeth blocked the idea.[27]

After the service at St Paul's, Elizabeth thanked Howard and his senior officers for their part in the victory, greeting them by name and praising them as 'men born for the preservation of their country'. All who had served in the campaign, she declared 'well merited of her and the Commonwealth'. And yet, a fawning report Camden printed in his *Annales*, saying that 'those that were wounded and indigent she relieved with noble pensions,' is demonstrably false.[28] The opposite is true. She had promised at Tilbury to reward her men for their loyalty and service and gave them her word as a Prince that she would never fail them. But it was not a promise she would keep.

In this, Burghley, as Lord Treasurer, eagerly colluded. The Exchequer, as he was several times forced to remind the queen, was empty. Debts were fast mounting, and he was struggling to raise huge loans, using as an intermediary the Genoese financier Horatio Palavicino, who had negotiated the largest of Leicester's borrowings. To secure credit from German lenders, Burghley told Palavicino he was willing to pay an interest rate of up to 10 per cent. His response to demands that he should settle the arrears of pay due to the brave mariners and soldiers, both living and dead, was savage. 'I marvel', he told Walsingham callously, 'that where so many are dead on the seas the pay is not dead with them or with many of them.'[29]

Elizabeth knew that the fatality list from the campaign far exceeded the hundred or so mariners who had been killed in the fighting itself. Thousands more had died from a virulent typhus epidemic that had begun on the 700-ton royal navy ship *Elizabeth Jonas* and had swept through the rest of the fleet. This one ship alone had a crew of five hundred: by the end of August, all but a handful of them were dying in the gutters of Margate.[30]

Howard did what he could to help the survivors, paying for their food and beer from his own purse and selling his gold and silver plate to buy them clothing. He warned his fellow privy councillors that the epidemic was so virulent and widespread it would soon threaten the queen's safety more than the might of Spain. The men, 'who well hoped after this so good service to have received their whole pay and finding it to come but this scantly unto them', were near to mutiny. At Tilbury, Elizabeth had been feted by her soldiers. Now, Howard said, they cursed her: such neglect 'breeds a marvellous alteration'. To Walsingham, Howard remonstrated, 'It were too pitiful to have men starve after such a service . . . and if men should not be cared for better than to let them starve and die miserably, we should very hardly get men to serve.'[31]

When his pleas went unanswered, Howard appealed to Elizabeth directly. 'The infection', he explained, 'is grown very great and in many ships, and now very dangerous, and those that come in fresh are soonest infected. They sicken the one day and die the next.' But her ears were shut.[32] Determined to brook no opposition, she ordered her privy councillors to arrest and hang a company of soldiers who had walked, limping and barefoot, to London to demand their pay. One victim, as he climbed the hangman's ladder and the rope was put about his neck, shouted out angrily to the crowd: 'The gallows are the pay they give us for going to the wars.'[33]

Most of those who took up arms for the queen would never receive a penny. Such behaviour contrasts strikingly with that of King Philip, who paid in full his soldiers' arrears of pay almost without fail, even if settlement could often be tardy. Unlike Elizabeth, Philip considered payment to be a moral obligation, a matter of honour. He also, through his agents, paid large sums by way of ransoms to Englishmen who had snatched Spaniards from the Armada ships they had successfully boarded.[34] Of course, for Elizabeth, the harsh reality was that she had little to give, other than what she could raise by slashing her personal expenditure. This she did not do. In fear of a mass insurrection, Burghley issued several threatening proclamations on her instructions, imposing martial law and ordering the apprehension of 'all soldiers, mariners and vagrant persons' as should be found wandering about the countryside. Such 'disloyal persons' were to be punished 'with all convenient extremity'.[35]

Suddenly, a new scare began. Pope Sixtus was still attempting to convert the young Scottish king, James VI, to Catholicism, and alarm bells rang loudly in London when Walsingham discovered that the Duke of Parma had proposed a fresh attack on England by way of

Scotland. As bait, he offered James the prospect of a Spanish bride, with a view to landing six thousand Spanish troops on the shores of the Firth of Forth in readiness for a *coup d'état*.[36]

In July 1586, when James had ratified the terms of his league with Elizabeth in exchange for a handsome pension, she had extracted a promise from him not to marry 'without her advice and privity'. It was a tactic she had tried before in Scotland: in 1564, her clumsy attempts to marry James's mother off to Leicester as a way of controlling her for the rest of her life had spectacularly misfired. The idea then had been that the newly-weds would live at Court with the English queen in a *ménage à trois*.[37] It was the silliest notion Elizabeth ever had. But steering James into a marriage favourable to England was a policy that might just work. Clearly, it was the candidate that counted: find the right one, and the Scottish problem could be solved, perhaps for ever.

A marriage between James and Anne, the younger daughter of King Frederick II of Denmark and his wife, Queen Sophie, had first been mooted in 1584, when James was eighteen. The Danes proved receptive, but Elizabeth lobbied for Catherine of Navarre, sister to Henry of Navarre, the Huguenot claimant to the French throne. She wanted to bind James into her policy of backing Henry against the Cardinal of Bourbon and the Guises in the succession struggle in France.[38] By late 1587, she was pushing insistently for Catherine.

But she met resistance from several quarters. As Walsingham's agent reported, 'This king is not as Her Majesty is: any [of] his subjects being gentle or noble may speak his mind frankly to him.' Not only could they, they often did, and at all hours of day or night. Opposition came chiefly from those Scottish lords who loathed the English for their handling of Mary Queen of Scots. 'Have they not cut off your mother's head?' they demanded shrilly of James. 'Marry, sir, they will give you a poor pension to make Your Majesty their pensioner to your more disgrace and shame to all princes that know it . . . You were better not [to] live to be a king than to receive such shame.'[39] They knew that the ever-impoverished James was reluctant to risk his English pension. Money was a continually tricky issue for him: without bribes or rewards, it was hard for him to balance or defeat the competing factions.[40]

Despite the death of the hard-drinking, hunting-mad King Frederick early in 1588, most likely from alcohol poisoning, it looked for a time as if things might go Elizabeth's way. On paper, Catherine of Navarre was by far the stronger candidate. But, by Christmas, the pendulum had swung in the opposite direction after the Edinburgh Parliament granted James £100,000 Scots (around £25 million sterling in modern values), dropping the strongest of hints that he should seek a Danish bride.[41] To counter Anne's advantage, Elizabeth piled on the pressure after Walsingham found proof that the Earl of Huntly, a Catholic opponent of the Anglo-Scottish league and one of James's leading favourites, was deeply implicated in the Duke of Parma's continuing plots to land Spanish troops in Scotland.[42]

Elizabeth forwarded the incriminating documents straight to James, but he refused to react.[43] Now almost twenty-three, he was too insecure not to keep open lines of communication to the Catholic powers.[44] He wanted Huntly close to him, and some were whispering that his interest was of a more personal nature. When, to silence Elizabeth, he did at last send Huntly briefly to prison, he visited him every day, brought him dinner and kissed him.[45] Rumours of his sexual predilections quickly reached London. As Burghley's man in Edinburgh warned, anyone sent north across the frontier to reason with James 'should be no young man'.[46]

Uncertainty about Scotland continued, but worse was to come. On 30 July 1589, a courier arrived from France with the shocking news that, eight days earlier, King Henry III had been assassinated. Driven more than fifty miles from Paris by the forces of the Duke of Guise, while Elizabeth had been preoccupied with the Armada, Henry had reached a temporary truce with the Catholic League, but then struck back. Early in the morning of 13 December 1588, he had summoned Guise to his study at Blois and had him cut down by the royal guards and his body burned to ashes and thrown into the Loire. Next day, Louis of Lorraine, Cardinal of Guise, the Duke's brother, was strangled. Now just over seven months later, Henry had been fatally stabbed in retaliation in his army camp at Saint-Cloud, six miles west of Paris, by Jacques Clément, a Dominican monk. He died around two o'clock the next morning.[47]

A civil war was erupting in France, with Philip II planning to throw his weight behind the forces of the Catholic League to wipe out the Huguenots. Elizabeth was desperate to assist Henry of Navarre, whom Henry III had named as his heir on his deathbed, on the condition that he would soon convert to Catholicism. James, meanwhile, had decided to marry Anne. He had been warned that Catherine, who was thirty, was 'old and crooked and something worse if all were known'.[48] Anne, it was pointed out to him, was just fourteen. A stunningly beautiful, sensual girl who loved music and dancing and was already a fluent linguist, she was said to be itching to marry him.[49] From James's viewpoint, this was exactly the sort of woman who could help him to quash the burgeoning rumours of his sexual tastes.[50]

Burghley did his best to persuade James to put 'in some suspense' his plans to make a Danish marriage.[51] When he failed, Elizabeth accepted defeat with unusual grace. Chiefly, this was a matter of keeping up appearances. As Walsingham cautioned her, she should not allow it to become known how far she had opposed the match with Anne, since this would upset Denmark as much as James.[52] In any case, once Henry of Navarre was forced to commit all of his resources into fighting to secure the throne of France, he was obliged to draw on his sister's personal revenues of 40,000 crowns a year. Without the attraction of a pension or a substantial dowry from France, James was hardly likely to marry Catherine. And as Burghley's Scottish agent succinctly explained, if the king had given his word to the Danes, it had to be kept.[53]

The paradox was that James had committed himself to marrying Anne but could not afford the costs of his wedding garments or the necessary refurbishments to Scotland's dilapidated palaces to welcome his bride. As Burghley's man scoffed, 'His plate is not worth £100, he has only two or three rich jewels and his guard is unpaid.'[54] If he were not to be disgraced, he needed Elizabeth's help.

With frosty hauteur, Elizabeth declared that she would 'allow' James's Danish marriage, because the Scots were 'resolved' to go through with it: in reality, she did not have the power to stop it.[55] She agreed to present James with gold and silver plate worth £2,000, along with a small allowance to help him make his mother's old apartments at Holyrood ready for Anne.[56] Her strategy was to control James through the power of the purse, after which she would work directly on Anne.

Anne's journey to Scotland took far longer than anyone could have envisaged. Her wardrobe and entourage were huge: sixteen ships would be needed to transport them. According to an eyewitness, one of her coaches was so fine it had 'no iron in it but all silver'.[57] But after her flotilla left harbour on 5 September 1589, it was battered by storms. Three times she set sail for Scotland, and three times she would be driven back. At last, after fifty days of agonizing seasickness, she was cast ashore on the coast of Norway and took refuge in Oslo. There, she resolved to postpone her voyage until the spring while her ships were repaired.

Unaware that Anne had not arrived at Holyrood as planned, Elizabeth handed over her gifts of gold and silver plate to the Scottish ambassador, spitefully timing their delivery so as to ensure that they would not arrive in Edinburgh until just after what she still believed was the intended wedding day. She then sent James a letter signed, 'Your most assured loving sister and cousin', in which she upbraided him for the unexpected 'speed' of his 'bargain' with the Danes. Unable to resist swiping at him, she informed him that he had only himself to blame for a situation in which 'my messengers come after the solemnities.'[58]

James wisely did not rise to the bait: with the wedding postponed, Elizabeth's sarcasm, in any case, backfired. Instead, in what seemed to the uninformed to be a spontaneous romantic gesture, he left at once for Oslo to pledge his love to Anne. His madcap dash across the North Sea in the thick of the equinoctial gales has often been seen as a supreme act of chivalry. In reality, his intention was to thwart fresh, highly embarrassing rumours that the delay in Anne's arrival was because she had somehow discovered that he was virile with men but impotent with women.[59]

Barely had James left Scottish waters than the country was ablaze with rumours that Huntly and his friends were now eagerly plotting a coup, to be bankrolled by Parma. Letters, it was said, had been sent to Spain, and promises made 'for subversion of religion within the realm'.[60] The rumours were false, but the Scottish Council's assurances did not satisfy Elizabeth. Believing Huntly to be a dangerous threat, she wrote to James, scolding him and urging him in the strongest terms to order his officers to 'apprehend in time (I pray God not too late) all such as any way they may suspect or know to be partakers of this faction'. Her letter concluded with a stark warning: 'Believe no more to dandle such babies as may, ere they come to honesty, shake your chair.'[61]

James would not listen. He had no intention of becoming the English queen's poodle. His attentions were fixed on Anne, and on 23 November they were married in the Great Hall of the Old Bishop's Palace at Oslo.[62] When the long Nordic winter was finally over, James prepared to lead his bride back to Scotland, by which time he had already spent more than a third of her considerable dowry of £150,000 Scots. Their ships finally set sail on 21 April 1590, and Anne was crowned and anointed Queen of Scotland in the abbey church at Holyrood on Sunday, 17 May. Even before the newly-weds had arrived, Elizabeth was writing to Anne, assuring her of her affection and declaring how 'it will give me singular pleasure to gratify you in whatever manner I may know to be agreeable to you.'[63]

Shortly after Anne's coronation, Elizabeth wrote to her again, to tell her that she would presently be sending the Earl of Worcester to Edinburgh. One of very few noblemen under the age of fifty she unreservedly trusted, he was sent to inform James that he was to be admitted to the much-coveted Order of the Garter. But Worcester would also be carrying a special message for Anne.[64]

The ploy clearly worked, since the teenager was soon replying in gratitude, neatly signing herself, 'Your most affectionate sister and cousin, Anna R', and declaring:

> If it please you to do us the honour to employ us in any thing which may turn to your contentment, as you may freely do, as well in respect of the near neighbourhood of the kingdoms wherein God has established us, as of the sex which is common to us both ... we shall endeavour by all good and honourable effects and offices to show you the desire that we have, not only to entertain, as hereditary, that friendship begun between the late King our father of happy memory and you, but to increase it and render it closer and more assured, for the universal good of this island.[65]

Anne's letter could not have pleased Elizabeth more. At last, as it now appeared to her, Scotland had a queen with whom she could do business: someone who was both Protestant and compliant; someone she felt she could rely on to keep James up to the mark. For all his waywardness, James was still best qualified by dynastic right to succeed to the English throne. When she had fenced with him over his refusal to deal quickly and effectively with the Catholic factions in Scotland, she believed it was only because she had his own best interests at heart. Anne, she imagined, would surely see this, even if he could not.

As the summer of 1590 approached, it seemed to Elizabeth that James had married the right wife after all, and that a fresh chapter was about to open in relations with Scotland, one in which she could finally put to rest her fears about the influence of King Philip and the Jesuits. Such hopes would later prove to be unfounded, but for quite different reasons from those anyone at the time might have supposed.

1. The 'Siena Portrait' of Elizabeth holding a sieve, an emblem of virginity, by Quentin Metsys the Younger, *c.*1583

2. An unknown woman, one of Elizabeth's Bedchamber or Privy Chamber staff, possibly the young Kate Carey, daughter of Lord Hunsdon and Elizabeth's cousin once removed, English School

3. The likelihood is strong that this woman is Katherine Carey, Elizabeth's first cousin, wife of Sir Francis Knollys, but if so and the painting was done in 1562, the age given may be incorrect. Such mistakes are quite common in Tudor portraiture as ages or dates were often repainted, moved or added by later owners or art restorers. By Steven van der Meulen

4. Mary Queen of Scots, by Nicholas Hilliard, c.1580

5. Anne of Denmark, studio of
Nicholas Hilliard, after 1603

6. Lettice Knollys, English School,
after 1603

7. Elizabeth corrects the second version of her reply to Parliament's petition in 1586 urging her to execute Mary Queen of Scots, showing interlineations and scorings-out

8. A copy of the warrant for the execution of Mary Queen of Scots, prepared by Robert Beale for the personal use of the Earl of Kent, one of the officiating commissioners present at Fotheringhay Castle

9. Robert Dudley, Earl of Leicester, in his mid-thirties, by Steven van der Meulen

10. Sir Francis Walsingham, by
John de Critz, *c.*1585

11. 'The Family of Henry VIII', a copy of a painting
Elizabeth gave to Walsingham in *c.*1572, while he was serving
as ambassador to France, after Lucas de Heere

12. William Cecil, Lord Burghley, wearing the robes of a Knight of the Garter and carrying the Lord Treasurer's staff of office, English School, after 1572

13. Philip II, with the Order of the Golden Fleece on his chest and holding a rosary in his left hand, by Sofonisba Anguissola, c.1573

7.   On the Attack

Leicester's death would not automatically guarantee the rise to power of his stepson Robert Devereux, Earl of Essex. Proud, with a supreme confidence in his own abilities and a sense of the honour due to him as his birthright, the young Earl had the temperament of a racehorse and was said to be 'full of humours', acting by fits and starts. A mass of contradictions, he projected himself to his followers as a man of action, yet he could be curiously effete. Narcissistic and notoriously prone to melodrama if crossed, he would vanish for days to brood or sulk in his study or bedchamber, where he nursed psychosomatic illnesses most likely brought on by stress.

As depicted in 1590 by William Segar in a fine portrait now in the National Gallery of Ireland, Essex had the beginnings of a pointed moustache, a style then in vogue with French aristocrats, but not yet the beard that he would grow some years later to perfect his image as a military man. Although raised and educated as a royal ward in Burghley's relatively sober household after his father's death, he was spoilt and something of a dandy. Even as a first-year student at Trinity College, Cambridge, he was allowed to spend £12 (£12,000 today) on a tawny velvet outfit with two pairs of matching shoes. His insistence on fine blue livery coats for all his servants testified to his incurable flamboyance and taste for expensive finery.[1]

With Leicester now gone, Sir Christopher Hatton, who at forty-seven had been made Lord Chancellor on the death of Sir Thomas Bromley, joined Burghley and Walsingham as one of the queen's three pre-eminent elder statesmen. To telegraph to the world a new, more serious conception of himself, Hatton chose to abandon his trademark jewel-encrusted hat topped with a feather in favour of a plain, flat, black velvet cap just like Burghley's.[2] This left Essex to battle it out with Ralegh for primacy among the younger, brasher generation of courtiers. Their struggle was bitterly fought.

In the week before Christmas 1588, Essex had challenged Ralegh to a duel, a move that the Privy Council sought to 'repress' and have 'buried in silence that it may not be known to Her Majesty', as both Burghley and Hatton so disliked Ralegh for his maverick ways they preferred to back Essex by default and cover up for him.[3] Others, chief among them the queen's cousin Lord Hunsdon, whose youngest son, Robert, had come to blows with Ralegh during a tennis match, willingly connived with them in such deceptions.[4] But the eventual outcome was uncertain, for Ralegh did not intend to give up on his bid to succeed Leicester in Elizabeth's esteem.

And he had grounds for hope. For in spite of Essex's endless boasts of her favour and the talk of his followers about her late-night card sessions with him, it was obvious that he lacked an intimacy with her of the sort previously enjoyed by his stepfather. The clearest signal of this was that she was unwilling to give him a pet name. In affectionate moments she addressed him as 'Robin', but she would never call him 'Rob' or her 'Sweet Robin'. No one, it seemed, would be able to replace her beloved 'Eyes'.[5]

She did, however, set him on the road to some measure of financial security. By early 1588, she had given him a long lease of York House, another of the great city mansions on the Strand, conveniently close to Leicester House. Traditionally, this was the Lord Chancellor's courtesy residence, but Hatton had no need of it, for he already had his own grand town house at Ely Place in Holborn. Then, on 12 January 1589, Elizabeth went considerably further, granting Essex his stepfather's highly lucrative lease of the farm of the customs on sweet wines.[6] But this was never enough: he had already accumulated staggering debts and his creditors were demanding repayment. He therefore naïvely set out to win acclaim as a Protestant hero in the war with King Philip. He felt sure he could clear his debts through plundering the Spanish king's territories and treasure at the same time as he led his men to glorious victories. Like Ralegh, he began studying maps and plans and reading books on Greek and Roman military strategy.[7]

Since the defeat of the Armada, Sir Francis Drake had been busy canvassing support for a speedy counter-attack on Spain that would land English troops on the Spanish mainland. Burghley had a more modest proposal. He merely wanted to send ships to strike at the weather-beaten remnants of the Armada as they struggled home between Ireland and Spain. For a while, it was Elizabeth's plan that seemed most likely to prevail. Her aim was to send Drake to intercept and attack King Philip's treasure ships somewhere in the mid-Atlantic: the value of the treasure could amount to as much as £3 million (£3 billion today). Even if just one or two ships could be detached from the convoy and captured with their vast chests of bullion, that would be enough. On no account did she want to commit herself to a risky military expedition on the Spanish mainland.[8]

But as Elizabeth's grief for Leicester distracted her attention, Drake came up with an ambitious, if awkward, conflation of these competing ideas. By this stage, he had teamed up with his old friend Sir John Norris, a veteran of the Netherlands campaign. Rather than risk a major naval battle with the warships that Philip always sent to the Azores to escort his treasure convoys on the final stages of their journey, Drake and Norris planned to sail initially to the ports of Santander and San Sebastian on the north coast of Spain, where the warships that had survived the disastrous Armada campaign were refitting, then loot and burn them in a surprise attack. That accomplished, Drake and Norris aimed at nothing less than a full-blown invasion of Portugal, with the object of deposing Philip as king and putting a rival on the throne. If time and resources permitted, they would then seek out the Spanish treasure convoy in the mid-Atlantic after making a commando raid on one of the islands of the Azores, which they could turn into a temporary base just for the duration of the campaign.[9]

Dom António, Prior of Crato and the illegitimate grandson of King Manuel I of Portugal, had been thirsting for revenge ever since Philip had won the contest for the disputed succession and been crowned king in 1581. Fleeing to Paris with the Portuguese Crown Jewels, Dom António had sought asylum in England. He now lived in Stepney, a few miles east of London. Elizabeth had blown hot and cold towards him, sheltering and indulging him only so long as he had money to spend and it suited her.

On balance, Elizabeth believed that trying to restore the Portuguese claimant was a waste of time and money. But Walsingham strongly disagreed, and Burghley was soon converted to the plan, maintaining it to be England's one and only opportunity to detach Portugal with its large fleet and vastly lucrative trade with the East Indies, West Africa and Brazil from Philip's clutches and inflict a knockout blow on the Spanish king before he could rearm.

By late December, Burghley had won the queen round to his viewpoint.[10] At last, she consented to the expedition, but only with the firm proviso that it was to have just two strategic goals: 'the one to distress the King of Spain's warships, the other to get the possession of some of the Islands of Azores, thereby to intercept the convoys of the treasure that doth yearly pass that way'. Only *after* those aims had been achieved were Drake and Norris even to contemplate invading Portugal. What the queen did not know was that Dom António had secretly offered Drake and Norris massive trade concessions in West Africa and Asia if they would restore him to the Portuguese throne.[11] The expedition was to be privately equipped and financed, with the queen providing £20,000 and six royal navy ships. The profits would be split between the investors in proportion to the size of their stakes. Essex strongly backed the idea and was eager to join the venture. He knew that Elizabeth was unwilling to allow any of her noblemen to put their lives at unnecessary risk, but he did not intend to let that stop him. Headstrong and impulsive, he decided that if he could not inveigle her into granting her consent, he would defy her and leave without it.[12]

On Friday, 4 April 1589, Drake and Norris sailed from Plymouth with 120 ships carrying some 19,000 men, along with Dom António and his supporters. Although expressly forbidden by Elizabeth from joining them, Essex defied her, galloping off from London between five and six on the evening of the 3rd. His brazen defiance was a calculated risk. If he could make a name for himself as a soldier, win treasure and fame and confound King Philip in the process, he was confident he would conquer the queen. After covering 220 miles in a bare thirty-six hours, changing horses regularly along the way, he put to sea on the queen's galleon *Swiftsure*, whose captain, Sir Roger Williams, knighted by Leicester in the Netherlands, had been waiting for him.[13]

In a fury when she learned of his deception, Elizabeth sent her kinsman Sir Francis Knollys post-haste to Plymouth to recall him, but he arrived too late: Essex had already sailed. Her next move was to write Essex a blistering letter, echoing in its idioms the earlier broadside she had sent his stepfather when he had defied her and accepted the position of Governor-General of the Netherlands:

> Your sudden and undutiful departure from our presence and your place of attendance, you may easily conceive how offensive it is, and ought to be, unto us. Our great favours bestowed on you without deserts hath drawn you thus to neglect and forget your duty, for other constructions we cannot make of these your strange actions. Not meaning, therefore, to tolerate this your disordered part, we gave directions to some of our Privy Council to let you know our express pleasure for your immediate repair hither which you have not performed as your duty doth bind you, increasing greatly thereby your former offence and undutiful behaviour in departing in such sort without our privity, having so special office of attendance and charge near our person. We do therefore charge and command you forthwith upon receipt of these our letters, all excuses and delays set apart, to make your present and immediate repair unto us, to understand our farther pleasure. Whereof see you fail not, as you will be loath to incur our indignation and will answer for the contrary at your uttermost peril.[14]

She could hardly have been plainer. No less cutting was a second letter she dictated to Walsingham then corrected in her own handwriting, to be forwarded to Drake and Norris at the earliest opportunity. The captain of the *Swiftsure* was to be severely punished by martial law, preferably hanged from the yardarm, for conniving in a crime close to mutiny: 'And if Essex be now come into the company of the fleet, we straightly charge you that, all dilatory excuse set apart, you do forthwith cause him to be sent back hither in safe manner.'

> Which, if you do not, you shall look to answer for the same to your smart [at your peril], for these be no childish actions, nor matters wherein you are to deal by cunning of devices, to seek evasions, as the customs of lawyers is. Neither will we be so satisfied at your hands.

In her dictation, we hear Elizabeth's authentic voice. 'For as we have authority to rule', she thundered:

> so we look to be obeyed, and to have obedience directly and surely continued unto us, and so look to be answered herein at your hands. Otherwise we will think you unworthy of the authority ye have, and that ye know not how to use it.[15]

As Walsingham sardonically quipped to the clerk called upon to make a neat copy of the document for the queen's signature, 'The draft of the letter is in as mild terms as may be, considering how Her Majesty standeth affected.'[16]

Elizabeth, for all her insistence on absolute obedience, was about to discover just how difficult it was for a woman ruler to assert control over the execution of policy in wartime. Drake and Norris headed for Coruña, where they believed some two hundred or so of Philip's more valuable supply ships lay at anchor.[17] When they arrived, however, they found only five Spanish vessels to loot.[18] Instead of retracing their steps and attacking the Armada warships refitting in the Biscay ports, they sailed directly for Lisbon, where they linked up with Essex, who had gone straight there, suggesting that there had been collusion between them from the outset. Their aim now was to loot and burn the merchant ships in the harbour of the Portuguese capital, then put Dom António on the throne: exactly what Elizabeth had said they should not even consider before fulfilling the expedition's strategic aims.

Essex was the first to land. He waded up to his shoulders in the foaming surf under the guns of the castle of Peniche, some sixty miles from Lisbon, where it was considered safest to disembark. Once the castle had been captured and claimed for Dom António, Norris mustered his army and led it on a slow and arduous march south across the rocky coastland to Lisbon, while Drake sailed around to meet him with the heavy artillery as quickly as the wind would allow. After marching for almost a week in the scorching heat, the soldiers, sick and weary, reached the westerly suburbs of Lisbon, but they found the city's main defences impregnable. Supplies were fast running low, as Dom António had persuaded Norris that, to protect his reputation, nothing should be taken from the Portuguese, only from the Spanish. But soon things were desperate. With the English troops no longer in a condition to begin a long siege, Norris gave Dom António an ultimatum: either he could raise reinforcements and supplies from the local population within a week or the army would withdraw.

Drake, meanwhile, went off at a tangent when he saw how securely the narrow, winding stretches of the Tagus estuary leading to the port of Lisbon were defended. Unwilling to risk transporting the heavy cannon and ammunition the army so badly needed past the well-equipped forts and batteries, he preferred to attack ships at anchor at the mouth of the estuary instead. He quickly captured sixty German hulks laden to the brim with wheat, copper, wax, masts and ships' cables.

With characteristic bravado, Essex fought off a Spanish ambush on the English camp, but Dom António's efforts to raise reinforcements were greeted with a sullen silence. When, in the intense heat, dysentery began to rampage through the army, Norris had no alternative but to order a retreat. On 8 June, one short week after Drake and Norris had summoned a Council of War to debate with their captains what should be done, all but twenty of their best ships set a course back to Plymouth, taking with them as many of the prize ships captured during Drake's raids as were still seaworthy.

Before leaving Lisbon, Essex rode up to the city gates and drove a lance into them in a symbolic, if pointless, act of defiance, challenging the Spanish governor to a duel. Unsurprisingly, his invitation was declined. He then reportedly threw his own belongings out of a carriage so that he could carry wounded soldiers back to the fleet. But not even such acts of chivalry could disguise the utter failure of the expedition.

Drake planned a desperate dash for the Azores with the rump of the fleet before returning home, but his flagship sprang a leak. When a fierce gale scattered the rest of his ships, he, too, hastened for Plymouth. Out of those who sailed on the expedition, more than six thousand died of disease or were killed.[19]

Elizabeth could scarcely conceal her exasperation. 'They went to places more for profit than for service,' she tartly declared on receiving Drake and Norris's letters, brought by a merchant vessel from off the coast of northern Spain.[20] Essex arrived home well in advance of the rest of the fleet, on 24 or 25 June, when Elizabeth was with the Privy Council at Nonsuch Palace, about to set out on her summer progress. He anxiously sent on ahead his younger brother Walter, with whom he was especially close, to test the waters. On 9 July, by which time Drake and Norris had also returned, he himself rode to Nonsuch to face the music.[21] He knew he was in serious trouble. A victualling ship from England had tracked him down while he was anchored off the mouth of the Tagus and had delivered Elizabeth's scathing letter of rebuke, now two months old.[22]

Essex's followers were 'in desperate suspense' as to what would become of him. They feared his hopes of greatness had been strangled at birth by his folly in defying the queen.[23] Some believed that all he had to do, like Leicester after his inglorious recall from the Netherlands, was to wait until her mood had changed. Others knew better. Quite apart from the strategic debacle, all those who had invested in the venture, especially the queen, had lost large sums of money – this not least when the German merchant ships captured at Lisbon had to be returned with their cargoes to their owners after angry diplomatic protests.[24]

Essex found Elizabeth at Nonsuch, but she froze him out. Whereas she awarded gold chains of honour to several participants in the expedition for their good services, she pointedly ignored him. She could not bring herself to banish him from Court, as she had first planned to do; on cool reflection, she was gradually coming round to believing him more foolhardy than treacherous, his defiance, as she later said, 'but a sally of youth'.[25] And yet she realized that by allowing him to escape a harsher punishment she was exposing her own vulnerability. He needed to be taught a sharp lesson. Doubly so, because he had provoked pain in her; for that, he must be made to suffer in return.

Her retribution was finely calculated. By the simple step of presenting a gold chain to Ralegh, who had contributed men and ships to the expedition but had not actually sailed with them, and by passing over Essex, she stung the proud Earl in a manner he found quite intolerable.[26] While his stepfather would have known that this was one of her classic methods of control and taken his medicine quietly, Essex's nature was such that he preferred to pick over the sore until it festered.[27]

By the time the Court moved on to Oatlands on 17 August, Essex's spin doctors were falling over themselves to pluck victory from the jaws of defeat. One spun the lie that the Earl 'hath chased Mr Ralegh from the Court and hath confined him into Ireland'.[28] This might have been more convincing if not for the fact that Ralegh was away in London at the time, attending to his affairs at Durham House.[29] When he did later visit his Irish estates, Ralegh made it plain that he did so in full confidence of his position at Court, boasting, 'I am in place to be believed not inferior to any man.'[30] The tension between the two rivals was approaching breaking point. 'There was never', chanted the Court gossips, 'such emulation, such envy, such backbiting, as is now at this time.'[31]

Jubilant over the subtle way she had taught Essex that she was his sovereign and expected his obedience, Elizabeth was in an upbeat mood over Christmas. So cold was the weather that the Thames froze over, and she spent the festive season at Richmond, which, unlike Greenwich, was easily accessible by coach when her barge could not cut a passage through the thick ice.[32] Whether Essex had yet stopped sulking when he resumed his place beside her chair on New Year's Day and leading courtiers presented her with their seasonal gifts is not recorded, but Sir John Stanhope, a gentleman of the Privy Chamber and the author of a series of chatty newsletters, observed Elizabeth to be in high spirits, dancing and singing and performing the galliard with its high leaps and jumps six or seven times every morning.[33]

Eager for a swift return to the centre of affairs, Essex sought to make Walsingham the arbiter of his destiny. Mixing business with pleasure, he began assiduously courting the spymaster's twenty-two-year-old daughter, Frances, Philip Sidney's widow. Sexually precocious, with a winning smile and long, elegant fingers, she was one of the women of the Court most sought after for her looks. Precisely when Essex began sleeping with her is uncertain, but they secretly exchanged wedding vows in the spring of 1590 when she knew she was already pregnant. Discretion was essential, for Essex was all too well aware that the queen would be enraged if she found out, as she had made it plain she considered Walsingham and his wife and daughter to be far inferior socially to the exalted Earl.[34]

Essex shamelessly courted Frances for political advantage. He was never seriously in love with her and, after their marriage, she would have to endure his growing notoriety as a philanderer. Within eighteen months, he was said to be pursuing the queen's maids of honour. One of them, Elizabeth Southwell, Kate Carey's granddaughter, would become pregnant by him.[35] The penalty for jeopardizing what the queen regarded as her quasi-parental duty to protect the younger female members of her Bedchamber and Privy Chamber staff from male lasciviousness could be severe. Elizabeth took a dim view of illicit sex, and where marriage was concerned what mattered most to her was that a couple were suitably matched socially; that her courtiers recognized their marriages were a matter for *her* to negotiate – conjointly with the girl's father, should he still be alive – and that courtships should not lead to pre-marital pregnancy.[36] Essex broke every one of these rules. In the short term, he would successfully shield himself by bribing Thomas Vavasour, another of the queen's servants and an older man, to confess to the paternity of Southwell's baby and face imprisonment. But his secret marriage to Frances Walsingham and his seduction of Southwell were time bombs waiting to explode.[37]

Essex's hope that his father-in-law would serve as a lever to advance his career quickly went awry. Frequently sick for some years, Walsingham was much troubled by 'the stoppage of my water' and a 'defluction into one of my eyes'.[38] In August 1589, he wrote to Burghley, 'I have caused these [letters] enclosed, sent me by your Lordship, to be read to me, being advised by my physicians to keep my bed, waiting whether I shall be visited with another fit of my fever.'[39] He was able to retain his seat in the Privy Council, but on 1 April the following year he suffered a stroke. For some time since he had successfully trapped Mary Queen of Scots, he had wanted to retire. Now, that moment had arrived, and he petitioned the queen to allow him to step down after his many years of service. His clerk wrote next day to reassure him: 'I told Her Majesty of your last night's fit', he explained, 'whereunto she answered that shortly she would call another to the place, so that I hope when a full presence of councillors shall be here the effect of her resolving will take place.'[40]

Four days later, Walsingham was dead. At ten o'clock the next evening, he was quietly buried at St Paul's, 'without any such extraordinary ceremonies as usually appertain to a man serving in my place'. These were the careful instructions he had set out in his will. (The reason had nothing to do with his Protestant convictions: he had stood surety for Philip Sidney's debts to the tune of £17,000, which he could not repay.)[41] If Elizabeth felt any grief at his passing, she hid it well. Much of her could never forgive him for his role in the trapping and destruction of Mary Stuart.

On 30 June, Burghley wrote to Count Giovanni Figliazzi, one of Walsingham's important Italian contacts and the Florentine ambassador to Madrid:

> I cannot otherwise think but you have afore this time heard, or else I am sure you shall hear, before this letter can come to your hands, of the death of Mr Secretary Walsingham, who left this world the 6th of April as we account by ancient custom: whereby, though he hath gained a better state, as I am fully persuaded, for his soul in heaven, yet the Queen's Majesty and her realm and I and others his particular friends have had a great loss, both for the public use of his good and painful long services and for the private comfort I had by his mutual friendship.

Anxious for their future as their career prospects dimmed, many of Walsingham's former protégés joined Essex's followers and advised their new leader to 'seek a domestical greatness', gradually working his way up the ladder at Court in the old-fashioned manner, by hard graft in a series of offices. But this was never Essex's way. As the Court gossips remarked, the Earl was 'impatient of so slow a progress'.[42] Restless, precocious, presumptuous, he wanted instant glory, to rise from zero to hero just like a character from one of the Arthurian chivalric legends or Spenser's *Faerie Queene*.

Twice Essex burned his fingers playing at politics in the year after his return from Lisbon. On the first occasion, he made an abortive overture to James VI, a move as naïve and clumsy as it was potentially treasonable. Sending a messenger to James carrying letters from himself and his elder sister, Penelope, the queen's god-daughter, he used the alias Ernestus and described himself as a 'Weary Knight' who accounted it 'a Thrall that he now lives in'. Offering the Scottish king his 'service and fidelity', he pointed out that since Elizabeth was now fifty-six – he called her Venus and James Victor – she might soon die. Essex's intermediary, however, proved indiscreet and unreliable, and soon the whole affair had been reported to Burghley by his agent in Edinburgh. Appalled by Essex's recklessness, Burghley and Hatton decided that the incident was best hushed up before whispers of it reached the queen. As yet, they were still backing Essex as the antidote to Ralegh.[43]

Then, acting out of a sense of misdirected honour, Essex attempted to persuade Elizabeth to rehabilitate William Davison and appoint him to Walsingham's vacant position. But when Davison petitioned the queen, he met with a resounding rebuff. She could never overcome her loathing for the man she still blamed for allowing the signed death warrant for Mary Queen of Scots to leave his possession. For the time being, she refused to promote anyone in Walsingham's place, throwing an additional burden on to the shoulders of Burghley and Hatton. As Elizabeth grew older, she found it increasingly difficult to appoint new men to important positions. Partly this was because she could not bring herself to face up to the prospect of her own mortality; partly it reflected a distaste for change and for forging new working relationships.[44]

Frustrated in his hopes for rapid advancement at home, Essex turned his mind once again to the prospect of military glory overseas. Ever since Henry III's assassination, he had been closely following the fortunes of the Huguenot leader Henry of Navarre, now Henry IV, who was locked in an unrelentingly merciless civil war with the Catholic League and its ally Philip II. Once tantalizingly close to recovering Paris from the Leaguers, by the end of August 1589 Henry had been driven back to the port of Dieppe in Normandy, where he was boxed in. To rescue him, Elizabeth lent him £22,000 in gold and silver coins and four thousand English troops, initially for a month. She gave the command not to Essex, but to Lord Willoughby, who had done the difficult job of replacing Leicester in the Netherlands with considerable skill, paving the way for the queen to reduce her forces there to a bare minimum of auxiliaries. Under the command of Sir Francis Vere, a veteran of Leicester's expedition, these auxiliaries reinforced the armies of the new Dutch leader, Count Maurice of Nassau, William of Orange's son.[45]

By the time Willoughby's reinforcements landed in Normandy, Henry had fought his way out of Dieppe. Helped by Willoughby, whose stay in France was extended to three months, he recaptured several fortresses between Normandy and the Loire over the course of a gruelling winter campaign. In March 1590, he was further able to inflict a crushing defeat on the Leaguers at the Battle of Ivry, thirty miles west of Paris, reopening the way to the capital.[46]

Henry's triumph was like a scorpion with a sting in its tail. King Philip now ordered the Duke of Parma to march from the Netherlands to defend Paris from a Huguenot siege. By late July, Parma's vanguard was beyond Amiens and, within two weeks, he was on the outskirts of Paris. For another month, Henry tried to hold him off, while dreaming of defeating him in a pitched battle, but the odds were stacked against him. By mid-September, he was forced to begin a retreat. Paris was still in the hands of the Leaguers, and Parma would soon make the long, slow march back to the Netherlands. Then, to Elizabeth's horror, three thousand Spanish troops landed on the right bank of the Loire and hastened north to the Blavet estuary in Brittany. There, they constructed a heavily fortified deep-water naval base ready for a force of Spanish warships, conjuring up the nightmare of a new Armada. As if in concert, the Leaguers once again took over large tracts of Normandy, establishing a stronghold in Rouen and more than doubling the size of its garrison.[47]

Essex had begun a correspondence with Henry IV even before Willoughby's forces landed in France. When the French king addressed him warmly as '*Mon Cousin*', and in terms that indicated he took him seriously, the Earl was deeply gratified.[48] He had discovered a cause which he could not only believe in passionately but which offered the prospects of plunder and martial glory, too. He began to cultivate the new French ambassador to London, Jean de la Fin, Sieur de Beauvoir-la-Nocle, visiting his house and feeding him intelligence. Meanwhile, he pressed Elizabeth to allow him to fight in France, stepping up his lobbying in November 1590 after Henry sent Viscount Turenne, chief gentleman of the *Chambre du Roi*, to visit her before travelling on to Germany to recruit mercenaries.[49]

Elizabeth warmly welcomed Turenne, preparing lodgings for him in the Dean's house when he came to see her at Windsor Castle and building a temporary banqueting house at Whitehall to receive him after he had attended the Accession Day tilts.[50] But it was Essex who provided Turenne and his entourage with the bulk of their lavish entertainment, throwing open York House to them and feasting them, even offering to contribute £1,000 towards the cost of hiring German *Reiter* (cavalry). He raised the money by selling lands that had been in his family for over a century.[51]

Admiringly observed by Turenne from a place of honour in Elizabeth's open-air gallery above the Whitehall tiltyard, Essex staged a dramatic entry into the lists on the queen's Accession Day to the applause of a large crowd seated on specially erected stands.[52] He was clad in shiny black armour, loosely covered by a surcoat intricately embroidered from top to bottom with pearls. Riding in a stately chariot pulled by coal-black steeds, he sat erect with his back to a driver dressed as 'gloomy Time'. His squires and pages were also dressed in black, bearing aloft his tilting lances, which were disguised as the staves that mourners carried at funerals.[53]

Elizabeth pretended hardly to notice her brash young favourite. Instead, she showered most of her attention on her young god-daughter Aletheia, daughter of Lord Talbot and his wife, Mary Cavendish, who was spending the day with her. According to Richard Brakenbury, the queen's senior gentleman usher, she was seen 'often kissing' the six-year-old Aletheia, 'which Her Majesty seldom useth to any, and then amending her dressing with pins . . . and so into the privy lodgings'.[54]

Elizabeth's seeming indifference to Essex stemmed from the fact that she had only just learned of his secret marriage. She had made the shocking discovery entirely by chance in the course of an impromptu visit to Somerset House, when she had been informed on arrival that Frances Walsingham, 'waited on as the Countess of Essex', had vacated the building a few days before. As Sir John Stanhope informed Aletheia's father, 'If she could overcome her passion against my Lord of Essex for his marriage, no doubt she would be much the quieter.'[55]

Modelling his tactics on his stepfather's before him, Essex came up with a solution that, for the moment, was enough to calm down the angry queen. According to Stanhope, he promised her that, in future, 'my Lady [the Countess] shall live very retired in her mother's house'.[56] For the first time since his return from Portugal, he had hit the right note. Within a month, Stanhope could report that the queen had partially relented and 'her favour holdeth in reasonable good terms to the Earl of Essex'.[57]

After months of indecision while she weighed up the pros and cons, Elizabeth finally informed Beauvoir, the French ambassador, that she would support a short, sharp, decisive blow to defeat the Leaguers and oust the Spaniards from France. As in 1588, however, she was unwilling to commit herself prematurely to a costly, risky conflict that might last for years. Unlike Essex, who thirsted for glory and yearned for instant results, she looked at the war against Spain and the Catholic League in the round and regarded England's role in northern France as that of an army of reserve, to be used cautiously and sparingly. She knew that Henry IV's war aims were different from her own. He hoped to defeat Parma in a set-piece battle and recapture Paris. Her goal, by contrast, was to secure the Channel ports of Le Havre, Caen and Dieppe, as well as the Blavet estuary, which is why she offered to focus her troops on the liberation of Normandy and Brittany.[58]

In April 1591, Elizabeth sent Sir John Norris with three thousand troops to reinforce Henry's meagre strength in Brittany. Half of his men were seasoned auxiliaries from the Netherlands, where they had been fighting under Vere's command alongside the Dutch. She then detached from their number a company of six hundred, whom she placed under the command of Sir Roger Williams and diverted to assist Henry elsewhere.[59]

No sooner had her forces arrived in France than she had second thoughts and wrote to Henry, who had just recaptured Chartres, urging him to march into Normandy and besiege Rouen before

Parma could return with his army. If he would agree, she would supply him with 3,400 extra troops and give them two months' pay.[60] With Rouen safely in his hands, she thought he could expel the Leaguers from the coastal zone once and for all, after which he could safely launch a sustained defence of Brittany.

From the moment an expedition to Rouen was first mooted, Essex staked his claim to lead the army. He thought it had all the makings of the glorious triumph for which he and his followers yearned. He had been deeply jealous of Lord Willoughby when the older, more experienced man had been chosen to relieve the siege of Dieppe, but Willoughby was now tired and sick and only too pleased to support Essex in his bid to replace him.[61]

Elizabeth was sceptical at first.[62] She knew that allowing Essex to lead such an important campaign would be a clear signal, both at home and abroad, that he was more than just another young favourite. It would mean that, eclipsing Ralegh, she would be seen to have marked him out as someone upon whom she must increasingly rely as she grew older, who would expect to join her Privy Council on his return. It is sometimes said that she gave him the command only after he had pleaded with her three times on bended knee, on each occasion for at least two hours, and that her decision was solely the result of an ageing woman's infatuation for a bewitching young man.[63] Romantic as this may be, it is wrong: what clinched her decision was Burghley and Hatton's emphatic support for the mission and for Essex's leadership.[64]

After much frantic correspondence between Burghley and Beauvoir, some written at three o'clock in the morning, Elizabeth at last relented. On 25 June, she agreed that Essex could serve as Lieutenant-General of her forces in France, a decision he had cheekily anticipated five days before when he began the mobilization of his tenants.[65] But she made one condition. She had recently recalled Sir Edward Stafford from his position as ambassador to France, his debts cancelled by a grateful queen unaware of his treachery as 'Julio'. His replacement was Sir Henry Unton, a protégé of Hatton, who was given strict orders to act as Essex's minder. Widely travelled and a natural linguist, Unton was to supervise and advise the Earl and send Burghley regular reports. He was instructed in particular to ensure that the main

Huguenot army was fully deployed alongside the English forces and that Essex did not indulge in a series of futile and dangerous heroics. Unton was to be assisted in this challenging role by Sir Thomas Leighton, a veteran of several military campaigns and also a fluent French speaker.[66]

Elizabeth, still far from confident that she could rely on Essex, meant to leave no room for ambiguity. His written instructions, issued on 21 July, required him to consult at all times with Leighton so as to avoid anything that proved to be 'inconvenient or over desperate to the manifest overthrow of our people'. He was to discuss strategy jointly with Henry and, if the two men were separated, Unton was to act as his liaison: on no account should Essex make important decisions on his own.[67]

Next, she wrote directly to Henry, in fluent French. Not mincing her words in a letter she had no hesitation in handing over to Essex to deliver to cause him maximum embarrassment, she cautioned the French king that her Lieutenant would do him worthy service, provided he was carefully kept in check:

> If, which most I fear, the rashness of his youth does not make him too precipitate, you will never have cause to doubt his boldness in your service, for he has given too frequent proofs that he regards no peril, be it what it may, and you are entreated to bear in mind that he is too impetuous to be given the reins. But, my God, how can I dream of making any reasonable requests to you, seeing you are so careless of your own life. I must appear a very foolish creature, only I repeat to you that he will require the bridle rather than the spur.[68]

This was hardly a glowing testimonial but, on Burghley's advice, Essex swallowed his pride and wrote at once to thank the queen for her 'gracious letter to the king in my behalf'.[69] Aware that Burghley had played a prominent part in his nomination through his dealings with Beauvoir and in his daily audiences with the queen, Essex continued to show him ostentatious deference and respect.[70] Unfortunately, after the Earl arrived in France, not even Burghley would be able to rescue him from an imbroglio that would surpass even that of Drake and Norris in Portugal. And when the newly chosen queen's Lieutenant returned to Court, he would find a disquietingly changed landscape, one that he came increasingly to resent and would strive with his whole being to disrupt.

A whole new phase was about to begin, one in which, step by step, the lines would begin to be laid down for a deadly, destructive feud between Essex and his rivals. And Elizabeth would be unable to stop it.

8. The Visible Queen

When on Elizabeth's Accession Day in 1590 Essex had made his dramatic entrance into the tiltyard in a chariot driven by a coachman dressed as 'gloomy Time', the *mise en scène* was meant to glorify the watching queen. Based on a well-known scene in Petrarch's *I Trionfi*, a standard allegorical sequence in Renaissance pageantry, the message was that carnal Love is overcome by Chastity, and Death itself by Fame, Time and Eternity.[1]

The celebrations in 1590 saw the idea of the Virgin Queen, first tentatively glimpsed in the Norwich entertainments scripted in 1578 by Thomas Churchyard, move towards a fully fledged 'cult' of Gloriana. Sir Henry Lee, the chief theatrical impresario of the tilts, who within two years would commission the famous 'Ditchley Portrait' of Elizabeth, in which a comparatively lifelike image of a fast-ageing monarch was successfully wedded to an icon of cosmic power, had decided to retire.[2] As his replacement, the queen had chosen the younger, dapper, fitter Earl of Cumberland, who had brought the news of the Armada's defeat to Tilbury. Lee staged a magnificent closing ceremony to mark his departure, one that sought to deify the post-menopausal queen both as a 'Vestal Virgin' and a goddess incarnate. As a vestal maiden she could be both pure and sexually alluring, but as a goddess she was a 'Virgin Mother', a second Madonna, 'whom neither time nor age can wither'.[3]

Lee's inspiration was a recently established portrait type of Elizabeth holding a sieve, of which the most explicit realization is a version found rolled up in an attic in the Palazzo Reale, Siena, in 1895. Based on a face pattern taken from a chalk drawing done from life by the Italian Mannerist Federico Zuccari during a visit to London in 1574, the 'Siena Portrait' was commissioned in 1583 by Sir Christopher Hatton from a Flemish artist, Quentin Metsys the Younger. (Hatton makes a cameo appearance in a small courtly scene in the upper-right-hand corner of the painting, wearing his distinctive white hind badge on his cloak.)[4]

The sieve was a well-known emblem of virginity. When her chastity was questioned, one of the Roman vestal virgins, the beautiful Tuccia, had proved her purity by carrying water in a sieve from the Tiber to the Vestal Virgin Temple in the Roman Forum without spilling a single drop. Lee's achievement was to interweave this theme with the idea of Elizabeth's quasi-divinity. In his version of the story, Tuccia's victory over her sexuality became a victory over the Fall and its consequences, even over death itself. Elizabeth's motto was *Semper Eadem*, 'Always one and the same'. Now, Lee would give that motto an entirely fresh spin.

As the closing ceremony began, Lee moved slowly forward towards the open-air gallery in which the queen sat with her god-daughter Aletheia, ready to surrender his staff of office and armour to Cumberland. To the sound of ravishingly sweet music played and sung by Robert Hales, the queen's favourite lutenist, a trapdoor opened in the floor before them to reveal a pavilion formed from a hundred yards of white taffeta, rising, as if by enchantment, from the void. An exact scale model of the Vestal Virgin Temple, operated by hidden clockwork and complete with what looked like columns of porphyry, the pavilion was round, with oil lamps burning before an altar bedecked with the finest cloth of gold. By the door of the pavilion stood a crowned pillar entwined with eglantine, from which was suspended a placard inscribed in golden letters with a Latin prayer 'Of Eliza' composed by Lee:

> Pious, powerful, most blessed of virgins, defender of faith, peace and nobility, to whom God, the stars and Virtue have a devotion exceeding every other. After so many years, so many jousts, this old knight, his soul prostrate at your feet, fastens on his sacred armour. He prays, by the blood of his Redeemer, that you might have a life of peace, empire, fame, eternity, immortality. You have moved the farther column of the Temple of Hercules. A crown surpassing all other crowns, for she to whom the heavens most happily bestowed a crown at birth, will, on her death, be borne beatified into heaven.[5]

Everything in this ceremony interlocked. In Italian Renaissance iconography, the crowned pillar beside the temple door stood for chastity, fortitude and empire, and eglantine for virginity. On the altar were 'certain princely gifts' which three vestal virgins, clad all in white, presented to the queen. As the Roman poet Horace had made plain, these maidens were synonymous with the safety and longevity of the City of Rome.

Lee's choreography, taken from an Italian theatrical handbook by Vincenzo Cartari, rested on the assumption that, when the Temple of Vesta was founded, four virgins were chosen. Now, the fourth and most celebrated of them all, Tuccia with her sieve, was to be Elizabeth herself.[6]

Lee knew his queen. She had no difficulty in understanding and appreciating the abstruse imagery in this spectacular entertainment. Lee adored Elizabeth and genuinely sought to honour her, but his sycophantic iconography would soon be cynically exploited by younger courtiers in the hope of advancing their careers. The promise of gaining offices, perquisites and grants of land was well worth the effort of hypocritically flattering an ageing spinster.

In the spring of 1591, Elizabeth began to plan the route for her most grandiose summer progress since a tour of East Anglia she had undertaken with Leicester in 1578. Besides leisure and recreation, her aim was to make herself visible to friends and foes alike, while saving money, since it was the 'privilege' of hosts to entertain their queen in style. At the same time, her privy councillors could investigate issues of concern in each locality at first hand.[7]

Conventionally, these itineraries began a week or two after the hay harvest in May, when the roads were dry and there would be enough food for the queen and her courtiers' many horses. They ended a fortnight or so before the law courts at Westminster reopened for business in the first week of October. Distances travelled were restricted for practical reasons: Elizabeth and her nobles rode in coaches pulled by six horses capable of moving up to 400lbs over makeshift tracks or highways pitted with deep potholes. She took her own bed, tapestries, bed hangings and linen, gold and silver plate, household goods and cookery utensils with her everywhere she went. These, and her courtiers' vast quantities of luggage and the clothes, tents and equipment needed by a small army of her servants were transported on up to three hundred carts. As a result, rarely could the royal entourage travel more than ten or twelve miles per day.[8]

The queen's grandfather, Henry VII, had gone as far north as Lincoln, Nottingham and York on his first and most ambitious progress in 1486, and as far west as Gloucester and Bristol. Her father, accompanied by an even larger retinue, had paid a visit to York in 1541, but Elizabeth never crossed the River Trent. At various times she intended to go to York, and also to Ludlow on the borders of Wales, but the furthest north she ever reached was Grimsthorpe Castle in Lincolnshire in 1566 and Chartley in Staffordshire in 1575.

When travelling between his network of palaces and hunting lodges, Henry VIII would rely on the monasteries to provide him and his entourage with overnight lodgings. After he expelled the monks and seized their lands between 1536 and 1540, he stayed at the houses of the nobility and gentry, a policy Elizabeth followed. It was considered to be a great honour to entertain the monarch: Hatton would wait almost twenty years in vain for the woman he called his 'holy saint' to visit his palatial mansion at Holdenby in Northamptonshire.[9] But it was also ruinously expensive, costing a minimum of £1,000 a week. Apart from the vast quantities of beef, lamb, veal, game, fish, wine, beer and other victuals of all types needed to feed the hungry courtiers and their servants, costly gifts and rewards had to be presented to the queen and her principal officers. And in the evenings, candlelit masques and pageants were expected, followed by exotic banquets replete with sweet white wine and sugar candies in the shape of everything from mermaids, lions and pigeons to drummers, forts and vipers.

If Elizabeth decided to go hunting, the costs could substantially increase. While staying at Berkeley Castle in Gloucestershire in 1574, she had spitefully decided to humiliate her host, Henry, Lord Berkeley, with whom Leicester had quarrelled. She particularly loathed Berkeley's wife, Katherine, the sister of Thomas, Duke of Norfolk, who had been executed in 1572 after the Ridolfi Plot. Katherine had made the serious mistake of bludgeoning her henpecked husband into outbidding the queen for a lute of mother-of-pearl that both women coveted. Piqued by the mere sight of the Berkeleys once she arrived at their castle, Elizabeth went out hunting in their deer park and, instead of shooting a token number of her host's stags, as was the polite custom, she slaughtered his entire herd. Faced with such losses,

Berkeley had no option but to convert the land to other uses as soon as she and her courtiers had departed, as he could not afford to restock it with deer.[10]

In early May 1591, Elizabeth took herself off to Burghley's estate at Theobalds, where she stayed for ten days. Once a manor house surrounded by a moat, the property had been transformed over twenty years of building works into one of the grandest stately homes in England. Burghley had purchased it in 1564, partly to create an estate for his younger son, Robert Cecil, since Burghley House, near Stamford, the family's principal ancestral seat – it, too, had been totally rebuilt – was earmarked for Robert's elder, less talented brother, Thomas.

Theobalds advertised Burghley's wealth and power; above all, his position as the queen's chief and longest-serving adviser. Complete with a grand Italian-style stone loggia adjoining the Great Hall with tower staircases at either end, the living accommodation consisted of three principal courts, the finest and innermost of them named the Conduit, or Fountain Court. A near-perfect quadrangle with four square towers, this was where the recently completed state apartments intended for Elizabeth's use could be found.[11]

Burghley had created two superlative gardens at Theobalds: a Great Garden, its most remarkable feature an Italianate grotto coated on the inside with shimmering metallic ore and studded with crystals; and a Privy Garden, complete with neo-classical arcades, fountains, pools and water courses, even a 'great sea' with an island graced with a swan's nest at its summit. The secret weapon of his head gardener, John Gerard, was the hothouse, of which there were many, filled with exotic plants and shrubs shipped in from places as far away as Brazil, Peru and Japan. Thanks to Gerard, Burghley could enjoy multiple varieties of roses, carnations and pinks, along with oleander, yucca and hibiscus plants grown from seed. He imported orange, lemon and pomegranate trees from southern Europe, and Burghley (not Ralegh, as legend has it) would be the first man in England to serve Elizabeth with a dish of sweet potatoes, home grown from New World seed.[12]

Arriving on 10 May, Elizabeth was greeted with a pageant and shown to her apartments. These included a vast new Presence Chamber, sixty feet in length and thirty wide, with a jewelled fountain from which fresh water gushed into 'a large circular bowl or basin supported by two savages'. On the ceiling were the signs of the zodiac, beneath which the sun and planets rotated, driven by a (silent) mechanical device. Around the walls were replicas of trees with birds' nests hidden in their branches, so artfully contrived that when Burghley's steward opened the windows to let in the fresh air, real birds flew into the room, perched themselves on the branches and began to sing.[13]

Burghley, his beard and hair now white, had gone to such vast expense because this was no ordinary visit by the queen. He was seventy-one and horribly overworked: ever since Walsingham's death, he had craved retirement. So frequent and painful had his attacks of gout now become, he was regularly confined to bed, unable to travel, or even sometimes to write, for two or three days on end. He had to ride around his gardens on a mule to admire the ornamental trees and plants.[14] But before he could retire, he wanted to secure a leading role at Court, preferably as Walsingham's successor, for his twenty-eight-year-old son Robert, who was married to the queen's god-daughter Elizabeth Brooke, daughter of Lord and Lady Cobham. (That had been a wise marriage as much for Burghley as for Robert, since the Cobhams were among the chief minister's most dependable allies in Elizabeth's Privy Council and Bedchamber.)[15] With the Earl of Essex's efforts to thrust William Davison into Walsingham's vacant position thwarted, the door seemed open for Robert.

To advance his suit, Burghley worked hand in glove with his son and a hired poet to devise the pageant to greet the queen on her arrival. When she reached the gates of Theobalds, an 'actor' dressed as a Hermit stepped forward. 'I am a Hermit', he declared, 'that this ten years space/ have led a solitary and retired life/ here in my cell, not past three furlongs hence.' He spoke a 'Welcome' in blank verse, playfully explaining how Burghley was no longer able to receive the queen himself, as he had retired to a hermit's cell on account of his worldly grief and cares. Instead, he had yielded pride of place to his son Robert. 'Therefore, I wish for my good founder's sake', the actor concluded, 'That he [Robert] may live with his first-born son/ Long time to serve Your Sacred Majesty/As his grandfather faithfully hath done.'[16]

As Burghley knew all too well, Elizabeth hated surprises, so he had warned her to expect something along these lines. Unfortunately for the ailing statesman, forewarned is forearmed: she was afflicted by one of her recurrent migraines during this visit, so answered the actor with a prepared speech of her own in the form of a mock 'charter', giving full vent to her own peculiar brand of sardonic humour. Read aloud on her behalf, the 'charter' addressed the Hermit as 'the disconsolate and retired Sprite, the hermit of Theobalds', with the clear implication that her message was aimed less at the 'actor' than at Burghley – 'Sprite', meaning 'Spirit', was a pun on her chief minister's nickname. Taking the form of a legal judgement in the Court of Chancery, the gist was that the actor-hermit should retire to his cell, 'too good for the forsaken, too bad for our worthily beloved Councillor', and Burghley should return to his post. She had no intention of allowing him to retire. For all their many differences over the years, she preferred to keep working with the devil she knew. As queen, she would have to soldier on to the end, and she saw no reason why he should not do the same. It was the price he would have to pay for the many benefits he had enjoyed for so long.[17]

All the same, age and experience had brought a high degree of mutual respect to them both. Elizabeth did, accordingly, grant Burghley something of what he asked for. After breakfast on the final day of her stay, she knighted Robert Cecil, a move generally taken to mean that, before long, she would advance him to the Privy Council, if not quite yet to Walsingham's more senior position of principal secretary, for which she clearly thought him too inexperienced. That did not stop Burghley, who had to continue to share the load of much of Walsingham's former role with Hatton, from continuing to drop the broadest of hints. As a prelude to the ceremony in which Robert was dubbed a knight, he arranged for a second pageant, in which a postman carrying letters for the queen from the Emperor of China knocked at the door and asked for 'Mr Secretary Cecil'.[18]

Elizabeth decided that from July to September she would tour Surrey, Sussex and Hampshire with a view to a possible rendezvous with

Henry IV in Portsmouth, if Burghley could arrange it. By 10 July, Lord Hunsdon, whom she had made her Lord Chamberlain in 1585, was busy organizing the stops she would make along the way.[19] On the 19th, she visited Burghley's house on the Strand to watch Essex parade his cavalry before departing for France.[20] Then she moved the Court to Nonsuch, in readiness for the first of the more extended visits she would make this year.

On 2 August, the day before she left Nonsuch for Sir William More's house at Loseley in Surrey, Elizabeth admitted Robert Cecil to the Privy Council. In the end, it was Hatton's intervention that brought this about. Described by Sir Henry Unton in a letter from Dover as Cecil's 'chiefest undertaker', Hatton had been lobbying the queen on his behalf for several months in the hope of winning her round.[21]

After a brief stop at Farnham, the queen reached her first major destination, Viscount Montague's house at Cowdray in Sussex, on the 14th. There, she would be entertained in several hastily land-scaped garden settings for six days, but all was not quite what it appeared to be. Her motive for the stay, normally taken by her biographers as a vote of confidence in her host, was in fact closer to the opposite. Her marginalization of Montague, one of the most prominent Catholics in the realm and a man at the centre of a clandestine network of those loyal to the old faith, had begun as early as 1559, when he had made a defiant speech in Parliament attacking Burghley's proposals to dismantle Mary Tudor's reunion with Rome and replacing it with a Protestant Religious Settlement.[22] The gulf had widened in 1570 after the Northern Rising and the pope's decree declaring the queen to be excommunicated and deposed, when all Catholic peers were viewed by her with the greatest suspicion. By carefully distancing himself from the Jesuits and by regularly accompanying Elizabeth in procession to chapel at one or other of her palaces (although he never stayed for the services), Montague had warded off disaster. But he occupied a no-man's-land. As a pro-Spanish peer who was an outspoken critic of the Dutch, his position further deteriorated after 1585, when he was dismissed from his leadership role in county government.[23]

Elizabeth arrived at Cowdray 'with a great train' at eight o'clock precisely on Saturday evening, just in time to frustrate the illicit weekly Mass that Montague allowed to be celebrated in his private chapel for the Catholic members of his household and others living nearby. She was greeted by loud music and a pageant in which one of the Viscount's retainers, clad in armour and standing between two gatekeepers 'carved out of wood', made a speech comparing the walls of Cowdray to the walls of Thebes. The retainer held a club in one hand and a golden key in the other. The choreography was a scaled-down version of a show Leicester had put on in 1575 for Elizabeth at Kenilworth, when she had famously been welcomed by a 'gatekeeper' dressed as Hercules, who had at first attempted to deny her entry but then yielded to her 'rare beauty and princely countenance', handing over both his club and his key. Montague's gatekeeper acted rather differently: he relinquished his key but held firmly on to his club. Whether this was just a faux pas on the man's part or whether the Viscount deliberately meant to signal to the queen that he was far from powerless and deserved to be treated with greater respect has been debated ever since.[24]

After rising late on Sunday morning, Elizabeth ate a hearty breakfast of roast fowl and beef; her entourage managed to get through three oxen and 140 geese just for this one meal. The next day, she went hunting in the park with the Viscount's sister Mabel. Both women shot with a crossbow from a stand at deer herded into a fenced enclosure, while serenaded by singers who performed verses set to music in the background. The verses flattered the queen as the 'goddess and monarch of this happy Isle' whose 'eyes are arrows, though they seem to smile.'

> Behold her locks like wires of beaten gold,
> Her eyes like stars that twinkle in the sky,
> Her heavenly face not framed of earthly mould,
> Her voice that sounds Apollo's melody,
> The miracle of time, the whole world's story,
> Fortune's queen, Love's treasure, Nature's glory.[25]

The highlight of the queen's stay came later in the week. On Wednesday, in the cool of the evening, she strolled through the gardens to the sound of sweet music and was led to a 'goodly fishpond', where she saw an actor dressed as an 'angler' engaging in a fierce debate with a second 'fisherman' about the evils of society. Following a tirade from the 'angler' against unscrupulous London merchants and rack-renting landlords, the second 'fisherman' praised the queen as a goddess whose 'virtue doth make envy blush', after which he loyally laid all the fish of the pond at her feet.[26] On Thursday, she and her courtiers feasted, seated in the 'privy walks' and 'alleyways' of the gardens, the queen served at a separate table while her courtiers ate together at a table forty-eight yards long.[27] Once the plates were cleared, a group of 'country people' – largely Montague's tenants – danced before her until dusk 'in a pleasant dance with tabor [small drum] and pipe'. In an intriguing breach of protocol, the Viscount joined in, a move clearly meant to paint him as no 'carp' or rack-renter but as an old-fashioned aristocrat whose 'good lordship' made him a pillar of his local community.[28]

When Elizabeth departed early on Friday morning, heading for Portsmouth, all seemed to be well. She even instructed Lord Admiral Howard to knight Montague's second son and son-in-law before she left. But, conspicuously, two rising Sussex gentry were knighted at the same ceremony, zealous Protestants who, unlike the Viscount's kinsmen, would be sworn in as county magistrates within the year, completing Montague's political eclipse.[29]

Behind closed doors at Cowdray, the Privy Council had agreed the texts of two of the harshest royal proclamations against Catholics of Elizabeth's reign.[30] When finally published in October, they would trigger a purge of prominent individuals, male and female, nobleman or commoner, suspected of sheltering or protecting Jesuits and seminary priests or smuggling them in or out of the country. Such 'venomous vipers' – Montague and his extended family had provided safe-houses for Catholic priests for many years – were no longer merely to pay their now hefty monthly fines for failing to attend church (these fines had been increased by Parliament in 1581 to £20 a month), they were to be locked up in prison as 'the abettors and maintainers of traitors'.[31]

Reflecting on the queen's stay after her departure, Montague remarked wryly, 'It hath been told Her Majesty that it was dangerous coming for her to my house, and she was advised at her peril to take heed how she came to me to Cowdray this summer past.'[32] In fact, no sooner had the courtiers left than the vultures pounced. Within weeks, Burghley would receive a letter from a shady informer, one 'Robert Hammond *alias* Harrison', who boasted how he had infiltrated the Viscount's retinue, only to find many Catholics there 'whose secret malice to Her Majesty and [the] State I can well witness'. Hammond offered to testify for the queen, and soon royal commissioners would be nominated for the county of Sussex, who were to interrogate under oath all those suspected of infringing the new proclamations and report their findings to Burghley. Escape for Montague came just in the nick of time, when he died of natural causes at the age of sixty-three a week after the two proclamations were published.[33]

Around eight o'clock in the evening on 26 August, Elizabeth reached Portsmouth, where she hoped to rendezvous with Henry IV for at least a few hours.[34] But she would be disappointed. After waiting in vain for two full days, she rode out in her coach to view the Downs from a specially constructed platform, then moved five miles north to Southwick. From there, she went on to examine the fortifications at Porchester Castle, before at last abandoning hope of a meeting and setting out for Southampton. Once there, she terrified her privy councillors by emphatically announcing that on 6 September she would make an impromptu visit 'with very few' of her attendants to Carisbrooke Castle on the Isle of Wight, sailing across the choppy waters of the Solent in a pinnace. To Burghley's immense relief, she changed her mind the night before.[35]

Gradually retracing her steps and on something of a whim, Elizabeth made a three-night stay at the Earl of Hertford's house at Elvetham in Hampshire, arriving in the late afternoon of Monday, 20 September. Despite having barely six weeks' notice of her arrival, Hertford was determined to receive her in princely style.[36] As with her visit to Cowdray, the queen's motives deserve close scrutiny. A royal visit to Elvetham was fraught with hazard for Hertford, since the place was never his principal home, merely one of several smaller manor houses he happened to own, set in grounds 'of no great receipt' and without a deer park. In fact, all of the facilities needed for the lodging and entertainment of a vast royal entourage were lacking.[37]

Although he was one of Burghley's protégés and a staunch Protestant, Hertford was deeply suspect. Shortly before Christmas 1560, he had secretly married Katherine Grey, sister of the ill-fated Jane Grey and the next of the so-called 'Suffolk' line with a claim to the throne under Henry VIII's last will. Katherine owned up to the marriage in August 1561, by which time she was heavily pregnant. In a fury, the queen sent the couple to the Tower, where their elder son, Edward, Lord Beauchamp, was born and a second son, Thomas, conceived, despite strict royal instructions to their gaoler that the couple be kept apart. In 1562, their marriage was annulled and their children declared illegitimate (and thus barred from the succession) by Archbishop Parker, who had reluctantly investigated the case at the queen's command. The annulment, pronounced in the Court of Arches, was justified on the technical grounds that the officiating clergyman could no longer be found and that the one witness to the wedding other than him was now dead. Urged on by the queen, the Court of Star Chamber fined Hertford the punitive sum of £15,000 the following year for his presumption in 'deflowering' a royal virgin.[38]

In 1571, three years after Katherine had starved herself to death while held in isolation under closely guarded house arrest, Hertford was partially rehabilitated and his fine reduced. He was allowed to return to Court, where he fell in love with Frances, sister of Lord Admiral Howard and sister-in-law of Kate Carey. For almost seven years they would secretly live together. In 1585, after a number of failed attempts, Howard successfully interceded with Elizabeth on his sister's behalf. 'Many persuasions she used against marriage,' the happy bride-to-be informed her betrothed when given the good news, saying also 'how little you would care for me'.[39] But despite briefly promising to do what she could for Hertford, the queen was only marginally less grudging about his second marriage than about the first.

Once made aware that Elizabeth would stay at Elvetham, Hertford and his wife lost no time in setting three hundred labourers to work preparing the house and its grounds for the royal visit. In just over a month they turned the estate into the equivalent of a film set. To house the courtiers, some twenty-two temporary (mainly timber) structures of various kinds were hastily erected and decorated with boughs and flowers, notably a 'room of estate' for the nobles and a large hall 'for entertainment of knights, ladies and gentlemen of chief account'. For the queen herself, an elaborate walled annexe with its own courtyard and a separate wardrobe building were constructed, with a 'long bower' attached to it for her guards.[40]

Outdoors, an Arcadian scene was created through a mixture of hasty landscaping and illusion. At its heart was a huge artificial lake, freshly dug in the shape of a crescent moon and surrounded by potted trees and foliage. Large enough to encompass three islands, a pinnace and several smaller boats, the lake was five hundred feet wide. According to an official description later printed for Hertford and sold in London – complete with a woodcut illustration of the lake – the islands alone had a combined surface area of ten thousand square feet.[41]

The lake was to be the stage for an ingenious water pageant, although the spectacle was almost spoiled by torrential rain. Fortunately, the sky lightened at the last minute and the rain stopped. After dining in her 'room of estate', Elizabeth came down to the lake, where actors dressed as the gods of woods and waters first declaimed cringingly fawning verses, then engaged in a farcical mock-battle in which they either somersaulted into the water or were ducked. Afterwards, Elizabeth (now addressed as 'sacred Sybil') was called upon to christen a ship that would sail in Her Majesty's name and 'attempt a golden fleece'.[42]

All this was said to be in honour of Cynthia, or Phoebe (or Belphoebe, as Spenser calls her in *The Faerie Queene*). Both were alternative names for the moon goddess Diana. Cynthia, now extolled as 'the wide Ocean's Empress', was commonly represented by a crescent moon, hence the shape of the lake. In classical literature the moon was firmly linked with virginity, sexual allure and female power. During the Middle Ages it became a standard motif in the iconography of the Virgin Mary and a symbol of the Immaculate Conception.[43]

The controlling idea of the 'lake' entertainment was that Cynthia's worth 'breeds wonder; wonder holy fear;/ And holy fear unfeigned reverence'.[44] Elizabeth is 'Beauty's queen'. Her lunar power can excite erotic desire: in this context, she is the sexually provocative Venus, who (according to one version of the myth) was born from the severed genitals of Uranus that were cast into the sea. But she is also Gloriana, invested, as in Spenser's *Faerie Queene*, with the sun-like brightness of majesty. In this mode, she is a 'second sun', whose warmth fuels a golden age free from storms, doubts and fears, like the Woman Clothed with the Sun in the Book of Revelation, who has the moon under her feet and a crown of seven stars on her head. As an actor in the pageant declaimed:

> What second sun hath rays so bright,
> To cause this unacquainted light?
> Tis fair Eliza's matchless grace,
> Who with her beams doth bless this place.[45]

As Gloriana, Cynthia and Venus all rolled into one, therefore, Elizabeth guarantees Elysium and at the same time both sparks and freezes erotic desire. Transcending age and time, she combines an idyll of eternal happiness with perfect love and perfect chastity in a mystically divine union.[46]

On the penultimate day of her stay, Elizabeth was awoken at nine o'clock in the morning by three musicians dressed in rustic attire who sang a May Day greenwood ditty outside her window. In the afternoon, she watched a game of five-a-side volleyball. Later that evening, she was treated to a breathtaking firework display, followed by a sumptuous 'banquet' of white wine and sugar candy, served in a gallery in the garden lit by a hundred torches.[47]

On Thursday morning, once Elizabeth was fully dressed and made up, a spellbinding masque was performed in a privy garden below her apartments that may have been an inspiration for Titania's scenes in Shakespeare's *A Midsummer Night's Dream*. After a fanfare of cornets, the Fairy Queen and her acolytes appeared. Dancing before Elizabeth, they offered their homage, after which the fairies sang a six-part song accompanied by a lute and a consort of viols:

Eliza is the fairest Queen
That ever trod upon this green.
Eliza's eyes are blessed stars,
Inducing peace, subduing wars.
Eliza's hand is crystal bright,
Her words are balm, her looks are light.
Eliza's breast is that fair hill,
Where virtue dwells, and sacred skill,
O blessed be each day and hour,
Where sweet Eliza builds her bower.

So delighted was Elizabeth by this performance, she twice asked for it to be repeated.[48]

Shortly afterwards, she climbed into her carriage, and the royal entourage began its weary journey back to the capital. As she passed by the lake on the way out, she was met by a poet who delivered farewell verses. 'For how can summer stay, when the sun departs?' was his constant refrain.[49]

For their sheer extravagance and variety, the Elvetham pageants surpassed any other entertainments on Elizabeth's summer progresses, apart from the awesome spectacles Leicester had laid on for her at Kenilworth. On that famous occasion, an entire village had to be demolished to make way for the construction of a vast artificial lake, and dozens of workmen toiled for weeks, applying a special gum to the needle-like leaves of thousands of rosemary plants so they could be individually coated with gold leaf to glint in the torch-light.[50]

Hertford's hospitality and building works, whose combined costs exceeded £6,000 (£6 million today), were a triumph. And yet he gained nothing for his trouble. At their parting, the queen had assured him that 'his entertainment was so honourable, as hereafter he should find the reward thereof in her special favour.'[51] If her intention had been to make him and his wife feel inconsequential, he had overcome the challenge in style. But neither honours nor rewards ensued. On the contrary, to Burghley's dismay, she would put Hertford back in the Tower within four years on suspicion of reviving his family's claim to the throne, leaving his wife Frances – 'very meanly attired' and said to have gone 'stark mad' – begging Elizabeth for mercy at the outer door of the privy lodgings at Whitehall Palace but refused an audience.[52] This time, her brother and her sister-in-law could not help her; only later did Elizabeth write Frances a letter reassuring her that she did not regard her husband's offence as 'more pernicious [and] malicious than as an act of lewd and proud contempt against our own direct prohibition'. She addressed Frances in familiar terms as 'Good Francke', but how comforting that was to a distraught wife she left entirely to the imagination.[53]

This was indeed a visible queen, but a visible queen with bite; an ageing one maybe, but one keen to show that she was still very much in control. And no one, from long-serving councillors to lesser courtiers, would ever be allowed to forget it.

9.   The Enemy Within

On Monday, 6 July 1590, after returning to Greenwich in her coach from a three-day stay at Lord Chancellor Hatton's London house at Ely Place, Elizabeth, decidedly jittery about the issue she was about to broach, wrote a letter in her very best handwriting to James VI in Edinburgh:

> Let me warn you that there is risen, both in your realm and mine, a sect of perilous consequence, such as would have no kings but a presbytery and take our place while they enjoy our privilege with a shade [i.e. with the colour, with the pretence] of God's Word, which none is judged to follow right without by their censure they be so deemed. Yea, look we well unto them. When they have made in our people's hearts a doubt of our religion and that we err if they say so, what perilous issue this may make I rather think than mind to write.[1]

Elizabeth had been rattled by Hatton's report to her of the existence of a highly organized group of Protestant sectaries who called themselves presbyterians. They had not merely dared to criticize her Religious Settlement, they had set out to replace it with a more radically Calvinist alternative. In her opinion, these so-called divines, all second-generation Calvinists, many of them trained or inspired by Theodore Beza, Calvin's successor at the academy in Geneva, were heretic schismatics who threatened the values of God-appointed monarchy. Just as much as Philip II and the pope, they sought to turn loyal subjects into traitors.

The presbyterians' chief distinguishing tenet was their belief that the church should be governed on a quasi-democratic basis by pastors, doctors, elders and deacons elected by their congregations, and that all ministers of the Gospel were of equal status. For them, no place existed in the church hierarchy for the queen as the 'Supreme Governor of the Church', as the 1559 Settlement had established, or even for archbishops and bishops. Such opinions, Elizabeth claimed, would turn the church into a social leveller, subverting her authority.

She had long privately held that the Religious Settlement, pushed through Parliament by Burghley and his allies in 1559 against vocal opposition and passing by only three votes in the House of Lords, had gone further towards Protestant doctrine than she would ideally have preferred, but she was young then and had only recently been crowned. She had accepted Burghley's Settlement, even if she had set about diluting it somewhat by stealth. When, for instance, Archbishop Parker ordered 'idolatries' such as images, paintings and candlesticks to be stripped out of the parish churches 'to the intent that all superstition and hypocrisy . . . may vanish', she had ostentatiously reinstated the crucifix and candlesticks in her own chapel. That shocked the Calvinists, but there was more to come. Elizabeth was notably sceptical of the value of regular sermons, even though preaching the Word of God lay at the very heart of the Protestant view of salvation.[2] In spite of such concerns, though, she was fully determined to unite her people around the Settlement, believing this was in everyone's best interests. That meant enforcing conformity and obedience to her own Church of England, the church initially purged and reformed by her father Henry VIII after he married her mother and broke with Rome.

Hatton had first broached the issue of the presbyterian threat more than a decade before the queen's letter to James. Shortly before he was promoted to the Privy Council in 1577, he had cautioned her that Parker's successor as archbishop of Canterbury, Edmund Grindal, whom she had appointed on Burghley's advice, was a covert fifth columnist, colluding with the presbyterians and encouraging their so-called 'prophesyings'. These were regular (often monthly) Scripture-study meetings, open to the laity as well as to clerics, to the poor as well as to the elite, at which abuses, ignorance and corruption in the official church were attacked and debated.[3]

Whereas Grindal had sought to use the prophesyings as a Trojan horse to stimulate a wider public appreciation of the role of a godly pastoral ministry in the church and a better understanding of cutting-edge Calvinist theology, Elizabeth condemned such exercises as illicit and dangerously revolutionary. Frequented by those she denounced as 'puritans' (she was one of the very first to coin this term of abuse), the prophesyings were, she believed, simply opportunities for malcontents, behaving as self-appointed local commissariats, to criticize her and the church she loved. This they had no business to do.

Twice she had summoned Grindal to an audience, ordering him to suppress the illegal gatherings: for 'down she would have them'.[4] When he refused, she threw him out of the Privy Chamber, straining relations between them to breaking point. He even, notoriously, dared to send her a 5,400-word letter informing her that, although she wore princely robes and there was 'no earthly creature to whom I am so much bounden', she was a mere woman who should leave matters of religion to those who knew about such things. Among his choicest observations was 'Remember, Madam, that you are a mortal creature.'[5]

No one could speak to Elizabeth like that and expect to get away with it. For five months, there had been a deafening silence, during which, behind the scenes, she battled it out with Burghley and Leicester, who closed ranks in a valiant attempt to save the unlucky archbishop's career. In 1577, she finally got her way and Grindal was disgraced and suspended. She then suppressed the prophesyings herself.[6]

When Grindal died, in 1583, Elizabeth ignored Burghley and promoted John Whitgift, bishop of Worcester, to be her new primate in the church. Three years later, she fast-tracked him to membership of the Privy Council. Significantly, Whitgift had secured the nomination while Leicester was absent in the Netherlands. His chief qualifications were his attacks on the presbyterians, whom he castigated in print and in the pulpit as anarchists and republicans.[7]

After the defeat of the Armada, Whitgift and Hatton became close allies. At Court, Leicester had been the highest-placed protector of the puritans. His death opened the way to a campaign, odious to Burghley and Walsingham, both long-standing puritan sympathizers, aimed at enforcing strict conformity to the 1559 Settlement upon clergy who were either outright Calvinists or Calvinist supporters.[8] In London, the attack was led by Bishop John Aylmer, once Jane Grey's tutor, but who had now changed sides and was Whitgift's

henchman and a cheerleader for the anti-puritans.[9] Ably assisted by
the most zealous of his apparatchiks, the inquisitor Richard Bancroft,
Aylmer clamped down on, and put on trial, anyone who failed to
satisfy Whitgift's new and more stringently devised criteria for religious orthodoxy. This was despite Burghley's impassioned plea that
the articles and questions used by Bancroft in his interrogations were
'so full of branches and circumstances, as I think the Inquisitors of
Spain use not so many questions to comprehend and to trap their
prey'. Unfortunately for Burghley, Elizabeth backed Whitgift and
Aylmer to the hilt.[10]

Several of Whitgift's intended victims fled to Scotland, where they
were embraced by the Kirk and tolerated by James in revenge for a
personal attack on him by Bancroft.[11] In her letter to James written
after her stay with Hatton at Ely Place, Elizabeth urged the Scottish
king to send them back at once:

> I pray you, stop the mouths or make shorter the tongues of such
> ministers as dare presume to make orisons [prayers] in their pulpits
> for the persecuted in England for the Gospel. Suppose you, my dear
> brother, that I can tolerate such scandals of my sincere government?
> No. I hope, howsoever, you be pleased to bear with their audacity
> towards yourself, yet you will not suffer a strange [i.e. foreign,
> meaning Elizabeth herself] king receive that indignity at such cater-
> pillars' hand, that instead of fruit, I am afraid will stuff your realm
> with venom.

Her letter ended with an appeal to James 'not to give more harbour
room to vagabond traitors and seditious inventors, but return them
to me or banish them [from] your land'.[12]

Elizabeth believed her hard-line approach to be justified by the
sensational clandestine distribution over the past two years of seven
scurrilous tracts ridiculing Whitgift and Aylmer. Printed on a portable press that was constantly on the move and written by a relay of
up to three, or perhaps as many as four, separate authors under the
pseudonym of Martin Marprelate, these lampoons were supremely
witty and irreverent, packed at every turn with mockery, parody
and merciless satire at the expense of the bishops. Imitating the idioms of the stage and the vocabulary of the gutter, the Marprelate

tracts scandalized the queen and the elite, and (it should be said) most of the puritans, too. Who exactly wrote them will never be known for certain: two country squires with seats in Parliament, Job Throckmorton and George Carleton, are among the names most regularly proposed. The tracts were liberally spattered with references to stews, brothels, strumpets, 'trulls' (concubines) and 'whorehunters', and among an inventive range of punning word-play was 'bumfeg', used as a verb to mean 'flog', 'Catekissing' for 'catechizing' and the graphically lewd 'fykckers' for 'vicars'.[13]

One of the later tracts, usually known as 'Martin Junior', included a eulogy to the most eloquent presbyterian of all, Thomas Cartwright. No other puritan would be mentioned so often, or with such obvious approval.[14] Once a Cambridge professor of divinity, he had given a celebrated course of lectures in 1570 on church discipline as it was set forth in the Acts of the Apostles, only to be dismissed from his post when Whitgift was the university's Vice-Chancellor. Now out of a job, Cartwright had taught alongside Theodore Beza in Geneva, gaining first-hand experience of presbyterianism. Later, he ministered to the merchant congregation of the English church in Antwerp, where Calvinism had taught itself to be astonishingly resilient in the face of persecution. On his return to England in 1585, he had the bewildering experience of being arrested by Aylmer and released shortly afterwards by an indulgent Burghley. Early the following year, Leicester found him what seemed to be a safe haven as master of his hospital in Warwick.[15]

Once back in England, Cartwright made his name as a puritan controversialist. He repeatedly confronted Whitgift in print, arguing that the government of the church should be purely autonomous, without interference from the civil magistrate or Parliament, and that episcopacy was not an institution of apostolic foundation. By denying that the queen could be the 'Supreme Governor of the Church', and by demanding that religion be removed from her supervision entirely, he infuriated Elizabeth. Daringly, he questioned in print whether monarchy was God-given, claiming instead that Parliament and the people granted rulers their authority, and it was thus to Parliament that the queen was properly accountable. He even insisted that, as a woman ruler, Elizabeth was not, as she always believed herself to be, an absolute sovereign, but shared her authority with her privy councillors and Parliaments.[16]

In early September 1589, directly after a lengthy audience with Elizabeth, Hatton had set out to arrest and prosecute Cartwright, along with eight other puritan leaders. His aim was to convict them, first, of charges of religious heterodoxy before a tribunal of ecclesiastical commissioners headed by Whitgift, and then of sedition in the Court of Star Chamber.[17] These were to be exemplary trials, modelled on Henry VIII's show trials at the time of his break with Rome: the aim was to crush radical Protestant dissent root and branch. As Hatton justified the move to Parliament, the puritans were 'of a very intemperate humour': their disaffection annoyed the queen even more than that of the Catholics. They lacked 'all grounds of authority' but 'they affect an unspeakable tyranny.' In short, they were felons and traitors in all but name.[18]

Elizabeth was counting on Hatton to prove that Cartwright and his friends had been involved in what she denounced as a 'conventicle', or seditious conspiracy, so that they could be imprisoned, perhaps even hanged. But the proceedings before the ecclesiastical commissioners dragged on for more than a year. Whitgift, who had scoured the highways and byways of Surrey and Kent with Lord Cobham, a noted anti-puritan, searching for 'Martin Marprelate', failed abysmally to deliver the necessary knockout blow. As a result, it was not until the week beginning Monday, 10 May 1591 that the prisoners were finally before the Star Chamber, where Hatton presided over a hand-picked panel of privy councillors and justices.

Hatton chose the date to begin the Star Chamber hearings with a certain dark finesse: he timed it to be the very same week in which Burghley, still one of Cartwright's secret admirers for his views on the sovereignty of Parliament, would be otherwise engaged, entertaining the queen at Theobalds. He did this knowing that if a judge missed the first ten days of a trial, as Burghley inevitably would while the queen was his guest, he was disqualified from sitting in the case later on.[19]

When asked by the Queen's Attorney, Sir John Popham, whether Elizabeth could be the Supreme Governor of the Church, as Parliament had enacted in 1559, Cartwright's brilliant lawyers stonewalled the court. Thereafter, Cartwright and his co-accused repeated time and time again their mantra that they 'were not bound to answer'. The most they would do was to 'acknowledge Her Majesty's supreme authority according as in Her Highness's Injunctions and laws in that behalf is expressed'.[20] These were weasel words: although from the opposite side of the religious divide, they conceded little more than Thomas More had famously done when Henry VIII had put him on trial for treason in 1535. More had told his judges then that Henry might have broken with the pope and declared the monarch to be the Supreme Head of the Church, but whether either step was valid in law or theology was a matter for the whole of Christendom to resolve.[21]

Next, Cartwright was questioned as to whether the form of government established by the Settlement was in conformity with the Word of God and whether the sacraments were rightly and justly administered. He refused to answer. Finally, he was asked whether the rites and ceremonies laid down in the Book of Common Prayer were 'such as no person ought therefore to make any schism, division or contention, or withdraw himself from the church'. Seeing the trap, he at once replied that no one should 'make any schism or withdraw himself'. On the other hand, whether the Elizabethan church's form of government, or its rites and ceremonies were lawful 'as they are used', he did not consider himself bound to answer, since the question 'is a matter of judgement, not of fact'.[22]

With the examinations and cross-examinations of the defendants and witnesses taking so much longer than he had envisaged, Hatton could brief Elizabeth only rarely during the summer and early autumn of 1591. The need to pin specific criminal offences on the puritan leaders was considered to be of sufficient importance to keep the Star Chamber in special session during the normal summer break. Hatton managed a flying visit to Cowdray to confer with the queen in mid-August, but he was unable to join her at Portsmouth or Elvetham, instead sending a jewel in the shape of a bagpipe, 'which she weareth on her ruff and with [which] doth she make much sport, remembering your Lordship by the name of her "Mutton".'[23] He kept in touch with the main body of the Privy Council, which travelled with the queen on her progress, by letter, using Robert Cecil as his intermediary.[24]

In the end, Elizabeth would be cheated of a victory and denied the proof she had demanded of a great puritan conspiracy. The case against Cartwright and his co-accused began to collapse in October, when Hatton, the driving force behind the prosecution, was no longer able to control the diabetes from which he had suffered for a number of years. He died at Ely Place on 20 November, from what Camden in his *Annales*, probably accurately, called 'a flux of his urine'.[25] A few days before, Elizabeth had visited him and gently fed him broth. He was just fifty-one.

On 11 December, Popham sent Burghley a confidential memo on the status of the case in response to a motion from the prisoners' lawyers asking for bail. Popham was still confident of a conviction, believing he had witness testimony proving that Cartwright and his friends had plotted to 'win the people' over to their cause. In Elizabeth's eyes, such rabble-rousing constituted sedition pure and simple.[26]

But the Queen's Attorney was too bullish. Around New Year 1592, the Star Chamber judges halted the prosecutions. On 9 January, the queen's kinsman Sir Francis Knollys, a privy councillor whose puritan sympathies were even stronger than Burghley's and who had attended every session of the trial with growing repugnance, explained that the decision had been taken for lack of evidence. Otherwise, 'Cartwright and his fellows had been hanged before this time.'[27] Now turning eighty and plagued by failing eyesight, Knollys had a thick skin – his ancestral badge was an elephant – so he cared little if his opinions reached the ears of the queen.[28]

Later, Knollys wrote again to Burghley, filling in the blanks. Shortly before Hatton had died, he explained, the Chief Justice of England, Sir Christopher Wray, himself no friend of puritans but a man who believed in fair play, had rounded on the ailing Lord Chancellor in the Star Chamber. He had urged Hatton to drop the case until he 'should have matter to prove some seditious act *de facto* to be committed'. Wray convinced his fellow judges that Hatton had no grounds in law for a guilty verdict.[29] What most irked Knollys, however, was that, although Cartwright was never convicted of anything, he and his fellow puritans were left to rot in prison on grounds of suspicion alone.

Elizabeth's dilemma was that she wanted to be both a Protestant defender of the faith and an upholder of the ideals of God-appointed monarchy at the same time. Cartwright's case proved this was impossible. Seeing that her Protestant credentials would be at risk if the outside world came to think she had victimized men of Cartwright's distinction for reasons of sheer prejudice, she washed her hands of the affair. It is striking that when Knollys politely asked to discuss these issues with her in confidence, she slammed the door in his face.[30]

With some difficulty, Burghley engineered the release on bail of the Star Chamber prisoners. But if this was a significant defeat for the queen, she prevailed elsewhere. When Chief Justice Wray died a few days before Cartwright's discharge, she promoted Popham to the vacancy, choosing a rising star in the legal profession, Sir Thomas Egerton, another anti-puritan, to replace him as Queen's Attorney. And in the spring of 1593, Whitgift secured her firm backing in Parliament for a savage law against the puritans.[31] The new law would ensure that, for the rest of Elizabeth's reign, Protestants who boycotted services in their parish churches on grounds of conscience, attended unlicensed gatherings 'under colour or pretence of any exercise of religion' or questioned the queen's authority would first suffer imprisonment, then banishment abroad. Dissident Protestants were now to be lumped alongside Catholics as the enemy within. To escape these sanctions, Cartwright fled to Guernsey, with Burghley's covert assistance, putting himself beyond Whitgift's reach.

It would take a 'madman' (or so Burghley privately described him) to salvage Elizabeth's reputation as a Protestant defender of the faith. At the climax of Cartwright's trial in the Star Chamber, an illiterate Northamptonshire maltster, one William Hacket, otherwise said to be a lunatic, proclaimed himself to be Jesus Christ and announced that the end of the world was nigh. A convert to puritanism, Hacket had come to believe he was a reincarnation of the Old Testament prophet Daniel after wrestling with the fiercest of the lions in the queen's menagerie at the Tower of London without being mauled. A week or so later, he declared himself to be the 'king of Europe'. It was, he declared, his intention, with two accomplices, to free Cart-wright from prison, kill Whitgift and overthrow the queen.

Swiftly arrested by the royal pursuivants in his lodgings, Hacket was tried and convicted of treason. Dragged on a hurdle drawn by horses to a gallows in Cheapside, near St Paul's, he continued to pro-test that he was the new Messiah, then 'fell to railing and cursing of the Queen's Majesty most villainously'.

For the horrified Londoners watching the scene, it was enough. From now on, dissident puritans, whoever they were and wherever they came from, were to be tarred with the brush of blasphemy and insurrection.[32]

With the draconian new law against puritans on the statute book, Elizabeth made it clear to her privy councillors that she was deter-mined to be seen to be acting even-handedly. Whitgift's attack on 'seditious sectaries' was thus to be accompanied by an equal, if not greater, assault on dissident Catholics.[33] This approach had most likely informed her decision to visit Cowdray, when she had arrived just in time to frustrate Viscount Montague's weekly Mass and where her privy councillors had drafted harsh new anti-Catholic proclamations.

Her most effective and notorious Catholic-hunter was her chief pursuivant, Richard Topcliffe. A vicious, desperately insecure man with pronounced psychopathic tendencies, Topcliffe doubled as her rack-master. Several times accused by his victims of ransacking their houses without due cause or of torturing them without the necessary warrants, he was a menacing and divisive figure who almost everyone knew about but preferred to forget. The earliest known document describing him as 'Her Majesty's servant' dates from 1573, and there has been much debate as to how much, or how little, Elizabeth coun-tenanced his activities.[34] Almost universally, her biographers, following Camden's *Annales*, have distanced her from him. In reality, strong archival evidence exists that she knew him personally, thor-oughly approved of his activities and received reports directly from him rather than through intermediaries.

Unscrupulous, self-seeking and venal, a sharp dresser who boasted of his 'watchful eyes' and took delight in his luridly serpentine handwriting, Topcliffe was a Nottinghamshire man. Orphaned at the age of twelve, he was brought up by an uncle and trained as a lawyer. He does not appear to have ever been called to the bar but, in or about the year 1557, when he was approaching twenty-five, he married (unhappily) Jane, the daughter of Sir Edward Willoughby of Wollaton, whose niece Margaret was one of Elizabeth's attendants during Mary Tudor's reign.[35]

First employed by Leicester during the reprisals following the Northern Rising to carry messages to the queen, Topcliffe was also on cordial terms with the Earl of Shrewsbury, Mary Queen of Scots's custodian, to whom he began writing chatty newsletters from London and the Court. In 1578, he told Shrewsbury how, during one of her summer progresses at which he was present, Elizabeth had drawn his attention to 'sundry lewd popish beasts' who were known to be frequenting the spa at Buxton. In reply, Topcliffe had informed her of 'one Dyrham, or Durande', a man he claimed was 'a detestable popish priest' and a sexual predator 'lurking in those parts', and offered to trap him.[36]

Shortly after the arrival of a Jesuit mission to England in 1580, Topcliffe's career came into its own. He began volunteering information to Burghley and Walsingham about the seditious activities of Jesuits and seminary priests. He scoured London's prisons, looking for men he could employ as spies and informers, and secured warrants from the Privy Council to torture suspects, sometimes for hours on end, in a 'strong room' in his house near the churchyard of St Margaret's Church in Westminster.[37] When the Throckmorton Plot was discovered in 1583, Elizabeth sent him on a special mission to 'the North parts' to round up political Catholics on a hit list she had prepared.[38] And in September 1586, there was more direct contact between them, when she called him in to see her and asked him to supervise the delivery of a herd of bucks she was sending as a gift to the hunting-mad James VI.[39]

Topcliffe's victims, many of them innocent, told gruesome stories about him. One of the most bizarre came in November 1591, submitted as a written complaint to William Waad, clerk of the Privy Council, by the seminary priest Thomas Pormort. Among his more spine-chilling claims, Pormort alleged that, while racking him, Topcliffe had indulged in salacious sexual fantasies. According to what still survives of Pormort's damaged manuscript, Topcliffe claimed to be 'familiar' with the queen: he had, he said, many times fondled her nipples and breasts and put his hands up her skirt. He had 'felt her belly' (vagina) and told her that she had 'the softest belly of any womankind'. She had (allegedly) said to him, 'Be not these the arms, legs and body of King Henry', to which Topcliffe answered, 'Yea.' Afterwards, the queen supposedly gave him one of her white stockings, 'wrought with silk', as a love token.[40]

Submitted in confidence solely to impeach Topcliffe and so as not to slander the queen, Pormort's claims about his tormentor's sexual fantasies are likely to have been substantially true. For, on a freezing-cold morning in February 1592, when Pormort was about to mount the gallows in St Paul's Churchyard, Topcliffe suddenly halted the proceedings and forced his accuser to 'stand in his shirt almost two hours upon the ladder' while he demanded that he retract these damning claims, which Pormort refused to do.

Waad, however, took no further action. Rabidly anti-Catholic himself, he was destined to be Topcliffe's ally rather than his scourge. Beyond that, he feared what might happen if the queen were to become involved. Even those at the centre of power were unsure as to where exactly she stood on the question of Richard Topcliffe. Who knew what she might do to anyone who dared to call him to account?[41]

The smoking gun proving Elizabeth's acquiescence in some of Top-cliffe's worst atrocities lies buried in Burghley's papers. When, in October 1591, the anti-Catholic proclamations drafted at Cowdray were published, Robert Southwell, a thirty-year-old English Jesuit schooled in Douai (then in the Netherlands) and trained as a priest in Rome, composed a rebuttal. This was entitled 'An Humble Supplica-tion to Her Majesty'. Too explosive to publish, Southwell's tract was passed in manuscript from hand to hand like samizdat literature: it would be printed surreptitiously in 1600, bearing a false date of 1595.[42] The work was incendiary, because it made the most lucidly persuasive case yet for the legitimacy of a loyalist, non-political form of Catholicism. While Burghley had maintained since 1559 – long before the papal decree of 1570 excommunicating Elizabeth and declaring her to be deposed – that Catholics were, by definition, traitors, Southwell argued that the queen's subjects were bound in conscience 'under pain of forfeiting their right in Heaven . . . to obey the just laws of their princes'.[43] It was not Catholics, but Calvinists, he argued, who believed that monarchs could be excluded or deposed on religious grounds. Here he aimed a cutting blow at Burghley.

Topcliffe longed to lay his hands on Southwell and bring him to the gallows. But the young Jesuit had a powerful protector. He had found a secure refuge in a house in Spitalfields, a suburb of London just outside the walls to the east of Bishopsgate Street, belonging to Anne Howard, Countess of Arundel, a Catholic convert. So long as he stayed in her lodgings he would be safe. But he made the mistake of venturing outdoors. On the feast of St John the Baptist (24 June), 1592, at ten in the morning, he met a young Catholic gentleman, Thomas Bellamy, in Fleet Street and set out for Bellamy's father's house, Uxenden Hall, near Harrow in Middlesex, some fifteen miles away. He celebrated Mass there before lodging for the night.

Shortly after midnight, Topcliffe, accompanied by a gang of armed men, smashed his way in. He knew Southwell would be there: his informer was none other than Thomas Bellamy's twenty-nine-year-old sister, Anne. Six months before, she had been denounced for her devout Catholic beliefs to Bishop Aylmer and imprisoned in the Gatehouse Prison at Westminster. There, Topcliffe raped her and made her pregnant. In a subterfuge worthy of Iago in Shakespeare's *Othello*, Topcliffe then offered to secure her release and 'protect' her and her baby by marrying her off to one of his assistants, Nicholas Jones. To bait the trap, Topcliffe promised Anne that, if she became his informant, her family would not be harmed, a promise he conspicuously failed to keep.[44]

As soon as Southwell had been apprehended, an elated Topcliffe wrote to inform Elizabeth of his prize. His letter, later filed among Burghley's papers, was explicit. As Topcliffe confided, his quarry was securely held in his 'strong chamber', shackled to the wall. It gave him great pleasure, he continued, to enclose Southwell's first testimony under interrogation. She would plainly see he had answered 'foully and suspiciously'. To take his investigations further, Topcliffe requested the queen's authorization to 'enforce' the prisoner 'to answer truly and directly'. 'May it please Your Majesty', he asked, 'to see my simple opinion?' He felt himself 'constrained in duty to utter it'.

Topcliffe advised Elizabeth that torture should begin at once:

> To use any means in common prisons either to stand upon or against the wall (wherein above all things exceeds and hurteth not) will give warning. But if Your Highness's pleasure be to know anything in his heart, [then] to stand against the wall, his feet standing upon the ground and his hands but as high as he can reach against the wall like a Trick at Trenchmore [a morris dance], will enforce him to tell all and the truth proved.

Specifically, Topcliffe recommended that Southwell be stretched out against the wall using 'hand gyves' (iron gauntlets). Speed was of the essence, or the prisoner's accomplices, 'such as be deeply concerned in his treacheries', might flee.[45]

Although the queen's reply was purely verbal, given at a private audience in the Privy Chamber and not written down, the fact that Topcliffe went on within a few days to torture Southwell in exactly the manner he had recommended, and without a further warrant from Burghley or his colleagues, as the law required, is the chilling proof that she gave her consent in the full knowledge of what he was about to do. Topcliffe would not have dared to act as he did had the queen forbidden it, and she was far from squeamish. At the time of the Ridolfi Plot, she had ordered two of Burghley's men, this time in writing, to torture suspected conspirators on the rack 'until they shall deal more plainly, or until you shall think meet [appropriate]'.[46]

Here, some highly curious facts may be illuminating. Southwell's mother, Bridget, née Copley, was one of the queen's kinsfolk. She and Anne Boleyn's father were second cousins, and she was said in 1583 to have been Elizabeth's 'old servant of near forty years continuance', although in what capacity is uncertain.[47] In Mary Tudor's reign, Bridget's brother, Thomas, an ardent Protestant, had bravely championed Elizabeth's claim to the throne in the House of Commons, for which he was arrested.[48] Then, a few years later, when Elizabeth was queen, he had married a Catholic heiress and converted to Rome. By the time Robert Southwell was in Topcliffe's hands, his uncle Thomas was dead. But his treachery had not been forgotten, as he had lived on for many years in exile at Rouen, from where he had regularly attacked the queen in libels and in print.[49]

Could it be that, for Elizabeth, who all her life was so keenly attuned to family loyalties, Robert Southwell's case was personal? Could it be that she was dealing not just with a hated Jesuit but with one whose uncle she felt had personally betrayed her, hence her willingness to demand the harshest possible retribution?

Topcliffe's distinctive style of torture – as he had claimed in his letter to Elizabeth – was considerably more painful than the traditional rack. Using iron gauntlets to stretch out his victims against the wall like elastic for hours on end, he would leave them there until they seemed to be on the point of death. He then took them down and revived them, only to hang them up again. So intense was the pressure that, in almost every instance, a vein or artery would burst, causing a sudden discharge of blood. At his trial, Southwell would claim that Topcliffe had tormented him like this as many as ten times: so excruciating was it, he said, that ten separate executions would have been preferable.[50]

Transferred for a month to the Gatehouse, Southwell was deliberately housed in a pauper's cell, in conditions so disgusting that his whole body was soon stinking and crawling with lice. After his friends protested loudly to the queen, he was escorted by his guards to one of the gloomiest cells in the Tower, where he was kept in solitary confinement for two and a half years.[51] At last, on Thursday, 20 February 1595, he was led by soldiers into the Court of Queen's Bench in Westminster Hall, to be tried before Chief Justice Popham, his wrists lashed together tightly with a cord.

Charged with treason under an Act passed by Parliament in 1585 that had declared all Jesuits and seminary priests to be traitors, Southwell was asked to plead guilty or not guilty. 'I am a Catholic priest', he replied, 'and I thank God for it, but no traitor; neither can any law make it treason to be a priest.' This was a formula Popham refused to accept. Only when the prisoner withdrew the subversive imputation that the law enacted by Parliament was invalid and pleaded simply, 'Not guilty of treason', could the case begin.[52]

The jury would take less than a quarter of an hour to find South-well guilty. The next day, he was dragged to the gallows at Tyburn in the fields to the west of the city, where common criminals were hanged. There, Elizabeth's macabre instructions to the hangman were that, as in 1585, in the failed assassin Dr William Parry's case, the prisoner should be cut down from the gallows the moment the ladder was kicked away, after just one swing of the rope. Long before he had stopped breathing, Southwell was to be forced to endure the torment of being disembowelled while still fully conscious, the hangman hacking the flesh and bone back beyond the ribs so that the dying man could see his heart and bowels burning in the fire even as he finally expired.

In this, the queen was simply following her father's method of dealing with inconvenient monks and priors. Except that, this time, things went awry. Allowed to speak a few words from the scaffold before he mounted the ladder, Southwell silenced his audience – who clearly expected something very different from a Jesuit – by praying for the queen and her councillors, just as Thomas More had done in her father's reign. 'May she enjoy all gifts of nature and grace' was Southwell's imprecation: 'all helps of friends and faithful councillors, whereby she may reign to God's glory and after this life be [an] inheritor of the kingdom of heaven.'

On hearing this, the crowd cried out with one voice, demanding that Southwell should not be cut down from the gallows and disembowelled until he was actually dead. And the hangman obliged. It was a rare moment of human compassion in a brutal world of bloodshed and religious violence.[53]

Camden airbrushed almost all of these events from his *Annales*. It was one thing to attack the frantic delusions of William Hacket, to whom he devoted several inflammatory pages, but to mention Cartwright or Southwell – and, most of all, Richard Topcliffe – was clearly quite another. Never, at least so far, had the Kafkaesque elements of Elizabeth's forgotten years been more glaringly on public display.

10.   Catastrophe in France

On Monday, 2 August 1591, while the case against Cartwright was still very much alive, the twenty-five-year-old Earl of Essex landed at Dieppe, ready to assume his command in Normandy. Splendidly clad in jewel-encrusted apparel and preceded by a dozen pages in gold-embroidered, orange velvet coats, he greeted his army of 3,400 men near the quayside. His mission, he confidently predicted, would provide him with the breakthrough he needed to succeed his step-father, Leicester, as the country's chief war leader.[1]

The reality would be crushingly different. Despite the bond that drew Essex and Elizabeth together, his career was not her priority. Her orders were clear and concise, her objectives limited. Working alongside Henry IV, he was to recapture Rouen from the Catholic League. He was then to make the town a regional base from which Henry's forces could guarantee the security of the Channel ports of Normandy, so that they could not be used in a future invasion of England. Afterwards, there was to be a brief, decisive assault to drive the Spaniards out of the Blavet valley in Brittany and send them back to Spain. That was all.

But by presuming that Henry shared her aims, Elizabeth miscalculated. Never really sold on the idea of besieging Rouen, the French king had set his sights on defeating the Duke of Parma's army in a pitched battle, and on recovering Paris. She had misread his character. Unlike Philip II, who could juggle many balls and keep them high in the air, as Elizabeth was being forced to do herself, Henry liked to focus on one thing at once and perform it to 'all his powers'. Compromise was not yet in his vocabulary. At thirty-eight, short of stature but immensely strong, with ruddy cheeks and a high fore-head, he was energetic and courageous, accessible and familiar, long on promises but short on delivery. Lengthy speeches and protracted Council meetings he could not abide: a man of action like Essex himself, he tended to strike first and think afterwards.[2]

His current preoccupation was to capture Noyon, on the border of Picardy, which he told Elizabeth was necessary to protect the main route from Brussels to Paris and to prevent strategic towns such as Saint-Quentin falling into Spanish clutches, should Parma choose to invade again.[3] Forbidden by their orders from joining the siege, Essex's forces were left twiddling their thumbs. The Earl therefore marched his men to Arques, four miles inland from Dieppe, to set up camp, where he conferred with Sir Henry Unton, who reminded him that his commission would expire in two months' time and that Elizabeth would not pay her soldiers for a day longer.[4]

Two weeks later, Noyon surrendered, and Sir Roger Williams, whom Elizabeth had put in charge of the six hundred troops sent from Brittany, rode in with letters from Henry inviting Essex to a man-to-man rendezvous at Compiègne, fifty miles north-east of Paris.[5] Taking just two hundred cavalry, Essex defied the queen's instructions by embarking on a perilous ride, travelling incognito through enemy lines for three long, scorchingly hot days, with both horses and men plagued by flies.

After four highly pleasurable days of feasting, entertainment, music and dancing, Essex left Compiègne 'much troubled' for his mission. To obey Elizabeth's instructions would not be so easy. Henry's enthusiasm for the siege of Rouen was lukewarm. Instead, the French king had decided to march into Champagne, where, as he claimed, his German *Reiter* would mutiny, unless they were paid.[6] The most he could do to help Essex, he said, was 'shortly' to detach from his main army twelve thousand men, under Marshal Biron, his most trusted and experienced general, and send them into Normandy. If Essex and Biron were to strike camp ready to besiege Rouen, he would join them as soon as he could.[7]

Essex feared Elizabeth's likely reaction, but felt he had to give way. As he informed Burghley, he was guided by reasons 'which though I dare neither censure nor allow, yet I assure your Lordships I cannot impugn'. On the other hand, Henry and Essex had struck up an obvious rapport at Noyon. They had talked animatedly late into the night of how they might defeat the Leaguers in a series of joint operations, and competed in a leaping contest, which Essex won.[8]

★ ★ ★

Elizabeth scolded Henry for his inaction on 18 August in her own handwriting and in fluent French:

> Do you really think, *mon frère*, that these are the ways to treat a prince who allows her subjects to risk their lives to defend your kingdom? Do those who hazard their lives to defend you deserve to be made prey to the enemy? If the Channel ports are lost, how will you protect the rest of your territory? From where will all the aid come when these areas will be hemmed in so that reinforcements cannot be sent to you? I am astounded at these reveries.[9]

A fortnight later, after hearing about what she described as Essex's 'dangerous and fruitless' ride to Compiègne, she flew into a fury again. So enraged was she that Henry and her Lieutenant had wasted precious time on feasting and on leaping contests, she said – as Robert Cecil reported – she wished Essex dead 'so that her troops may not miscarry'.[10]

Matters did not improve when the Leaguers set an ambush for Essex on his return journey from Compiègne. Thanks to the sharp eyes of his scouts, he circumvented the danger and was able to get word to his forces to meet him at Pavilly, some fifteen miles northwest of Rouen.[11] Now within striking distance of his main target, Essex was unable to begin a siege before Biron brought reinforcements. And since idly waiting was never his way, he rashly attacked Pavilly. But in a desperate fight lasting several hours, he lost his brother Walter, who was hit in the face by a musket-ball. Essex was grief-stricken, describing Walter as 'the half arch of my house'. Much worse, the following afternoon, a cooking fire in a house adjoining the English munitions dump at Pavilly caused an explosion that destroyed the entire village. Some soldiers were killed; the rest ran for their lives. Unable to handle these setbacks psychologically, Essex collapsed for several days, which required deft footwork from Unton, who had to keep the queen unawares until he recovered. This was despite Unton's own sickness from leptospirosis, also known as black jaundice, and caused by animal urine polluting the water supply at Dieppe.[12]

Reluctantly ordering a retreat to his earlier camp at Arques, Essex sought to salvage his reputation by besieging Gournay-en-Bray.

Biron, whose troops had finally arrived in Normandy, joined in a siege lasting ten days. Lying on marshy ground between rolling hills some thirty miles to the east of Rouen, Gournay was the final staging post on the main road from Picardy that Parma's forces had to take, should they attempt to relieve Rouen once it came under attack.

On 26 September, the town surrendered after an early-morning bombardment by Essex's artillery left two large breaches in the walls.[13] This success came not a moment too soon: a day or so earlier, Elizabeth had demanded his recall. In a vituperative rant dictated to Burghley, who did his utmost to tone it down in three different drafts, she castigated Essex for not doing more to induce Henry to keep his promises. All this, she said accusingly, had shown 'as much dishonour to us as could be to ourselves and our nation, whereof you have for yourself, if you be not blinded with the French qualities, no small part'.[14] Already, she was deeply suspicious, even jealous, of the growing friendship between Henry and Essex. Was it, she asked him, that her favourite would so much rather serve a king than a 'mere' queen?[15]

But her tirade had barely begun. She saw, she said, no reason why her forces should remain in France for a moment longer. Essex must return at once, handing over his command to Sir Thomas Leighton, a man she unreservedly trusted and whom she had already instructed to shadow him at all times. And she went on to humiliate Essex still further. He was himself to write to the perfidious French king to inform him of his recall. 'You may add', she witheringly concluded, that her troops had 'spent their time by reason of the said king's delays both unprofitably and to the dishonour of us and themselves, whereof you may write how sorry you are to have so great a part to your own disgrace.' In a postscript, she further sniped that Essex should by now plainly understand the reasons for her dissatisfaction with him, 'if you be not senseless'.[16]

As luck would have it, Essex had just sent Robert Carey, one of his junior officers, back to England to report on the victory at Gournay and plead for an extension to his commission. Carey left Dieppe on the 27th, missing the courier passing in the opposite direction with Essex's letters of recall by no more than twenty-four hours.

After four days, Carey, spattered with mud, rode into the courtyard at Oatlands shortly after dawn, long before the queen was up and dressed. Losing no time, he went first to sound out Burghley, who warned him that she was furious with Essex and had ordered his recall. Burghley cautioned Carey to 'look out for himself' as, by now, Elizabeth was regaling anyone who dared to suggest that Essex's commission should be extended with the spiteful accusation that, if her favourite was furtively lobbying behind her back to tarry longer in France, then clearly he 'had so small desire to see her' again that she would 'requite' him in kind by 'crossing him in his most earnest desire'.[17] Unton had sent his own message to the queen, backing Essex's request for an extension, and when Burghley tried to step in she railed at him, to the point where the gout-ridden Lord Treasurer snapped, saying, 'By God, Madam, I would have written as he did, and so done, except you meant to make him stand for a cipher.' To this, she retorted, 'Well, I will have him know his error and, if you do it not, I will.'[18]

Shortly after ten o'clock that morning, Carey was granted an audience with the queen. He reported in his *Memoirs* that Elizabeth 'burst out into a great rage against my Lord and vowed she would make him an example to the entire world, if he presently left not his charge and returned'. Her mood lightened, but only fractionally, when she read Essex's letter giving his account of the capture of Gournay. She seemed, said Carey, 'to be meanly well contented'.[19]

In a decidedly high-risk strategy, Carey informed her that Essex feared that accusations of cowardice would be levelled against him if he were to leave France before completing his mission. His sense of dishonour would then be such that he would have no alternative but to retire permanently from Court. 'I know', said Carey, 'his full resolution is to retire to some cell in the country.'

Elizabeth was unimpressed by this feeble attempt at emotional blackmail. With a sweep of the hand, she tetchily ordered Carey to leave her, only to send for him again in the afternoon.[20] By then, she had read Essex's letter more carefully and had consulted Burghley, who informed her that Biron, as Unton had now separately confirmed, was talking of attacking Rouen without further delay.[21] Henry, admittedly, was still making excuses. But despite her ally's studied invisibility, Elizabeth yielded, scribbling a letter to Essex in which she informed him that, on account of 'the winning of Gournay in so short a time, whereof we are very glad', and because, it seemed, the siege of Rouen was about to begin 'and like well to succeed', then, 'for these considerations', he could remain in France with his forces for one more month – provided that Henry himself shouldered the cost. Essex, however, was to understand that her decision was solely in the interests of the war effort. It was not to please him and 'not to pleasure the [French] King at all'. And the Earl was to take note that there were to be no more 'dangerous' or 'rash' manoeuvres. Humble him though she might, she did not want him to die.[22]

A drawn-out black comedy ensued. Carey raced back across the Channel to France with the queen's letters countermanding Essex's recall. He landed in Dieppe shortly before midnight on 8 October, just two hours after Essex, facing up to what he believed to be a juggernaut, caught the tide aboard 'a little skiff' bound for England, obeying Elizabeth's original instructions to return. Disembarking at Rye in Sussex, he at first lacked the courage to confront her directly, sending a servant to announce his return. Bawled out by the queen, the man returned to Essex, who wrote to her in apparent humility, 'I see Your Majesty is constant [determined] to ruin me; I do humbly and patiently yield to Your Majesty's will', before declaring, more theatrically, 'I appeal to all men that saw my parting from France, or the manner of my coming hither, whether I deserved such a welcome or not.'[23]

As with his stepfather after his recall from the Netherlands, Elizabeth was icy when Essex made his belated entrance to Richmond Palace, but was quickly reconciled to her wayward favourite. Several days of 'jollity and feasting' ensued, after which her Lieutenant confidently rejoined his army at Dieppe, only to find morale and supplies at rock bottom and disease rampaging through the companies. Malaria, first in evidence in the marshy ground around Gournay, coupled with dysentery and outbreaks of bubonic plague, had halved his forces.[24] But not all the news was bad: Biron was mopping up small towns in the vicinity of Rouen, and there was talk that Henry, still dallying in the vicinity of Sedan in the Ardennes, was finally preparing to march west. Of particular relief was the fact that he had sent five thousand crowns from the treasury at Caen (worth around £1.6 million today) to help pay and supply the English soldiers.[25] When the queen's allowance had run out, Essex had been forced to pay his men from his own pocket to the tune of £14,000, plunging him ever more deeply into debt.[26]

Hoping to repair his losses, Essex entreated Burghley to send more men and money.[27] A few days later, he sent Sir Roger Williams to Richmond to argue his case before the queen.[28] To Williams's astonishment, Elizabeth agreed to send a thousand soldiers from her auxiliaries in the Netherlands and another four hundred and fifty from England, whom she would pay for one month. Her confidence in Essex had been restored since his brief return to Court, and with Rouen in her sights she softened, no longer subjecting him to tirades of abuse.[29]

But the siege of Rouen proved to be slow and intractable. Situated on a gentle slope on the right bank of a sweeping curve in the fast-flowing Seine, the old administrative and judicial capital of Normandy was protected by thick ramparts, deep ditches and formidable towers. Accessible only through heavily fortified gates, it housed a population of around 75,000 in its many half-timbered buildings, as compared to London's 186,000.[30] Stoutly defended by the Leaguers since 1589, it was further protected by a recently restored fort at the top of the nearby Mont Sainte-Catherine. There, André Brancas, Sieur de Villars, the local Leaguer commander, had reinforced the garrison to some six thousand fighting men and stationed forty large cannon with a plentiful supply of shot.

Essex and Biron agreed to begin the siege before dawn on 29 October, when their forces would make a commando-type raid on the surrounding villages under cover of darkness. Biron was late, and his troops came under fire, but by the end of the day Essex's men were safely lodged on Mont aux Malades to the north-west of the city, close to a building, once a flourishing leper house, that was now the site of a popular fair held in September each year.[31] A fanciful scheme to build a floating artillery platform from which to pound the city's ramparts on their weakest, riverside section came to nothing, so Essex's men began to dig trenches near the foot of Mont aux Malades, overlooking the Cauchoise gate into the city.[32] From this vantage point they could fire their muskets at any of the Leaguers who dared to venture out.[33]

To Elizabeth's exasperation, however, there was still no sign of Henry. On 8 November, she dictated a chivvying letter to him in English, which she had translated by one of Burghley's clerks. The next day, she replaced it with a thundering, much shorter diatribe she wrote herself in French:

> From our enemies we were expecting nothing but bad faith, and now that our friends treat us in exactly the same way, what difference do we find? I am astounded that someone who is so much in need of our assistance should repay us, his most assured ally, in such base coin. Do you imagine that my sex deprives me of the courage to resent such a public affront?[34]

In fact, as she dictated her letter, Henry really was at last on his way to Rouen. When he arrived, Essex and Biron went out to kiss his hand at his camp midway between the city and Mont Sainte-Catherine. At a Council of War, a decision was taken to concentrate the attack upon the Sainte-Catherine fort. After the generals dispersed, Essex stayed on, while Henry dined, 'talking and discoursing of many matters', presumptuously wearing his cap while the king's advisers stood bareheaded. Riding back to Mont aux Malades, he narrowly escaped a hail of small artillery fire from the Leaguers. Two bullets whistled past his head, 'for I might sensibly feel the wind of the bullets in my face'.[35]

A week later, Essex went on a second, desperate visit to see Elizabeth. He found her this time at Whitehall Palace, where she had just watched the closing ceremony of that year's Accession Day tilts from a newly refurbished gallery.[36] There, he appealed to her for a further extension of his stay and for more money and reinforcements, as a freak spell of cold weather and fresh outbreaks of disease had hit him hard: his men were close to mutiny and deserting in droves.[37]

Burghley was more shocked by the suddenness of Essex's unauthorized return than by his requests.[38] What he could not know was that, to support his pleas, Essex lied, vastly exaggerating his success so far in the siege: it was only this that persuaded a grudging Elizabeth to consent to pay his troops for two more months. Led to believe that valuable plunder might be had by pillaging Rouen and by intercepting the heavy chests of money and valuables that the citizens were removing and sending for safety to their relatives elsewhere in France, she even ordered four royal navy pinnaces to blockade the Seine.[39]

Leaving Whitehall for Dover on 5 December, Essex was back in Normandy by the 14th.[40] With Burghley's support fast waning, however, it would only be a matter of days before the queen had second thoughts. By the 17th, Unton was in receipt of a letter in which Burghley warned him of 'Her Majesty's dislike of the King's letters and demands for further aid'. She was now convinced that her French ally was attempting to fleece her.[41]

The trigger for Essex's final recall was a report that many of his blue-blooded officers had succumbed to plague.[42] Two days before Christmas, Elizabeth wrote him a handwritten rebuke, recapitulating all her earlier criticisms and ordering him to repatriate as soon as possible any surviving 'gentlemen of good quality dear to their parents and blood' before they, too, were struck down. Cuttingly, she then suggested he return himself, 'if you shall at last be so well advised as to think how dishonourable it is for you to tarry with so mean a charge, after so many men consumed so little to the purpose they were sent for, with many other absurd defects which blemish the honour of the place you hold under us as our general'.[43]

On Christmas Eve, in hastily scribbled orders, she recalled her delinquent favourite without any further excuses or delays.[44] Her instructions were steely:

> We have thought good no longer to suffer you to continue there to so small purpose to the needless hazard of all such as are with you there in our service whom we sent as auxiliaries to aid a French king and not to be drawn to every dangerous desperate attempt which the king shall and hath moved you to undertake and that which you do continually come into, as by our Treasurer's letters you shall perceive by divers particularities ... We therefore, both in regard of our own honour and your particular reputation, do require you, upon the sight hereof, to make your speedy return.[45]

Unbeknown to Elizabeth, even as she was signing the letter, Henry and Essex would join forces in a daring attack on the Mont Sainte-

Catherine fort, successfully ousting the Leaguers from their defensive positions until a counter-attack next day reversed their gains.[46] Three days later, Essex decided to lead his men in a last decisive, all-out surge over the walls of the fort at dead of night, using scaling ladders supplied by Biron. Blatantly defying the queen's instructions that he take no personal risks, he crossed the ditch and ordered his men to raise their ladders, only to find that they were eight feet too short.[47]

Much, much worse, the Earl had personally ordered his soldiers to wear white shirts over their armour so they could see one another more easily in the dark. But this also made them visible to the enemy, whose sniper fire picked them off one by one as they ran away.[48] It was a final, ignominious blow. For Essex, the Normandy adventure was a catastrophe, and he knew it. In Unton's wonderfully deadpan assessment, these setbacks 'killeth our hope of Rouen'.[49]

On Tuesday, 10 January 1592, after surrendering his command and taking leave of Henry, Essex hastened to Dieppe for the last time.[50] Downcast and weary, he was far from the dashing figure he had been five months earlier, even if, to keep up appearances, his pages still wore their fine orange livery coats. He had conspicuously failed on the battlefield, but it would not be long before his spin doctors would be rewriting history to make things appear very different. Nor could he resist melodrama. In a farewell gesture worthy of a Victorian gothic novelist, he drew his sword and kissed the blade as his ship sailed out of the harbour and unfurled its sails.[51]

On the Saturday following, Essex reappeared in the Privy Chamber at Whitehall and danced with the queen. Shortly afterwards, she recalled Sir John Norris from Brittany. A highly experienced commander but a disillusioned man, he cursed her for her neglect of his mission in the Blavet valley. While all her attention had been on Rouen, she had turned his company, he confided to Burghley, into 'the forgotten army'. He had suffered no defeat, but neither could he capture more than a few minor towns, most of which the Leaguers had quickly recovered. By the time winter had set in, more than half his men had died in the mud in their boots, either from cold or from a 'new sickness', most likely plague but quite possibly a new strain of influenza.[52]

Just as Elizabeth had failed to offer assistance or support to her brave mariners and soldiers after the 1588 Armada campaign, she gave no thought, shockingly, to Norris's men, or to the ordinary foot soldiers in Essex's field army still stranded in Normandy. Rather than ordering their repatriation with their officers, she cheerfully left them to return home under their own steam or else forage off the land in northern France until she needed them again. By never giving them their arrears of pay, she left them destitute. Six months would pass before she offered any of these soldiers the prospect of a passage home. Instead, all of her attention was on the Duke of Parma, who had once again marched into Picardy, at the head of a new, crack Spanish division. The fear was that he was making his way towards Aumale, on Normandy's eastern border, which made it almost certain he was heading for Rouen.

Intent on a set-piece battle, Henry rode out with seven thousand cavalry to confront his old enemy, but he positioned himself badly and was shot in the groin while leading his troops across a bridge. Within ten days, he would recover sufficiently to mount his horse, but his brief incapacity gave Parma the opportunity he needed. The Spanish forces pressed ahead towards Rouen, which they successfully relieved on 10 April after ambushing Biron's camp. Any lingering hope Elizabeth had of capturing Rouen was now gone.[53]

Henry attempted several times to force Parma into a pitched battle, but failed. Then, while besieging Caudebec, a fortified town on the Seine, Parma was himself shot by a musketeer. The bullet entered his right arm below the elbow and lodged above the wrist. As the wound gradually began to fester, he withdrew his army, hotly pursued by Henry. By early June, he was safely back in the Netherlands, but five months later he died of heart failure.[54]

The Dutch celebrated Parma's death with fireworks and dancing in the streets. While the Duke had been absent in France, the armies of their new leader, Count Maurice, ably reinforced by Vere's auxiliaries, had stormed Steenwijk in Overijssel. Now they laid siege to Geertruidenberg in north Brabant. Henry, meanwhile, had another obstacle to overcome. With Norris no longer in command of the English forces in Brittany, Henry's army there was heavily defeated. Once again, it seemed as if Spain might take control of the entire province. When Henry appealed for Norris's return, Elizabeth prevaricated.[55] Only on receiving credible intelligence that Philip II might stake a claim to Brittany for his daughter, the Infanta Isabella, did she relent, sending Norris back with money and fresh supplies to begin a guerrilla campaign against the Spanish bases around Blavet.

On 30 June, after tense negotiations, Elizabeth entered into another treaty with the French king. She promised to supply him with four thousand more troops, some artillery and a large quantity of munitions. In return, he agreed to repay her costs, which were estimated at £3,200 a week.[56]

Then, as in a Greek tragedy, more bad news came. Spanish forces had captured Épernay, on the left bank of the Marne, enabling them to dominate an area crucial to the provisioning of Paris. Desperate to recover the town, Henry had ridden out after supper along the opposite riverbank to reconnoitre. Against orders, Biron followed him, but a cannonball fired from a tower set off an explosion of blood and bone that left him among the dead. It was, Henry informed Elizabeth in ciphered French, 'one of the very worst blows I could have had'.[57]

In the ensuing year-long stalemate, Elizabeth's relations with Henry were scarred by mutual mistrust. He saw her as unreasonable, stingy and half-hearted; she came to fear that he would never repay his debts. She suspected that, to defeat the Catholic League and recover control of the whole of his kingdom, he could before long be tempted to betray her by fulfilling his promise to the dying Henry III of converting to Catholicism.

Outwardly, she maintained good relations, sending the French king a portrait miniature of herself by Nicholas Hilliard and a scarf she had supposedly embroidered. In return, he sent her an African elephant to join the lions, tigers and a porcupine in her menagerie at the Tower. She regarded the elephant as a massive inconvenience: its food – some had to be specially imported – cost her around £150 a year. Shirking the expense, she quickly farmed out the animal to its Flemish keeper: in exchange for paying for its upkeep, he was allowed to keep all profits from exhibiting it to the public.[58]

By the spring of 1593, Elizabeth could only watch from the sidelines as events in France slid out of her control. Vast tracts of Normandy and the area around Paris would be devastated by the rival armies.

With food becoming scarce and peasant revolts more frequent, Henry's subjects were weary of the civil war and longed for peace.[59]

Philip II took his chance. For the very first time, he made a direct personal intervention in French politics, audaciously suggesting that the Infanta should marry the eldest son of the assassinated Duke of Guise. The Estates-General would then elect them king and queen of France in place of Henry, who would be declared a heretic and a usurper like Elizabeth.[60]

Henry decided he had had enough. And he saw a way out. On Sunday, 15 July 1593, St Swithin's Day, he solemnly processed into the royal Abbey of Saint-Denis, the burial place of the kings of France for eight hundred years, and was received into the Catholic Church. Clad all in white and carrying a candle, he knelt at the entrance to the choir and was escorted to the high altar by the archbishop of Bourges. There, he professed that he would live and die in the Catholic religion, after which he attended Mass. And as a great bonfire was lit on the hill of Montmartre to announce his conversion to the citizens of Paris, he issued a proclamation in which he recognized the Catholic Church as the 'true church of God'.[61] Not forgetting the loyal supporters who had sacrificed so much for him on the battlefield for so many years, Henry took pains to induce many Catholic noblemen to sign a document promising never to raise arms against the Huguenots. Although sceptics on both sides of the religious divide mocked him by falsely attributing to him the cynical aphorism 'Paris is well worth a Mass', his move cut support for the League by three quarters as moderate Leaguers all over France switched sides.[62]

For more than a year, Lorenzo Guicciardini, the chief adviser of Ferdinando de' Medici, Grand Duke of Tuscany, had dropped hints to Elizabeth that her ally might convert. A loyal Catholic, but notoriously anti-Spanish, the Grand Duke had already spoken of marrying his sister or niece to the French king and of providing a dowry of 4 million gold pieces and 600,000 crowns a year.[63] Alerted in this way nine months before the day of the ceremony in Saint-Denis, Elizabeth had cautioned Henry about the dangers of his possible apostasy: 'If a ruler does not have his eyes firmly fixed upon the King of Kings without any distraction, how can he expect to achieve either success or stability in his affairs?'[64]

When the blow fell, it struck her like a sudden bereavement all the same. Her reaction showed that she really did believe that God had been on her side when the Armada was defeated. Henry's conversion now put that in jeopardy. Confronted by the news, she was in denial for months, simply stunned. '*Ah quelles douleurs! O quels regrets!*' ('Ah what griefs! Oh what regrets!') she exclaimed. She then berated the French king for a decision that she believed flew in the face of God:

> Is it possible that any worldly respect should efface the terror with which the fear of God threatens us? Can we with any reason expect a good outcome from an act so iniquitous? He who has preserved you many years by his hand – can you imagine that he would permit you to walk alone in your greatest need? Ah, it is dangerous to do evil to make good out of it; I still hope that a sounder inspiration will come to you.[65]

Three months later, Elizabeth ordered the rump of her forces in northern France to embark for home, declaring herself to have been shamefully abused by her faithless ally. Then, after intense lobbying by Burghley, she modified her instructions. Now, only the sick and wounded were to return. The able-bodied from Brittany were to remain there, to help repel another two thousand Spaniards who had recently landed at Blavet, and those still in Normandy were to be shipped first to Sandwich in Kent, where they were to be held strictly under guard, 'lest those that remained should run away', before being sent to Ostend to reinforce the English auxiliaries in the Netherlands.[66]

Elizabeth had found the French campaign deeply frustrating. In 1588, with her policy of peace at any price in tatters and the Spanish fleet sailing for the Channel, she had largely, and wisely, left Lord Admiral Howard and Sir Francis Drake to combat the threat on their own terms. By contrast, she had never fully trusted Essex and had thought she could govern him at a distance. In this she was wrong. Despite incurring bills for the war effort on land exceeding £100,000 (worth £100 million today), she had found herself powerless to exert the degree of control that she had expected.[67]

For if Essex had been an unbridled horse, so, too, had Henry. That she considered herself the senior partner in their alliance as the more established and experienced monarch did not mean he would follow her instructions. In Scotland, King James had several times gone his own way; now Henry was doing the same. At this moment, she was quite unsure what her future relationship with him would be. Revealingly, she had signed her last letter to him, 'Your most assured sister if it be of the old fashion; with the new I have nothing to do'.[68]

As for her daredevil young favourite, the fiasco at Rouen did not necessarily mean the end of his military career. Elizabeth might long to dismiss him for insubordination in the same way as, thirty years before, she had yearned to call Burghley to account for his thinly veiled attempts to force her into marriage or into naming an heir in Parliament, but she could not quite bring herself to do so. Unable yet to cut him adrift, still prepared to reward and support him, granting him fresh resources even as he wasted her money, she seemed blind to the trouble she was fomenting.

One thing, though, she had learned the hard way: recent events in France had cured her of any notion that an aggressive European land campaign could work in her best interests. She would think harder and longer next time.

11. 'Good Queen Bess'

In the City of London, the summers of 1592 and 1593 were long, hot and turbulent. With overseas trade and domestic demand for goods and services gravely depressed by the effects of the long war with Spain and its ally the Catholic League, unemployment began to soar throughout the country, especially among the young. Economic stagnation was made worse by sharply rising prices and the hefty taxes needed to pay for the war effort. In the years of peace, taxes had been low, but with Leicester's expedition to the Netherlands and the coming of the Armada, they soared to unprecedented levels. It was almost inevitable that, before long, the anguish and frustration of those struggling to make ends meet would explode into violence.[1]

Trouble began at eight o'clock on a sultry Sunday evening in early June 1592, when, with almost two hours to go before dusk, an angry crowd of feltmongers' apprentices armed with cudgels and daggers swarmed out of Bermondsey High Street in Southwark and joined forces with a disgruntled rabble of young unemployed men and war veterans. Only the quick thinking of London's mayor, Sir William Webb, saved the day. Rushing from his house and crossing London Bridge with the sheriff and his constables, Webb arrested the ringleaders and dispersed the throng. Writing to Burghley next day, he argued for leniency, claiming that the spark had been an apprentice's wrongful arrest. Debt collectors had burst into the man's lodgings with daggers drawn and dragged him off to the Marshalsea in front of his terrified landlady, who stood clutching a baby in her arms. The rioters had planned to storm the prison and free the inmates. Webb believed the best way to calm the situation was to rectify the injustice done to the young man as quickly as possible.[2]

Suspicion that a further riot was planned for Midsummer's Day was strong enough to warrant the proclamation of a curfew. In an effort to stifle further disorders, the Privy Council closed playhouses and other places of public entertainment such as bear-baiting rings and bowling alleys until the New Year, and charged the justices of the peace for Middlesex and Surrey (the counties adjacent to London) to coordinate their patrols with those of the mayor and aldermen.[3] Writing again to Burghley, Webb urged the queen's chief minister to be on his guard against racial and ethnic tension caused by foreigners who had migrated to London for purely economic reasons. He pointed to the Dutch Calvinists who had recently arrived and set up businesses in the city, although many were already free to practise their religion and trades at home.[4] His warning chimed with one of the city's longest-standing grievances, namely that second-generation Huguenot immigrants posed a threat to English merchants. Whereas their parents, fleeing France after the St Bartholomew Day's Massacre in 1572, had been happy to integrate fully into London society, these younger Huguenots were rediscovering their national identity as Frenchmen and discriminating against true-born Englishmen. After serving apprenticeships and becoming freemen in their adopted city, they would take on their own, exclusively immigrant apprentices before selling on lower-priced goods they had imported directly from their French relatives, so putting Englishmen out of their jobs. And as if that were not enough, they had begun investing in residential property, forcing up prices and dividing their properties into tenements to maximize rents.[5]

Six weeks later, in the scorching heat of August, plague struck the city, silently killing its victims as, finally, sick and wounded soldiers returned home in droves from the war zones in Normandy and Brittany. Once back on English shores, they gravitated to the capital, most of them lacking their arrears of pay, only to roam the streets, desperately seeking work or charitable relief and spreading diseases they had picked up while in France. For this menacing new threat, the queen and her advisers were utterly unprepared.[6]

As summer turned to autumn and the heat abated, the Privy Council forbade discharged soldiers from entering the city and ordered the Lord Mayor's Feast to be cancelled. Almost as fearful of contagious diseases as her father, although less of a hypochondriac, Elizabeth threw a cordon sanitaire around her Court, restricting access to a radius of two miles. Only her privy councillors, their clerks and a reduced number of her own servants were to be allowed

in, whether she was in London or on one of her summer progresses.
Anyone else attempting entry could be imprisoned.[7] Heralds read out
royal proclamations in Cheapside and at the gates of Whitehall, closing the central law courts at Westminster and ordering the judges to
hear only the most urgent cases, at Hertford Castle, some twenty-
five miles north of the city.[8]

For a time, these measures helped to control the epidemic, reducing
deaths to some thirty a week, but the following spring the heat and
the plague returned, turning London into a nursery of infection. At
Elizabeth's insistence, plague orders were published, requiring houses
afflicted by disease to be quarantined, their street doors marked
clearly with a red cross. The Privy Council shut the theatres again,
for fifteen months this time. Other than royal command performances, plays were to be staged only outside a radius of seven miles
(later cut to five) from St Paul's – and, even then, only if the neigh-
bourhood was free of the pestilence.[9]

In an effort to reduce tension after an outcry in Parliament about
the plight of the war veterans, Elizabeth reluctantly offered temporary relief to the most badly maimed. They were granted the sum of
two shillings weekly, almost enough to buy bread and some cheese,
and those too weak or crippled to claim the money in person could
send nominees to collect it. But to cut dramatically the numbers of
discharged soldiers and mariners in London and its suburbs, this relief
was made payable to them only at their birthplaces.[10] The measure
helped, but the underlying disquiet remained. The threat of violence
returned in April and May when young unemployed men began to
roam the streets in gangs, threatening bloodshed against foreigners.
Under cover of darkness, they began distributing what the authorities regarded as a vicious wave of seditious libels, which were either
handed out as broadsheets to passers-by or pasted up on walls or
nailed to posts at street corners as printed 'placards'. Crammed with
slogans and doggerel verses, these so-called 'libels' stirred up xenophobia by turning immigrants into convenient scapegoats for poverty
and recession. Some even had pictures of gallows with immigrants
hanging from them with ropes around their necks, their feet dangling in the air.[11] They revived memories of Evil May Day, a notorious

episode early in Henry VIII's reign when more than a thousand young English-born apprentices driven by just such xenophobia had run riot, wielding cudgels and ransacking houses and warehouses in the immigrant communities. Principally, their target had been the hated money-lenders from Lombardy in northern Italy, whom they attacked, until they were famously called to order by Sir Thomas More, then undersheriff of London. His eloquence alone, according to the London chroniclers, had stemmed the worst of the violence.[12]

The summer of 1593 would turn out to be the hottest and driest of the century. Just in London alone, some eighteen thousand people – roughly a tenth of the urban population – died over the course of the year, two thirds from plague. Such high mortality was merely the tip of an iceberg: twice as many were known to have succumbed to infection but managed to survive. In the Tower, several prisoners died in their cells from heat exhaustion.[13] Wealthy merchants and their families sought refuge in the country, closing the city for business. Elizabeth herself would shortly flee with a small group of women and courtiers to the safety of Windsor Castle. Even there she could not feel completely secure: she was terrified when a page of Kate Carey's younger sister, Philadelphia, Lady Scrope, died of plague in the castle keep.[14]

That only two apprentice riots occurred that summer was as much due to fear of the plague as to strong governance.[15] Determined to avoid a repeat of Evil May Day, Burghley and his colleagues searched high and low for the authors and printers of the offending libels, but in vain.[16] Around the same time, the queen's Master of the Revels, Sir Edmund Tilney, heavily censored the first draft of a controversial stage play whose working title was *Sir Thomas More*. Intended for when the theatres reopened and most likely conceived by a playwright or patron with unwelcome Catholic sympathies, the play contained a number of highly inflammatory and topical passages. In these, More did not simply calm the May Day rioters but was a man whose moral fibre was considerably greater than that of the king who executed him for resisting the break with Rome and opposing his marriage to Elizabeth's mother.[17]

Fully attuned to the double risk of fresh mob violence and the queen's wrath, given her legendary resolve to protect her parents' reputations from slander, Tilney picked up his blue pencil. He knew all too well that less than a year had elapsed since Elizabeth, writing in fluent Italian, had chivvied Ferdinando de' Medici, Grand Duke of Tuscany, into suppressing the first edition of a book by Girolamo Pollini, a Dominican friar from the monastery of Santa Maria Novella in Florence, which had defamed both her parents. Drawing on salacious passages excerpted from a biography of More by his favourite nephew William Rastell, a work now known only from fragments and one which for some years had been clandestinely circulated in manuscript, Pollini claimed that Anne Boleyn was actually Henry VIII's own daughter by an illicit liaison with her mother, Lady Elizabeth Boleyn. In her letter to Duke Ferdinando, Elizabeth had railed furiously against 'such horrible calumnies and lies', keeping up the pressure until he publicly burned copies of the book.[18]

Since much of the inspiration for the play of *Sir Thomas More* had come from Rastell's writings and those of his fellow Catholic exiles in Louvain and Douai, Tilney purged from the script all references to prison breakouts, street brawls and apprentice riots, along with a still more daring passage in which, in idioms not dissimilar to those Shakespeare would shortly use of Sir John Falstaff, the queen's father was lampooned as a glutton by day and a lecher by night.[19] Stripped of its bite, the play became a mere shell. Quite possibly in the hope that it might be resurrected, it was then handed over to fresh playwrights for script doctoring. Shakespeare was one of them: his proposed revisions still survive in a rare example of his handwriting, interleaved with the original, censored version of the script. But even *his* powers of invention were insufficient to rescue a play so denuded of its story arc.[20]

As Elizabeth hid away with her much-reduced Court, invisible to her subjects and seemingly impervious to their suffering, she would become unnerved, then numbed by her inability to respond to extreme socio-economic forces so obviously beyond her control. In late June, she renewed her efforts to contain the plague by ordering prayers to be said in the churches and by insisting that Bartholomew Fair and the annual feasts of the London livery companies be cancelled.[21] The loss of the feasts was hardly important – the rich could enjoy other things – but the Fair mattered greatly to ordinary Londoners. Held in mid-August in the fields beyond Smithfield, outside the city walls, and complete with horseracing and rabbit coursing, wrestling, juggling, peddlers, dancing and market stalls, it was their recreational highlight of the year. The mayor and aldermen insisted it posed no tangible threat to public health as long as those in contact with known plague victims were kept away. Elizabeth flatly rejected this assertion but was unable to counter the mayor's argument that the wholesale trades conducted by merchants and entrepreneurs during the Fair were critical to the economic survival of the city's clothiers. When Burghley threw in his weight on the mayor's side to help stave off bankruptcies, the queen finally yielded, agreeing that the event could take place but only if drastically curtailed.[22]

Shortly afterwards, she succumbed to a run of severe episodes of intense depression. It just so happened that the very worst of the plague coincided precisely with Henry IV's shock conversion to Catholicism. Elizabeth concluded that God had unleashed the epidemic on England and northern France to punish Henry for his apostasy and herself for conniving in it. Utterly persuaded by this apocalyptic interpretation of events, she spiralled downwards into a dark 'melancholy' lasting several months.[23] So committed was she to the principles of her father's break with Rome, she believed the French king's perfidy made him a traitor to God and an 'unnatural' brother to herself. Christian rulers conventionally addressed each other as 'brother' or 'sister', and in her remonstrations to Henry over the course of that summer she pointedly declared that, from now on, she could see herself only as his 'bastard' sibling, a remark replete with resonances relating to her own troubled childhood and feuds with her half-sister Mary, who had many times denounced Anne Boleyn as a filthy whore.[24]

A month or so after she passed the landmark of her sixtieth birthday, Elizabeth made a concerted effort to reconcile the setback of Henry's apostasy with her own religious faith.[25] She spent her days reading the Bible, the writings of the ancient Church Fathers and Greek and Roman philosophy (chiefly Seneca's *Moral Essays*). She held regular audiences with Archbishop Whitgift, her preferred adviser on anything to do with the church or matters of conscience.

She also began, and completed, a line-by-line translation from Latin into English of *The Consolation of Philosophy* by the early-sixth-century writer Anicius Manlius Severinus Boethius.[26]

The son of a Roman aristocrat, Boethius was an ardent student of ancient Greek philosophy and Christian theology, who had become first consul and later master of ceremonies to the Ostrogothic King Theodoric the Great at Ravenna. Accused as a co-conspirator for defending a fellow senator suspected of treason, he wrote *The Consolation* while under house arrest before his execution. Elizabeth may well have seen a link between Boethius and herself, recalling the terrifying time when she had been imprisoned on suspicion of treason after the failure of Wyatt's rebellion. During the months she had spent under tight guard at Woodstock in Oxfordshire after her release from the Tower, she had passed her time by reading voraciously and making literary translations of the Latin classics. It was during this highly formative time that she had first encountered Boethius.[27] Now, nearly forty years later, as she struggled to cope with Henry's conversion to Catholicism, she came once again to interpret contemporary events as a test of character imposed on her by God. She clearly believed that humans, even kings, who persisted in their 'iniquity' would be severely punished. She had also come to believe that God had called on her to be an instrument for the salvation of northern Europe. This was why Henry's defection hit her so hard: she suspected he had shunned the clear light of Protestantism in favour of the dark forces of Catholicism entirely for worldly advantage. It was a step on the road to hell.

Elizabeth suppressed much of Boethius's dialogue, preferring to deploy her own authorial voice to emphasize that God is the only certain hope of human existence. His foreknowledge, the one sure attribute of his divinity, allows him to understand everything, including events that spring from human free will. Her manuscript, half of which survives in her own handwriting and half in a version dictated to a clerk, suggests that, after the watershed of her sixtieth birthday, she found herself battling with the same questions of the interrelationship between human affairs and divine Providence that have troubled theologians and philosophers throughout Christian history. How could a loving God, if he can look into our hearts and has complete foreknowledge of the future course of events, allow evil-doers to flourish in the world? Like Boethius, she consoled herself with the belief that evil men would never be happy, whatever their worldly success, while the virtuous, regardless of their fortunes, would be blessed.[28]

In the spring and summer of 1594, the unseasonably hot plague years gave way to months of storms and torrential rain.[29] Barns, church steeples and entire houses were flattened, and in the forests of Worcestershire and Staffordshire nearly five thousand oak trees were felled in a single day. In Sussex and Surrey, a sudden inundation of hail and unrelenting rain caused flash floods that swept away houses, cattle, iron-mills and the coal heaps ready to fire their furnaces. The deluges continued until the end of July, ruining the crops. A brief respite in August enabled a meagre harvest to be gathered in, but during September the monsoon rains returned, causing dozens of rivers to burst their banks and roads and bridges to be destroyed. Grain prices doubled almost overnight, to 6s. 8d. for a bushel of wheat,* and 5s. for a bushel of rye.[30]

Scarcity of food and high prices encouraged rioting, muggings, lootings and arson attacks in the capital involving up to five hundred people at a time, chiefly apprentices and the young unemployed. Street brawls escalated without warning into mass violence. In an attempt to force speculators hoarding grain to sell it in local markets at fair prices, the Privy Council issued a series of so-called 'dearth orders', but these were widely ignored. Enforcement was so patchy that, to a majority of ordinary Londoners, it could only appear as if Elizabeth was markedly more interested in her own entertainment than in their plight.[31] By now, the Lord Chamberlain, Lord Hunsdon, had recruited Shakespeare's company of actors to help satisfy her appetite for new plays. During the festive season, he brought them to Greenwich Palace to perform two comedies for her, for which he paid them £20. One play may have been Shakespeare's *The Comedy of Errors*; the other is unknown.[32]

Elizabeth lived in great luxury, cosseted, cared for, her every whim

---

* £330 in modern values for around 70lbs of wheat.

satisfied, all financed by the receipts of taxation and the profits from excise duties and the Crown lands. The choicest foods on which she dined were, by the royal prerogative, requisitioned from local markets at artificially low prices set by her officials rather than at market rates. Cocooned within the gilded bubble of her palaces, she feared social revolution but did little to help prevent it beyond exhorting others to action.[33] She continued to maintain a cordon sanitaire around herself, personally drafting another proclamation excluding onlookers from her vicinity on pain of arrest and imprisonment.[34] Hard on this came yet another, limiting by name, for the very first time, those who might gain admission through her palace gates on the pretext of seeking justice or to petition the Privy Council.[35] Finally, she forbade the public from continuing to visit her menagerie in the Tower to view the elephant presented to her by Henry IV.[36]

Out of touch with the horrendous conditions experienced by the overwhelming majority of her people, Elizabeth did not believe it was her responsibility to take systematic steps to alleviate their hardship. Instead, she saw her remit in terms of the promises she had made when she swore her coronation oath: to offer her people justice in the law courts, to defend the Church of England and to defend her realm from foreign invasion. That was all. And yet in her father's reign Thomas More had argued in *Utopia* (1516) that, first and foremost, it was the duty of rulers to protect the welfare of their citizens.[37] By Elizabeth's day, so-called 'commonwealth' writers routinely took this line, but she did not adapt to their way of thinking. Her motto, *Semper Eadem*, remained her yardstick. All she wanted was for the recent apprentice riots and other civil disturbances to end, and she expected the mayor, civic magistrates and the leaders of the merchant guilds to keep control of the capital's streets in her name.

Inevitably, falling wages and skyrocketing prices caused serious rumblings of mass discontent. While courtiers and city speculators prospered through fraud, bribery and, especially, by supplying inferior clothing, equipment and foodstuffs to the royal navy or the land forces overseas, the poor continued to suffer. Addressing her troops at Tilbury in 1588, Elizabeth had boasted that she regarded the trust of her 'faithful and loving people' as her greatest 'strength and safeguard'. But, once the immediate scare was over, what looked like her heartless refusal to pay her brave mariners and soldiers their arrears of pay had rankled with the victims of her neglect.

Her rhetoric, first used at her encounter with King Philip's ambassador, the Count of Feria, would never change. In December 1597, she would inform a visiting French ambassador that it was simply unbelievable how much her people loved her and how she loved them no less than they her.[38] Lupold von Wedel, the queen's starstruck Christmas guest in 1584, tells us that, when she rode in an open carriage through the streets of London, she used a stock mantra. To all whom she passed, she cried out, 'God save my people!' – to which, somewhat optimistically, he expects us to believe they chirruped heartily in reply, 'God save your grace!'[39]

Feria's celebrated dispatch and the queen's own rhetoric apart, the primary sources of the myth of 'Good Queen Bess' were the fawning glosses in the English editions of Camden's *Annales* introduced by his bestselling translator Robert Norton. Thanks to Norton's fantasies, it was made to appear how, from her accession until she breathed her last, Elizabeth, wherever she went, was greeted by the 'hearty applause and well-wishings of her people'. This, Norton added, was because of 'her singular clemency and goodness', gracious attributes that would inspire her people to 'continue and increase their love towards her even to her dying day'. Soaring ever higher towards hyperbole, Norton even managed to claim that never in the whole of human history, from the days of Herodotus to the modern era, had any people 'embraced their prince with more hearty and constant affection, more dutiful observance and more joyful acclamations than they did her during the whole course of her life'.[40]

Smouldering resentment of the queen first sparked into open revolt in 1595, when the years of excessive heat, plague and flood were followed by the second of what turned out to be four disastrous harvests in a row. The wholesale price of butter rose from £2 10s. to £4 a barrel, and ling (a common, cod-like fish much eaten by the poor) from £3 to £5 5s. a hundredweight. In London, speculators were caught offering three large hen's eggs for two pence (close to £8 today) and a pound of butter for seven pence. Rumours were rife that the price of wheat would soon soar from 7s. to 16s. a bushel, while wages plummeted to their lowest levels since records began. Near-starvation among the inhabitants of the upland or moorland sheep-farming regions of England and Wales, who grew crops under marginal conditions and were forced to buy grain in nearby markets, encouraged a flood of internal migration from the most depressed regions to the capital. Now thousands of 'sturdy beggars' (as the civic authorities liked to call them) roamed the streets by day and slept in doorways and church porches by night, joining the already bulging ranks of war veterans and young unemployed in begging for work and food.[41] Meanwhile, the seemingly endless recession smothered most of what was left of the legitimate clothing trade.[42]

Another flashpoint was military conscription. Able-bodied recruits had long come to dread the queen's service overseas and would do almost anything to avoid the draft.[43] 'I assure you', Burghley had warned Sir Henry Unton, Elizabeth's ambassador to Henry IV, after Essex's return from his ill-fated expedition to Rouen, 'the realm here is weary to see the expense of their people for foreign services, hav-ing presently in sight great necessity of domestical forces to withstand foreign attempts daily prepared against this realm.'[44] Muster-masters were forced to accept the very lowest in society for the army. In counties such as Oxfordshire and Berkshire, and not just in London, they simply emptied the gaols to secure recruits. Even experienced privy councillors were quick to conclude that 'rogues, vagabonds and other idle, dissolute and masterless persons' were the perfect can-non fodder, seemingly unaware that the very process of labelling a man a vagrant helped to make him one in the eyes of the local magis-trates. Few officials in charge of musters were immune to bribery, and it is easy to see from where Shakespeare's inspiration would come for the Gloucestershire scenes in *Henry IV, Part II*.[45]

Clamouring in vain for butter and fish at the same low prices at which the queen purchased them for her palaces, a group of London apprentices twice stormed the market stalls in Southwark in June and took what they wanted. Others pulled down the pillories in Cheap-side and Leadenhall and threatened to kill the newly appointed mayor. He was none other than Sir John Spencer, who as sheriff in 1584 had been humiliated by the Privy Council on Elizabeth's orders after he had arrested her favourite musicians. As the heat of summer returned and tempers frayed again, a horrified Spencer would be confronted by the nearest thing to a reprise of Evil May Day for almost a century. In the late afternoon of Sunday, 29 June, a mob said to be several thousand strong marched on Tower Hill, emboldened by a trumpeter who was a war veteran. Planning first to arm themselves by ransacking the nearby gunmakers' shops, the rioters intended to pillage the houses of the wealthier merchants, especially foreigners, and to hang Mayor Spencer from a gallows they had set up outside his magnificent house in Bishopsgate.[46]

About seven o'clock in the evening, Spencer, having raised a well-armed posse, rode to Tower Hill with his ceremonial sword carried before him, the blade unsheathed, to quell the insurrection. He was met by a hail of stones, and his sword was snatched away from his sword-bearer under his very eyes. Not without injuries, but fortunately without serious bloodshed, the posse managed to disperse the crowd and Spencer recovered his sword. Dirty and dishevelled, his ego sorely bruised but his authority intact, the mayor made his way back to the Guildhall to scribble an urgent postscript to Burghley at the bottom of a letter he had written earlier in the day, triumphantly announcing that his men had apprehended the ringleaders and sent them to prison.[47] Charged at the Guildhall with levying war against the queen on a very dubious interpretation of the treason legislation, five of the rioters were swiftly convicted by a jury of much-relieved property-owning citizens and were led away, shackled in irons, to be dragged on hurdles to the gallows.[48]

Seriously alarmed by the commotion on Tower Hill, Elizabeth summoned her privy councillors to an emergency audience at Greenwich Palace. On 4 July, she dictated her terms of reference for what Burghley then turned into arguably the most savage proclamation of her reign, one that she demanded be 'duly observed upon pain of her indignation'. Using the somewhat specious justification that 'sundry sorts of base people', notably 'wandering idle persons of [the] condition of rogues and vagabonds', had been spotted among the rioters disguised as war veterans, she ordered martial law to be imposed throughout London and its suburbs on an indefinite basis.

A supreme military judge known as a Provost Marshal was to have unlimited discretion 'to apprehend all such as shall not be readily reformed and corrected by the ordinary officers of justice'. In the most serious cases, suspects of no fixed abode whom the Provost Marshal's officers had caught roaming the streets were to be hanged from the gallows 'by order of martial law', without the need for a trial or an appearance in court.[49]

A set of equally draconian, more specific orders drawn up under Burghley's supervision assigned to the Provost Marshal a detachment of thirty cavalry, who were to be equipped with pistols, swords and daggers.[50] Patrolling the streets night and day, they were to haul all suspicious characters to account, in the first instance before a special commission consisting of London and Middlesex magistrates sitting twice a week at the Old Bailey, near Newgate Prison.[51]

Burghley's orders stressed the right of the Provost Marshal to sentence and hang summarily anyone found writing or disseminating a seditious libel or placard. And yet, despite his insertion of a last-minute clause into the document offering a handsome bounty to anyone providing information that would lead to such a drastic outcome, no one was caught.[52]

Hearing cases throughout the summer, the special commissioners ordered many offenders to be whipped or imprisoned. Others were ordered to leave London and return home to their birthplaces. Only gentlemen and their wives and Elizabeth's servants – such as her purveyors, pursuivants, grooms, messengers and musicians – or others who could be vouched for by gentlemen were allowed to walk the streets after sunset. Everyone else was to be subject to the curfew.[53]

Although Mayor Spencer, fearing the mob, had strongly urged Elizabeth to proclaim martial law, these extreme measures sparked fears that she intended more generally to override the established courts of law. The result was a strongly worded protest from the judges of the Court of Queen's Bench.[54] Frustrated at what they took to be an affront to Magna Carta and due process of law, they sent a memo to the queen (unfortunately, only part of it survives) reasserting their right to summon before them any prisoners they chose to free from summary detention on writs of habeas corpus and to demand to know the cause of their arrest.[55]

A fortnight later, Sir Thomas Wilford, a Kentish man who had served with distinction in the Netherlands and in Normandy, was appointed Provost Marshal. Anxious not to provoke a second clash with the judges, Burghley did his best to rein in the queen's desire for exemplary hangings, ensuring that Wilford's commission was drafted so as to encourage him to proceed, wherever possible, 'in ordinary manner', using the city's existing magistrates and constables rather than military men. According to the final version of Wilford's commission, only 'desperate offenders' so incorrigible, so 'notoriously culpable' and careless of the law that they 'care not for any ordinary punishment' were to be hanged.[56]

In September, Wilford's commission was quietly withdrawn and Mayor Spencer took back control of the city's affairs, by which time civil order had largely been restored. At Spencer's request, the commissioners appointed to sit at the Old Bailey continued to meet for at least another year, their remit whittled down to clearing the city's highways and alehouses of the underclass so conveniently stereotyped by its social superiors as rogues, vagabonds and whores.[57]

Elizabeth did not herself revisit the topic of law and order directly. Instead, she watched approvingly as the Privy Council, acting on its own initiative, sharpened its enforcement weapons against unruly vagrants. During 1596 and 1597, Burghley and his fellow councillors, controversially, would order entire shiploads of beggars, vagrants, thieves, pimps and cutpurses from London and its criminal underworld to be forcibly rounded up and deported for military service in Ireland or the Netherlands. To organize these purges, they established a fresh team of Provost Marshals whose exclusive role was to seek out anyone caught loitering in the streets and escort them to the ports.[58] Demobilized war veterans caught begging for lack of pay were to be arrested and sent straight back to the front line. For the first time, loitering became a serious crime, leading to an outcry in Parliament.[59]

Most scandalously to modern eyes, the queen did not blink when, in 1596, a Lübeck merchant, Caspar van Senden, put forward an extraordinary scheme to capture and forcibly deport as many people of black African descent as he could find living in England, shipping them to Spain or Portugal to be sold as slaves or exchanged for English prisoners of war. No one knows precisely how many black Africans had been brought to England by this time, but from the 1540s onwards some London merchants had made fairly regular voyages to 'Barbary' (Atlantic Morocco), and in the 1560s Sir John Hawkins of Plymouth and his elder brother William had made their names infamous by trading for African slaves with backwoods Portuguese merchants.[60] As a commercial venture, van Senden's plan failed, but the fact that Elizabeth approved it and is on record as saying that she 'doth think it a very good exchange', will do nothing to enhance her reputation as 'Good Queen Bess' in the twenty-first century.[61]

12.   The Quest for Gold

Finding his star waning at Court while those of his rivals waxed, Sir Walter Ralegh decided that the time had come to make or break his fortune. For some years, Elizabeth had promised that he would succeed Hatton as Captain of the Queen's Guard, but Hatton had clung to the post like a clam. Only on Hatton's death had Ralegh at last secured the office, which enabled him to attend the queen in the Privy Chamber, carrying an ebony baton tipped with gold.

Ralegh was a genuine patriot, and one of the most original minds of his generation. When Elizabeth had made it plain that she would not adopt his grand strategy for colonization and conquest in the Americas, he switched tack to privateering, transforming himself into the closest thing to a conquistador that England would produce. A quick thinker eager to operate on the largest possible canvas, he lobbied Elizabeth and Burghley to change their naval tactics: instead of trying to intercept and plunder Philip's treasure ships in mid-Atlantic off the Azores, as the queen had ordered Drake and Norris at the time of their ill-fated expedition to Portugal, the convoys should be throttled at the dispatching end. That should either be done by raids on the Panama Isthmus, where much of Philip's treasure from his Peruvian silver mines was sent for shipment to Spain, or by blockading the coast of Cuba or the Straits of Florida. And Ralegh knew his queen. If anything would win her support, it was the promise of riches. He threw stardust in her eyes, offering her the beguiling prospect of booty so vast it would make the war against Philip self-financing.[1]

Ralegh had first learned all there was to know about privateering as an adolescent, from his half-brother Sir Humphrey Gilbert and his mother's kinsmen, the staunchly Protestant Champernownes of Modbury in Devon.[2] After the outbreak of the Wars of Religion in France in 1562, the Champernownes were in the vanguard of Channel privateering, a practice developed largely by the English during the Hundred Years War and sanctioned by international law. Governments issued 'letters of marque' to merchants claiming to have suffered losses at the hands of foreign nationals. These letters authorized them to recoup their losses by 'reprisal', and their scope was soon enlarged to include not just enemy ships but neutral ships carrying enemy cargoes.[3]

Covertly aided by Walsingham between 1568 and 1572, the Champernownes had helped to organize a joint fleet with the Huguenots of La Rochelle that sailed under letters of marque and reprisal issued by the Huguenot leaders. Armed with these documents, the West Country men cheerfully plundered ships from all nations, but chiefly from Spain, returning to Plymouth for supplies and to sell off the loot.[4] Long before the outbreak of war with Spain in 1585, they had expanded their horizons, crossing the Atlantic and venturing as far as the West Indies in search of what Drake would euphemistically call 'some little comfortable dew from heaven'.[5] And when in 1581 the Portuguese Cortes had ousted Dom António and recognized Philip as the lawful king, the privateers gained a munificent new patron. From his lodgings in Stepney, the Portuguese pretender issued his own letters of reprisal, which empowered them to capture both Spanish and neutral ships and their cargoes. The legality of these Portuguese commissions might be highly dubious but, as international law was in its infancy, they could never be tested.[6]

Privateering would become an official weapon of Elizabethan warfare in 1585 after Philip placed an embargo on English and Dutch shipping in Iberian ports and attempted to seize the *Primrose* at Bilbao. The Privy Council instructed Lord Admiral Howard to issue letters of reprisal to all English merchants who suffered depredations from Spanish actions. Proof of losses would soon become little more than a legal fiction as ventures were undertaken by all who fancied the chance of making their fortune. Increasingly, private 'men-of-war', mostly converted merchantmen financed and equipped by speculators and investors, took to sea with a view to snatching prizes whenever the opportunity arose, offering little more than a token nod in the direction of the queen. Between 1589 and 1591 alone, privateers captured some three hundred merchantmen, seizing plunder worth in excess of £400,000.[7]

By 1591, when Ralegh turned his attention in earnest to privateering, more than two hundred such voyages had already taken place. Now he aimed to mastermind the most daring venture so far: an expedition to Panama, whose target was nothing less than Philip's treasure convoy. Mortgaging his estates and pooling the resulting cash with that of a few friends and business associates, he set about recruiting stakeholders, notably the queen, a syndicate of London merchants and the Earl of Cumberland. If even three or four of Philip's ships could be captured with their cargoes, the gains would be immense.[8]

At first, Elizabeth gave Ralegh permission to assume command of the expedition, but then she changed her mind. With her beloved Leicester gone and Essex away on the Rouen campaign, she wanted a handsome man beside her to attend and entertain her. She never really loved Ralegh, but he kept her amused. When she told him he might accompany the expedition as far as Cape Finisterre but then must return, he had no alternative but to find a replacement for the rest of the venture. For that he turned to Sir Martin Frobisher, the first Englishman to enter the Hudson Strait and an intrepid explorer with strong connections to the Muscovy Company, who had already made three attempts to locate the fabled north-west passage linking the Atlantic and the Pacific oceans. He was to take command of the queen's ships once they were at sea, while Sir John Burgh, who had fought under Lord Willoughby in the Netherlands and for Henry IV at the Battle of Ivry, would take over Ralegh's flagship, the *Roebuck*, and its pinnaces.[9]

In February 1592, Ralegh was ready to set sail, but he was prevented by fierce westerly gales that lasted for months. Only on 6 May was he at last able to put to sea. By then, he feared for the success of the expedition. With supplies fast diminishing and the season already too far advanced to reach the Caribbean, he worried about how he could repay the creditors who had financed the enterprise.[10] Worse was to come: he had barely left Falmouth harbour and reached the open sea when Frobisher came alongside his ship on a small boat and informed him that he must return to Court immediately. A scandal was about to break, and Ralegh was at its centre.[11]

Ever the inveterate maverick, Ralegh disobeyed. Only after he had seen the last of his ships out past Cape Finisterre would he return to face Elizabeth's fury. Intercepting some merchant vessels sailing between Sanlúcar de Barrameda in southern Spain and Antwerp, on one of which was an escaped English prisoner of war, he discovered that Philip had ordered the treasure convoy not to sail that year, on account of the gales. On the other hand, the prisoner also brought the news that no fewer than five great carracks (huge, multi-deck merchant ships of more than a thousand tons) were expected to arrive from the Portuguese East Indies between the end of July and the middle of August, sailing round the Cape of Good Hope and up the West African coast.[12]

Armed with this fresh intelligence, Ralegh split his fleet into two. Frobisher was ordered to cruise up and down in Spanish waters and prevent Philip's warships from leaving port, while Burgh was instructed to sail towards the Azores to intercept as many of the carracks as he could. Only then did Ralegh return home, in a borrowed ship, reaching Plymouth in the third week of May. It was time to face the queen.[13]

Events would take a more sinister turn than Ralegh had imagined. His offence was to have secretly married Bess Throckmorton, one of Elizabeth's Privy Chamber intimates. The daughter of Sir Nicholas Throckmorton and thus a kinswoman of the queen, Bess had begun sleeping with Ralegh around Christmas 1590. All the signs point to it being a love match. Dancing attendance on the queen was one thing, but now, at thirty-seven, Ralegh hoped for a son and heir, just as Leicester had before him when he married Lettice Knollys. Ten years younger than her husband, Bess was one of the Court beauties, a mature woman with a will and mind of her own. This was no flighty teenager bewitched by her swaggering beau, even if Ralegh had recently taken to wearing a double-pearl earring in his left ear, to bring out what one biographer has called his 'dark Celtic virility'.[14] When Bess had become pregnant by the end of the summer, the couple were quietly married.

Two days after the queen's Accession Day in November, Bess's brother Arthur heard of his sister's predicament and offered to help.

Slipping away from Court on the pretext of sickness, she went to his house in Mile End, east of London, where she was safely delivered of a son. Arthur recorded the date in a remarkable diary found in 1950 by a carpenter in an outhouse: it was Wednesday, 29 March 1592, 'between two and three o'clock in the afternoon', just over a month before the baby's father set sail from Falmouth. Towards the end of April, Bess left her child with a wet nurse at Enfield in Middlesex, twelve miles north of London, and resumed her duties in the Bedchamber as though nothing had happened. But it was not long before her secret seeped out.[15]

If Ralegh ever supposed he could brazen it out with the queen, he was sadly mistaken. The revelation came when her ears were already tingling. A fortnight before Bess's clandestine wedding, London had been buzzing with reports of scandals involving the queen's maids of honour. First to break was the news that an illegitimate son had been born to Elizabeth Southwell. Essex's paternity would be kept safely hidden for several more years, although the curious fact that the infant was whisked away by Lettice Knollys to be brought up quietly in Staffordshire inevitably invited rumours.[16]

The queen then caught Leicester's illegitimate son by Douglas Sheffield, the young Robert Dudley, kissing Margaret Cavendish in the Presence Chamber. Barely a week later, another of her maids, Katherine Legh, was found to have given birth to a daughter in a corner of the Maids' Chamber. Thoroughly disgusted at such behaviour, Elizabeth dismissed Mrs Jones, the 'mother of the maids', sending her and Legh's seducer, Sir Francis Darcy, one of Essex's acolytes, to the Tower.[17]

Ralegh fatally compounded his own offence by lying. As his relationship with Bess had come under scrutiny even before he sailed for Cape Finisterre, Robert Cecil, whose antennae were twitching, had put feelers out in a letter meant to elicit a candid exchange of confidences. But when Ralegh replied, confirming that he still meant to accompany his ships, despite having ceded overall command of the expedition to Frobisher, he prevaricated, telling Cecil, 'I mean not to come away, as they say I will, for fear of a marriage and I know not what.'

If any such thing were, I would have imparted it unto yourself before any man living. And therefore, I pray, believe it not, and I beseech you to suppress what you can [in] any such malicious report. For I protest before God, there is none on the face of the earth that I would be fastened unto.[18]

It was never wise to lie to a Cecil. On 28 May, Bess's baby was brought by his nurse to Durham House, where his father dandled him on his knee for the first and possibly the only time: the child would die before a year was out. Three days later, Elizabeth had Ralegh committed to Robert Cecil's custody under house arrest. A day or so later, he was back at Durham House, in the charge of Cecil's close ally Sir George Carew. From there, Ralegh wrote melodramatic letters to anyone who would listen and staged a suitably theatrical scene for Carew in which he swore passionately that his heart would break unless he could catch a glimpse of his goddess the queen.[19]

On 3 June, Elizabeth sent Bess to live with Sir Thomas Heneage and his wife, Anne, at their house in London, near Aldgate. Heneage, Leicester's scourge in the Netherlands and now a privy councillor, could be trusted to clip the new Lady Ralegh's wings. As to how the queen intended to deal with the two impetuous lovers in the longer term, she kept her own counsel.[20]

Essex alone was willing to petition Elizabeth for Ralegh. Much of their former rivalry melted away in these months, as Essex stood as godfather to Ralegh's son and nominated Ralegh for election to the Order of the Garter, a conspicuously futile gesture but one that made his point.[21] Never really able to understand what went on inside Elizabeth's head, Essex simply could not see why Ralegh's secret life should jeopardize his career simply because she insisted on behaving as a surrogate parent to women who were old enough to make their own decisions.

Everyone was on tenterhooks. No one could predict how the queen would react next. When Mary Shelton, another woman of the Bedchamber, had made a runaway marriage with the young widower John Scudamore in 1573 or early 1574, Elizabeth had exploded. So extreme was her fury, she had physically attacked Shelton, breaking the girl's finger. As Eleanor Brydges, a maid of honour and an eye-witness, told the Earl of Rutland, 'The Queen has used Mary Shelton very ill for her marriage. She hath dealt liberally, both with blows and evil words and hath not yet granted her consent. I think in my conscience never woman bought her husband more dear than she had done.' The incident had to be hushed up, and everyone was made to pretend that a falling candlestick had caused the accident.[22] After his own bruising experience following his marriage to Douglas Shef-field, Sir Edward Stafford had declared Elizabeth to be 'angry with any love'.[23]

Stafford's view was understandably jaundiced. From the queen's perspective, what Bess had done was tantamount to perjury. When she was first admitted to the Bedchamber, she had sworn to serve her royal mistress 'faithfully and honestly', and by that Elizabeth under-stood the girl to have also promised to be chaste. If they conducted themselves in a manner she considered to be appropriate, Elizabeth could positively assist her Bedchamber servants or their offspring in their love suits. Contrary to all expectations, she would shortly inter-vene on behalf of Elizabeth Gorges, the daughter of one of her favourite attendants, Helena Snakenborg, Marchioness of North-ampton, and her second husband, Sir Thomas Gorges, who had hit a brick wall in negotiations with their future in-laws.[24]

Unfortunately, by first sleeping with and then secretly marrying Ralegh after becoming pregnant, Bess had wounded the queen at her most vulnerable points. Not only had her kinswoman gone behind her back and allowed herself to be 'vilely debauched' by Ralegh, she had dared to marry a man from whom Elizabeth expected undying devotion.[25] Ralegh, more so even than Leicester or Hatton before him, owed his career to the queen. She was filled with a sense of betrayal. To add insult to injury, barely two months before Bess's baby was born, she had settled a generous ninety-nine-year lease of Sherborne Castle and its exquisite estates on Ralegh.

Just as in Leicester's case, when he had secretly married Lettice Knollys, there was no instant royal tantrum, no hasty exchange of harsh words. Ominously, when Elizabeth managed to bridle her temper, it proved to be all the more lethal. The storm broke on Monday, 7 August, when she ordered Ralegh and Bess to be sent under guard to the Tower and placed in separate cells.[26] Writing to Anthony Bacon, Burghley's invalid nephew and a brilliant linguist who was shortly to become Essex's chief spin doctor and intelligencer, Sir Edward Stafford gloated: 'If you have anything to do with Sir Walter Ralegh, or any love to make to Mistress Throckmorton, at the Tower tomorrow you may speak with them, if the countermand come not tonight, as some think will not be, and particularly he that hath charge to send them thither.'[27]

The lovers' fate was sealed by all absence of the slightest expression of contrition. Now that Ralegh was turning forty, a contemptuous self-reliance, combined with distaste for the humiliations he felt he had to endure in pandering to the vanity of an ageing, irascible spinster, was taking over his character. Demanding pen and paper in the Tower, he turned the iconography of the Elvetham water pageant completely on its head, daring to choreograph himself explicitly in verse as the wide, restless sea and Elizabeth as the unapproachable, tyrannical Cynthia, the chimerical, vindictive moon goddess who irrationally tortures men for their honest love.[28]

For her part, Bess seemed blissfully unaware that humble submission coupled with the most grovelling apology was the only possible route to pardon and reconciliation in the eyes of the queen. Despite her many months spent in relatively close proximity to Elizabeth since her admission to the Bedchamber eight years before, she stubbornly clung to the belief that she had done nothing wrong. Writing to sympathetic friends whom she hoped would show her letter to the queen, she protested, 'I assure you truly, I never desired nor never would desire my liberty without the good liking nor advising of Sir Walter Ralegh: it is not this imprisonment, if I bought it with my life, that should make me think it long if it should do him harm to speak of my delivery.' And she signed herself, 'Ever assuredly in friendship, E.R.'[29] The initials were meant to show that she believed she had a valid marriage but were deliberately provocative, for they mimicked the queen's own cipher.

What would save Ralegh and Bess was, almost literally, the pungent scent of booty in Elizabeth's nostrils. Just five weeks after she had sent them to the Tower, she heard that a Portuguese carrack captured by Ralegh's fleet of privateers had been safely piloted into Dartmouth harbour with a prodigiously rich cargo. Already some of the loot had been siphoned off and sent to Exeter, hidden in sacks or under men's cloaks.[30] Bags of pearls and pots of aromatic musk used in perfume and as an aphrodisiac had even found their way to London. As Robert Cecil, who rode post-haste to Exeter on his way to Dartmouth, complained to Burghley, you could smell the looters a mile off. No fewer than two thousand dealers had flocked to Devon to snap up bargains. An eyewitness quipped that it was like Bartholomew Fair all over again.[31]

This time, luck seemed to be on Ralegh's side. After the splitting of his fleet, Sir John Burgh's squadron had sailed for the Azores, where they found the first of the great Portuguese carracks already within sight. When the vessel evaded him during a storm, Burgh positioned his ships so as to intercept a second carrack that was thought to be close behind. Shortly after midday on 3 August, he saw the *Madre de Dios* on the horizon, returning from Kochi, on the west coast of India. Rated at 1,600 tons and 165 feet long from prow to stern, her main mast towering 121 feet high, she was a floating castle. It took over six hundred men to handle her. With no fewer than seven decks, one above another, and two thirds of her tonnage represented by the weight of the exotic goods she was carrying, she would prove to be by far the richest prize captured by English privateers over the long course of the war.[32]

After a fierce and bloody gun battle lasting from noon until dusk, the vast ship was overwhelmed and its surviving crew forced to surrender. Ralegh's men were the first to board, and an orgy of plunder ensued. Ransacking the upper decks by candlelight, they helped themselves to the more portable and valuable cargo: gold, silver, emeralds, diamonds, rubies, pearls and amber (commonly set in amulets and thought to attract lovers). Only narrowly did they avoid a catastrophic explosion, when, bearing their candles aloft, they burst into an armoury packed with gunpowder.[33]

Over the ten or so days that followed, many of the bulkier, heavier goods, as many as could be shifted at sea, were unloaded on to ten other ships so as to lighten the carrack. With Spanish warships still

lurking off the coast of Brittany, near the Blavet estuary, it was essential that the privateers and their prize made as swift a homeward
journey as possible. Many of the smaller ships made for Plymouth
rather than Dartmouth, where much of the loot embezzled at sea,
valued at £250,000, was sold off at ridiculously low prices. Only
when Cecil, sent by the Privy Council to inventory the spoils, finally
reached the quayside at Dartmouth was the sheer volume of the haul
apparent. Among other wares, there were 537 tons of spices, 8,500
hundredweight of pepper, large chests of cloves, cinnamon and nut-
meg, fifteen tons of ebony, two enormous crosses of gold and a large
brooch studded with diamonds meant for King Philip which the
looters had missed. Other items included carpets, tapestries, silks and
fine fabrics, Chinese porcelain, hides, coconuts, frankincense, dyes
such as cochineal and indigo, ivory and elephant's teeth (ground to a
fine powder and used in the treatment of leprosy).

On Cecil's instructions, the houses of local people and inns where
the wealthier dealers lodged were raided in a concerted effort to salvage as much of the embezzled cargo as possible. His men found
jewellery, notably pearls, diamonds and an armlet of gold, and a fork
and spoon of crystal with rubies. Overall, the value of the recovered
cargo was assessed at £141,120 (£141 million today), still an astonishing sum.[34]

Ralegh's sailors, meanwhile, were running riot all over the West
Country, spending their money on drink and women. Informed that
no one but he would be able to discipline them, Elizabeth reluctantly
signed the order for his conditional release. Barely six weeks after he
had arrived at Tower Wharf and been led across a narrow drawbridge
used for important prisoners, Ralegh walked out of the Tower
through the main gateway.[35] He was escorted on his journey down to
Dartmouth by a 'keeper' – one 'Mr Blount', possibly Sir Christopher
Blount, his sworn enemy and Essex's stepfather. He claimed self-
pityingly that he was still the queen's poor captive but, to all intents
and purposes, he was now a free man.[36]

Naturally, there was more to Ralegh's release than first meets the
eye. He alone, the mastermind of the whole extraordinary venture,
could adequately explain to Robert Cecil and his officials the costs

the various investors had incurred in equipping the privateers and the share of the booty that was rightfully theirs. On the face of it, this was a simple enough task, but Ralegh knew it would not turn out that way, guessing from the outset that Elizabeth would steal a march on her fellow speculators by claiming the lion's share of the loot.[37]

He was absolutely right. Enraged at the scale of embezzlement, the queen at first contemplated seizing the whole of what remained of the fortune, and Ralegh could hardly stop her. To muzzle him, she was quite capable of threatening to frame him for theft, along with Sir John Burgh, whom she had already accused of carrying off large quantities of precious stones, amber and musk. She would be undeterred by the inconvenient fact that Ralegh had been in the Tower, and not at sea, when the worst of the thefts had taken place. His men, after all, had played a leading part in ransacking the upper decks of the carrack. It was surely therefore *his* fault that roughly two thirds of the booty (in value, if not in volume) had been so carelessly frittered away.[38]

Her greed exposed her character at its most rapacious. Remembering her searing reaction to the sending of the death warrant for Mary Queen of Scots and wary of falling foul of her in that way ever again, Burghley warned Sir John Fortescue, his deputy in the Exchequer responsible for cash flow, to advise her that, since the country was at war, she had a right by royal prerogative to allocate shares of the booty at her sole discretion. Her decision was final and 'must be the Law in the cause'. There could be no appeal.[39]

But Fortescue was decidedly uncomfortable. Describing it as a 'tickle matter', he cautioned Burghley that it would 'utterly overthrow all service if due regard were not had of my Lord of Cumberland and Sir Walter Ralegh, with the rest of the adventurers, who would never be induced to further adventure if they were not princely considered of'.[40]

The upshot was a compromise, but one weighted heavily in the queen's favour. Although, as Ralegh reminded Burghley, Elizabeth had risked only 'the tenth part' of the costs of the expedition, she now proceeded to dictate the distribution of the profits irrespective of how much individual investors had staked.[41] Whereas she had put at risk just two ships and £1,800, she awarded herself more than £70,000, or 50 per cent of the gains. Cumberland, who had risked £19,000, got his original investment back, plus a profit of £18,000, almost doubling his money.[42] The syndicate of city merchants, who had staked £6,000, received a similar rate of return. However, Ralegh, who had contributed £34,000, was handed back only his stake and a modest profit of £2,000, way out of proportion to the formula applied elsewhere. Elizabeth arrived at this figure by drastically discounting the costs of fitting out the ships he had provided, and she took no account of the £11,000 he had been forced to pay in interest charges on his borrowed money, as she did with others. At a stroke of her pen, she turned Ralegh's meagre 'profit' into a hefty loss.[43]

Still smarting from his marriage, she then banished him from Court, suspending him indefinitely from his office as Captain of the Guard. Bess was released from the Tower on 22 December, and the two retired to Sherborne to lick their wounds in time for Christmas.[44] Ralegh had bought their freedom by sacrificing between £16,000 and £32,000 of the profits Cecil calculated were due to him.[45] Anticipating this outcome some weeks before the final settlements of accounts, he joked with his customary braggadocio that this was 'more than ever any man presented Her Majesty with as yet'.[46]

If Ralegh was down, he was far from out. Debarred from Court and forced to seek a seat in Parliament as a humble burgess for the village of Mitchell in Cornwall rather than as the senior knight of the shire for Devon, he knew that his only viable route back to royal favour was to return to sea. He consoled himself after the death of his firstborn with the fact that Bess had become pregnant again: the elder of their two surviving sons would be baptized Walter, or 'Wat' for short, in Lillington parish church, a few miles south of Sherborne, on All Saints' Day in 1593.[47]

For some years, Ralegh had been preoccupied by stories circulating among Spanish conquistadors of a legendary empire known as El Dorado, ruled by a descendant of the royal line of the Incas. El Dorado was thought to be home to the mines from where the wealth of the Inca and Aztec civilizations had been sourced; it was said that there men powdered themselves with gold dust after bathing in turpentine. And with Thomas Harriot still the chief impresario of his team of technical advisers, Ralegh set him to work to draw up a new plan of exploration and discovery. A variant of the original grand strategy of 1585 that had so signally failed to impress the queen, it placed a much greater emphasis on prospecting for gold.[48]

According to legend, the lost empire lay in Guiana, on land that today is part of Venezuela and Colombia, between the mouths of the Orinoco and Amazon rivers. Hidden away deep in the tropical jungle somewhere near the source of the Orinoco was a city of gold called Manoa, whose ruler dined off gold and silver plate, had chests and trunks full of bullion and precious stones and who relaxed in a pleasure garden packed with life-sized sculptures of fishes, animals, birds, flowers, herbs and trees, all made of gold. An explorer, Don Pedro Sarmiento de Gamboa, captured by one of Ralegh's privateers, had told him of this magical place and informed him that Don António de Berrío, the governor of the Spanish colony of Trinidad, had made no fewer than three expeditions into the jungle in search of gold.[49]

Stuck at home with Bess at Sherborne, Ralegh's imagination fed his gambler's streak and persuaded him to sail to Trinidad and begin a search for El Dorado. Success would not only bring him the wealth and fame that he believed were rightly his, it would restore him to his place of honour. Bess did her best to dissuade him, even writing to Robert Cecil: 'Now sir, for the rest, I hope you will rather draw Sir Walter towards the East than help him forward toward the sunset, if any respect to men or love to him be not forgotten.'[50]

But Cecil and Lord Admiral Howard were both keen to take their cut should Ralegh be as good as his word. They bought shares in his expedition, while Ralegh amassed his own stake by selling land and borrowing £60,000. He pulled off this seemingly impossible feat at a time when his own credit was in disarray by borrowing on the security of a kinsman, the successful London financier William Sanderson.[51] Vastly overconfident, Ralegh unscrupulously milked his gullible relative, offering spurious promises of repayment. Ultimately the man was ruined.[52]

On Thursday, 6 February 1595, Ralegh sailed from Plymouth, heading for the Canary Isles with some two hundred mariners and a hundred and fifty soldiers aboard five ships. Among the soldiers was his nephew John, Sir Humphrey Gilbert's son. Six weeks later, they all reached Trinidad, where Ralegh launched a night-time commando raid on the sleepy Spanish garrison and captured none other than Berrío himself. By wining and dining, charming and beguiling his exalted prisoner, Ralegh coaxed from him invaluable intelligence that he believed would enable him to succeed where others had failed.[53]

Navigating a route through the shallow, sandy channels of the delta in cockleshell rowing boats, Ralegh led a hundred of his fittest men up the crocodile-infested Orinoco, battling a blazing sun, torrential showers and adverse currents. In a journey fraught with peril, braving unrelenting attacks from snakes and insects and with their supplies of food and clean water fast diminishing, his party travelled some 250 miles inland, convincing themselves that they were about to become as rich as Croesus. Although Ralegh did find what he believed to be gold-bearing rock on a cliff face not far from the River Caroní, a tributary of the Orinoco, he lacked the tools needed to break it. It was only on his return that he discovered that many of the stones he and his men were able to gather would prove to be disappointingly valueless.[54]

Elizabeth did not think about Ralegh much while he was away, but he thought of her constantly. On arrival in Trinidad, he had shown the local chiefs her portrait while he sang her praises. And in an extraordinary encounter on the south bank of the Orinoco, some three miles to the east of its junction with the Caroní, he pitched a tent and conversed through an interpreter with the Orenoqueponi King Topiawari, declaring (disingenuously) that a Virgin Queen, no less, had sent him to protect the indigenous people from the atrocities of the cruel Spaniards.[55]

Despite all his bravery and derring-do, Ralegh returned empty-handed to Plymouth in September to be greeted with delight by Bess alone.[56] From Sherborne, an estate he had been so solicitous to acquire but which he now described as 'this desolate place', he urged Robert Cecil to sponsor a follow-up expedition in which both men could recoup their losses.[57] He sent Cecil a lengthy report that he had written either on his return voyage or shortly after landing at Plymouth. A thrilling action-adventure story surpassing anything written in a later age by Rudyard Kipling or Henry Rider Haggard, it was a heady mixture of fact and fiction. Published early the next year in a carefully edited version overseen by Cecil under the title *The Discoverie of the Large, Rich and Bewtiful Empire of Guiana*, it was, to all practical effects, the prospectus for a sale of shares in a second venture.[58]

In a patriotic appeal intended for the queen's ears, Ralegh urged Cecil never to forget that, unless more were done to make England's war effort self-financing, King Philip would prove to be invincible and the Protestant cause throughout Europe would be crushed. 'We must not look to maintain war upon the revenues of England,' he fervently exclaimed.[59]

But Elizabeth's ears were shut fast. Only with the arrival of sudden, terrifying news that a second *Gran Armada* was in an advanced state of preparation and that Calais was under attack by Spanish forces would Ralegh's career rise, phoenix-like, from the ashes. Then, like the chameleon he had undoubtedly become, he would, once more, be able to reinvent himself and return to the El Dorado of her favour.

13. Conspiring against the Queen

From sunrise until four o'clock in the afternoon of Thursday, 28 February 1594, an event took place at the Guildhall in London that had tongues wagging all over England. Dr Roderigo Lopez, for the past twelve years Elizabeth's chief physician, stood trial before a panel of fifteen special commissioners on a charge of plotting to poison her. For this heinous act of treachery, he had been offered the vast sum of 50,000 crowns or gold escudos (worth roughly £18 million now).[1] Asked how he would plead after the long indictment was read out, he replied, 'Not guilty'. Twelve jurors, all citizens of London, were then sworn in and the lawyers for the prosecution began to make their case.

Seven or eight hours later, the jurors were asked to deliver their verdict. 'Guilty of high treason' came the instant reply. Lopez, who was denied legal representation, as custom in treason trials dictated, was asked if he knew any reason why the court should not proceed to judgement. He replied starkly, 'I have nothing to say that I've not said before.' He had been closely questioned in the Tower, and everything he and the witnesses in the case had said had been repeated in court.

Without further delay, the prosecution asked the court to deliver its sentence. Lopez was condemned to be led away back to his cell in the Tower, and from there to be dragged on a hurdle to the gallows at Tyburn, where he was to be hanged, drawn and quartered.[2] Except that Elizabeth halted the execution the day before it was due to take place. As late as the beginning of June, he was still alive. Why the delay? Did the ageing queen believe her doctor was innocent, or was she finally losing her touch, unable to decide whom to believe, Lopez or his accusers?

The baptized son of a converso Jew who had risen to become King John III of Portugal's chief physician, Roderigo Lopez had graduated from the University of Coimbra, famous for its teaching of the use of Arabic and Asian medicines and strong drugs. Fluent in five languages, he had fled to London to escape from the hated Inquisition when he was in his mid-thirties, shortly after Elizabeth's accession.

14. One of the new documents showing Elizabeth suing abjectly for peace as late as 20 June 1588, a month after the Armada had set sail

15. The cipher used by Elizabeth's peace commissioners at Bourbourg in 1588 to report their negotiations with the Duke of Parma's representatives

16. Portrait of a man often said to be Sir Francis Drake,
by Isaac Oliver, c.1590

17. Robert Devereux, Earl of Essex, depicted as 'The Young Man among the Roses', by Nicholas Hilliard, *c.*1588

18. Robert Devereux, Earl of Essex, depicted with the spade-shaped beard he grew in 1596 at Cádiz, in a sketch by Isaac Oliver that would become a pattern for engravers

19. Sir Walter Ralegh, showing the battle for Cádiz in the background, attributed to William Segar. Ralegh carries a cane, a sign of a 'grievous blow' he suffered to his leg during the fight, *c.*1598

20. The 'Armada Portrait' of Elizabeth, the Woburn Abbey version,
circle of George Gower, *c.*1588

21. Elizabeth aged fifty-nine, by Isaac Oliver. This image was intended to provide a face pattern for engravers, hence its seemingly unfinished state, 1592

22. Elizabeth's letter of instructions, with her famous official signature at its head, to Lord Willoughby, the Earl of Leicester's successor in the Netherlands, concerning the towns of Dordrecht and Geertruidenberg, 30 March 1588

23. Robert Vaughan's posthumous portrait of Robert Dudley, Earl of Leicester, 1588, with background scenes of the defeat of the Armada and of the Battle of Zutphen

24. Thomas Cockson's engraving of Robert Devereux, Earl of Essex, 1600, with background scenes alluding to events at Cádiz and in the Azores, Rouen and Ireland. Essex is controversially acclaimed as 'Virtue's honour, Wisdom's nature, Grace's servant, Mercy's love, God's elected'

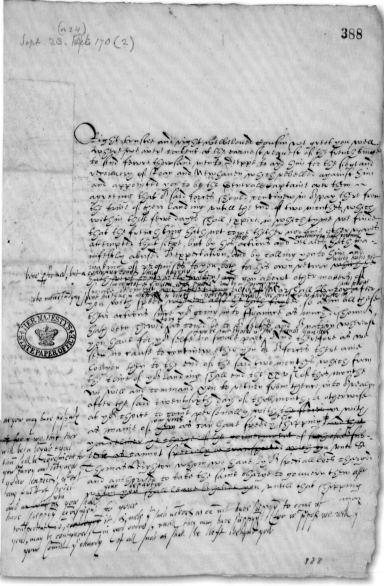

25. A draft, heavily corrected by Burghley, of one of Elizabeth's letters to the
Earl of Essex, recalling him from Rouen. The letter goes on to instruct Essex to
write to Henry IV to tell him 'how sorry you are to have so great a part to your
own disgrace'. The queen then snipes that Essex should understand the reasons
for her dissatisfaction 'if you be not senseless', 23 September 1591

Conforming outwardly in religion by attending his local parish church but reputedly faithful to Judaism in secret, Lopez was appointed house physician at St Bartholomew's Hospital in London and quickly won a reputation as a society doctor – one of several unsubstantiated allegations was that he performed illegal abortions.[3] Married to Sara Añes, the daughter of the queen's grocer, who was also of Portuguese Jewish descent, he rented a tenement in the parish of St Andrew's, Holborn.[4]

With the help of an anonymous celebrity patient, who was almost certainly the Earl of Leicester, Lopez received a grant of denization and became a naturalized Englishman. Soon, Walsingham was another of his patients. And, in 1581, Elizabeth appointed Lopez as her own chief physician at a salary of £50 a year. He was now one of very few men allowed into her Bedchamber and the only one allowed to see her without a wig or cosmetics. When he was accused of plotting the queen's assassination, he was living in some style with his wife and daughter in a house in Mountjoy Inn, near Aldgate, where Elizabeth's great-grandmother Margaret Beaufort had once lodged.[5]

While, however, Lopez was well known by his Portuguese friends to be 'a man in great credit with the queen', he was up to his neck in the murky world of politics and espionage.[6] When Dom António sought asylum also in 1581, Lopez petitioned Leicester to help get him into England and then acted as his informal ambassador and financial agent.[7] Four years later, when Dom António fell sick during a visit to the West Country, Elizabeth ordered Lopez, then attending her at Nonsuch Palace, to ride post-haste to Plymouth to do what he could for him.[8] But after the fiasco of Drake and Norris's bungled attack on Lisbon in 1589, Elizabeth largely went cold on Dom António, who was forced to live in poverty in Windsor before moving to France to eke out a living on a meagre pension. As his prospects grew dimmer, his followers began to melt away. Some even put out feelers to King Philip, offering their services to a man they had hitherto denounced as a vile usurper.

From Burghley's perspective, the situation was threatening, but also an opportunity. The opportunity lay in the relative ease with which the Portuguese could be recruited as unofficial English agents, or better still as counter-spies, working for him; the risk was that they might become Philip's spies or begin selling information gleaned from Elizabeth's courtiers or privy councillors.

Lopez, who wisely never put anything in writing if it could possibly be avoided, began his espionage career in earnest in 1589, when he began feeding Walsingham information on Spanish intentions after the failure of the Armada.[9] Using the code name the Merchant, he introduced Burghley to the shadowy circle around a fellow Portuguese exile and head of the Jewish community in London, the physician Hector Nuñez. Among them was Manuel de Andrada, a close confidant of Dom António based in London, who was ostensibly loyal to the pretender but was actually a double agent regularly in touch with Bernardino de Mendoza, Philip's ambassador in Paris.[10]

By 1591, even as Burghley lobbied Elizabeth to allow the Earl of Essex's expedition to Normandy, it was already clear that the costs of the long war with Spain were fast spiralling out of control. Elizabeth's drawn-out peace negotiations of 1588 with the Duke of Parma, abandoned only once it was known in England that Philip had ordered his Armada to set sail, had made a deep impression on Burghley. Everything that had happened since then had confirmed his belief that, deep down, the queen still wanted peace. He therefore decided to do the unthinkable: to enter into clandestine negotiations with Philip on his own account – just in case. And the Portuguese exiles were the ideal agents to make such secret overtures.[11]

Andrada travelled from London to Madrid on his way to the Escorial, using the code name David, in the spring of 1591. Peddling Burghley's line that Elizabeth wanted a general peace, he secured an audience with Philip.[12] In a vivid account, Andrada described the sixty-four-year-old king, whose hand he was invited to kiss, as being tormented with arthritis and sitting in a black velvet chair in which his attendants shuttled him about.[13] But, predictably, Philip was interested in extending the hope of peace only to lull Elizabeth into a false sense of security while he rearmed. At a subsequent interview, two of his closest advisers, Cristóbal de Moura and Juan de Idiáquez, both hawks renowned for condoning assassinations, promised Andrada a generous reward if he would eliminate Dom António, either by killing him or by arranging for him to be kidnapped.

At the second of these interviews, Andrada – purely, as he later claimed to Burghley, to 'sound out' Philip's inclinations – asked what might be available should someone be willing to assassinate Elizabeth. De Moura answered warily, but to point Andrada in the right direction he (or just possibly, Philip; the sources differ) gave him a gold ring set with a diamond and a large ruby worth over £100. This came as a gift for Dr Lopez or his daughter as a token of the Spanish king's high esteem. Already, it seems, Lopez was a name to conjure with at Philip's Court.[14]

Since Andrada meant to sell his services to the highest bidder, it is likely that he secured these interviews by offering to double-cross Burghley. But things went badly awry. His ship foundered off the coast of Saint-Malo on his return journey to London and he was forced to make his way overland through France before hitching a lift at Le Havre on a Flemish sloop. Intercepted and searched by three of Henry IV's patrol vessels near Dieppe, he attracted the attention of Ottywell Smith, an English merchant driven out of Rouen by the Leaguers, who was one of Burghley's most reliable informants. Writing on 6 July 1591, Smith warned the Lord Treasurer that Andrada had been caught carrying a bundle of highly incriminating documents, along with letters of credit to receive money from Philip in Flanders. And this despite professing himself loyal to the queen.[15]

On landing at Rye, on the south coast of England, Andrada was quickly arrested. He immediately wrote to Burghley, pleading to be called to account only by him or 'some other person whom Her Majesty hath great trust in'.[16] Burghley sent his servant Thomas Mills, accompanied by Lopez, to question Andrada and search his luggage.[17] Then, in the second week in August, Burghley made what would turn out to be a costly error. He himself met Andrada.[18] It was a short meeting. Andrada falsely reported that Philip had agreed to the idea of a general peace in principle, but Burghley did not believe him: he had just read the documents confiscated at Dieppe.[19]

Covering his tracks for fear he would be in trouble for his unauthorized diplomacy, Burghley sought an audience with Elizabeth. Carefully minimizing his role in the proceedings, he reported disingenuously that Andrada had arrived unexpectedly, claiming to be sent by Philip to make overtures for peace. What should he do? Somewhat bemused, the queen ordered Burghley to send Thomas Mills to put fresh, more detailed interrogatories to the now imprisoned Andrada, to which the double agent was to give written answers, either in French or Italian, but not in Portuguese, which neither she nor Burghley could read.[20]

Eventually released from prison and put under surveillance, Andrada went to lodge with Lopez, but on 24 April 1593 he slipped away from London late in the evening and fled to Calais and then Brussels. He would never return.[21] He was spotted at Vlissingen in December and in Amsterdam shortly afterwards, still posing as one of Dom António's diplomats but in reality fully exposed for what he had long ago become: a dangerous spy in Philip's pay. The one outstanding niggle in Burghley's mind was that Lopez had been far too friendly with him and might have been told of Burghley's secret overtures to Philip. It was a worrying loose end.[22]

The sensational accusation that the queen's chief physician was a traitor would be levelled not by Burghley but by a triumphant Earl of Essex, making his debut as a serious politician. It took him a discouragingly long time to hit this mark, since, after the debacle of the scaling ladders at the siege of Rouen, his career had languished in the doldrums. In the twenty or so months since his return from France, Elizabeth had chiefly used him as a stage prop at official ceremonies such as the reception of visiting ambassadors.[23]

To give him credibility as a co-host, she permitted him to occupy Leicester's vacant lodgings at her palaces and to move into Leicester House on the Strand, which he renamed Essex House. She loaned him furniture (all his stepfather's possessions and artworks had been auctioned off) and even ordered her bailiffs to give him the keys to Leicester's country retreat at Wanstead. But she ignored all his pleas for patronage and career advancement for himself and his friends.[24]

On account of the plague, Elizabeth celebrated Christmas 1593 with a much-reduced Court. She moved from Windsor Castle to Hampton Court shortly after finishing her translation of *The Consolation of Philosophy*, but she was still suffering bouts of depression. When Robert Carey arrived on Boxing Day, he found the lords and ladies dancing, as usual, in the Presence Chamber but the queen in a bad mood and refusing to leave her Bedchamber.[25] Forced to emerge on Twelfth Night to receive Bernard of Anhalt, the younger brother of Prince Christian of Anhalt, who had commanded Henry's German *Reiter* at the siege of Rouen, she watched a play in the early evening and stayed up to see the dancing afterwards until one in the morning.[26] She 'appeared there in a high throne', as an eyewitness, the spy Anthony Standen, one of Walsingham's shadier veterans, reported, 'richly adorned, and as beautiful . . . as ever I saw her'. Beside her, tall, svelte and clean-shaven, apart from his pointed moustache, stood the Earl of Essex, 'with whom she often devised in sweet and favourable manner'.[27]

Standen's report is sometimes misread to mean that a sexually frustrated, sexagenarian spinster openly flirted with Essex, a man less than half her age, kissing or caressing him.[28] Lytton Strachey's entire theory that 'her heart melted with his flatteries, and, as she struck him lightly on the neck with her long fingers, her whole being was suffused with a lasciviousness that could hardly be defined' depends on this solitary reference.[29]

But 'to devise' in Tudor speech normally means 'to plan, contrive, design, converse', not to kiss or caress. It can also mean 'consider, scan, survey, examine, look at attentively', and something along these lines is likely to be what Standen had in mind. Undoubtedly, Elizabeth liked having Essex around her. She needed the reassurance of his attentions. He made her feel young again, but, for all her attachment to him, he was not like his stepfather, whom she had several times kissed or fondled in public. Only recently, she had quarrelled violently with Essex, which was hardly surprising, as the Court was ablaze with rumours that he, too, had become Dr Lopez's patient and was being treated for a highly embarrassing venereal disease.[30]

Most likely, she enjoyed dangling him on a string, forcing him to dance attendance on her. We do not know what they spoke about that evening, but this was almost exactly the moment when Essex began lobbying her to appoint his new confidant and adviser, the brilliant forensic lawyer and polymath Francis Bacon,* to the sensitive post of Queen's Attorney, which was about to be vacated by Sir

---

* The younger brother of Anthony Bacon, who by now had become Essex's chief intelligencer.

Thomas Egerton. If indeed he raised the topic that evening, she would have answered him evasively. She had no intention of promoting Bacon. She was too irked with him, because, posing as a taxpayers' champion, he had dared to criticize the scale of her war taxation in Parliament.[31]

Keen to advance his bid for power and influence, Essex concluded that only a spectacular intelligence coup would convince Elizabeth that he could beat Burghley and Robert Cecil at their own game. Some ten weeks earlier, he had heard whispers from those still loyal to Dom António that Lopez, coaxed by Andrada, had offered to kill the queen for a large sum of money in some sort of ingeniously undetectable way.[32] To advance his plan, Lopez was said to be in secret communication with King Philip's advisers via yet another Portuguese double agent, Esteban Ferreira da Gama, whom Essex had tracked down and questioned. The Earl did not yet have much by way of proof, but he suspected a conspiracy. He remembered that he had spotted Lopez in furtive conversation with da Gama earlier that summer at Wanstead.[33] And, after all, where political assassinations were concerned, Philip had form: memories of the brutal murder of William of Orange were still fresh.

It was typical of Essex that he should have fired his ammunition prematurely. A few days after Twelfth Night, having notified Cecil and Lord Admiral Howard of his suspicions, he marched into Elizabeth's Privy Chamber and accused Dr Lopez of hatching a plot to assassinate her. When he burst in, febrile with excitement, she thought he had gone mad. She scolded him witheringly, calling him a 'rash and temerarious youth'. He had no business, she said, to venture into a matter 'which he could not prove', against a man 'whose innocence she knew well enough'.[34]

She even accused him of levelling this accusation maliciously, to take revenge for the rumours of his venereal disease. The good doctor, she said, had already been questioned once by Burghley and his son. Cecil had searched Lopez's house, but nothing incriminating could be found. Essex, she fumed, had acted presumptuously. His unwelcome intervention had put her honour at stake: she must now see justice done, and he should leave her presence, go home and recover his senses.

Returning to the Strand, Essex locked himself in his study, slamming the door. There he sulked for over an hour before retiring to his bedchamber, where he remained for two days. Only when he had calmed down did he realize that all was not lost. When questioned, Lopez had said that yes, he had indeed dabbled in what might look like a conspiracy with Andrada and Ferreira da Gama, but he was simply out to recover from King Philip the considerable sums he had personally spent on behalf of the Portuguese pretender, who was unable to repay a penny. Burghley and his son were convinced that Lopez was innocent. As Cecil jotted down in a brief note to his father, 'In Lopez's folly, I see no point of treason intended to the queen, but a readiness to make some gain to the hurt of Dom António.'[35]

But Essex was convinced of the doctor's guilt. Since Walsingham's death, he had recruited several of his father-in-law's spies and cryptographers, notably Thomas Phelippes, the man who had infamously added the ciphered postscript to the 'bloody letter' of Mary Queen of Scots. Phelippes had been inveigled into working for Essex by Francis Bacon and William Sterrell, an expert at penetrating the networks of English Catholic exiles in Flanders.[36]

Sterrell (whose aliases were Henry St Main, Mr Franklin and Robert Robinson) had long been on the track of a cell of Catholic exiles who were promoting the idea of a false peace with Elizabeth so that they could kill her. At the time, the trail had led nowhere, causing Essex and Phelippes huge embarrassment, but after a courier for one of Sterrell's informers chanced on a suggestive scrap of evidence during a trip to Antwerp, one Manuel Luis Tinoco, a Portuguese spy, friend of Andrada and close associate of Ferreira da Gama, came firmly into the spotlight.[37]

Tinoco, Phelippes confirmed, had sneaked out of England in July 1593 for the Continent, supposedly on a mission for Dom António.[38] Hoping to keep himself safely under the radar, he went to see Philip's senior advisers in Brussels, taking with him documents from Andrada. To secure a passport from Burghley for the return journey to Dover, he pretended to have recently escaped from prison in Morocco and claimed he had important information to offer.[39] Granted a passport shortly after Christmas, Tinoco made his return around the third week of January 1594, when he was intercepted on the road to London by an increasingly vigilant Essex.[40]

When searched, he was found to be carrying letters from Brussels addressed to da Gama, ordering him to take over from Andrada the organization of a plot to kill Elizabeth.[41] The letters confirmed that King Philip had agreed to the assassination, which Lopez had told da Gama in their furtive conversation at Wanstead he was willing to do for the sum of 50,000 crowns by poisoning the queen's syrup.[42] Tinoco also carried letters of credit, to be shown to Lopez 'for his assurance', which proved that the ever-cautious Philip required the bounty to be paid by merchants in Antwerp, so as not to be attributable to him and on no account before the deed was done. This evidence was damning.[43]

On Monday, 28 January, Essex wrote in jubilation to Anthony Bacon:

> I have discovered a most dangerous and desperate treason. The point
> of conspiracy was Her Majesty's death. The executioner should have
> been Dr Lopez; the manner by poison. This I have so followed, as I
> will make it appear as clear as the noon day.[44]

At first, Lopez was detained in Essex's custody at Essex House, where he was guarded by the Earl's steward, Sir Gelly Meyrick. Held in isolation while Tinoco and Ferreira da Gama were also arrested, the doctor was left to stew until Essex had compiled a full dossier of charges.

When Elizabeth was shown the dossier on Tuesday, the stakes rose considerably. She reluctantly allowed Essex to transfer all three prisoners to the Tower. Questioned by Essex, Tinoco now revealed that Cristóbal de Moura had previously sent Lopez a valuable jewel (the ring set with a diamond and a ruby). He even explained the meaning of some crucial code words in a seemingly innocent document that had so far baffled Essex. 'Musk' and 'Amber' referred not to imported goods but to a projected Spanish attack on the English fleet; the 'Pearl' was Elizabeth, and 'the price of the Pearls' meant the sum that was to be paid for poisoning her.[45]

Shortly after dawn the next day, Essex and Robert Cecil began interrogating Lopez. Peppering his admissions 'with oaths, protestations and profane speeches', the doctor protested that his part in the conspiracy was no more than a feint designed to 'cozen' (cheat) the Spanish king so as to recoup his disbursements on Dom António's behalf. He had never meant to kill Elizabeth. It was common knowledge, he said, that she never touched syrups: she or her Bedchamber servants had only to be asked for confirmation and all would become clear. And it is true, Elizabeth never contradicted Lopez's claim.[46]

Essex, however, was convinced that Lopez was lying and he was determined to prove it. The doctor admitted that he had indeed been sent a jewel by de Moura, which he claimed his wife had sold for half its true value.[47] He also disarmingly confirmed that he had 'caused da Gama to offer his services to the king of Spain' for a large sum of money – Anthony Bacon considered this alone to be enough to hang him.[48]

But if Essex believed this investigation would provide him with an opportunity to unseat Burghley and his son from their dominant positions of influence, he was sorely mistaken. No sooner had he shown the queen his dossier proving that her chief physician had a definite case to answer than – to cut him down to size – she spitefully warned him that he could expect to lose out to Burghley in the competition to nominate the next Queen's Attorney. She then taunted him further, saying she was listening intently to her chief minister's request that Cecil should be given the lion's share of Walsingham's old position as her principal secretary, the very role that Essex so desperately coveted for himself.[49]

To add insult to injury, Robert Cecil dropped the veneer of civility. In a coach they shared on their way back from the Tower to the Strand after interrogating Lopez, he goaded Essex, gloating that Elizabeth intended to appoint a new Queen's Attorney very shortly and asking him if he had any suggestions. Tetchily, Essex replied that he wondered why Cecil should ask him this question, since it was common knowledge that he was backing Francis Bacon. 'Good Lord,' said Cecil insouciantly. 'I wonder your Lordship should go about to spend your strength in so unlikely and impossible a matter.' He went on to suggest that it was as simple as ABC to know that Elizabeth meant to appoint Burghley's candidate, Sir Edward Coke, Bacon's rival and the more obvious choice – as indeed she soon did.[50]

★ ★ ★

Essex may have been wounded by these encounters, but he was far
from conceding defeat. During February, Burghley's attacks of gout
had once more confined him to bed. This time, the severe, unrelenting pain compounded his sense of vulnerability: a cascade of
revelations from da Gama and Tinoco, who turned queen's evidence,
dramatically increased the risk that his secret meeting with Andrada
three years before would become more widely known.[51] Burghley
was gradually reconciling himself to the fact that, almost fifty years
since he had begun to serve the teenage Elizabeth, he was finally losing his grip. Too weak to scribble more than a few lines, let alone
ride, he left his reputation in the hands of his son, who dashed to and
fro between the Tower and Elizabeth's Privy Chamber clutching
papers, passing through the Presence Chamber 'like a blind man, not
looking upon any'.[52]

What Essex always considered to be his biggest breakthrough in
the case came on 18 February, when da Gama confessed to having
received two letters from Lopez, dictated from the doctor's own lips,
both addressed to de Moura in Madrid. Da Gama had undertaken to
see them delivered, and their contents, as he carefully described them,
tied the assassination plot securely to Lopez.[53] Five days later, Tinoco
confirmed that, when he had met Philip's advisers in Brussels, they
had assured him that Lopez had 'offered and bound himself to kill the
queen with poison'. 'All this', he said, 'I certify to have passed in great
truth and certainty, and do affirm it under mine oath.'[54]

On 25 February, Essex interrogated Lopez for the last time. The
prisoner was threatened with the rack and told to tell the whole
truth. He admitted 'for the discharge of his conscience' that he had
plotted with da Gama to poison the queen for 50,000 crowns but
stuck resolutely to his story that he had never intended to go through
with it, since his sole aim was to cozen King Philip. On this point, he
refused to budge, and there the matter rested, as Essex was only too
well aware that Elizabeth would never allow him to torture her
trusted physician. Gossip in the streets of London held that Lopez
had been tortured 'divers times upon the rack', but this was untrue.
He was merely shown 'the instruments of torture' in an attempt to
terrify him into revealing all he knew.[55]

When, despite lacking Lopez's signed confession to a charge of conspiracy to murder, Essex declared his belief that he had enough evidence to convince a jury, Cecil, surprisingly, agreed. Although he and his father still privately maintained that Lopez was innocent, they intended now to do their utmost to send the doctor speedily to the gallows. Far from intervening to save the man's life in the interests of justice, they wanted him dead before Essex, who was getting too close for comfort, unearthed any trace of Burghley's clandestine peace diplomacy. On Burghley's advice, Elizabeth even allowed Essex and Cecil to sit in judgement at the Guildhall as two of the fifteen trial commissioners, despite their prominent role in compiling the case for the prosecution.[56]

At Lopez's trial, the Solicitor-General, Sir Edward Coke, put on a bravura performance, his eye firmly fixed on his imminent promotion to Queen's Attorney:

> For the poisoning of Her Highness, this miscreant, perjured, murdering traitor and Jewish doctor hath been proved a dearer traitor than Judas himself . . . The bargain was made, the price agreed upon and he did undertake it. The fact was deferred but until payment of the money was assured. The letters of credit for his assurance were sent, and before they came to his hand . . . God most mercifully and miraculously revealed and prevented it.[57]

Further spiced with anti-Semitism in the shape of a report that Lopez's 'conversion' to Christianity had never been more than a sham, Coke's rhetoric all but guaranteed a guilty verdict.[58]

Once the verdict was pronounced, Cecil lost no time in ordering Sir Thomas Windebank, the senior clerk standing in as the queen's confidential secretary, to inform her that while 'the vile Jew' had pleaded not guilty, 'the most substantial jury that I have seen have found him guilty in the highest degree of all treasons, and judgement [is] passed against him with an applause of all the world.' Cecil clearly believed that Elizabeth would need this depth of reassurance to be convinced that her doctor should be sent to the gallows.[59]

Breaking any promises to treat da Gama and Tinoco leniently in exchange for turning queen's evidence, Cecil resolved to convict and hang them, too. Interrogated afresh in early March, they had little more to say, and a trial date was set for the 14th.[60] Da Gama pleaded not guilty, but changed his plea when confronted by the prosecution's evidence. Tinoco pleaded guilty from the outset, then asked for mercy. Both were sentenced to death 'for the highest and most horrible and detestable treasons', though quite how they could have been considered to be traitors when they were Portuguese and had never, unlike Lopez, been naturalized or sworn to Elizabeth's service was left unexplained. They were returned to the Tower, where they were to await their final journey with Lopez to Tyburn.[61]

And yet nothing happened. Far from being hanged in the usual way, all three prisoners were alive and well a month later, safely in the custody of Sir Michael Blount, the Lieutenant of the Tower.[62] Uneasy about the verdicts, Elizabeth refused to give her final assent to the men's deaths. At one point, she set a date and time, the morning of Friday, 19 April at nine o'clock, but at the last moment she changed her mind and ordered the executions to be postponed indefinitely.[63]

Her indecision caused consternation. Lord Buckhurst, the privy councillor who in 1587 had dared to tell her that she would end up looking like a murderer if she summarily hanged the unfortunate William Davison, at once protested to Cecil. Only two days were left, he reminded him, before the authority of the fifteen trial commissioners would lapse. If the doctor and his co-conspirators were not hanged by then, new commissioners would have to be appointed and all three trials begun again.[64]

Elizabeth's thinking at last became clearer. As Cecil reported it, she had forbidden Sir Michael Blount from allowing the condemned men to be taken from their cells to execution until she instructed otherwise. She still believed in Lopez's innocence: to save the life of her doctor, she would use her royal prerogative to stay the due process of law. This, a worried Cecil reported, would create a public outcry, as Londoners were baying for blood.[65]

Slyly, Cecil now persuaded the judges of the Court of Queen's Bench to extend the powers of the trial commissioners on their own authority.[66] But Elizabeth was too quick for him. When he began a fresh move to have the condemned men sent to the gallows, she stepped in again, ordering Blount not to allow Lopez to be executed on pain of dire punishment, however many death warrants he received.[67]

Burghley and Cecil broke the deadlock in an underhand way. Joining forces with Essex and commandeering Lord Hunsdon and Lord Admiral Howard, whose opinions on sensitive matters the queen always respected, they confronted Elizabeth on 1 June at Lady Anne Gresham's house at Osterley in Middlesex, where she had just begun her summer progress. When they all insisted, one by one, that the law be put into effect, Elizabeth yielded to the principle. But that was the easy bit. She did not, at the same time, countermand her restraining order to Blount.[68]

To circumvent this final hurdle, Burghley and Cecil used a legal trick. Applying on 4 June to the judges of the Court of Queen's Bench, they secured writs ordering Lopez, da Gama and Tinoco to be brought into Westminster Hall within ten days to answer certain questions. When on the 7th the prisoners appeared, they were first asked if they had anything to add to what they had said before, which none did.[69] No one seriously imagined that they would: the objective was simply to take them out of Blount's jurisdiction. They were then remanded back to prison, but this time they were not sent to the Tower. Cecil, Burghley and Essex had colluded in advance with the most senior judges to make sure that the condemned men would instead be sent to the Marshalsea, where no restraining order from the queen was in force.[70]

The very next morning, the condemned men were frogmarched to London Bridge and dragged from there to Tyburn. On the scaffold, Lopez vehemently protested his innocence, declaring that he loved the queen and Dom António as much as he loved Jesus Christ. Coming from a man who was universally believed to be a practising Jew and almost certainly was, his words only excited the ribald jeers of the angry crowd.[71] It can be no coincidence that, in these very months, London's best-known theatrical impresario, Philip Henslowe, staged multiple performances of a revival of Christopher Marlowe's *The Jew of Malta*.* With its dramatic scenes of poisoning by a Jew who dissembled in religion and possessed a secret knowledge of drugs very closely

* The theatres reopened in April and May 1594 after the plague.

akin to that taught at the University of Coimbra, the play packed out the Rose Theatre for weeks. A rough draft of Shakespeare's *Merchant of Venice* may even have been sketched out around this time.[72]

Elizabeth had hoped to spare her chief physician's life. Outmanoeuvred by her councillors for the first time since the execution of Mary Queen of Scots, she must have been privately exasperated, but she chose not to exact reprisals. Whatever Lopez had meant to her, he was not a queen. She could console herself with the fact that, after all, he might, conceivably, have been guilty. For among Essex's more tantalizing discoveries was a report that Lopez was planning to retire to Istanbul and had already made arrangements with his Jewish in-laws there to purchase a house.[73]

Essex appeared to be the victor in this affair. By unmasking what had all the hallmarks of a dangerous conspiracy and driving its architects to the gallows, he had proved he was a force to be reckoned with. He had shown to his own satisfaction his mastery of intelligence matters, oblivious to the fact that Burghley and his son had deliberately allowed themselves to be outflanked on this occasion. Now it seemed that nothing could stop him from succeeding Burghley as the queen's chief minister. A meteoric career as a statesman, as well as a military man, would surely open up before him.

But would Elizabeth let him and, even if she did, could he restrain his ambition sufficiently to work harmoniously with his fellow privy councillors and so retain her trust? Or would his hunger for glory bring him to the brink of catastrophe?

14. Games of Thrones

While the headstrong Earl of Essex was busy interrogating Dr Lopez, an event of the utmost significance was taking place at Stirling Castle in Scotland. Shortly after three o'clock on the morning of Tuesday, 19 February 1594, Prince Henry, the first child of Anne of Denmark and James VI, was born. In Edinburgh, bonfires were lit in the streets and church bells rung. To demonstrate their loyalty and fidelity, the town council ordered that all good citizens should make their way to the Kirk to join in a public service of thanksgiving to God for sending them a male heir to guarantee the survival and stability of the Scottish monarchy.[1]

South of the border, the repercussions were very different. Whereas Anne and James now had a healthy son, Elizabeth was a barren spinster. As she had no biological heir, the Tudor dynasty would die with her. Since the ratification of the Anglo-Scottish league in July 1586, James, naïvely, had drawn what seemed to him to be the obvious inference that she would nominate him to succeed her. But when he failed to curb to her satisfaction the actions of his favourite, the Earl of Huntly, whom Burghley's spies caught plotting to assist a Spanish invasion of the British Isles for a second time in 1592, she slashed his annual pension from £5,000 to £2,000, throwing her intentions into doubt.[2]

She then went one step further and began talking openly to her privy councillors of reneging on her league with James.[3] So angry with him was she for his failure to call Huntly to account that, three days before Christmas in 1593, she berated him in the manner of a bossy nanny:

> To see so much, I rue my sight that views the evident spectacle of a seduced king, defying counsel and wry-guiding kingdoms. My love to your good and hate of your ruin breeds my heedful regard of your surest safety. If I neglected you, I could wink at your worst and yet

withstand my enemies' drifts. But be you persuaded by beguilers, I will advise you void of all guile and will not stick to tell you that if you tread the path you go in, I will pray for you but leave you to your harms.[4]

He was, she railed, leading himself and all who depended on him to damnation.

She had already lived longer than any English monarch since Edward III. And yet, to Burghley's despair, she still could not bring herself psychologically to name her successor. In fact, she refused as obstinately now as she had while Mary Queen of Scots was alive. Her reasons were the same: she believed that identifying a successor by name would hasten her own death. With painful memories of the threats she had faced in Mary Tudor's reign still prominent in her mind, she had once stated, 'I know the inconstancy of the people of England, how they ever mislike the present government and have their eyes fixed upon that person that is next to succeed.'[5]

One of her most celebrated mantras was 'Think you that I could love my own winding sheet?'[6] And no one could forget the ongoing tribulations of the unfortunate Peter Wentworth, who had come close to asking her to do just that.[7] A noted parliamentarian and pres-byterian sympathizer on cordial terms with Burghley, he had first put his thoughts on the succession down on paper shortly after the execution of Mary Queen of Scots. He fell foul of Elizabeth in the summer of 1591, when he started lobbying Burghley and his friends to persuade the queen to summon a special session of Parliament in which all titles and claims to the succession could be discussed. Although he did not say as much, Wentworth clearly envisaged a scenario in which Parliament would confirm the succession of a staunchly Protestant candidate, removing the decision from Eliza-beth's hands. The question was: who?[8]

Privately, Burghley agreed that the queen should settle the succes-sion, but he had burned his fingers so many times on this explosive issue that he refused to intercede. Wentworth recorded the chief minister's excuse: Elizabeth, he said, wanted all discussion of 'that question' to be suppressed 'so long as ever she lived'.[9] Merely men-tioning the topic forced her to confront the prospect of her own mortality and the devastating question of who would wear her crown and jewels once she was laid in her coffin. Ever since her brush with smallpox in 1562, she had lived in the knowledge that her councillors were serving her with an eye firmly fixed on a future without her. Even her beloved 'Sweet Robin' had kept in touch clandestinely with Mary Queen of Scots, sneaking off to the spa at Buxton while she was taking the waters there to keep on good terms with her – just in case. Now Elizabeth particularly feared that if she named a successor, even one her advisers could all agree on, she would be assassinated or forced to abdicate.

In despair, Wentworth switched his lobbying to Essex and had already begun to attract his attention through the physician Dr Thomas Moffett, when Moffett's carelessness in arranging for the copying of a dossier supplied to him by Wentworth led to the contents being leaked.[10] The storm had broken just as Elizabeth was leaving Nonsuch Palace for Viscount Montague's house at Cowdray. In a state of stunned disbelief that her death and the succession were 'the talk of cobblers and tailors' (as she graphically put it), she had ordered Wentworth's arrest and had his house searched for other incriminating papers. Closely questioned by the Privy Council, he was sent to the Gatehouse Prison for four months, then put under house arrest.[11]

Finally granted his freedom, Wentworth began lobbying friends in the House of Commons to join him in forcing a debate on the taboo subject, whether the queen liked it or not. Two days after the opening of Parliament in February 1593, he dared to organize a secret meeting at which he discussed with his puritan friends how they might engineer just such a debate. Aghast at his subversion, Elizabeth sent him to the Tower. There he would remain, despite Burghley's best efforts to secure his release on bail, for the rest of his life.[12]

Elizabeth was known as far away as Venice to be increasingly prone to sickness.[13] Persistent rumours early in 1594 that she was mortally ill or even dead drove third-tier courtiers and officials into unwise speculation about a successor. One story traced back to stallholders at the bustling markets of St Nicholas' Shambles to the west of St Paul's had the queen being carried out of her Bedchamber in a coffin at dead of night and rowed downstream to a secret funeral at Greenwich.[14]

Incurable insomnia coupled with migraine attacks, severe depression and sudden mood swings were Elizabeth's most frequent afflictions around this time, but she also had recurrent chest and throat infections, gastric disorders, sore eyes and chronic periodontal problems caused by her addiction to sugar in its various forms.[15] Although not yet quite sixty-one, her face was grey and marred by deep wrinkles, the unavoidable effects of age, compounded by the seriously harmful effects of the cosmetics she applied so thickly every day.

Not only did wrinkles furrow her neck and cheeks, her teeth had turned yellow or black, and she had lost most of her hair. Like Mary Queen of Scots, Elizabeth had worn hair extensions, and then wigs, since her early thirties. To disguise the wrinkles on her neck, she either wore a starched cambric (fine linen) ruff or high collar, or put on elaborate pearl choker necklaces or jewelled gold collars. To mask her bad teeth she sometimes placed a perfumed silk handkerchief in her mouth. Soon, to make herself look taller than she really was and also to keep up with the latest Italian fashions, she would order from her shoemaker, Peter Johnson, the first shoes that are described as having high heels and arches: the heels were probably made of wood.[16]

To achieve her ivory-like complexion, her women would wash her face up to three times a week with a liquid made from egg white, powdered eggshell, alum, borax, camphor oil, lemon juice, white poppy seeds and plant extracts, all mixed together in spring water. The ointments that maintained the myth of her pristine skin included ceruse, vinegar, turpentine and quicksilver. The brilliant rouge dye used to colour her cheeks and lips came from cochineal or vermilion. Several of these ingredients were highly toxic and corrosive: ceruse, for instance, was white lead (a compound of carbonate and hydrate of lead); quicksilver was liquid mercury; and vermilion was red crystalline mercuric sulphide. Alum, too, depending on its form, could severely irritate the skin and the mucous membranes. Applied over many years, the queen's cosmetics could be expected to trigger allergies, dermatological complaints, memory loss and sensory impairments.[17]

And, as the queen aged, so, too, did Burghley. After Mildred, his beloved wife to whom he was married for over forty years, died in 1589, his health had never been quite the same. Now nearing seventy-five and mocked behind his back by some of Essex's supporters, he was regularly crippled by bouts of arthritis in his hands, arms and knees, as well as by gout in his toes. The pain could sometimes be so agonizing that the old man was heard to cry aloud.[18] A throbbing in his writing hand and an inability to focus his eyes, despite using spectacles, prevented him from working as he had in his youth. He was still as mentally agile as ever but was forced to retire to bed for days at a time.[19] 'My aching pains so increase that I am all night sleepless,' he lamented to his son, Robert. 'If this continue, *I* cannot . . . I can hardly read what I have written, not being able to bow my head to my paper.'[20]

Others around him were fast failing as well. Sir Thomas Heneage, whom Elizabeth had made Chancellor of the Duchy of Lancaster despite his advancing renal condition, looked 'very ghastly' and within eighteen months would be felled by a stroke.[21] Lord Hunsdon, the queen's oldest living relative, was another veteran of the Privy Council stricken by arthritis. He valiantly soldiered on as Lord Chamberlain for another two years. But the old order was under attack from all sides.

Elizabeth greeted the birth of an heir in Scotland with stony silence. Although James promptly invited her to be his son's godmother and named him Henry after her father and grandfather – a choice loudly signalling his own ambition to sit on her throne – she did not deign to reply.[22] Still smarting from his refusal to discipline Huntly, she had no intention of breaching royal protocol in order to attend the christening celebrations in person and declined to say who would represent her.

Instead, she ratcheted up a policy she had begun two years before and secretly backed James's arch-enemy, Francis Stewart, Earl of Bothwell, as a stalking horse to counter Huntly. The Protestant nephew of the third husband of Mary Queen of Scots and a rabble-rouser with a well-earned reputation for violence, sorcery and generally stirring up trouble, Bothwell was adroit at exploiting the old Scottish convention that nobles could walk unannounced into the royal Bedchamber at almost any hour of day or night to 'advise' the king, and this despite James's attempts to bar him.[23] Two days after Christmas in 1591, he had famously besieged James and Anne in their apartments, attempting to smoke James out by lighting a fire before breaking down the queen's door with hammers. Pursuing Bothwell on his horse, James fell into a freezing river, where he almost drowned.[24] Equally sensationally, Bothwell had harangued James, sword in hand, for several hours in July 1593. Arriving late one evening in the king's Bedchamber at Holyrood while James was sitting on his close stool (lavatory), he attempted to broker a role for himself as Huntly's replacement.[25]

In the spring of 1594, Elizabeth ordered her Scottish agents to incite Bothwell to wage a private war against Huntly, offering him bribes to raise the necessary troops. In reply, James announced his intention to prosecute the queen's stalking horse and proclaim him an outlaw. Mustering 2,400 troops himself, James attempted to ambush Bothwell, whom Burghley's man in Scotland wittily nicknamed 'Robin Hood', for his ability to disappear into forests. But he mishandled the assault and the royal forces fled. However, Bothwell's days as the joker in Anglo-Scottish politics would soon be numbered.[26] When Huntly and his allies invited him to switch sides and join them, since he could not beat them, and when the Kirk, rightly questioning his Protestant zeal, condemned him from the pulpit, Elizabeth had no choice but to make an embarrassing retreat, professing once again her support for James and appointing the Earl of Sussex, a handsome young nobleman and protégé of Essex, to ride to Stirling with her christening gifts. And when, in return, James agreed to punish Huntly and Bothwell on equivalent terms, a decidedly smug Elizabeth abandoned her stalking horse to his fate, since she had no longer any use for him.[27]

With Anglo-Scottish relations in so delicate a state, Essex seized this opportunity to renew the clandestine contact with James he had first attempted so disastrously after his return from Lisbon in 1589. His chief intelligencer, Anthony Bacon, was an 'ancient friend' of the Scotsman David Foulis, one of James's regular confidants and special envoys. In Foulis's correspondence with Bacon, which was conducted in French, Essex was Plato or '28', and James Tacitus or '10'.[28]

This time, Essex meant to keep Burghley and his son completely in the dark. He was still smouldering after a series of run-ins with Burghley, of which the most bruising had led to a tersely worded message from Elizabeth informing him that, if he wished to continue to petition her to reimburse the £14,000 he had laid out from his own pocket to pay his troops during the later stages of his expedition to Normandy, he should kindly make his application through Robert Cecil.[29]

With his fencing with Cecil fast morphing into a feud, Essex was determined to gain an advantage over his pen-pushing rival. In the longer term, that would mean building up a good working relationship with James. Astutely, he recognized that his best bet was to exploit James's low opinion of Burghley, knowing that James was well aware that Burghley, more than Elizabeth, had been his mother's nemesis.[30]

Once Essex convinced himself that he could gain the upper hand, his attitude to Cecil became more actively aggressive. Under the delusion that his own wayward flashes of genius were superior to his rival's dogged persistence, he wrote him off as a lackey and joked semi-blasphemously about 'the father and the son', as if – like the Holy Trinity – Cecil and Burghley were indivisible. Anthony Bacon encouraged him in these smears, lampooning Cecil and calling him 'a little pot soon hot', just like Petruchio's manservant Grumio in Shakespeare's *The Taming of the Shrew*.[31]

More woundingly, Anthony's brother Francis went a step further and cruelly mocked Cecil's puny physique, making him appear as the living embodiment of Caliban in *The Tempest*: a slave, savage and deformed, 'a born devil, on whose nature/ Nurture can never stick'.[32] For whereas Essex was tall and well-proportioned, Cecil stood little more than five feet and was a hunchback. (To boost his self-esteem, he kept a pet parrot who entertained his guests by strutting up and down his dinner table.) Elizabeth nicknamed him 'Elf' and sometimes 'Pygmy'. He claimed not to mind but, privately, he found his nicknames hurtful and demeaning. After receiving a letter addressed by the queen to 'Pygmy', he told his father poignantly, 'Though I may not find fault with the name she gives me, yet seem I only not to mislike it because she gives it.'[33]

In the long interval during which Elizabeth had refused to acknowledge James's invitation to be his son's godmother, the Scottish king had thrown caution to the wind. In one of the rudest letters he ever wrote, he seized upon her insult that he was 'a seduced king' and cast it back at her. Quipping that all he had to do was to repeat her own words but change the sex, he sent her a diatribe:

> So many unexpected wonders, madame and dearest sister, have of late so overshadowed my eyes and mind and dazzled so all my senses as in truth I neither know what I should say nor where at first to begin. But thinking it best to take a pattern of yourself since I deal with you, I must, repeating the first words of your last letter, only the sex changed, say 'I rue my sight that views the evident spectacle of a seduced queen.' For when I enter betwixt two extremes in judging of you, I had far rather interpret it to the least dishonour on your part, which is ignorant error.

He went on to call her to account for her underhand dealings with Bothwell and for denying that she had been secretly financing him. And he quoted a famous line from Virgil's *Aeneid*: 'If I cannot bend the powers above, I will appeal to those of hell.'[34]

Elizabeth did not take kindly to getting a taste of her own medicine.[35] And no sooner had James sealed and dispatched his broadside than he repented of it.[36] So, with his secret channel of communication to Essex already up and running, he begged him to intervene on his behalf: it is a rare example of direct contact, although, significantly, the letter was merely to be shown to Essex and then returned to Edinburgh, where it still survives.[37] Gratifying the Earl, as Henry IV had done on the eve of the Normandy campaign, by addressing him as his 'Right trusty and well-beloved cousin', James urged Essex to do all he could to defend the Anglo-Scottish league and thus, by inference, to champion his claim to succeed Elizabeth. He professed his friendship in the warmest of terms. 'I look, milord, that a nobleman of the rank ye are of, will move and assist the Queen with your good advice, not to suffer herself to be [de]filed and abused any longer with such as prefer their particular and unhonest affection to the Queen's princely honour and peace of both the realms.'[38] By this, Essex plainly understood that James meant Cecil and Burghley, and it would not be long before the Earl would himself be denouncing Cecil and his minions as 'flatterers' and 'upstarts', serving the queen solely for their own corrupt advantage.

James laboured under the misapprehension that Essex would be able to intercede for him. To Essex, on the other hand, the Scottish king's letter seemed to hold out the prospect of a brilliant future after Elizabeth. Through Anthony Bacon, Foulis had already made it plain that it was James's intention to grant the Earl some spectacular reward in exchange for assisting his smooth accession to the English throne. Nothing could be put on paper but, from this point onwards, Essex began to line himself up for a position of power in the next reign. Beguiled by such intoxicating thoughts and scorning the danger, he would soon be receiving intelligence from Scotland several times a week.[39]

In early August 1594, with the Earl of Sussex packing his luggage ready to ride north for Prince Henry's baptism, Elizabeth decided that the best way to keep the errant King James on side was to renew her friendly exchanges with Queen Anne. Arthritis in her right hand prevented her from writing herself but, after sending for Robert Cecil's clerk and dictating a letter, she made several amendments in what she liked disparagingly to call her 'skrating', or scribbling, hand.[40]

'It was no small contentment unto us', Elizabeth's letter began, 'when we were informed by our ambassador of the favour which God hath bestowed upon you in making you mother of a young prince and heir apparent to our dear brother and cousin the King of Scots.' Disingenuously blaming a diplomatic muddle for her tardy reply to James's offer, she declared how delighted she was to be asked 'so honourably and kindly' to be godmother to Anne's baby. Addressing the Scottish queen as 'our dearest sister', but continuing to use the royal 'we' rather than slipping into the first person singular, as she often did when talking intimately to other women, she added that, besides her gifts, Sussex would be delivering her 'unfeigned well wishes' both for the child and his mother. Ending on an elegiac note, she assured Anne that memories of her late father, Frederick II, remained as affectionately in her thoughts as ever. She ended by wishing 'all prosperous increase to the young Prince, whom nature's bond by his father as well as his noble derivation on both sides hath tied us to hold most dear'.⁴¹

But Elizabeth's actions belied her words. She envied Anne her youth, her good looks and, most of all, her son. When, after delivering the letter, Sussex handed over her gifts, everyone could see that they had a good deal more show than substance. Chief among them 'a fair cupboard of silver overgilt, cunningly wrought, and some cups of gold massy' (i.e. a cabinet of silver plate, dressed up to look more valuable than it really was because it was skilfully gilded and mixed up with some genuine gold goblets), they were conspicuously outclassed by the gifts from other Protestant states, even those of the hard-pressed Dutch. They were not even in the same league as her gift at James's own baptism in 1566, when she had sent a font of solid gold weighing 333 ounces that was the talk of Europe.⁴²

Anne, who was fast learning how to hold her own in the maelstrom of international politics, parried the English queen. Replying in her own hand and writing in Lowland Scots, which she had mastered in just four years, she assured Elizabeth seemingly without irony that, after examining her gifts closely, she fully understood 'how lovingly and worthily you have conceived of us and of our son'. 'We are', she said, 'moved by the greatness of such courteous affection . . . rather the more, seeing it has pleased God to bless us in our son, so near in blood belonging to yourself.'⁴³ Signing herself 'your most loving and affectionate sister and cousin, Anna R', she made it crystal clear, nonetheless, that it would be only a matter of time before her son would rule the whole of the British Isles, insinuations all the more offensive to Elizabeth as, in his sermon at the baptism, the archbishop of Aberdeen had spoken for more than an hour on the topic of James's descent from the kings of England. This was a theme taken to its extreme conclusion in a further set of celebratory verses, personally approved by James and published by his official printer in Edinburgh, that audaciously styled the Scottish ruler as 'King of all Britain in possession'.⁴⁴

Practically shaking with rage, Elizabeth ordered Burghley to instruct his agent at Holyrood to deliver a sharp note of protest to James, demanding an immediate apology, 'considering her portion is the greatest part of Britain and his the less'. James, however, was unrepentant, observing that, being descended as he was, he 'could not but make claim to the crown of England after the decease of Her Majesty'. He would continue to do so whether she liked it or not.[45]

So firmly convinced was Essex that he had secured a glittering future for himself, he was genuinely dumbstruck, a year later, to receive a peremptory summons from an icy Elizabeth. Ushered into her presence in the Privy Chamber at Richmond Palace early on Monday, 3 November 1595 and not emerging until the late afternoon, he was asked to explain how an inflammatory book, *A Conference about the Next Succession to the Crown of England*, came to be dedicated to him. When she pointed with her finger to the 'Epistle dedicatory', he turned 'wan and pale'. For it said there, extolling him by name:

> No man is in more high and eminent place or dignity at this day in our realm than yourself, whether we respect your nobility or calling or favour with your prince or high liking of the people, and consequently no man [is] like to have a greater part or sway in deciding of this great affair [the succession] . . . than Your Honour, and those that will assist you and are likest to follow your fame and fortune.

These, an eyewitness remarked, were 'dangerous praises of his valour and worthiness, which doth him harm here'.[46]

That was a wonderfully deadpan understatement. For some months, Essex's Catholic enemies had been circulating malicious rumours that he was aiming for the Crown himself.[47] Worse, he had only just managed to overcome his belated exposure as the real father of Elizabeth Southwell's illegitimate son: the storm that had erupted over this sensational disclosure triggered a series of bitter quarrels between Essex and the queen. She was particularly incensed that, by imprisoning Thomas Vavasour for the offence, she had wronged an innocent man.[48]

A Conference about the Next Succession to the Crown was the equivalent of a stick of dynamite thrown into Elizabeth's coach. A sequel to an earlier, much shorter tract by the same author published in Antwerp in 1593 entitled *News from Spain and Holland*, it was intended to create an urgent sense of impending crisis about who should be the queen's heir. In this, it brilliantly succeeded, making the succession the hottest of hot topics. Elizabeth greeted it with undisguised horror: its fake dedication was a deliberate ploy to discredit Essex. The book's author, writing under the pseudonym of R. Doleman, was known by John Harington, the queen's favourite godson, to be Robert Parsons, the exiled superior of the English Jesuits.[49] Parsons had first drafted *A Conference* in 1593 while living in Valladolid, at a seminary he had founded there – an early copy was presented to Philip II. In the summer of 1595, two thousand copies were published in Antwerp. And when smuggled into London, they caused a run on the bookshops.[50]

With the Catholic Mary Queen of Scots dead and her son, James VI, a Protestant, the Jesuit Parsons stole the Calvinists' clothes and argued – not unlike the younger Burghley, when he had tried for so many years to exclude Mary – that it was within the power of the 'Commonwealth' (by which Parsons meant Parliament) to determine the succession on its own. Bad or incompetent rulers like King John or Richard II had in the past been called to account or deposed, and Parliament might, for good reasons, choose to debar an otherwise lawful successor in order to 'remedy the inconveniences of bare succession alone'.[51]

Parsons then ran his eye over the rival claimants to the throne in the style of a racing tipster, playing mischievously on the anti-Scottish xenophobia he knew to be rife in England. Native-born Englishmen, he said, would never consent to be ruled by a barbarian Scot and, as a foreigner, James VI was arguably prevented from inheriting the Crown by English law. In any case, as the son and heir of the executed Mary Queen of Scots, the small print of the Bond of Association of 1584 barred him on the grounds that his mother had been an accessory to the Babington Plot. (These were familiar debating points long contested by lawyers on both sides of the Scottish border.)[52]

Next, Parsons turned to the nineteen-year-old Arbella Stuart, James's English-born cousin.[53] Elizabeth had invited her to Court in

1587, but the following year banished her to deepest Derbyshire, leaving her isolated and unable to build up a following. The two women had clashed after Elizabeth had deliberately staged a scene in which Arbella was forced to stand for hours in the Presence Chamber at Whitehall, waiting to gaze in awe upon the queen when she emerged from the Privy Chamber in all her cosmetically enhanced splendour. Under the misapprehension that, when she finally appeared, she would 'pronounce me an eaglet of her own kind', Arbella went along with this charade. When, however, Elizabeth at last caught sight of her teenage kinswoman with her reddish fair hair, beautiful bright blue eyes and pale skin untouched by the ravages of time, she was gripped by jealousy in much the same way as King Lear in an early version of the play (not William Shakespeare's):

> And yet as jealous as the princely Eagle,
> That kills her young ones, if they do but dazel [gaze]
> Upon the radiant splendour of the Sun.[54]

Seeking to sow hatred and division among the Protestants, Parsons then artfully pitched the claims of James and Arbella against those of the so-called 'Suffolk' line who had been named by Henry VIII as the heirs to the Crown if all his children should die without progeny. With Jane, Katherine and Mary Grey all now dead, Parsons focused on the staunchly Protestant Earl of Hertford and his two sons. Naturally, he concluded that Hertford was disqualified by reason of his father's divorce. So was the Earl's elder son, Lord Beauchamp, by virtue of the illegitimacy Archbishop Parker had pronounced in the Court of Arches in 1562. Ingeniously, however, Parsons argued that, far from being illegitimate, too, Thomas, the younger son, was born in lawful wedlock as, before he was conceived, both of his parents had confessed their marriage vows before the Privy Council. Thomas, therefore, had as good a claim as Arbella and a better one than James, since he was male and born in England. Here Parsons sought to make as much mischief as he could: Elizabeth still deeply mistrusted Hertford and his family, despite their professions of loyalty and obedience to her in their Elvetham pageants, whereas whispers had been heard that Burghley secretly favoured their cause.[55]

Before turning to the Catholic options, Parsons tied up some loose ends. Margaret Clifford, now Dowager Countess of Derby, was yet another descendant of the 'Suffolk' line via her mother, Eleanor Brandon. A wilful, self-indulgent, profligate woman, she had been separated from her husband for more than twenty years after quarrelling violently with him. Exiled from Court by Elizabeth for her indiscretions, she had just one of her four sons alive by the summer of 1595, the thirty-four-year-old William, recently married to Burghley's granddaughter, Elizabeth de Vere. He was undoubtedly legitimate, but, despite Parsons' best efforts, he refused to involve himself with the succession and, as time went on, his case was not helped by rumours of his wife's infidelities with both Essex and Ralegh.[56]

Among the Protestants, this left only Henry Hastings, Earl of Huntingdon. Better known as the Puritan Earl, he was directly descended from Edward III on both his parents' sides and a lineal descendant of George, Duke of Clarence, a younger brother of King Edward IV, the last rightful Yorkist king. His wife, Katherine, was Leicester's youngest sister and a woman close to the queen. During the Northern Rising of 1569, he had been a joint custodian of Mary Queen of Scots and, afterwards, he had served loyally as President of the Council of the North. Huntingdon was also close to Burghley and Essex, but his lack of descent from Henry VII stood against him and he had no ambition for the Crown.[57] More fatally, from Parsons' viewpoint, he died childless barely six weeks after *A Conference about the Next Succession to the Crown* hit the streets of London.

At last, Parsons cut to the quick. In what might have seemed to many readers a breathtaking non-sequitur, he suddenly announced that Philip II was Elizabeth's rightful successor. This was on the convoluted grounds that the Spanish king was the true dynastic heir of John of Gaunt (1340–99),* Edward III's eldest surviving son, the founder of the House of Lancaster, from whom Henry VII, Elizabeth's grandfather, had derived his own somewhat tenuous claim to rule.[58]

---

* Gaunt's daughter Philippa by his first wife, Blanche of Lancaster, had married King John I of Portugal, one of Philip II's ancestors. A daughter, Catherine, by Gaunt's second wife, Constance of Castile, had gone on to marry King Henry III of Castile, an ancestor of Philip's father, Charles V.

Hereditary right was not, however, insisted Parsons, momentarily shifting his ground, the only or even the most important factor in determining the succession to kingdoms. He argued that the defence of true religion was just as important, combined with an ability to defend the realm from foreign invasion.[59] He knew well enough that, by this late stage, not even the most hawkish of Philip's advisers believed that a ruler who for the last few years had rarely left the hallowed portals of the Escorial would be willing to succeed Elizabeth in person.

Failing him, therefore, Parsons' preferred candidate was the Spanish king's daughter, the Infanta Isabella. Backed by her father, who had already sought in vain to make her queen of France, she would have the combined military and naval power of Spain and Portugal behind her. Purely on these grounds alone, as Parsons trumpeted, she was 'by her title and her father's goodwill' most likely to 'bear it away'.[60]

Anyone reading *A Conference* today would think it a chaotically structured polemic, the work of a fantasist with the mind of a demented magpie. But when it first appeared in London it seemed almost apocalyptic, since it shattered a taboo. No one had dared before to publish so extensively on a topic Elizabeth had always insisted was off limits. So outraged and, more to the point, so rattled was she by the book's appearance that she ordered her palace gates to be slammed shut and a search of all her courtiers' lodgings made by torchlight to see how many copies could be found. Those that were uncovered were instantly burned. Seasoned observers knew that she regarded the mere possession of this book as treasonable: to discuss its existence, let alone its contents, was a serious risk.[61]

Bowing to the inevitable, Essex resigned himself to a lengthy period of disgrace, both with the queen and with James, who was even angrier than she was.[62] On reflection, the Earl knew that he had seriously misplayed his hand, ignoring crucial warnings: Anthony Bacon had discovered the gist of the offending book from his continental spies shortly after it had first appeared in Antwerp.[63] So had Robert Beale, the man who had delivered the death warrant for Mary Queen of Scots to Fotheringhay, who still kept an eagle eye on international events.[64]

But rather than taking credit for being the first to unmask Parsons and his book, as he had with the Lopez Plot, and then preparing Elizabeth (and James) for the more unwelcome aspects of its disclosures, Essex had kept silent, too embarrassed by the fake dedication.

After his gruelling audience with the queen, Essex returned to the Strand, where he withdrew to his bedchamber to nurse another of his psychosomatic illnesses. Two days later, it was said that 'he continues very ill', and he would remain in seclusion for at least another week.[65] Unnerved by the ferocity of the attacks on him, Essex was also painfully aware of the high stakes involved in his clandestine advocacy of James, who was so obsessed with *A Conference* that he was unable to part with his copy. As one of Burghley's spies reported, the book 'is so charily kept by the King as that it cannot by no means be wanting from him that keeps it above one night'.[66] James, in a visible state of agitation, was seen pacing about his bedchamber up to three times a day, clutching the book. Already there were rumours that he was seeking advice, with a view to answering it.[67] Meanwhile, a news blackout had been imposed in Scotland. So gravely did James regard the threat of Parsons' book, he proclaimed that 'no man shall write anything or news out thereof upon pain of death.'[68]

Essex, too close for comfort to the offending tome through no fault of his own, knew that he was walking barefoot on shards of glass. Early in 1596, he would turn pale again on hearing reports that the incorrigible but happily Protestant Wentworth had replied to Parsons. Communicating his polemic from the Tower in the form of multiple copies of a long, handwritten 'letter' ostensibly to his 'privy friends', Wentworth at last explicitly defended James's right to be Elizabeth's successor. Up until this point, he had carefully hedged his bets, wary of James's Catholic friends, such as the Earl of Huntly. Now, desperate to counter Parsons, Wentworth unconditionally endorsed James's candidacy, ironically citing in his support Elizabeth's words of 1561 to the Scottish secretary Maitland of Lethington, when she had declared James's mother to have a near-invincible right of succession to the English throne on grounds of blood.[69]

Fortunately for Essex, Wentworth made no appeal to him in his tract, nor did he make further overtures to Dr Moffett. As he prudently noted, the topic was 'dangerous' and the times 'ticklish'.[70] He took care because *A Conference*, circulating underground in so many copies, was slowly fuelling what, regardless of Elizabeth's commands, would gradually ripple outwards into a daring public debate. Just as dangerously, it would feed a growing appetite among London theatre-goers for plays on the theme of dynastic civil wars, usurpation and the nature of legitimacy.[71] Almost certainly, the issues raised by Parsons were the inspiration for Shakespeare's *King John* and *Richard II*. Both, strikingly, were written out of sequence in the canon of his English history plays. Both were about royal succession, dynastic ambition, civil war and usurpation, and each is replete with Shakespeare's most visceral reflections on the action of history and the legitimacy of kingship.[72]

No longer was the divinity of kings a topic reserved only for princes to consider in private. Now, it seemed, anyone could join in the conversation. Since her very first encounter with the Count of Feria all those years ago, Elizabeth had played on the trope of the broad popular support she claimed to enjoy. Suddenly, with large numbers of ordinary people avidly discussing the succession and doing this flatly against her commands, her attitude changed and 'popularity' became a dirty word. For Elizabeth and James equally, Parsons had opened an almighty can of worms.

15.   A Counter-Armada

The Earl of Essex's response to the furore over Parsons' fake dedication was typically melodramatic. He depicted himself as the victim of a Court conspiracy. 'I am so handled by this crew of sycophants, spies and delators', he complained, 'as I have no quiet myself nor much credit to help my friends.'[1]

And yet the queen soon came to realize that Parsons had shamelessly libelled him, and her attitude softened. Stricken with remorse, she came to visit him on his sickbed and fed him broth.[2] Before a week was out, she was ordering letters from her ambassadors abroad to be delivered straight to him at Essex House. He alone was to answer them. As the Court gossips marvelled, 'The harm [that] was meant him [is] by Her Majesty's gracious favour and wisdom turned to his good and strengthens her love unto him.'[3]

Essex was jubilant, but his joy was short-lived. With the queen's Accession Day fast approaching and Burghley ill at his house on the Strand, the power-hungry Earl made the mistake of arriving in the tilt-yard at Whitehall Palace flaunting his credentials as her next chief minister. To script his lines, he retained Francis Bacon, who devised a glittering pageant on the theme of Essex's undying passion for the queen. Falling into three parts performed before and after the supper break, it featured the characters of 'a melancholy, dreaming Hermit' representing Learning, 'a mutinous, brainsick Soldier' representing Fame and 'a busy, tedious Secretary' representing Experience. Each sought to persuade Essex to strive for self-fulfilment and to serve their mistress, Philautia, the goddess of Self-Love, for whom they sought to win him.

Through his squire, the Earl rejected their entreaties, rebuking them for their selfish illusions and protesting that 'this knight would never forsake his mistress's love.' This was on the grounds that Elizabeth's virtue 'made all his thoughts divine', her wisdom 'taught him all true policy', and her beauty and worth 'were at all times able to make him fit to command armies'.[4]

The drafts of the surviving fragments of the script include a marginal note from Bacon urging Essex to apply the allegory unashamedly to his own ends.[5] Since glory in war and politics were the qualities he sought to make his own, he should telegraph to Elizabeth that his only aim in pursuing them was to serve her more faithfully.

Although it became the talk of London, the pageant badly misfired. The spectators saw Essex's production as little more than a crude attack on his chief rivals.[6] By the Hermit, they assumed he meant to lampoon Burghley (unsurprisingly, in view of the chief minister's earlier pageant on that same theme at Theobalds). They took the pen-pushing Secretary to be Robert Cecil, and suspected the mutinous Soldier to be the hot-headed Sir Roger Williams, who had served Essex at the siege of Rouen but who harboured his own ambitions as a general and military strategist.[7]

Least impressed of all was the woman in whose honour the entertainment was staged. Elizabeth grew tetchier and tetchier as the night wore on. Not only had Essex upstaged her on her Accession Day, he had put on a show that, for all its prodigious cost, was the most overwrought and pretentious spectacle she had ever endured. Far from creating the impression that he was suppressing his ambition in her honour, he had achieved precisely the opposite effect. He was, it seemed, showing his true colours as a courtier who, for all his fair words of love, loyalty and constancy, loved himself more than her: and *that* her vanity could not tolerate.

Rising from her seat the moment the show ended, Elizabeth was overheard muttering loudly that 'If she had thought there would have been so much said of her, she would not have been there that night.' She then went straight to bed.[8] She might have been angrier still had she caught sight of another of Bacon's notes, in which he reminded the Earl that it was 'the Queen's unkind dealing, which may persuade you to self-love'.[9]

A few weeks before the pageant, Essex had described Elizabeth as a sphinx whose riddles he could not unravel.[10] Unlike his stepfather, whose ambition and sexual indiscretions she eventually found it within herself to forgive, or the faithful Christopher Hatton, whose love and constancy had kept him single for the whole of his career, to the point where he was forced to refute claims that he was sleeping with the queen, Essex never really understood her.[11]

The fact that he was serving a woman ruler had begun to create serious difficulties for Essex.[12] Burghley in his youth had never masked his doubts, telling Elizabeth that 'to serve Your Majesty in anything that myself cannot allow must needs be an unprofitable service.' Now, however, in his old age, 'sore sick' and 'with pain of head, heart and hand', and deaf to the point where visiting ambassadors had to shout loudly at him, he longed to live out his remaining days in peace and had finally come round to accepting his sovereign on her own terms. In the spring of 1596, he would address to Robert Cecil what would become the quintessence of his political creed in his declining years:

> I do hold and will always [take] this course in such matters as I differ in opinion from Her Majesty as long as I may be allowed to give advice. I will not change my opinion by affirming the contrary for that were to offend God to whom I am sworn first. But as a servant I will obey Her Majesty's commandment, and no wise contrary the same, presuming that she being God's chief minister here, it shall be God's will to have her commandments obeyed.[13]

This was never Essex's way. If Elizabeth would not yield to his petitions or flattery, then he would try to cajole her, even force her to submit to his will.[14] With his hunger as urgent as ever for a fresh military command and for promotion to the full responsibilities of Walsingham's former position, the importunate Earl began bombarding her with verses and sonnets, some to be sung by her favourite lutenist, Robert Hales. Inevitably, he could not resist etching into them thinly veiled protests against what he believed to be her ill-treatment of him, stereotyping her as his cruel, inconstant mistress, as in the double-edged line: 'And if thou should'st by Her be now forsaken,/ She made thy Heart too strong for to be shaken.'[15]

Soon, he would go further, declaring, 'I shall never do her service but against her will.'[16] In his frustration, he began plotting behind her back, giving secret directions to Sir Henry Unton, sent once more as the queen's ambassador to France, despite a serious riding accident, in an attempt to force her to ratchet up the war effort. Whereas Elizabeth had instructed Unton, though to little avail, to complain to Henry IV that she had been assisting him for far longer than she had ever intended, Essex incited him to stir her into action by feeding the French a false report that her true plan was to make a secret unilateral peace with Spain. Playing with fire, he even urged Unton to warn Henry that it was the tight-fisted Lord Treasurer and his son who opposed further military aid for the French king.[17]

Such flagrant transgressions did not go unobserved. Unton, however in awe of Essex for his relationship with the queen and his high status, regarded Burghley as his chief point of contact with the Privy Council: he kept him fully briefed about the disinformation he was reporting on the Earl's behalf, even if he did not always disclose its exact source.[18]

But, for the moment, Essex's greatest offence in Elizabeth's eyes was his attempt to reap the maximum rewards from his costly pageant by circulating highlights from the script among his friends and admirers and having a portrait miniature of himself painted in his tournament garb by Nicholas Hilliard. In this image, most likely meant to be distributed in life-sized and half-sized copies by lesser artists, Essex stands wearing gold-filigreed armour, his right hand casually resting on his waist, his left hand on the table with his matching helmet. On his sword-belt, and woven in and out of the skirt of his armour, was inscribed the *impresa*, or badge, he sported on that day, a single diamond with the Latin motto *Dum Formas Minuis* ('While you fashion it, you diminish it'), referring to the cutting and shaping of diamonds by a jeweller. The glove Elizabeth gave him as a favour at the beginning of the tournament is clearly visible, tied to his upper right arm with a large ribbon, a symbol of his claim to be her champion, whether she wanted it or not.[19]

What Essex most sought was another chance to prove his martial valour in war. Already entering its eleventh year, the struggle was gathering momentum again after a relative lull of almost two years. In 1595, Henry IV had declared outright war against Spain. He felt confident to do so, as Brittany was largely back in his control after a successful guerrilla campaign by Norris's auxiliaries, whom the queen had then recalled. But, despite all his best efforts, Henry had lost ground in Picardy and Champagne to crack divisions of the Army of Flanders slipping across the frontier, ably led by their new commander, Don Pedro Enríquez de Azevedo, Count of Fuentes. First, Fuentes stormed Doullens and massacred its garrison. Turning eastward, he then marched off and laid siege to the important fortress of Cambrai. More threateningly, rumours abounded that the incoming replacement as the Spanish governor in the Netherlands, Archduke Albert of Austria, was planning a sweeping attack on Calais as part of a plan to gain at least partial control over the English Channel.[20]

Philip, meanwhile, was rebuilding his navy. Throughout the summer of 1595, Elizabeth had been confronted by a succession of scares that he was preparing to launch a second *Gran Armada*. It was in these circumstances that she grudgingly entertained a fresh plan of attack. Although for ever cured of the notion that an aggressive European land campaign could work in her best interests, she was willing to consider a cheaper seaborne alternative. Developed by Burghley, in consultation with Lord Admiral Howard and Sir Francis Drake, the plan was modelled on Ralegh's idea of throttling Philip's supply of treasure at the dispatching end in Panama or off the coast of Cuba.[21]

Essex talked down the plan.[22] Adamant that victory could be won only by taking the struggle to the beating heart of Philip's worldwide empire, he began lobbying Elizabeth for a direct attack on the Spanish mainland and ports. Nothing less than a full-scale counter-Armada, he argued, would be sufficient.

In August 1595, after weeks of fruitless discussion, Elizabeth put both proposals on ice, approving instead a much smaller privateering venture to be jointly led by Drake and Sir John Hawkins. They were to sail to the Caribbean with twenty-seven ships and 2,500 men to capture and loot a 350-ton treasure ship, the *Begoña*, that was known to lie stranded in Puerto Rico. According to eyewitness reports, the cargo was worth two and a half million ducats (some £800 million today).[23]

But after leaving Plymouth, Drake and Hawkins quarrelled. In late September, Drake, ever the daring, improvising opportunist, tried unsuccessfully to capture Las Palmas on the island of Gran Canaria, and further bickering ended only on the late afternoon of 12 November, when the English ships came to weigh anchor off the coast of Puerto Rico.[24] By then, Hawkins was already gravely ill. He died hours later and was buried at sea.[25] Undeterred, Drake launched his attack, but the Spaniards were ready for him. The master seafarer who had played the leading role in the defeat of the 1588 Armada had his stool shot from under him as he sat on deck eating his supper.[26]

Now, Drake decided to revert to Burghley's plan of intercepting a treasure fleet at its principal departure point. But he reached Nombre de Dios, at the northern end of the jungle track across the Panama Isthmus, only to find the town had been evacuated. He ordered his men to march over the mountain pass to Panama City, but they were repulsed by Spanish snipers and forced to return. All he could do was burn Nombre de Dios and the ships in its harbour before taking to sea again.

By January 1596, dysentery was rampaging through the English fleet. Drake was stricken by the deadliest form of the disease and died on the morning of the 27th. He was buried the next day at sea, not 'slung atween the round shot', as in Sir Henry Newbolt's famous ballad, written in 1885, but sealed in a lead coffin. The survivors made a footfall at Portobelo to replenish their water barrels and then set a mournful course for home. After battling the winter gales and a Spanish ambush off the coast of Cuba, some thirteen of the original twenty-seven ships finally slipped through the Straits of Florida into the Atlantic, the last of them reaching Plymouth in early May.

Elizabeth considered the expedition yet another fiasco. Far from making a handsome return on her investment, she had lost two of her finest seamen and was left nursing losses in excess of £32,000.[27] Worse still, at dawn on 30 March, while Drake's ships were sailing home, Archduke Albert unexpectedly diverted his crack divisions from La Fère, near Saint-Quentin in Picardy, and laid siege to Calais.[28] The artillery bombardment of the walls was so intense the queen could actually hear the thunder of the Spanish cannon from her barge on the Thames.[29]

Henry protested that he could no longer sustain the burden alone and threatened to make a separate peace with Spain if Elizabeth did not offer him fresh aid, and quickly.[30] Grudgingly, she began negotiations for a new treaty, ratified in May, by which, in a secret clause, she undertook to provide the French king with four thousand men to fight in Picardy and Normandy. This was the very least she could get away with – a commitment she promptly halved. Confirmed by mutual oaths, the treaty specified that neither ruler would make peace without the other's consent.[31]

By then, Calais had fallen and even Burghley was advocating a more aggressive war strategy.[32] Intelligence had reached him by way of Genoa that a hundred or more of Philip's galleons from the Biscay ports were preparing to sail for Calais or Marseilles, where they were to be joined by warships from Lisbon.[33] What finally gave Essex the chance for which he had waited so long was the threat of a second *Gran Armada* using Calais as a base. For once showing a degree of tact, he joined forces with Lord Admiral Howard and handed Elizabeth a fully worked-out plan to send a counter-Armada to Spain.[34]

Determined to outflank all opposition, Essex set about mending his fences with Robert Cecil. Meanwhile, Lord Howard sent for Ralegh, whose naval expertise he considered indispensable.[35] Still languishing at Sherborne Castle, dreaming of a second expedition up the Orinoco, Ralegh at first dragged his heels. According to Anthony Bacon, this was not through 'sloth or negligence, but upon pregnant design, which will be brought forth very shortly'.[36]

Ralegh gambled that the queen would refuse to allow Lord Howard and Essex to leave her side, leaving the way open for him to command the entire venture. In this, he was mistaken. Howard's command was never in question. And although Elizabeth changed her mind twice before allowing Essex to go, she finally agreed that he could. He certainly meant to make the most of it. His chance, he was convinced, had come to assert his masculinity by forcing upon her his own, more realistic (as he imagined) conception of how the war should be waged.[37]

The detailed plan of attack was Howard's contribution, and it was he who selected Cádiz as the target. Security throughout was tight; few of the officers, let alone the men, knew their exact destination until they arrived. The fleet consisted of one hundred and twenty ships: seventeen warships from the royal navy, a squadron of eighteen lent by the Dutch States General and the rest armed merchantmen or transport vessels hastily requisitioned. Aboard were 1,300 mariners and 6,300 soldiers, accompanied by 1,000 gentlemen volunteers. Sir Francis Vere, still serving in the Netherlands as the captain of the English auxiliary forces, was summoned, with nine hundred of his veterans, and a further thousand experienced troops were provided by the Dutch.[38]

Elizabeth appointed Howard and Essex as Lords General in overall command, with equal, overlapping authority. Vere was given operational control over the army, while Ralegh was to direct the fleet. A Council of War, made up of these four and a few of their immediate subordinates, was to decide in more detail how the mission should be conducted.[39]

Elizabeth's vision for the venture, once again, was strictly limited. In her final written instructions, badly scorched in a fire in 1731 and now only partly legible, she ordered the Lords General to attack and destroy Philip's warships at Cádiz, taking care to salvage any naval supplies and equipment that she could recycle. Casualties were to be avoided, and (in a clause directed at Essex) she made it explicit that no 'desperate or doubtful actions of offence in a strange country' were to be committed. The temptation to create a more permanent military and naval base was to be firmly resisted. If any towns had to be levelled, the women, children and 'aged men not able to bear arms' should be spared. If, however, any of Philip's carracks or treasure ships happened to come within range, they were to be seized with their cargoes as a way of financing the whole operation.[40]

On Thursday, 3 June 1596, Lord Howard led the fleet out of Plymouth Sound with Essex chasing up the loiterers. They sighted Cádiz on the 20th, when Essex's bid to land troops in a surprise assault on the west side of the town was thwarted by perilously high waves, but at dawn the next day the vanguard of the fleet, commanded by Ralegh, entered the bay and launched a naval attack. Some seventy Spanish ships lay at anchor, including a dozen or so warships, four of which were brand-new, eighteen galleys, three treasure ships and a flotilla of thirty-four large merchantmen about to depart for the West Indies. On board the merchant ships were munitions, cash, wine, oil, silks, cloth of gold and other commodities said to be worth an eye-watering 12 million ducats (£3.5 billion in modern values).

This was more than ten times the queen's ordinary annual revenue.[41]

Seeing Ralegh's vanguard advancing, Diego de Soto, the captain of the Spanish galleons, raised the alarm. By the time the main body of the English fleet had entered the bay on the morning tide, the Spanish had moved their ships closer in, towards the inner harbour, guarding the entrance by stationing their biggest warships astride it in a defensive line. The English engaged the warships in a gun battle lasting eight hours, policing this passageway until two of Philip's galleons were grounded as the tide gradually ebbed. When a third had to be abandoned after an exploding barrel of gunpowder set it on fire, the smaller, lighter English vessels were able to pound all three to pieces. As the tide rose again, more of the larger Spanish ships attempted to make for the safety of the inner harbour but ran aground. The English pounced, capturing two of Philip's fine new warships, along with 1,200 cannon, and sinking or burning the rest. In the melee, Ralegh received 'a grievous blow in my leg, larded with many splinters which I daily pull out'. For months afterwards, he walked with a cane, a sign of his war wound.[42]

Essex, meanwhile, thirsting for glory, made a catastrophic misjudgement. Neglecting the poorly defended merchantmen with their priceless cargoes, he impetuously rushed two thousand troops ashore to the beat of a drum. When the great wooden gates of the city were slammed in his face, he gained entrance by sending an advance party to scale the medieval wall, leaving Vere's veterans to batter down the gates. After a fierce fight, the town hall was seized, as well as a munitions dump, a sugar warehouse and the customs house. By sunset, Essex and Vere were the masters of the streets.

The next day, the Spaniards who had taken refuge overnight in the castle negotiated ransoms. The city was then apportioned among the English and Dutch officers and systematically plundered by the soldiers. Elizabeth's instructions, superficially at least, were obeyed. Lord Howard afterwards declared that no women were raped or children or old men harmed, but the Spaniards told a different story.

The queen's generals had delivered the most complete and dramatic victory of the long war. The glaring loose end was the thirty-four merchantmen. Against Ralegh's sage advice, Essex wasted a whole day entertaining ransom offers from the owners of their cargoes. Fearing that the English would seize their ships regardless, Don Luis Alfonso Flores, the supreme commander of the *flota*, then ordered them to be set on fire and scuttled. The ensuing inferno lasted three days and nights, as 12 million ducats went up in smoke. Only twelve of Philip's galleys escaped. After rowing deep into the recesses of the inner harbour and dismantling a bridge, their crews were able to drag them along a creek running between the port and the open sea to safety.

But with the victory won, the struggle, from Essex's viewpoint, was barely beginning. Having captured Cádiz, what should he do with it? Elizabeth had never wavered in her instructions. No captured Spanish towns were to be held on any account as bases for future English operations.

And yet this was exactly what Essex suggested. Shortly before leaving Plymouth, he had sent a long letter to his fellow privy councillors indicating his inclination on strategic grounds to defy the queen's orders. He pleaded with them to coax her into allowing him to establish a permanent bridgehead at Cádiz. Once garrisoned with up to three thousand men, he said, it would function as 'a continual diversion and . . . as it were, a thorn sticking in his [Philip's] foot'.[43] Instead of giving the Spanish king a single blow from which he might soon recover, Essex aspired to establish footholds on the Iberian coast, supplied from England by sea. Possession of these towns and their valuable seaports – he elsewhere proposed Lisbon as a prime target – would allow the royal navy to blockade the coastline. Cut off from his treasure fleets, Philip would be strangled into submission. Only in this way, Essex argued, could Elizabeth become 'an absolute Queen of the Ocean'.[44]

With unusual passion even for him, Essex now commended his ideas to his fellow officers in the Council of War. An integrated military and naval strategy such as his, he vociferously maintained, was beyond the imagination of an ageing spinster who had never left English shores. It was up to her generals, experienced men of war such as themselves, to take the initiative while they still could.

Elated at its success so far, the Council at first agreed to delay the fleet's return home until the queen could be consulted. But their initial enthusiasm gave way to serious doubts as Essex began to exhibit disturbing signs of paranoia and hubris. In the end, the Council decided that Cádiz should be razed to the ground and burned. Only the churches and monasteries were to be spared.[45]

In London, Burghley and his son strenuously opposed Essex's plan. With considerable relish, they showed the Earl's letter to a furious queen, thereby securing the outcome for which they had hoped for so long. Within a fortnight, she would announce Robert Cecil's appointment to the vacant post of principal secretary, despite having faithfully promised Essex that she would do nothing of the kind while he was away.[46] When the news reached Cádiz, the Earl was beside himself. He interpreted Elizabeth's change of heart as nothing less than a personal betrayal. Unable to mask his emotions, he groaned and sulked, 'exceedingly dejected in countenance and bitterly passionate in speech'.[47]

On 5 July, the very same day Cecil took his oath as the queen's new principal secretary, Essex sailed to Faro in southern Portugal with the intention of looting the town. But the inhabitants saw him coming and, by the time he arrived, they had fled, clutching their valuables. All that was to be found worth plundering was a collection of rare books and manuscripts from the bishop's library, most of which the Earl would eventually present to Sir Thomas Bodley's newly founded library at Oxford.[48]

On returning to sea, Essex urged Lord Howard to allow him to sail to the Azores with a dozen ships to intercept a combined convoy of Portuguese and Spanish treasure ships that was expected. Since a diversion of exactly this sort had been authorized by the queen, Howard agreed, but he was vigorously contradicted by Ralegh. This split in the Council of War stemmed from Essex's catastrophic failure to capture the cargoes of the merchantmen in the harbour at Cádiz before the ships were set on fire. As a result, the soldiers had scooped the lion's share of the available booty, leaving the mariners with little more than scraps. Defending Essex, Sir Francis Vere rounded on the mariners for neglecting to plunder the ships, but Ralegh protested, rightly, that Essex had failed to give them the necessary orders.[49]

In a fit of pique, Essex demanded that each member of the Council of War set down his opinion in writing as to the propriety of his conduct, so he could later exonerate himself before the queen. This was typical of his conceit: he was a man who had to be proved right every time.

Disembarking at Plymouth on Tuesday, 10 August, Essex raced to see Elizabeth, demanding that his colleagues who had attacked him in the Council of War be censured, especially Ralegh.[50] In this he would partially succeed, but only because it turned out that he had all along been right about the incoming treasure convoy. By being denied the chance to sail for the Azores, he had missed it by a mere two days. Mortified by this failure and the untold wealth that had once again slipped through her fingers, Elizabeth was furious with Ralegh.[51]

But she was angrier still at how small a proportion of the plunder taken by the soldiers at Cádiz had been handed over to her officials. She had contributed in excess of £50,000 (£50 million in modern values) to the costs of the expedition. Cádiz, she had been reliably informed, had been stripped of everything of value, down to the very last farthing. And yet all she had to show for it were the two captured warships, some 1,200 cannon, a paltry amount of coin and gold and silver plate and small quantities of jewellery, silks, sugar, ginger, hides, bells and armour.[52]

All the more galling, thanks almost entirely to Essex's fatal misjudgement, was the loss of the cargoes of the thirty-four merchantmen. If only that sort of money had become available to her, Elizabeth believed, the whole course of the war might have been very different.[53]

On 8 September, Burghley and his son humiliated Essex in front of the queen in a carefully staged, widely publicized scene over his failure to account adequately for the missing booty. 'This day I was more braved by your little cousin than ever I was by any man in my life,' he grumbled to Anthony Bacon. Most telling was that Elizabeth did nothing to save him. In an effort to defend himself, Essex struck back by accusing Cecil's ally Sir George Carew of embezzling 44,000 ducats' worth of plundered gold, but he fell flat on his face when he failed to prove the charge.[54]

Unlike Ralegh, who stood uncharacteristically aloof from the infighting, still hoping to be allowed back to Court as Captain of the Guard, Essex's response was to recruit a new spin doctor. He chose Henry Cuffe, a brilliant Oxford scholar weary of the dreaming spires, a man said to harbour 'secret ambitious ends of his own', who offered to concoct a highly partisan account of the expedition.[55] Closely supervised by Essex, who meant to use the piece to foist upon Elizabeth his own conception of how the war should be waged, the tract, artfully disguised in the form of a private letter from a soldier in the field to Anthony Bacon, was to be published under the title *A True Relation of the Action at Cádiz the 21st of June under the Earl of Essex and the Lord Admiral*.[56]

But there was a mole at the heart of Essex's entourage. Caught out by Cecil with a small fortune in undeclared spoils, Sir Anthony Ashley became a turncoat, pleading for his pardon and leaking a draft of Cuffe's tract to the queen to save his skin. So irate that, for once, she struggled to find words to express her feelings, Elizabeth ordered it not to be printed, on pain of death. Essex was forced to restrict its circulation to handwritten copies sent to his friends and supporters at home and abroad.[57]

Cecil pushed home his advantage, daring to have Essex's correspondence from abroad intercepted and copied before it was returned to the courier and delivered to Essex House. Suspecting this sinister turn of events, Anthony Bacon fed the Earl's sense of grievance by telling him he was being baited by dogs like a bear in a pit.[58]

Never prepared to admit that he might be losing the battle for power and fame, Essex made the spade-shaped, military-style beard he had grown at Cádiz his personal trademark. From now on, he adopted a fixed facial image to remind everyone of his victory.[59] The prime version, hanging at Woburn Abbey, was created by the fashionable Court artist Marcus Gheeraerts the Younger. Painted from life in the closing months of 1596, in the portrait Essex affects a regal bearing, as if he were himself a king, his head and shoulders leaning slightly forwards, and dressed in a white satin doublet and hose, sporting the insignia of the Order of the Garter and clutching his sword. In the background is a view of Cádiz in flames. The image is that of a man who felt himself born to greatness and at liberty to ignore Elizabeth's commands.[60]

Numerous variants of this portrait type survive in full-length, half-length and head-and-shoulders versions, suggesting that, as with Hilliard's depiction of him in his tournament garb, Essex meant his new image to be widely disseminated. A portrait miniature by another rising young artist, Isaac Oliver, also featuring Essex's spade-shaped beard, would be copied even more frequently. Now at the Yale Center for British Art in New Haven, Connecticut, the composition is especially telling. Deliberately left unfinished, it was drawn in grey ink and gouache on parchment laid on to card as a pattern for replication, chiefly in printed engravings.[61] The victor of Cádiz, it is clear, had embarked on a visual propaganda campaign that outclassed anything ever imagined by the queen. She, it is now understood by art historians, rarely distributed her image in any significant quantities, except perhaps in miniature, and then usually for diplomatic ends, leaving it to her courtiers to propagate her brand as part of the 'cult' of Gloriana.[62]

Foreseeing all too clearly the dangers inherent in this unrelenting campaign of self-advertisement, Francis Bacon urged his patron to tread warily. In a penetrating letter of advice written on 4 October, he begged Essex to disabuse himself of the notion that he could bend the queen to his will over the conduct of the war. Rather than antagonizing her, he must do all he could to win her love through gracious speeches and (where necessary) unctuous flattery – but flattery that avoided any suspicion of hypocrisy, something Essex's verses and sonnets, with their double-edged innuendo, had so far failed to achieve.[63]

Warming to his theme, Bacon urged Essex to model himself on the examples set by Leicester and, still more, Hatton, favourites who had learned how to flatter Elizabeth with effortless warmth and (as it seemed to her) unimpeachable sincerity. Spin doctoring, confessed Bacon – and here he spoke with the voice of a master craftsman – was a matter of calculating how one's message was likely to be received. Essex had got it all wrong. Unlike Leicester, he was cultivating his image as a man of war even at moments when this was entirely inappropriate. Time and place were of the essence. He should remember that Elizabeth was a ruler who 'loveth peace. Next, she loveth not charge.' 'You say the wars are your occupation and go on in that course; whereas, if I might have advised your Lordship, you should have left that person at Plymouth.'[64]

Given the queen's inclinations and opinions, Bacon concluded, Essex could only appear to her to be an unbridled horse – the very phrase she had used of him on the eve of the Rouen campaign. Imagining her to be listening in like a fly on the wall, Bacon had her judge Essex to be 'a man of a nature not to be ruled; that hath the advantage of my affection, and knoweth it; of an estate not grounded to his greatness; of a popular reputation; of a military dependence'. 'I doubt', warned Bacon, delivering his punchline, 'whether there can be a more dangerous image than this represented to any monarch living, much more to a lady of Her Majesty's apprehension?'[65]

It was a brilliant vignette. And of all the dangers he enumerated, the greatest and most threatening to Essex was his quest for fame or popularity. For this, said Bacon, he must quickly learn to lose his appetite. 'Take all occasions', he cautioned, 'to speak against popularity and popular courses vehemently.'[66] The Earl had to learn – Bacon might have added like Coriolanus in Shakespeare's eponymous play, had the play yet been written – to know the distinction between civilian and military conduct, and to act appropriately in each of those spheres.

This was the sagest counsel Essex would ever receive. Some doubt exists as to whether Bacon actually sent this letter or merely drafted it and consigned it to a drawer but, if he did send it, his advice fell on deaf ears.[67] For the moment, Elizabeth still found herself psychologically bound to Essex, even as she chose to blame and furiously upbraid him. It would not be long, however, before the spell would be broken, even if she still expected him to stand beside her chair on New Year's Day, or Twelfth Night, as his stepfather had done before him. A tragedy was in the making, but before then the war would still require Essex's services and he would live to fight another day.

16.   One Last Chance

On his return from Cádiz, a crestfallen Essex set about reversing the shattering blow he believed he had suffered while fighting for the queen. In a matter of months, Robert Cecil had gained the coveted role of the queen's principal secretary, the route to succeeding his father as Elizabeth's chief minister. Then, when the ailing Lord Hunsdon died, Cecil had secured for his father-in-law, Lord Cobham, the influential post of Lord Chamberlain, which gave him overall control of access to the queen. Archbishop Whitgift's close friend ever since they had hunted for the author of the Marprelate tracts together, Cobham would have proved to be a formidable enemy to Essex had he not sickened and died in March 1597, six weeks after his daughter suffered a fatal miscarriage. Cecil, understandably, was stunned and for a while unravelled by the shock of his wife's sudden death. Ralegh, who never lacked human sympathy in such tragic circumstances, wrote him a moving letter of condolence:

> Sir: Because I know not how you dispose of yourself, I forbear to visit you, preferring your pleasing before mine own desire. I had rather be with you now than at any other time if I could thereby either take off from you the burden of your sorrows or lay the greatest part thereof on mine own heart. In the meantime I would but [re]mind you of this, that you should not overshadow your wisdom with passion but look aright into things as they are . . . Sorrows draw not the dead to life but the living to death, and if I were myself to advise myself in the like I would never forget my patience till I saw all and the worst of evils, and so grieve for all at once, lest lamenting for some one, another might yet remain in the power of destiny of greater discomfort. Yours ever beyond the power of words to utter, W. Ralegh.[1]

Money troubles slowed Essex down. Debts in excess of £10,000, chiefly arising from the huge sums he had invested in his Normandy and Cádiz expeditions, were about to fall due, whereas his guaranteed annual income was rarely higher than £2,500 from rents and £3,500 from the lease of the farm of the customs on sweet wines. Up until now, he had been regularly bailed out by gifts from the queen, a few as generous as £2,000 or £4,000, and had bridged the gap by converting grants worth £1,000 a year into one-off payments, one of which yielded as much as £38,000.[2]

In June 1596, however, Burghley had intervened. He persuaded Elizabeth shortly after Essex sailed for Cádiz that no more immediate warrants for grants signed off by her alone were to be processed, whether for Essex or for anyone else. From now on, warrants must be countersigned by three or four privy councillors, of whom he was always to be one. It was an audacious move, usually interpreted by Elizabeth's biographers to reflect a decline in her mental powers with the onset of age.[3]

But, in reality, it had nothing to do with her losing her grip. Burghley's timing was politically charged. For his new orders were issued immediately after he had shown the queen Essex's letter addressed to his fellow privy councillors signalling his intention to defy her orders and capture Cádiz as a permanent garrison town. Not surprisingly, in the light of her rooted hostility to the proposal, Elizabeth raised no objection to Burghley's move to save her money. While she found it difficult to resist the dashing young Earl in person, she knew she had spoiled him over the years, but now all this must come to an end. She could afford to indulge him only if she were prepared to assume a financial burden beyond the resources of her kingdom which she could not sustain. It was, though, entirely consistent with her devious ways of doing unpleasant things that she would disavow responsibility for the sudden block on her patronage, instead blaming her advisers, whose shoulders were broad.

Smarting from this blow, Essex, whose growing paranoia about Robert Cecil clouded his judgement, meant to expose the Lord Treasurer and his son for the corrupt dealings he believed were at the root of his humiliation. As he boasted to a steadily growing cabal of disaffected aristocrats and swordsmen who clustered around him at Essex House like hornets around a honey jar, 'I will perhaps jerk some of our gallants with their own rods, and then the queen shall see truth and fraud opposite one against the other, yet that I do not persecute my very enemies but as I am forced.'[4]

Chief among Essex's latest recruits were Henry Wriothesley, Earl of Southampton, and Lord Henry Howard, the younger brother of the Duke of Norfolk executed in 1572 after the Ridolfi Plot. Angry, idle, fashionable, rich, effeminate and bisexual, Southampton, still in his mid-twenties, was one of William Shakespeare's patrons, the man to whom Shakespeare had dedicated his Ovidian narrative poems *Venus and Adonis* and *The Rape of Lucrece*. For more than three years, Southampton pursued an on-off love affair with Elizabeth Vernon, one of the queen's maids of honour, whom (having initially broken off the relationship) he hastily married after getting her pregnant.[5]

Henry Howard, who had just turned fifty-six, was a crypto-Catholic supporter of Mary Queen of Scots. Five times Burghley had him arrested and imprisoned on suspicion of treasonable conspiracy while Mary was alive. Older, wiser, subtler, less partisan than Southampton, and far more slippery, he had long been out of favour with Elizabeth and was consumed by frustrated ambition. Regularly the first to be admitted to Essex's bedchamber in the morning, he managed the Earl's more sensitive correspondence, replacing Anthony Bacon when Bacon became terminally ill.[6] An ardent student of the lute and, like Elizabeth, an avid patron of the Catholic musician William Byrd, Howard drafted detailed political advice for Essex, ferreting out rumours and laconically describing himself as a 'sponge' from which the Earl could wring the lurid details of Court intrigues. All the same, he knew how to stay on the right side of Cecil, towards whom he would steadily gravitate as Essex's political paranoia became more pronounced.[7]

A third high-born supporter was Lord Rich, the husband of Essex's elder sister, Penelope, and once the wealthiest and most eligible bachelor in England. Virile, rash, opinionated and with a penchant for duelling, Rich loathed Burghley and did not seem to mind when another of the Earl's aristocratic friends, Charles Blount, Lord Mountjoy, took Penelope as his lover. Famously tall and handsome, with a freckled complexion and balding fair hair, Mountjoy had the makings of a high-flyer. Whether he would achieve his potential remained to be seen.

★ ★ ★

It did not help Essex that Elizabeth, now sixty-three and travelling longer distances only in her coach or barge, rarely ventured very far from her principal palaces of Whitehall, Greenwich, Richmond, Hampton Court and Nonsuch. The courtiers whose houses she regularly visited, usually just for dinner, narrowed to Burghley at Theobalds, Robert Cecil on the Strand, Whitgift at Lambeth and Lord Admiral Howard and his wife, Kate Carey, in Chelsea, a group that to Essex resembled a hostile praetorian guard. His suspicions only increased when, while still not deigning to favour him with a pet nickname, Elizabeth bestowed one on Whitgift after a visit to Lambeth for dinner, calling him her 'Little Black Husband'.[8]

Over the winter of 1596–7, Essex's response to his omission from the queen's choice of hosts was to sulk and brood. One day when she dined at Chelsea Manor, a fine country estate beside the Thames owned by the Crown and given to Kate Carey by Elizabeth as a sign of her special favour, he kept to his chamber and refused to come out.[9] On another occasion, after Cecil spent the whole day closeted with her 'in private and secret conference', he took to his bed for a fortnight, even though he was not sick. Up to a point, this type of emotional blackmail could still work for him: the queen, piqued by his absence, sent for him several times until, finally, he emerged from his chamber 'in his gown and night cap'. How much she really wanted to see him, rather than prove to herself that she could still make him dance to her tune, is hard to judge.[10]

In a more constructive effort to recover Elizabeth's favour, Essex posed as a reformed character, turning his back on sexual transgressions and embracing religion, making regular appearances at Matins and Evensong in church.[11] His attempt to reinvent himself appears not to have lasted long. Shortly before Christmas 1596, Anne Bacon, the mother of Francis and Anthony, upbraided him in a blistering broadside (after first approvingly recording his 'change of mind'), on account of his alleged flagrant 'backsliding'.[12]

Bacon's source was her friend Dorothy Stafford, now the longest serving of Elizabeth's Bedchamber women, who had informed her that Essex had embarked on an adulterous liaison with the unhappily married young Elizabeth Stanley, Countess of Derby, Burghley's granddaughter and Robert Cecil's favourite niece. Bluntly urging

Essex as a man of honour to abstain from 'carnal dalliance', Bacon charged him with 'infaming a nobleman's wife and so near about Her Majesty', then prayed that God 'by his grace' might speedily intervene to prevent 'some sudden mischief', a circumlocution undoubtedly meant to warn him to beware at all costs of getting the Countess pregnant.

Essex indignantly denied the charge, but his reply showed how vulnerable he was to such attacks. 'What I write now', he declared, 'is for the truth's sake and not for mine own: I protest before the majesty of God, and my protestation is voluntary and advised, that this charge which is newly laid upon me is false and unjust. And that since my departure from England towards Spain, I have been free from taxation of incontinency with any woman that lives.'[13]

Unfortunately, the rumour was not wholly unfounded as, four months later, when the Countess returned to Court for Easter, Essex slept with her.[14] And there was more because, just a few days earlier, the queen had physically attacked two of her more sexually precocious maids of honour, Bess Brydges and Bess Russell, showering them with 'words and blows of anger'. Their offence was secretly 'taking physic', then creeping through the privy galleries to watch Essex playing tennis.[15] The link between those charges suggests she believed the two young women had gone to watch Essex armed with pre-coital contraceptives, typically vaginal suppositories made of bitter almonds blanched and ground.[16]

Essex would get one last chance to prove his worth against Spain. Now past seventy, Philip II had vowed to be avenged for the sack of Cádiz. Stricken by gout and arthritis to the point where he was almost immobile and a valet had to massage his legs and feet in bed for up to an hour each morning, he had been overheard to protest that he would sell everything he owned, even down to his last candelabra, to get even with Elizabeth.[17]

So determined was he to wreak fire and havoc that, acting impulsively for perhaps the first time in his life, he had ordered a second *Gran Armada* to put to sea, on 13 October 1596, far too late in the season for the expedition to have above average prospects of success.[18] This was one of those rarer moments when Philip felt so provoked he lost sight of his long-established strategic goals in search of instant results. The best-informed monarch in the world, he was still vulnerable to his own personality traits, chiefly his compulsive tendency to micromanage his commanders.

Originally equipped to capture Brest in Brittany, the new Spanish fleet of some 126 ships, including sixty warships carrying fifteen thousand soldiers, had been instructed to make for Ireland or, if the winds were adverse, for Milford Haven in Wales.[19] Should the fleet arrive in one piece, the threat of invasion was potentially greater than in 1588, as the queen's ships were refitting at Chatham when the news of the earliest sightings off Cape Finisterre arrived. But on the night of 17 October, the Armada was severely battered by a south-westerly gale, losing thirty-two large vessels and many smaller craft. The surviving ships limped into Ferrol and Coruña, unable to continue their journey north, where they were joined by a flotilla of forty warships and pinnaces carrying 4,500 troops which had been immobilized by storms off the coast near Vigo.[20]

Even before Christmas, while Essex was still under a cloud over his failure to account adequately for the plunder from Cádiz, Lord Howard and Burghley had begun meeting privately at Burghley's house on the Strand to consider their next move on the chessboard. They quickly agreed in outline a plan for a fresh offensive to put the rest of Philip's Atlantic fleet out of commission. But who should be put in command? Howard professed himself too old: he had recently celebrated his sixtieth birthday and had no wish to expose himself to the rigours of another long and perilous maritime venture. Elizabeth was willing to consider Essex, but the Earl insisted the mission should be turned into another fully-fledged counter-Armada of the sort attempted the previous year. When the queen flatly forbade this, Essex sulked. Then, behind her back, he plotted with Ralegh and Cecil to put the idea into practice on a smaller scale. The final terms of this arrangement, which Cecil inveigled Elizabeth into approving if with the gravest of reservations, were secretly thrashed out on 18 April 1597 in a deal made during a clandestine dinner that Essex, Cecil and Ralegh shared at Essex House.[21]

According to this deal, Essex was at last to be given the freedom to capture and garrison a major port in Spain as a permanent base for

English ships to blockade the Spanish coast, just as he had always wanted. Ralegh was to serve as his deputy and would be allowed back to Court, where he would resume his old position as Captain of the Guard. His support was further bought with a government contract to victual six thousand men for three months, so drawn that he could be sure of a handsome profit. Cecil was to scoop the lucrative office of Chancellor of the Duchy of Lancaster, said to bring in a profit of at least £2,500 a year (£2.5 million today), while Lord Howard would be given valuable land grants in exchange for his non-interference. Everyone gained something.[22] And so full of bonhomie at their own ingenuity did the three rivals become, a point was reached where they were soon all sniggering over a risqué joke about the deposed King Richard II, undoubtedly at the queen's expense and sufficiently hilarious to make Essex 'wonderfully merry'.[23]

The loser in this sordid little conspiracy was to be Elizabeth. Except that she saw straight through them. Deeply suspicious of their sudden unexplained rapprochement, she withdrew her consent. Summoning her councillors to an audience in the Privy Chamber on 18 or 19 May, she berated them for urging the necessity of another campaign while failing to prove that any new or specific threat existed. 'I will not make wars', she angrily exclaimed, 'but arm for defence.' This, she insisted, was fundamental to her ideal of monarchy for, as in 1588, she was no warrior queen. She then spoke at length about the vast sums she had laid out both on land and at sea. She was particularly irked with Burghley for first proposing another large-scale expedition, 'seeing no great occasion'.[24]

What changed Elizabeth's mind was news of further reversals in France. Under Count Maurice, the Dutch had steadily transformed themselves into an effective fighting force since their victories at Steenwijk and Geertruidenberg. They had stormed Groningen and come close to winning almost full control over the seven northern Dutch provinces after routing a Spanish army in the field near Turnhout in January 1597. But, as yet, they were unable to reach across the frontier and impede Spanish operations in Picardy, where Henry IV was struggling badly. Early in March, quite shocking reports arrived in London that Amiens had fallen to Archduke Albert's troops, complete with forty cannon and a large munitions store, giving the enemy a bridgehead to cross the Somme a mere eighty or so miles from Paris. In this dire situation, the French king sent envoys across the Channel to urge Elizabeth to grant him fresh aid, even this time offering to allow her to keep Calais as a security for the repayment of his debts if only she would send an army to recover the town.[25]

Elizabeth was deeply unimpressed, replying that she could not afford to do more than she was doing already.[26] Her rebuff provoked Henry into resolving privately to throw everything he had into a final campaign to recover Amiens, after which he would make peace with Philip, regardless of his treaty with the English queen and his oath to uphold it. Marching to besiege Amiens just as Elizabeth was rebuking Burghley for giving his support to Essex's combined military and naval strategy, Henry also put out his first tentative feelers in Rome for indirect negotiations with Spain.

The catastrophe at Amiens, however, spurred Elizabeth into reversing her decision to block Essex's new attack on Spain. Reports had reached her that King Philip had now managed to refit over a hundred and fifty ships at Ferrol, Lisbon and Coruña, ready to put to sea again with sixteen thousand soldiers. On 20 May, shortly after clashing with her privy councillors, she wrote to the Dutch States and Count Maurice, asking to borrow back a thousand of Sir Francis Vere's veteran auxiliaries and requesting the loan of fifteen flyboats suitable for landing troops ashore instead of the twenty warships they had offered to lend her.[27]

Essex, meanwhile, put together a fleet of a hundred and twenty ships and came up with an ingenious plan to muster six thousand extra soldiers without drawing further on Vere's auxiliaries or the rump of the queen's troops still in France. They were to be drawn from the ablest men in the local militias, who never expected to serve outside their native counties. To conscript them for overseas service was unprecedented and almost certainly illegal, but Essex was undaunted by constitutional niceties. He needed soldiers – and this was the easiest way to recruit good ones.[28]

Elizabeth signed Essex's new commission as Lieutenant-General with her customary bold pen strokes at Greenwich Palace on 4 June, and followed up with more specific instructions eleven days later. His first priority was to be the destruction of all Philip's ships in the harbour at Ferrol, after which she suggested that Essex might sail to the Azores and capture the island of Terceira. Should it be possible to intercept Philip's New World treasure fleet or the Portuguese carracks expected to arrive from the East Indies to pay for the expedition, so much the better.[29]

In contrast to her orders for the attack on Cádiz the previous year – the much-amended wording of this clause shows that she acted with obvious misgivings – the queen gave Essex her official sanction to seize and fortify *any* place within Philip's dominions.[30] From the final version of her instructions, though, it seems she was already having second thoughts. Her preference, clearly, was for Essex to capture and fortify Terceira and nowhere else, and even then only if he could be certain that the garrison he left there could safely defend itself without regular supplies from England.[31] As hungry as ever for Spanish silver, Elizabeth opted for Terceira because Philip's treasure fleets regularly regrouped there before embarking on the final stage of their journey to Spain.

The queen's concession that Essex might, at his discretion, seize and fortify any place on Spanish shores, even if she preferred Terceira, had obviously been wrung out of her. At last, the Earl believed he had a realistic prospect of achieving his grand military ambition. And he could have no excuse for failure this time. As he later boasted, punch-drunk with a consuming sense of his own impregnability, 'When I had defeated that force [at Ferrol], I might go after whither I list, and do almost what I list; I mean in any places along the coast.'[32]

Unfortunately for him, his hopes were crushed by the appalling summer weather. Shortly before the expedition set sail from Plymouth on 10 July, Essex was in high favour with the queen. As a good-luck token for his voyage, she sent him a portrait miniature of herself, an unusual gesture. He wrote back in ecstasy, thanking her 'for bestowing on me that fair angel that you sent to guard me'.[33] But barely had the fleet reached the coast of Brittany than it was battered almost to pieces by a severe north-westerly gale. Ralegh returned with the timbers of his flagship smashed to splinters in several places. So determined was Essex not to abandon the voyage that he tried to ride out the storm, delaying a return until the last moment, barely making it to Falmouth, with even his most experienced mariners laid low by excessive vomiting. Once back on land, many seized the chance to run away.[34]

Elizabeth, grudgingly, allowed the Earl to try again, but her confidence and patience were fast waning. And in a letter that now survives only as a copy, she reminded him to beware of the daredevil arrogance of youth. 'Eyes of youth', she began in one of her more Shakespearean sentences, 'have sharp sights, but commonly not so deep as those of elder age, which makes me marvel less at rash attempts and headstrong counsels, which give not leisure to judgement's warning nor heeds advice, but makes a laughter at the one and despise[s] with scorn the last.'

> Trust not to the grace of your crazed vessel that to the ocean may fortune [to] be too humble. Foresee and prevent it now in time, afore, too late, you vex me too much with small regard of what I scape [*sic*] or bid. Admit that by miracle it would do well, yet venture not such wonders where such approachful mischief might betide you. There remains that you, after your perilous first attempt, do not aggravate that danger with another in a farther off climate . . . Let character serve your turn, and be content when you are well, which hath not ever been your property.

Essex had been put on notice that he was not to fail this time.[35]

Once more, however, foul weather kept the fleet in port while plague rampaged through the ranks of the soldiers. With his supplies running low, Essex was forced to dismiss all his troops apart from Vere's thousand veterans, the absolute minimum needed for an attack on Ferrol. Then, suddenly and inexplicably, Elizabeth's mood lightened. Cecil could write reassuringly, 'The queen is so disposed now to have us all love you, as she and I do every night talk like angels of you.'[36] (It was a true report but, beneath the mask, Cecil had an evil intent, since he had already guessed that the Earl was destined to fail.)[37]

Hoping to reap advantage of Elizabeth's mood swing, Essex rode post-haste to Greenwich with Ralegh to see if she would approve a last-minute change of plan. Now, he wanted to sail directly to the

Caribbean to intercept Philip's treasure ships at the dispatching end, as Ralegh had always longed to do. His timing was inopportune. Gone was Elizabeth's sunny disposition. Instead, the two men found her writhing in agony from arthritis in her right hand. Unwilling to modify her existing instructions, she tetchily ordered her Lieutenant to implement them as best he could. It was he who had sought this command. After all the expense she had incurred in allowing him to get this far, he must shoulder the blame if things went wrong.[38]

It was never in Essex's nature to turn back from an enterprise once begun but, by the time he finally headed for the Bay of Biscay on the night of 17 August, he had to face the unpalatable fact that his expedition was most likely doomed. When, on first glimpsing the Iberian coast, his fleet was dispersed by yet another storm, he decided to abandon the attack on Ferrol and sail directly to the Azores, where he planned to lie in wait for Philip's treasure fleet.

This was exactly the sort of stopgap plan, made on the spur of the moment, that he had once scathingly described as little better than 'idle wanderings upon the sea'.[39] Now, he was trapped into it himself, making his choice because he was deceived by clever Spanish disinformation that the Ferrol fleet already had its orders to meet the treasure convoy in mid-Atlantic.[40] His decision transformed the nature of the expedition. From this point onwards, it was devoid of anything resembling a coherent plan. Everything would come down to luck and quick thinking. A naval venture of this type placed an overwhelming burden on its leader, but Essex was no seaman like Drake or Ralegh. His experience had largely been acquired on land.

He made a litany of mistakes. On arrival at Terceira, he was shocked to be informed that Philip's fleet was still lying safely at anchor in the harbour at Ferrol. Even knowing that, he refused to return to patrol the Spanish coast, backing a hunch that a third Armada would not be seaworthy until the following spring. He then issued a whole series of ambiguous, contradictory, over-complex orders to his mariners for cruising between the islands of the Azores.[41]

Tempers quickly frayed. At Faial, where he had sailed in search of plunder, Essex's shortcomings led to a violent split with Ralegh that would never be healed. The Earl's supporters, incited by his hot-headed steward Sir Gelly Meyrick, had shrilly demanded that Ralegh be charged with mutiny and then hanged for landing troops to burn and sack the town before Essex had arrived to give the orders. The incident proved hugely destructive as Ralegh's supporters came to his defence. When Essex, distracted by the quarrel, then failed by a mere three hours to intercept the Spanish treasure fleet as it approached Terceira, he squandered his last chance of retaining Elizabeth's favour. Twelve million ducats (coincidentally, the same amount the Earl had lost at Cádiz by not taking the thirty-four merchantmen before they were scuttled), laden on six ill-defended ships of no more than three hundred tons apiece, slipped through his fingers. His consolation prize was to capture a ship belonging to the Governor of Havana, which had strayed from the *flota*, accompanied by two frigates. On board were 400,000 ducats (around £128 million today), ample to cover the expedition's costs but nothing like enough to satisfy the queen.[42]

The *coup de grâce* came when Essex limped home in October, only to discover that the vanguard of a Spanish fleet had recently been sighted reconnoitring near Falmouth. While he had been cruising between the islands of the Azores, Philip had sent his third *Gran Armada* from Ferrol with orders to seize a Cornish port and establish a military base there, just as Essex sought to do at Lisbon or Cádiz.[43] By now, the Spanish king was confined to his sickbed, tended lovingly by the Infanta, who moved into the vacant queen's apartments at the Escorial adjacent to Philip's own. By spooning broth down her ailing father's throat, it was she who kept alive his hopes that, before he died, he might still triumph over the heretic bastard queen he had once thought of marrying.[44]

Little had Essex known as he set sail homewards that his ships and this third Armada, each unaware of the other, were on a collision course. By 12 October, the bulk of the Spanish fleet lay off the coast of Blavet, waiting for troops to board. Quite oblivious to the impending threat, the Privy Council was horrified to receive on the 26th a scribbled note from Sir Ferdinando Gorges, the captain of the harbour defences at Plymouth, informing them that Spanish ships had been sighted.[45]

By then, luckily, the threat was minimal. A sudden, powerful north-easterly gale had scattered the Armada and forced it to make for home with similar losses to the year before. When Essex landed at Plymouth, he would nonetheless be appalled to discover that he had missed the Spanish warships by a relatively short distance. His hope of a decisive victory was once again thwarted, his limitations as a war leader cruelly highlighted.[46]

Arriving in London on 5 November, Essex briefly visited the Court at Whitehall, then retreated straight to his bedchamber to sulk, declining to attend Parliament, which the queen had summoned to secure the fresh taxes she needed to finance the war. He even failed to put in an appearance in the tiltyard on Accession Day.[47] He had just learned that Elizabeth had sent him an icy rebuke in a letter he had not received while still at sea for his failure either to attack Ferrol or to intercept the treasure fleet.[48]

Her dissatisfaction was plain:

> When we do look back to the beginning of this action which hath stirred so great expectation in the world and charged us so deeply, we cannot but be sorry to foresee already how near all our expectations and your great hopes are to a fruitless conclusion.

For his lamentable performance, she declared, 'We should think ourselves in much worse case than when the action did begin, not only in point of honour and charge, but also for safety.'[49] At one moment, she even threatened that, if she could be sure he was to blame for missing Philip's treasure fleet as it approached Terceira, she 'would have struck off his head'.[50] As the Court gossips chorused in glorious understatement at the news, she was 'not well pleased with him for his service at sea, wherein it is alleged he might have done more than he did'. She did, however, quickly seize all the treasure he had captured from the Governor of Havana's ship for the royal coffers, before it slipped away into the hands of the mariners and soldiers.[51]

Most cuttingly of all, Essex discovered that, while he had been away fighting, the queen had promoted Lord Admiral Howard to be Earl of Nottingham, with a pension of £100 a year. This promotion gave the newly created Earl precedence over Essex in the House of Lords and also in royal processions. To rub salt in the wound, Nottingham was a royal title: previous incumbents had included Richard, Duke of York, the younger son of Edward IV; and Henry Fitzroy, Henry VIII's illegitimate son by his mistress Elizabeth ('Bessie') Blount. To crown it all, the wording of Nottingham's patent of creation seemed to give him all the credit for the victory at Cádiz.[52]

In an unashamedly hierarchical society, precedence really mattered. As Ulysses puts it in Shakespeare's *Troilus and Cressida*, 'Take but degree away, untune that string,/ And hark what discord follows.'[53] Essex felt his honour had been infringed, his triumph at Cádiz stolen from him. His towering sense of entitlement began to eat away at him and destroy him. He even challenged Nottingham, or any of his sons, to a duel.[54] His ego cut to the quick, he insisted that Elizabeth either amend the patent or that Nottingham surrender it.[55] When these provocative demands yielded no result, he went on strike, refusing to carry out the duties of his various offices and petulantly indicating that he would not return to the queen's service until she gave him some superior reward to salve his pride.[56]

Essex withdrew to his country estate at Wanstead for over a fortnight in a sulk: he seemed to be provoking the queen to a direct test of wills.[57] His insolence encouraged Cecil and Ralegh, once again working together, to renew all their old antagonisms to him. Whereas they had made their peace with Essex at the time of their clandestine dinner, now they went about traducing him as a dangerous maverick.[58] To compound matters, the Earl's brief affair with Burghley's granddaughter, the Countess of Derby, suddenly became public knowledge, infuriating the queen, uniting all the Countess's many relatives against Essex and marginalizing him even further.[59] All of this severely dented his carefully crafted image as a serious politician and war leader.

Weary of Essex's unremitting harassment, Nottingham left Court for his Chelsea estate, declaring himself sick and taking his wife, Kate Carey, with him.[60] Elizabeth urged Ralegh to mediate but, when Essex declined to cooperate, the stand-off continued.[61] When Essex finally returned to Court, he chose to boycott the Privy Council.

For once, Elizabeth decided to end the quarrel the easy way.[62] Much against her better judgement, she allowed Essex to exercise the post of Earl Marshal, which she had kept vacant since the Earl of

Shrewsbury's death in 1590. This uneasy promotion put him in charge of the College of Arms, making him the chief officer responsible for organizing royal coronations, marriages, christenings and funerals.[63] His duties would be purely ceremonial but, by virtue of Henry VIII's 1539 Act for the Placing of the Lords, they allowed him to recover his former precedence over Nottingham in the seating arrangements in the House of Lords.[64]

Elizabeth had indulged him. She knew better, but it seemed to be the least bad option for now. The one thing she knew was that she could not afford to lose Nottingham or Kate Carey: it seems they had become too close to her personally. And she failed to see why Nottingham should be demoted from his new honours merely to appease Essex. Even then, Essex quibbled over the small print of his patent, rejecting the wording first suggested by Cecil and insisting on his own alternatives. He volubly protested, 'I reach at nothing to which I lay not a true claim.'

It was far from the end for Essex, but this was the episode that first signalled his enduring estrangement from the queen and his colleagues in the Privy Council. From this point onwards, there would be no turning back. Ever since his stepfather's death, he had sought to make himself an indispensable war hero and Burghley's heir as chief minister. But all he had achieved was to infuriate the queen and make himself generally odious. And when Elizabeth took umbrage, those who had given her offence tended fairly quickly to suffer damaging reprisals.[65]

It would take barely six months for Essex to receive his comeuppance. The moment arrived when Elizabeth sought to choose a new Lord Deputy for Ireland on the death from typhus of Thomas, Lord Burgh. After sounding out Nottingham, Cecil and Essex in the Privy Chamber at Greenwich Palace, she proposed Sir William Knollys, Essex's uncle. He was, she declared, 'the fittest of any' to be sent over as chief governor to the Tudor equivalent of Siberia. But Essex obstinately dissented, eager instead to get rid of Sir George Carew, whom the Earl had unsuccessfully accused of stealing 44,000 ducats' worth of plundered gold at Cádiz. Losing his temper and quite forgetting where he was when the queen refused to budge, Essex gave her a scornful look, then turned his back on her in a calculated gesture of contempt. Such effrontery on the part of a subject and a man to whom she had given so much sent her into an apoplexy. Unable to restrain herself, she struck him across the face and told him to go and be hanged.

Instinctively, Essex reached for his sword and had to be forcibly restrained by Nottingham. Escorted by guards from the Privy Chamber, Essex swore a great oath, informing the queen and his thunderstruck colleagues that 'he neither could nor would put up [with] so great an affront and indignity, neither would he have taken it at King Henry the Eighth his [*sic*] hands.'[66]

To say that to Elizabeth, who revered her father, despite all that he had done to her mother, was fatal enough. But Essex had not quite finished. He then, according to Ralegh's account, compounded his offence by muttering in her hearing as he left the room that 'her conditions were as crooked as her carcass.' Ralegh reckoned that to say this to a woman was as bad as to tell a king that he was wicked or a coward. 'It is one and the same error.'[67]

In a well-intentioned letter of advice, Sir Thomas Egerton, now promoted on the death of Sir John Puckering from his post of Queen's Attorney to be Keeper of the Great Seal, urged the Earl to apologize to the queen and plead for her forgiveness. 'You are not yet so far gone', he said, 'but you may well return. The return is safe, the progress dangerous and desperate. In the course you hold, if you have any enemies, you do that for them which they could never do for themselves.'[68]

But Essex refused to listen. 'You must give me leave to tell you', he replied, 'that in some cases I must appeal from all earthly judges; and if in any, then surely in this, when the highest judge on the earth hath imposed upon me the heaviest punishment without trial or hearing.'

> Nay, when the vilest of all indignities is done unto me, doth religion enforce me to sue? Doth God require it? Is it impiety not to do it? Why, cannot princes err? Cannot subjects receive wrong? Is an earthly power or authority infinite? Pardon me, pardon me, my good lord, I can never subscribe to these principles.[69]

By asking these rhetorical questions and then seemingly answering them with a resounding 'No,' Essex made himself vulnerable to a charge of atheism, since it could be made to appear that he was denying the God-given authority of kingship. From now on, far more even than Ralegh, who had dreamed of the success of his Roanoke colony or of tapping the untold riches of El Dorado, the reckless Earl came to inhabit a fantasy world of his own making. If ever Elizabeth, ageing or not, had found him irresistible and longed to make him a surrogate for her beloved Leicester to remind her of her youth, it was no more. She was a queen as well as a woman: he was quite mistaken in imagining that he could conquer her by the sheer force of his will. The spell that had bound them together was finally broken. It simply remained to discover how precisely the drama would end.

17.   Seeking Détente

By the time Essex returned to Plymouth from the Azores in October 1597, the war with Spain had dragged on for longer than the First and Second World Wars combined. The fiscal burden on Philip II had become unsustainable. The Spanish king had never fully understood his own finances. Despite silver and gold arriving regularly from the New World, he had to endure a series of financial crises brought about by almost constant warfare, colossal military spending and ever-increasing debt repayments. In its written advice in November 1596, his Council of Finance estimated that he would have to lay out 11 million ducats (around £3.2 billion in modern values) over the following thirteen months and could expect Spain's accumulated deficit to approach 16 million ducats by the end of 1598 and 26 million by 1599.[1] With such amounts far exceeding his ability to pay the interest or restructure his loans, Philip declared bankruptcy.

His approach was ingenious. He simply told the Italian and German bankers operating in the markets of Antwerp, Genoa and Seville that their credit agreements, or *asientos*, with him infringed the canon law of usury and were to be replaced by Spanish state securities, or *juros*, carrying a much lower rate of interest. The inevitable result was a run on the banks, a sudden collapse in liquidity, violent exchange-rate fluctuations and large-scale paralysis in international trade.

And yet, the psychological effects of bankruptcy were far greater. No longer could Philip pose convincingly as the hammer of the heretics and the upholder of the Spanish-Habsburg world order. He had defaulted before – in 1557, 1560 and 1575 – but this time the amounts involved were much larger and it was obvious that Spain could not continue to regard its New World assets as inexhaustible. For the first time since the beginning of the war, Philip had to confront the possibility of defeat. So far, he had flatly repudiated any suggestion of peace with Elizabeth or the rebellious Dutch. But his councillors' advice was firm. 'The objective of wars', they declared sententiously, 'is peace, always provided the proper conditions may be obtained.'[2]

Henry IV was also eager for peace. The catastrophic loss of Amiens in March 1597 had seriously compromised his campaign to reunify France. Throughout the ensuing summer, he had struggled desperately to recover the town from its Spanish garrison before Archduke Albert ordered the main body of his forces across the border from the southern Netherlands into Picardy.

On 9 September, Henry was able to write jubilantly to Elizabeth announcing that, with the assistance of her auxiliaries, he had finally recovered Amiens.[3] Albert, severely weakened by the effects of Philip's bankruptcy, had been unable to raise a large enough relief force to hold the town. By letting Count Maurice and the Dutch take full control of the seven northern provinces of the Netherlands, he had mustered 20,000 infantry and 4,500 cavalry, whereas Henry, by a herculean effort, managed to scrape together sufficient funds to support an army of 23,000 infantry and 5,500 cavalry for just long enough to win a victory.[4]

Peace talks between France and Spain could now begin in earnest under the auspices of Alexander de' Medici, the legate of the new pope, Clement VIII. Notwithstanding his oath to Elizabeth not to entertain a peace proposal without consulting her, Henry felt he was unable to continue fighting unless the English and the Dutch would join him in a final, costly, all-out offensive to clear all the remaining Spaniards from the war zones, including Brittany. And that was well-nigh impossible.

Philip, for his part, fully aware that he was fast approaching death, was eager to clear the path for his only surviving son, nineteen-year-old Philip, the fourth child of his last wife, Anne of Austria. As the bedridden king gradually came to terms with the harsh reality that Spain was no longer as supremely powerful as it had been at the time of the abdication of his own father, Charles V, he knew that his son would only be able to rule effectively without the distractions of this crippling conflict across northern Europe.

Making overtures to Albert shortly after recovering Amiens, Henry discovered enough common ground to persuade him that it was time to take counsel with his allies. To Elizabeth, he sent André Hurault, Sieur de Maisse, a former French ambassador to Venice. Arriving in London on 22 November 1597, de Maisse, an experienced lawyer-diplomat, delivered a very similar message to one Henry had sent to the Dutch States General. Unless, he said, the English queen was willing to engage in a full-scale land war to evict the Spaniards from France and the Netherlands rather than wage a sea war against Spain's Atlantic naval power, Henry would feel obliged to make peace whether she liked it or not.[5]

Never someone who reacted well to an ultimatum, Elizabeth was in no hurry to make up her mind. She veered instinctively towards détente but still bitterly remembered Philip's perfidy in 1588, when he had allowed her talks with the Duke of Parma's representatives at Bourbourg to drag on fruitlessly until a month after the first *Gran Armada* had set sail from Lisbon. Towards Henry, she had mixed feelings. He, too, was perfidious – she had never forgiven him for his conversion to Catholicism – but foremost in her mind were the debts of her French and Dutch allies, which, allowing for accumulated interest, had soared to £1.6 million.[6] Whether or not she decided to entertain a peace proposal would most likely depend on the prospects for repayment of a significant proportion of these debts.

De Maisse's arrival therefore began a lengthy process of debate and deliberation, as much in the queen's own mind as in the Privy Council.[7] And a fresh dimension was added when, shortly after de Maisse presented his credentials, Philip betrothed his daughter, the Infanta, to Archduke Albert and announced that he would shortly be transferring sovereignty over the old Burgundian lands of Franche-Comté and the Netherlands to the couple as Isabella's dowry.[8] Elizabeth cautiously welcomed this news, which seemed to offer a chance that the southern provinces of the Netherlands would recover at least some of their ancient liberties. Remembering an Italian joke with vaguely obscene connotations she had learned as an adolescent, she twice quipped *per molto variar natura è bella* ('Nature's beauty comes from these sorts of surprises').[9]

The result was that de Maisse, who had a keen eye for detail and was a shrewd judge of character, stayed in England for over six weeks, keeping a fascinating diary in which he recorded the details of his audiences with the queen. This was hitherto known only from brief, paraphrased extracts in French and from a questionable early-twentieth-century translation, but a complete French text has now been rediscovered in a manuscript in the Bibliothèque Nationale in Paris and, for the first time, more accurate descriptions of his encounters with the queen can be given.[10]

Elizabeth gave de Maisse six audiences, but he never knew very far in advance when she would see him. She would send for him only when she was ready, laying on her coach or barge to fetch him. Once, she cancelled their meeting at the very last moment. Later, de Maisse discovered she had looked in the mirror and decided her appearance was too ghastly for her to receive him.[11]

Age had increased rather than tempered her vanity. In times of stress, she would lash out at the younger, prettier members of her Bedchamber staff, accusing them of insolence or insubordination. Shortly before de Maisse's arrival, she had caused a series of ugly scenes in the Privy Chamber, accusing Mary Howard, one of her maids of honour, of wilfully neglecting her duties, whereas the girl's true offence was flaunting her good looks and fine clothes and flirting with Essex.[12] As John Harington famously put it, when Elizabeth smiled, 'it was a pure sunshine that everyone did choose to bake in if they could; but anon came a storm from a sudden gathering of clouds, and the thunder fell in wondrous manner on all alike.'[13]

The defective English translation of de Maisse's diary has persistently been used by Elizabeth's biographers to make it seem as if the sixty-four-year-old queen had taken to dressing like a whore for hire, flaunting her naked bosom to make it appear that, although her prospects of marriage and childbearing were long past, she was still sexually provocative. 'I'm not ready to die just yet, Mr Ambassador', she told de Maisse at one of their encounters, 'and am not as old as everyone thinks.'[14] But the original French text makes plain what was really going on: as a fluent Italian speaker and lover of all things Italian, Elizabeth was determined to prove to this former ambassador to Venice that she could outplay the Italians at their own game. Flirtatious and distant in confusingly equal measure during their talks, she often spoke to him in Italian rather than French.

For their first meeting, she wore a loose white-and-carnation-col-
oured dress made from a fabric de Maisse called 'silver gauze'. (Most
likely this meant either that the silk was embellished with puffs of
white gauze or else that tiny silver or silver-gilt metal strips were
interwoven into it so that it sparkled.) The dress had open sleeves
lined with red taffeta, and a high collar at the back, flecked with tiny
rubies and pearls. For at least two years, gowns with a closed front,
low neckline, open sleeves and exactly such a collar, much in vogue
in Italy, had made their way to London. Commonly, the sleeve open-
ings could be fastened with ribbons or gold buttons, or adorned with
other miniature pendant sleeves, leaving just a hint of the lining visible. It would appear from de Maisse's description that the queen's
sleeves were of this type, and he adds the fascinating detail that she
constantly fidgeted with her pendant sleeves when speaking.[15]

According to the defective English translation, Elizabeth had
dressed to kill, flaunting her sexuality:

> She kept the front of her dress open, and one could see the whole of
> her bosom, and passing low, and often she would open the front of
> this robe with her hands as if she was too hot . . . Her bosom is some-
> what wrinkled as well as [*several words are missing in the manuscript here,
> replaced by seven dots*]* the collar that she wears around her neck, but
> lower down her flesh is exceeding white and delicate, so far as one
> could see.[16]

But the original French in the Bibliothèque Nationale manuscript is
quite emphatic that it was only *toute sa gorge et assez bas* that de Maisse
could see, so *la gorge* and 'enough' or 'sufficiently below it'.[17] And
while *la gorge* in twenty-first-century French usually means 'throat',
but can indeed sometimes refer to 'bosom', as the translator assumes,
we can confidently say that, during the sixteenth century, the second
of these meanings had not yet come into being. Our guide is the
expert etymologist and lexicographer Randle Cotgrave. He had
lived for many years in France and, in his monumental *Dictionarie of
the French and English Tongues*, finally published in 1611, he explains

---

* The fact that words are missing at this point was not disclosed by the translator.
See below.

that *la gorge* normally means 'the throat or gullet, most properly the bottom of the mouth, or the most deep and inward part thereof'.* But in the case of a woman, it means the outward and upper part of the flesh 'between the neck and the pappes'. 'Pappes' is the sixteenth-century English word for a woman's mammary glands or bosom. And Cotgrave confirms with reassuring specificity that the correct French word for 'bosom' during his lifetime was *le sein* (as it still is today) and not *la gorge*.

What did de Maisse mean by saying, according to the translator, 'lower down her flesh is exceeding white and delicate, so far as one could see'?[18] The answer is: very little. The translator fails to inform us that immediately before this passage several words are missing in the French manuscript. Instead, he attempts to supply them. He adds the words 'one can see for', to make the sentence read: 'Her bosom is somewhat wrinkled as well as *one can see for* the collar that she wears round her neck, but lower down her flesh is exceeding white and delicate, so far as one could see.' For almost a century, these words have been attributed to de Maisse as if he had recorded them. But all we know about what he *actually* said is that, *below the collar* around the queen's neck, her flesh was 'exceeding white and delicate, so far as one could see'. Given the solid fact as confirmed by modern-costume experts that Elizabeth was commissioning Italian and especially Venetian-style dresses around the time of de Maisse's visit, the most credible explanation is that her gown was cut down to the cleavage in the latest Italian style.[19] In other words, even supposing de Maisse *had* managed to catch a glimpse of her bosom, this was not a sign of sexual desperation but a reflection of the fact that she had always loved haute couture.

Similar confusions about women's fashions pervade the other descriptions. Describing de Maisse's second audience, the defective translation claims the queen wore a gown of black taffeta trimmed with gold lace in the Italian style with a 'petticoat of white damask' and a matching chemise, which she left open at the front so that 'one could see all her belly, and even to her navel'. 'When she raises her

---

* In the case of birds, especially birds of prey, *la gorge* could also refer to a meal, or 'gorgeful'.

head, she has a trick of putting both hands on her gown and opening it, insomuch that all her belly can be seen.'[20]

Once again, the original French does not support these luridly erotic suggestions. The word 'chemise' in the context of Italian gowns means a jerkin, or an embroidered bodice. As to a 'petticoat', the manuscript does not use this word but refers merely to 'the garment beneath'. Beneath her chemise in the 1590s, a lady of fashion wore a silk under-bodice, or 'a shirt or smock', cut no lower than the top of the cleavage, and usually both the chemise and the smock had slashes at the front, towards the centre. Four of the five Italian gowns that are accompanied by fully detailed tailoring specifications in Elizabeth's costume accounts called for a 'double bodice' of precisely this sort. As the queen put her hands to her side as she raised her head, therefore, the decorative guards of the gown would have parted slightly, half opening to reveal the garments beneath. And it was merely through their slashes that de Maisse would have been able to glimpse small parts of the queen's *estomach* ('stomach') down as far as the *nombril* ('navel') – for that was considered chic. With the chemise worn directly over the smock, however, acres of bare flesh would never be seen.[21]

The same misapprehension mars the translator's account of de Maisse's third audience. On this occasion, he reports Elizabeth as wearing 'a white robe of cloth of silver, cut very low and her bosom uncovered'. For once, de Maisse does use the word for 'bosom' (*le sein*).[22] But what the original French confirms is that her low neckline was 'cut or made hollow and into a half-round' in the Italian manner (the correct sixteenth-century meaning of the word *échancré*). It is a proven fact that a fashionable neckline of this type would indeed have left the top, and only the top, of the cleavage visible.[23] But this was not a provocation. Elizabeth would be shown wearing almost exactly this type of décolletage in her famous 'Rainbow Portrait', painted a few years later, and no one has ever claimed it was erotic or indecent.

Besides describing her attire, de Maisse put on record a vivid, if hardly flattering, impression of Elizabeth's appearance in his diary:

On her head . . . she wore a great reddish-coloured wig, with a great
number of spangles of gold and silver, and hanging down over her
forehead some pearls . . . As for her face, it is and appears to be very
aged. It is long and thin, and her teeth are very yellow and unequal,
compared with what they were formerly, so they say, and on the left
side less than on the right. Many of them are missing so that one cannot understand her easily when she speaks quickly.[24]

This complements Paul Hentzner's similar description of the queen
at Greenwich in 1598:

Her face [is] oblong, fair but wrinkled; her eyes small, yet black and
pleasant; her nose a little hooked, her lips narrow and her teeth black
(a defect the English seem subject to for their too great use of sugar)
. . . She wore false hair, and that red; upon her head she had a small
crown.[25]

Both accounts conform closely to an unusually arresting, recently
rediscovered portrait of the queen made by Marcus Gheeraerts the
Younger's studio, painted when she was sixty-two or sixty-three.
Purchased by a wealthy American, Mrs Ruth Coltrane Cannon, from
a New York dealer in 1958, the painting was later given to the Garden
Club of North Carolina to adorn the entrance of its Elizabethan Garden at Manteo on the eastern side of Roanoke Island. (There it
remained until 2008, when it was spotted by a visiting academic, who
recognized its significance.)[26]

A stark and compelling reworking of the upper half of the portrait that Gheeraerts had painted for Sir Henry Lee in 1592 to adorn
his house at Ditchley in Oxfordshire, the 'Manteo' painting depicts
the ageing queen with unflattering realism.[27] Her face is covered in
folds and wrinkles. She gazes down haughtily at the viewer, showing
off her elongated, slightly hooked nose. Her dark eyes are piercing,
her lips pursed, and no attempt is made to disguise the fact that the
crown and pearls on her head are pinned to a thick auburn wig. A
few wisps of natural grey hair are visible underneath, peeping out at
the sides. Like her mother, the queen has a long, thin neck. A closer
scrutiny of the portrait suggests evidence of the dermatological damage caused by the powders and creams she used to smooth and blanch

her skin and the rouge she used to colour her lips and cheeks. Around the mouth, her cheeks seem pinched: perhaps evidence of her missing teeth.

The survival of the 'Manteo Portrait' confounds those who have insisted that Elizabeth's extreme sensitivity to her appearance led her to order the destruction of all realistic depictions of her in old age. As one famous art historian put it in a quotation regularly taken out of context, 'all likenesses of the Queen that depicted her as being in any way old and hence subject to mortality' were to be sought out and destroyed.[28] This assessment was based on a Privy Council order of 1596, but scrutiny of the original document, tucked away in the Privy Council's records, makes clear that only images (this probably meant face patterns, woodblocks or copper plates) used by 'divers unskilful artisans' were 'to be defaced and none to be allowed'. Evidently, the Council's intention was to regulate the burgeoning problem of the mass manufacture of *debased* images of the queen, chiefly engravings put out by London and Antwerp printers. There is no mention of banning realistic images by *skilful* artists that were faithful to the queen's true likeness. It would, in any case, have been logistically impossible for privy councillors to enter hundreds of private houses and confiscate unwelcome images of the queen, simply because they made her look her full age.[29]

When, in 1592, Isaac Oliver, a brilliant protégé of Nicholas Hilliard who would go on to marry Marcus Gheeraerts's half-sister Sara, had produced a miniature of the queen, painted from life, he had intended it to be a model for engravers, hence its unfinished state. His sketch was utterly realistic. The queen looks every one of her fifty-nine years.[30] No doubt she did not much care for the result, since she gave Oliver no further commissions. But, equally, no attempt was made to ban the engravings based upon Oliver's image. Quite the reverse. The pattern was used extensively, among others by John Woutneel, a prolific book- and print-seller from the Netherlands who had settled in London. He sent Oliver's template to one of the most famous engravers in Europe, Crispijn de Passe, who produced a series of copper plates based on it for more than a decade, only slightly softening the queen's facial appearance.[31]

Admittedly, the preferred face pattern of Elizabeth's final years is one that would become known as the 'Mask of Youth'. Mainly the work of Hilliard, whose studio produced over twenty miniatures in this style, beginning in 1594, this image consciously abandoned any attempt to depict the reality of a woman in her sixties. Instead, Elizabeth's features were airbrushed back to become those of a young woman in her late twenties or early thirties.[32] The apotheosis of this most famous face pattern would be the 'Rainbow Portrait' of the queen, most likely commissioned from Gheeraerts by Robert Cecil in 1602 to mark her visit to his fine new house on the Strand, with its glorious gardens running down to the Thames.[33]

At the reception Cecil laid on for her, Elizabeth was eulogized in verse as Cynthia, Phoebe and Flora (the goddess of flowering and blossoming plants), and a pageant was staged, at the climax of which a messenger arrived in Turkish dress to present the queen with a rich, imperial mantle.[34] She is depicted in the portrait wearing a ruby-jewelled crown with a crescent moon on the top and clutching a rainbow in her right hand, above which appears the legend *Non sine sole iris* ('No rainbow without the sun').

In other words, Elizabeth is the sun queen (Phoebe was the grandmother of Apollo, the sun god). She is also the moon goddess, with all the associated motifs of female power, virginity and sexual allure. Embroidered on her gown, flowers are in bloom – symbols of fertility and rebirth. A twisted serpent on her sleeve, the symbol of wisdom, has a red, heart-shaped jewel hanging from its jaws, indicating that she rules from the head and not the heart. Finally, the viewer's gaze is held by her sumptuous mantle, one side of which is made of pale silk woven with a fine silver stripe and the other of orange satin, the colour of the sun. Quite possibly an exact representation of the gift carried by the actor playing the part of the Turkish courier, it is adorned with eyes and ears, to indicate her hold over her subjects.[35]

And yet, for all de Maisse's frankness about the effects of her age, there was still something he found awesome about Elizabeth.[36] Almost immediately after describing her rotting teeth, he found himself declaring her to be as tall and elegant as she was perfectly poised. Her hands, in particular, were very beautiful. She could not resist showing them off to him, removing her gloves so that he could admire her long, slender fingers.[37]

Elizabeth may have been old, but she had not lost her touch: beguiling the French ambassador with her small talk, she made sure that he left the country no wiser as to her intentions concerning détente than he had been on arrival. Burghley was more forthcoming. The old Lord Treasurer badly wanted peace. When de Maisse made a final visit to his house on the Strand to say farewell, Burghley told him that he wished for nothing else save that before his death, adding in a whisper, *Nunc dimittis*,* before reminding Henry's envoy that what Elizabeth saw as the chief obstacle was the lack of progress over the question of the French and Dutch war debts.[38]

Elizabeth now decided she would test the waters for herself by sending special envoys to speak directly to Henry. De Maisse suspected double-dealing. Mistrustful of Burghley, whom he described as proud, presumptuous and instinctively hostile to French interests, he was worried that secret bilateral talks between England and the Archduke might already have begun.[39] He was especially disturbed that it took more than a month after his departure from London on 5 January 1598 before the queen's special envoys would land in Dieppe. Robert Cecil led the delegation, and it did not include Essex. Elizabeth, wary of the Earl's commitment to waging an aggressive war against Spain in alliance with the French and the Dutch, had refused to let him go. To buy him off, Cecil was forced to beg the queen to offer him a gift of cochineal captured during the Azores expedition worth £7,000 and sell him another £50,000 worth at eighteen shillings per pound, when the market price was thirty to forty shillings. Desperate for as much ready cash as he could lay his hands on to appease his creditors, Essex accepted, but he also began taking bribes.[40]

When Cecil arrived in France, he set out for Rouen and from there made his way to Paris, seemingly unaware that peace negotiations between Henry IV's diplomats and those of the Archduke were already well advanced at Vervins in Picardy.[41] Watching closely from the sidelines, Essex wrote Cecil a five-page letter urging him to keep

---

* From the famous evensong canticle 'Now let thy servant depart in peace.'

the war alive, since 'from Spain there can be no peace meant.'[42] But the pressure for peace was intense, notably from wealthy merchants and investors who had originally made their fortunes in the Iberian trade. Cecil himself had shareholdings in several mercantile ventures, and many London and Bristol merchants had already resumed trading clandestinely at Seville, claiming Scots or Irish nationality.[43]

By 14 March, the peace terms Henry sought had been secretly approved by Philip. France was to recover all of its lost territory, including Calais and Blavet, and the Spanish king agreed to offer a six-month period of grace to Elizabeth and the Dutch while they considered their positions. No longer willing to wait for his allies to make up their minds as to whether or not to join in the negotiations, Henry ordered his diplomats to conclude a peace on these conditions 'without insisting any longer upon the desires or humours of our neighbours for whom the king has had too much regard'.[44]

Three days later, Cecil met Henry face to face at Angers in the Loire Valley.[45] Deadlock ensued as the French king insisted on a peace and Cecil countered by reminding him that he was bound by oath not to make a separate one without his allies, and that the Dutch States General wanted neither a peace nor a truce. Resolved to continue the fight until Spain gave in, the Dutch at once appealed to Elizabeth for thirteen thousand infantry to invade the heart of the southern Netherlands so that a victory could be won.[46]

Elizabeth, however, had no intention of being bounced into anything by anyone. Burghley, weak in body as his health collapsed once more but still strong mentally, had already set about planting spies inside the Archduke's Court at Brussels. Now, Burghley took his revenge for the damage done in 1588 by 'Julio': he found a highly placed mole willing to make him copies of all the most secret correspondence between Albert and Philip II relating to the peace negotiations. Just as 'Julio' had provided Philip with every last detail about Elizabeth's overtures to the Duke of Parma's representatives at Bourbourg, so this time Burghley was able to show Elizabeth every move on Philip's chessboard.

To pull off this extraordinary intelligence coup, Burghley had re-employed Walsingham's former expert cryptographer, Thomas Phelippes, who was prudently distancing himself from Essex. For so spectacularly assisting Essex in uncovering the Lopez Plot, Burghley had spitefully sent Phelippes to prison, ostensibly because of debts owed to the queen. Anthony Bacon had secured his release and, when Burghley pretended to forgive Phelippes, he was able to plug into the cryptographer's network of informants. One of these, John Petit, an Oxford-educated canon of Liège whose mother was English and who filed his reports using the monogram 'J. P. B.', had an agent at the very heart of the Archduke's entourage. The result was a steady flow of intercepted correspondence between Brussels and Madrid, most of it in cipher.[47] This was where Phelippes came into his own. The cipher was fiendishly difficult to decrypt, but Phelippes, who ran his agents in Brussels under the alias of Pieter Halyns, cracked it.[48]

To protect his sources, Burghley disingenuously claimed that the originals of these intercepted documents had, by a miraculous stroke of luck, been plucked from the sea by some passing Dover fishermen, having been thrown overboard by Spanish sailors whose ship was taken by Dutch warships as they left the harbour at Calais.[49] No one, least of all the queen, believed a word of it. She knew Burghley's methods well enough by now, but all that mattered to her was the contents of the intercepted letters, which confirmed her worst fears: that Henry meant to make a separate peace with Spain. Taking no chances, however, Burghley made sure to silence Phelippes by promptly sending him back to prison once his job was done.[50]

Without delay, Elizabeth dictated and signed peremptory instructions to Cecil and Dr John Herbert, the secretary to the English delegation in France, ordering them to demand that Henry inform her of his true purpose. Her letter was sharp and imperious, but at the very last moment she sweetened her tone by scribbling a note in her own hand, saying, 'God bless you both with his grace for your best.'[51]

Cecil secured a second audience with Henry, in his study on 6 April at Nantes. Without standing on ceremony, he asked the French king point-blank whether he sought war or peace and demanded that he prove his good faith by answering honestly. He then reminded him yet again that he had taken an oath not to make a separate peace behind Elizabeth's back.

Put on the spot, Henry protested that either he must ruin himself or offend the queen. 'My necessities', he declared, 'are such as I cannot stand out, for I should get by the hazard of war no more than I should have with assurance of peace.' Only he could know where his own best interests lay, and it had become clear to him after the catastrophe at Amiens that he must make peace or face utter ruin. Had not many of the Huguenots failed to come to his aid at Amiens, fearful of his conversion to Catholicism? And had not Elizabeth refused to send him the necessary reinforcements? 'Well,' he concluded, 'it is now past. And am I like a man clothed in velvet that hath not meat to put to his mouth?'

When Cecil answered that however often he invoked the vocabulary of ruin, such words could never justify his breathtaking breach of faith, Henry angrily retorted, 'I care not for the world's satisfaction.' His conscience, he resumed, was a sufficient witness, and if the world chose to abuse him, so be it. 'As for the queen, she has done very favourably for me, and yet her succours might have been better employed than they were, for I never had them in time, nor half the number.'[52]

For Cecil, this criticism of Elizabeth was close to blasphemy. Daringly, he brought the interview to an abrupt close by asking for his passport home. His excuse was that he had no commission from the queen to join in the Treaty of Vervins, least of all without the consent of her Dutch allies. Wary of incurring her wrath, he had no wish to be seen to be condoning the peace negotiations, although this did not stop him from handing over to Henry a memo outlining the terms on which he believed, unofficially, she might be willing to agree to a peace.[53]

Before Cecil left Nantes on 15 April, Henry sought to draw the sting of the peace by publishing the Edict of Nantes. This gave all the king's subjects (as he declared) 'a general law, clear, precise and absolute to be applied in all disputes that have arisen among them' and assured to the Huguenots a large measure of religious toleration within certain areas.[54] Although the Edict fell far short of the more extreme demands of the loyal Protestants who had risked their lives and careers fighting for him during his darkest hours, only to see him convert to Catholicism, it mended his fences with them sufficiently to ensure their compliance and allow them to be re-employed in public capacities.

Henry then sought to buy time with Elizabeth by promising Cecil that he would not ratify the Peace of Vervins before forty days were out. This would give her enough time to send Cecil back to France with new instructions, or to continue the war if she so chose, either alone or alongside her Dutch allies.[55] At least it would have, if Henry had not almost immediately broken this promise, too, and signed the treaty with Spain on the 22nd, protesting that he had already given the English and Dutch three months to make up their minds and claiming he could not afford to delay a moment longer.[56]

Eventually given his passport, Cecil left France on the 27th by way of Caen and Ouistreham, landing on the Isle of Wight two days later. A coach was waiting for him in Portsmouth, and between ten and eleven o'clock at night he reached Whitehall, where he went directly to see the queen.[57]

To say that she was disappointed with Henry is a grave understatement. Despite a recurrence of the arthritis that had made her so tetchy with Essex and Ralegh shortly before they had sailed for the Azores, Elizabeth sat down and wrote him a blistering letter:

> If you search among the affairs of men to seek out the very worst iniquity and the thing by which this earth on which we live is most brought to ruin, it is breach of faith, mistrust of friendship, loss of love – especially where there is absolutely no justification for it. Whatever they may say, I am never quick to think evil of someone I hold in high regard, and yet I can do no more than roundly assure you and ask you to consider that if there were a mortal sin called ingratitude, then among men it would be justly called the sin against the Holy Ghost.

If he succeeded in securing favourable terms for himself from Spain, he had only her to thank. She therefore demanded, without prevarication or deceit, a prompt and truthful response, enlightening her as to just what it was he had done for her in his peace treaty.[58]

'Forsake not an old friend, for a new one will not be like him' was the famous aphorism put into her mouth by Camden in his *Annales* when summing up her diatribe. To a considerable degree, it captures the mordant tone of her letter, but the reader of the original French text, still preserved in the archives, will search in vain for this quotation.[59]

By the time Henry's conciliatory reply arrived, Elizabeth had calmed down. As a fellow practitioner of realpolitik, it was difficult to quarrel with his argument that the 'public necessity' of France had forced him to act. And, with the peace now proclaimed throughout France, there was little point in mutual reproaches.[60] Strikingly, it was the queen's religious faith that restored her spirits. 'That [same] God who hath hitherto enabled us to prevail against all malice whatsoever', she confided to Sir Thomas Edmonds, Unton's replacement as ambassador to France, 'will bless our kingdom and people still with like success.'[61] Now, Elizabeth made it clear that the key to her actions would be the behaviour of the Dutch. Her concern for their fate owed little to moral principle and everything to her desire to get back the huge sums she had lent them.

When, in May, envoys from the States General at last arrived at Greenwich Palace, she upbraided them for demanding reinforcements to continue the war. 'God alive! God alive!' she exclaimed. 'How am I to defend myself? What repayment shall I get?' Already, she said, she had helped the Dutch to fight Spain for longer than the Trojan War had lasted: she had been a fool to give them and the French so much costly aid.[62]

After some two months of insistent diplomacy, the Dutch States finally agreed to acknowledge an outstanding debt to the queen of £800,000 (£800 million in modern values), of which they would immediately begin to repay half, at the rate of £30,000 a year. The balance was to be left to a future treaty once all parties had made peace with Spain. From this point onwards, the Dutch were also to pay for half the cost of the three thousand or so English auxiliaries who continued to fight for Count Maurice. This would still leave the queen with a considerable annual commitment for the other half, running to at least £40,000.[63]

Elizabeth, meanwhile, rejected an impassioned plea from Essex to continue the war, declaring that she meant only to delay peace negotiations.[64] In a characteristically ambiguous way, she kicked the bigger issues into the long grass. Despite yearning for an end to the years of war, she could not find it in her to make overtures to her old adversary, as she had in 1588. She was no more prepared than he was to end a costly and exhausting war with the slightest tarnish on her honour.

Instead, she preferred merely to slim down drastically her commitments. From this moment onwards, she intended Protestant England largely to become a sleeping partner in the struggle for the soul of Europe. Her mistrust of Philip was implacable, and she had come to suspect that she would not be able to begin peace negotiations with Spain in her lifetime. As things stood, the cessation of hostilities in France, combined with Archduke Albert's more conciliatory attitude, meant that, once the Dutch had offered at least partial repayment of their debts, she could choose to step back and satisfy her conscience, at the same time shaving more than £120,000 a year from her regular outgoings.[65]

Burghley now lay mortally ill at his house on the Strand. In April, he had secured the queen's permission to be absent from Court by reason of his 'want of health and weak estate of body yet remaining' from his 'late great sickness'. He had returned in July, but was very frail. At the end of the month, he tried to get out of bed but was too weak to sit up. His throat was swollen and sore, and he found it impossible to swallow without pain. There is no reliable account of his final days, but the news from France and Holland must have brought him delight, since it seemed at long last as though the European land war that had cost the queen so dearly and destroyed so many ordinary soldiers' lives would end less with a bang than with a whimper. He also had the satisfaction of knowing that, during the final stages of their haggling with the Dutch envoys, his fellow privy councillors had been led by his son. Essex was in deep disgrace, and he would remain so throughout the summer.[66]

Burghley died shortly before seven o'clock on the morning of Friday, 4 August, just two days before the treaty with the Dutch was signed. He was seventy-seven years old. His last words were said to have been 'Lord, receive my spirit; Lord, have mercy on me.'[67] Not long before, the queen had ridden in her coach to see the man who had first become her backstairs fixer almost exactly fifty years before.[68] On this, her last farewell, she fed him broth 'with her own princely hand, as a careful nurse', as Burghley thankfully recorded in his parting letter to his son. His final words to Robert, 'Serve God by serving of the Queen for all other service is indeed bondage to the Devil,' were replete with unintended irony, given the twists and turns of his earlier career.[69] In more ways than one, it was the end of an era. And Elizabeth knew it.

Elizabeth was enjoying the final few days of her summer progress at Nonsuch late in September 1598 when the news filtered down via Paris, Venice and The Hague that Philip II was dead. After more than two months of unrelieved torture from his arthritis, the seventy-one-year-old Spanish king had taken the last rites of the Catholic Church in his study-cum-bedroom at the Escorial and died with his son and heir, the future Philip III, and the Infanta at his bedside. So severely afflicted by bedsores was he in these last, lingering days that his doctors were forced to wriggle underneath his bed and cut holes in his mattress from below to drain out the pus.[1]

The Venetian ambassador to Madrid observed that Philip's twenty-year-old son had the same prominent Habsburg jaw as his father and grandfather before going on to praise him as a man of peace: 'affable, grave, temperate, beloved by those who serve him'.[2] His assessment, many times repeated, helped to foster a myth that Philip was mild-mannered and agreeable, a keen horseman who loved music and magnificence and believed that the Spanish monarchy's dignity was best preserved by peace, pomp and parade.[3]

In reality, the new king of Spain was nothing of the sort. He demanded that force be met with force, agreeing with Don Baltasar Álamos de Barrientos, who wrote a steely memorandum to him on his accession, advising:

It would be neither proper nor profitable to make peace with England: nor would any such peace be firm, for this Crown has been extremely offended by *that woman*. She is a schismatic and utterly contrary to our religion, and will consequently never trust us; peace with her will be very unsure.[4]

Philip III needed little persuasion. His feelings for the heretic bastard queen were no warmer than his father's; he did, however, recognize the extent of Spain's human and material losses since the failure of the *Gran Armada* of 1588. After his father's bankruptcy, nothing on such a scale could be attempted again. Instead, the Treaty of Vervins presented an opportunity for the young king to open a new, limited front in the war against Elizabeth, one where he believed he could win a lasting victory. The result was a policy in which he decided to attack Ireland, England's soft underbelly. He believed far fewer troops would be needed, as it was said in Spain that the English defences in Ireland outside Dublin were no more than rudimentary, while the Gaelic Irish were loyal Catholics almost to a man. The Protestant Reformation had made minimal inroads into Ireland. Henry VIII had even failed to dissolve many of the more remote Irish monasteries. Still better from the Spanish viewpoint, Ireland was now in open rebellion and had been for the last four years.[5]

The revolt had begun in 1594 as little more than a regional uprising in the northern province of Ulster led by the wily and ambitious Hugh O'Neill, Earl of Tyrone, but by the summer of 1598 much of Gaelic Ireland had been set aflame. Elizabeth's Lord Deputy, based in Dublin, Lord Burgh, had mounted a strong offensive, building a new fort on the River Blackwater three miles north of the garrison town of Armagh to guard the main road to Dungannon.[6] He had then fallen fatally ill on his return from revictualling it. Seeing his opportunity, Tyrone tripled the stakes, demanding liberty of conscience for all Catholic Irishmen and redress for English offences against the Irish over the past fifty years. When he was rebuffed, Tyrone laid siege to the Blackwater fort. On 14 August, after ambushing a relief force in the thick woods south of Armagh, his forces killed some two thousand English troops at the Battle of the Yellow Ford.[7] It was the greatest victory ever achieved by Irish arms against the English and seemed to threaten the complete loss of Ireland.[8]

And the reverberations echoed still further through the British Isles as Elizabeth increasingly suspected King James of colluding in Tyrone's rebellion. Her quarrels with James had entered a new phase some two years into the revolt, when he had condoned a cross-border raid into England by the Laird of Buccleuch, who rescued one of the queen's closely guarded prisoners in a midnight assault on Carlisle Castle.[9] Elizabeth retaliated by slashing his pension again, and when negotiations for a new treaty for the regulation of the border did not go her way, she fumed to her ambassador in Edinburgh, 'I wonder how base minded that king thinks me that with patience I can digest this dishonourable slur. Let him therefore know that I will have satisfaction, or else.'[10]

In January 1598, Anglo-Scottish relations further deteriorated when Elizabeth levelled a raft of obscurely phrased but stinging accusations against James for criticizing her in the Scottish Parliament:*

> I do wonder what evil spirits have possessed you, to set forth so infamous devices void of any show of truth . . . I see well we two be of very different natures, for I vow to God I would not corrupt my tongue with an unknown report of the greatest foe I have, much less could I detract my best-deserving friend with a spot so foul as scarcely may ever be outraised . . . I never yet loved you so little as not to moan your infamous dealings which you are in mind. We see that myself shall possess more princes' witness of my causeless injuries, which I could have wished had passed no seas, to testify such memorials of your wrongs. Bethink you of such dealings, and set your labour upon such mends as best may. Though not right, yet salve some piece of this overslip. And be assured that you deal with such a king as will bear no wrongs and endure no infamy.[11]

After this, James began to ignore her, claiming, 'It becomes me not to strive with a lady, especially in that art wherein their sex most excels' (i.e. in trading insults).[12]

Elizabeth's misgivings about James's intentions in Ireland were fuelled by his secret overtures to the European Catholic powers and by highly disturbing reports that Anne of Denmark was very close to converting to Catholicism. Up until Prince Henry's christening, Anne had been safely Protestant, but afterwards her chief gentlewoman, the French-born Henrietta, Countess of Huntly, had slowly but surely begun to convert her.[13] Late in 1596, a St Andrews clergyman noted for his attacks on the anti-English, pro-Spanish Earl of Huntly and his wife preached a sermon denouncing Anne as a renegade 'papist'. 'As to the queen,' he declared, 'we have no cause to pray

---

* The precise words that provoked this outburst have never been traced.

for her. We hear no good of her. She will never do us good. It may be she [will] trouble us all shortly.'[14]

James positively revelled in this growing appreciation of Anne's apostasy: he found it an invaluable diplomatic tool in his quest to persuade the Catholic powers that he was the best candidate to succeed Elizabeth. Pope Clement VIII prayed for his conversion, and James went out of his way to foster this hope. Shortly before Philip II's death, the Scottish king had sent Lord Robert Sempill to Madrid to rebuild commercial links between Scotland and Spain, armed with secret instructions to secure recognition of James's title to the English throne.[15] After Philip III's coronation, Sempill's mission encouraged the new king's advisers to consider sending an ambassador to Edinburgh with instructions to work towards partitioning the British Isles into pro- and anti-Spanish spheres of influence. When Elizabeth learned of this, she raged against James, whom Cecil had also caught out drumming up Catholic support for his claim to the throne in Venice, Florence and Paris.[16]

Elizabeth put two and two together and made five. Relying on warnings she had received from Tyrone's former mentor, the Earl of Ormond, coupled with a leaked copy of a letter purportedly from James to the rebel leader, she convinced herself that James was in league with Tyrone and conspiring with Spain.[17] She suspected him of joining clandestinely with Tyrone in a grand pan-Britannic conspiracy in which both men hoped to profit from her death. Prompted by dark hints from Cecil, she even harboured suspicions that there might be a plot, centred on James and Catholic Ireland, to force her to abdicate.

After their fatal encounter in the Privy Chamber on 30 June or 1 July 1598, when the Earl of Essex had insolently rejected her nomination of Sir William Knollys as Lord Burgh's successor in Ireland, Elizabeth at first decided to leave him to sulk and feign illness at his country estate at Wanstead. 'He hath played long enough upon me,' she said. 'I mean to play awhile upon him and to stand as much upon my greatness as he hath done upon [his] stomach.'[18] But after news came in of the catastrophe at the Blackwater fort, she decided to recall Essex and make him live up to his proud boasts over so many years to be a true military leader. It was a coolly calculated gamble on her part, a toss of a coin she knew she could not lose. Heads, she would recover Ireland, and Essex his career. Tails, Essex would destroy himself, and she could distance herself from the disaster.

But before she gave Essex the command in Ireland, he would have to submit and apologize for the offence he had caused her. Until then, she refused to admit him to her presence.[19] There seemed slender prospect of this after the Earl sent her a letter complaining of 'the intolerable wrong you have done both me and yourself'.[20] His friend and admirer Sir Henry Lee tactfully urged him to come to his senses:

> Your honour is more dear to you than your life, but yet may it please your Lordship to consider these circumstances. She is your sovereign, whom you may not beat [treat] upon equal conditions . . . I grant your wrongs to be greater than so noble a heart can well digest, but consider my good Lord how great she is with whom you deal . . . What advantage you have in yielding when you are wronged, what disadvantage by facing her whom (though you deserve never so much) yet you must rely upon for favour.[21]

The impasse was resolved only when Essex succumbed to a bout of genuine fever. Anxious for his welfare, Elizabeth sent one of her own physicians to treat him, and by 10 September he was sufficiently recovered to attend a Council meeting for the first time since their spectacular row.[22] He met her privately two days later to kiss her hand. After that, it was said that, at least for the moment, he was 'in as good terms as ever he was'.[23] Although he lost out hands down to Cecil and his allies in the redistribution of offices after Burghley's death, Elizabeth was still prepared to accept his service when it suited her, but strictly on her own terms.

By 20 October, the Court gossips were confidently placing their bets on Essex going to Ireland.[24] But while, by December, it was certain that he would be sent there, a heated debate was taking place over the conditions of his appointment, which Essex contested clause by clause. Elizabeth signed his commission on 25 March 1599, granting him wider powers than any of his predecessors. In one notable clause she authorized him either to prosecute or conclude the war at his discretion, and even to come to terms with Tyrone. After endless discussion, he had finally convinced her that his expedition aimed at nothing less than 'the saving of one of Her Majesty's kingdoms' and, to do this, he needed a free hand.[25]

Given the sweeping nature of this last clause, the Earl secured a licence from the queen permitting him temporarily to put a deputy in place so that he might return and consult her at such times as he should find cause, 'as well to see our person as to inform us of such things as may be to our important service'.[26] He left London on the 27th and landed in Dublin just over two weeks later, feeling distinctly queasy after an unusually stormy passage across the Irish Sea. With him sailed twenty thousand infantry and two thousand cavalry, the largest English army ever sent to Ireland.[27]

The key to the Earl's initial plan of campaign was to dispatch amphibious forces to Lough Foyle in the far north, well behind Tyrone's lines, with the aim of establishing a new English garrison there.[28] Modelled on his earlier template for Cádiz, the idea was to create a permanent military bridgehead that could readily be relieved and provisioned by sea. Before he died, Lord Burgh had intended to march to Lough Foyle to establish exactly such a garrison. The problem for Essex was that Cecil and his allies in the Privy Council had in the meantime diverted the necessary forces and supplies much further south for the defence of Dublin.[29]

This diversion of resources was undertaken despite confidential warnings Cecil had received from his chief intelligence officer in Dublin, Sir Geoffrey Fenton, suggesting that a strong garrison at Lough Foyle would be essential for the reconquest of Ulster.[30] Essex had pledged himself to an immediate attack on Tyrone before leaving England, but the profound lack of support he received from Cecil and his allies invites the conclusion that they were setting him up to fail.[31]

Unable to establish the garrison, Essex dissipated the prime campaigning months of May and June in a southerly march through Leinster towards Waterford and from there into Munster, capturing the supposedly impregnable Cahir Castle, relieving a fort at Askeaton and driving the rebels into the woods and mountains.[32] His sweep through southern Ireland was approved by the Privy Council. It safeguarded Munster from the threat of attacks from Spain and from

Tyrone, but it also wasted valuable time, money and supplies.[33] In particular, Essex was much delayed by a dire shortage of carriage horses, which had to be sent from England. Despite repeated warnings from his own officials, Cecil refused to treat this question with anything like the seriousness it deserved, stonewalling Essex by pretending that the queen 'will not be content to be put to any new charge for that'.[34]

Early in July, Essex returned to Dublin to file a decidedly hysterical report to the queen outlining the difficulties he had so far faced. Now in the hands of his physicians, with his body (as he claimed) 'indisposed and distempered' by the harsh conditions he had endured, he found his spirit crushed by the tenacity of Irish resistance.[35] Already seething over the spiralling cost of his expedition, Elizabeth was exasperated by a series of damning reports she had received from Cecil outlining Essex's demands for further 'liberal supplies of men, money and victual', the appointment of his younger protégé, the Earl of Southampton, as his General of the Horse – she flatly refused to confirm this nomination – and delays in confronting Tyrone. 'O miserable employment and more miserable destiny of mine', Essex wailed to the Privy Council, 'that makes it impossible for me to *please* and *serve* Her Majesty at once.'[36]

In a scorching diatribe she dictated on 30 July, Elizabeth instructed Essex to march north without any more excuses or delay: he was to attack Tyrone in his heartland of Ulster. But by the time her letter reached him, his forces had shrunk to fewer than six thousand infantry and five hundred cavalry.[37] Many had slipped away home to England; others were feigning sickness; some had defected to the rebels. Essex's thoughts quickly turned to how he might parachute himself out of Ireland and return to Court to confront not Tyrone but his enemies on the Privy Council, whom he believed to be subverting him at every turn. For a single madcap moment he even toyed with the idea of going over to Wales with two thousand or three thousand troops and marching on Whitehall to purge the evil councillors who were poisoning the queen's mind against him.[38]

In a typically extravagant gesture, with his forces diminishing by the hour, Essex then invited Tyrone to fight him in single combat. After a game of high-stakes poker, he finally accepted the fifty-four-year-old Irishman's offer of a parley. On 7 September, the two men came face to face on the opposite banks of a river at Ballaclinch ford near the town of Louth, between Ardee and Dundalk. With Essex's horse at the water's edge and Tyrone's standing belly-deep midstream, as the river was too wide at this point to shout across, they talked alone for half an hour. Playing for time, but also genuinely torn between a new accommodation with Elizabeth and one with Spain, it would appear from what he said about it afterwards that Tyrone demanded freedom of conscience, liberation of the Irish from English domination and a full pardon as the price of a settlement. Essex refused.[39]

At last, a rolling truce was agreed upon that was to last for six weeks at a time. Renewable until 1 May 1601, the truce was to be terminable earlier by either side at two weeks' notice. Tyrone, who swore an oath to observe it, also offered his eldest son as a hostage as a sign of his good faith. Afterwards, the rebel leader boasted to Philip III's agent in Ireland that he had almost persuaded Essex to turn against Elizabeth, but this was surely bluster. Like Ralegh, Essex was a genuine patriot who would never have been able to reconcile himself to colluding with Spain.[40]

And yet, however honourably intended, the murky circumstances of the truce left Essex, who now disbanded what was left of his army, open to damaging smears. Francis Bacon later summed up the extent of his vulnerability. Just as 'the secrecy of that parley', as he put it, gave Essex 'the more liberty of treason, so it may give any man the more liberty of surmise what was handled between them'.[41] Almost certainly, Essex's overriding aim was to protect Elizabeth from the threat of a Spanish invasion of Ireland. The danger was that his enemies would find it easy to feed a distorted account of the purpose of the truce directly into Elizabeth's fears of a grand pan-Britannic conspiracy.[42]

But that was still to come. On reading Essex's first reports of the truce, Elizabeth was not unduly concerned, believing it to have been 'seasonably made (though now it seems that in many provinces the rebels make use of it), as great good hath grown to the most of Her Majesty's subjects by it'.[43] But from the outset she expressed a justified anxiety over the lack of witnesses to the parley. 'For comeliness, example and for your own discharge', she chivvied Essex a mere ten days after his rendezvous with Tyrone, 'we marvel you would carry it no better.' But this was chiefly because Tyrone was as slippery as he was duplicitous. 'To trust this traitor upon oath', she parried, 'is to trust a devil upon his religion.'[44]

The fact is that Elizabeth had far more on her mind in the summer and early autumn of 1599 than Essex's Irish expedition. Since mid-June, rumours that Philip III was intent on sending a fourth *Gran Armada* had triggered a panic throughout southern England. Sixty great warships and a hundred and twenty other ships with three thousand soldiers on board were said to be victualled and ready to sail from Coruña.[45]

In response, the queen appointed the Earl of Nottingham, who was still Lord Admiral, to be Lieutenant-General of the Kingdom with supreme command by land and sea. Working closely with Cecil, he dispatched a full complement of royal navy ships to patrol the Channel approaches and the southern coast of Ireland, while another forty or so armed merchantmen and pinnaces were requisitioned as support vessels. An improvised barrage was hastily created across the Thames, near Barking, by scuttling eighty-three small ships half laden with ballast. The coastal defences were strengthened and the county militias from Cornwall to Norfolk put on full alert. As in 1588, plans were made to assemble a field army some twenty-five-thousand-strong, drawn from the southern counties, to defend the queen and Court if the Armada landed. A serious failure of intelligence left the Privy Council entirely unaware that the Spanish fleet's true destination was to be Ireland.[46]

Several false alarms brought turmoil to London as heavy iron chains were once again hung across the streets and the city gates locked and bolted. In early August, a rumour spread like wildfire that Spaniards had landed at Southampton and were marching towards London. This had arisen from a mistake during the night of the 6th, when lookouts on the Isle of Wight had spotted a flotilla of ships passing eastwards along the Channel and fired the beacons. In fear of her life, Elizabeth was driven at high speed in her coach to St James's Palace, where she took refuge, exactly as in 1588. Several days would elapse before she could be certain that these mysterious vessels in the Channel were no more than innocent merchantmen plying their trade, and she could safely emerge.[47]

At the very last moment, Philip III's ships sailed not northwards for England or Ireland, but southwards for the Azores, where a formidable fleet of Dutch warships lay in wait for the New World treasure convoys.[48] Unaware of the change of plan, the queen resumed an intriguing diplomacy she had pursued intermittently since 1587, when, after vigorous lobbying by Walsingham and the London merchants for the best part of two years, she had appealed to Sultan Murad III of Turkey to open up a new front in the war. Her aim then was to distract the Spanish navy by inciting Murad to attack Spain on its Mediterranean flank.[49]

Strongly encouraged by Walsingham, Elizabeth had from the very outset justified her initiative on religious as well as strategic grounds, arguing that both Protestantism and Islam were haters of idolatry.[50] Perhaps surprisingly for a woman who, by the time of her translation of Boethius, had come to interpret contemporary events as a test of character imposed on her by God, she had no compunction about setting the Muslim 'infidels' against the Christians of Spain. For their part, a number of London merchants trading in Venice and Turkey had joined forces to form the Levant Company, chartered in 1592. Lobbying the queen continually to open up diplomatic and therefore improved commercial relations with the Sultan, they were able to make huge profits from exporting raw iron and munitions to the Ottoman empire, returning from Istanbul and Aleppo with spices, raw silk, cotton, indigo, carpets, apothecary wares, currants, sugar and sweet wines.[51]

Begged by Elizabeth for support at the time of the great crisis of 1588, the Sultan had excused himself, saying that he lacked the resources to wage war simultaneously in Persia and the western Mediterranean.[52] When, however, the Persian war ended in 1590, Burghley and the queen had tried again to unleash Ottoman forces against Spain, channelling much of their diplomacy through Dr Lopez. The most influential westerner in Istanbul, the Portuguese Jewish merchant Don Solomon Abenaes was Lopez's kinsman. And it was largely through Don Solomon that Burghley and the queen spent much of the next three years urging Murad and his advisers to attack Spanish possessions in southern Italy.[53] In fact, the queen's links to Don Solomon may go some considerable way to explain her decision to stay Lopez's execution warrant.[54]

Unfortunately, Murad always replied that he had more pressing problems than Spain. Chief among them were the episodic upheavals in his tributary principalities beyond the Danube, either in Moldavia, the last Christian outpost in the Balkans, or in Hungary, where in 1593 the Ottomans resumed war against the Habsburgs.[55] When, two years later, Mehmed III, Murad's eldest son and heir by the Albanian-born Sultana Sāfiye, mounted the throne, Elizabeth wrote again (her letter is lost but its contents can be worked out from the reply). An offer of amity was swiftly returned by the Grand Vizier, Sinān Pasha, but it came with a sting in the tail. After reminding the queen that the Hungarian war was the new Sultan's top priority, Sinān Pasha invited her to send *him* troops and money first. When Edward Barton, Elizabeth's newly appointed first resident ambassador in Istanbul, provided her with a translation of this document, he tactfully omitted that last passage.[56]

A superficially more enticing offer followed in the summer of 1596 on the back of Philip II's second *Gran Armada*, which was at first thought to be directed against Calais or Marseilles. In a reassuring letter to the queen, the Sultan explained that he would not want her war effort to be compromised by a Spanish attack on Marseilles: if the town fell, he would send a fleet to relieve it and restore it to France. Once again, self-interest lay at the heart of the Turkish response, as Marseilles, along with Venice, was the chief hub for imports of Ottoman goods into western Europe.[57]

No sooner had the ink dried on the Sultan's letter than he left Istanbul for Hungary at the head of an army of thirty thousand, accompanied by Barton, who followed in a coach with his luggage, carried by thirty-six baggage camels provided at Mehmed's expense. For the next three years, Anglo-Ottoman diplomacy slumbered and the Sultan's letters to Elizabeth were restricted to reporting Turkish victories in central Europe.

Then, in 1599, at the height of the fresh crisis created by the threat of a fourth Spanish Armada, Elizabeth decided to write, woman to woman, to Mehmed's mother, Sāfiye. Her approach made perfect sense, because the Ottoman state, during both Murad III and Mehmed III's reigns, notoriously, was ruled mainly from the harem. Elizabeth had employed very similar tactics on Barton's advice six years earlier in 1593, using Sāfiye as her intermediary in an attempt to influence the direction of the Hungarian war.[58] At that time, her letter had been accompanied by a few handsome gifts, paid for by the Levant Company. These consisted of 'a jewel of Her Majesty's picture' (possibly a Hilliard miniature) set with rubies and diamonds, three great gilt plates, ten garments of cloth of gold and a very fine case of glass bottles, silver and gilt.[59]

Elizabeth's letter of 1593 has disappeared, and Burghley, maddeningly, kept no copy, but even if this is likely to have been far from a candid personal correspondence, Sāfiye replied courteously and effusively. 'Let there be a salutation so gracious', she had declared in the course of a raft of diplomatic compliments, 'that all the rose-garden's roses are just one petal from it and a speech so sincere that the whole repertoire of a garden's nightingales is but one stanza of it.' Advised by Barton that 'a suit of princely attire being after the Turkish fashion' would be the ideal gift, Sāfiye sent the queen a fine gown of cloth of gold, together with a kirtle of cloth of silver and 'a girdle of Turkey work, rich and fair'.[60]

When, in 1599, acting on the advice of Barton's replacement as ambassador, Henry Lello, Elizabeth wrote again, she sent more gifts. As before, the queen's letter is lost, and the gifts, a richly upholstered coach for Sāfiye and a magnificent mechanical organ for her son, were to be paid for by the Levant Company. Elizabeth's Ottoman diplomacy did not extend so far as spending her own money.

Sāfiye sent two letters in reply, each to similar effect, reassuring Elizabeth that she would not cease to intervene on her behalf with her son, not least to the benefit of mutual trade, and thanking her for the coach. The gift was presented to her on 11 September by Lello's secretary, Paul Pindar. 'It has arrived and has been delivered,' reported Sāfiye. 'It had our gracious acceptance.'[61]

As Lello later informed the queen, Sāfiye received the gift 'very gratefully'. She 'made a great demonstration of joy', handsomely rewarding the coachman. She then proceeded to ride out with her son in the coach 'often times'. Afterwards, she 'sent to me to send her the queen's picture to behold, which I have here given order to make by one that came with the ship' – by which he probably meant Rowland Buckett, the organ-painter.[62] She also 'did take a great liking to Mr Pindar, and afterwards she sent for him to have his private company, but their meeting was crossed [prevented]'.[63]

The queen's gifts had travelled on the *Hector*, which had sailed from Gravesend, along with the organ-maker Thomas Dallam, a coachman Edward Hale and their assistants.[64] The coach, built in Cow Lane, near Smithfield in London, was modelled on the queen's own.[65] Said to be worth £600 and thus more valuable than the organ, it closely resembled another built in 1604 with ironwork by Elizabeth's former locksmith, Thomas Larkin, and with decorations by Marcus Gheeraerts the Younger. A gift from James I to Tsar Boris Godunov of Russia, this coach is still intact and now preserved in the Armoury Museum in Moscow.

Also crated up on board the *Hector* during the six-month voyage was the Sultan's organ.[66] Dallam and his assistants toiled day and night to repair it on arrival in Istanbul, as it had been severely damaged by heat and storms during its journey. At last assembled in the Topkapi Palace, the instrument stood sixteen feet high and was adorned with 'very curious work of gold and other rich colours'. Four or five feet above the keyboard was a twenty-four-hour striking clock, framed by the organ's pipework, cased in Corinthian columns carved from gilded oak. Higher up was a platform with angels holding silver trumpets to their lips, and above that a cornucopia of baroque wood-carving surmounted by a holly bush on which silver thrushes and blackbirds perched.

Every hour, on the hour, once the clockwork was wound up and a pin moved, a peal of bells went off, after which the trumpeters sounded a *tantarra*. The organ then played a series of voluntaries, all by itself, the keys of the instrument going up and down. When the music stopped, the thrushes and blackbirds burst into song and flapped their wings.[67]

Mechanical instruments were a particular favourite of Elizabeth's. Before Dallam left Gravesend, she had made him set up the organ at

Whitehall for a bespoke performance. And while in the Privy Chamber, he would have seen 'a certain jewel' specially made for her by her resident instrument-maker and tuner, Edmund Schetz: 'a pair of virginals with three thousand rich stones' that came complete 'with trees, branches, herbs, flowers, weeds, birds, beasts and such like of perfect sterling silver'. When Elizabeth played the instrument, as Schetz helpfully recorded, the birds and animals moved 'without rattling or any noise' so that it seemed as if Orpheus by his melodies had 'made the brute beasts to rejoice'.[68]

So entranced was the Sultan with his gift, he asked Dallam to repeat the mechanical display and then to give a brief solo recital. The second of these requests struck terror into Dallam, since it meant turning his back on the Sultan, which he had been warned that 'no man on pain of death might do'.[69] Fortunately, Mehmed was sufficiently delighted by Dallam's virtuoso performance to overlook the breach of protocol, rewarding him with forty-five pieces of gold. In fact, he was so overcome he begged Dallam to stay with him for ever, offering him two royal concubines or any two virgins he cared to select for himself as wives. Dallam managed to extricate himself only by the skin of his teeth.[70] But before he could return home, he had to dismantle the organ and move it to Mehmed's favourite spot, a pavilion on the shore of the Golden Horn known as the Pearl Kiosk, where he liked to relax.[71]

On 18 October, a week before Dallam finished his second reassembly of the organ, the *Hector* left Istanbul and began its homeward journey.[72] To Sāfiye's dismay, it departed without the letters and further gifts she had prepared for Elizabeth, which included a gown of cloth of silver, a matching pair of sleeves, gold-embroidered handkerchiefs and a crown studded with pearls and rubies.[73] Liaising with Sāfiye's chief gentlewoman Esperanza Malchi, a Venetian Jewess, Lello arranged for Paul Pindar to travel to Greece with Dallam and his assistants on a Turkish vessel, and from there to cross to the island of Zante, where he could rejoin the *Hector*. Pindar's task was to deliver Sāfiye's messages and gifts safely to London.[74]

Pindar finally reached Dover in mid-May 1600. When he handed over the gifts to the queen in the Privy Chamber at Greenwich Palace, she was said to be 'very well' and enjoying herself as if she had stripped twenty years from her true age. 'This day she appoints to see a Frenchman do feats upon a rope ... Tomorrow, she hath commanded the bears, the bull and the ape to be baited in the tiltyard. Upon Wednesday she will have solemn dancing.'[75]

Whatever triggered her sunny mood, though, it was not Sāfiye's gifts. Elizabeth barely glanced at them. With the threat from Spain's fourth Armada finally dissipated, but with Tyrone's revolt now commanding ever more of her time and attention, she had lost all interest in the prospect of opening up a new front in the Mediterranean. Pressure from the London merchants had also largely evaporated. For the sensational news had just arrived from Aleppo that a flotilla of Dutch merchant ships had successfully sailed to the East Indies around the Cape of Good Hope, defying Portuguese claims to exclusive rights to navigation in the region. Once the astronomical value of the cargoes they had returned with became known, the London merchants forgot about Turkey and rapidly switched their attention to Asia.[76]

It was another nail in the coffin of the more fully joined-up ways of devising a war strategy that men like Walsingham, Ralegh and Essex had pioneered. Since the assassination of William of Orange in 1584, all three, in their radically different ways, had advocated a more aggressive, better coordinated strategy for dealing with Spain and Catholicism, one that at the same time could transform England's economic and commercial position in the world, but always the queen had proved to be the obstacle. Now, it was to be a matter of defeating Tyrone as quickly as possible, and at almost any cost, before Philip III sent a fifth Armada to land in southern Ireland.

19.   Defying the Queen

With Burghley joining Leicester, Walsingham, Hatton and Hunsdon in the grave, Elizabeth's bouts of black depression multiplied. Crippling arthritis in her right hand and arm, and severe toothache prevented her from writing and forced her to postpone audiences at short notice. In moments of remission, she gave full play to her old sardonic humour. '*Mortua sed non sepulta!*' she would exclaim with macabre aplomb ('Dead but not yet buried!')[1]

Robert Markham, John Harington's cousin, was struck by the impact of Burghley's death on the queen:

> There is little heed to be had to show of affection in state business . . .
> If my Lord Treasurer had lived longer, matters would go on surer. He
> was our great pilot, on whom all cast their eyes and sought their
> safety. The queen's highness doth often speak of him in tears, and
> turns aside when he is discoursed of. Nay, [she] even forbiddeth any
> mention to be made of his name in the Council.[2]

Others spoke to similar effect. 'I do see the queen often,' Robert Sidney, Leicester's nephew and Philip's younger brother, confided to Harington. Another veteran of the Battle of Zutphen, Sidney divided his time between the queen's service in the Privy Chamber and in the Netherlands, where he served as the governor of Vlissingen, one of a handful of so-called 'cautionary towns' the Dutch had granted Elizabeth as security for the loans she had provided. 'She doth wax weak since the late troubles,' he declared, 'and Burghley's death doth often draw tears from her goodly cheeks. She walketh out but little, meditates much alone and sometimes writes in private to her best friends.'[3] Sidney had once looked to Essex to advance his career but had become disillusioned by the Earl's inability to help him. His position at Vlissingen had required him to correspond regularly with Burghley and his son, and he had taken this opportunity to build bridges to Robert Cecil. After Essex sailed with his army to Ireland, Sidney distanced

himself further from him and his acolytes, as they became the subject
of frenzied speculation, mainly hostile. 'The queen is not well
pleased. The Lord Deputy [Essex] may be pleased now, but I sore
fear what may happen hereafter,' Markham commented, before adding menacingly, 'Essex hath enemies; he hath friends too . . . but
when a man hath so many showing friends, and so many unshowing
enemies, who learneth his end here below?'[4]

Meanwhile, the threat of a new Spanish invasion in southern Ireland and the murky circumstances of Essex's parley with Tyrone at
Ballaclinch ford made Elizabeth increasingly jumpy. What exactly,
she wondered on reflection, was it that Essex had *really* promised the
rebels in that ill-advised encounter?

In a sign of her growing impatience, she had instructed Essex to
march immediately north to Ulster and attack Tyrone in his lair. In
the same letter, she had also flatly and unambiguously countermanded her original licence that he might temporarily put a deputy
in his place and return to Court to consult her when he should find
cause. 'Our will and pleasure is, and so we do upon your duty command you', she had ordered in language ominously reminiscent of
her rebuke to Leicester, when he had accepted the position of Governor-General of the Netherlands, 'that notwithstanding our
former licence provisionally given . . . you do now in no wise take
that liberty.'[5]

Now, if Essex wished for any reason to leave his post, he would
first have to secure Elizabeth's explicit consent. Only after receiving
a royal warrant of approval with clear instructions for his deputy
might he leave Ireland, 'without which we do charge you, as you
tender our pleasure, that you adventure not to come out of that kingdom by virtue of any former licence whatsoever'.[6]

Nine weeks later, Essex defied these orders and returned in haste
to London. Utterly convinced – not without reason, in view of their
refusal to establish a garrison at Lough Foyle – that his enemies on the
Privy Council were setting him up to fail and that disaster was imminent, he believed his only way of turning the course of events in his
favour was to see the queen unannounced and put his case in person.

Almost completely isolated from his fellow privy councillors
thanks to his egotism, he was paying the price for his failure to build

and retain a network of supporters at the heart of the Court. For all his dubious liaisons with the queen's maids of honour, he had even failed to build allies among the women of the Privy Chamber, relying purely on the shaky foundations of his favour with the queen. And whereas he had once been backed by Burghley, Hatton and Hunsdon, he had antagonized them and those who had risen to take their places, chiefly Cecil, Nottingham and Lord Buckhurst, whom the queen had appointed to Burghley's old post of Lord Treasurer.[7]

Reaching Whitehall shortly before dawn on Friday, 28 September 1599, Essex took a boat across the chilly, misty Thames to Lambeth. There, he commandeered horses waiting for their owners and started riding as fast as he could to Nonsuch, where Elizabeth was relaxing for a few days.[8] By sheer chance, Lord Grey, a bitter enemy of the Earl of Southampton, Essex's confidant, was also at Lambeth that morning. Refusing a request to let Essex break the news of his return himself to the queen, Grey rode straight to Nonsuch and reached the palace shortly before ten in the morning, fifteen minutes before Essex. This gave him just enough time to let Cecil know that Essex was on his way, but not enough to double the queen's guards or to warn her.[9]

Elizabeth, who was by her own admission 'no morning woman', was just getting up. Not yet dressed, without the make-up her women painstakingly applied to disguise the wrinkles and blemishes of old age, wigless and with what remained of her wispy grey hair hanging around her face, this was the queen whom no man was ever meant to see.

Suddenly, the door burst open and Essex barged into the room. Mud-spattered and filthy from his breakneck ride from Lambeth, he threw himself at the shocked queen's feet, kissed her hand and began to harangue her. Unable to judge whether this violation might be the beginning of some sort of coup and imagining that his followers had overcome her guards and taken control of the palace, Elizabeth kept her nerve. She did not panic. Her words, as reported by Robert Sidney's Court agent, gave him 'great contentment'. Emerging from the bedroom a short while afterwards so that he could make himself presentable while the queen's horrified women worked their customary magic on her, he remarked how he thanked God that, having suffered so 'much trouble and storms' in Ireland, he had found a 'sweet calm' at home.[10]

An hour or so later, he returned to the queen and was closeted with her until the early afternoon. As far as he was concerned, all was well, 'her usage very gracious towards him'. He was fatefully wrong. That afternoon, in his third interview with Elizabeth that day, he found 'her much changed'.[11] Once she realized that this was no coup, she turned on him, icily berating him for defying her orders not to leave Ireland 'at so great hazard' without her prior warrant and making her displeasure only too clear. Although neither of them realized it at the time, this would be their very last meeting.

Between ten and eleven o'clock that night, an order came from the queen that Essex should remain in his chamber.[12] The following afternoon he was told to present himself to a hastily convened Privy Council meeting. While he was received with great courtesy, it was clear from the outset that his career was in jeopardy. Made to stand bareheaded at the far end of the table like a prisoner, he was sternly rebuked for his flagrant defiance of the queen's orders in abandoning his post, for his 'presumptuous letters written from time to time', for his 'overbold' approach to the queen, as well as for his 'rash manner of coming away from Ireland'. So serious were the charges, the clerks of the Council, normally always present, were asked to leave the room.[13]

Essex carried himself well. Citing chapter and verse during a long interrogation lasting some three hours, he attempted to justify himself. When, after a short discussion among themselves, the councillors reported back to the queen, she told them she would ponder the Earl's responses and 'pause and consider of her answers'. On a question as serious as this – for she considered Essex's unlicensed return to be little short of lese-majesty – she had no intention of making a snap decision.[14]

By Monday, she had made up her mind: Essex was taken to London and incarcerated in York House on the Strand while evidence was gathered against him. 'The time is now full of danger,' warned the Court gossips. 'Be very careful what you write here or what you say,' Robert Sidney's agent advised him. 'I must beseech your lordship to burn my letters or else I shall be afraid to write ... If you write by post, take heed what you write, for now letters are intercepted and stayed.'[15]

While Essex had been awaiting Elizabeth's decision on Sunday, her fury had been mounting to the point where she was so angry she refused him permission even to write to his long-suffering wife, Frances, who had just given birth to a daughter.[16] Still smarting from the deep humiliation she had suffered when he had burst into her bedchamber unannounced, she could not bring herself to forgive him. This time, he had gone too far. Harington, who saw her shortly afterwards, reported her saying, 'By God's Son, I am no Queen; that man is above me: who gave him command to come here so soon? I did send him on other business.'[17]

Essex was kept at York House in Lord Keeper Egerton's custody while the Privy Council considered potential charges. On 29 November, he was summoned to the Star Chamber to be given a vituperative dressing-down.[18] The seven charges included wasting the queen's money, 'tarrying' in England for two months instead of crossing to Ireland the moment he was directed to go there, parleying with Tyrone without authority, not prosecuting the war against Tyrone when he had first arrived and relinquishing his post and returning home when he had been forbidden to do so.[19] He defended himself ably, but his answers concerning Tyrone were considered sufficiently ambiguous to warrant his imprisonment while further evidence was assembled.

In preparation for the worst, Essex's secretary, Edward Reynolds, instructed Henry Cuffe, by now the Earl's most assiduous spin doctor, to search through his private papers to find anything that might help 'clear any of those points' about his conduct in Ireland.[20] Essex's attitude and demeanour, though, worried Reynolds. If he wanted 'an end of his troubles', Reynolds confided to Cuffe, the best approach would be to 'use humble respect to Her Majesty'; but 'if he contest[s] and speak[s] in a high style' he would 'plunge himself further, and overthrow his fortune for ever'. Humble submission, however, would never come easily to a man who had questioned whether princes might 'err'.[21]

The strain made Essex ill. Unlike some of his earlier, psychosomatic, illnesses, which had waxed and waned according to the queen's temper and his own, this one was genuine. He became weak and was confined to bed: his legs swelled, his strength was dissipated. Doctors were summoned, but an appeal to the queen for an examination by her own chief physician, Dr Brown, fell on deaf ears, although she reluctantly allowed the Earl's physicians to consult Brown, provided he did not see Essex himself.[22] A month later, when it looked as though Essex might actually die and was about to make his will, she relented, sending Dr Brown and granting the Earl permission to walk in the garden.[23] As yet, her vindictiveness did not stretch to allowing him to die: when his condition deteriorated further, she dispatched eight doctors to his bedside, sent broth to aid his recovery and commanded that he should be carried into Egerton's own bedchamber, as it was more comfortable.[24]

Even so, his family despaired for his life. Frances, desperate to see him, despite the shameless neglect he had shown her when at the height of his career, was finally allowed to visit him, although only during the daytime; at night, she returned to Walsingham House.[25] His sister Penelope begged for the same privilege, but Elizabeth froze her out.[26] Essex's mother, Lettice Knollys, tried to win the queen's sympathy by sending her a gown worth £100, but in vain.[27] Elizabeth even refused ostentatiously to accept the Earl's New Year's gift, while handsomely rewarding Cecil for his.[28] And when some well-meaning but ill-advised preachers in London offered public prayers for the Earl, they were threatened with prosecution for sedition in the Star Chamber.[29]

Throughout his six weeks of illness, Essex's enemies on the Privy Council continued to collect evidence against him, but they found nothing damning enough to justify a treason trial. Essex then handed them evidence of his own making by commissioning from Thomas Cockson, one of the finest art engravers in London, an equestrian portrait of himself in armour modelled closely on Robert Vaughan's posthumous image of his stepfather, which had famously included an inscription below background scenes of the defeat of the Armada and the Battle of Zutphen. In imitation of this design, Essex had himself depicted against similar background scenes of his triumphs in Cádiz and the Azores, and, less plausibly, Rouen and Ireland. But whereas the inscription below Leicester's portrait had merely listed his titles and honours, Essex's acclaimed him as 'Virtue's honour, Wisdom's nature, Grace's servant, Mercy's love, God's elected'. More provocatively still, the Earl chose to circulate among his friends copies of his exchange of letters with Egerton the previous year in which he had asked, 'Why, cannot princes err? Cannot subjects receive wrong? Is an earthly power or authority infinite?'[30]

The publication of Cockson's engraving with its description of Essex as 'God's elected', coupled with his letter to Egerton, was enough to support the charge of lese-majesty of which Elizabeth so clearly believed him to be guilty. So, when his health had sufficiently recovered, he was summoned to a trial in the Court of Star Chamber: the case was set to begin on Thursday, 13 February 1600. The Star Chamber could not inflict the death penalty, but it could impose unlimited fines and life imprisonment. For Essex, who valued his honour more than his life, death would be preferable.

Essex was at last persuaded by his friends to appreciate the gravity of his position. For once prepared to humble himself, he wrote to the queen in just the sort of obsequious terms she liked.[31] Drafted by Reynolds, in whose handwriting the only surviving text of the letter is preserved, he said that he was 'humbly and unfeignedly' willing to acknowledge his offence; he had undergone her indignation 'patiently'; he begged 'that this cup may pass' from him. And he appealed to her vanity, entreating her to consider 'how much more it will agree with your princely and angel-like nature to have your mercy blazed by the tongue of Your Majesty's once happy, but now most sorrowful orator, than to have a sentence given to ruin and disable him who despiseth life when he shall be made unfit for your service'.[32]

It worked. Just as Elizabeth had been unwilling to leave him to die, so she was unwilling completely to destroy him. The spell that had bound her to him had been broken when he had impudently turned his back on her and insulted her shortly before he had been sent to Ireland. But, for all that, she decided to stop a trial she might not be able to control once it started.

Her intervention came at the very last moment, on the evening of

12 February. By then, Cecil had returned to his house in the Strand from Richmond to prepare for the hearing the following day. The queen, who was also at Richmond, told Thomas Windebank, still acting as her confidential secretary, while also serving Cecil, to contact him verbally and by letter. She was 'loath', she explained beguilingly to Windebank, who had the difficult job of relaying her exact words, 'to let slip' the Star Chamber proceedings, but if Cecil, Nottingham, Buckhurst and Chief Justice Popham 'did think that that might be done at some other time and place with her honour', then so be it. Otherwise, naturally, she 'would not have forborne tomorrow, and this Her Highness's will is Your Honour should impart to her said Council'.[33]

Packed with weasel words, her statement was carefully designed to create the impression that in stopping the trial she had merely given way to advice, so keeping her fingerprints off the decision. As Cecil had so insightfully mused in a memo he had written when he had found himself in a not dissimilar position a few years earlier: 'This argueth the queen would have her ministers do that she will not avow.'[34]

Even then, reluctant to commit herself to anything on paper, she called Windebank back, perused his letter three or four times 'before it were closed [sealed]', then ordered him not to send it, saying, 'My Lord Admiral and they knew her pleasure and meaning sufficiently, and therefore that she needed not to write.'[35]

Unlike William Davison at the time of the sending of the death warrant for Mary Queen of Scots, Windebank knew exactly where he stood and what to do. Racing to the stables and mounting his horse, he rode 'haste-post-haste' into London to warn Cecil that he should call off the trial – at least for now, until the queen's mood changed.[36]

Essex's gratitude was suitably effusive. 'I acknowledge, upon the knees of my heart, Your Majesty's infinite goodness in granting my petition', he began in another letter drafted for him by Reynolds, which again would not disappoint Elizabeth. 'God that hath all hearts in witness', he continued, knew 'how faithfully I do vow to dedicate the rest of my life . . . in obedience, faith and zeal to Your Majesty'. And he protested 'I shall live and die your most humble vassal.'[37]

Of course, his problems were far from over. Although he was allowed to return to Essex House in March, he would now be a prisoner of Sir Richard Berkeley, who kept all the keys to the house, slept in the very next room and had orders from the queen to allow no one to visit without her permission.[38] In an effort to alleviate his plight, Essex threw himself on Elizabeth's mercy in a series of self-pitying letters. In him, he assured her, she had 'a servant whose humble and infinite affection cannot be matched'; in her, he had 'a lady, a nymph or an angel, who, when all the world frowns upon me, cannot look with other than gracious eyes'. All he wanted on this earth, he declared, was to 'expiate my former offences' and 'recover Your Majesty's more than gracious favour'.[39]

Yet still he was not a free man. He was not at Court, and his enemies on the Council continued to pursue him. In this, they were cheered on relentlessly from the sidelines by Ralegh, who, with Cecil's help, had recovered much of Elizabeth's lost favour and been fully rehabilitated to his old position as Captain of the Guard. Their moment came in May 1600, when a London printer, possibly incited by Henry Cuffe, attempted to publish a vigorous defence of all Essex's actions since the siege of Rouen, a work Essex had begun writing on his voyage home from Cádiz in 1596 and which he had already circulated widely in manuscript among his friends and admirers.[40]

Couched in the form of a letter to Anthony Bacon and entitled *An Apologie of the Earle of Essex against Those Which Jealously and Maliciously Tax Him to be the Hinderer of the Peace and Quiet of His Country*, the book gave Cecil his chance. Coming hard on the heels of Cockson's provocative engraving and despite Essex's efforts to defuse the situation by insisting that the printed version of his *Apologie* had not been authorized by him, it seemed to the queen as if he was once again courting fame and popularity in a manner she most despised and feared.[41]

On 5 June, therefore, by royal command, Essex was brought back to York House as a prisoner to face a whole day's interrogation by eighteen special commissioners, including Cecil, Egerton, Buckhurst, Nottingham and Archbishop Whitgift. A repeat of his former tactic of writing an abject letter to the queen shortly before the commissioners met failed, and this time the case was heard.[42]

Essex was charged with failing to prosecute the Ulster campaign as directed, dishonourable parleying with Tyrone and defiantly returning to Court. His sentence, pronounced by Egerton, was to be stripped of his offices of state and remain under house arrest until Elizabeth decided otherwise.[43] While she thought about it, she allowed the Earl to recuperate at his wife's country house at Barn Elms, on the south bank of the Thames, near Richmond. On 1 July she relieved him of Berkeley's supervision. On 26 August, after much deliberation, she finally declared she was prepared to grant him his freedom. But she refused to see him, and she banished him from Court for ever, declining to listen to his appeals to return, no matter how often he wrote, flattered and begged.

As the weeks passed without an audience, Essex became increasingly convinced that Elizabeth would not renew his highly lucrative lease of the farm of the customs on sweet wines, which was due to expire in October 1600. This lease had been the mainstay of his finances since the concession had first been granted to him in 1589, and without it he would be utterly ruined. Quite realistically, he took renewal as a key indicator of whether he would ever regain his former positions. When questioned later, his friend and confidant Sir Charles Danvers recalled that Essex had told him that 'by the renewing [of] it, or taking it from him, he should judge what was meant him.'[44]

He would soon find out. After reportedly saying that an 'ungovernable beast must be stinted of his provender', Elizabeth chose not to continue the lease, nudging Essex further towards the edge of the precipice.[45] In conversation with Danvers, he had spoken of taking his cause into Parliament, where he might muster his followers should the lease not be renewed, but he thought better of it and instead suggested 'sending emissaries' into Ireland, where the queen had appointed his close ally and his sister Penelope's lover, Lord Mountjoy, to be the new Lord Deputy.[46]

Elizabeth had first outlined Mountjoy's task to him at Richmond in October 1599. He was to finish the work that Essex had failed to do by defeating Tyrone and defending Ireland against Spanish invasion.[47] Over the course of the next eighteen months, Mountjoy would successfully reverse most of the earlier English losses with far smaller resources than the Earl had been given. While delighted by his friend's success, however, it would greatly rankle with Essex that the Privy Council allowed his successor to tighten the noose on Ulster and north Connacht by establishing a strong military garrison behind enemy lines at Lough Foyle – the very strategy he was himself denied.[48]

The sinister aspect of Essex's plan for 'sending emissaries' into Ireland emerges from the fact that, starting in 1598, he had renewed in earnest the clandestine correspondence with James VI begun four years earlier through the Scotsman David Foulis. According to Cuffe, his intent 'hath been principally that by assuring that prince of his good affection', he might improve James's prospects of succession (and of course his own career) and at the same time 'hinder the designs of the Infanta of Spain'.[49]

Ignorant of the true extent of Essex's slide towards disaster, James totally overestimated his potential value. The letters that passed between them at this stage no longer survive and are known only from reports by Essex's intimates extracted under interrogation, but as the Earl fell deeper into disgrace his plans for both Scotland and Ireland began to stray into waters that were at best questionable and at worst treasonable. Working hand in glove with Mountjoy, Essex reassured the Scottish king that he would fully support his claim to the throne after Elizabeth's death. In a decidedly murky manoeuvre, he then promised him that a mechanism would be devised by which his accession might, under certain unspecified circumstances, be contrived while the queen still lived.[50]

One possible stratagem secretly discussed between Essex and Mountjoy was that the new Lord Deputy should leave Ireland safely guarded, then cross over to England with an army of four thousand or five thousand men to join a force that Essex himself would raise.[51] At the same time, James, as Essex imagined, 'would enter into the cause'. Whether this meant actually invading England or merely giving a show of strength on the border, he did not specify. When Sir Henry Lee, Essex's friend and admirer, hurriedly rode to James to sound him out, though, nothing came of it: the canny Scottish king made soothing noises but chose not to commit himself to anything so hazardous.[52]

With Essex now free but banished from Court, he was far from out of danger, as he was prevented from reaching the queen to plead his cause: he still arrogantly believed that, if he could only see her and talk to her, he could bend her to his will. The problem was how to get past Ralegh as Captain of the Guard. Never known for his patience, Essex tried again for outside help, sending the Earl of Southampton to Ireland and calling once more on Mountjoy to prepare an invasion force. But, to Southampton's astonishment and dismay, Mountjoy refused. Seeing the extent of the collapse of Essex's fortunes and the danger to himself, he 'utterly rejected' the venture.[53] Acting to save Essex's life while he was still a prisoner or to assist the putative heir to the throne, he declared, was one thing. But if what was at stake now was merely to 'restore his fortune only . . . and to satisfy my Lord of Essex's private ambition', he would not risk his own skin 'by discovery of the former project'.[54]

Mountjoy could hardly have been more candid. Accordingly, the increasingly desperate Essex changed tack, asking Mountjoy simply to write a letter that he might show to the queen, denouncing his enemies, now identified as Cecil, Ralegh and the handsome young Lord Cobham, Cecil's brother-in-law, who had succeeded to the barony on his father's death.[55] Essex meant to present this letter personally to Elizabeth, to which end he asked Mountjoy to send him 'divers captains and men of quality, such as he could spare'.[56] Their role was to secure the Court against Ralegh's men, whom Essex knew were under orders to deny him admission should he seek to attempt an entry. With the help of these captains, Essex would arrest Cecil and Ralegh. He would then be able to make his way freely through the Privy Chamber and into Elizabeth's presence once more.[57]

As before, Mountjoy prudently declined to get involved. So, as Christmas approached, feeling himself boxed firmly into a corner, Essex tried one last approach to James.[58] A trusted intermediary, 'Norton the bookseller', who frequently travelled to Scotland on business and would arouse no particular suspicion, collected a letter penned by Essex and took it to James.[59] In the smuggled note, Essex melodramatically alleged that Cecil and his allies were suborning his servants, stealing his papers, forging letters and negotiating with Spain to put the Infanta on the throne. He went on to assure James that he was 'summoned of all sides to stop the malice, the wickedness and madness of these men, and to relieve my poor country that groans under her burden'. The Scottish king, he said, could best protect his own interests by sending an ambassador to Elizabeth calling for her agreement to his accession, and asking her at the same time to reinstate Essex to all his former offices. He proposed the Earl of Mar for this delicate mission. And as Cuffe later claimed under interrogation, Essex even wrote a list of instructions and general information to present to Mar when he arrived in London.[60]

The Earl of Mar would indeed be sent by James, but only when it was too late. Around noon on Sunday, 8 February 1601, Patrick Brewe, one of the wardens of the Goldsmiths' Company, was standing outside his house in Lombard Street in the City of London.[61] Suddenly, he saw Essex, flanked by the Earls of Southampton, Rutland and Bedford and closely followed by Sir Christopher Blount, riding down Cheapside at the head of some three hundred of their supporters, all armed with rapiers. In the ensuing investigations, Brewe repeated what he had heard Essex cry out to the startled Londoners: 'God save the Queen's Majesty, and pray for her, and pray to God to bless and keep her, and to keep this city from the Spaniards, for the Crown of England is sold to strangers.'[62] Thomas Curson, a London armourer, confirmed that Essex had shouted to anyone who would listen that 'the Crown of England was sold to Spain.'[63]

Although neither Brewe nor Curson knew it at the time, they were witnesses to the final act in the drama that was Essex's life. Robert Cecil, addressing his fellow privy councillors in the Star Chamber a few days later, would describe the Earl as 'traitorous', 'more like a monster than a man', someone who had been clandestinely plotting treason for many years.[64] A Catholic fifth columnist, a sympathizer of Robert Parsons and the Jesuits, he was out to dethrone Elizabeth and restore the old faith. After reaching a secret deal with Tyrone during their infamous parley, he had conspired to raise the city on the false report that his own life was in danger as a prelude to capturing the queen and the Court and making himself king. Assiduously cultivating 'popularity', 'insinuating himself into the favour of the people', he had postured as a successful war leader so as to build up a military following. After he had 'removed' all those privy councillors loyal to Elizabeth, he would 'put beside [depose]' the queen herself. For his grand finale, he would then make the whole of England the prey of Irish kerns.[65]

But was Essex really a traitor to Elizabeth? Arrogant, stubborn, narcissistic and presumptuous he certainly was. He took the smallest slights as intense personal attacks and would always find it difficult to give way to the will of others, even that of the queen. In his mind, his opinions were not merely of value, they were always right. He had said as much in his *Apologie*: when, at various points in his career, he had flouted Elizabeth's orders, he had always done so, he protested, on grounds of 'necessity' and the 'public good'. And, in his mind, it had to be he, not his anointed sovereign, who defined such a 'necessity'.

But defiance and treason are two very different things. Essex had always been his own worst enemy. He acted foolishly and impetuously and had crossed the line in his scheming with James. But would he go so far as to claim the throne for himself? And why was it that privy councillors, over the ensuing weeks and months, would make so much of an allegation that Essex had set out 'to make this time seem like the time of King Richard II . . . to be reformed by him as by Henry IV'?[66]

What did Elizabeth have to do with Richard II, whose arbitrary rule and belief in the God-given sanctity of kingship had brought him and England to catastrophe?

20. 'I am Richard II'

When on that fateful Sunday, 8 February, Essex led some three hundred of his supporters down Cheapside crying out that 'the Crown of England is sold to Spain', his actions were inspired by the fear and mistrust he felt for those he considered to be his mortal enemies. His broad intentions can be worked out from the interrogations begun once he and his key supporters were safely in the Tower. From the moment Robert Cecil began to read this sworn evidence, it was obvious that, for several weeks, the Earl had, at the very least, been plotting with his friends to regain what he saw as his rightful place in Elizabeth's affections.[1]

Sir Charles Danvers confessed that, shortly before Christmas, the Earl had begun weighing up how he might gain access to Elizabeth without unduly startling her or being intercepted by Ralegh's guards.[2] Sir John Davies, who had accompanied Essex on his defiant return from Ireland and ridden with him to Nonsuch, testified to the same effect.[3] Sir Ferdinando Gorges, a cousin of Ralegh knighted for his bravery at the siege of Rouen, went on to disclose that Essex had summoned a hundred or so of his supporters – among them Davies, the Earl of Southampton, Danvers and Gorges himself – to meet at Drury House off the Strand on Tuesday, 3 February to hatch a plan.[4] Evidently, Essex did not want to risk such a large gathering at his own house on the Strand, as he knew it to be under close surveillance. (The carefully selected venue, on what is now Drury Lane, was the home of Sir Robert Drury, a well-trusted ally who had sailed on the Cádiz expedition and fought alongside the Earl in Ireland.)

Several of those present confessed that their discussions that day had been lengthy, often confused and increasingly heated. Broad tactics for capturing the Court had been worked out, with the various participants allocated the specific areas they should occupy while Essex and Southampton made their way to Elizabeth. Gorges claimed to have expressed doubts about what he felt was turning uncomfortably into a *coup d'état*. He had 'utterly disliked that course', he said, and expressed 'horror' at it. All, though, had agreed that to seize the Tower and its munitions was the only way to 'alter the government' and force the queen to summon a Parliament that would impeach Cecil and his minions. Where they disagreed most violently was over the timing: should they first 'attempt' the Tower or the Court – or both together? Or should they first 'stir' Essex's many friends in the City of London?[5]

Essex, according to Gorges, was almost entirely motivated by an unshakeable belief in his fame and his popularity with the Londoners. Forced to cope on a daily basis with the devastating social consequences of a relentless economic recession triggered by the long war, the mayor and aldermen had been deeply uneasy about the queen's failure to act since the summer rioting of 1595. Now, rather than attack her personally, they blamed her failings on corruption and abuses of power in high places, putting Cecil and his allies in the frame. In the meeting at Drury House, the most heated part of the argument had been over whether to centre Essex's protest around capturing the Court or to present the queen with a petition of grievances, asking her to remove those whom Essex and many of the Londoners (if for very different reasons) called her 'evil councillors'. At one moment, the confusion between these conflicting aims had become so intense that, in a moment of exasperation, Southampton had blurted out: 'Then we shall resolve upon nothing, and it is now three months or more since we first undertook this.'[6]

What *was* crystal clear from the sworn testimony is that Essex had not at first planned to do anything at all on the weekend of his madcap ride along Cheapside. Instead, circumstances had changed so dramatically at the last moment, or so he had come to think, that he felt he could delay no longer.

Essex had spent Saturday morning playing tennis, which hardly suggests he was planning a coup for the next day.[7] That same afternoon, several of his supporters, including his steward, Sir Gelly Meyrick, had eaten together around noon at the home of a man called Gunther near Temple Bar beside the Strand. They were then rowed across the Thames to attend a performance by the Lord Chamberlain's Men, whose resident playwright was William Shakespeare, at the Globe Theatre. A latecomer, Captain Thomas Lee, one of Essex's kinsmen who had served under him in Ireland, just managed to slip in before the play began.[8]

That afternoon, Cecil had convened a secret emergency meeting of the Privy Council at Lord Buckhurst's house. He was deeply uneasy, as his spies watching Essex House had reported muskets being oiled, ready for use.[9] The councillors decided to bring the Earl in for questioning, ostensibly to discuss rumours that a fifth Spanish Armada was in preparation. As suspicious of them as they were of him, Essex refused to go. Summoned for a second time, he refused again, declaring that he would be murdered on Ralegh's orders before even reaching Buckhurst's house.[10]

The same evening, Essex had invited his sister Penelope, his stepfather Sir Christopher Blount, Southampton, Davies and Danvers to a private supper party.[11] Afterwards, he called Blount and Davies separately into his bedchamber. He also spoke privately with Sir Gelly Meyrick, whom he summoned to Essex House and away from his own supper before a morsel had even touched his lips. Then, everyone was told to assemble in the Earl's 'withdrawing chamber', where they were joined by Sir William Constable, whose testimony to Cecil eight days later set his ears tingling. For Constable testified how Essex had declared that a plot had been laid by his enemies to draw him to Lord Buckhurst's house and assassinate him. As a result, the guards on Essex House would be doubled that night.[12]

Essex's conviction that he was about to be murdered was the immediate reason for his unbelievable act of folly. By six o'clock on Sunday morning, he was mustering an armed following at Essex House, indignantly protesting that there was a plot to kill him and that he meant to 'stand upon his strength'.[13] He intended to raise the city, where he believed his fame would guarantee him mass support and where he thought one of the sheriffs, Sir Thomas Smythe, would supply him with trained soldiers to face down Ralegh and his guards. It is a little-known fact that Essex would personally visit Smythe's house in Gracechurch Street early that morning: Smythe was seen talking to him in the street outside. What passed for a plan in the turmoil of Essex's consciousness was that the city's officers would go to Elizabeth to petition her on his behalf. He had drafted a template that he wanted the mayor and sheriffs to sign.[14]

Already, Cecil's spies had reported the mustering of armed men at Essex House. The queen's principal secretary could only assume that an armed insurrection was about to be attempted. Shortly before ten o'clock, therefore, a delegation of four officials from Whitehall – Lord Keeper Egerton, the Earl of Worcester, Sir William Knollys and Chief Justice Popham – arrived at Essex House. Egerton afterwards wrote a graphic eyewitness account of what they found there. The place, he said, was heavily defended and it was only possible to gain entrance through a small wicket gate. Brought directly to Essex in the courtyard, Egerton, the delegation's spokesman, told him that if he stated his grievances they would be reported to the queen, who would consider them and do him justice.[15]

Essex would have none of it. He suspected a trap and called for his bodyguards, loudly expostulating that he was to be murdered in his bed. When Egerton proposed that they withdraw and discuss the matter privately, things turned ugly. The Earl's supporters cried out, 'Away, my lord, away!' 'They abuse you, they betray you, they undo you, you lose time.'[16]

True to his office as Lord Keeper, Egerton ordered Essex's followers to lay down their weapons and disperse if they considered themselves loyal subjects of the queen. At this, the men in the courtyard shouted back 'All, all, all!' But as Essex began to lead the delegation into the safety of the house, the clamour intensified, some of the men shouting 'Kill them!' and 'Let us shop them up!'[17]

Once indoors, Essex took the four officials into his library ('book-chamber') and locked the door, which was immediately patrolled by heavily armed soldiers. It was clear they were now prisoners.[18] Leaving the room, Essex said he would be back in half an hour but, in reality, they would be locked up until almost four o'clock in the afternoon.[19] During that time, Essex would make his frantic attempt to raise the city.

At Whitehall, the Court was stricken by panic. Not even Cecil had expected Essex to act so rashly or so precipitately. Elizabeth was just about the only person in authority who kept her nerve. (It was said she managed to create the impression that she felt no more vulnerable than she would have done on hearing of a pub brawl in Fleet Street. Given that this was a credible alarm, it was an impressive piece of showmanship.)[20]

Ralegh's soldiers scurried to and fro, gathering up as many weapons as they could find in the Guard Chamber and storerooms of the armoury. Barricades of upturned coaches and carts were thrown across the main access routes to the palace and the back entrances. Nearby householders were ordered to hand over any weapons they had stockpiled and to reinforce the guards until help arrived.[21]

Essex's attempt to rouse the city, meanwhile, failed miserably. He was dismayed when everything fast descended into chaos. His aim had been 'to apprehend' the mayor and aldermen at St Paul's, where they would be attending the usual Sunday-morning civic sermon, meaning to ask them to carry his petition to the queen. But because he was delayed by the delegation, he arrived to find that Cecil had already mobilized the city's militia and instructed the mayor to send armed men to reinforce Ralegh's guards.[22]

When Essex and his followers then made their way along Fleet Street, past St Paul's and into Cheapside, shouting out their slogans, the astonished citizens had done nothing to prevent them, but nor had they assisted them. Essex largely met a bemused silence, occasionally interrupted by cries from some of the wilier citizens, who chose to pretend that he was reconciled to the queen and so cried out 'God save Your Honour!'[23] Catastrophe struck when the gates of the city were bolted and Essex and his men found themselves locked in.

By two o'clock in the afternoon, their number was fast dwindling as they realized their cause was lost. When the rump of a hundred or so approached Ludgate and St Paul's, hoping to return to Essex House, they were prevented by a heavy iron chain strung across the street, behind which stood a row of pikemen and soldiers armed with muskets. In the ensuing melee, Sir Christopher Blount was badly wounded in the head and his page killed, and still the way was blocked. Essex's only remaining option was to force a path down to the wharf at Queenhithe and flee to Essex House by river, which is exactly what he did.[24]

Essex rushed back into Essex House shortly before four o'clock, just a few minutes too late to prevent Sir Ferdinando Gorges from releasing the Whitehall delegation and so ending any chance that they might be used as bargaining counters.[25] As the Earl had left unambiguous instructions that the officials were to be held under guard until he personally sanctioned their release, Gorges's actions aroused considerable speculation, with 'remorse' or 'cunning' being assumed. Because Gorges was Ralegh's cousin and Ralegh was Captain of the Guard, 'cunning' seems the likelier explanation, especially since Gorges would later avoid the death penalty by turning queen's evidence.[26]

Essex's freedom would be short-lived. Although Essex House was not designed to withstand a siege, some fifty or so of his diehard supporters managed to hold it until a little before six o'clock, when two cannon were brought on carts from the Tower.[27] Then, Elizabeth intervened. She demanded that the stand-off end at once and said she would not go to bed until it had. She sent Lord Admiral Nottingham along the Strand to take charge. He had no compunction in threatening to blow up the house unless Essex surrendered.[28] Sir Gelly Meyrick went up on the roof, heavily armed, ready to fire at anyone who came near the front gate. But such gestures were futile: no one could resist the sheer firepower of the cannon.[29]

Nottingham agreed to offer a two-hour truce only when informed at the last moment that Essex's sister Penelope and his wife, Frances, were in the house. After that, he would wait no longer. The queen must be obeyed. Essex briefly considered going down fighting, 'the sooner to fly to heaven', but was eventually persuaded to surrender. The Thames, often treacherous at night and at high tide, was impassable downriver, so he was taken to Archbishop Whitgift's house at Lambeth, then escorted the next morning to the Tower in a closed barge. A hundred or so of his followers were then arrested and sent to prison.[30]

The event Cecil called 'this dangerous accident' was not yet quite over.[31] Four evenings later, Captain Thomas Lee, Essex's kinsman and the man who had just managed to slip into the Globe Theatre before the play began, would be caught loitering in the lobby outside the entrance to Elizabeth's Privy Chamber, armed with a dagger. His manner was said to be very strange, 'with a stern countenance, his colour very pale, yet so sweating as very many drops of sweat appeared on his face'.[32] When he asked if the queen was yet at supper, he was arrested, tried the next day and found guilty of high treason. The fact that Essex had employed him as an intermediary with Tyrone helped seal his fate.[33]

After that, things looked bleak for Essex. But they were not yet bleak enough in the eyes of Cecil or Ralegh. Due process of law would have to be observed and, if Essex were to be tried for treason, Cecil would have to construct a watertight case for the prosecution. The jurymen would be Londoners, many of whom did not think Essex should die, even if they had conspicuously failed to back his uprising. Such men would need convincing. Writing to Cecil, Ralegh did not mince his words. 'If you take it for a good counsel to relent towards this tyrant, you will repent it when it shall be too late. His malice is fixed, and will not evaporate by any [of] your mild courses, for he will ascribe the alteration to Her Majesty's pusillanimity, and not to your good nature.'[34] Ralegh still bitterly remembered his showdown with Essex at Faial in the Azores after Sir Gelly Meyrick had accused him of mutiny and demanded that he be hanged.

Cecil's final round of interrogations began with Augustine Phillips, one of Shakespeare's fellow actors and the company manager. His darkest suspicions were stirred by what Gelly Meyrick had confessed about the play performed at the Globe Theatre, which would now become the chief focus of the investigations. Phillips confirmed that, a day or so before the play's performance, a group of Essex's followers had been to find the players and asked them to put on a bespoke performance of 'the play of the deposing and killing of King Richard the Second to be played the Saturday next'.[35] When the actors protested that the play was 'so old and so long out of use', they were overruled. It was to be that or nothing, and they were offered forty shillings to perform it on top of their 'ordinary' rate for a command performance of £10.

The play Essex's supporters had requested was Shakespeare's *Richard II*, first written and performed in 1595 or 1596, during the furore over the publication of Robert Parsons' *A Conference about the Next Succession to the Crown*.[36] The play opens with Henry Bolingbroke,

Earl of Derby and Duke of Hereford, challenging Thomas Mowbray, Duke of Norfolk, to trial by single combat. At the very last
moment, Richard intervenes and forbids the fight, sending both
combatants into exile. Bolingbroke goes to France. From there, he
returns unexpectedly with an army, and then deposes and later mur-
ders Richard, along with his corrupt minions and parasites, Bushy,
Bagot and Green. Whether Bolingbroke consciously orders Richard
to be murdered or does so more insidiously, by dropping broad hints,
is left ambiguous. Finally, Bolingbroke has himself proclaimed King
Henry IV.

Superficially, to insist on seeing a play portraying the dethroning
and killing of a God-appointed king on the day before mounting an
armed insurrection at the heart of England's capital city was evidence
of a dastardly conspiracy. The inconvenient fact for Cecil was that
the trigger for Essex's ride into the streets came only *after* the show.
On both the day the special performance was commissioned and the
day it was given, no *specific* rising had yet been planned by Essex or by
anyone else.[37]

Neither had Essex been in the audience, but Cecil ignored that, too.
For him, the resonances between Essex and Bolingbroke had become
just too alluring. Both were descended from John of Gaunt, Edward
III's eldest surviving son. Essex had been known as Viscount Hereford
until his father's death in 1576. Bolingbroke, like Essex, had been keen
to cultivate fame and popularity in London. And there was more:
when Elizabeth had promoted Lord Admiral Howard to the earldom
of Nottingham in 1597, Essex had challenged him to a duel. Howard
was directly descended from Thomas Mowbray, Duke of Norfolk.
Most crucially of all, Bolingbroke and Essex had both returned home
unexpectedly from overseas, Bolingbroke with an army from France,
and Essex, it was alleged, with the intention of summoning one from
Ireland. As for the corrupt parasites Bushy, Bagot and Green, 'the caterpillars of the commonwealth/ Which I have sworn to weed and
pluck away', as Bolingbroke puts it in the play, substitute Cecil, Ralegh
and the young Lord Cobham, Cecil's brother-in-law.[38]

As Cecil spun his spider's web around Essex, determined to trap and
devour him, an earlier incident involving Essex and a literary work

took on a fresh and highly sinister meaning. Shortly before the Earl had left to take up his command in Ireland, the lawyer John Hayward had published a book entitled *The First Part of the Life and Raigne of King Henrie the IIII*. A highly coloured account of Bolingbroke's deposition of Richard II in 1399, the book described the corruption of Richard's government in ways that seemed uncannily similar to the complaints the Earl had been levelling against Cecil and his allies ever since his return from Cádiz. Furthermore, the book began with a fulsome dedication to Essex, written in such a way as to appear to be an incitement to his political ambitions.[39]

An instant bestseller, Hayward's book had been the talk of London. Furious at what she believed to be its innuendoes, Elizabeth sent its author to the Tower, where he would remain until after her death. Her 'Little Black Husband' Whitgift ordered the offending dedication to be excised from all copies of the book (although not a single copy surviving today lacks it), and 1,500 copies of a 'corrected' second edition still awaiting binding were seized and burned.[40]

Gone were the days when Cecil and Ralegh exchanged a risqué joke with Essex about the deposed King Richard II, as they had done after their clandestine dinner on the eve of the Azores expedition. As Cecil now framed the case, Essex had deserted his post in Ulster, poised to summon an army from Ireland. His 'wicked purpose' was to give those loyal servants closest to the queen the treatment meted out by Bolingbroke to Bushy, Bagot and Green. After that, Essex would 'deal' with Elizabeth as Bolingbroke had 'dealt' with King Richard and 'set the Crown of England upon his own head'.[41] Hayward's book was thus, in Cecil's opinion, Essex's manifesto in his bid for the throne.[42]

Cecil arranged with Chief Justice Popham to put Essex and his chief ally, the Earl of Southampton, on trial for treason at Westminster Hall on Thursday, 19 February. In the interim, an important loose end had to be cleared up. Immediately after his dash back to Essex House following his failed attempt to rouse the city, Essex had hurriedly burned his papers. Or had he? What tore away at Cecil's brain was the question of what had been inside a little black taffeta bag that the Earl always wore around his neck. When he had rushed in, he had taken a key out of the bag, using it to unlock a small iron chest containing a book about his troubles that he had written himself. This he reluctantly burned, along with a list of names he carried in his pocket and the contents of another chest, which he had to break open, as the key was lost. But there had been a paper inside the bag as well as the key. It was said to be quite small, only about a quarter of a sheet, and with just six or seven lines 'not of his own hand, but written by another man'.[43]

Interrogated in the Tower as to the contents of the bag, the Earl's spin doctor Henry Cuffe testified explosively that the missing paper had been a ciphered message from James VI.[44] If it still existed, Cecil was determined to find it. He ordered Sir John Peyton, the newly appointed Lieutenant of the Tower, to subject Essex to the supreme humiliation of a full body search. Peyton did as he was bid, searching the Earl's person, 'his body and legs, naked' in addition to his shirts and other clothing, but he found nothing. What Cecil was looking for but never managed to find was written proof of collusion between Essex, James and Tyrone over the future of Ireland and the succession. Had he found it, the course of British history might have been very different.[45]

As prominent aristocrats, Essex and Southampton were entitled to be tried by their peers in the Lord Steward's Court. (Chief Justice Popham and his fellow judges were present throughout to advise on points of law.) A special platform was constructed for the trial in the shape of a square, with raised seating on opposite sides covered in green cloth for the peers. Nine earls were present, among them Nottingham and Worcester, and sixteen barons. Buckhurst presided as acting Lord Steward, seated on a raised chair at the upper end of the square beneath a canopy of state. Sir Edward Coke, flushed with success after his bravura performance in the trial of Dr Lopez and now well ensconced as Queen's Attorney, sat opposite him on a low bench, flanked by Francis Bacon, his junior for the day. As at Lopez's trial, Coke would prove himself a master of hostile advocacy. Bacon, too, hungry for promotion, would stick the knife into his old patron at every opportunity.[46]

Although it was a long trial, lasting from eight in the morning until seven at night, guilty verdicts were a foregone conclusion. Both defendants were condemned to death and returned to the Tower to await execution. Southampton's sentence would later be commuted to life imprisonment on the grounds that Essex had led him astray.[47] Stripped of his lands and title, he was to be imprisoned at the queen's pleasure. Essex melodramatically refused to plead for mercy, declaring that it would be beneath his dignity. When Buckhurst offered him the opportunity, as the law required, he replied, 'I had rather die than live in misery.'[48]

More important than the trial itself is what happened afterwards. Still obsessed by the missing contents of Essex's black taffeta bag, Cecil demanded more information on the Earl's activities in Ireland. To fish for it, he sent a preacher, Dr Thomas Dove, Dean of Norwich, to the Tower, carefully primed to encourage Essex to confess everything so that he could die with his conscience clear. When that failed, Cecil redoubled his efforts, sending Dr Abdias Assheton, one of the Earl's own chaplains, who knew precisely how to touch Essex's emotions and play on his weaknesses. Assheton did a psychological demolition job on the Earl, destroying his sense of heroic failure and prompting a flood of fresh evidence that led to the conviction of his stepfather, Christopher Blount, along with Charles Danvers, John Davies, Sir Gelly Meyrick and Henry Cuffe.[49]

Typically, Essex cast the blame on his followers. Meyrick and Cuffe would be hanged at Tyburn, Blount and Danvers beheaded on Tower Hill. Unfortunately for Cecil, Assheton failed to extract any useful information about what had really happened in Ireland. Or, if he did, Cecil suppressed it on the grounds that it implicated the new Lord Deputy Mountjoy, who was getting the upper hand against Tyrone and the rebels and thus much too valuable to lose. It may be no coincidence that Elizabeth would send Mountjoy a personal letter of pardon without ever stating explicitly what it was he was supposed to have done wrong.[50]

Shortly after eight o'clock on the morning of Ash Wednesday (25 February), Essex was beheaded in the inner courtyard of the Tower before a small group of witnesses handpicked by the queen.[51] In innumerable biographies of Elizabeth it has been suggested that she found herself psychologically unable to sign his death warrant. After several days of indecision following his trial, so the story goes, she signed it on 23 February, then countermanded the order the next day, so strong still was her emotional tie to Leicester's stepson.[52] Camden in his *Annales* says that 'she wavered in her mind' thanks to 'her former affection and favour towards him'.[53]

In truth, her bond to him had long been severed and, if she wavered, it was only for a couple of hours. She signed his death warrant on the afternoon of Shrove Tuesday (24th), as soon as Cecil was satisfied that Assheton could prise no more information from him.[54] Cecil told the constable of the Tower that the signed warrant would arrive before nightfall. Later, he instructed Sir John Peyton that Essex was to be told after finishing his supper that he would die the following morning.[55]

Camden says that Elizabeth sent one 'Sir Ed. Cary' to the Tower to reprieve Essex. Later, she sent 'a fresh command by Darcy that he should be put to death'.[56] Sir Edward Carey, a kinsman of Sir Robert Carey, was one of her longest-serving grooms of the Privy Chamber; Edward Darcy was a much younger colleague.[57] The crucial detail Camden omits is that Carey was sent on his mission in the early evening, just as Elizabeth was coming down from her Bedchamber to the Great Hall at Whitehall to watch a play by the very same Lord Chamberlain's Men who had performed *Richard II* at the Globe barely three weeks before. She sent Darcy to the Tower to reinstate the warrant the minute the play was over.[58]

The title of this play, almost certainly by Shakespeare, is, maddeningly, not recorded. During it, however, Elizabeth decided that Essex must die. Hubristic, egotistical, selfish, ungrateful, immature, incapable of compromise and with a towering sense of his own entitlement, his focus was himself and always had been. The worst of his many mistakes had been to mutter in Elizabeth's hearing that 'her conditions were as crooked as her carcass' after she had struck him across the face.

In August 1601, six months after Essex mounted the scaffold, Elizabeth would give an audience to the noted lawyer and antiquary William Lambarde. Recently appointed the Keeper of the Rolls and Records in the Tower of London, he had come to her Privy Chamber at Greenwich Palace to present her with what he called a *Pandecta Rotulorum*, an inventory, or 'digest', of the records in his charge.[59] As he went through the list with her, reign by reign, beginning with King John, she asked him to explain what some of these documents were, and what some of the more obscure Latin terms and names used in them meant. Lambarde seems to have immensely relished showing off his expertise, until they reached Richard II's reign, when a lightning bolt struck. '*I* am Richard II,' Elizabeth suddenly announced sententiously, 'know ye not that?' She then went on to add, 'He that will forget God will also forget his benefactors; this tragedy was forty times played in open streets and houses.'[60]

Fully aware that she was speaking of Essex, Lambarde responded stoutly but tactfully. 'Such a wicked imagination was determined and attempted by a most unkind gentleman, the most adorned creature Your Majesty ever made.' The conversation then switched back to the safer ground of the Tower records, until Elizabeth brought it back to Richard. Had Lambarde seen 'any true picture or lively representation of his countenance and person'? Lambarde said no, prompting her to offer to ask the keeper of her gallery at Whitehall to show him a portrait she had recently acquired. The conversation ended with Elizabeth remarking, 'In those days force and arms did prevail, but now the wit of the fox is ever on foot, so as hardly a faithful and virtuous man may be found.'[61]

She was no fool. Had she come to suspect that Essex's enemies had plotted to destroy him ever since that terrible day when he turned his back on her and she struck him across the face? Had she guessed that they set him up to fail in Ireland, then tempted him to some suitably rash action on his return? But then he had, after all, invited it: had she not herself called him a 'rash and temerarious youth' to his face and an unbridled horse behind his back?

For nearly four hundred years, Elizabeth's words have been endlessly dissected. Doubt has even been cast on Lambarde's transcript of their conversation, but these have recently been dispelled by the discovery of a fresh version whose authenticity is beyond question.[62] By saying 'He that will forget God will also forget his benefactors,' the queen clearly meant that Essex's conduct was, in her eyes, as much a failure to respect *her* royal status as a failure to respect God. When she said, 'this tragedy was forty times played in open streets and houses,' she was obviously not referring to Shakespeare's play but to the fact that Essex and others of his acquaintance had wantonly overreached themselves in criticizing her manner of rule 'in open streets and houses'.[63] She particularly suspected Thomas Smythe, whose house in Gracechurch Street Essex had visited early on that fateful Sunday morning. In retaliation, she had dismissed Smythe from his post as sheriff and sent him to the Tower.[64]

But her words must also in part be taken at face value. When she said, '_I_ am Richard II, know ye not that?', it would seem she really did suspect that, had Essex succeeded in taking Whitehall and the Tower, he would have 'dealt' with her as Bolingbroke had 'dealt' with Richard. It was a suspicion that brought home to her that monarchy, even if divine, was also transient and mortal. The institution might live on, but its incumbents changed and she soon must die.

And when that time drew nigh, would she, too, feel, like Bolingbroke in the closing scene of Shakespeare's play, that her own hands were drenched in blood?[65] She had told Burghley that, if she signed the death warrant for Mary Queen of Scots, she would be condoning a regicide. The 'divinity of kingship' would for ever be attenuated, making the monarchy accountable to Parliament and threatening a twilight world darkened with threats, confusion and moral ambiguities.

Like Bolingbroke, she had killed a God-appointed ruler. It was a heavy load she would carry to the grave.

21. The Queen's Speech

Ever since the Treaty of Vervins, cries for peace with Spain had steadily become more strident.[1] Robert Cecil, with his own mercantile
investments to think of, had led the peace party in the Privy Council.
And, as the long anxious months went by, the queen's resolve never
to make peace with Spain in her lifetime had slowly begun to waver.
In September 1599, a bare fortnight after Archduke Albert had made
his triumphant entry into Brussels with his new bride, the Infanta
Isabella, he had put out an olive branch, assuring Elizabeth of his
desire for peace. Lying through his teeth, Albert added that he had
received full authority from his new brother-in-law, the Spanish
King Philip III, to discuss terms.[2]

Elizabeth swiftly reassured Count Maurice and the States General
that she would do nothing without them.[3] She already knew their
response: they adamantly opposed a settlement with Spain. Barely
was his father cold in the grave than Philip had imposed a trade
embargo on the Dutch, aiming to hit them where it hurt most. And
she knew only too well, as they did, that Albert's olive branch had
been triggered not by goodwill but by mutinies in his armies.[4]

On the afternoon of Sunday, 9 March 1600, Lodewijk Verreycken,
the Archduke's special envoy, requested an audience at Richmond
Palace.[5] To his dismay, Elizabeth gave him a bruising reception, fencing irritably with him. For his part, Verreycken was overconfident.
Rather than preparing for the interview, he had been wined and
dined by Lord Buckhurst and attended a performance of Shakespeare's *Henry IV, Part I*.[6]

Deeply vexed with Verreycken for talking down to her as if a
peace was a virtual certainty, Elizabeth quibbled that his letters of
credence were signed only by Albert and not by Philip. She then
ostentatiously changed the topic to the appalling weather, asking
him how the Infanta was coping with her move from the Escorial to
freezing Brussels.[7] Afterwards, Cecil, Nottingham and Buckhurst

tore his proposals to shreds. When Verreycken demanded that the
queen's remaining auxiliary troops be withdrawn from the Netherlands and that all trade between England and the Dutch should cease,
he was greeted with a deafening silence. Curious to see if a deal could
still be done, the privy councillors asked whether Philip would concede English merchants free passage to the trade of the East Indies,
but Verreycken refused. Nor was he able to promise that no Spanish
aid would be given to Tyrone's rebels.[8]

Verreycken was sent back to Brussels with a demand that the Archduke should fundamentally revise the peace terms and was offered a
month to provide an answer. The result was a much-heralded peace
conference at Boulogne in May, when Spanish, Flemish and English
delegates finally sat down together.[9] The Dutch held their breath, but
the negotiations were doomed to fail. Elizabeth's instructions to Sir
Henry Neville, the new ambassador to France who led the English
delegation, ran to ten closely written pages and made it clear that
there was to be no compromise over the auxiliaries and no agreement
to a hostile move against the Dutch States. Neville was also told to
stipulate that free trade to the East Indies would be considered a lit-
mus test of a 'true amity' with Spain, without which the two
countries must remain at war.[10]

With peace once more off the agenda, Philip made fresh plans to
invade Ireland, where Mountjoy was fast boxing the rebels into their
Ulster homeland. Just as the Spanish delegates to the Boulogne conference were on their way to file their report in Brussels, Tyrone,
who had a price of 4,000 marks (£2.6 million today) put on his head,
made a loud appeal for Spanish aid. Without delay, Philip consulted
the Council of State. 'We think that to protect and help these Catholics will be an act most worthy of Your Majesty's greatness' was the
unanimous reply. 'Your Majesty will be able to copy what the queen
does through the rebels of Holland and Zeeland, and at a very small
cost.'[11] Juan de Idiáquez, one of the hawks who had encouraged the
Portuguese double agent Manuel de Andrada to incite Dr Lopez to
poison the queen, argued for a fifth Armada to be sent to southern
Ireland to bring Elizabeth to her knees. His fellow councillors urged
caution: Spain could barely find enough money to pay the Arch-

duke's troops and an expedition that went off at half-cock would jeopardize the very interests that Philip hoped to protect.[12]

But Philip sided with de Idiáquez. On Monday, 24 August 1601, a fifth Armada set sail from the port of Lisbon, destined for Ireland. On board a fleet of thirty-three ships, nineteen of them warships and the rest armed merchantmen and transport vessels, were 4,500 soldiers under the command of Don Juan del Águila. The expedition would be jinxed from the beginning. Many of the mariners were foreign conscripts, pressed into service by a last-minute raid on foreign shipping. They could not understand their officers and had no loyalty to the king or to the cause. As one of Águila's naval commanders complained, 'When the action came, I had more need to protect myself from the enemy I was carrying with the Armada than from the enemy without . . . Once in Ireland, many of them left me for the enemy.'[13]

A shortage of victuals combined with a disagreement as to the Armada's final destination sowed further confusion. Was the fleet to undertake the slower, much riskier Atlantic route to Ulster around the west coast of Ireland or the quicker, safer one to the southern coast between Cork and Waterford? If the former, food would be short. If the latter, Águila's troops would be left with the almost impossible task of marching across the hostile terrain to join up with the rebels.[14]

As luck would have it, a storm decided the issue by scattering the fleet. Not until the evening of 21 September, after an atrocious journey lasting more than three times longer than anyone had predicted, would Águila make dry land, at Kinsale to the south-west of Cork. By then, he had only 1,700 men and they were on half-rations. After a week, the number rose to 3,400, as the stragglers drifted in. Sir George Carew, a fine soldier and Cecil's key informant in Ireland, was the closest of Mountjoy's senior officers to the invading Spaniards and he marched from Cork to assess the threat. Soon Mountjoy followed him. On the 29th, the Lord Deputy rode with a few of his men to reconnoitre the area around the town of Kinsale, which the Spaniards had fortified. It took him a month to pull together his field army but, by the end of October, he had laid siege to the hungry Spaniards with seven thousand men, who would soon be reinforced by two thousand raw conscripts and three hundred cavalry from England, with another three thousand conscripts to follow.[15]

Tyrone would first try ravaging Leinster in an attempt to force Mountjoy to abandon the siege of Kinsale.[16] When that failed, he continued to march southwards, elated to find a new threat ravaging the English ranks – an unidentified zoonotic disease that killed 2,500 soldiers and put 2,000 more out of action. Carew wrote to Cecil in dismay: it was beginning to look as if Mountjoy could end up trapped in a pincer movement between the Spaniards and the Ulstermen with a much-reduced fighting force.[17]

Carew's fears proved to be unwarranted. Although Tyrone had almost 10,000 men at his disposal, the Spaniards would dwindle to fewer than 2,500 fit for combat. With his proud soldiers soon thinking themselves lucky to be eating dogs and cats when they could find them, Águila appealed to Tyrone not to delay. And, shortly after dawn on Christmas Eve, the battle began.[18] Caught between firm ground and a bog by an English cavalry charge that broke his lines, Tyrone would have no choice but to flee. Seeing that the rebels' cause was in tatters, the Spaniards declined to sally forth from Kinsale, fearing a massacre. By dusk, a thousand Irish lay dead and eight hundred were wounded, as against only a handful of English.[19]

Elizabeth's last Parliament assembled on Tuesday, 27 October 1601 in the dark shadow of these events. She had summoned Parliament for one reason alone, and that was to secure the 'subsidies' (taxes) she needed to continue Mountjoy's campaign.[20] She needed money more desperately now than ever before. Despite her financial accord with the Dutch, the States General had just saddled her with another bill for £385,000 to pay for the auxiliaries who continued to fight for Count Maurice, while Tyrone's revolt had so far cost her in excess of £1 million. In 1593, as Cecil recalled in a starkly worded memo, Parliament had granted her £486,000. In 1597, it offered almost as much, some £474,000 over three years. All this and more was spent. The queen had paid the difference partly by selling some of her jewels, partly by selling Crown land, partly by imposing forced levies on wealthy foreign merchants.[21]

When she had summoned Parliament, it was her firm intention

26. Sir Walter Ralegh captures Don António de Berrío, the governor of the Spanish colony of Trinidad, during a night-time commando raid, 1595

27. The meeting on the south bank of the Orinoco between Sir Walter Ralegh and King Topiawari, 1595

SERO, SED SERIO

28. Robert Cecil, by John de Critz, *c.*1606. His motto,
Sero, Sed Serio, means 'Late, but in earnest'

29. James VI of Scotland and I of England, by Nicholas Hilliard, *c.*1610

30. Henry IV of France before the walls of Paris, 1594, French School

31. Elizabeth aged sixty-two or sixty-three, studio of
Marcus Gheeraerts the Younger, *c.*1596

32. Archduke Albert of the
Netherlands and Infanta Isabella
Clara Eugenia of Spain and
Archduchess, *c.*1600

33. The most widely circulated
image of the ageing Elizabeth.
Based on Isaac Oliver's face
pattern of 1592, it was engraved
by Crispijn de Passe, 1596

34. This closely observed image by Jan Rutlinger, a German-born engraver at the Tower Mint, offers the truest likeness of the shape of the queen's face and nose and of her long, slender fingers, *c.*1585

NON SINE SOLE
IRIS.

35. The 'Rainbow Portrait' of Elizabeth with the face pattern
known as the 'Mask of Youth' in which the queen's features were airbrushed
back to become those of a young woman in her late twenties or early
thirties, by Marcus Gheeraerts the Younger, 1602

36. Elizabeth's monumental tomb in the north aisle of
Henry VII's Chapel in Westminster Abbey, commissioned by
James I and completed in 1606, engraved by Magdalena or
Willem de Passe, c.1620

that the session should be over by Christmas.[22] It would be, but if she thought all would go smoothly, she was mistaken. Barely had the Commons elected John Croke, the new Recorder of London, as their Speaker, when some of the bolder members, weary of struggling to cope with the severe impact of the economic recession in their constituencies, began to complain about abuses of power in high places.[23] They would consider the queen's request for money, they said, but first they expected their grievances to be redressed.[24]

Mindful of the queen's desire for speed, Cecil urged members not to trouble themselves 'with any fantastic speeches or idle bills', but he was soon forced to eat his words.[25] Several speakers protested that the poor had been forced to suffer while venality, embezzlement, tax evasion and bribery thrived among courtiers and the elite. Among other scandals, it had recently come to light that Burghley, while Lord Treasurer, had covered up a whole raft of financial improprieties. One, in the Exchequer, involving the teller Richard Stonely, had cost the queen tens of thousands of pounds. Another, in the Court of Wards, had cost £20,000. A third, probably the largest fraud to be detected, centred around Sir Thomas Sherley, the queen's treasurer of war in the Netherlands, who was believed to have siphoned off sums approaching £20,000 a year for almost fifteen years to fund his high living and private speculations. When the queen finally caught up with him, he was already bankrupt.[26]

Ralegh joined those criticizing such abuses. 'I like not', he said, 'that the Spaniards our enemies should know of our selling our pots and pans to pay subsidies. Well may you call it policy . . . but I am sure it argues poverty in the state.' He then proceeded to attack courtiers and wealthy landowners for tax cheating. Estates worth £3,000 and £4,000, he alleged, were being routinely undervalued by their owners for tax purposes as being worth no more than £30 and £40 – 'it is not the hundredth part of our wealth.'[27]

To this, Cecil, himself now known to be one of the courtiers fiddling his taxes, replied evasively:

Touching the Spaniards' knowing of the sale of our pots or pans, which should be a matter of policy, to which the gentleman on my left hand (Ralegh) took exceptions: I say it's true; and yet I am mis-

taken, for I say it is good the Spaniards should know how willing we
are to sell our pots and pans and all we have to keep him out. Yet I do
not say it is good he should know we do sell them; that is, I would
have him know our willingness to sell (though there be no need) but
not of our poverty in selling, or of any necessity we have to sell them,
which I think none will do, neither shall need to do.[28]

Members then turned their attention to the explosive issue of
Elizabeth's monopoly grants. While some monopolies took the form
of genuine patents or copyrights to protect new inventions or industrial processes, most were designed simply to corner the market in
lucrative commodities, causing prices to rocket. Others granted their
beneficiaries exclusive rights over certain types of trade that enabled
them to extort large payments for the sale of licences to genuine
craftsmen. The queen gave these grants as rewards to courtiers or as
payments in lieu for services to the Crown. But they were frequently
used also to make debt repayments to her creditors or else shamelessly sold to the highest bidder for an annual rent.[29]

Among the more notorious examples were monopolies for the
brewing of beer for export, for the import of currants, for the manufacture of paper, glass, starch, stone pots and bottles, saltpetre or felt
hats. Some monopolists controlled the sale and distribution of such
essentials as lead, tin, salt, aniseed, vinegar and blubber oil. Others
regulated the trades in leather tanning, charcoal burning, the smoking of pilchards, the salting and packing of fish, and so on. Grants
Elizabeth had specifically given as rewards to courtiers included
Ralegh's lucrative monopoly on the retail sale of wine and the licensing of vintners, one for the import and sale of certain frequently
prescribed drugs given to Dr Lopez and a third for the import, manufacture and sale of playing cards given to Edward Darcy, the groom
of her Privy Chamber who had carried her final instructions for
Essex's execution to the Tower.[30]

The queen's grants rested exclusively on the royal prerogative, so
could not be challenged in the ordinary courts of law without her
consent. Over the winter of 1597–8, she had called in some fifteen
monopolies for scrutiny after receiving numerous complaints, but
nothing was done. Instead, the critics were forced to apologize and

plead for their pardon on the grounds that her royal prerogative was 'the chiefest flower in her garland and the principal and head pearl in her crown'.[31] The beneficiaries had the strong arm of the Privy Council and the Star Chamber behind them. Shortly before Parliament met in 1601, a test case challenging the lawfulness of Darcy's monopoly for the sale of playing cards had been filed in the Court of Common Pleas. When Darcy reported this to the queen, she immediately ordered her privy councillors to send a so-called 'Letter of Assistance' to Sir Edmund Anderson, the chief justice of the court, ordering him to cease the hearings. The case was stopped in its tracks.[32]

The attack on monopolies turned ugly when several members of the House of Commons submitted draft bills to reform them, then demanded to have them read. When the Speaker tried to smother them, tempers flared until finally a bill was allowed to go forward.[33] As Francis Moore, a Berkshire lawyer, declared, 'I cannot utter with my tongue, or conceive with my heart, the great grievances that the town and country for which I serve suffer by some of these monopolies: it bringeth the general profit into a private hand; and the end of all is beggary and bondage to the subject.' Moore came perilously close in his speech to criticizing the queen: 'Out of the spirit of humility, Mr Speaker, I do speak it: there is no act of hers that hath been, or is more derogatory to Her own Majesty, or more odious to the subject, or more dangerous to the Commonwealth, than the granting of these monopolies.'[34]

Richard Martin, a London lawyer and member for Barnstaple, rose in his support. 'I speak for a town that grieves and pines, and for a country that groaneth under the burden,' he began. 'The principal commodities both of my town and country are engrossed into the hands of these bloodsuckers of the Commonwealth.' 'What shall become of us', he asked, when 'the fruits of our own soil, and the commodities of our own labour, which with the sweat of our brows (even up to the knees in mire and dirt) we have laboured for, shall be taken from us by warrant of Supreme Authority, which the poor subject dares not gainsay?'[35]

Martin's speech was echoed time and time again over the next few days. To prick Cecil's complacency, Sir Robert Wroth, one of the most experienced members of the House, read out a list of the monopolies granted in the last three years. Barely had he begun than a quick-thinking young lawyer, William Hakewill, interjected, 'Is not bread there?' 'No,' he said at once, answering his own question, 'but if order be not taken for these, bread will be there before the next Parliament,' which forced Cecil hurriedly to concede that some change would be essential.[36]

What made this session of Parliament so sinister in Elizabeth's eyes, however, was not just what was said in the Commons chamber, but the fact that a noisy public demonstration, one that seemed suspiciously well organized, took place in the lobby outside. Sir Edward Hoby, a member for Rochester – he was one of Cecil's cousins but no government stooge – complained of 'a multitude of people at the door who said they were Commonwealth's men'. These agitators, he said, shouted for members 'to take compassion of their griefs, they being spoiled, imprisoned and robbed by monopolists'.[37]

Ordered by the Speaker to disperse, the protesters refused. Sir William Knollys, newly made a privy councillor, was sent to deal with them. As they left the precincts, Cecil stood up in a great passion, demanding, 'What meaneth this? Shall we suffer it?' But nobody rose to second him. Finding himself isolated, so united was the House against the monopolists, he had little choice but to sit down again.[38]

The idea that royal policy could be shaped by popular protests in the streets or demonstrations outside Parliament was Elizabeth's ultimate nightmare, and yet she now had little choice but to bend if she wanted her taxes for the war in Ireland. But she would bend in her own way. On Wednesday, 25 November, therefore, the Speaker came to the House to deliver a message she had given him. It had come to her attention, she began, that 'divers patents that she had granted were grievous unto her subjects'. It had, she insisted, never been her intention to allow any grant that was bad in itself. 'And if in the abuse of her grant, there be anything that is evil . . . she herself would take present order for reformation thereof.' She meant to do this by issuing a proclamation.[39]

Cecil rose from his seat again to confirm what the Speaker had just said. To loud cheers, he promised that no more 'Letters of Assistance' would be granted. Cleverly slithering into the idioms of his opponents, Cecil now stigmatized the monopolists. 'Why', he asked, should anyone seek to 'give anything in reason for these caterpillars' satisfaction?'[40]

Before sitting down, Cecil delivered an impassioned warning to members against allowing what was discussed in Parliament to become known outside the House. 'I fear', he remonstrated, 'we are not secret within ourselves. Then must I needs give you this for a future caution. That whatsoever is subject to public expectation cannot be good, while the Parliament matters are ordinary talk in the street. I have heard myself, being in my coach, these words spoken aloud: "God prosper those that further the overthrow of these monopolies."' There were evil men in London, he continued, who 'would be glad that all sovereignty were converted into popularity'.[41]

This, undoubtedly, was Elizabeth speaking. Since the beginning of the session, fresh riots had thrown London and Kent into turmoil over military conscription for Ireland, nursing her fears that the embers of Essex's uprising were still smouldering. For fear of a surprise attack on Whitehall, she had begun carrying a sword inside the palace.[42] And now, for the very first time in her life, she was being forced to bow to public pressure and account to Parliament for her actions and those of her courtiers and ministers, and over a matter that she believed belonged exclusively to her royal prerogative.

But all was not yet lost. She planned to satisfy the Commons' grievances in a purely minimalist way. She neither intended to allow them to continue with their bills to reform monopolies, nor did she intend to promise to make no more grants.

The queen's proclamation, published three days later, simply rescinded twelve of the most widely detested monopolies. They included those for starch, salt, vinegar, pots and bottles, blubber oil and the salting and packing of fish. All the rest were to remain in force exactly as they were before. As Cecil had promised, no more 'Letters of Assistance' were to be issued. Beyond that, the queen retained the principle of her prerogative power intact: she was free to make as many more grants of monopoly in the future as she chose. If anyone should 'seditiously or contemptuously' call that into question, she said, she would enforce her power to the extremity of the law. And that meant a show trial in the Star Chamber.[43]

In response, the House decided to send the Speaker to her, accompanied by a dozen or so members, to express their thanks for listening to their grievances. Cecil announced that she would receive this deputation on the afternoon of Monday, 30 November. 'And, if it please you', she had said, 'to come with a convenient number of forty, fifty or a hundred, they shall all be welcome.'[44]

Elizabeth meant to grasp this opportunity with both hands and deliver a speech they, their children and grandchildren would always remember. This was not, however, purely to smooth over the unrest. What most concerned her was that the Commons had not as yet granted her the taxes she so badly needed. To win them over, she would need to sweet-talk their deputation. She found the whole idea of pandering to Parliament utterly repellent, but it would have to be done.

She first sketched out a rough draft of her speech, later sending a handwritten fair copy to Sir Henry Savile, Provost of Eton, with whom she had been reading some Greek texts.[45] Then, shortly after three o'clock on Monday afternoon, the eighty or so members of the Commons' deputation crammed themselves into the Council Chamber at Whitehall. The Speaker began by expressing their gratitude for the recent proclamation. 'We come not, Sacred Sovereign,' he began obsequiously, bowing three times, 'one of ten to render thanks, and the rest to go away unthankful; but all of us . . . do throw down ourselves at the feet of Your Majesty.'[46]

In reply, Elizabeth gave her speech, famously known by her biographers as her 'Golden Speech'. And yet, what exactly she said depends largely on who is reading the sources. Unlike the Tilbury speech, where the differences between the competing versions are less pronounced, this one exists in no fewer than seven radically different texts. Three are from the seventeenth century. One was printed in 1628 during the parliamentary struggle with Charles I over the Petition of Right, when it was intended to be a model of how a ruler should defer to Parliament. Another was reputedly found in the study of William Dell in 1642, when he was secretary to Archbishop Laud.[47] A third version, Camden's in the *Annales*, is an invention, despite being printed as if it were a verbatim report.[48]

The text that can be linked most closely to the queen is her own first draft.[49] She liked it well enough, once the speech had been delivered, to send it to her official printer, Robert Barker, who published it as a pamphlet emblazoned with the royal arms.[50] In that edition, it masquerades as 'being taken [down] verbatim in writing by A. B. as near as he could possibly set it down'.[51] But this is a common literary device and means little – 'A. B.' is likely to be a phantom. The only member of the Commons with these initials was Anthony Blagrave, an obscure country gentleman, and member for Reading.[52]

Surprisingly, the language of this officially published text is leaden rather than golden. Unlike Elizabeth's speech at Tilbury, it retains the royal 'we' until just over halfway through, rather than slipping colloquially into the first person singular from the outset. The style is ornate and old-fashioned. 'As nothing is more dear to us than the loving conservation of our subjects' hearts,' she begins, 'we trust there resides in their conceits of us no such simple cares of their good whom we so dearly prize that our hand should pass aught that might injure any, though they doubt not it is lawful for our kingly state to grant gifts of sundry sorts to whom we make election.' Things barely improve as she gets into her stride. 'You must not beguile yourselves, nor wrong us', she continues, 'to think that the glozing [gilded, flattering] lustre of a glittering glory of a king's title may so extol us that we think all is lawful what we list, not caring what we do.'[53]

The classic version of the speech is supplied by Hayward Townshend, a young kinsman of Francis Bacon and member for Bishop's Castle in Shropshire. In its favour is the fact that Townshend knew shorthand and so was in a position to take notes at speed.[54] He had played a prominent role in the debates on monopolies.[55] And, almost certainly, he was present on the day when the speech was delivered. In this version, Elizabeth, speaking exclusively in the first person and seemingly unaware that the overwhelming majority of her people were still struggling with the crippling effects of high prices, harvest failures, poverty and disease, plays more fully than ever on the trope that she has their love and support:

> I do assure you, there is no Prince that loveth his subjects better or whose love can countervail our love. There is no jewel, be it of never

so rich a price, which I set before this jewel, I mean your love: for I do more esteem of it than of any treasure or riches . . . And, though God hath raised me high, yet this I count the glory of my crown: that I have reigned with your loves. This makes me that I do not so much rejoice that God hath made me to be a Queen as to be a Queen over so thankful a people.[56]

In all the variants of this speech, Elizabeth stoutly maintains that she has never sought to pillage or oppress her subjects:

Of myself, I must say this, I was never any greedy scraping grasper, nor a straight, fast-holding prince, nor yet a waster. My heart was never set on worldly goods, but only for my subjects' good. What you do bestow on me, I will not hoard it up, but receive it to bestow on you again. Yea, my own properties I count yours, and to be expended for your good.[57]

She goes to great lengths to protest that she has been misled by the evil monopolists, who, like false physicians coating their fake medicines with sugar, have persuaded her to grant them privileges by pretending that their bitter pills are sweet and beneficial cures of social ills. For condoning these deceptions, she squarely blames her privy councillors.[58]

Like all sixteenth-century monarchs defending their prerogative against the encroachments of representative institutions, Elizabeth stresses her accountability to God. 'I have ever used to set the Last Judgement Day before my eyes, as so to rule as I shall be judged to answer before a higher judge.' She has been compelled, she says, to act against the monopolists 'for conscience's sake', for which reason, ingratiatingly, if demonstrably insincerely, she offers her thanks to the Commons for saving her from 'the lapse of an error, only for lack of true information'.[59]

Townshend's reconstruction of the queen's speech concludes on a patriotic note. 'There will never queen sit in my seat with more zeal to my country, care for my subjects, and that sooner with willingness will venture her life for your good and safety than myself. For it is not my desire to live nor reign longer than my life and reign shall be for your good.'

And there is an echo of the Tilbury speech:

> Shall I ascribe any thing to myself and my sexly weakness? I were not worthy to live then, and of all, most unworthy of the great mercies I have had from God, who hath ever yet given me a heart, which never yet feared foreign or home enemy. I speak it to give God the praise, as a testimony before you, and not to attribute any thing to myself . . . That I should speak for any glory, God forbid.[60]

Was this the speech Elizabeth actually gave or the one Townshend thought she ought to have given? Speaker Croke gives us a clue. When he and his fellow members of the Commons returned to Parliament the following day to present their report, he gave a summary of what she had said for those who had been unable to hear it. In this version, Elizabeth rejoices to be a queen over 'so thankful a people'. She has never been a 'greedy griper or fast holder'. She says she 'ever set the Last Judgement before her eyes, and never thought arose in her, but for the good of her people'. If her grants had been abused, 'it was against her will' and she hopes God will not blame her. 'Had it not been for these her good subjects, she had fallen from lapse into error.' Finally, 'the cares and troubles of a crown are known only to them that wear it.' She has been forced to act 'for conscience's sake'. She is 'not allured with the royal authority of a King, neither did she attribute anything to herself, but all to the glory of God'.[61]

Croke's report largely vindicates Townshend's rendering. It would appear that Elizabeth had followed her usual custom in addressing Parliament. After sketching out a first draft to shape the lines of her speech, she put it aside to create the illusion of speaking off the cuff. Townshend may well have edited and improved the speech for greater impact when he turned his shorthand notes into a fuller transcript. But, as recently as July 1597, Elizabeth had put on a spectacular display of her oratorical skills. When Paul Dzialynski, a visiting Polish diplomat, criticized her in public for allowing English privateers to plunder the ships of other nations trading with Spain, the furious queen gave him a dressing-down in what Cecil called 'one of the best answers extempore in Latin that ever I heard'.[62] Public speaking was her forte: like many talented political leaders, she could rise to the occasion and speak eloquently and persuasively. Given the discovery of the queen's first draft, however, and the considerable discrepancies between it and Townshend's version, the reader is left to infer that she was a much finer orator than writer.

The queen's speech did the trick. On Saturday, 5 December, four days after Speaker Croke had made his report to the whole assembly of the Commons, the House voted in the taxes Elizabeth had demanded, offering a formula that Cecil later calculated could yield as much as £600,000.[63] But, beneath the surface, everything was not quite what it appeared to be.[64] Not all members were satisfied with the relatively narrow concessions she had made, or with her promises alone. Three had already moved that what she had so far offered by way of reform of the hated monopolies should now be entered into the Journals of the House as a matter of record. One was Gregory Donhault, member for Launceston in Cornwall and Lord Keeper Egerton's secretary, otherwise a prime candidate for a plum promotion as a Master in the Court of Chancery. For his temerity, the queen turned on him once the session of Parliament was ended and vindictively denied him his promotion.[65]

In a similar vein, after members had left London and returned home for Christmas, another complaint against Edward Darcy's monopoly of the sale of playing cards would be brusquely swept aside on the grounds that Elizabeth had no intention of reforming any monopolies other than those specifically listed in her proclamation. In an unusually draconian decree, the Privy Council ruled that those 'obstinate and undutiful persons' who had attempted to annul Darcy's grant were to be arrested and imprisoned if their criticisms were not immediately withdrawn. They must also pay Darcy hefty compensation for any infringement of his rights. Their only remedy would be to take the case to the Court of Queen's Bench for trial.[66]

Despite this rebuff, Darcy's critics refused to back down. No longer were Elizabeth's subjects prepared to accept her absolute right to dictate in what goods they could trade or what products they could import or manufacture as an aspect of her God-appointed royal prerogative. Directly after the Privy Council hearing, Thomas Allen, a London haberdasher, manufactured and sold large quantities of his own playing cards and challenged Darcy to sue him, which he did.

The result was a victory for Allen. Chief Justice Popham, torn between conflicting loyalties but realizing his duty to the law of the land was greater than his obligation to defend the indefensible, ruled that Allen should be allowed to sell his cards. He then added, somewhat disingenuously, that Elizabeth had been 'deceived in her grant'. She had meant it to be 'for the public good', but Darcy had used it to line his pockets by charging exorbitant prices for his cards.[67]

On the face of it, this was a landmark decision, except it did nothing to stop the flow of further grants. If ever from now on a genuine craftsman wished to challenge a monopoly, then on every and each occasion he would have to bring his case to court and risk expensive and potentially dangerous litigation. For all her smooth talk, Elizabeth was not prepared to surrender any of her most cherished ideals. She had been forced to bite her lip and issue a proclamation against monopolies to secure the taxes she needed for Ireland. But she was still determined to defend the rights and privileges of her Crown. In her proclamation, she conspicuously maintained that the twelve offending monopolies were to be made void 'of her mere grace and favour', and not because Parliament had compelled her to take action.[68] Her father, she knew, would be shuddering in his grave at the very thought of this attenuation by Parliament of the ideal of God-appointed monarchy. She did not believe herself to be accountable to her people. The problem was that others now did.

22. On a Knife's Edge

Elizabeth was eager to prove that age did not hinder her. After Essex's execution, she had purposefully adopted a carefree attitude when showing herself in public to prove 'she was not so old as some would have her'.[1] Glimpses of physical weakness were first apparent in the autumn of 1600, when she made a half-day visit to Robert Sidney's town house at Baynard's Castle, near Blackfriars. Barely had she arrived there than she seemed visibly tired and, despite sitting down to dinner, she consumed little more than 'two morsels of rich comfit cake' before drinking 'a small cordial from a gold cup'. 'Two ushers did go before [her], and at going upstairs she called for a staff and was much wearied in walking about the house.'[2]

One of her favourite techniques for appearing younger, as Burghley's former clerk John Clapham would record after her death, was overdressing. 'In her latter time,' he explained, 'she was always magnificent in apparel, supposing haply thereby, that the eyes of her people, being dazzled with the glittering aspect of those accidental ornaments would not so easily discern the marks of age and decay of natural beauty.'[3] Another piece of showmanship was to orchestrate her public appearances with great care. 'She would often show herself abroad at public spectacles, even against her own liking,' Clapham added, 'to no other end but that the people might the better perceive her ability of body and good disposition, which otherwise in respect of her years, they might perhaps have doubted.'[4]

Good impressions mattered desperately to her. When the twenty-eight-year-old Virginio Orsini, Duke of Bracciano, arrived at Whitehall Palace on Twelfth Night 1601, she put on a virtuoso performance for him. The pampered nephew of Ferdinando de' Medici, Grand Duke of Tuscany, whom she had memorably persuaded to burn Girolamo Pollini's infamous book about her parents, Orsini had been chosen to escort his cousin Marie de' Medici, with whom he had a scandalous affair, on her journey from Italy to marry Henry IV of France. After the wedding, Orsini had crossed over from Calais to stay with Filippo Corsini, his uncle's London agent, before proceeding to Brussels to pay court to Archduke Albert.[5]

Keen that he should kill off reports in Brussels that she was already at death's door, Elizabeth had ordered her councillors to fête Orsini like a prince. The Lord Chamberlain's Men, Shakespeare's company, were booked to put on a Twelfth Night play. To be quite sure all would go well, she gave Lord Admiral Nottingham the job of 'taking order generally with the players' to ensure that something was chosen 'that shall be best furnished with rich apparel, have great variety and change of music and dances, and of a subject that may be most pleasing to Her Majesty'.[6] Some have suggested that Nottingham selected *Twelfth Night*, but this claim is hotly disputed: it may well have been, except the only reasons for thinking so are the coincidences of the play's title with the date of its performance, the name of one of the principal characters, Count Orsino, Duke of Illyria, and the fact that the play includes musical interludes (it does not feature dances).[7]

Elizabeth played her own part that day to perfection. Decked out in so many jewels that Orsini was amazed they did not weigh her down, she received him graciously, enchanting him by conversing in perfect Italian. While she dined in state, Orsini was served a delicious meal in a separate chamber, after which he accompanied her as far as her outer Bedchamber. There, she treated him to an afternoon recital by her finest musicians, the star of the show being the lutenist Robert Hales.[8] Following a supper party hosted by the Earl of Worcester, Orsini was again escorted to meet the queen and to accompany her to the play. Arriving in the Great Hall to the sound of trumpets, she introduced Orsini to the women of the Court, after which the play began.[9]

On his second visit three days later, Orsini was amazed when the sixty-eight-year-old queen offered to dance for him. When the French envoy de Maisse had been with her three years earlier, she had told him that she had learned the art of 'dancing high' as a teenager, a skill for which her women nicknamed her 'the Florentine', adding that she danced no longer, merely moving her legs and arms to and fro in time with the music.[10] But, for Orsini, she danced a galliard, 'very comely, and like herself, to show the vigour of her old age'.[11] An independent witness reports that her dances were 'both measures and galliards'.[12] The galliard, with its high leaps and jumps, was a particularly athletic dance, said to be taxing even for much younger women.

And yet, despite doing her utmost to live up to the image her more sycophantic courtiers chose to promote of a goddess incarnate 'whose beauty adorns the world, and whose wisdom is the miracle of our age', there were soon worrying signs that Elizabeth really was ageing.[13] And, with the succession unresolved, these were perilous times. Her confidence in the men around her had been shattered by Essex's treachery. If he could betray her, then who next? As John Harington confided to a friend, 'Every new message from the city disturbs her, and she frowns on all the ladies.' She 'disregardeth every costly cover [dish] that cometh to the table', preferring to eat 'manchet and succory potage [fine white bread and chicory soup]'. She 'walks much in her Privy Chamber.' She 'stamps with her feet at ill news, and thrusts her rusty sword at times into the arras in great rage'.[14]

More seriously, as she went to open Parliament in October 1601, she stumbled as she alighted from her coach. She would have fallen over 'if some gentlemen had not suddenly cast themselves under that side that tottered and supported her'.[15] Who was to succeed her if she suddenly died? Thomas Wilson, one of Robert Cecil's protégés, identified no fewer than twelve competitors. Chief among them, he declared, were James VI, Lord Beauchamp (the Earl of Hertford's elder son), Arbella Stuart and the Infanta. 'Thus you see', he concluded dryly, 'this crown is not like to fall to the ground for want of heads that claim to wear it.'[16]

Gossip in the streets and taverns of London mingling with justified fears for the future were a toxic combination. In the Star Chamber, Lord Keeper Egerton complained of the 'railing open speeches [and] false, lying, traitorous libels' circulating in the metropolis and of 'divers vile persons, seditious in religion and factious in disposition'.[17] A key destabilizing factor was the queen's own unrelenting refusal to allow even her privy councillors to discuss the taboo topic. This prevented them from mounting any sort of effective counter-propaganda to Robert Parsons, who continued to churn out tracts in favour of the Spanish Infanta, and had the perverse effect of driving the debate underground. 'I am in fear to write of it to discover such a great secret of state', Harington confided in a note to himself, 'and yet I smile at mine own fear . . . My study walls may accuse me. But "over shoes, over boots" as they say: as long as I do not print nor publish it, I break no law.'[18]

Harington, like many, favoured James. Not least because, in addition to their eldest son, Prince Henry, James and his wife now had two other children: Elizabeth, born in 1596, and Charles, born in 1600. If James were to become king, the future of the monarchy appeared secure. Harington indicated just how widespread the preference had become for James:

> God hath blessed our sovereign with a prosperous reign and a long life
> . . . Long may she live to his glory: but when so ever God shall call
> her, I perceive we are not like to be governed by a lady shut up in a
> chamber from all her subjects and most of her servants, and seen sel-
> dom but on holy days; nor by a child that must say as his uncle bids
> him . . . but by a man of spirit and learning, of able body, of under-
> standing mind, that in the precepts he doth give to his son shows what
> we must look for, what we must trust to. Thus [say] friends that dare
> [to] talk one to another.[19]

But nothing was decided, and thus nothing could be presumed, certainly not after Elizabeth summarily imposed a sentence of indefinite imprisonment on a certain Valentine Thomas, an itinerant English Catholic said to be a professional horse thief. As early as 1598, he had been captured near Morpeth in Northumberland and brought to London, where in a fit of derangement he accused James of inciting him to kill the queen.[20] Thomas's case raised the tricky issue of the Bond of Association and the Act for the Queen's Surety. By their terms, any claimant to the throne who could be proved to have been the instigator or intended beneficiary of a plot to assassinate the queen was to be disqualified. Although introduced when fears about Mary Queen of Scots were at fever pitch, the legislation still stood. James had been sufficiently anxious about this to write to his ambassador in England, requesting an accurate copy of the Act.[21]

What worried him even more as time went by was that Elizabeth obviously thought the allegation might be true.[22] James sent her a strongly worded protest, only to receive a frosty reply in which she denied ever giving credit to the accusation. '[I] charge you in God's name to believe', she retorted, 'that I am not of so viperous a nature to suppose or have thereof a thought against you, but shall make the deviser have his desert more for that than for aught else.' All the same, after Cecil learned of Essex's little black taffeta bag purportedly containing a ciphered message from James about Ireland and the succession, she meant to keep Thomas on ice in the Tower as an insurance policy against James until she died.[23]

After Essex's uprising, James had hurriedly sent the Earl of Mar and the lawyer Edward Bruce south, ostensibly to congratulate Elizabeth on her narrow escape. In reality, he wished to be cleared of all charges of collusion either with Thomas or Essex.[24] Specifically, Mar and Bruce were to remind Elizabeth of what James chose optimistically to call 'her old promise that nothing shall be done in her time, in prejudice of my future right'. Over and above that, besides generally ingratiating themselves and countering his detractors, they were to threaten Cecil and his allies with the dire retribution they could expect to receive once James became king, should they dare to attempt to block him.[25]

'When the chance shall turn,' James snarled, 'I shall cast a deaf ear to their requests; and whereas now I would have been content to have given them by your means a pre-assurance of my favour . . . so now, they contemning it, may be assured never hereafter to be heard, but all the queen's hard usage of me to be hereafter craved at their hands.'[26]

Elizabeth was not easily fooled. Mentally as sharp as ever, she saw straight through Mar and Bruce's sycophancy and rejected all their demands.[27] Braving the pain from a fresh attack of arthritis, this time in her right thumb, and writing to James in her own hand, she upbraided the Scottish king for his presumption in assuming that he or his advisers could bend her to his will:

Let not shades deceive you which may take away best substance from you, when they can turn but to dust or smoke. An upright demeanour bears ever more poise than all disguised shows of good can do. Remember that a bird of the air, if no other instrument, to an honest king shall stand instead of many feigned practices.[28]

She was particularly annoyed by James's request to be granted some English estates, so that he could bypass the legal objections to his succession on grounds of his Scots nationality.[29] 'We hope to hear no more of any of these matters,' she remonstrated, 'which are so unworthy of our dispute who have and do resolve to nourish and perform all princely correspondency.'[30]

In these dark, doubtful, dangerous days, the border between loyalty and treachery was becoming blurred. Elizabeth would have been incandescent had she known that, by the time Mar and Bruce arrived in London, Essex's former intelligencer, the slippery Lord Henry Howard, had begun clandestinely corresponding with James and his agents on his own account.[31] Deftly realigning himself on Cecil's side, Howard in these letters leaked a heady mixture of news and Court gossip, and in a vitriolic piece of character assassination warned James to beware of the 'accursed duality' of Ralegh and the young Lord Cobham.[32] Ralegh and Cobham hatched 'cockatrice eggs . . . daily and nightly' at Durham House, he now wrote melodramatically, 'where Ralegh lies in consultation'.[33] Neither Ralegh nor Cobham had secured advancement to the Privy Council after Essex's execution. Envious of the ease with which Cecil had taken command after Burghley's death, they were hungry for change. Howard feared their possible influence on James.[34]

Such self-interested mischief-making fuelled James's suspicions that Ralegh and Cobham were plotting to exclude him from the throne. To turn Cecil irrevocably against Ralegh and Cobham – both his former allies when Essex was alive – Howard deluged him with slander, insidiously persuading him that Ralegh and Cobham could not be trusted and were organizing a 'mutiny' against him.[35] Abandoning scruples and honour, he even advised him to 'snare the ambition' of Ralegh and Cobham into some 'rash direction', tempting them into treason so they could be destroyed like Essex. It was a truly Machiavellian insinuation.[36]

Not daring to return to Scotland to face their sovereign's wrath after Elizabeth had refused all James's demands, Mar and Bruce took a monumental gamble. Cheered on by Howard, they made overtures directly to Cecil. Their gamble paid off. In May 1601, they arranged a rendezvous at the Duchy of Lancaster offices on the Strand, at which Cecil satisfied them that Essex's allegations that he was out to exclude James from the succession and had sold his soul to the Infanta were wholly false. As proof of his goodwill, Cecil inveigled Elizabeth into restoring James's annual pension to its original level of £5,000, agreed at the ratifying of their league in July 1586, to be paid in regular, twice-yearly instalments.[37]

After weighing up the risks and opportunities for a fortnight or more, Cecil next agreed to correspond with James in return for the king's future favour.[38] In their secret communications, conducted in English and Scots and partially ciphered, James was '30', Cecil '10', Howard '3' and Elizabeth '24'.[39] Letters were carried to and fro by Cecil's chief intelligencer and spy in Scotland, George Nicolson, who was duped into acting as a postman and referred to in the letters as 'the pigeon'.[40] To evade scrutiny by the customs men at the English border post at Berwick-upon-Tweed, letters from Edinburgh travelled south in the diplomatic bag, sealed and labelled as addressed to French Huguenot noblemen. Replies from London came along the same route.

Although James and Cecil did occasionally pen their letters personally, most of their correspondence was handled through intermediaries, chiefly Howard and Bruce. This was to lessen the risk of detection.[41] As Cecil mused sanctimoniously:

> If her Majesty had known all I did . . . her age and orbity, joined to the jealousy of her sex, might have moved her to think ill of that which helped to preserve her. For what could more quiet the expectation of a successor, so many ways invited to jealousy, than when he saw her ministry, that were most inward with her, wholly bent to accommodate the present actions of the state for his future safety, when God should see his time?[42]

He was only too well aware of the danger of discovery by the queen. When one of his secretaries began taking too close an interest in his correspondence, the man was dismissed.[43]

Mostly, Cecil's advice to James was purely tactical. He took great care to avoid any unambiguous suggestion of treason should any one of his letters be lost or intercepted. In particular, he declined to voice an opinion as to the rightful successor, merely doing what he could to assist James. 'The subject', he remarked, 'is so perilous to touch amongst us, as it setteth a mark upon his head for ever that hatcheth such a bird.'[44]

For all their author's reserve, however, James would find Cecil's letters invaluable. What they offered him was an intimate knowledge of how best to handle the queen. James, Cecil advised, should bear in mind that, for princes in possession, '[j]ealousy stirreth passion, even between the father and the son.'[45] He might well have mentioned another of Elizabeth's celebrated mantras: 'Princes cannot like their own children.'[46] To best nurture his claim, James should avoid 'needless expostulations' in his dealings with the queen or 'over much curiosity' about her real intentions. To win the good opinion of a woman 'to whose sex and quality nothing is so improper', he should avoid appearing 'too busy' on his own behalf. Especially, he should shun the 'general acclamation of many', which she famously abhorred. Anyone, concluded Cecil, who sought to win over the hearts and minds of 'the vulgar' sort of people, 'little understands the state of this question'.[47]

In return, James offered Cecil the prospect of a golden future. '[I shall] rule all my actions for advancing of my lawful future hopes by your advice,' he warmly declared, 'even as [if] ye were one of my own councillors already, being justly moved to this confidence in you'.[48] But his promise of patronage came at a price: there could be no question of peace with Spain, the policy pursued however fitfully and ineffectually by the queen at Boulogne. Such a peace made before he was king, James believed, would be 'most perilous' to his 'just claim', since it would allow more open debate in England of a 'Spanish title' and greatly assist Philip III and Archduke Albert in advancing the Infanta's claim.[49]

Cecil immediately took the hint. Within months, he would be boasting to James that '[the] scandal which followed the late Earl of Essex for his greediness of war . . . is most[ly] transferred to me.' From now on, Cobham would champion the cause of peace, not Cecil.[50]

★ ★ ★

Philip III, meanwhile, was planning his final throw of the dice. Assiduously lobbied by the English Catholic exiles, he was seriously considering putting the Infanta Isabella, his half-sister, on Elizabeth's throne. He was utterly opposed to James, whom he suspected, not without reason, of plotting with Henry IV and Pope Clement to engineer an anti-Spanish alliance.[51] Confirmation from Rome that Anne of Denmark had taken her vows as a Catholic and was secretly receiving Mass added to his anxiety.[52] Equally disturbing was a flurry of reports that Henry and James were planning a Franco-British alliance to drive the Spanish Netherlands into submission to the Dutch Protestants. This threat was made all the more real by rumours that James had recently received firm offers of support from the Dutch, Denmark and several Italian states, including Florence and Venice.[53] An otherwise trivial incident fuelled Philip's fears. One day when James was about to go out hunting, he had taken a reliquary set in a necklace from his wife's neck and put it around his own to ward off accidents. It was doubtless an innocent, playful gesture, but to Philip its significance was deep and worrying.[54]

Eager to exclude James and any other candidate who was likely to have French sympathies from the English throne, Philip had several times consulted the Council of State. For a while, the councillors were unable to agree but, after lengthy deliberations, their choice fell unanimously on the Infanta.[55]

Philip had ratified the nomination in February 1601.[56] The fly in the ointment was that Isabella's husband, Albert, as everyone would come to realize too late, was impotent. Isabella was then thirty-five and still capable of bearing children, but rumours were soon rife in Brussels that Albert, who was forty-two, suffered from erectile dysfunction and had not been able to consummate the marriage. His confessor was reported as saying that, in all his life, Albert had never yet succeeded in bedding a woman.[57] All the signs, therefore, were that the couple would never have children, a fatal drawback, since any settlement of the English succession in the Spanish interest would need to be cemented by the promise of an heir. Philip knew all too well the problems created by his father's unproductive union with Mary Tudor.

To Philip's frustration, Albert himself expressed fatal misgivings when told that Spain would back his wife's claim.⁵⁸ Already overburdened by the pressure of keeping Count Maurice's armies at bay, neither Albert nor Isabella wished to take on this new battle. They would rather capitalize on their current status as independent sovereigns, whereas the Spanish Council of State had recommended that, if Isabella became Queen of England, the Netherlands must return to the direct overlordship of Spain. Albert far preferred the simpler option of a rapprochement with James, which would turn the screw on the Dutch and guarantee his own survival in Brussels.⁵⁹

In Valladolid, where Philip was gradually moving his Court, opinion in the Council of State slowly began to fragment. Some voices continued to champion Isabella; others argued that it would be better to win over James with bribes. In no respect would he be an ideal choice, but it might be worth ordering the Archduke to send a special envoy to Edinburgh to open up talks, a move that was bound to infuriate Elizabeth.⁶⁰ If all went well, the envoy could be replaced by an ambassador and full diplomatic relations restored. At least one councillor suggested that James might be inveigled into sending his heir Prince Henry to be educated at Valladolid in exchange for Spanish support. Unpalatable as the union of the crowns of England and Scotland might be, it could just be acceptable if guided by a monarch who was mortgaged to Spain.⁶¹

But with a Spanish victory in Ireland a distant prospect after the failure of Águila's expedition, Philip felt morally obliged not to put another heretic on Elizabeth's throne. He was stridently supported by Count Olivares, his father's former ambassador to the crockery-throwing Pope Sixtus V, who had recently returned to Spain from a posting as Viceroy of Naples. Taking his seat in the Council in October 1602, Olivares argued that England and Scotland must be prevented from uniting under a staunchly Protestant king such as James must inevitably become. To believe he could be bound to Spain by bribes was wishful thinking. The best way forward, to his mind, was to reach a compromise with the French and the pope over a mutually agreed Catholic candidate, who could be imposed by force. This should be managed so that Spain did not appear to lose face by withdrawing its support for the Infanta. A move of this kind was all the more urgent, as Henry IV was threatening to annex Franche-Comté and thus to block one of the principal arteries of the so-called Spanish Road, the route over the Alps and through the old Burgundian dominions along which Spanish troops had marched to defend the southern Netherlands against the Dutch.[62]

When news of Tyrone's rout in Ireland and the failure of the fifth Armada finally arrived in Valladolid, Philip was genuinely shocked. Seeing no hope of swift reinforcements, Águila had been forced to surrender. Elizabeth was so overcome with relief, she at once scribbled a personal message to Mountjoy above her signature at the head of a more formal letter she had just dictated thanking him for his good service.* 'We can but acknowledge your diligence and dangerous adventure', she purred, 'and cherish and judge of you as your careful sovereign.'[63] This was code for saying she had chosen to erase permanently from her memory all suspicions of his clandestine dealings with Essex.

So anxious was Mountjoy to be rid of the invading Spaniards, he allowed them to march out of Kinsale with all the honours of war.[64] Adverse winds interrupted their departure: several weeks would elapse before the last of them set sail. Tyrone, meanwhile, rode as fast as he could towards Ulster, holding out in the woods for just over another year. By the summer of 1602, though, many of his relatives and officers were desperate and offering terms. Coaxed by Mountjoy, Elizabeth accepted a form of submission in which, one by one, the rebel captains swore on oath that she was 'the only true, absolute and sovereign lady of this realm of Ireland, and of every part and of all the people thereof'. They were then granted back their lands.[65]

Tyrone, an expert at guerrilla warfare, held out until the very end. Elizabeth had always insisted that she would never grant a pardon to a rebel who had cost her so many lives and almost £2 million so far to defeat. At the end of 1602, Tyrone offered to parley, but she angrily refused, demanding his unconditional surrender. Her decision caught Mountjoy in a vice. By now desperately short of men and munitions,

---

* Elizabeth almost without exception placed her signature at the top of her official correspondence, above the first line of text.

he was bound to fall back on diplomacy. In an awkward balancing act, he informed Tyrone that he would continue to petition the queen on his behalf, but 'I will cut your throat in the meantime if I can.'[66]

In Cecil's eyes, the stalemate in Ireland was a worrying loose end. Munster and Leinster had been quickly pacified and Connacht largely so. But until Ulster was under the Lord Deputy's full control, it was always possible that Tyrone might make a comeback and the dying embers of the revolt flare up yet again.[67]

Throughout the spring and summer of 1602, Elizabeth set herself a punishing schedule, determined to prove to the world that she was still very much alive. She began with a visit to the May Day festivities in Richmond, continuing with a summer progress that included stays at the homes of more than twenty of her courtiers, within a thirty-mile radius of London. Sometimes she simply went for dinner; at other times she stopped overnight. She dined twice at Lambeth with Archbishop Whitgift. At Eltham in Kent, she stayed for a day or so with Sir John Stanhope, a protégé of Cecil and a notably accomplished flatterer. She was then regally entertained for three days by Egerton at Harefield, his estate on the Middlesex and Buckinghamshire border.[68]

The progress ended at Oatlands, where she lavishly welcomed some visiting ambassadors. Among those offered sumptuous hospitality were Christophe de Harlay, Comte de Beaumont, the new French envoy, and his wife, Anne Rabot, a wealthy heiress.[69] 'Blessed be God,' Cecil exclaimed in a letter to Carew, 'I saw not Her Majesty so well these dozen years!'[70] And the Earl of Worcester valiantly kept up the pretence of her well-being. 'We are [at] frolic here in Court,' he said, with 'much dancing in the Privy Chamber of country dances before the Queen's Majesty, who is exceedingly pleased therewith'. 'Irish tunes are at this time most pleasing,' he added, 'but in winter, "Lullaby", an old song of Mr Byrd's [William Byrd], will be more in request, as I think.'[71]

But, shortly after Christmas, rumours began to circulate that the woman who had ruled England for forty-four years was reduced to sitting on cushions on the floor. Now in her seventieth year, she was clearly very ill. For some months, the diplomatic grapevine had been buzzing with tales of her poor health. One claimed she was very sick because of 'a sore in her breast' and 'cannot live long'; another that she was 'in very bad health'; a third that she had already been pronounced dead; a fourth that she had been 'very ill' but had made a full recovery.[72]

For a while, she was able to dissemble. When the Venetian ambassador to London, Giovanni Scaramelli, left an audience with her at Richmond on Sunday, 6 February 1603, he believed her to be in the finest of health. She pulled off this trick partly by speaking to him throughout in fluent Italian, partly by her dress. Scaramelli waxed lyrically to the Doge and the Senate about her silver-and-white taffeta gown trimmed with gold, her elaborate headdress with pearls the size of small pears, her wig with its red fluorescent colour 'never made by nature', her large diamonds and even larger rubies, her elaborate pearl bracelets.[73]

But John Harington and others close to her knew the cold truth. When he had seen her two days after Christmas, Harington had noticed a profound deterioration. Writing to his beloved wife, Mary, whom he affectionately called 'Sweet Mall', he said he found Elizabeth 'in most pitiable state'. She was eating little and, when she put a golden cup to her lips and tried to drink, 'her heart seemeth too full to lack more filling.' Although she rallied enough to ask him what he had been writing, her reply, when he began to read some of his verses, 'to feed her humour', was poignant: 'When thou dost feel creeping time at thy gate, these fooleries will please thee less; I am past my relish for such matters.'

Still worse, she began suffering from intermittent bouts of memory loss. She sometimes sent for people, only to dismiss them 'in anger' when they arrived. 'But who', Harington mused sorrowfully, 'shall say "Your Highness hath forgotten?"'[74]

The killer blow would be the death of a woman who had served her faithfully for well over forty years and ended up, as it was now said, her closest female friend. This evidently referred to Kate Carey, Countess of Nottingham. The precise nature of her relationship with the queen remains infuriatingly obscure: the loss of Kate's family papers is to blame. But it was said that Elizabeth fell into a deep 'melancholy' when the news was brought to her, complaining of pains in her head, aches in her bones and continual cold in her legs, so that none of her privy councillors except Cecil dared to approach her.[75]

Kate died at her London home on Thursday, 24 February after suffering numerous 'fits'.[76] She was no more than fifty-seven.* Her youngest brother, Robert, claimed he had not seen the queen so afflicted since the execution of Mary Queen of Scots. 'No, Robin, I am not well,' she had answered in response to his solicitous enquiries. Her heart, she said, was 'sad and heavy', and then, to Carey's great alarm, she gave 'forty or fifty great sighs'.[77]

Kate had been one of Elizabeth's gentlewomen since she was barely fifteen and a maid of honour before that. Although her younger sister Philadelphia Scrope was still alive and in the Privy Chamber, it was said she had never been as intimate with the queen as Kate. All those closest to Elizabeth before or shortly after she came to the throne were now gone. To lose Kate was yet another intimation of her own mortality. Had she not already lived longer than her father, her grandfather Henry VII and her siblings?

But if Elizabeth was preparing to die, who was to succeed her? Tyrone had yet to submit and was still pursuing his guerrilla war in Ulster. And what of Spain's fresh search for a Catholic candidate for her throne? Momentous, menacing uncertainties faced the country and the state: the course of events rested on a knife's edge.

* The year of her birth is not recorded, but was somewhere between 1545, when her parents married, and 1550.

23. The Final Vigil

On Wednesday, 16 February 1603, Elizabeth finally accepted that if she was to keep Ireland safely in her possession before she died, she would have to come to terms with Tyrone. She considered it to be her sacred duty to preserve the monarchy in the same state as she had received it at her coronation. Believing death to be fast approaching, she dictated a letter to Mountjoy in which she conceded that she must yield:

> We conceive the world hath seen sufficiently how dear the conservation of that kingdom and people hath been unto us, and how precious we have been of our honour that have of late rejected so many of those offers of his, only because we were sorry to make a precedent of facility to show grace or favour to him that hath been the author of so much misery to our loving subjects. Nevertheless because it seemeth that there is a general conceit that this reduction may prove profitable to the state by sparing the effusion of Christian blood . . . we are content to lay aside anything that may herein contrary our own private affections and will consider that clemency hath as eminent a place in supreme authority as justice and severity.[1]

Even then, she hobbled her Lord Deputy. 'We require you to be careful to preserve our dignity in all circumstances,' she cautioned. '[Tyrone] shall have his life and receive upon his coming-in such other conditions as shall be honourable and reasonable for us to grant him.' As Mountjoy complained to his secretary when they pored over her letter together, this meant no more and no less than that he was 'to send for Tyrone, with promise of security for his life only' in exchange for his humble submission. Anything else needed Elizabeth's personal approval.[2]

After sleeping on it, she dramatically changed tack, writing again the following day offering Mountjoy more flexibility. Now, he might offer Tyrone his life, liberty and pardon. Religion was to be excluded from the conversation, but even on this sensitive point, she made it clear that the rebel leader need have 'little fear of prosecution' if he remained a Catholic. He must surrender his lands in Ulster but, once his garrisons and fortified places had been demolished and free traffic assured, he might have them back. The queen's one sticking point was that he must resign his title and take a different one. The name of Tyrone, indistinguishable as it was from the cause of revolt, was to be proscribed for ever.[3]

The following day, Cecil echoed and amplified Elizabeth's instructions. In a postscript that plainly underlined her vulnerability and inner turmoil, he explained that she 'was in a conflict with herself'. She believed she was on a slippery slope to Hades if she discussed terms with a traitor; on the other hand, talks with Tyrone were the only way to pacify Ireland. Well aware that Tyrone would never abandon his ancestral title, Cecil advised Mountjoy first to make a show of obedience to her orders, making sure his efforts were recorded in writing. Choosing his words with extreme caution for fear they might be misinterpreted by the queen, Cecil then privately urged the Lord Deputy to strive for a settlement by whatever means he saw fit, underhand if necessary. Sometimes, he revealingly confided, 'honest servants must strain a little when they serve princes.' It was a latitude he had never allowed his hated rival Essex.[4]

Elizabeth's downward slide, meanwhile, continued. 'I am not sick, I feel no pain, and yet I pine away,' she was reputed to have said.[5] The agony from her arthritis was briefly in remission, but she was suffering from an extreme 'melancholy' and refusing to move from Richmond to Whitehall.[6] She had little appetite for food. She was plagued by her old insomnia, even though she managed to snatch an hour or two of sleep during daylight hours. She then came down with bronchitis, called in the sources 'an inflammation from the breast upwards'.[7]

On Tuesday, 15 March, a visiting Dutch diplomat, writing in French, sent a more detailed report to the States General. The queen, he said, had been ill for more than fifteen days. For ten or twelve of them, she had been unable to sleep. For the last three or four, she had managed four or five hours a night. She had begun to eat again but would not hear of medicine. A sudden 'defluxion' of foul matter into her throat had almost choked her. Said to be caused by mouth abscesses (*quelques petites apostumes dans la bouche*) rather than by phlegm or catarrh, this particular episode (if it happened this way) would have been linked to her periodontal problems. For almost half an hour, she could scarcely speak.[8]

Cecil had waited until the 9th before briefing his spy and chief intelligencer in Edinburgh, George Nicolson, alias 'the pigeon', who carried the secret correspondence between Cecil and James VI up and down the Great North Road. 'All flesh', he warned, 'is subject to mortality.' In a doomed attempt to pre-empt rumours of her imminent demise, he declared the queen to be 'free from any peril'. But 'I must confess to you that she had been so ill disposed these eight or nine days as I am fearful lest the continuance of such accidents should bring Her Majesty to future weakness, and so to be in danger of that which I hope mine eyes shall never see.'[9]

When Robert Carey, Kate's youngest brother, saw Elizabeth ten days later, she was in seclusion in her inner Bedchamber.[10] Hearing that she had expressed a desire to attend chapel the next morning, he waited hopefully with the other courtiers, expecting her to take her usual place. But she did not appear. Instead, she said she would hear the service from her privy closet, a small space with a clerestory window squeezed in off a narrow gallery linking the chapel to the Privy Chamber. Like her father, she always made her real devotions there, after which she would show herself in public in the chapel.

But, at the last moment, she changed her mind again. When the familiar liturgy began, she listened to it prostrate on cushions set out for her in the Privy Chamber, 'hard by the closet door'.[11] This was eerily like her old adversary Philip II, who, when dying, had listened to the chanting of the monks and priests at the altar in the monastic church at the Escorial through an interior window in his bedchamber.

After that, Elizabeth rapidly deteriorated. Eating less and stubbornly refusing to go to bed for two days and three nights, she sat immobile on a stool in her nightgown, staring into space. She 'had a persuasion that if she once lay down, she would never rise', said the well-informed John Chamberlain.[12] Elizabeth Southwell thought she knew why. In a dream some nights before, affirmed Southwell, the queen said she had seen a ghoulish apparition of herself 'in a light of fire', and she feared a similar nightmare if she returned to bed, taking it to be a terrible portent of the torments of hell.[13]

If her women had only seen such a thing, the queen had continued, they would not try to persuade her to sleep as they did. When Cecil dared to force her to take to her bed, she berated him, calling him 'Little man, little man' and reminding him that 'must' was a word 'not to be used to princes'. 'If your father had lived,' she is said to have growled, 'ye durst not have said so much: but thou knowest I must die, and that maketh thee so presumptuous.'[14]

Southwell's somewhat lurid, repeatedly recycled account must be questioned, coming as it does from someone who, in 1605, would convert to Catholicism and flee the country disguised as a page in order to marry her new (and already married) lover, Robert Dudley, Leicester's illegitimate son by Douglas Sheffield.[15] While the queen's alleged put-down of Cecil was highly characteristic of a woman who had cruelly nicknamed him 'Elf' and 'Pygmy', Southwell's assertion that her source was her great-aunt Philadelphia Scrope does not ring true: Scrope would have been unlikely to keep such a sensational snippet from her brother Robert Carey, and he does not mention it in his otherwise effusive *Memoirs*. Another of Southwell's stories of the discovery of a playing card, the queen of hearts, nailed to the bottom of Elizabeth's chair is even more implausible. The card had supposedly been hammered straight through the forehead, suggesting a plot to kill the queen through sorcery in the inner Bedchamber.[16]

Kate Carey's bereaved husband, Lord Admiral Nottingham, at last managed to coax the queen into her bed.[17] When she spurned all medication, he was sent for as a last resort. He had not seen Elizabeth since Kate's death, which he had taken badly, absenting himself from Court and shutting himself up in his own chamber to mourn in private.[18]

The diarist John Manningham, who sometimes dined with one of the queen's chaplains, Dr Parry, reported that she had been troubled by 'melancholy' on and off for more than three months. Her physicians, he said, were certain that she could have lived many more years if only she had taken medicine, chiefly for her chest.[19] It was as though she had given up: she seemed to be 'weary of life', as she had reputedly told de Beaumont, the French ambassador.[20]

By Wednesday, 23 March, when Robert Carey saw her for the last time, it was clear that she was wasting away. Speechless by midday, she rallied a little during the course of the afternoon, demanding some broth, but by the evening she was sinking fast.[21] And she knew it. Just as her father, when facing death, had called for Archbishop Cranmer, so she now summoned Archbishop Whitgift, the man she had nicknamed 'Little Black Husband'.

At about six o'clock that evening, no longer able to speak, she made signs that he should be sent for, along with her almoner and chaplains. Carey was allowed to kneel beside her bed. '[I] sat upon my knees full of tears to see that heavy sight,' he wrote.[22] The queen 'lay upon her back, with one hand in the bed, and the other without', and he listened as she did her best to respond to Whitgift's gentle questions about her faith in God by 'lifting up her eyes, and holding up her hand'. Although a great queen, Carey heard the archbishop say, she would soon have to 'yield an account of her stewardship to the King of kings'.[23]

When, after he had been 'long in prayer', Whitgift stopped, the dying queen made a sign which Carey's sister Philadelphia Scrope understood. Elizabeth wanted the archbishop to continue praying. By now, Whitgift was exhausted, his knees 'weary', for he was over seventy himself and would die from a stroke within a year. Stalwart to the last, he prayed for another half an hour, and then another. By then, Elizabeth, too, had tired and the archbishop was at long last able to rise from his knees and leave her. Carey left with him. 'By this time it grew late, and everyone departed,' he tells us, 'all but her women that attended her.' They did not have to attend her for long: she died peacefully at about three o'clock on Thursday morning.[24] Among a small packet of letters found beside her bed tied up with ribbon, the writing slightly blotted from her tears, was Leicester's final letter to her, on to the back of which she had scribbled in her own distinctive handwriting 'his last letter'.[25]

The queen's body was barely cold before what Carey called 'false lies' began to circulate as to whether she had named her successor.[26]

Speechless by Wednesday midday, she had been able to make only signs.[27] Possibly relying on information from his sister Philadelphia, Carey claims in his *Memoirs* that, on her last afternoon, Elizabeth had made a sign for her Privy Council to be summoned to her bedside. Then, when James's name was mentioned, she put her hand to her head.[28]

Whether she meant to signal her assent to James as she touched her head because that was where she wore her crown, or whether she was just touching it because it hurt her, is open for debate. In the light of a newly discovered final letter she sent to James shortly before Kate Carey's death, it is most unlikely that Elizabeth meant to make things easy for the Scottish king. Battling against her arthritis to write in her own hand, she sarcastically mocked his over-enthusiastic response to Spanish overtures for a rapprochement with the Catholic powers. She had always known, she remarked reproachfully, that 'you had no particular love to me.' In fact, she said, James's eagerness to treat with Catholics had dishonoured her and everything she had ever stood for.[29]

Psychologically, too, it seems doubtful that she named her successor. She had airily swept aside such requests for so many long years. 'I care not for death,' she had told members of Parliament in 1566, when they had pleaded with her to do so. 'For all men are mortal. And, though I be a woman, yet I have as good a courage answerable to my place as ever my father had. I am your anointed queen. I will never be by violence constrained to do anything.'[30]

The meaning of Elizabeth's gesture on that final afternoon will always remain enigmatic, but to smooth James's path to the throne and so advance their careers and their fortunes in the new reign, the privy councillors standing around her bedside conspired to interpret it as an explicit designation of James. 'By putting her hand to her head when the King of Scots was named to succeed her,' wrote Carey, 'they all knew he was the man she desired should reign after her.'[31]

The 'false lies' Carey denounced in his *Memoirs* were first fed by Cecil and Nottingham to Scaramelli, who describes how, 'with tears and sighs', Elizabeth begged her advisers to care for her realm and to bestow the Crown on the candidate they judged to be most deserving. This, she purportedly said, 'in her secret thought', had all along been James, for the Scottish king was far better entitled than she had ever been to rule, 'both in right of birth and because he excelled her in merit having been born a king, while she was but a private person'. James, she implausibly added, was all the more credible as her heir 'in that he brought with him a whole kingdom, while she had brought nothing but herself, a woman.'[32]

Scaramelli's colleague Marin Cavalli, the Venetian ambassador to France, elaborated on this fairy tale. He would have us believe that, shortly before she died, Elizabeth found her speech miraculously restored, enabling her to name James as her successor and explain her reasons. She then made something of a speech, exhorting her councillors to be loyal to the new king, before handing Cecil a 'casket' intended for James which contained all manner of papers, one being 'A Memorial on the Methods of Governing Well'.[33]

The most finely detailed, widely credited of these fictions sprang from the pen of Sir Robert Cotton, the historian and antiquary who helped his good friend and former schoolmaster William Camden to research the *Annales*. Cotton reports that Elizabeth, first 'falling into speech' with Nottingham on or about 14 January, had protested, 'My seat hath been ever the throne of kings, and none but my next heir of blood and descent should succeed me.'[34] Prompted by Nottingham to repeat this to Cecil and Egerton on 22 March – conveniently for them, the last day on which she fully retained the power of speech – she was said to have repeated, 'I told you my seat had been the seat of kings, and I will have no Rascal to succeed me, and who should succeed me but a king.' Cecil, claims Cotton, asked her to explain more precisely what she meant: 'Whereunto she replied that her meaning was a king should succeed her, and who, quoth she, should that be but "Our cousin of Scotland."' Cecil asked her whether that was 'her absolute resolution'. To that, she purportedly retorted, 'I pray you trouble me no more, I'll have none but him.'[35]

Wary of offending James when finishing up in manuscript the second instalment of his *Annales* in 1617, Camden included this story, which appears in all the printed versions of his work.[36] His narrative is taken as fact by many of Elizabeth's biographers. But the story is flatly contradicted by de Beaumont's far more credible dispatches to

Henry IV and his principal secretary, Nicolas de Neufville, Sieur de Villeroy.[37] Now rediscovered in their original, accurate French texts and crammed with verifiable detail, they show that this meticulous French diplomat, who was either a guest at Court or travelling to Richmond every single day to garner news, had access to the highest-placed sources. Writing to Villeroy on the late evening of 22 March, de Beaumont was adamant that Elizabeth had made no will and named no successor.[38] And, late in the day following her death, he confirmed this in another dispatch to his opposite number in Valla-dolid.[39]

And yet, two weeks after his first report and ten days after the second, de Beaumont would recount a radically different version of events. The shift came directly after Cecil and Nottingham summoned him and spun him a yarn. Elizabeth, a few days before her death, these councillors now claimed, had told them 'in confidence' that she recognized no other successor but James. She did not 'want her kingdom to fall into the hands of scoundrels, that is to say of Rascals (*c'est à dire des Canailles*)'. When, later, they asked her to attest her wishes before other privy councillors, she – being unable to speak – had made a sign by putting her hand to her head.[40]

The reference to *des Canailles* (the 'Rascals') strongly suggests that Cecil and Nottingham, speaking two weeks after the events they claimed to be describing, were working to a script. Cotton, Camden and John Manningham were deceived, but de Beaumont was always sceptical.[41] Why had the queen's declaration about not wanting her throne to fall into the hands of rascals only now become known?

Elizabeth died before she knew the outcome of Mountjoy's mission. Armed with her second letter to him, he had been able to track Tyrone down to his hideout in the great forest of Glenconkyne and entice him to a rendezvous with the offer of three weeks' safe conduct. On the eve of the meeting, a messenger, riding 'haste-post-haste' from London and making an unusually swift crossing over the Irish Sea, arrived late at night with a report of the queen's death. He was led instantly to Mountjoy's secretary and sworn to keep this sensational news absolutely secret from all except the Lord Deputy himself.[42]

Mountjoy decided to press ahead urgently before news of the queen's passing leaked out. Kneeling before him on Wednesday, 30 March, the rebel leader made his humble submission on oath to Elizabeth and received his pardon, oblivious of the fact that she was already dead.[43] Swearing allegiance to the English monarchy, he promised to renounce foreign alliances, especially with Spain, to resign his ancestral title and to put his lands at the disposal of the Crown. A secret memorandum records that, shortly before the ceremony, Mountjoy had signed an irrevocable agreement promising to restore Tyrone's title and all of his lands save for some two thousand or so acres.[44]

It was the closest of finishes. Had Elizabeth died a month or so earlier, Tyrone's supporters might well have rallied and he could have played a confident pan-Britannic game from a position of strength as a broker for Ireland's future with James. He might even have taken a decisive role in determining the English succession itself. At the very least, he might have secured Catholic toleration in Ireland. With the convert Henry IV now secure on the French throne and James married to another convert to Catholicism, that would have seemed entirely feasible.[45]

In Valladolid, meanwhile, the Spanish Council of State had been sharply split for months over how hard to press Henry IV and the pope to agree a compromise Catholic candidate for Elizabeth's throne.[46] While Philip III greeted the news of the death of the heretic bastard queen with jubilation, his satisfaction was bittersweet. Briefly, the Council debated compelling James to declare himself a Catholic by force as the alternative to a last-ditch, highly risky attempt to make the Infanta Queen of England. In a fit of wishful thinking, Philip ordered his forces to be put in readiness so that 'the King of Scotland or any other contender for the English throne might see how much help such forces might be if they were with him, and if not, how much of a threat'. There was even rash talk of capturing or demanding secession of the Isle of Wight as a bargaining tool.[47]

The Constable of Castile knew better. A former Governor of Milan and Captain-General of the Spanish forces allied to the French

Catholic League, he drew on his extensive military and naval experience. Besides, his mother, Lady Jane Dormer, the widow of the same Count of Feria who had met Elizabeth on the eve of her accession and judged her to be 'a very vain and clever woman', had for many years been a supporter of James, to whom she had written several times, urging him to embrace Catholicism. She had told her son precisely how badly the Scottish king would be likely to react to Spanish intimidation.[48]

The Constable's proposal, eventually adopted in a modified form, was to set aside 200,000 gold escudos (roughly £75 million today) as bribes to secure goodwill in England once James was crowned. It was a case of sheer necessity: through his quiet diplomacy with France and Rome over several years, and most especially by pretending until the very last moment that he planned to join his wife in converting to Catholicism, James had outwitted the Catholic powers. And Philip, for all his efforts and expenditure, had proved himself incapable of identifying a viable candidate of his own.[49]

When Cecil had first used that fatal word 'mortality' in his letter to his 'pigeon' George Nicolson on 9 March, he and his allies began preparing for a smooth transition of power to James.[50] Noblemen within a radius of fifty miles were summoned to Richmond. Promising them honours and rewards to win their loyalty, Cecil made a pact with them to prop up the privy councillors' authority until it could be renewed by the new king, for, technically, their power would legally expire when Elizabeth breathed her last.[51] At Court, the queen's guard was doubled.[52] In London, the city watches were put on maximum alert, large public gatherings outlawed, dissident Catholics rounded up and theatres closed.[53] Cecil had Arbella Stuart moved from Derbyshire to Woodstock in Oxfordshire and placed under close guard as an added precaution.[54]

On Saturday, 19 March, Cecil sent James a draft of the proclamation the Privy Council would issue announcing his accession. It was, observed the Scottish king's intermediary Edward Bruce, now Lord Kinloss, 'set of music that soundeth so sweetly in the ears of "30" [King James] that he can alter no notes in so agreeable a harmony'.[55] To the consternation of foreign ambassadors, the ports were then closed as part of a more general information blackout. Neither people nor letters were allowed to leave the country.[56] Scaramelli managed to circumvent this by sending his dispatches 'by many different routes in the hope that one copy' would get through.[57] Other envoys were not so lucky.

Determined to be the first to deliver the news of James's succession to Scotland if he could, Robert Carey had bribed a Court insider to send him word the moment Elizabeth died. When the messenger arrived at his lodgings, breathless, shortly before half-past three on the morning of Thursday the 24th, Carey rushed to the palace to check, but the gates were securely bolted. Luckily, he managed to talk his way in. Led to the Privy Chamber, where the councillors were huddled in close session, he was ordered point-blank not to leave the precincts 'till their pleasures were farther known'.[58]

Quietly slipping away all the same and evading the guards, Carey rode to London and set off shortly after nine on the four-hundred-mile ride to Edinburgh, bearing a blue sapphire ring given to him by his sister Philadelphia. Changing horses many times along the way and surviving an ugly fall near Norham, the last village in northern Northumberland before the frontier, he reached Holyrood late on Saturday evening, just after James had retired.

Carey was immediately led up to the king's bedchamber and saluted him by his new title of King of England, Scotland and Ireland. He then handed him the ring, which James had sent to Philadelphia Scrope sometime before so that it could serve as proof of Elizabeth's death ahead of any official notification.[59] From James's own detailed description of the encounter early the next morning, it is clear that Carey did *not* give him any reason to believe that Elizabeth had designated him as her heir by a deathbed gesture, further proof perhaps of the murky ambiguity of that reputed sign.[60]

At Richmond Palace on the early morning of the 24th, Cecil, flanked by his fellow privy councillors, proclaimed James to be king an hour or so before first light. All then rode to London, where at ten o'clock the proclamation was read again in a stage-managed ceremony at the gates of Whitehall. Shortly afterwards, four earls, four peers, the whole Privy Council, the judges, and the mayor and aldermen processed through the city in their scarlet robes, led by trumpeters, heralds and the Garter King of Arms. Once more, Cecil proclaimed James to be king, this time at Temple Bar, then at St Paul's, at Ludgate, in Cheapside and in Cornhill. It was then ordered that the proclamation be printed for general distribution throughout the realm.[61]

In London, the crucible of the nation, says an eyewitness, 'The proclamation was heard with great expectation and silent joy, no great shouting.' But, by evening, all that had changed. Now, there were bonfires in the streets and the church bells pealed. 'No tumult, no contradiction, no disorder in the city: every man went about his business as readily, as peaceably, as securely as though there had been no change, nor any news ever heard of competitors,' John Manningham recorded in his diary.[62]

And yet nothing could be taken for granted. Rumours of plots hatched by the Jesuits and the Catholic exiles were as rife as ever. One story doing the rounds was that Archduke Albert and the Infanta had been proclaimed King and Queen of England in Brussels and that Catholics all over Europe were mobilizing to assist them.[63] Secret cells of well-placed fifth-columnists were said to be active in Sussex and the north.[64] In York, it was reported that many of the citizens expected their houses to be ransacked.[65]

Such swirling undercurrents were enough to persuade the Privy Council to order local magistrates to arrest all 'letter carriers', suspicious persons, strangers, rumour-mongers 'tending to the disturbance of the common peace' and dubious-looking foreigners. Sermons were to be preached from the pulpits on Sundays, admonishing the people and calling them to their true obedience to the newly proclaimed King James.[66] Most dangerous were those rumours that claimed James had turned Catholic. One sinister report had it that James had already promised the pope that, if he succeeded Elizabeth, he would grant Catholic toleration in England as well as Ireland. Not only that, all those exiled by Elizabeth for their religious faith and stripped of their estates over the years would be welcomed home and invited to reclaim their lands.[67]

To counter such reports, Cecil's agents put out their own stories, and soon the printing presses would be pouring out pamphlets and verses praising the new king and welcoming him to his new kingdom.

According to these, James was a grown man, an experienced ruler with a strong dynastic claim. Unlike the late queen, he was male and blessed with a wife and children to safeguard the succession. The panegyric was predictable, if expressed in execrable rhyme:

> Let all the true and noble hearts,
> Wherewith England abounds:
> Unto their king, of rarest parts,
> Be loyal subjects found.
> Sing they melodious harmony,
> Sing welcome, welcome heartily.
> Therefore rejoice, rejoice therefore, rejoice and sing,
> For it hath pleas'd God to give us a King.[68]

In accordance with Elizabeth's dying wishes, her corpse was not embalmed.[69] Those of most monarchs, and the very wealthy, were embalmed after their deaths to keep the cadaver in a reasonable state of preservation. Professional embalmers would cut the corpse open from throat to groin, remove the entrails, which could be buried separately, then wash the cavities with vinegar before stuffing them with salt and spices. The body would then be carefully wrapped in cerecloth, a special cloth made of fine linen or silk soaked in molten wax. After that, it could be dressed in all its finery for display in state before interment.[70]

Elizabeth was not alone in refusing to be embalmed. Mary, Countess of Northumberland, had stipulated in 1572 that no embalmer was to be allowed near her corpse: 'I have not loved to be very bold afore women, much more would I be loath to come into the hands of any living man, be he physician or surgeon.'[71] For Elizabeth, the Virgin Queen, the same sentiments may well have applied, but practicalities meant that the process of decomposition would have to be delayed. Cerecloth, if correctly applied, would work for a month or so, but not much longer. Unfortunately, those wrapping Elizabeth's cadaver did a botched job, charging the full fee but embezzling a proportion of the cloth with which they had been supplied, which meant that the seals were not properly airtight.[72]

The queen's body was moved by night on a black-draped barge lit by torches along the Thames from Richmond to Whitehall. There it was placed on a bed of state, but no funeral could take place without the new king's assent.[73] And James declared himself to be in no hurry to complete his journey south – all the more so when a fresh plague epidemic struck London, killing thousands.

On 6 April, James protested from the safety of Berwick-upon-Tweed on the border that he would 'do all honour that we may unto the queen defunct'.[74] His sincerity may be doubted, as he assiduously refused to put on mourning dress for the woman who had left him a throne. Neither would he allow Queen Anne, his courtiers, or foreign ambassadors and their retinues to wear black in his presence. The Marquis de Rosny, Henry IV's special envoy, sent to congratulate James on his succession, left Paris supplied with fine mourning attire only to be told on arrival that 'no one, whether ambassador, foreigner or English, was admitted . . . in black.' He had no choice but to order all his retinue 'to change their apparel, and provide themselves others as well as they could'.[75]

Between the queen's last breath and the lowering of her body into her tomb, it was as though she had never died. As Scaramelli reports, 'The Council waits on her continually with the same ceremony, the same expenditure, down to her very household and table service, as though she were not wrapped in a fold of cerecloth, and hid in such a heap of lead, of coffin, of pall, but was walking as she used to do at this season, about the alleys of her gardens.'[76]

In the end, the funeral could be delayed no longer.[77] On Thursday, 28 April, four days after Easter, the cortège, half a mile long, beginning with 260 poor women recruited from local almshouses, clad in black and walking in rows of four, their heads covered with linen handkerchiefs, made its way towards Westminster Abbey. Next came the officers of the late queen's household, the mayor and aldermen of London and the judges. Behind them walked the Privy Council, the bishops, the archbishop of Canterbury and the nobles in order of their rank, followed by the queen's women. Ralegh, as Captain of the Guard, brought up the rear, marching at the head of his soldiers, five in a row, all pointing their halberds downwards, draped in black.[78]

A symbolic riderless horse, the palfrey of honour, was led by the Earl of Worcester, who had replaced Essex as Master of the Horse. The French ambassador, de Beaumont, enveloped in a hood and long, black mourning cloak, also walked in the procession, his train six yards long. Scaramelli refused to attend, excusing himself on the grounds that entering a Protestant church might offend the pope and jeopardize his soul.[79]

Elizabeth's body took pride of place in the ceremony. Her purple-velvet-covered coffin lay on an open chariot pulled by four great horses, each trapped in black velvet emblazoned with the arms of England and Ireland. On the top of the lead-lined wooden coffin, now firmly sealed, was a skilfully crafted wooden effigy of the queen dressed in her Parliament robes, with a crown on her head and a sceptre in her hand. An eyewitness described the carefully painted model as 'very exquisitely framed to resemble the life'.[80] Six knights wearing their coats of arms supported a canopy above the chariot, while twelve barons, six to each side, held aloft heraldic banners around the coffin in a blaze of colour. Immediately behind them walked the woman chosen by Cecil to be the chief mourner, the Marchioness of Northampton, flanked by his chief allies, Nottingham and Buckhurst, wearing deepest black.

James had suggested his cousin Arbella Stuart as chief mourner on the grounds that she was his closest living relative, but Arbella had refused. Since she had been snubbed by Elizabeth and packed off to Derbyshire for so many years, she said 'she would not after her death be brought upon the stage for a public spectacle.'[81]

Inside the abbey, the funeral service began with a sermon, followed by a eulogy read by the late queen's almoner, Anthony Watson, bishop of Chichester. Psalms and prayers ensued, after which the coffin and Elizabeth's effigy were lowered into her tomb in the crypt beneath the altar of the Henry VII Chapel.[82] Only later would her mortal remains be moved by James to their present location in a specially constructed monumental tomb in the north aisle of the Chapel.[83]

James was still on his leisurely journey south on the day of the queen's funeral. By then, he and his Scottish entourage had reached Hinchingbrooke House, near Huntingdon, where he spent the day hunting and feasting with his intimates on the finest meats, game, fish and wines, 'the like . . . not seen in any place before since his first setting forward out of Scotland'.[84] Afterwards, James was greeted by the masters of the Cambridge colleges, bowing low in their scarlet gowns and doffing their caps.

Hinchingbrooke House was owned by the uncle of the future regicide and Lord Protector of England, Oliver Cromwell, and where young Oliver often played as a boy.

Epilogue

On the morning of Elizabeth's death, Robert Cecil sent James a copy of the proclamation of his title as king and pressed him to renew the Privy Council's authority, which he did.[1] As the new king's cavalcade made its snail-like way south from Edinburgh and James was besieged by suitors seeking offices or knighthoods, or simply yearning for change, Cecil and Lord Henry Howard strained every nerve to keep Ralegh and Cobham – the 'accursed duality', as Howard had nicknamed them – out of sight.[2] They failed, however, to prevent James, who continued to hold the memory of Essex and his supporters in high esteem, from releasing the Earl of Southampton from the Tower.[3]

In April, James fully restored Southampton to his lands and title.[4] Essex's family was not forgotten either. When his widow, the much-slighted Frances Walsingham, married Richard Burke, Earl of Clanricarde, an Irish nobleman she had taken as her lover, James created him Viscount Tunbridge. Essex's twelve-year-old son, Robert, who had barely known his father and was left an orphan when his mother moved away, was brought to Court and made a page to Prince Henry. Within a year, he, too, received back the lands and titles due to him. Last but not least, Essex's sister Penelope married her lover Lord Mountjoy, this within days of securing a scandalous divorce on the grounds of her own confessed adultery.[5]

And yet, Cecil appeared to have little to worry about. Before leaving Holyrood, James had scribbled him a message: 'How happy I think myself by the conquest of so faithful and so wise a councillor, I reserve it to be expressed out of my own mouth to you.'[6] Working hand in glove, Cecil and Howard planned to shape the new government in their own interests.[7] Thus, at the first meeting of the Privy Council since Elizabeth's funeral, held at Whitehall on Easter Monday, Mountjoy was sworn in as a new member.[8] Nine days later, at Burghley's old house – now Cecil's – at Theobalds, where James spent his final nights on his journey southwards, Howard took the councillor's oath, as did the Earl of Mar and Edward Bruce, Lord Kinloss, James's intermediaries for his secret correspondence with Cecil.[9] That same day, James invited Cecil, Nottingham and Buckhurst to appoint the officers of the new royal household in consultation with his Scottish advisers. Cecil could do little to limit the number of Scots flooding into James's Court, especially in the Bedchamber. But he and Nottingham could at least keep out their own rivals.

Not for nothing did James tell his privy councillors that he would 'be moved to multiply our princely favours to you accordingly in such sort as all the faithful subjects of the land shall be encouraged by your example'.[10] Cecil would rise in remarkably short order to be Lord Cecil of Essendon, Viscount Cranborne and Earl of Salisbury. Buckhurst was made Earl of Dorset and Lord Treasurer for life. Howard became Earl of Northampton. Nottingham, too, was showered with grants, his cupidity egregious even by the standards of James's Court. Finally, Mountjoy was created Earl of Devonshire and Egerton made Lord Chancellor, with the title of Baron Ellesmere, in which capacity he cheerfully advised James that 'whatsoever the king directed in any case he would decree accordingly.'[11]

When James decided to do what Elizabeth had failed to finish and correct the abuses of monopolies, things followed a similar pattern.[12] Cecil made sure that Egerton was put in charge, with powers to limit the scope of these investigations.[13] He then turned the spotlight on those he wished to punish. Ralegh's monopoly for the sale of wine was among the first to be called in, causing his credit to collapse. The haberdasher Thomas Allen, whose plucky campaign against Edward Darcy's monopoly for playing cards had resulted in a legal victory in court, was threatened with the Tower if he did not 'utterly relinquish the same' and allow Darcy to enjoy his former privileges.[14] Ralegh, to his fury, was even sent a peremptory notice to quit Durham House, which he had occupied for almost twenty years. His wine licence, once revoked, would be granted to Nottingham.[15]

On Sunday, 8 May, at a special session of the Privy Council, Ralegh appeared by Cecil's special command and was informed that James meant to strip him of his office of Captain of the Guard.[16] Ostensibly, the move was innocent: James, long used to Scottish bodyguards, wanted them in England, too.[17] Except that Sir Thomas Erskine, the Earl of Mar's cousin and another of Cecil's confidants, was chosen as the new Captain.[18]

Malicious rumours were soon mysteriously put about that Ralegh and Cobham had plotted Essex's downfall by forging letters.[19] The Comte de Beaumont, still the resident French ambassador, conjectured that what lay at the root of all these stories was a villainous intrigue masterminded by Cecil to destroy Ralegh and Cobham. When Ralegh requested an audience with James in a bid to exonerate himself, he was curtly refused.[20]

James made his ceremonial entry into London to the cheers of the adoring crowds on the morning of Wednesday, 11 May. Carrying the sword of state in the procession was Essex's young son, Robert. By then, Elizabeth's portraits had been cleared away and replaced by more politically correct images of the king's mother, Mary Queen of Scots.[21] After a brief unofficial visit to Whitehall to feast his eyes on the old queen's jewels and gold and silver plate, James took possession of the Tower and was treated to a 250-gun salute.[22] He slept there for only a single night before leaving in the royal barge early the next morning for Greenwich, where he felt safer from the plague.[23]

With Cecil and Howard pulling so many of the levers of power, it was only a matter of months before the careers of Ralegh and Cobham would be destroyed.[24] Through his spies, Cecil learned of a madcap plot involving some forty conspirators, among them Cobham's wayward brother George Brooke, to kidnap James on Midsummer Night (24 June) and imprison him in the Tower until he granted religious toleration for Catholics and purged Cecil from the Privy Council.[25] Under interrogation, Brooke (strangely, a Protestant himself) claimed to be an *agent provocateur* working for James (his claim was never vindicated but may have been true). All that mattered, however, was that he went on fleetingly to accuse Cobham of something far more serious – and, this time, the charges appeared to have more substance to them.

The gist of these new allegations was that Cobham, dismayed by his exclusion from power, had talked to Ralegh of removing 'the king and his cubs' and putting Arbella Stuart on the throne. After multiple interrogations, Cobham confessed that he was to be paid the astonishing sum of 600,000 crowns (around £100 million today) by Archduke Albert's envoy, Charles de Ligne, Comte d'Aremberg, who had arrived in London to congratulate James on his accession. Cobham was to travel to Brussels, then Valladolid or Madrid, to collect the money. He was to return via Jersey, from where he and Ralegh were to direct a rebellion.[26]

Cobham and Ralegh spoke of putting Arbella on the throne, but whether they meant to *act* on their conversations is a quite different matter. To extricate himself after his arrest, Ralegh turned on Cobham.[27] In retaliation, Cobham turned on Ralegh, accusing him of offering to sell state secrets to the Archduke for a pension of £1,500.[28]

Brought to trial in November in Winchester, where Sir Edward Coke led the case for the prosecution, Ralegh put on a bravura performance. He admitted listening to Cobham's loose talk but vehemently denied a conspiracy. He demanded the right to confront Cobham face to face and, when this was denied him, he pulled out of his pocket a letter in Cobham's hand smuggled to him while in prison:

> Seeing myself so near my end, for the discharge of my own conscience and freeing myself from your blood, which else will cry vengeance against me, I protest upon my salvation I never practised with Spain by your procurement. God so comfort me in this my affliction as you are a true subject for anything that I know.[29]

Coke then produced an affidavit from Cobham that confirmed his original accusation, which the jury believed.[30] Ralegh and Cobham were found guilty and condemned to death, but James spared their lives, in Cobham's case only after he had tempered mercy with a touch of sadism, waiting until the very moment Cobham was about to face the executioner.

Cobham was to spend the next fourteen years in the Tower: he would die of a stroke within a year of his release. Ralegh spent thirteen years there, writing, studying history and geography, doing scientific experiments, even advising the heir to the throne, the teenage Prince Henry, on navigation and the rudiments of shipbuilding.[31] Finally, in 1616, he would be freed on licence to lead a second expedition up the Orinoco in search of El Dorado and its fabled gold mines.[32] The profligate James desperately hoped that Ralegh's new venture would rescue the Crown's finances from catastrophe. But when Ralegh returned empty-handed after allowing his company to kill a number of Spanish colonists and burn their settlement, frustrating James's pro-Spanish diplomacy, the original death warrant was put into effect.

Concluding his *Annales* in 1617, William Camden failed to write Elizabeth's obituary. He chose merely to remark that in her final years her courtiers 'ungratefully in a manner forsook her', preferring to 'curry favour' with the new king: 'they adored him as the rising Sun, and neglected her as being now ready to set.'[33] A more outspoken eyewitness, Godfrey Goodman, observed that 'the people were very generally weary of an old woman's government.' 'After a few years,' however, 'when we had experience of the Scottish government, then . . . in hate and detestation of them, the queen did seem to revive. Then was her memory much magnified.'[34]

By the middle of James's reign, Elizabeth's gender, so fraught a subject in her lifetime, would become immaterial. With those around her so often regarding a queen as inferior to a king, she had been forced, as the years went by, to devise methods of reducing her vulnerability. Writing in the 1620s, Sir Robert Naunton, who had spied in Holland, France and Spain for Essex before shifting his allegiance to Cecil, famously wrote of her, 'The principal note of her reign will be that she ruled much by faction and parties, which herself both made, upheld and weakened as her own great judgement advised.'[35] Persistently cited by her biographers as one of the shrewdest assessments ever made of Elizabeth's style of ruling, the passage is thoroughly misleading, as it maps the political practices of James's last decade back on to hers.

Elizabeth's methods of control were different. Sometimes she deliberately distanced herself from what she had done, shifting the blame on to others. Most spectacularly, she denied all responsibility for the regicide of Mary Queen of Scots, ruthlessly destroying William Davison's career and reputation. Then again, there was her weasel-worded halting of Essex's first trial in the Star Chamber after his defiant return from Ireland. As Cecil had remarked of such ploys,

'This argueth the queen would have her ministers do that she will not avow.'

Her privy councillors did not always agree on policy, and she could exploit these differences to reduce risk and let time work to her advantage, especially where the debate concerned a policy that she did not really like. In a valedictory speech to Parliament at the end of the 1601 session, she had turned this tendency into a virtue, claiming she had always made her advisers fully debate *pro* and *contra*, 'as all princes must that will understand what is right'.[36] Where personality clashes at Court caused friction, she manipulated them to divide and rule, a method that worked well in controlling Ralegh and Essex. She could also play on her courtiers' fears of what it would be like if she were no longer there. This method was especially effective against Burghley, who knew that James despised him as his mother's nemesis.

She was only human, and a marked susceptibility for the sort of unctuous flattery Hatton had mastered to perfection and for dashing young men were her main weaknesses: these could, and sometimes did, cloud her judgement. Hatton, fortunately, was too loyal and devoted to betray her. Ralegh she handled better than Essex, never allowing him to become a privy councillor. Although it is true that Essex, at first, had the backing of Leicester, Hatton and Burghley as a counterweight to Ralegh, she indulged him for far too long before cutting him off. If she had ever thought that he could be a surrogate for his stepfather, she was sadly mistaken.

After the deaths of Walsingham, Leicester, Hatton and, later, Burghley, it was Robert Cecil, Nottingham, Buckhurst and Archbishop Whitgift who took centre stage as the advisers she trusted implicitly, leaving Essex to struggle to assert his primacy as a war leader. With the arrival of this close-knit circle at the heart of her Court, Elizabeth would discover that her technique of playing individuals off against each other did not work so well. Yet, even at the height of the deadly feud between Essex and Cecil, she would never lose control of her Court. Knowing that the final choice was always hers, her ministers were forced to iron out their differences before making any final recommendation. To attempt to approach her individually, as Essex would so often do, would almost always prove to be counter-productive. It was a mistake her own 'Sweet Robin', her beloved 'Eyes', had never made, for all his many faults.

Towards the end, her Court could feel claustrophobic, even oppressive. The wise watched what they said or wrote, for letters could be read and intercepted. 'Danger goeth abroad, and silence is the safest armour,' wrote Robert Markham in a letter to John Harington shortly before Harington's departure with Essex for Ireland.[37] On his return, Harington summed up the situation in an epigram: 'Who liveth in Courts must mark what they say;/ Who liveth for ease had better live away.'[38]

The queen's vanity and temper added to the often feverish atmosphere of the Court. She could lash out at anyone from maids to privy councillors if in the mood to do so, and there were times when she was best avoided. In her correspondence with James, she could be so vituperative that they several times ended up having a slanging match. Once, when emerging from her presence with 'ill-countenance', Hatton advised Harington not to ask her for anything. 'If you have any suit today, I pray you put it aside. The sun doth not shine.'[39] But often these outbursts were more directed towards keeping other people in their place than might appear at first sight. And, if Elizabeth had a sharp tongue, she did not indulge in the wholesale bloodbaths that had scarred her father's reign as nobleman after nobleman, courtier after courtier, minister after minister, had mounted the scaffold for alleged treason. Her Court was a safer place than his, despite the atrocities of her chief pursuivant, the perverse and paranoid Catholic hunter, Richard Topcliffe.

With uncanny accuracy, Henry VIII had predicted two areas in which a female ruler would be particularly vulnerable: war and the succession. Whereas he had personally led his armies into battle on two noted occasions, Elizabeth could not. She might address her troops with martial vigour, but war was essentially a male preserve. Yet, for almost twenty years, she successfully held off the might of Catholic Spain. Without her military and financial aid, Henry IV and the Dutch would have succumbed, but her victory had as much to do with luck and Philip II's own failings as with her leadership. Encouraged by heroic dreams of martial glory, Leicester would defy her in the Netherlands, Ralegh at the beginning of his aborted expedition to Panama, Essex in Portugal, Rouen and Ireland. Moreover, during both his Cádiz and Azores campaigns, Essex either seriously deviated from or consciously chose to misinterpret his instructions, believing he knew better than she did.

Once she had given him his head and he had failed her, she was determined never again to allow him (or Ralegh) to talk her into an aggressive military and naval strategy. This, together with her more obvious financial concerns, helps explain her generally defensive approach to the war effort. Broadly speaking, her war aims centred more on survival and safety than on victory.

Reflecting wistfully on the war effort after James had made peace with Spain in 1604, Ralegh would declare, 'If the late Queen would have believed her men of war as she did her scribes, we had in her time beaten that great empire in pieces, and made their kings of figs and oranges, as in old times. But Her Majesty did all by halves.'[40] This most memorable of quotations is frequently used by her biographers to argue that Elizabeth's caution and female dithering stripped the war effort of the strategic vision and unstinting allocation of resources needed to win. Had the war been run more aggressively by a leader with a fully integrated approach to military and naval strategy, or so Ralegh claimed (meaning, of course, someone like him), it would quickly have become self-financing and the brave military men whom she had marginalized could have revolutionized the country's future.

Elizabeth held such thinking to be a chimera. Her minimalist, almost entirely defensive approaches were, she confidently believed, not second best but the only way to match the tolerance of taxpayers to the measures needed to protect Protestant England from the Catholic powers. In any case, the idea that she was more than usually cautious or indecisive where the war effort is concerned comes less from the facts than from contemporary stereotypes about the alleged weakness and capriciousness of women and wives. Sometimes, she would deliberately exploit such tropes. Sometimes, she would invert them to resounding effect rhetorically, as when, at Tilbury, she protested, 'I know I have the body but of a weak and feeble woman, but I have the heart and stomach of a King, and of a King of England too.'

It is, of course, entirely true that she hated risk. And when unable to extricate herself from difficult corners, she preferred to wait and see what time might do to rescue her. In the case of her great adversary, Philip II, such caution generally passed for admirable prudence, but for Elizabeth the opposite almost always held true. Nothing was more dangerous in her eyes than military over-extension. She was already lending vast sums to Henry IV and the Dutch, on top of her own massive expenditure at sea, in northern Europe and latterly in Ireland, and yet she managed to leave James with Crown debts of only £365,000. It was James, not she, who, in under ten years of peace, would drive the country to the edge of bankruptcy.

In her last, chiding letter to James, Elizabeth would give us her side of the story. Set down for posterity as her political testament as much as it was intended for James, she laid out in the clearest terms the aims she had attempted to uphold since the outbreak of the Dutch revolt. Everything, she said, went back to the offer she had received in 1576 from the States General to be their sovereign. She had been confronted with a profound moral dilemma: how to reconcile the legitimacy of the Dutch cause with her ideal of God-appointed monarchy. Throughout the long war, it had never been her intention to steal or encroach on another ruler's territory. Rather than breach her principles, she said, she had tried to broker a settlement between Spain and the Dutch, designed to help the Dutch to recover their ancient liberties and free themselves from an occupying army. When Philip II had refused to negotiate, she had offered the Dutch purely defensive assistance. For that, Philip had declared war on her. Afterwards, she had been forced to help Henry IV to prevent France from falling into the Catholic tyrant's hands. She had done no more, no less, than attempt to restore the status quo in northern Europe. In return, Philip had sought to have her deposed and killed, and to conquer her realm.

'Deserved I such recompense, as many a complot, both for my life and my kingdom?' she asked. 'Ought not I to defend [myself] and bereave him of such weapons?' The whole root of the quarrel, she declared, lay in the fact that proud Philip had cast aside the covenants his father, Charles V, had made with the Dutch, subjecting them to the cruel, direct rule of Spaniards. 'I would not [have] dealt with

others' territory, but they hold those by such covenants.' By breaching them, Philip had brought war on himself. Had they not existed,
she would never have defended rebels in a 'wicked quarrel' with their
lawful prince.[41]

The succession had presented her with a second, more practical
dilemma. To assure the continuation of the dynasty, she would need
an heir, and that meant marriage, with all the vexing problems of
finding a suitable husband and risking having to submit herself, and
her country, to his authority, as her half-sister had done. Opting to
remain single, on the other hand, could lead to chaos or even to civil
war. When still of childbearing age, she had been lobbied repeatedly
to marry or name an heir. Scandalously, Burghley had covertly mobilized his allies in Parliament against her and even toyed with the idea
of establishing a statutory mechanism by which the throne might
pass only to a Protestant if she were suddenly to die. The menopause
had liberated her, as there was no point in urging marriage upon a
barren woman, but it also highlighted the succession issue all the
more acutely. Unlike her privy councillors, Elizabeth believed she
would end up weaker, not stronger, if she named an heir rather than
leaving the question in limbo. While at one level her attitude was
deeply irresponsible, it was firmly rooted in her searing experiences
in her half-brother's and half-sister's reigns. Things might have been
different as she approached her late sixties had she actually liked
James but, judging by her tetchy letters to him, she found his waywardness and presumption exasperating. She preferred to promise
nothing and leave all to time.

Time worked in her favour in the end, though it took its toll on a
personal level. As the post-menopausal queen began to age, she left it
to her courtiers to promote the 'cult' of Gloriana by commissioning
ever more flattering and iconographically abstruse portraits as small
armies of labourers toiled for a month or more at a time to create
outdoor Arcadian fantasies during her summer progresses. Unlike
her father, she was never mesmerized by her own legend, but she did
come to believe after 1588 that God was a Protestant and on her side.
When she berated Henry IV after his conversion to Catholicism for
making a choice that she felt flew in the face of God and told him that
he and perhaps *she* (for continuing to support him) might find herself

paying the price, she made it clear that her religious convictions were central to her ways of thinking. She felt that God had called on her to be an instrument for good for the salvation of northern Europe.

While being wooed by handsome younger men like Ralegh or Essex appealed to her vanity, she increasingly came to appear ridiculous to her younger courtiers. So intense did the 'cult' of Gloriana become, it introduced a toxic element into Court culture. Courtiers really had to believe the queen was a second Madonna: Essex shattered the taboo when he muttered in her hearing that 'her conditions were as crooked as her carcass.'

For the vast majority of her subjects, whom Elizabeth always referred to in the abstract as her 'people' and whose love and support she had claimed to hold since she came to the throne, the Court was another world. She told members of Parliament poetically in 1601, 'I have . . . been content to be a taper of true virgin wax to waste myself and spend my life that I might give light and comfort to those that live under me' – but in this she was deluding herself.[42] To most of her people, as they struggled against often impossible odds to live their lives, she was a distant image or just a name. The social and economic effects of the long war hit them hard, and yet she expected the civic and county magistrates to take the measures necessary to restore equilibrium rather than taking them herself. All this was made far worse when thousands of severely wounded or sick mariners and soldiers, destitute and unpaid, began returning from the war zones. Her reward to those who had fought in the 1588 Armada campaign was to leave them to die in the gutters. For those who fought on land with Essex and Sir John Norris in northern France, she showed pity for the blue-blooded officers but not the ordinary foot soldiers, whom she left to starve or find their own way home. She was always a terrible snob.

In her final years, she was often ill, but until Kate Carey's death she was mentally as agile as ever. Only Cecil managed to hoodwink her, for the best part of two years. Claims by several biographers that she somehow found proof of the secret correspondence going up and down between London and Edinburgh before she died are not supported by the evidence.[43] How far she guessed that Cecil deliberately set up Essex to fail in Ireland is impossible to judge.

If asked to pronounce a verdict on herself, Elizabeth would have regarded her ultimate test not as the 1588 Armada or its successors but the execution of Mary Queen of Scots. Her chief aim had been to preserve the ideal of God-appointed monarchy. She had always maintained that if she were to sign her Scottish cousin's death warrant, the monarchic ideal would be attenuated. England would descend into the wild, untamed, primordial world of King Lear on the heath. It was her misfortune to rule at a time when the vagaries of dynastic succession competed with the ideal of an exclusively Protestant commonwealth. When Elizabeth spoke in her own voice, hereditary rights took priority over religion; when Burghley did the talking, it was always the other way round. The Wars of Religion in France and the heroic struggle of the Calvinists in the Netherlands were mainly to blame. On both sides of the religious divide, many could be found who were happy to justify assassination plots, elective monarchy or worse.

By 1601, Elizabeth had found Parliament dangerously fractious, as her subjects demanded change. Her ultimate nightmare was the thought of that 'multitude of people . . . who said they were Commonwealth's men' crowding the lobby outside the House of Commons and staging a public demonstration to force Parliament to 'take compassion of their griefs'. This was 'popularity' with a vengeance, conjuring up Essex and the 'tragedy' he had brought down upon her that 'was forty times played in open streets and houses'. Such demands implied that the monarchy should become accountable to Parliament, and Parliament to the people – both anathema to Elizabeth.

Ralegh, a master-wordsmith, shall have the last word. Justifying himself to his accusers at his trial at Winchester, he brilliantly captured Elizabeth's situation in the final weeks and months of her long reign. She had, he said, become 'a lady whom time hath surprised'.[44] It was not just grief for Kate Carey that killed her, if indeed the reports are true that mourning for Kate had brought about her final decline. Elizabeth was also mourning for the death of England – or the version of England and its ideals that she and her father had always imagined. She might not have changed, but the world had.

This is her tragedy.

Abbreviations

AGR	Archives Générales du Royaume, Brussels
AGS	Archivo General de Simancas
APC	*Acts of the Privy Council of England, New Series*, ed. J. R. Dasent, 46 vols. (London, 1890–1964)
Bath MSS	*Calendar of the Manuscripts of the Most Honourable The Marquess of Bath*, 5 vols. (London, 1904–80)
BIHR	*Bulletin of the Institute of Historical Research*
Birch, *Memoirs*	*Memoirs of the Reign of Queen Elizabeth from 1581 till Her Death*, ed. T. Birch, 2 vols. (London, 1754)
Birch, *Hist. View*	*An Historical View of the Negotiations between the Courts of England, France, and Brussels, from the Year 1592 to 1617*, ed. T. Birch (London, 1749)
Bodleian	Bodleian Library, Oxford
BL	British Library, London
BNF	Bibliothèque Nationale de France, Paris
Bond	*The Complete Works of John Lyly*, ed. R. W. Bond, 3 vols. (Oxford, 1902)
Camden	W. Camden, *The History of the Most Renowned and Victorious Princess Elizabeth, Late Queen of England*, 3rd edn (London, 1675)
CCM	*Calendar of Carew Manuscripts Preserved in the Archiepiscopal Library at Lambeth*, ed. J. S. Brewer and W. Bullen, 6 vols. (London, 1867–73)
Chamberlain	*Letters Written by John Chamberlain during the Reign of Elizabeth I*, ed. S. Williams, *Camden Society*, Old Series, 79 (1861)
Chambers	E. K. Chambers, *The Elizabethan Stage*, 4 vols. (Oxford, 1923)
CKJVI	*Correspondence of King James VI of Scotland with Sir Robert Cecil and Others in England during the Reign of Elizabeth I*, ed. J. Bruce, *Camden Society*, Old Series, 78 (1861)
Collins	*Letters and Memorials of State: Collections Made by Sir Henry Sydney, Knight of the Garter, Lord President of the Marches of Wales, etc.*, ed. R. Collins, 2 vols. (London, 1746)
CP	Cecil Papers, Hatfield House (available on microfilm at the BL and Folger Shakespeare Library)
CSPC	*Calendar of State Papers, Colonial*, ed. W. N. Sainsbury, 45 vols. (London, 1860–1970)
CSPD	*Calendar of State Papers, Domestic, Edward VI, Mary, Elizabeth I and James I*, ed. R. Lemon and E. Green, 12 vols. (London, 1856–72)
CSPD Mary	*Calendar of State Papers, Domestic Series, of the Reign of Mary I, 1553–1558*, ed. C. S. Knighton (London, 1998)
CSPF	*Calendar of State Papers, Foreign*, ed. W. B. Turnbull, J. Stevenson and A. J. Crosby, 25 vols. in 28 parts (London, 1861–1950)
CSPSM	*Calendar of State Papers Relating to Scotland and Mary, Queen of Scots, 1547–1603*, ed. J. Bain and W. K. Boyd, 13 vols. (London, 1898–1969)
CSPSp, 1st Series	*Calendar of Letters, Despatches, and State Papers Relating to the Negotiations between England and Spain*, ed. G. A. Bergenroth, P. de Gayangos and M. A. S. Hume, 13 vols. (London, 1873–1954)

CSPSp, 2nd Series	*Letters and State Papers Relating to English Affairs Preserved Principally in the Archives of Simancas*, ed. M. A. S. Hume, 4 vols. (London, 1892–9)
CSPV	*Calendar of State Papers and Manuscripts Relating to English Affairs in the Archives and Collections of Venice and in Other Libraries of Northern Italy*, ed. R. Brown, G. Cavendish-Bentinck and H. F. Brown, 38 vols. (London, 1864–1947)
CUL	Cambridge University Library
De L'Isle and Dudley MSS	*Report on the Manuscripts of Lord De L'Isle and Dudley Preserved at Penshurst Place*, 6 vols. (London, 1925–66)
De Maisse	*A Journal of All That Was Accomplished by Monsieur de Maisse, Ambassador in England . . . Anno Domini 1597*, ed. and trans. G. B. Harrison and R. A. Jones (London, 1931)
Devereux	*Lives and Letters of the Devereux, Earls of Essex, 1540–1646*, ed. W. B. Devereux, 2 vols. (London, 1853)
D'Ewes	*The Journals of All the Parliaments during the Reign of Queen Elizabeth*, ed. S. D'Ewes (London, 1682)
DIB	*Dictionary of Irish Biography*, ed. J. McGuire and J. Quinn, 9 vols. (Cambridge, 2009) and http://dib.cambridge.org/
EAC	*Elizabeth I: Autograph Compositions and Foreign Language Originals*, ed. J. Mueller and L. S. Marcus (Chicago, 2003)
ECW	*Elizabeth I: Collected Works*, ed. L. S. Marcus, J. Mueller and M. B. Rose (Chicago, 2000)
EHR	*English Historical Review*
Ellis	*Original Letters, Illustrative of British History*, ed. H. Ellis, 3 series, 11 vols. (London, 1824–46)
FF	Ancien Fonds Français
Finch MSS	*Report on the Manuscripts of Allan George Finch, Esq., of Burley-on-the-Hill, Rutland*, 5 vols. (London, 1913–70)
Foedera	*Foedera, Conventiones, Litterae et Cuiuscunque Generis Acta Publica inter Reges Angliae et Alios Quosuis Imperatores, Reges, Pontifices, Principes vel Communitates*, ed. T. Rymer, 20 vols. (London, 1726–35)
Folger	Folger Shakespeare Library, Washington DC
Guildhall	Guildhall Library, London
Hakluyt	*The Principal Navigations, Voyages, Traffiques and Discoveries of the English Nation*, ed. R. Hakluyt, 2 vols. in 1 (London, 1599)
Hardwicke State Papers	*Miscellaneous State Papers from 1501 to 1726*, ed. P. Yorke, 2nd Earl of Hardwicke, 2 vols. (London, 1778)
Harington	J. Harington, *Nugae Antiquae. Being a Miscellaneous Collection of Original Papers in Prose and Verse, Written . . . by Sir John Harington*, new edn, 3 vols. (London, 1792)
Harleian Miscellany	*The Harleian Miscellany, Or, A Collection of Scarce, Curious, and Entertaining Pamphlets and Tracts, as Well in Manuscript as in Print, Found in the Late Earl of Oxford's Library*, 2 vols. (London, 1808)
Harrison	*The Elizabethan Journals. Being a Record of the Things Most Talked of during the Years 1591–1603*, ed. G. B. Harrison, 3 vols. in 1 (London, 1938)
Hartley	*Proceedings in the Parliaments of Elizabeth I*, ed. T. E. Hartley, 3 vols. (Leicester, 1981–95)
Hatfield MSS	*Calendar of the Manuscripts of the Most Honourable the Marquis of Salisbury Preserved at Hatfield House*, 24 vols. (London, 1883–1976)
Haynes	*A Collection of State Papers . . . left by William Cecil, Lord Burghley*, ed. S. Haynes (London, 1740)
HEH	Henry E. Huntington Library, San Marino, California
HLQ	*Huntington Library Quarterly*

HMC	Historical Manuscripts Commission
HJ	*Historical Journal*
HR	*Historical Research*
JEH	*Journal of Ecclesiastical History*
JMH	*Journal of Modern History*
LASPF	List and Analysis of State Papers, Foreign, ed. R. B. Wernham, 7 vols. (1964–2000)
Lambeth	Lambeth Palace Library
Laughton	*State Papers Relating to the Defeat of the Spanish Armada, Anno 1588*, ed. J. K. Laughton, 2 vols. (London, 1894)
Lettenhove	*Relations Politiques des Pays-Bas et de l'Angleterre sous le Règne de Philippe II*, ed. K. de Lettenhove, 11 vols. (Brussels, 1882–1900)
Lettres de Henri IV	*Recueil des Lettres Missives de Henri IV*, ed. M. Berger de Xivrey and J. Guadet, 9 vols. (Paris, 1843–76)
Lodge	*Illustrations of British History, Biography and Manners . . . Exhibited in a Series of Original Papers Selected from the Manuscripts of the Noble Families of Howard, Talbot and Cecil*, ed. E. Lodge, 2nd edn, 3 vols. (London, 1838)
LQE	*The Letters of Queen Elizabeth*, ed. G. B. Harrison (London, 1935)
LQEJ	*Letters of Queen Elizabeth and King James VI of Scotland*, ed. J. Bruce, Camden Society, Old Series, 46 (1849)
LSP, James VI	*Letters and State Papers during the Reign of King James VI*, ed. J. Maidment (Edinburgh, 1838)
MS	Manuscript
Murdin	*A Collection of State Papers . . . left by William Cecil, Lord Burghley*, ed. W. Murdin (London, 1759)
Nichols	*The Progresses and Public Processions of Queen Elizabeth . . . Illustrated with Historical Notes*, ed. J. Nichols, new edn, 3 vols. (London, 1823)
NA	National Archives, London
ODNB	*The New Oxford Dictionary of National Biography*, ed. C. Matthew and B. Harrison, 60 vols. (Oxford, 2004) and http://www.oxforddnb.com/public/index.html
RO	Record Office
Rutland MSS	*The Manuscripts of His Grace the Duke of Rutland, Preserved at Belvoir Castle*, 4 vols. (London, 1888–1905)
RQ	*Renaissance Quarterly*
SCJ	*Sixteenth-Century Journal*
Secret Corr.	*The Secret Correspondence of Sir Robert Cecil with James VI, King of Scotland*, ed. D. Dalrymple (Edinburgh, 1766)
SHR	*Scottish Historical Review*
Spedding	*The Letters and the Life of Francis Bacon*, ed. J. Spedding, 7 vols. (London, 1861–74)
SR	*Statutes of the Realm*, ed. A. Luders, T. E. Tomlins and J. Caley, 11 vols. (London, 1810–28)
State Trials	*A Collection of State Trials and Proceedings for Treason and Other Crimes and Misdemeanours from the Reign of King Richard II to the Reign of King George II*, 3rd edn, 6 vols. (London, 1742)
Stow, 1592 edn	J. Stow, *The Annales of England* (London, 1592)
Stow, 1605 edn	J. Stow, *The Annales of England . . . Continued until This Present Year 1605* (London, 1605)
Stow, 1631 edn	*Annales, Or A General Chronicle of England, Continued and Augmented . . . unto the End of This Present Year 1631* (London, 1631)
Townshend	*Historical Collections, Or An Exact Account of the Proceedings of the Four Last Parliaments of Q[ueen] Elizabeth*, ed. H. Townshend (London, 1680).

TRHS	*Transactions of the Royal Historical Society*
TRP	*Tudor Royal Proclamations*, ed. P. Hughes and J. F. Larkin, 3 vols. (London, 1964–9)
Unton	*Correspondence of Sir Henry Unton, Knight, Ambassador from Queen Elizabeth to Henry IV, King of France in the Years 1591 and 1592*, ed. J. Stevenson (London, 1847)
Winwood	*Memorials of Affairs of State in the Reigns of Q[ueen] Elizabeth and K[ing] James I . . . from the Original Papers of the Right Honourable Sir Ralph Winwood*, ed. E. Sawyer, 2 vols. (London, 1725)
Wright	*Queen Elizabeth I and Her Times*, ed. T. Wright, 2 vols. (London, 1838)

Manuscripts preserved at NA are quoted by the call number there in use. The descriptions of the classes referred to are as follows:

C 76	Chancery, Treaty Rolls
E 112	Exchequer, King's Remembrancer, Bills, Answers, etc.
E 192	Exchequer, King's Remembrancer, Private Papers and Exhibits, Supplementary
E 351	Exchequer, Lord Treasurer's Remembrancer and Pipe Offices, Declared Accounts (Pipe Office)
KB 8	King's Bench (Crown Side), Bag of Secrets
LC 2	Lord Chamberlain's Department, Special Events
LC 5	Lord Chamberlain's Department, Miscellanea
PC 2	Privy Council, Registers
PROB 11	Prerogative Court of Canterbury, Registered Copy Wills
REQ 2	Court of Requests, Proceedings, Henry VII to Charles I
SO 3	Signet Office, Docquet Books
SP 11	State Papers, Domestic, Mary
SP 12	State Papers, Domestic, Elizabeth
SP 15	State Papers, Domestic, Addenda, Edward VI to James I
SP 46	State Papers, Supplementary
SP 52	State Papers, Scotland, Series I, Elizabeth I
SP 53	State Papers, Scotland, Series I, Mary, Queen of Scots
SP 59	State Papers, Scotland, Border Papers
SP 63	State Papers, Ireland, Elizabeth I to George III
SP 70	State Papers, Foreign, General Series, Elizabeth I
SP 77	State Papers, Foreign, Flanders
SP 78	State Papers, Foreign, France
SP 83	State Papers, Foreign, Holland and Flanders
SP 84	State Papers, Foreign, Holland
SP 94	State Papers, Foreign, Spain
SP 97	State Papers, Foreign, Turkey
SP 98	State Papers, Foreign, Tuscany
SP 99	State Papers, Foreign, Venice
SP 101	State Papers, Foreign, Newsletters
SP 102	State Papers, Foreign, Royal Letters
SP 103	State Papers, Foreign, Treaty Papers
STAC 5	Court of Star Chamber, Proceedings, Elizabeth I

Notes and References

Preface

1 Camden's debt to Burghley and Robert Cecil is from BL, Additional MS 36294, fo. 24. Burghley's role as the teenage Elizabeth's backstairs fixer is from J. Guy, *The Children of Henry VIII* (Oxford, 2013), pp. 136–7.

2 The criticisms expressed here are my own, but similar conclusions were reached by C. Haigh, 'Introduction', in *The Reign of Elizabeth I*, ed. C. Haigh (London, 1984), pp. 6–11. For the dates and circumstances of composition of Camden's *Annales*, see P. Collinson, 'One of Us? William Camden and the Making of History', *TRHS*, 6th Series, 8 (1998), pp. 151–63. For a discussion of the limitations of Camden's work, see P. Collinson, 'William Camden and the Anti-Myth of Elizabeth: Setting the Mould?', in *The Myth of Elizabeth*, ed. S. Doran and T. S. Freeman (London, 2003), pp. 79–93.

3 See, for instance, *Annales, Or, The History of the Most Renowned and Victorious Princesse Elizabeth*, trans. R. Norton (London, 1635), sig. b; P. Collinson, 'Elizabeth I and the Verdicts of History', *HR*, 76 (2003), p. 480.

4 L. Strachey, *Elizabeth and Essex* (London, 1928; repr. 1971), pp. 22–4.

5 V. Woolf, 'The Art of Biography', in *Selected Essays*, ed. D. Bradshaw (Oxford, 2008), pp. 116–23.

6 Strachey, *Elizabeth and Essex*, p. 11.

7 For an earlier attempt to advocate this line, see J. E. Neale, 'The Sayings of Queen Elizabeth', *History*, 10 (1925), pp. 212–33.

8 Only the State Papers, Domestic, are covered by the Victorian printed calendars for the last years of the reign. After July 1589, the State Papers, Foreign, cease to be calendared, and, instead, increasingly rudimentary, consolidated digests of documents cover the years until December 1596. Thereafter, nothing before 1603 is printed, leaving major sub-collections to be searched by trial and error, including State Papers, France, Spain, Holland, Germany, Italy, Portugal, Russia and Turkey. A significant quantity of Burghley's and Robert Cecil's correspondence now at Hatfield House for the years after 1583 is abstracted in HMC, *Hatfield MSS*, III–XIV, and some selected documents are printed in full by Murdin. However, large swathes of highly important papers in the BL, Cotton, Lansdowne, Harleian and Additional collections (to name but four) are not printed or calendared at all.

9 E 351/542–3. See also BL, Harleian MSS 1641–2. There is much more in the enrolled accounts than is apparent from Chambers, IV, pp. 77–116, which is concerned almost exclusively with performances of plays and entertainments. The itinerary and related data in M. H. Cole, *The Portable Queen: Elizabeth I and the Politics of Ceremony* (Amherst, MA, 1999), pp. 180–235, are chiefly derived from Chambers and flawed in several respects. See my review in *Albion*, 33 (2001), pp. 641–2.

Introduction: A Virgin Queen

1 *Letters of the Kings of England*, ed. J. O. Halliwell, 2 vols. (London, 1848), I, pp. 297–320; J. Guy, *A Daughter's Love: Thomas and Margaret More* (London, 2008), pp. 219–64.

2 J. Guy, *The Children of Henry VIII* (Oxford, 2013), p. 76.

3 G. R. Elton, *Policy and Police: The Enforcement of the Reformation in the Age of Thomas Cromwell* (Cambridge, 1972), pp. 176–7.

4 *Records of the Reformation: The Divorce, 1527–1533*, ed. N. Pocock, 2 vols. (Oxford, 1870), II, p. 386.

5 M. Levine, *Tudor Dynastic Problems, 1460–1571* (London, 1973), p. 74.

6 *Foedera*, XV, pp. 112–14.

7 *Foedera*, XV, pp. 110–17; 'The State of England AD 1600 by Thomas Wilson', ed. F. J. Fisher, *Camden Society*, 3rd Series, 52 (1936), pp. 8–9.

8 E. W. Ives, *Lady Jane Grey: A Tudor Mystery* (Oxford, 2009), pp. 137–68.

9 Inner Temple, London, Petyt MS 538, vol. 47, fo. 317.

10 G. Redworth, '"Matters Impertinent to Women": Male and Female Monarchy under Philip and Mary', *EHR*, 112 (1997), pp. 597–613.

11 J. M. Richards, 'Mary Tudor as "Sole Queen"? Gendering Tudor Monarchy', *HJ*, 40 (1997), pp. 895–924.

12 'The Count of Feria's Despatch to Philip II of 14 November 1558', ed. M. J. Rodríguez-Salgado and S. Adams, *Camden Society*, 4th Series, 29 (1984), p. 331.

13 C. Jordan, 'Women's Rule in Sixteenth-Century British Political Thought', *RQ*, 40 (1987), pp. 421–51; P. Collinson, 'The Monarchical Republic of Queen Elizabeth I', *Bulletin of the John Rylands Library of Manchester*, 69 (1987), pp. 394–424.

14 'It is not in England so dangerous a matter to have a woman ruler as men take it to be. For, first, it is *not she* that ruleth, but the laws, the executors whereof be her judges, appointed by her, her justices of the peace and such other officers . . . She maketh no statutes or laws but [in] the honourable court of Parliament . . . What may she do alone wherein is peril?': J. Aylmer, *An harborowe for faithfull and trewe subiectes* (London, 1559), sigs. B2v, G3, H3v.

15 P. E. J. Hammer, '"Absolute and Sovereign Mistress of Her Grace"? Queen Elizabeth I and Her Favourites, 1581–92', in *The World of the Favourite*, ed. J. H. Elliott and L. W. B. Brockliss (London, 1999), p. 40.

16 BL, Additional MS 35830, fos. 158–9; *Hardwicke State Papers*, I, p. 174.

17 Northamptonshire RO, Fitzwilliam of Milton MSS, Political MS 102 (unfoliated).

18 BL, Cotton MS, Julius F.VI, fos. 167–9v; BL, Additional MS 48035, fos. 141–6v; S. Alford, *Burghley: William Cecil at the Court of Elizabeth I* (London, 2008), pp. 90–94; Guy, *Children of Henry VIII*, pp. 179–83. That the committee both existed and met has been proved by Simon Adams, 'Elizabeth I's Former Tutor Reports on the Parliament of 1559', *EHR*, 128 (2013), pp. 43–7. Although not intrinsically Calvinist, since Elizabeth insisted on retaining bishops, traditional dress for the clergy and a number of the rites and ceremonies that her father had still cherished after he broke with Rome, the 1559 Settlement – theologically, at least – had Calvinist leanings unwelcome to the queen.

19 BL, Lansdowne MS 102, fo. 1; BL, Lansdowne MS 103, fo. 3; Alford, *Burghley*, pp. 110–11.

20 *Hardwicke State Papers*, I, p. 167.

21 S. Doran, 'Elizabeth I's Religion', *JEH*, 51 (2000), pp. 711–12; R. Bowers, 'The Chapel Royal, the First Edwardian Prayer Book and Elizabeth's Settlement of Religion, 1559', *HJ*, 43 (2000), pp. 320–21; P. Collinson, *Elizabethan Essays* (London, 1994), pp. 87–118; Guy, *Children of Henry VIII*, pp. 134, 137–8, 152, 161, 167, 174, 179–85.

22 S. Alford, *The Early Elizabethan Polity: William Cecil and the British Succession Crisis, 1558–1569* (Cambridge, 1998), pp. 97–119, 142–57, 225–32; M. Taviner, 'Robert Beale and the

Elizabethan Polity', University of St Andrews Ph.D. (2000), pp. 56–60; Alford, *Burghley*, pp. 124–38.

23 BL, Cotton MS, Cotton Charter IV.38 (2); CP 138/163; HMC, *Hatfield MSS*, XIII, pp. 214–15.

24 For a description of the Privy Chamber at Hampton Court, see *The Diary of Baron Waldstein*, ed. G. W. Groos (London, 1981), p. 151; *Paul Henztner's Travels in England during the Reign of Queen Elizabeth*, ed. H. Walpole (London, 1797), pp. 56–8; G. von Bülow and W. Powell, 'Diary of the Journey of Philip Julius, Duke of Stettin-Pomerania, through England in the Year 1602', *TRHS*, New Series, 6 (1982), p. 55.

25 S. Thurley, *The Royal Palaces of Tudor England* (London, 1993), pp. 135–43; S. Thurley, *Whitehall Palace* (London, 1999), pp. 37–64.

26 A. Johnson, 'William Paget and the Late-Henrician Polity, 1543–1547', University of St Andrews Ph.D. (2003), pp. 36–41.

27 *The English Court: From the Wars of the Roses to the Civil War*, ed. D. Starkey (London, 1987), pp. 71–118.

28 J. H. Astington, *English Court Theatre, 1558–1642* (Cambridge, 1999), pp. 96–110, 161–9.

29 LC 2/4/3, fos. 53v–63; LC 2/4/4, fos. 45–7; BL, Lansdowne MS 3, fo. 191; BL, Lansdowne MS 29, fo. 161; BL, Lansdowne MS 34, fo. 76; BL, Lansdowne MS 59, fo. 43; *The English Court*, ed. Starkey, pp. 147–72; C. Merton, 'The Women Who Served Queen Mary and Queen Elizabeth: Ladies, Gentlewomen and Maids of the Privy Chamber, 1553–1603', University of Cambridge Ph.D. (1992); J. Arnold, *Queen Elizabeth's Wardrobe Unlock'd* (Leeds, 1988), pp. 99–104; A. Whitelock, *Elizabeth's Bedfellows: An Intimate History of the Queen's Court* (London, 2013), pp. 17–29.

30 *Relations Politiques de la France et de l'Espagne avec l'Écosse au XVIe siècle*, ed. A. Teulet, 5 vols. (Paris, 1862), II, p. 203.

31 For lists of names and fees of the queen's musicians as well as special one-off payments to visitors, see E 351/541–3, *passim*. For Elizabeth's own account of her credentials as a dancer and love of the Italian style of dancing, see de Maisse, p. 95. For Lucretia de Tedeschi, alias di Conti, who was paid from Michaelmas 1568 onwards, see SP 12/287, no. 64.

32 Nichols, I, pp. xxxvi–xxxvii, 118–19.

33 'Journey through England and Scotland made by Lupold von Wedel in the Years 1584 and 1585', ed. G. von Bülow, *TRHS*, 2nd Series, 9 (1895), pp. 223–70; *Diary of Baron Waldstein*, pp. 59, 147, 159–63; *Thomas Platter's Travels in England, 1599*, ed. C. Williams (London, 1937), pp. 192–7, 200–202; *Report on the Pepys Manuscripts Preserved at Magdalene College, Cambridge*, ed. E. K. Purnell (London, 1911), p. 190; E 351/541 (entries from Mich. 1571–2); E 351/542 (entries from Mich. 1591–2, 1592–3, 1593–4, 1595–6); E 351/543 (entries from Mich. 1596–7, 1597–8); SP 12/287, no. 64; W. Nagel, *Annalen der englischen Hofmusik: von der Zeit Heinrichs VIII, bis zum Tode Karls I* (Leipzig, 1894), p. 29; *Elizabeth I*, ed. G. Ziegler (Washington DC, 2003), p. 88.

34 BL, Egerton MS, 2806, fo. 70; Arnold, *Queen Elizabeth's Wardrobe Unlock'd*, pp. 104–108; C. C. Stopes, 'Elizabeth's Fools and Dwarfs', *The Athenaeum*, no. 4477 (16 Aug., 1913), p. 160; Whitelock, *Elizabeth's Bedfellows*, pp. 84–7; I. H. Habib, *Black Lives in the English Archives, 1500–1677: Imprints of the Invisible* (Aldershot, 2008), pp. 72–3. I remain to be convinced that 'Thomasina' was a black African female, as some scholars assert. I am grateful to Dr Miranda Kaufmann for drawing my attention to the growing numbers of black servants in Tudor England.

35 Arnold, *Queen Elizabeth's Wardrobe Unlock'd*, pp. 139–41; Whitelock, *Elizabeth's Bedfellows*, pp. 24–7.

36 HMC, *Bath MSS*, IV, p. 186.

37 Arnold, *Queen Elizabeth's Wardrobe Unlock'd*, p. 110.

38 That privacy came at a cost would be discovered by King Henry III of France. In 1584, tired of being constantly badgered by a steady stream of petitioners and competing religious factions, he modelled his Court on Elizabeth's and withdrew to his inner cab-

inet, or study, where he isolated himself from reality until he was finally assassinated. See *CSPF*, 1584–5, pp. 184–5; M. Chatenet, *La Cour de France au XVIe siècle* (Paris, 2002), pp. 139–40, 147–54.

39 N. Mears, *Queenship and Political Discourse in the Elizabethan Realms* (Cambridge, 2005), pp. 40–66; N. Mears, 'Politics in the Elizabethan Privy Chamber: Lady Mary Sidney and Kat Ashley', in *Women and Politics in Early Modern England, 1450–1700*, ed. J. Daybell (Aldershot, 2004), pp. 67–82.

40 Haynes, p. 602.

41 For example, SP 52/10, nos. 62–3.

42 For example, SP 12/17, no. 1; *Hardwicke State Papers*, I, pp. 180–86.

43 Harington, II, pp. 316–17.

44 For example, SP 52/8, nos. 70 (Burghley's draft); BL, Cotton MS, Caligula B.X, fos. 261–2v (final version as sent). SP 52/12, no. 20 (Burghley's draft); SP 52/12, no. 19 (final version as sent).

45 *CSPSp, 2nd Series*, 1558–67, p. 669.

46 *Correspondence of Matthew Parker, DD*, ed. J. Bruce and T. Thomason Perowne (Cambridge, 1853), p. 223. My thanks to Stephen Alford for this reference.

47 Collins, I, pp. 7–8; HMC, *De L'Isle and Dudley MSS*, II, p. 2.

48 My tally includes letters now preserved only as drafts or office copies but which are annotated on the back as 'written with her own hand' or 'of her own hand' (see, for example, SP 78/36, fos. 8–9v; SP 52/51, no. 75). R. Allinson has a higher total of 3,000 letters written by the queen, but this includes letters merely signed 'E.R.', not all of which may have been personally dictated. See R. Allinson, *A Monarchy of Letters: Royal Correspondence and English Diplomacy in the Reign of Elizabeth I* (New York, 2012), p. xii.

49 For example, SP 52/8, nos. 53–5 (drafts with amendments); BL, Cotton MS, Caligula B.X, fos. 218–19 (final version as sent). On one notorious occasion, Elizabeth and Burghley issued rival instructions to Sir Nicholas Throckmorton. See SP 52/13, nos. 81, 83 (Elizabeth's as dictated to Burghley); SP 52/14, no. 1 (Burghley's own memo to Throckmorton).

50 Sotheby's sale of 15 July 2014, lot 403.

51 *CSPSp, 1st Series*, 1554, pp. 166–7.

52 Guy, *Children of Henry VIII*, pp. 154–61; 'The Count of Feria's Despatch', ed. Rodríguez-Salgado and Adams, p. 342, n. 31.

53 M. T. Crane, '*Video et Taceo*: Elizabeth I and the Rhetoric of Counsel', *Studies in English Literature*, 28 (1988), pp. 1–15; F. Teague, 'Elizabeth I: Queen of England', in *Women Writers of the Renaissance and Reformation*, ed. K. M. Wilson (Athens, GA, 1987), p. 522.

54 Key recent writings include *The Reign of Elizabeth I: Court and Culture in the Last Decade*, ed. J. Guy (Cambridge, 1995); P. Hammer, *Elizabeth's Wars* (London, 2003); *Doubtful and Dangerous: The Question of Succession in Late-Elizabethan England*, ed. S. Doran and P. Kewes (Manchester, 2014); A. Gajda, 'Political Culture in the 1590s: The "Second Reign" of Elizabeth I', *History Compass*, 8 (2010), pp. 88–100.

55 S. Doran, 'Juno versus Diana: The Treatment of Elizabeth's Marriage in Plays and Entertainments, 1561–1581', *HJ*, 38 (1995), pp. 257–74.

56 H. Hackett, *Virgin Mother, Maiden Queen* (London, 1995), pp. 96–8, 119–23, 177–8, 186–91.

Chapter 1: A City in Fear

1 *The Order of My Lord Mayor, the Aldermen and the Sheriffes* (London, 1629), pp. 7–8.

2 I. W. Archer, *ODNB*, s.v. 'Sir John Spencer'.

3 S. Rappaport, *Worlds within Worlds: Structures of Life in Sixteenth-Century London* (Cambridge, 1989), pp. 54–60.

4 Camden, pp. 134–5; T. Norton, *To the Quenes Maiesties Poore Deceived Subjectes of the North Countrey* (London, 1569), sig. A5v–6; *A Treatise of Treasons against Q. Elizabeth and the Croune of England* (London, [1571–2]), *passim*; C. Sharp, *The Rising in the North: The 1569 Rebellion* (Shotton, 1975; new edn), *passim*; K. Kesselring, 'Rebellion and Disorder' in *The Elizabethan World*, ed. S. Doran and N. Jones (London, 2011), pp. 381–3.

5 *ECW*, pp. 125–6; S. Doran, 'The Political Career of Thomas Radcliffe, 3rd Earl of Sussex, 1526?–1583', University of London Ph.D. (1977), pp. 243–309.

6 SP 12/48, no. 61.

7 G. Parker, 'The Place of Tudor England in the Messianic Vision of Philip II of Spain', *TRHS*, 6th Series, 12 (2000), pp. 167–221.

8 D. MacCulloch, *Thomas Cranmer: A Life* (London, 1996), Appendix 2, pp. 637–8.

9 J. Guy, *'My Heart is My Own': The Life of Mary Queen of Scots* (London, 2004), pp. 134–352.

10 Guy, *'My Heart is My Own'*, pp. 437–97.

11 SP 11/6, fos. 25–31; SP 11/14, fos. 47–55; *CSPD Mary*, nos. 229–35. See also BL, Cotton MS, Titus B.II, fos. 114–16; Parker, 'Messianic Vision of Philip II', pp. 192–5.

12 *SR*, IV, i, pp. 526–8; Parker, 'Messianic Vision of Philip II', pp. 187–220.

13 Guy, *'My Heart is My Own'*, pp. 467–9.

14 BL, Cotton MS, Vespasian F.VI, fo. 64.

15 Guy, *'My Heart is My Own'*, pp. 149–69.

16 'Lethington's Account of Negotiations with Elizabeth in September and October 1561', in *A Letter from Mary Queen of Scots to the Duke of Guise, January 1562*, ed. J. H. Pollen (Edinburgh, 1904), Appendix 1, p. 39.

17 SP 52/10, no 62; BL, Cotton MS, Caligula B.X, fos. 301–5.

18 Guy, *Children of Henry VIII*, pp. 161, 167; R. Harkins, 'Elizabethan Puritanism and the Politics of Memory in Post-Marian England', *HJ*, 57 (2014), pp. 899–919.

19 G. D. Ramsay, *The End of the Antwerp Mart: The Queen's Merchants and the Revolt of the Netherlands*, 2 vols. (London, 1975–86), II, pp. 51–3.

20 Guy, *Children of Henry VIII*, pp. 155–75.

21 S. Doran, *Monarchy and Matrimony: The Courtships of Elizabeth I* (London, 1966), pp. 22–5; H. Kamen, *Philip of Spain* (London, 1997), p. 72.

22 SP 77/1, no. 37; Lettenhove, VIII, pp. 157–62; Lodge, II, pp. 135–7; S. Adams, 'Elizabeth I and the Sovereignty of the Netherlands, 1576–1585', *TRHS*, 14 (2004), pp. 309–17.

23 Doran, *Monarchy and Matrimony*, pp. 130–94.

24 The old idea, derived chiefly from Camden's *Annales*, that Burghley and Walsingham pursued dramatically different policies on the Netherlands is not borne out by the evidence.

25 Lettenhove, X, pp. 518–22, 533, 558–64, 567–80.

26 Philip claimed the Portuguese throne on the death of the gravely ill Cardinal Henry, who in 1578 had succeeded his nephew, the young Sebastian I, after he was killed fighting the Ottoman Turks at the battle of Alcazar-el-Kebir in Morocco.

27 Ellis, 1st Series, III, p. 52; Doran, *Monarchy and Matrimony*, pp. 154–94.

28 *CSPSp*, 2nd Series, 1580–86, pp. 226–7.

29 *Les Mémoires de M. le Duc de Nevers*, ed. Le Sieur de Gomberville, 2 vols. (Paris, 1665), I, pp. 552–3.

30 Camden, p. 268; *CSPV*, 1581–91, pp. 23–4; *Mémoires de M. le Duc de Nevers*, I, p. 552.

31 G. Parker, *The Army of Flanders and the Spanish Road, 1567–1659* (Cambridge, 1972), pp. 239–41.

32 *Foedera*, XV, p. 792.

33 *CSPF*, 1583 and Addenda, pp. 20–22; HMC, *Hatfield MSS*, III, no. 29; W. T. MacCaffrey, *Queen Elizabeth and the Making of Policy, 1572–1588* (Princeton, 1981), pp. 283–5, 300–301.

34 SP 12/163, nos. 4, 21–3, 28, 47, 48, 53, 55; KB 8/45; Stow, 1592 edn, pp. 1189–90; S. Alford, *The Watchers: A Secret History of the Reign of Elizabeth I* (London, 2012), pp. 134–5.

35 S. Carroll, *Martyrs and Murderers: The Guise Family and the Making of Europe* (Oxford, 2009), pp. 242–55; Alford, *The Watchers*, pp. 45–92, 152–66.

36 C. Read, *Mr Secretary Walsingham and the Policy of Queen Elizabeth*, 3 vols. (Oxford, 1925), II, pp. 381–6.

37 SP 12/163, no. 65; SP 12/171, no. 86; *Harleian Miscellany*, III, pp. 190–200; J. Bossy, *Under the Molehill: An Elizabethan Spy Story* (London, 2001), pp. 65–124.

38 *CSPSp, 2nd Series*, 1580–6, pp. 513–14.

39 *CSPF*, 1583–4, nos. 647–8.

40 SP 78/12, no. 1; *Marie Stuart et Catherine de Médicis*, ed. A. Chéruel (Geneva, 1975), p. 328; 'Journey through England and Scotland made by Lupold von Wedel in the Years 1584 and 1585', ed. G. von Bülow, *TRHS*, 2nd Series, 9 (1895), p. 262.

41 E. Saulnier, *Le Rôle Politique du Cardinal de Bourbon, 1523–1590* (Paris, 1912), pp. 103–25; M. P. Holt, *The French Wars of Religion, 1562–1629* (Cambridge, 2005; 2nd edn), pp. 123–6.

42 *Harleian Miscellany*, III, p. 200–201.

43 SP 12/168, no. 1; SP 12/190, no. 44; Stow, 1592 edn, pp. 1190–91.

44 Expelled from England by Edward I in 1290 when their houses were sold and goods and debts confiscated by the Crown, Jews had been allowed back by Henry VIII in the 1530s, when he broke with Rome.

45 SP 12/173, nos. 25, 47, 47 (I); *Chamber Accounts of the Sixteenth Century*, ed. B. Masters (London: London Record Society, 1984), nos. 77, 83, 227; D. Lasocki and R. Prior, *The Bassanos: Venetian Musicians and Instrument Makers in England, 1531–1665* (Aldershot, 1995), pp. 78, 243–4.

46 Chamberlain, pp. 50, 109.

47 SP 12/173, nos. 25, 47, 47 (I).

48 Walsingham's letter is lost, but its contents can be worked out from Spencer's reply, SP 12/173, no. 47.

49 The location of the Court can be tracked in E 351/542 (entries from Mich. 1584–5); Lodge, II, pp. 246–7.

50 E 351/541 (entries for 1572).

51 SP 12/173, no. 47.

52 SP 12/173, no. 47.

53 STAC 5/H6/1, STAC 5/H10/21, STAC 5/H33/23, STAC 5/H38/10, STAC 5/H41/6.

54 E 351/542 (entries for 1584).

Chapter 2: Crisis and Betrayal

1 *CSPF*, 1584–5, p. 79.

2 SP 83/23, no. 28; SP 12/173, no. 65.

3 SP 12/173, no. 94.

4 E 351/542, m. 66v.

5 SP 84/1, no. 56; S. Adams, 'Elizabeth I and the Sovereignty of the Netherlands, 1576–1585', *TRHS*, 14 (2004), pp. 317–19; S. Adams, 'The Decision to Intervene: England and the United Provinces, 1584–1585', in *Europa y la monarquía católica: Congreso Internacional "Felipe II (1598–1998), Europa dividida, la monarquía católica de Felipe II" (Universidad Autónoma de Madrid, 20–23 abril 1998)'*, ed. José Martínez Millán, 3 vols. (Madrid, 1998), I, pp. 19–31.

6 BL, Lansdowne MS 43, fos. 127–8; *Household Accounts and Disbursement Books of Robert Dudley, Earl of Leicester, 1558–61, 1584–86*, ed. S. Adams, Camden Society, 5th Series, 6 (1995), p. 228; Camden, pp. 306–308; J. Bossy, *Under the Molehill: An Elizabethan Spy Story* (London, 2001), pp. 96–9, 132–4; S. Alford, *The Watchers: A Secret History of the Reign of Elizabeth I* (London, 2012), pp. 139–92.

7 BL, Harleian MS 285, fos. 123–5; BL, Harleian MS 168, fos. 102–5; SP 84/1, no. 61; Adams, 'The Decision to Intervene: England and the United Provinces, 1584–1585', pp. 19–31.

8 Adams, 'The Decision to Intervene: England and the United Provinces, 1584–1585', pp. 23–4. For the misleading claims, see C. Read, *Lord Burghley and Queen Elizabeth* (London, 1965), pp. 311–15. The confusing passage is Camden, pp. 319–21.

9 SP 103/33, no. 82; BL, Harleian MS 285, fos. 196–7v.

10 Hakluyt, II, pp. 112–14; S. Adams, 'The Outbreak of the Elizabethan Naval War', in *England, Spain and the Gran Armada, 1585–1604*, ed. M. J. Rodríguez-Salgado and S. Adams (Edinburgh, 1991), p. 45.

11 T. Stocker, *A Tragicall Historie of the Troubles and Civile Warres of the Lowe Countries* (London, 1583), sig. a.iiiv.

12 BNF, MS FF 15970, fo. 14; S. Adams, *Leicester and the Court: Elizabethan Essays* (Manchester, 2002), p. 139.

13 J. Guy, *The Children of Henry VIII* (Oxford, 2013), pp. 98–101.

14 S. Adams, *ODNB*, s.v. 'Mary Sidney'. Geoffrey Fenton, later Secretary of State for Ireland, dedicated his translation of the Italian novellas of Matteo Bandelli to Mary under the title *Certaine Tragicall Discourses written oute of Frenche and Latin* in 1567, and William Painter dedicated the first volume of his rival collection under the title *The Palace of Pleasure* to her brother Ambrose Dudley, Earl of Warwick, in 1566. In 1579, Fenton dedicated his final and most ambitious work, an English translation of Guicciardini's *Storia d'Italia*, to Elizabeth.

15 SP 12/159, no. 1; BL, Lansdowne MS 18, fo. 74; A. Riehl, *The Face of Queenship: Early Modern Representations of Elizabeth I* (New York, 2010), p. 55.

16 A. Bryson, '"The Speciall Men in Every Shere". The Edwardian Regime, 1547–1553', University of St Andrews Ph.D. (2001), p. 198.

17 'The Count of Feria's Despatch to Philip II of 14 November 1558', ed. M. J. Rodríguez-Salgado and S. Adams, *Camden Society*, 4th Series, 29 (1984), p. 316.

18 SP 70/5, fos. 183–4.

19 *CSPSp, 2nd Series*, 1558–67, pp. 57–8, 263.

20 'A "Journal" of Matters of State Happened from Time to Time . . . until the Year 1562', in *Religion, Politics and Society in Sixteenth-Century England*, ed. S. Adams and G. W. Bernard, *Camden Society*, 5th Series, 22 (2003), p. 66.

21 C. Skidmore, *Death and the Virgin* (London, 2010), pp. 203–306, 377–8.

22 Hartley, I, pp. 44–5.

23 Camden, p. 27.

24 Hartley, I, p. 45.

25 Hartley, I, pp. 146–7, 472–3.

26 Haynes, p. 99.

27 Haynes, p. 99.

28 Haynes, pp. 89–90; Guy, *Children of Henry VIII*, pp. 117–23.

29 Lord Herbert of Cherbury, *The Life and Reign of King Henry the Eighth* (London, 1682), pp. 410–12.

30 S. Doran, *Monarchy and Matrimony: The Courtships of Elizabeth I* (London, 1966), pp. 195–218. See also N. Mears, 'Counsel, Public Debate, and Queenship: John Stubbe's *The Discoverie of a Gaping Gulf*, 1579', *HJ*, 44 (2001), pp. 629–50; Guy, *Children of Henry VIII*, pp. 49, 114–15, 186–93.

31 SP 78/5, nos. 123–9; *CSPSp, 2nd Series*, 1580–86, nos. 173, 186.

32 BNF, MS FF 15970, fo.14r–v; Adams, *Leicester and the Court*, p. 139.

33 J. Harington, *A Tract on the Succession to the Crown*, ed. C. R. Markham (London, 1880), p. 40.

34 BNF, MS FF 15970, fo.14r–v.

35 Adams, *Leicester and the Court*, pp. 139–40.

36 E. Goldring, 'Portraiture, Patronage and the Progresses: Robert Dudley, Earl of Leices-

ter and the Kenilworth Festivities of 1575', in *The Progresses, Pageants and Entertainments of Queen Elizabeth I*, ed. J. E. Archer, E. Goldring and S. Knight (Oxford, 2007), p. 164.

37 LC 2/4/3, fo. 52v.

38 'A Letter from Robert, Earl of Leicester, to a Lady', ed. C. Read, *HLQ*, 9 (1936), pp. 15–26.

39 HMC, *Bath MSS*, V, pp. 205–206; LC 2/4/3, fo. 53v.

40 SP 12/148, no. 24; S. Adams, *ODNB*, s.v. 'Douglas Sheffield'; S. Adams, *ODNB*, s.v. 'Dorothy Stafford'.

41 Adams, *ODNB*, s.v. 'Lettice Knollys'.

42 Camden, p. 227.

43 Camden, pp. 232–3.

44 Adams, *ODNB*, s.v. 'Robert Dudley', citing Kent History and Library Centre, MS U1475/L2/4, item 3.

45 'The Letter of Estate', ed. D. C. Peck, *Notes and Queries*, 28 (1981), p. 30.

46 *CSPSp, 2nd Series, 1580–86*, p. 477.

47 HMC, *Bath MSS*, V, p. 44.

48 SP 12/172, no. 37.

49 SP 12/29, no. 61; Adams, *ODNB*, s.v. 'Robert Dudley'.

50 S. Adams, '"The Queenes Majestie . . . is now become a great huntress": Elizabeth I and the Chase', *Court Historian*, 18 (2013), pp. 158–60.

51 Walsingham's letter is lost, but the contents can be inferred from Leicester's reply, see BL, Harleian MS 285, fo. 131; for the full sequence of events, see *Household Accounts . . . of Robert Dudley*, ed. Adams, Appendix II.

52 SP 12/182, no. 1.

53 SP 12/182, no. 24.

54 BL, Harleian MS, 285, fos. 196–7v; *Household Accounts . . . of Robert Dudley*, ed. Adams, Appendix II; *Correspondence of Robert Dudley, Earl of Leicester, during his Government of the Low Countries, in the Years 1585 and 1586*, ed. J. Bruce, Camden Society, Old Series, 27 (1844), pp. 20, 57–63, 166, 238–9; W. T. MacCaffrey, *Queen Elizabeth and the Making of Policy, 1572–1588* (Princeton, 1981), pp. 352–74.

55 *Correspondence of Robert Dudley, Earl of Leicester*, ed. Bruce, pp. 12–15, 63.

56 For a good example of Elizabeth's use of Heneage for a second opinion and its consequences, see Haynes, p. 602.

57 BL, Cotton MS, Galba C.VIII, fo. 27v; *Correspondence of Robert Dudley, Earl of Leicester*, ed. Bruce, p. 110.

58 BL, Cotton MS, Galba C.VIII, fos. 22–6; SP 84/6, no. 110.

59 *Correspondence of Robert Dudley, Earl of Leicester*, ed. Bruce, p. 112.

60 *Correspondence of Robert Dudley, Earl of Leicester*, ed. Bruce, pp. 209–11.

61 Camden, p. 328.

62 *CSPF, 1585–6*, pp. 527, 570, 628, 674–5; *CSPF, 1586–7* (Pt. 2), pp. 3–4, 45, 57, 143–4, 202–5.

63 SP 84/9, no. 112.

64 SP 77/1, no. 93 (fos. 199–200), and the draft at no. 94 (fos. 205–206). The translation of this passage in *LQE*, pp. 176–8, is fanciful.

65 See *EAC*, no. 1; Guy, *Children of Henry VIII*, pp. 111, 113, 139, 178.

66 BL, Cotton MS, Galba C.IX, fo. 200; printed in *LQE*, pp. 175–6.

67 SP 84/9, no. 38; Adams, *Leicester and the Court*, pp. 147–8.

68 *CSPF, 1586–7*, pp. 164–5, 168, 202.

69 Camden, p. 330; Adams, *ODNB*, s.v. 'Robert Dudley'.

70 SP 12/198, no. 19.

Chapter 3: Brave New World

1 Ralegh's 'blackamore' is from *Household Accounts and Disbursement Books of Robert Dudley, Earl of Leicester, 1558–61, 1584–86*, ed. S. Adams, Camden Society, 5th Series, 6 (1995), pp. 178, 210.

2 *CSPSp, 2nd Series*, 1580–86, p. 501.

3 'Journey through England and Scotland made by Lupold von Wedel in the Years 1584 and 1585', ed. G. von Bülow, *TRHS*, 2nd Series, 9 (1895), pp. 250–55; J. Arnold, *Queen Elizabeth's Wardrobe Unlock'd* (Leeds, 1988), p. 6.

4 H. Nicolas, *Memoirs of the Life and Times of Christopher Hatton, K.G.* (London, 1847), pp. 16–30; Murdin, p. 588.

5 *Correspondence of Robert Dudley, Earl of Leicester, during his Government of the Low Countries, in the Years 1585 and 1586*, ed. J. Bruce, Camden Society, Old Series, 27 (1844), p. 113.

6 *CKJVI*, p. 18; A. L. Rowse, *Ralegh and the Throckmortons* (London, 1962), pp. 175–8.

7 J. Guy, *The Children of Henry VIII* (Oxford, 2013), pp. 98–100, 109, 111, 117–22, 137–8, 155, 166, 169–71, 178, 189; C. Merton, *ODNB*, s.v. 'Katherine Astley [née Champernowne]'.

8 Haynes, p. 100.

9 R. Rapple, *Martial Power and Elizabethan Political Culture* (Cambridge, 2009), pp. 51–85, 82–4.

10 SP 63/80, no. 82.

11 R. Rapple, *ODNB*, s.v. 'Sir Humphrey Gilbert'.

12 P. E. J. Hammer, '"Absolute and Sovereign Mistress of Her Grace"? Queen Elizabeth I and Her Favourites, 1581–92', in *The World of the Favourite*, ed. J. H. Elliott and L. W. B. Brockliss (London, 1999), p. 43.

13 H. Nicolas, *Memoirs of the Life and Times of Christopher Hatton, K.G.* (London, 1847), pp. 275–8.

14 *APC*, XI, pp. 384, 388–9, 421; SP 12/219, no. 33; Hammer, '"Absolute and Sovereign Mistress of Her Grace"?', p. 46.

15 Hakluyt, III, pp. 4–5.

16 E. T. Jones, 'Alwyin Ruddock: "John Cabot and the Discovery of America", *HR*, 81 (2008), pp. 224–54.

17 Hakluyt, I, pp. 231–2.

18 Hakluyt, I, pp. 232–3, 245–6; *CSPV*, 1555–6, no. 269.

19 Hakluyt, I, pp. 246–7.

20 Hakluyt, III, pp. 135–7; M. Nicholls and P. Williams, *Sir Walter Ralegh in Life and Legend* (London, 2011), pp. 12–13; K. R. Andrews, *Trade, Plunder and Settlement* (Cambridge, 1984), pp. 187–90.

21 Hakluyt, III, pp. 143–54; J. LeHuenen, 'The Role of the Basque, Breton and Norman Cod Fishermen in the Discovery of North America from the 16th to the End of the 18th Century', *Arctic*, 37 (1984), pp. 520–27.

22 Hakluyt, III, p. 154.

23 G. Parry, *The Arch-Conjurer of England: John Dee* (London, 2011), pp. 41, 84–6, 88–90, 111.

24 Hakluyt, III, pp. 151–61; Andrews, *Trade, Plunder and Settlement*, pp. 193–7.

25 Hakluyt, III, pp. 243–5.

26 *The Letters of Sir Walter Ralegh*, ed. A. Latham and J. Youings (Exeter, 1999), p. xliii and nos. 6, 8, 14.

27 SP 12/169, nos. 36–7; *CSPC, America and West Indies*, Addenda 1574–1674, pp. 24–5; Hakluyt, III, pp. 135–7, 243–5.

28 D. B. Quinn, 'Preparations for the 1585 Virginia Voyage', *William and Mary Quarterly*, 9 (1949), pp. 209–10.

29 C. Read, *Mr Secretary Walsingham and the Policy of Queen Elizabeth*, 3 vols. (Oxford, 1925), III, pp. 370–71.

30 A. Thevet, *The New-Found Worlde or Antarctike*, trans. T. Hacket (London, 1580), sig. *ij–*iijv; R. Kuin, 'Sir Philip Sidney and the New World', *Renaissance Quarterly*, 51 (1998), pp. 149–85.

31 Read, *Walsingham*, III, pp. 400–404; Kuin, 'Sir Philip Sidney and the New World', pp. 572–5; *CSPSp, 2nd Series*, 1580–86, pp. 384–5; *CSPC, America and West Indies*, Addenda 1574–1674, pp. 22–3.

32 *CSPSp, 2nd Series*, 1580–86, pp. 384–5.

33 Read, *Walsingham*, III, pp. 404–10.

34 J. W. Shirley, *Thomas Harriot* (Oxford, 1983), pp. 60, 80; P. Honan, *Christopher Marlowe, Poet and Spy* (Oxford, 2005), pp. 235–7.

35 *CSPC, East Indies, China and Japan*, 1513–1616, nos. 31, 35, 37, 42.

36 SP 12/167, no. 7; SP 12/170, no. 1; *The Original Writings and Correspondence of the Two Richard Hakluyts*, ed. E. G. R. Taylor, *Hakluyt Society*, 2nd Series, 76, 77 (1935), I, pp. 1–66; R. Hakluyt, *Divers Voyages touching the Discoverie of America* (London, 1582), sig. ¶–¶4.

37 Kuin, 'Sir Philip Sidney and the New World', p. 575.

38 SP 12/167, no. 7.

39 D. H. Sacks, 'Discourses of Western Planting: Richard Hakluyt and the Making of the Atlantic World', in *The Atlantic World and Virginia, 1550–1624*, ed. P. C. Mancall (Chapel Hill, 2007), pp. 410–53.

40 *Household Accounts . . . of Robert Dudley*, ed. Adams, pp. 180–81.

41 *Original Writings . . . of the Two Richard Hakluyts*, I, pp. 33–4.

42 D. H. Sacks, 'Cosmography's Promise and Richard Hakluyt's World', *Early American Literature*, 44 (2009), pp. 161–78.

43 *Original Writings . . . of the Two Richard Hakluyts*, II, pp. 214–18.

44 *Original Writings . . . of the Two Richard Hakluyts*, II, pp. 257–65; 'Discourses of Western Planting', pp. 426–7. See also M. Guasco, '"Free from the Tyrannous Spaniard?": Englishmen and Africans in Spain's Atlantic World', *Slavery and Abolition*, 29 (2008), pp. 1–22.

45 For example, *The Spanish Colonie* (London, 1583), sig. A3v–4; *Original Writings . . . of the Two Richard Hakluyts*, II, p. 261. My thanks to David Sacks for this information.

46 *Original Writings . . . of the Two Richard Hakluyts*, II, pp. 218–39, 268–73; 'Discourses of Western Planting', pp. 423–7.

47 *Original Writings . . . of the Two Richard Hakluyts*, II, pp. 239–46; 'Discourses of Western Planting', pp. 420–21.

48 *Original Writings . . . of the Two Richard Hakluyts*, II, pp. 283–9.

49 *Original Writings . . . of the Two Richard Hakluyts*, II, pp. 287, 289.

50 *Original Writings . . . of the Two Richard Hakluyts*, I, p. 34.

51 'Journey through England and Scotland', ed. von Bülow, p. 251.

52 Hakluyt, III, pp. 246–51; A. T. Vaughan, *ODNB*, s.v. 'American Indians in England'.

53 *Original Writings . . . of the Two Richard Hakluyts*, II, pp. 313–26; Quinn, 'Preparations', pp. 214–18.

54 *Original Writings . . . of the Two Richard Hakluyts*, I, p. 39.

55 *Original Writings . . . of the Two Richard Hakluyts*, I, p. 34.

56 Quinn, 'Preparations', pp. 231–2; Chambers, IV, pp. 101, 160; Rowse, *Ralegh and the Throckmortons*, p. 142.

57 *CSPSp, 2nd Series*, 1580–86, p. 532.

58 Quinn, 'Preparations', pp. 232–3.

59 Hakluyt, III, pp. 251–62; *The Roanoke Voyages, 1584–1590: Documents to Illustrate the English Voyages to North America under the Patent Granted to Walter Ralegh in 1584*, Hakluyt Society, ed. D. B. Quinn, 2nd Series, 104–5 (1955), I, pp. 158–99.

60 Hakluyt, III, pp. 263–6; *The Roanoke Voyages*, ed. Quinn, I, pp. 200–313; Andrews, *Trade, Plunder and Settlement*, pp. 207–11; Nicholls and Williams, *Sir Walter Ralegh*, pp. 45–70.

Chapter 4: Armada of the Soul

1 SP 12/174, no. 1.

2 SP 12/173, no. 85; see also Lodge, II, pp. 250–52.

3 SP 12/176, nos. 22, 28–31; CP 205/128; CP 210/17; HEH, Ellesmere MS. 1192, annotated and corrected by Burghley; BL, Additional MS 48027, fos. 248–51v; J. E. Neale, *Elizabeth I and Her Parliaments*, 2 vols. (London, 1969), II, pp. 44–57; G. R. Elton, *The Parliament of England, 1559–1581* (Cambridge, 1986), p. 362; P. Collinson, 'The Monarchical Republic of Queen Elizabeth I', *Bulletin of the John Rylands Library of Manchester*, 69 (1987), pp. 394–424; P. Collinson, 'The Elizabethan Exclusion Crisis', *Proceedings of the British Academy*, 84 (1993), pp. 51–92.

4 *SR*, IV, i, pp. 704–5.

5 Sotheby's sale of 7 Dec. 2010, lot 11. My warmest thanks to Dr Gabriel Heaton of the Books and MSS department for allowing me to see this astonishing cache of letters and documents in advance of the auction.

6 Sotheby's sale of 7 Dec. 2010, lot 11.

7 Sotheby's sale of 7 Dec. 2010, lot 11.

8 Sotheby's sale of 7 Dec. 2010, lot 11.

9 SP 11/4, no. 2; *ECW*, pp. 41–2; J. Guy, *The Children of Henry VIII* (Oxford, 2013), p. 156.

10 Sotheby's sale of 7 Dec. 2010, lot 11.

11 Sotheby's sale of 7 Dec. 2010, lot 11.

12 S. Alford, *The Watchers: A Secret History of the Reign of Elizabeth I* (London, 2012), pp. 193–209.

13 SP 53/18, no. 55.

14 Alford, *The Watchers*, pp. 210–32.

15 *CSPSp, 2nd Series*, 1580–86, p. 623; Alford, *The Watchers*, pp. 232–4; J. Guy, *'My Heart is My Own': The Life of Mary Queen of Scots* (London, 2004), pp. 490–91.

16 Murdin, p. 785.

17 *Hamlet*, 4, v, l. 138.

18 The proceedings at Fotheringhay and in the Star Chamber are from BL, Additional MS 48027, fos. 492–510, 540–54, 557v–68; BL, Cotton MS, Caligula C.IX, fos. 477–95; *State Trials*, I, pp. 143–64; HMC, *Hatfield MSS*, III, pp. 208–9; Alford, *The Watchers*, pp. 236–40; Guy, *'My Heart is My Own'*, pp. 487–94.

19 SP 12/195, no. 64.

20 SP 12/197, no. 5; E 351/542 (entries for 1588).

21 SP 12/194, no. 30.

22 *The Fugger News-Letters*, ed. V. von Klarwill, 2nd Series (London, 1926), nos. 155–8.

23 SP 12/197, nos. 6–7, 10, 15–18, 21–3; SP 15/30, nos. 2–6; Murdin, pp. 578–83.

24 For Burghley's early drafts envisaging either a public execution or an assassination under the terms of the Bond, see Murdin, pp. 574–5, 576–7. Copies of the final version of the warrant are from BL, Additional MS 48027, fos. 645–6; Lambeth, Fairhurst MS 4769.

25 The reports of the clandestine Council meeting, dispatch of the warrant and Davison's trial in the Star Chamber are from BL, Harleian MS 290, fos. 218–40; BL, Additional MS 48027, fos. 398–403, 636–50v, 666–90v; M. Taviner, 'Robert Beale and the Elizabethan Polity', University of St Andrews Ph.D. (2000), pp. 215–43.

26 BL, Additional MS 48027, fos. 639v–40; *The Letter-Books of Sir Amyas Paulet*, ed. J. Morris (London, 1874), pp. 359–62; Taviner, 'Robert Beale', pp. 210, 217–18.

27 Lambeth, Fairhurst MS 4267, fo. 19.

28 J. Harington, *A Tract on the Succession to the Crown*, ed. C. R. Markham (London, 1880), p. 41; Adams, *ODNB*, s.v. 'Dorothy Stafford'.

29 Ellis, 2nd Series, III, p. 117.

30 *Memoirs of Robert Carey, Earl of Monmouth* (Edinburgh, 1808), p. 116; Taviner, 'Robert Beale', p. 221.

31 Taviner, 'Robert Beale', p. 222.

32 CP 164/10; CP 164/15; Taviner, 'Robert Beale', pp. 224–5.

33 BL, Additional MS 48027, fo. 637v.

34 BL, Additional MS 48116, fos. 151–2; Taviner, 'Robert Beale', p. 227.

35 *CSPSM*, 1586–8, pp. 346–55; Taviner, 'Robert Beale', pp. 229–36.

36 SP 53/21, no. 27; *CSPSM*, 1586–8, pp. 343–4; Taviner, 'Robert Beale', pp. 228–9; Burghley continued to cast the blame on Davison in a second examination: BL, Additional MS 48027, fo. 702.

37 R. B. Wernham, 'The Disgrace of William Davison', *EHR*, 46 (1931), pp. 632–6.

38 Murdin, p. 786; J. Summerson, 'The Building of Theobalds, 1564–1585', *Archaeologia*, 97 (1959), pp. 107–26.

39 SP 12/202, no. 1; C. Read, *Lord Burghley and Queen Elizabeth* (London, 1965), pp. 377–9; S. Alford, *Burghley: William Cecil at the Court of Elizabeth I* (London, 2008), pp. 294–5, 297.

40 BL, Cotton MS, Caligula C.IX, fo. 212; *ECW*, pp. 296–7.

41 *Memoirs of Robert Carey*, pp. 12–13.

42 BL, Cotton MS, Caligula C.IX, fo. 212.

Chapter 5: No Warrior Queen

1 *CSPSp, 2nd Series*, 1580–86, no. 442; *CSPSp, 2nd Series*, 1587–1603, nos. 15, 60, 157.

2 HMC, *Hatfield MSS*, III, p. 70.

3 *Foedera*, XV, pp. 803–7.

4 *EAC*, pp. 57–67; J. Guy, *'My Heart is My Own': The Life of Mary Queen of Scots* (London, 2004), pp. 472–6.

5 *CSPSp, 2nd Series*, 1587–1603, nos. 17, 65, 115, 117. See also M. J. Rodríguez-Salgado, 'The Anglo-Spanish War: The Final Episode in the Wars of the Roses?', in *England, Spain and the Gran Armada, 1585–1604*, ed. M. J. Rodríguez-Salgado and S. Adams (Edinburgh, 1991), pp. 1–32.

6 The documents are printed, but the identification of 'Julio' and his aliases, along with the scale of his espionage, was overlooked until 1996. See *CSPSp, 2nd Series*, 1587–1603, pp. 118, 124, 133–4, 139–40, 142–3, 147, 148–9, 159–60, 173, 176, 178–9, 183, 189, 192, 194, 196–8, 209, 213–14, 223, 228–9, 230, 255–8, 261, 272, 278, 297, 303, 305, 314, 319–20, 352, 356, 369. For his aliases as 'the new confidant' or 'the new informant', see *CSPSp, 2nd Series*, 1587–1603, nos. 26, 47, 50, 62, 64–5, 85–7, 100, 420, 430. For his alias as 'the new friend', see *CSPSp, 2nd Series*, 1587–1603, nos. 71, 82, 90, 98, 109, 111, 121, 124, 260. His role and multiple identities were clinched by M. Leimon and G. Parker, 'Treason and Plot in Elizabethan Diplomacy: The "Fame of Sir Edward Stafford" Reconsidered', *EHR*, 111 (1996), pp. 1134–58.

7 The delay may be accounted for in part by the fact that these secret dispatches were among a large number of Spanish diplomatic documents carted off from the archives in Simancas to Paris in 1810 on Napoleon's orders during the Peninsular War. The greater part was returned in 1816, but a substantial section retained until 1941, when it was returned on Adolf Hitler's orders as part of his efforts to persuade General Franco to enter the Second World War on the side of the Axis Powers.

8 SP 78/17, no. 57.

9 SP 12/200, nos. 1, 2, 17.

10 SP 12/200, no. 17.

11 AGR, T 109/587/2 (a large unfoliated bundle of documents).

12 G. Parry, *The Arch-Conjurer of England: John Dee* (London, 2011), pp. 31–3, 48–50, 107–13.

13 AGR, T 109/587/2. For the iconography of Elizabeth as a peace-maker, see H. Hackett, 'A New Image of Elizabeth I: The Three Goddesses Theme', *HLQ*, 77 (2014), pp. 225–56.

14 SP 12/201, no. 15; SP 12/203, nos. 34, 37; *CSPSp, 2nd Series, 1587–1603*, no. 173.

15 *CSPSp, 2nd Series, 1587–1603*, no. 132.

16 SP 77/1, nos. 118, 126a (fos. 261–4); *CSPF, 1586–7*, pp. 388–90, 396–9, 435–7; *CSPF, 1586–8*, pp. 323, 335–7, 369–70.

17 S. Adams, 'Elizabeth I's Former Tutor Reports on the Parliament of 1559', *EHR*, 128 (2013), p. 37.

18 *CSPF, 1586–8*, pp. 385, 411; *CSPF, 1586–7*, pp. 388–90, 396–99, 435–7; *CSPF, 1587*, pp. 358–61, 375–6, 398, 466–7, 472–82; Camden, p. 407.

19 SP 77/1, fo. 354v.

20 SP 84/19, fo. 34.

21 *CSPSp, 2nd Series, 1587–1603*, no. 198.

22 E 351/542 (entries from Mich. 1587–8). The play, based on the ancient myth of Endymion and Diana, or Cynthia, the moon goddess of chastity, was printed in 1591; J. H. Astington, *English Court Theatre, 1558–1642* (Cambridge, 1999), pp. 196–7, 233.

23 *CSPF, 1588*, pp. 49–50.

24 SP 77/4, fos. 89–96; BL, Cotton MS, Vespasian C.VIII, fos. 18–21, 117–32; *CSPF, 1588*, pp. 25, 40, 43–6, 59, 98–9, 103–4, 128–131, 134, 144, 145–7, 173–4, 178–9, 190–91, 192–5, 206–7, 211–12, 220–21, 222–4, 229–30, 239–44, 239–46, 256–60, 261–4, 266–7, 324, 371, 376, 386–7, 403, 418–19, 423–4, 471–4, 485–8; Camden, pp. 407–10.

25 *CSPSp, 2nd Series, 1587–1603*, no. 283; Leimon and Parker, 'Treason and Plot', pp. 1149–50.

26 AGR, T 109/587/2.

27 *CSPSp, 2nd Series, 1587–1603*, no. 219; G. Parker and C. Martin, *The Spanish Armada* (London, 1992), pp. 114–32.

28 G. Parker, 'Queen Elizabeth's Instructions to Admiral Howard, 20 December 1587', *Mariner's Mirror*, 94 (2008), pp. 202–8.

29 *CSPSp, 2nd Series, 1568–79*, no. 564; S. Adams, *ODNB*, s.v. 'Katherine Howard, née Carey, Countess of Nottingham'; K. Bundesen, '"No Other Faction but My Own": Dynastic Politics and Elizabeth I's Carey Cousins', University of Nottingham Ph.D. (2008), p. 194.

30 Parker, 'Queen Elizabeth's Instructions', pp. 206–7.

31 *CSPSp, 2nd Series, 1587–1603*, no. 322.

32 R. Mulcahy, *Philip II, Patron of the Arts* (Dublin, 2004), pp. 632–4.

33 Laughton, I, pp. 159, 167–9, 179–80; Parker and Martin, *Spanish Armada*, pp. 30–32.

34 BL, Harleian MS 6994, fo. 120, printed by Laughton, I, pp. 150–51; the movements of Elizabeth and the Court are from E 351/542 (entries for March and April 1588).

35 Laughton, I, p. 285.

36 SP 12/212, no. 79; SP 12/213, no. 9.

37 N. A. Younger, 'War and the Counties: The Elizabethan Lord Lieutenancy, 1585–1603', University of Birmingham Ph.D. (2006), pp. 92–113; H. M. Colvin, *A History of the King's Works*, IV, Pt. 2 (London, 1982), pp. 410, 602–4.

38 *CSPSp, 2nd Series, 1587–1603*, no. 375.

39 SP 12/212, no. 80.

40 Camden, pp. 410–12; G. Parker, A. Mitchell and L. Bell, 'Anatomy of Defeat: The Testimony of Juan Martínez de Recalde and Don Alonso Martínez de Leyva on the Failure of the Spanish Armada in 1588', *Mariner's Mirror*, 90 (2004), p. 316; *Armada*, ed. M. J. Rodríguez-Salgado (London, 1988), pp. 233–8.

41 *CSPSp, 2nd Series, 1587–1603*, no. 396. For the chains, see nos. 182, 423.

42 Camden, pp. 412–14; Parker, Mitchell and Bell, 'Anatomy of Defeat', p. 316; *Armada*, ed. Rodríguez-Salgado, pp. 238–40.

43 N. A. M. Rodger, *The Safeguard of the Sea, 660–1649* (London, 1997), pp. 268–9.

44 Camden, pp. 414–15; *Armada*, ed. Rodríguez-Salgado, pp. 240–41.

45 Camden, pp. 415–16; *CSPSp, 2nd Series*, 1587–1603, nos. 451–2, 476, 478, 483; Parker, Mitchell and Bell, 'Anatomy of Defeat', pp. 316–17; *Armada*, ed. Rodríguez-Salgado, pp. 241–2, 263.

46 SP 12/213, no. 46; M. Christy, 'Queen Elizabeth's Visit to Tilbury in 1588', *EHR*, 34 (1919), pp. 43–61.

47 SP 12/214, no. 34; Christy, 'Queen Elizabeth's Visit', p. 47.

48 The sources are fully described and discussed in Christy, 'Queen Elizabeth's Visit', pp. 43–61; S. Frye, 'The Myth of Elizabeth at Tilbury', *SCJ*, 23 (1992), pp. 95–114; J. M. Green, 'I My Self: Elizabeth I's Oration at Tilbury Camp', *SCJ*, 28 (1997), pp. 421–45. Burghley's account (printed pseudonymously) is *The Copie of a Letter sent out of England to Don Bernardin Mendoza* (London, 1588), pp. 21–3. The arrangements at Ardern Hall are from E 351/542 (entries for August 1588). Frye's critique is undermined by her confusion between the Julian and Gregorian calendars. She gives 14 August as the date on which the interrogation of Don Pedro de Valdéz began, so claiming it post-dates the queen's visit to the camp, whereas it is correctly 4 August (Old Style), four days before the queen set out for Tilbury. See SP 12/214, nos. 21–2; Nichols, II, pp. 535–7.

49 D. Edwards, *ODNB*, s.v. 'Thomas Butler, 10th Earl of Ormond'.

50 *CSPSp, 2nd Series*, 1587–1603, nos. 430, 438, 457, 466.

51 J. E. Neale, *Elizabeth I and Her Parliaments*, 2 vols. (London, 1969), II, pp. 392–3, 427–31. There are especially good grounds for thinking that a fair copy of the queen's script for her closing speech in the 1601 Parliament is BL, Cotton Titus C.VI, fos. 410–11. See also below, chapter 21, for a discussion of the process by which the queen's 1601 speech to a parliamentary delegation on monopolies was composed.

52 For the variant versions of the speech, see the sources discussed in the papers by Christy, Frye and Green cited above. Sharpe's handwritten copy is from BL, Harleian MS 6798, fos. 87–8v.

53 BL, Harleian MS, 6798, fo. 87.

54 BL, Harleian MS 6798, fo. 87v.

55 *Isocrates*, ed. G. Norlin, 3 vols. (London, 1928), I, pp. 52–3; *ECW*, pp. 41, 95; J. Guy, *The Children of Henry VIII* (Oxford, 2013), pp. 139, 155–6, 191.

56 'The Count of Feria's Despatch to Philip II of 14 November 1558', ed. M. J. Rodríguez-Salgado and S. Adams, *Camden Society*, 4th Series, 29 (1984), p. 331.

57 *The Copie of a Letter*, p. 22.

58 *Memoirs of Robert Carey, Earl of Monmouth* (Edinburgh, 1808), p. 19.

59 SP 12/214, no. 50. The delivery is from BL, Harleian MS 6994, fo. 136, printed in Laughton, II, p. 69.

60 SP 12/214, no. 47.

Chapter 6: A Funeral and a Wedding

1 The queen's movements can be worked out from E 351/542 (entries from Mich. 1587–8, 1588–9).

2 *CSPSp, 2nd Series*, 1587–1603, no. 423.

3 SP 12/215, no. 65.

4 Folger MS, Additional 1006; *Elizabeth I*, ed. G. Ziegler (Washington DC, 2003), pp. 67–8.

5 SP 12/215, no. 65.

6 Wright, II, p. 393.

7 *Household Accounts and Disbursement Books of Robert Dudley, Earl of Leicester, 1558–61, 1584–86*, ed. S. Adams, *Camden Society*, 5th Series, 6 (1995), pp. 448–59; *A Brief Description*

of the Collegiate Church and Choir of St Mary in the Borough of Warwick (Warwick, 1763), pp. 61–4.

8 E 123/17, fo. 142.

9 C. L. Kingsford, 'Essex House, Formerly Leicester House and Exeter Inn', *Archaeologia*, 73 (1923), pp. 1–54.

10 P. E. J. Hammer, *The Polarisation of Elizabethan Politics: The Political Career of Robert Devereux, 2nd Earl of Essex, 1585–1597* (Cambridge, 1999), p. 130.

11 Hammer, *Polarisation of Elizabethan Politics*, pp. 34–5; Adams, *ODNB*, s.v. 'Lettice Knollys'.

12 *CSPSp, 2nd Series*, 1587–1603, nos. 432, 470.

13 *CSPSM*, 1586–8, no. 513.

14 E 351/542 (entries for 1588–9).

15 E 351/3223–5; E 351/542 (entries from Mich. 1588–9).

16 SP 12/218, no. 38; Stow, 1592 edn, pp. 1281–2; R. Strong, 'Elizabethan Pageantry as Propaganda', Courtauld Institute Ph.D. (1962), pp. 56–8.

17 Stow, 1592 edn, p. 1282; Camden, p. 418; Nichols, II, pp. 537–42; *National Prayers: Special Worship since the Reformation*, ed. N. Mears, A. Raffe, S. Taylor and P. Williamson, Church of England Record Society, 20 (2013), pp. 182–4.

18 Folger MS, L.a.39; Devereux, I, p. 186; HMC, *Bath MSS*, V, p. 216; P. E. J. Hammer, '"Absolute and Sovereign Mistress of Her Grace"? Queen Elizabeth I and Her Favourites, 1581–92', in *The World of the Favourite*, ed. J. H. Elliott and L. W. B. Brockliss (London, 1999), p. 46.

19 Devereux, I, pp. 187–8.

20 Hammer, *Polarisation of Elizabethan Politics*, pp. 13–75.

21 Camden, p. 417; National Maritime Museum, Coins and Medals, A6, B8.

22 The prime versions of the portrait are at Woburn Abbey, the National Portrait Gallery, London (NPG 541), and in the Tyrwhitt-Drake private collection. It is likely that, originally, the Tyrwhitt-Drake version was the master copy, but this can no longer be verified as it was heavily overpainted in the seventeenth century. See also J. Arnold, *Queen Elizabeth's Wardrobe Unlock'd* (Leeds, 1988), pp. 33–6; R. Strong, *The English Icon: Elizabethan and Jacobean Portraiture* (London, 1969), pp. 16, 182.

23 For the queen's true appearance, see the contemporary description in *England as Seen by Foreigners in the Days of Elizabeth and James the First*, ed. W. B. Rye (London, 1865), pp. 104–5. The shape of the nose in the engraving of the queen by Jan Rutlinger, *c*.1580–85, captures this description exactly.

24 SP 12/31, no. 25 (quotation from stamped fo. 46).

25 R. Strong, *Portraits of Queen Elizabeth I* (London, 1963), pp. 7–8, 17–22.

26 N. Hilliard, 'A Treatise Concerning the Arte of Limning', *Walpole Society*, I (1912), pp. 28–9.

27 SP 12/31, no. 25.

28 Camden, p. 418.

29 Laughton, I, pp. 284–5.

30 Laughton, II, pp. 96–7.

31 Laughton, II, p. 183.

32 Laughton, II, p. 138.

33 *CSPSp, 2nd Series*, 1587–1603, no. 562.

34 *CSPSp, 2nd Series*, 1587–1603, nos. 553, 554, 566, 574, 597, 598, 607; G. Parker, *The Army of Flanders and the Spanish Road, 1567–1659* (Cambridge, 1972), pp. 180–94.

35 SP 12/228, nos. 9, 10, 17, 22, 23; SP 12/229, no. 21.

36 *CSPSM*, 1586–8, nos. 384, 460, 545, 553, 554, 558, 570, 589.

37 J. Guy, *'My Heart is My Own': The Life of Mary Queen of Scots* (London, 2004), pp. 185–203.

38 *CSPF*, 1586–8, p. 369.

39 *CSPSM*, 1586–8, no. 602.

40 *CSPSM*, 1586–8, nos. 387, 407, 478, 568.

41 Only through an accord with Denmark could Scottish merchant ships pass freely through the narrow Øresund to and from the ports of the Baltic Sea, since the Danes claimed the right to levy a toll on every foreign ship that took this route, sending costs soaring.

42 *CSPSM*, 1586–8, nos. 384, 460, 584, 589.

43 *CSPSM*, 1586–8, no. 593.

44 J. D. Mackie, 'The Secret Diplomacy of King James VI in Italy Prior to His Accession to the English Throne', *SHR*, 21 (1924), pp. 267–82.

45 *CSPSM*, 1586–8, nos. 589, 593; *CSPSM*, 1589–93, no. 3.

46 *CSPSM*, 1589–93, no. 3.

47 SP 78/19, fos. 199–202v.

48 *CSPSM*, 1589–93, nos. 107, 115, 161, 163.

49 *CSPSM*, 1589–93, no. 160.

50 D. Stevenson, *Scotland's Last Royal Wedding: The Marriage of James VI and Anne of Denmark* (Edinburgh, 1997), pp. 1–16, 24–33.

51 *CSPSM*, 1589–93, no. 162.

52 *CSPSM*, 1589–93, no. 183.

53 BL, Cotton MS, Caligula D.I, fo. 363; *CSPSM*, 1589–93, no. 181.

54 *CSPSM*, 1589–93, no. 19.

55 *CSPSM*, 1589–93, no. 187.

56 *CSPSM*, 1589–93, nos. 113, 114, 226.

57 *CSPSM*, 1589–93, no. 160.

58 *LQEJ*, pp. 55–6.

59 Stevenson, *Scotland's Last Royal Wedding*, pp. 30–56.

60 D. Moysie, *Memoirs of the Affairs of Scotland, 1577–1603*, ed. J. Dennistoun, *Bannatyne Club*, 39 (1830), p. 81; *CSPSM*, 1589–93, nos. 261, 289–305.

61 *LQEJ*, pp. 57–9.

62 Stevenson, *Scotland's Last Royal Wedding*, pp. 30–56.

63 SP 52/45, no. 27.

64 SP 52/45, no. 54.

65 SP 52/45, no. 70.

Chapter 7: On the Attack

1 P. E. J. Hammer, *The Polarisation of Elizabethan Politics: The Political Career of Robert Devereux, 2nd Earl of Essex, 1585–1597* (Cambridge, 1999), p. 30.

2 Murdin, p. 588.

3 SP 12/219, no. 33; see also a garbled report in *CSPSp, 2nd Series, 1587–1603*, p. 504.

4 BL, Lansdowne MS 96, fo. 69; Hammer, *Polarisation of Elizabethan Politics*, p. 85.

5 P. E. J. Hammer, '"Absolute and Sovereign Mistress of Her Grace"? Queen Elizabeth I and Her Favourites, 1581–92', in *The World of the Favourite*, ed. J. H. Elliott and L. W. B. Brockliss (London, 1999), p. 49.

6 Hammer, *Polarisation of Elizabethan Politics*, pp. 72, 77.

7 Murdin, pp. 634–5.

8 Laughton, II, p. 167; R. B. Wernham, *After the Armada: Elizabethan England and the Struggle for Western Europe, 1588–1595* (Oxford, 1984), pp. 11–15.

9 SP 12/222, no. 89. See SP 12/224, no. 53 for a reprise of the final, consolidated aims of the expedition. Burghley's role was central by 23 December 1588; SP 12/219, no. 37. Wernham, *After the Armada*, pp. 15–21, 92–9.

10 SP 12/219, nos. 37, 45.

11 SP 12/222, no. 89.
12 Hammer, *Polarisation of Elizabethan Politics*, pp. 82–3.
13 Wernham, *After the Armada*, pp. 101–2.
14 Devereux, I, pp. 204–5.
15 SP 12/224, no. 10.
16 SP 12/224, no. 6.
17 SP 12/223, no. 64.
18 Lodge, II, pp. 359–66; Camden, pp. 429–30; Wernham, *After the Armada*, pp. 108–10.
19 Lodge, II, pp. 379–82; Camden, pp. 431–3; Hakluyt, II, ii, pp. 134–43; Devereux, I, pp. 198–204; G. B. Harrison, *The Life and Death of Robert Devereux, Earl of Essex* (London, 1937), pp. 36–44; Wernham, *After the Armada*, pp. 107–30.
20 Wernham, *After the Armada*, p. 114.
21 Murdin, p. 790.
22 Hakluyt, II, ii, p. 149.
23 H. Wotton, *A Parallel between Robert, Late Earl of Essex, and George, Late Duke of Buckingham* (London, 1641), pp. 2–3; Hammer, *Polarisation of Elizabethan Politics*, pp. 88–9.
24 Camden, p. 433.
25 Wotton, *A Parallel*, p. 3.
26 BL, Harleian MS 6845, fo. 100, is the key document, but it does not seem to me to prove that Ralegh sailed with Drake and Norris, as opposed to contributing ships and men; C. E. Mounts, 'The Ralegh–Essex Rivalry and *Mother Hubberd's Tale*', *Modern Language Notes*, 65 (1950), pp. 509–13.
27 Mounts, 'The Ralegh–Essex Rivalry', pp. 509–13.
28 Birch, *Memoirs*, I, p. 56.
29 *The Letters of Sir Walter Ralegh*, ed. A. Latham and J. Youings (Exeter, 1999), no. 33.
30 *Letters of Sir Walter Ralegh*, ed. Latham and Youings, no. 33.
31 Birch, *Memoirs*, I, p. 57.
32 Lodge, II, p. 352.
33 Lodge, II, p. 386.
34 Lodge, II, pp. 417, 422.
35 Hammer, *Polarisation of Elizabethan Politics*, pp. 95–6, 319–20.
36 SP 12/240, no. 17.
37 Hammer, *Polarisation of Elizabethan Politics*, pp. 95–6.
38 BL, Cotton MS, Galba D.I, fo. 248; *CSPSM*, 1586–8, no. 434.
39 BL, Harleian MS 6994, fo. 189.
40 SP 12/231, no. 62.
41 PROB 11/75, fo. 262v; BL, Lansdowne MS 96, fo. 69.
42 SP 12/239, no. 70.
43 Murdin, pp. 636–40; Hammer, *Polarisation of Elizabethan Politics*, pp. 91–2.
44 'Letters from Sir Robert Cecil to Sir Christopher Hatton, 1590–1591', ed. P. E. J. Hammer, *Camden Society*, 5th Series, 22 (2003), pp. 210–11; Hammer, *Polarisation of Elizabethan Politics*, pp. 101–2.
45 *LASPF*, 1589–90, pp. 245–55, 320–27; Camden, p. 436; Birch, *Hist. View*, p. 2; Wernham, *After the Armada*, pp. 131–57.
46 *LASPF*, 1589–90, pp. 257–78; Camden, pp. 436–7; Wernham, *After the Armada*, pp. 159–80.
47 *LASPF*, 1590–91, pp. 232–58, 297–311; Lodge, II, p. 423; Camden, pp. 442–4; Wernham, *After the Armada*, pp. 181–206.
48 *Recueil des lettres missives de Henri IV*, ed. B. de Xivrey, 9 vols. (Paris, 1843–58), II, p. 390.
49 *LASPF*, 1590–91, p. 296.
50 Lodge, II, p. 422; E 351/542 (entries from Mich. 1590–91); Wernham, *After the Armada*, pp. 265–6.
51 Lodge, II, pp. 419–20; Hammer, *Polarisation of Elizabethan Politics*, pp. 96–7.
52 Lodge, II, pp. 419–20; W. Segar, *Honor, Military and Civill, Contained in Four Books* (London, 1602), p. 197.

53 *The Poems of Sir Walter Ralegh*, ed. A. Latham (London, 1951), p. 11; R. Strong, 'Elizabethan Pageantry as Propaganda', Courtauld Institute Ph.D. (1962), pp. 122–4.

54 Lodge, II, pp. 418–19.

55 Lodge, II, p. 422–3; Devereux, I, pp. 211–12.

56 Lodge, II, p. 422.

57 Lodge, II, p. 433.

58 *LASPF*, 1590–91, pp. 297–316; Wernham, *After the Armada*, pp. 262–91.

59 *LASPF*, 1590–91, pp. 323–5.

60 *LASPF*, 1590–91, pp. 327–9; Camden, pp. 448–9, where the initiative is wrongly attributed to Henry IV. Henry made a similar proposal in September 1590, but it was not then pursued. See H. A. Lloyd, *The Rouen Campaign* (Oxford, 1973), pp. 37–8, 63–77.

61 The essential work here has been done by Hammer, *Polarisation of Elizabethan Politics*, pp. 97–104, to whom I am much indebted.

62 *LASPF*, 1591–2, p. 324.

63 Harrison, *Life and Death of Robert Devereux*, p. 47; Devereux, I, p. 215.

64 Hammer, *Polarisation of Elizabethan Politics*, pp. 98–9, 102–4.

65 Murdin, p. 796; Devereux, I, pp. 215–17.

66 SP 78/25, fos. 81–4; Unton, pp. 1–4.

67 Murdin, p. 797; SP 78/25, fos. 70–74.

68 SP 78/25, fo. 94; *LASPF*, 1591–2, p. 327; *LQE*, pp. 209–10.

69 SP 78/25, fo. 105.

70 SP 78/26, fo. 278.

Chapter 8: The Visible Queen

1 R. Strong, 'Elizabethan Pageantry as Propaganda', Courtauld Institute Ph.D. (1962), p. 123.

2 The description of the 'Ditchley Portrait' is from R. Strong, *Artists of the Tudor Court* (London, 1983), p. 124.

3 Strong, 'Elizabethan Pageantry', pp. 125–30; H. Hackett, *Virgin Mother, Maiden Queen* (London, 1995), pp. 144–54.

4 R. Strong, *Portraits of Queen Elizabeth I* (London, 1963), pp. 17, 66–9, and plates 9–10; F. A. Yates, *Astraea: The Imperial Theme in the Sixteenth Century* (London, 1975), pp. 112–17; *Dynasties: Painting in Tudor and Jacobean England, 1530–1630*, ed. K. Hearn (London, 1995), nos. 40, 100.

5 W. Segar, *Honor, Military and Civill, Contained in Four Books* (London, 1602), pp. 197–200; G. Peele, *Polyhymnia* (London, 1590), sig. B3v–B4v; Strong, 'Elizabethan Pageantry', p. 126.

6 Strong, 'Elizabethan Pageantry', pp. 125–30.

7 According to the Duke of Newcastle's advice to Charles II after the Restoration in 1660, the purpose of Elizabethan-style progresses was so that 'Your Majesty will do all you can to please your people both great and small, and to caress the great that hath power in their several counties.' 'Caress', however, also had an ironic meaning: to cajole or even perhaps intimidate, as well as to treat affectionately. See *A Catalogue of Letters and Other Historical Documents Exhibited in the Library at Welbeck*, ed. S. A. Strong (London, 1903), p. 226.

8 Some relevant detail can be found in M. H. Cole, *The Portable Queen: Elizabeth I and the Politics of Ceremony* (Amherst, MA, 1999), pp. 40–46. But the book is riddled with confusion about the nature and purpose of royal progresses.

9 H. Nicolas, *Memoirs of the Life and Times of Christopher Hatton, K.G.* (London, 1847), pp. 125–6, 155–6, 333–4.

10 J. Smyth, *The Berkeley Manuscripts: The Lives of the Berkeleys . . . in the County of Gloucester from 1066 to 1618*, ed. J. MacLean (3 vols., Gloucester, 1883–5), II, pp. 337–8, 378–9; L. Stone, *Family and Fortune: Studies in Aristocratic Finance in the Sixteenth and Seventeenth Centuries* (Oxford, 1973), p. 248. In Elizabeth's favour is that, on being afterwards informed of Dudley's malice towards him, she sent Lord Berkeley 'a secret, friendly advertisement', the closest thing to an apology to which she ever put her name.

11 J. Summerson, 'The Building of Theobalds, 1564–1585', *Archaeologia*, 97 (1959), pp. 107–26; S. Alford, *Burghley: William Cecil at the Court of Elizabeth I* (London, 2008), pp. 300–302.

12 T. Martyn, *Elizabeth in the Garden* (London, 2008), pp. 154–84.

13 Summerson, 'The Building of Theobalds', pp. 122–3. Further details of the pageant may be found in Bond, I, pp. 417–19; B. R. Smith, 'Landscape with Figures: The Three Realms of Queen Elizabeth's Country-House Revels', in *Renaissance Drama*, New Series, 8 (1977), pp. 78–9; G. Heaton, 'Elizabethan Entertainments in Manuscript: The Harefield Festivities (1602) and the Dynamics of Exchange', in *The Progresses, Pageants and Entertainments of Queen Elizabeth I*, ed. J. E. Archer, E. Goldring and S. Knight (Oxford, 2007), pp. 229–31.

14 J. Clapham, *Certain Observations Concerning the Life and Reign of Queen Elizabeth*, ed. E. P. Read and C. Read (Philadelphia, 1951), p. 81.

15 Nichols, III, p. 19. Brooke's mother was another veteran of the Court. Attending Elizabeth at regular intervals from 1558 until 1592, and with special responsibilities for the queen's choice of clothes, she was one of only a handful of confidantes known to be able to speak frankly to her: she had offered to intercede with the queen when Elizabeth had shut out Burghley in the anxious weeks after the execution of Mary Queen of Scots. See BL, Lansdowne MS 18, fo. 73; BL, Lansdowne MS 29, fo. 161; BL, Lansdowne MS 34, fo. 76; BL, Lansdowne MS 59, fo. 43; J. Arnold, *Queen Elizabeth's Wardrobe Unlock'd* (Leeds, 1988), p. 104; Alford, *Burghley*, pp. 311–13.

16 BL, Egerton MS 2623, fos. 15–16; J. P. Collier, *The History of English Dramatic Poetry to the Time of Shakespeare* (3 vols., London, 1879), I, pp. 276–8; Nichols, III, pp. 74–5; J. M. Sutton, 'The Retiring Patron: William Cecil and the Cultivation of Retirement, 1590–98', in *Patronage, Culture and Power: The Early Cecils*, ed. P. Croft (London, 2002), pp. 159–79; Alford, *Burghley*, pp. 312–13.

17 *Annals of the Reformation*, ed. J. Strype (4 vols., London, 1824), IV, pp. 108–109; SP 12/238, no. 159.

18 Nichols, III, pp. 76–8.

19 Nichols, III, pp. 81–4.

20 Murdin, p. 797; 'Letters from Sir Robert Cecil to Sir Christopher Hatton, 1590–1591', ed. P. E. J. Hammer, *Camden Society*, 5th Series, 22 (2003), p. 204.

21 Unton, p. 16; P. E. J. Hammer, *The Polarisation of Elizabethan Politics: The Political Career of Robert Devereux, 2nd Earl of Essex, 1585–1597* (Cambridge, 1999), p. 102.

22 M. C. Questier, *Catholicism and Community in Early Modern England: Politics, Aristocratic Patronage and Religion, c.1550–1640* (Cambridge, 2006), pp. 117–23; T. J. McCann, 'The Parliamentary Speech of Viscount Montague against the Act of Supremacy, 1559', *Sussex Archaeological Collections*, 108 (1970), pp. 50–57.

23 C. C. Breight, 'Caressing the Great: Viscount Montague's Entertainment of Elizabeth at Cowdray, 1591', *Sussex Archaeological Collections*, 127 (1989), pp. 147–66; Questier, *Catholicism and Community*, pp. 162–78, 196–9.

24 Bond, I, pp. 422–3; Breight, 'Caressing the Great', pp. 150–51. I have used the texts in Bond in preference to the confusingly presented versions in *Entertainments for Elizabeth I*, ed. J. Wilson (Woodbridge, 1980).

25 Bond, I, pp. 423–4.

26 A more complex reading is suggested by E. Heale, 'Contesting Terms: Loyal Catholicism and Lord Montague's Entertainment at Cowdray, 1591', in *Progresses, Pageants and Entertainments of Queen Elizabeth I*, ed. Archer, Goldring and Knight, pp. 188–206.

27 Nichols, III, p. 95.
28 Bond, I, pp. 427–9; Nichols, III, pp. 95–6. Heale maintains that the second 'fisherman' is ambiguously both a fisherman and a Catholic priest, and that the purpose of his dialogue with the 'angler' is to assert the loyalty of Catholics and the dangers of the real traitors: the 'privy carpers, ambitious climbers and immoral exploiters who operate unchecked within the Protestant state'. See Heale, 'Contesting Terms', pp. 203–4.
29 Bond, I, p. 429.
30 Breight, 'Caressing the Great', pp. 157–9.
31 *TRP*, III, nos. 738–9; Stow, 1592 edn, pp. 1290–91.
32 Questier, *Catholicism and Community*, p. 176.
33 BL, Lansdowne MS 99, fo. 163; SP 12/240, nos. 42–3; Questier, *Catholicism and Community*, pp. 177–8.
34 HMC, *Hatfield MSS*, IV, pp. 132–3; *LASPF*, 1591–2, p. 331; 'Letters from Sir Robert Cecil to Sir Christopher Hatton', ed. Hammer, pp. 236, 245.
35 'Letters from Sir Robert Cecil to Sir Christopher Hatton', ed. Hammer, pp. 209, 238, 246.
36 C. C. Breight, 'Realpolitik and Elizabethan Ceremony: The Earl of Hertford's Entertainment of Elizabeth at Elvetham, 1591', *RQ*, 45 (1992), pp. 20–49; H. H. Boyle, 'Elizabeth's Entertainment at Elvetham: War Policy in Pageantry', *Studies in Philology*, 68 (1971), pp. 146–66; Robert Cecil confirmed that the 'gestes' (i.e. itinerary for the queen's return journey to London in the form of a list of stops along the route) were still being revised and adjusted shortly before 4 September 1591: see 'Letters from Sir Robert Cecil to Sir Christopher Hatton', ed. Hammer, pp. 245–6.
37 Bond, I, p. 432; Breight, 'Realpolitik and Elizabethan Ceremony', p. 26; S. Adams, '"The Queenes Majestie . . . is now become a great huntress": Elizabeth I and the Chase', *Court Historian*, 18 (2013), p. 163.
38 SP 46/10; BL, Additional MS 33749; HEH, Ellesmere MS 2652, fo. 7; Haynes, p. 378.
39 HMC, *Bath MSS*, IV, p. 158.
40 Bond, I, p. 432; Boyle, 'Elizabeth's Entertainment at Elvetham', p. 147.
41 *The Honorable Entertainement Gieven to the Queenes Majestie in Progresse, at Elvetham in Hampshire, by the Right Honorable the Earle of Hertforde* (London, 1591); Bond, I, p. 433.
42 Bond, I, pp. 446–7.
43 H. Hackett, *Virgin Mother, Maiden Queen* (London, 1995), pp. 141–2, 174–8.
44 Bond, I, pp. 442–3.
45 Bond, I, pp. 443–4; Smith, 'Landscape with Figures', pp. 90–92; Hackett, *Virgin Mother, Maiden Queen*, pp. 139–40.
46 Breight, 'Realpolitik and Elizabethan Ceremony', pp. 31–2; Hackett, *Virgin Mother, Maiden Queen*, pp. 107–8, 139–42, 165.
47 Bond, I, pp. 447–9.
48 Bond, I, pp. 449–50.
49 Bond, I, p. 451.
50 Martyn, *Elizabeth in the Garden*, pp. 62–85.
51 Bond, I, p. 452.
52 Collins, I, pp. 358–60; HMC, *De L'Isle and Dudley MSS*, II, pp. 177, 183–4, 192, 197; HMC, *Hatfield MSS*, V, pp. 273–4; Breight, 'Elizabeth's Entertainment at Elvetham', pp. 37–40.
53 SP 12/254, no. 54.

Chapter 9: The Enemy Within

1 SP 52/46, fo. 5. This document is a copy, but the information about the queen's hand comes from the endorsement.

2 *Visitation Articles and Injunctions of the Period of the Reformation,* ed. W. H. Frere and W. M. Kennedy, 3 vols. (London, 1910), III, pp. 9, 16, 20; *CSPSM,* 1547–63, pp. 257, 289; *The Zurich Letters,* ed. H. Robinson (Cambridge, 1846; 2nd edn), p. 98; P. Collinson, *Archbishop Grindal, 1519–1583: The Struggle for a Reformed Church* (London, 1979), pp. 97–102; P. Collinson, *Elizabethan Essays* (London, 1994), pp. 87–118; D. Crankshaw and A. Gillespie, *ODNB,* s.v. 'Matthew Parker'.

3 P. Lake, 'A Tale of Two Episcopal Surveys: The Strange Fates of Edmund Grindal and Cuthbert Mayne Revisited', *TRHS,* 6th Series, 18 (2008), pp. 129–63.c

4 Northamptonshire RO, Fitzwilliam of Milton MSS, Political MS 70.c (reference kindly supplied by Patrick Collinson); Collinson, *Archbishop Grindal,* pp. 233–52.

5 BL, Lansdowne MS 23, fos. 24–9v; *The Remains of Archbishop Grindal, D.D.,* ed. W. Nicholson (Cambridge, 1843), pp. 376–90.

6 BL, Lansdowne MS 25, fos. 94–5.

7 This paragraph is, necessarily, a highly simplified summary of P. Lake, *Anglicans and Puritans? Presbyterianism and English Conformist Thought from Whitgift to Hooker* (London, 1988).

8 P. Collinson, *Richard Bancroft and Elizabethan Anti-Puritanism* (Cambridge, 2013), pp. 39–59. For the Scottish dimension, see J. Wormald, 'Ecclesiastical Vitriol: The Kirk, the Puritans and the Future King of England', in *The Reign of Elizabeth I: Court and Culture in the Last Decade,* ed. J. Guy (Cambridge, 1995), pp. 171–91.

9 Chief among them was Richard Bancroft, who doubled as Hatton's chaplain and Whitgift's inquisitor-general. Playing second fiddle was Dr Richard Cosin, who had been Whitgift's pupil at Trinity College, Cambridge. See Collinson, *Richard Bancroft,* pp. 83–147; J. E. Hampson, 'Richard Cosin and the Rehabilitation of the Clerical Estate in Late-Elizabethan England', University of St Andrews Ph.D. (1997), pp. 73–168.

10 SP 12/172, no. 1.

11 G. Donaldson, *Scotland: James V–James VII* (Edinburgh, 1971), p. 192.

12 SP 52/46, fo. 5.

13 L. H. Carlson, *Martin Marprelate, Gentleman: Master Job Throckmorton Laid Open in His Colors* (San Marino, CA, 1981), pp. 8–52, 178–209; Collinson, *Richard Bancroft,* pp. 60–82; P. Collinson, *The Elizabethan Puritan Movement* (Oxford, 1990), pp. 391–402; P. Collinson, 'Ecclesiastical Vitriol: Religious Satire in the 1590s and the Invention of Puritanism', in *Reign of Elizabeth I,* ed. Guy, pp. 150–70. Modern editions of the Marprelate Tracts are *The Marprelate Tracts 1588, 1589,* ed. W. Pierce (London, 1911) and *The Martin Marprelate Tracts: A Modernized and Annotated Edition,* ed. J. L. Black (Cambridge, 2008).

14 *Theses Martinianae* ([Coventry], 1589), sig. C1r–v.

15 Collinson, *Elizabethan Puritan Movement,* p. 295.

16 For the arguments on both sides, see *The defense of the aunsvvere to the Admonition against the replie of T.C. By Iohn Whitgift Doctor of Diuinitie* (London, 1574), pp. 180–83, 645–50.

17 SP 12/226, no. 4 (memo in Hatton's hand, headed 'From her Ma[jest]tie'). The plan evolved following disclosures from three of the printers of the Marprelate Tracts, trapped in August 1589 in a rented house near Manchester in Lancashire during a raid by the Earl of Derby's men, who were tortured on the rack in the hope that they would disclose the identity of the pseudonymous 'Martin'. See Carlson, *Martin Marprelate,* pp. 38–41. Neither Hatton nor Elizabeth was averse to the use of torture.

18 Hartley, II, pp. 414–24.

19 Collinson, *Elizabethan Puritan Movement,* pp. 409–18. Relying on a letter of Sir Francis

Knollys, Collinson argued that the Star Chamber proceedings began on 13 May, but in 1591 that was Ascension Day, when the courts did not usually sit. It is more likely that the case itself began earlier the same week, although the conference in the judges' dining-chamber to which Knollys refers could well have taken place on Ascension Day. See BL, Lansdowne MS 68, fo. 190.

20 BL, Lansdowne MS 68, fos. 98–101; BL, Lansdowne MS 120, fos. 84–8. A much fuller account of the prosecution than can be given here may be found in Collinson, *Elizabethan Puritan Movement*, pp. 418–31.

21 J. Guy, *A Daughter's Love: Thomas and Margaret More* (London, 2008), pp. 259–63.

22 BL, Lansdowne MS 68, fos. 98–101; BL, Lansdowne MS 120, fos. 84–8.

23 'Letters from Sir Robert Cecil to Sir Christopher Hatton, 1590–1591', ed. P. E. J. Hammer, *Camden Society*, 5th Series, 22 (2003), pp. 238, 246.

24 'Letters from Sir Robert Cecil to Sir Christopher Hatton', ed. Hammer, pp. 206–9, 213–14.

25 Camden, p. 458 (where the date is wrongly stated to be 20 September); H. Nicolas, *Memoirs of the Life and Times of Christopher Hatton, K.G.* (London, 1847), pp. 495–8.

26 BL, Lansdowne MS 68, fo. 43; Collinson, *Elizabethan Puritan Movement*, p. 427 (where the date is mistakenly given as the 12th). Knollys spoke metaphorically: Star Chamber could not impose the death penalty, only hefty fines, life imprisonment, flogging, the pillory, branding or banishment.

27 BL, Lansdowne MS 66, fo. 150; Collinson, *Elizabethan Puritan Movement*, p. 427.

28 For an insight into Knollys's state of mind during the case, see BL, Lansdowne MS 68, fo. 190.

29 BL, Lansdowne MS 68, fo. 97.

30 The request is from BL, Lansdowne MS 68, fo. 190.

31 *SR*, IV, ii, pp. 841–3; J. E. Neale, *Elizabeth I and Her Parliaments*, 2 vols. (London, 1969), II, pp. 280–97.

32 Stow, 1592 edn, pp. 1288–90; R. Bancroft, *Daungerous positions and proceedings published and practised within this I[s]land of Brytaine, vnder pretence of Reformation, and for the Presbiteriall discipline* (London, 1593), pp. 143–68; R. Cosin, *Conspiracie, for pretended reformation viz. presbyteriall discipline* (London, 1592), pp. 57–72; Collinson, *Richard Bancroft*, pp. 138–47; Collinson, *Elizabethan Puritan Movement*, pp. 424–5; A. Walsham, '"Frantik Hacket": Prophecy, Sorcery, Insanity and the Elizabethan Puritan Movement', *HJ*, 41 (1998), pp. 27–66.

33 For the earlier background to this 'even-handedness', see Lake, 'A Tale of Two Episcopal Surveys', pp. 136–42, 148–63. For Knollys's incredulity that 'puritans' could be considered to be as dangerous as 'papists', see BL, Lansdowne MS 66, fo. 150.

34 *The House of Commons, 1558–1603*, ed. P. W. Hasler, 3 vols. (London, 1981), III, pp. 513–15.

35 *House of Commons*, ed. Hasler, III, pp. 513–14. The suggestion that Topcliffe had known Elizabeth since the time of his marriage strongly chimes with his confident assertion to Robert Cecil in 1601 that, by then, he had served her for forty-four years. See HMC, *Hatfield MSS*, XI, pp. 224.

36 Lodge, II, pp. 121–2.

37 SP 12/152, no. 54; SP 12/165, no. 21; SP 12/175, no. 88; SP 12/190, no. 15; SP 12/230, no. 57; SP 12/235. no. 8; *APC*, XIII, pp. 360, 382–3; *APC*, XIV, p. 241; *APC*, XV, p. 122; *APC*, XVI, pp. 235, 273; *APC*, XVII, p. 205; *APC*, XIX, pp. 278, 370; *APC*, XX, pp. 100, 175, 204; *APC*, XXII, pp. 39–40, 41–2, 92, 213, 548; *APC*, XXV, pp. 237, 254; *APC*, XXVIII, pp. 165, 187.

38 E 351/542 (entries from Mich. 1583–4).

39 HMC, *Hatfield MSS*, XIII, p. 309.

40 *Unpublished Documents Relating to the English Martyrs*, ed. J. H. Pollen, *Catholic Record Society*, 5 (London, 1908), p. 210.

41 In 1595, the London merchant Francis Cordale was able to say of Waad, 'Popham, the

Chief Justice, is [away from London] in circuit, but Mr Waad in his absence keepeth the Papists in awe.' See SP 12/271, no. 107.

42 The date is proved by the fact that the 'Humble Supplication' refers to the trials of the seminary priests Edmund Jennings, Eustace White and Polydore Plasden on 4 December 1591, but not to their executions on the 10th. See *Unpublished Documents Relating to the English Martyrs*, pp. 205–9; *An Humble Supplication to Her Majestie* (n.p., [1600]), pp. 58–9.

43 *An Humble Supplication*, pp. 29–30, 59–60.

44 This summary of the facts is worked out from Richard Bellamy's subsequent petition to Burghley and from the reports of Catholic contemporaries. BL, Lansdowne MS 73, fos. 151–3; *Unpublished Documents Relating to the English Martyrs*, pp. 211–12; *Records of the English Province of the Society of Jesus*, ed. H. Foley, 7 vols. in 8 parts (London, 1875–83), I, pp. 349–60.

45 BL, Lansdowne MS 72, fo. 113.

46 BL, Cotton MS, Caligula C.III, fo. 242.

47 BL, Lansdowne MS 38, fo. 107. In addition, Bridget's mother, Elizabeth, was 'mother of the maids' to the maids of honour in Queen Mary Tudor's Bedchamber. See NA, LC 2/4/2.

48 *Journals of the House of Commons*, 85 vols. (London, 1742–1830), I, pp. 50–51.

49 *Letters of Sir Thomas Copley*, ed. R. C. Christie (London, 1897), pp. i–xx, *passim*; M. A. R. Graves, *ODNB*, s.v. 'Sir Thomas Copley'.

50 *Unpublished Documents Relating to the English Martyrs*, p. 335.

51 *Records of the English Province*, ed. Foley, pp. 357–62.

52 27 Elizabeth I, c. 2; *Unpublished Documents Relating to the English Martyrs*, pp. 333–5.

53 *Unpublished Documents Relating to the English Martyrs*, pp. 336–7; *Records of the English Province*, ed. Foley, pp. 371–5.

Chapter 10: Catastrophe in France

1 Devereux, I, pp. 222–3; P. E. J. Hammer, *The Polarisation of Elizabethan Politics: The Political Career of Robert Devereux, 2nd Earl of Essex, 1585–1597* (Cambridge, 1999), pp. 106–7.

2 R. Dallington, *The View of France* (London, 1601), sigs. G4–H4.

3 *LASPF*, 1591–2, p. 379; H. A. Lloyd, *The Rouen Campaign* (Oxford, 1973), pp. 105–13.

4 Lloyd, *Rouen Campaign*, p. 107.

5 *Journal of the Siege of Rouen*, ed. J. G. Nichols, *Camden Society*, Old Series, 39 (1847), pp. 13–14.

6 *LASPF*, 1591–2, p. 379; *Journal of the Siege of Rouen*, ed. Nichols, pp. 14–16.

7 *Memoirs of Robert Carey, Earl of Monmouth* (Edinburgh, 1808), p. 22; *Journal of the Siege of Rouen*, ed. Nichols, pp. 16–18; Lloyd, *Rouen Campaign*, pp. 112–13.

8 *Journal of the Siege of Rouen*, ed. Nichols, pp. 17–19; Devereux, I, pp. 225–9.

9 SP 78/25, fo. 210; BL, Cotton MS, Caligula E.VIII, fo. 235; Unton, p. 41.

10 'Letters from Sir Robert Cecil to Sir Christopher Hatton, 1590–1591', ed. P. E. J. Hammer, *Camden Society*, 5th Series, 22 (2003), pp. 215, 242.

11 'A Journal of the Siege of Rouen in 1591', ed. R. Poole, *EHR*, 17 (1902), pp. 529–31; *Memoirs of Robert Carey*, pp. 23–5; Lloyd, *Rouen Campaign*, pp. 114–16.

12 'Journal of the Siege of Rouen', ed. Poole, p. 531; *Memoirs of Robert Carey*, p. 26; 'Letters from Sir Robert Cecil to Sir Christopher Hatton', ed. Hammer, p. 237; Lloyd, *Rouen Campaign*, p. 116.

13 'Journal of the Siege of Rouen', ed. Poole, pp. 531–6; *Memoirs of Robert Carey*, pp. 27–9.

14 SP 78/25, fo. 388 (sent from Farnham, where Elizabeth lodged between 23 and 25 September). Earlier drafts are SP 78/25, fos. 344, 48. See also SP 78/25, fo. 352; *LASPF*,

1591–2, nos. 578–9; Hammer, *Polarisation of Elizabethan Politics*, p. 106.

15 Hammer, *Polarisation of Elizabethan Politics*, pp. 104–106; P. E. J. Hammer, *ODNB*, s.v. 'Robert Devereux, 2nd Earl of Essex'.

16 SP 78/25, fo. 388v.

17 *Memoirs of Robert Carey*, pp. 28–9; 'Letters from Sir Robert Cecil to Sir Christopher Hatton', ed. Hammer, p. 260.

18 'Letters from Sir Robert Cecil to Sir Christopher Hatton', ed. Hammer, p. 263.

19 *Memoirs of Robert Carey*, p. 29.

20 *Memoirs of Robert Carey*, pp. 30–31.

21 Unton, pp. 96–8.

22 Murdin, pp. 644–5; HMC, *Hatfield MSS*, IV, pp. 143–4; *Memoirs of Robert Carey*, pp. 30–31. SP 78/26, fos. 3–4, is a copy of a milder version of the queen's letter, sent to Essex by the Privy Council. It is endorsed 3 October, a day earlier than the date on the queen's letter. However, the endorsement is in a different hand and of a later date than the copy of the letter itself, and the correct date is almost certainly the 4th.

23 *Journal of the Siege of Rouen*, ed. Nichols, p. 28; Devereux, I, pp. 244–5.

24 *Memoirs of Robert Carey*, pp. 32–3; Lloyd, *Rouen Campaign*, p. 125.

25 *Journal of the Siege of Rouen*, ed. Nichols, p. 30, where the figure is wrongly given as 50,000 crowns.

26 *LASPF*, 1591–2, no. 301; Hammer, *Polarisation of Elizabethan Politics*, p. 227.

27 Devereux, I, pp. 250–53.

28 *Journal of the Siege of Rouen*, ed. Nichols, p. 31; *LASPF*, 1591–2, no. 602.

29 SP 78/26, fo. 152; *LASPF*, 1591–2, nos. 608–10; Lloyd, *Rouen Campaign*, pp. 125–6; R. B. Wernham, *After the Armada: Elizabethan England and the Struggle for Western Europe, 1588–1595* (Oxford, 1984), pp. 358–60.

30 P. Benedict, *Rouen during the Wars of Religion* (Cambridge, 1981), pp. 1–45. The figure of 186,000 includes the outparishes and suburbs of London. See S. Rappaport, *Worlds within Worlds: Structures of Life in Sixteenth-Century London* (Cambridge, 1989), pp. 56, 61.

31 *Journal of the Siege of Rouen*, ed. Nichols, pp. 31–2; Wernham, *After the Armada*, p. 356; Lloyd, *Rouen Campaign*, p. 146. The correct date is established by the *Journal*.

32 Lloyd, *Rouen Campaign*, pp. 147–51.

33 *Journal of the Siege of Rouen*, ed. Nichols, p. 39.

34 L. de Kéralio, *Histoire d'Elizabeth, Reine d'Angleterre*, 5 vols. (Paris, 1786–8), V, pp. 459–60. The abortive letter of 8 November is SP 76/26, fos. 140–42.

35 *Journal of the Siege of Rouen*, ed. Nichols, pp. 40–41; Lloyd, *Rouen Campaign*, pp. 153–4.

36 *Journal of the Siege of Rouen*, ed. Nichols, p. 47; E 351/542 (entries from Mich. 1591–2).

37 Unton, pp. 152, 165; *LASPF*, 1591–2, nos. 318, 328; Wernham, *After the Armada*, pp. 361–7.

38 Murdin, p. 797.

39 *LASPF*, 1590–91, nos. 620–21; Unton, pp. 175–6, 187–8.

40 Murdin, p. 797.

41 SP 78/26, fos. 303–4; Unton, pp. 203–5, 213–14.

42 SP 78/26, fo. 309.

43 SP 78/26, fos. 321–2.

44 Unton, pp. 251, 263–4.

45 Murdin, p. 651.

46 *Journal of the Siege of Rouen*, ed. Nichols, pp. 64–5; Unton, pp. 233–5; Devereux, I, pp. 270–72.

47 Unton, pp. 246–7; Lloyd, *Rouen Campaign*, p. 158.

48 *Memoirs of Robert Carey*, p. 39.

49 Unton, p. 246.

50 *LASPF*, 1591–2, no. 642; Devereux, I, pp. 274–5 (incorrectly dated).

51 Devereux, I, p. 275.

52 SP 78/27, fos. 61–2; *LASPF*, 1591–2, nos. 419–74; 'Letters from Sir Robert Cecil to Sir

Christopher Hatton', ed. Hammer, p. 236; Wernham, *After the Armada*, pp. 322–5, 335–8.

53 Lloyd, *Rouen Campaign*, pp. 161–8, 173–84; Wernham, *After the Armada*, pp. 376–99.

54 *LASPF*, 1592–3, no. 584; Birch, *Memoirs*, I, p. 99; Lloyd, *Rouen Campaign*, pp. 184–8.

55 *LASPF*, 1592–3, nos. 317–22; Wernham, *After the Armada*, pp. 400–409.

56 SP 103/7, fos. 308–9, 316; *LASPF*, 1592–3, nos. 116, 493; *Foedera*, XVI, pp. 151–3, 154–5, 167–9, 171, 173–5.

57 SP 78/28, fo. 234; *LASPF*, 1592–3, nos. 215, 217, 219.

58 *LASPF*, 1591–2, no. 672; *LASPF*, 1592–3, nos. 175, 512, 517–18; A. Keay, *The Elizabethan Tower of London* (London, 2001), pp. 27–8.

59 J. H. Salmon, *Society in Crisis: France in the Sixteenth Century* (London, 1975), pp. 276–306; M. P. Holt, *The French Wars of Religion, 1562–1629* (Cambridge, 2005; 2nd edn), pp. 123–52.

60 *LASPF*, 1592–3, no. 458; Holt, *French Wars of Religion*, p. 151; Salmon, *Society in Crisis*, pp. 268–70; Wernham, *After the Armada*, pp. 488–92.

61 *LASPF*, 1593–4, nos. 380–81.

62 Wernham, *After the Armada*, p. 491; Holt, *French Wars of Religion*, pp. 151–2; M. Wolfe, 'Protestant Reactions to the Conversion of Henry IV', in *Changing Identities in Early Modern France*, ed. M. Wolfe (Durham, NC, 1996), p. 379.

63 SP 98/1, fo. 83; *LASPF*, 1592–3, no. 630.

64 SP 78/29, fo. 182.

65 *EAC*, pp. 165–6; *ECW*, pp. 370–71 (I have made one small amendment to the translation); HMC, *Hatfield MSS*, IV, p. 343.

66 SP 12/246, no. 4; SP 15/32, fos. 181–2; *LASPF*, 1593–4, nos. 214–23, 251–77; Wernham, *After the Armada*, pp. 499–513.

67 *LASPF*, 1592–3, no. 494.

68 *EAC*, p. 166.

Chapter 11: 'Good Queen Bess'

1 I. W. Archer, *The Pursuit of Stability: Social Relations in Elizabethan London* (Cambridge, 1991), pp. 9–14.

2 BL, Lansdowne MS 71, fo. 28; S. Rappaport, *Worlds within Worlds: Structures of Life in Sixteenth-Century London* (Cambridge, 1989), p. 12.

3 *APC*, XXII, pp. 549–51; Harrison, I, pp. 142–3.

4 BL, Lansdowne MS 71, fo. 32.

5 *TRP*, III, nos. 754–5; Rappaport, *Worlds within Worlds*, pp. 54–5.

6 *APC*, XXIII, 177–8, 183–4, 195–6, 203–204, 220–21, 232–3.

7 SP 12/243, no. 5; *APC*, XXIII, p. 195; *TRP*, III, no. 750; Chambers, IV, pp. 347–8.

8 *TRP*, III, nos. 748, 750–52; Stow, 1592 edn, p. 1271.

9 *APC*, XXIV, pp. 21–3, 31–2, 209–12, 212, 343; Chambers, IV, pp. 313–14, 348–9.

10 *APC*, XXIV, pp. 178–80.

11 *APC*, XXIV, pp. 184, 187, 191–2, 200–201, 222; Harrison, I, pp. 236–9; Archer, *Pursuit of Stability*, p. 7.

12 E. Hall, *Henry VIII* [an edition of Hall's *Chronicle*], ed. C. Whibley, 2 vols. (London, 1904), I, pp. 157–61; Stow, 1592 edn, pp. 847–9; R. Holinshed, *The Third Volume of Chronicles* (London, 1577), pp. 841–4; Guildhall MS, Court of Aldermen, Repertory 3, fos. 143, 221.

13 Stow, 1592 edn, p. 1274.

14 *TRP*, III, nos. 758–60; *APC*, XXIV, p. 284; HMC, *Hatfield MSS*, IV, pp. 425–6; Birch, *Memoirs*, I, p. 133.

15 *APC*, XXIV, p. 488; Rappaport, *Worlds within Worlds*, p. 12.

16 *APC*, XXIV, pp. 187, 200–201. When identified, suspects were to be tortured until they confessed all they knew.

17 *The Book of Sir Thomas More*, ed. W. W. Greg (Oxford: Malone Society Reprints, 1961; 2nd edn); P. W. M. Blayney, '"The Booke of Sir Thomas Moore" Re-examined', *Studies in Philology*, 69 (1972), pp. 167–91; T. Merriam, 'The Misunderstanding of Munday as Author of *Sir Thomas More*', *Review of English Studies*, New Series, 51 (2000), pp. 540–81; G. Melchiori, '*The Booke of Sir Thomas Moore*: A Chronology of Revision', *Shakespeare Quarterly*, 37 (1986), pp. 291–308.

18 SP 99/1, fos. 197–8; P. Rebora, *L'opera di uno scrittore toscano sullo scisma d'Inghilterra e una lettera della regina Elisabetta, Archivio storico italiano*, 93 (1935), vol. I, pp. 233–54; M. Wyatt, *The Italian Encounter with Tudor England* (Cambridge, 2005), pp. 128–30, 260–61. Quite possibly, Pollini culled his material from the exiled Nicholas Sander's *De origine ac progressu schismatis Anglicani liber* ('Cologne' [i.e. Rheims], 1585), which also extracted its material on Anne Boleyn from Rastell.

19 *Book of Sir Thomas More*, ed. Greg, pp. I, 49–50. Rastell's source was Sir George Throckmorton, who had boldly spoken out in Parliament against Katherine of Aragon's divorce and had urged Thomas More to do the same. See J. Guy, *The Public Career of Sir Thomas More* (New Haven, CT, 1980), pp. 207–12. Throckmorton was the grandfather of Francis Throckmorton, executed in 1584 after the Guise invasion plot to which, inadvertently, he lent his name. Further information on Rastell's lost biography of Thomas More is from N. Harpsfield, *The Life and Death of Sir Thomas Moore, Knight, Sometymes Lord High Chancellor of England, Written in the Tyme of Queene Marie*, ed. E. V. Hitchcock, Early English Text Society, Original Series, 186 (1932), pp. ccxv–ccxix, 221–52.

20 Shakespeare's revisions can be seen in *Book of Sir Thomas More*, ed. Greg, pp. 73–9 and plate inset.

21 *APC*, XXIV, pp. 342–3, 347–8; *National Prayers: Special Worship since the Reformation*, ed. N. Mears, A. Raffe, S. Taylor and P. Williamson, Church of England Record Society, 20 (2013), pp. 203–4.

22 *APC*, XXIV, pp. 373–5, 448–9; *TRP*, III, no. 757; Stow, 1592 edn, p. 1274; Chambers, IV, pp. 348–9.

23 *APC*, XXIV, pp. 400–401. When Frederick, Duke of Wirtenberg, had received an audience with Elizabeth in 1592, she had repeatedly assured him, quoting St Paul, that 'If God be for us, who can be against us?' See *England as Seen by Foreigners in the Days of Elizabeth and James the First*, ed. W. B. Rye (London, 1865), p. 13.

24 *EAC*, pp. 165–6; *ECW*, pp. 370–71.

25 Camden, p. 475. Purportedly, it took Elizabeth just under a month, beginning in October 1593, to translate a Latin text that ran, in Boethius's original, to 25,000 words. See *Queen Elizabeth's Englishings*, ed. C. Pemberton (London, 1899), pp. ix–x.

26 Camden, p. 475. For the translation, see *Elizabeth's Englishings*, ed. Pemberton, pp. 1–120; *Elizabeth I: Translations, 1592–1598*, ed. J. Mueller and J. Scodel (Chicago, 2009), pp. 72–365.

27 F. Teague, 'Elizabeth I: Queen of England', in *Woman Writers of the Renaissance and Reformation*, ed. K. M. Wilson (Athens, GA, 1987), pp. 524, 528–9, 532–5; 'State Papers Relating to the Custody of Princess Elizabeth at Woodstock in 1554', *Norfolk Archaeology*, 4 (1855), pp. 161, 164, 168–9, 172, 175–6.

28 Elizabeth's (partly holograph) manuscript is SP 12/289, fos. 13–57, 64–83, 100–102.

29 *APC*, XXIV, p. 488.

30 Stow, 1592 edn, pp. 1274–9.

31 P. Slack, 'Books of Orders: The Making of English Social Policy, 1577–1631', *TRHS*, 5th Series, 30 (1980), pp. 1–22.

32 E 351/542 (payments for 1594–5); Chambers, IV, pp. 164–5.

33 The movements of the Court can be tracked in E 351/542 (entries, especially warrants for payment, for 1594).

34 *HMC, Hatfield MSS*, IV, p. 514.

35 *A Commandement that No Suiters Come to the Court for Any Priuate Suit except their Petitions be Indorsed by the Master of Requests* (London, 1594).

36 SP 84/48, fos. 249–50.

37 T. More, *Utopia*, ed. G. M. Logan and R. M. Adams (Cambridge, 2002; revised edn), pp. 30–34.

38 BNF, MS FF 15974, fo. 235.

39 'Journey through England and Scotland made by Lupold von Wedel in the Years 1584 and 1585', ed. G. von Bülow, *TRHS*, 2nd Series, 9 (1895), pp. 250–56.

40 *Annales, Or, The History of the Most Renowned and Victorious Princesse Elizabeth*, trans. R. Norton (London, 1635), sigs. b–c.

41 SP 12/253, no. 110; Stow, 1592 edn, pp. 1278–81; Archer, *Pursuit of Stability*, pp. 9–14; J. Sharpe, 'Social Strain and Social Dislocation, 1585–1603', in *The Reign of Elizabeth I*, ed. J. Guy (Cambridge, 1995), pp. 192–211; Rappaport, *Worlds within Worlds*, pp. 123–61; P. Slack, *Poverty and Policy in Tudor and Stuart England* (London, 1988), pp. 91–107.

42 Stow, 1592 edn, p. 1279; F. Consitt, *The London Weavers' Company* (Oxford, 1933), pp. 312–21; Harrison, II, p. 32; Rappaport, *Worlds within Worlds*, pp. 57–9.

43 *Foedera*, XVI, p. 195.

44 BL, Cotton MS, Caligula E.VIII, fo. 19; Unton, pp. 376–7; R. B. Wernham, *The Return of the Armadas: The Last Years of the Elizabethan War against Spain, 1595–1603* (Oxford, 1994), p. 2.

45 N. A. Younger, 'War and the Counties: The Elizabethan Lord Lieutenancy, 1585–1603', University of Birmingham Ph.D. (2006), pp. 185–96; E. P. Cheyney, *A History of England from the Defeat of the Spanish Armada to the Death of Elizabeth*, 2 vols. (London, 1914), I, pp. 284–7.

46 Stow, 1592 edn, p. 1280; SP 12/252, no. 94 (II–III); HMC, *Hatfield MSS*, V, pp. 248–50; BL, Lansdowne MS 78, fos. 159–61; Harrison, II, pp. 27–9, 30–31; Archer, *Pursuit of Stability*, p. 1.

47 Spencer's note can be seen scribbled as a postscript to BL, Lansdowne MS 78, fo. 159.

48 Stow, 1592 edn, p. 1280; R. B. Manning, 'The Prosecution of Sir Michael Blount, Lieutenant of the Tower of London, 1595', *BIHR*, 57 (1984), pp. 216–19, 222–3; Archer, *Pursuit of Stability*, p. 2.

49 BL, Lansdowne MS 66, fos. 241–2; SP 12/261, no. 70; *The Queenes Maiesties Proclamation for staying of all unlawfull assemblies in and about the Citie of London, and for Orders to punish the same* (London, 1595); *TRP*, III, nos. 735 (wrongly dated 1591), 769.

50 BL, Lansdowne MS 66, fos. 243–8; *Orders prescribed by her Maiesties commandement by advise of her Counsell, published in London, and other places neere to the same, for the observation of her Maiesties present Proclamation* (London, 1595).

51 BL, Lansdowne MS 78, fos. 126–33; Stow, 1592 edn, p. 1280.

52 BL, Lansdowne MS 66, fo. 243.

53 BL, Lansdowne MS 66, fos. 243–8; *Orders prescribed by her Maiesties commandement*; Stow, 1592 edn, p. 1280.

54 BL, Lansdowne MS 78, fo. 159.

55 SP 12/261, no. 69.

56 *Foedera*, XVI, pp. 279–80; L. Boynton, 'The Tudor Provost-Marshal', *EHR*, 77 (1962), pp. 437–55.

57 Chambers, IV, p. 318; G. Salgado, *The Elizabethan Underworld* (London, 1977), pp. 117–93.

58 *APC*, XXV, pp. 324, 330, 437–9; *APC*, XXVI, pp. 23–4, 118, 352; *APC*, XXVII, pp. 290–92.

59 *APC*, XXVII, pp. 283–4, 290–92; Archer, *Pursuit of Stability*, pp. 210–11, 254.

60 P. E. H. Hair and R. Law, 'The English in Western Africa to 1700', in *The Origins of Empire: British Overseas Enterprise to the Close of the Seventeenth Century*, ed. N. Canny (Oxford, 1998), pp. 241–9.

61 *APC*, XXVI, pp. 20–21; M. Kaufmann, 'Caspar van Senden, Sir Thomas Sherley and the "Blackamoor" Project', *HR*, 81 (2008), pp. 366–71.

Chapter 12: The Quest for Gold

1 *The Works of Sir Walter Ralegh, Knight*, 8 vols. (Oxford, 1829), VIII, p. 246.

2 J. Guy, *The Children of Henry VIII* (Oxford, 2013), pp. 98–100, 109, 111, 117–22, 137–8, 155, 166, 169–71, 178, 189; C. Merton, *ODNB*, s.v. 'Katherine Astley [née Champer-nowne]', 'John Astley'.

3 J. Sumption, *The Hundred Years War: Cursed Kings* (London, 2015), pp. 89–91.

4 N. A. M. Rodger, 'Queen Elizabeth and the Myth of Sea-Power in English History', *TRHS*, 6th Series, 14 (2004), pp. 153–7.

5 Rodger, 'Queen Elizabeth and the Myth of Sea-Power', p. 156.

6 K. R. Andrews, *Elizabethan Privateering* (Cambridge, 1964), p. 5; K. R. Andrews, *Trade, Plunder and Settlement* (Cambridge, 1984), pp. 102–15.

7 Andrews, *Elizabethan Privateering*, pp. 3–31; G. Parker and C. Martin, *The Spanish Armada* (London, 1992), p. 223.

8 Hakluyt, II, ii, pp. 194–5; W. R. Drake, 'Notes upon the Capture of the "Great Car-rack" in 1592', *Archaeologia*, 33 (1849), pp. 209–240; M. Nicholls and P. Williams, *Sir Walter Ralegh in Life and Legend* (London, 2011), pp. 76–7; R. B. Wernham, *After the Armada: Elizabethan England and the Struggle for Western Europe, 1588–1595* (Oxford, 1984), pp. 445–6.

9 *The Letters of Sir Walter Ralegh*, ed. A. Latham and J. Youings (Exeter, 1999), no. 41; Hak-luyt, II, ii, pp. 194–5.

10 *Letters of Sir Walter Ralegh*, ed. Latham and Youings, no. 43.

11 Hakluyt, II, ii, pp. 194–5.

12 SP 12/242, no. 48; *Letters of Sir Walter Ralegh*, ed. Latham and Youings, no. 44; HMC, *Hatfield MSS*, IV, p. 200; Hakluyt, I, ii, p. 195.

13 *Letters of Sir Walter Ralegh*, ed. Latham and Youings, no. 44.

14 R. Lacey, *Sir Walter Ralegh* (London, 1973), p. 147; A. L. Rowse, *Ralegh and the Throck-mortons* (London, 1962), pp. 129–88. See the portrait of Ralegh, attributed to the monogramist 'H' (Hubbard?), in the National Portrait Gallery, London.

15 Rowse, *Ralegh and the Throckmortons*, pp. 160–61; Nicholls and Williams, *Sir Walter Ralegh*, pp. 76–8.

16 HMC, *Hatfield MSS*, IV, pp. 153–4; P. E. J. Hammer, 'Sex and the Virgin Queen: Aris-tocratic Concupiscence and the Court of Elizabeth I', *SCJ*, 31 (2000), pp. 77–97; P. E. J. Hammer, *The Polarisation of Elizabethan Politics: The Political Career of Robert Devereux, 2nd Earl of Essex, 1585–1597* (Cambridge, 1999), pp. 95–6.

17 HMC, *Hatfield MSS*, IV, pp. 153–4, 154–5; Hammer, 'Sex and the Virgin Queen', pp. 80–90.

18 *Letters of Sir Walter Ralegh*, ed. Latham and Youings, no. 41.

19 *Letters of Sir Walter Ralegh*, ed. Latham and Youings, nos. 46–7; Bodleian, Ashmole MS 1729, fo. 177, printed in H. E. Sandison, 'Arthur Gorges, Spenser's Alcyon and Ralegh's Friend', *Publications of the Modern Language Association of America*, 43 (1928), pp. 657–8.

20 Rowse, *Ralegh and the Throckmortons*, p. 161; Nicholls and Williams, *Sir Walter Ralegh*, pp. 77–9.

21 Hammer, *Polarisation of Elizabethan Politics*, p. 116; Rowse, *Ralegh and the Throckmortons*, pp. 160–61.

22 HMC, *Rutland MSS*, I, p. 107; W. J. Tighe, 'Country into Court, Court into Country: John Scudamore of Holme Lacy and His Circles', in *Tudor Political Culture*, ed. D. Hoak (Cambridge, 1995), pp. 163–4; S. Adams, *ODNB*, s.v. 'Mary Scudamore [née Shelton]'.

23 SP 78/16, fo. 100; Hammer, 'Sex and the Virgin Queen', p. 81.

24 SP 12/260, nos. 25–6.

25 As far as Bess's finances were concerned, it was highly relevant that she was both an orphan and impoverished after she lost most of the £500 bequeathed to her by her

father as a future dowry in a property transaction that went wrong. This made her even more socially dependent upon the queen, her kinswoman.

26 Rowse, *Ralegh and the Throckmortons*, p. 162.

27 Quoted from Lambeth, MS 648 in J. P. Collier, 'Continuation of New Materials for a Life of Sir Walter Ralegh', *Archaeologia*, 34 (1852), p. 160; Birch, *Memoirs*, I, p. 79.

28 *The Poems of Sir Walter Ralegh*, ed. A. Latham (London, 1951), pp. 77–95.

29 HMC, *Finch MSS*, I, p. 34; Rowse, *Ralegh and the Throckmortons*, pp. 163–4; K. Robertson, 'Negotiating Favour: The Letters of Lady Ralegh', in *Women and Politics in Early Modern England, 1450–1700*, ed. J. Daybell (Aldershot, 2004), pp. 102–3. Bess wrote to the husband of her good friend, Elizabeth Finch, daughter of Sir Thomas Heneage, the queen's Vice-Chamberlain. It was perhaps unfortunate that father and daughter were estranged.

30 HMC, *Hatfield MSS*, IV, p. 232; BL, Lansdowne MS 70, fos. 102–104.

31 SP 12/243, nos. 16–17; Drake, 'Notes upon the Capture of the "Great Carrack" in 1592', p. 220.

32 Hakluyt, II, ii, pp. 194–5; Camden, p. 465.

33 BL, Lansdowne MS 70, fos. 227–8; HMC, *Hatfield MSS*, IV, p. 233; Drake, 'Notes upon the Capture of the "Great Carrack" in 1592', p. 219.

34 Hakluyt, II, ii, pp. 194–5; SP 12/243, no. 16; *Letters of Sir Walter Ralegh*, ed. Latham and Youings, no. 50; HMC, *Hatfield MSS*, IV, pp. 228, 230–31, 234–5, 254–5; Drake, 'Notes upon the Capture of the "Great Carrack" in 1592', pp. 222–3, 227–37; C. L. Kingsford, 'The Taking of the *Madre de Dios*, anno 1592', in *The Naval Miscellany, II*, ed. J. K. Laughton, Navy Records Society, 40 (1912), pp. 85–121; Wernham, *After the Armada*, pp. 447–9; Andrews, *Elizabethan Privateering*, pp. 43, 73.

35 BL, Lansdowne MS 70, fo. 88; Drake, 'Notes upon the Capture of the "Great Carrack" in 1592', pp. 225–7; *Letters of Sir Walter Ralegh*, ed. Latham and Youings, no. 52.

36 SP 12/243, no. 17.

37 *Letters of Sir Walter Ralegh*, ed. Latham and Youings, no. 51. Ralegh's books of account were kept by William Sanderson. See R. A. McIntyre, 'William Sanderson, Elizabethan Financier of Discovery', *William and Mary Quarterly*, 3rd Series, 13 (1956), pp. 184–201.

38 BL, Lansdowne MS 70, fos. 100, 117–18; HMC, *Hatfield MSS*, IV, pp. 233–4; Drake, 'Notes upon the Capture of the "Great Carrack" in 1592', pp. 231–2.

39 BL, Lansdowne MS 70, fo. 210; SP 12/244, no. 18; Drake, 'Notes upon the Capture of the "Great Carrack" in 1592', pp. 237–8.

40 BL, Lansdowne MS 70, fo. 210.

41 *Letters of Sir Walter Ralegh*, ed. Latham and Youings, no. 51.

42 The figures differ slightly in different documents. In an attempt to reconcile them, I have collated BL, Lansdowne MS 70, fos. 38–9, 40 with Ralegh's figures at fo. 217. See also Drake, 'Notes upon the Capture of the "Great Carrack" in 1592', pp. 238–40.

43 BL, Lansdowne MS 73, fos. 38–9; *Letters of Sir Walter Ralegh*, ed. Latham and Youings, no. 56; E. Edwards, *The Life of Sir Walter Ralegh*, 2 vols. (London, 1868), I, pp. 157–8.

44 Rowse, *Ralegh and the Throckmortons*, pp. 164, 168.

45 BL, Lansdowne MS 70, fos. 38–40. Ralegh said it was £40,000, but this must have been an exaggeration, as the official reckoning does not bear it out.

46 BL, Lansdowne MS 70, fo. 217; *Letters of Sir Walter Ralegh*, ed. Latham and Youings, no. 51.

47 Rowse, *Ralegh and the Throckmortons*, p. 179.

48 *Sir Walter Ralegh's 'Discoverie of Guiana'*, ed. J. Lorimer, Hakluyt Society, 3rd Series, 15 (2006), pp. xl–lx; Andrews, *Elizabethan Privateering*, pp. 196–7; E. G. R. Taylor, 'Harriot's Instructions for Ralegh's Voyage to Guiana, 1595', *Journal of the Institute of Navigation*, 6 (1952), pp. 345–51; J. J. Roche, *ODNB*, s.v. 'Thomas Harriot'.

49 *Sir Walter Ralegh's 'Discoverie of Guiana'*, ed. Lorimer, pp. xl–lx, 47–66; Nicholls and Williams, *Sir Walter Ralegh*, pp. 99–110; Lacey, *Sir Walter Ralegh*, pp. 202–9.

50 HMC, *Hatfield MSS*, IV, p. 485; Robertson, 'Negotiating Favour: The Letters of

Lady Ralegh', in *Women and Politics in Early Modern England, 1450–1700*, ed. Daybell, pp. 104–5.

51 Sanderson's wife, Margaret Snedall, was Ralegh's niece.

52 The complicated story of Ralegh's relationship with Sanderson and his finances for the Guiana expedition can be pieced together from McIntyre, 'William Sanderson, Elizabethan Financier of Discovery', pp. 197–201; J. W. Shirley, 'Sir Walter Ralegh's Guinea Finances', *HLQ*, 13 (1949), pp. 55–69.

53 *Sir Walter Ralegh's 'Discoverie of Guiana'*, ed. Lorimer, pp. 28–9, 65–87.

54 *Sir Walter Ralegh's 'Discoverie of Guiana'*, ed. Lorimer, pp. l–lxi, 12–13; Nicholls and Williams, *Sir Walter Ralegh*, pp. 102–8.

55 *Sir Walter Ralegh's 'Discoverie of Guiana'*, ed. Lorimer, pp. 26–30, 80–145.

56 HMC, *Hatfield MSS*, V, p. 396; *Letters of Sir Walter Ralegh*, ed. Latham and Youings, no. 86; *Sir Walter Ralegh's 'Discoverie of Guiana'*, ed. Lorimer, pp. 5–6.

57 *Letters of Sir Walter Ralegh*, ed. Latham and Youings, nos. 86–7.

58 *Sir Walter Ralegh's 'Discoverie of Guiana'*, ed. Lorimer, pp. xlvii–lxi; Nicholls and Williams, *Sir Walter Ralegh*, p. 111.

59 *Letters of Sir Walter Ralegh*, ed. Latham and Youings, no. 87.

Chapter 13: Conspiring against the Queen

1 SP 12/247, nos. 100, 102; BL, Additional MS 48029, fo. 162v; KB 8/52, Pts. 1–2; A. Dimock, 'The Conspiracy of Dr Lopez', *EHR*, 9 (1894), pp. 440–72. I first set forth the gist of my argument in this chapter in a television documentary, 'Conspiring against the Queen', Episode 3 of *Renaissance Secrets*, Series 2, screened on BBC 2, 12 November 2001.

2 KB 8/52, Pt. 1.

3 Lopez's secret Judaism is from SP 12/248, no. 16.

4 E. Samuel, *ODNB*, s.v. 'Roderigo Lopez'; *Leicester's Commonwealth*, ed. D. C. Peck (Athens, Ohio, 1985), p. 116; A. Stewart, 'Portingale Women and Politics in Late-Elizabethan London', in *Women and Politics in Early Modern England, 1450–1700*, ed. J. Daybell (Aldershot, 2004), pp. 84–5; A. Stewart, '"Every Soil to Me is Natural": Figuring Denization in William Haughton's Englishmen for My Money', *Renaissance Drama*, New Series, 35 (2006), pp. 62–5.

5 SO 3/1, fo. 516v; Dimock, 'Conspiracy of Dr Lopez', pp. 440–41; *Household Accounts and Disbursement Books of Robert Dudley, Earl of Leicester, 1558–61, 1584–86*, ed. S. Adams, *Camden Society*, 5th Series, 6 (1995), p. 332.

6 SP 12/238, fo. 98v.

7 *CSPSp, 2nd Series, 1587–1603*, pp. l–li, 74, and nos. 550, 556. My thanks to Professor Alan Stewart for advice on this point.

8 BL, Harleian MS 1641, fo. 15v; *Household Accounts . . . of Robert Dudley*, ed. Adams, p. 332.

9 SP 12/225, no. 21; SP 12/247, no. 102.

10 SP 12/238, nos. 68, 194; *CSPSp, 2nd Series, 1587–1603*, nos. 516, 519, 579.

11 *CSPSp, 2nd Series, 1587–1603*, pp. l–lii; SP 12/236, no. 159; SP 12/238, no. 68 (especially fos. 98v–9); SP 12/239, no. 152.

12 SP 12/238, no. 68; SP 12/248, no. 18; *CSPSp, 2nd Series, 1587–1603*, nos. 579, 588, 591. The truth has to be unpicked from the boasts and overblown claims made by Andrada to Lopez and Burghley.

13 SP 12/239, nos. 135–6, 150–51.

14 SP 12/239, nos. 136, 151 (translations into Italian and French for Burghley of the original Portuguese); BL, Additional MS 48029, fos. 162v; *A True Report of Sundry Horrible Conspiracies of Late Time Detected* (London, 1594), p. 8; Dimock, 'Conspiracy of Dr Lopez', pp. 446–7; D. Katz, *The Jews in the History of England, 1485–1850* (Oxford, 1994), pp. 74–5.

15 SP 78/25, fo. 8; SP 94/4, fos. 23–6, 33, 41–2. See also SP 12/239, nos. 72, 82–3.

16 SP 12/239, nos. 121–2.

17 SP 12/239, no. 123.

18 SP 12/240, no. 22.

19 SP 12/240, no. 22.

20 SP 12/239, no. 135 (shown to the queen); SP 12/239, nos. 142, 142 (I–II), 143, 149, 150–52.

21 HMC, *Hatfield MSS*, IV, p. 248; SP 12/248, no. 18.

22 SP 84/48, fo. 78; Dimock, 'Conspiracy of Dr Lopez', p. 448.

23 P. E. J. Hammer, *The Polarisation of Elizabethan Politics: The Political Career of Robert Devereux, 2nd Earl of Essex, 1585–1597* (Cambridge, 1999), pp. 111–51.

24 Hammer, *Polarisation of Elizabethan Politics*, pp. 71, 130–31; C. L. Kingsford, 'Essex House, Formerly Leicester House and Exeter Inn', *Archaeologia*, 73 (1923), pp. 1–54.

25 *Memoirs of Robert Carey, Earl of Monmouth* (Edinburgh, 1808), pp. 61–2.

26 *LASPF*, 1593–4, p. 486; Birch, *Memoirs*, I, p. 146.

27 Birch, *Memoirs*, I, p. 146.

28 See, for instance, A. Whitelock, *Elizabeth's Bedfellows: An Intimate History of the Queen's Court* (London, 2013), p. 278.

29 L. Strachey, *Elizabeth and Essex* (London, 1928; repr. 1971), pp. 22–4, 41–3.

30 R. Lacey, *Robert, Earl of Essex: An Elizabethan Icarus* (London, 1971), p. 201.

31 *The Letters of Lady Anne Bacon*, ed. G. Allen, *Camden Society*, 5th Series, 44 (2014), pp. 133, 140; Dimock, 'Conspiracy of Dr Lopez', p. 498.

32 *Letters of Lady Anne Bacon*, ed. Allen, p. 161; BL, Additional MS 48029, fo. 148.

33 Hammer, *Polarisation of Elizabethan Politics*, pp. 159–60; BL, Additional MS 48029, fos. 155v, 162v.

34 Birch, *Memoirs*, I, pp. 149–50; Hammer, *Polarisation of Elizabethan Politics*, pp. 138, 160–63.

35 CUL, MS Ee.3.56, no. 15. Although some words are scored out, Dom António's name is clearly visible beneath the penstrokes.

36 Birch, *Memoirs*, I, pp. 66–9, 98–140; *Letters of Lady Anne Bacon*, ed. Allen, p. 16; S. Alford, *The Watchers: A Secret History of the Reign of Elizabeth I* (London, 2012), pp. 285–97; P. Hammer, 'The Uses of Scholarship: the Secretariat of Robert Devereux, Second Earl of Essex', *EHR*, 109 (1994), pp. 26–51; Hammer, *Polarisation of Elizabethan Politics*, pp. 173–87.

37 SP 12/239, no. 120; SP 12/240, no. 12; SP 12/241, nos. 44–5; SP 12/242, no. 3; Hammer, *Polarisation of Elizabethan Politics*, pp. 153–62.

38 SP 12/248, no. 18.

39 SP 12/246, nos. 39, 39 (I–III), 45; Dimock, 'Conspiracy of Dr Lopez', pp. 448–55.

40 SP 12/247, no. 13.

41 SP 12/246, no. 25 (translations of both letters on the same folio).

42 BL, Additional MS 48029, fos. 155v–84v (another copy of this dossier is BL, Harleian MS 871, fos. 7–64); 'A True Report of the Detestable Treason, Intended by Dr Roderigo Lopez', in Spedding, I, p. 283; SP 12/248, no. 7 (I); Murdin, pp. 669–75.

43 SP 12/247, no. 102; 'A True Report', in Spedding, I, pp. 285–6. Spanish documents confirm the substance of this claim. See *Documentos inéditos para la historia de España: Publicados por los Señores Duque de Alba* [and others], 12 vols. (Madrid, 1936–57), I, p. 197; Dimock, 'Conspiracy of Dr Lopez', pp. 457–8.

44 Birch, *Memoirs*, I, p. 152.

45 'A True Report', in Spedding, I, p. 284; *True Report of Sundry Horrible Conspiracies*, pp. 8–16, 28–31; BL, Additional MS 48029, fos. 158v–84v; SP 12/247, nos. 19, 51, 58, 82–4; Dimock, 'Conspiracy of Dr Lopez', pp. 457–65.

46 BL, Additional MS 48029, fos. 158v–84v; 'A True Report', in Spedding, I, pp. 274–87.

47 Lopez's wife may not have sold the ring. It was later excepted from a partial restoration of goods that Sara Lopez, the doctor's widow, and her children received from the queen after Lopez's chattels were seized by the Crown. See CP 28/8–11; HMC, *Hatfield MSS*,

IV, p. 601; Dimock, 'Conspiracy of Dr Lopez', pp. 469–70.

48 BL, Additional MS 48029, fos. 161, 162v; *Letters of Lady Anne Bacon*, ed. Allen, p. 164.

49 Birch, *Memoirs*, I, p. 152; *Letters of Lady Anne Bacon*, ed. Allen, pp. 163–4; Hammer, *Polarisation of Elizabethan Politics*, p. 348.

50 *Letters of Lady Anne Bacon*, ed. Allen, p. 164.

51 SP 12/247, nos. 70, 82–4.

52 CUL, MS Ee.3.56, no. 17; Birch, *Memoirs*, I, p. 155. Burghley's few lines on the plot can be found at HMC, *Hatfield MSS*, V, pp. 54–5.

53 SP 12/247, no. 70; *True Report of Sundry Horrible Conspiracies*, pp. 27–8.

54 SP 12/247, no. 84; BL, Additional MS 48029, fo. 169; *True Report of Sundry Horrible Conspiracies*, pp. 28–30.

55 BL, Additional MS 48029, fo. 174; SP 12/247, no. 97.

56 SP 12/248, no. 16 and KB 8/52, Pt. 1.

57 SP 12/247, no. 102 (quotation at stamped fo. 167).

58 SP 12/248, no. 16.

59 SP 12/247, no. 97. For Elizabeth's location, see E 351/542 (entries for February and March 1594).

60 SP 12/248, nos. 12, 19, 20 (I), 22. On the eve of the arraignment, Chief Justice Popham, the president of the trial commission, was suddenly taken ill and had to withdraw. A replacement judge was quickly found and the trial went ahead as planned. See SP 12/248, nos. 26, 26 (I). (SP 12/248, no. 26 [I] is dated 'at Lincoln's Inn, this 14th of March', but the sense clearly shows that Attorney-General Egerton misdated the letter, since he refers to the scheduled date and time set for the case to begin. Also, the trial records prove that the case was heard on the 14th. SP 12/247, no. 103 [stamped fos. 172v–5]; KB 8/52, Pt. 1.)

61 SP 12/247, no. 103 (stamped fos. 172v–5); Dimock, 'Conspiracy of Dr Lopez', pp. 467–8, where the date is mistaken.

62 SP 12/248, no. 68 (II).

63 CP 26/30; HMC, *Hatfield MSS*, IV, p. 513.

64 CP 26/29; HMC, *Hatfield MSS*, IV, p. 512.

65 CP 26/30; HMC, *Hatfield MSS*, IV, p. 513. See also SP 97/2, fo. 261v.

66 KB 8/52, Pt. 1.

67 CP 26/39; HMC, *Hatfield MSS*, IV, p. 515. Elizabeth's instructions put Blount on the spot. He would obey her, he said, but what should he do about da Gama and Tinoco? Could they be executed on their own?

68 BL, Harleian MS 6996, fos. 160, 162. The date on fo. 160 is hard to read. It could be either 1st or 4th. I've inclined to the 1st, since the writs definitely emanated from the Queen's Bench on the 4th.

69 KB 8/52, Pt. 1 (*postea* section), where it is recorded that the accused *separatim dixerunt quod nihil aliud pro seipsis dicere.*

70 KB 8/52, Pt. 1 (*postea* section); BL, Harleian MS 6996, fo. 162.

71 Camden, pp. 484–5.

72 *Henslowe's Diary*, ed. R. A. Foakes (Cambridge, 2002; 2nd edn), pp. 21–4; Harrison, I, pp. 296–7, 302–3, 304, 306, 307; *English Professional Theatre, 1530–1660*, ed. G. Wickham, H. Berry and W. Ingram (Cambridge, 2000), pp. 328, 431–2; S. L. Lee, 'The Original of Shylock', *Gentleman's Magazine*, 246 (1880), pp. 185–200.

73 SP 97/2, fo. 261v. See also SP 97/2, fos. 211–14, 255, 263; SP 94/4, fos. 158–9; Stewart, 'Portingale Women and Politics', in *Women and Politics in Early Modern England*, ed. Daybell, p. 93.

Chapter 14: Games of Thrones

1 T. Birch, *The Life of Henry, Prince of Wales* (London, 1760), pp. 1–2; *National Prayers: Special Worship since the Reformation*, ed. N. Mears, A. Raffe, S. Taylor and P. Williamson, *Church of England Record Society*, 20 (2013), p. 206.

2 SP 52/50, no. 83; SP 52/53, no. 35; G. Donaldson, *Scotland: James V–James VII* (Edinburgh, 1971), pp. 189–93; R. B. Wernham, *After the Armada: Elizabethan England and the Struggle for Western Europe, 1588–1595* (Oxford, 1984), pp. 456–60.

3 SP 52/52, pp. 30–31 (this entry book of dispatches is paginated, not foliated).

4 SP 52/51, no. 75.

5 'Lethington's Account of Negotiations with Elizabeth in September and October 1561', in *A Letter from Mary Queen of Scots to the Duke of Guise, January 1562*, ed. J. H. Pollen (Edinburgh, 1904), Appendix 1.

6 'Lethington's Account', p. 41.

7 J. Harington, *A Tract on the Succession to the Crown*, ed. C. R. Markham (London, 1880), p. 40.

8 SP 12/240, no. 21; J. E. Neale, 'Peter Wentworth', *EHR*, 39 (1924), pp. 182–202. For a recent reappraisal of this question, see P. Kewes, 'The Puritan, the Jesuit and the Jacobean Succession', in *Doubtful and Dangerous: The Question of Succession in Late-Elizabethan England*, ed. S. Doran and P. Kewes (Manchester, 2014), pp. 48–57, 60–66.

9 *A treatise containing M. Wentworth's iudgement concerning the person of the true and lawfull successor to these realmes of England and Ireland* (Edinburgh, 1598), p. 3. Published as the final part of *A pithie exhortation to her Maiestie for establishing her successor to the crowne. Whereunto is added a discourse containing the author's opinion of the true and lawfull successor to her Maiestie* (Edinburgh, 1598). Both works, published posthumously by Wentworth's friends, derive from Wentworth's (now lost) manuscripts, each written much earlier. For a full explanation and reconstruction of these intriguing documents, see Neale, 'Peter Wentworth', pp. 182–202.

10 SP 12/240, no. 21 (I); P. E. J. Hammer, *The Polarisation of Elizabethan Politics: The Political Career of Robert Devereux, 2nd Earl of Essex, 1585–1597* (Cambridge, 1999), p. 168; Neale, 'Peter Wentworth', p. 184; J. E. Neale, *Elizabeth I and Her Parliaments*, 2 vols. (London, 1969), II, p. 255; Kewes, 'The Puritan, the Jesuit and the Jacobean Succession', in *Doubtful and Dangerous*, ed. Doran and Kewes, p. 53.

11 *APC*, XXI, pp. 392–3; SP 12/240, no. 21 (I).

12 HMC, *Hatfield MSS*, VII, pp. 284, 286, 303; Neale, 'Peter Wentworth', pp. 186–97; Neale, *Elizabeth I and Her Parliaments*, II, pp. 256–62; Kewes, 'The Puritan, the Jesuit and the Jacobean Succession', in *Doubtful and Dangerous*, ed. Doran and Kewes, pp. 54–7.

13 SP 101/95, fos. 121–2.

14 SP 12/247, no. 50; J. Stow, *A Survey of the Cities of London and Westminster*, 2 vols. (London, 1720), I, p. 75; R. B. Manning, 'The Prosecution of Sir Michael Blount, Lieutenant of the Tower of London, 1595', *BIHR*, 57 (1984), p. 216.

15 SP 78/32, fo. 393v; SP 78/36, fos. 10, 96; *Annals of the Reformation*, ed. J. Strype (4 vols., London, 1824), IV, pp. 331–2.

16 *Paul Hentzner's Travels in England during the Reign of Queen Elizabeth*, ed. H. Walpole (London, 1797), pp. 34–5; *England as Seen by Foreigners in the Days of Elizabeth and James the First*, ed. W. B. Rye (London, 1865), pp. 104–5; J. Arnold, *Queen Elizabeth's Wardrobe Unlock'd* (Leeds, 1988), pp. 214–15, 223–6; F. Moryson, *An itinerary written by Fynes Moryson Gent. First in the Latine tongue, and then translated by him into English* (London, 1617), Pt. III, iv, 1, p. 172.

17 *Cosmeticks or, the beautifying part of physick. By which all deformities of nature in men and women are corrected* [based on the writings of Johann Wecker (1528–86)] (London, 1660), pp. 17–25, 27–30, 53–5, 92–3; A. Whitelock, *Elizabeth's Bedfellows: An Intimate History of the*

Queen's Court (London, 2013), pp. 24–5, 190–91; A. Riehl, *The Face of Queenship: Early Modern Representations of Elizabeth I* (New York, 2010), pp. 57–8.

18 Collins, I, pp. 357–8.

19 Wright, II, pp. 440–44.

20 *CSPD*, 1595–7, p. 114; SP 12/254, no. 26 (the original document is now misplaced at the NA).

21 Hammer, *Polarisation of Elizabethan Politics*, p. 355.

22 W. Fowler, *A True Reportarie of the Most Triumphant, and Royal Accomplishment of the Baptisme of the Most Excellent, Right High, and Mightie Prince, Frederik Henry* (Edinburgh, 1594), sig. A3.

23 E. J. Cowan, 'The Darker Vision of the Scottish Renaissance: The Devil and Francis Stewart', in *The Renaissance and Reformation in Scotland*, ed. I. B. Cowan and D. Shaw (Edinburgh, 1983), pp. 125–37.

24 D. Calderwood, *The History of the Kirk in Scotland*, 8 vols. (Edinburgh, 1844), V, pp. 140–42, 144.

25 Calderwood, *The History of the Kirk in Scotland*, V, pp. 256–7.

26 SP 52/53, no. 20; SP 52/54, no. 118.

27 Calderwood, *The History of the Kirk in Scotland*, V, pp. 306–45; Birch, *Memoirs*, I, pp. 177–8; Cowan, 'Darker Vision of the Scottish Renaissance', in *Renaissance and Reformation*, ed. Cowan and Shaw, pp. 133–6; Donaldson, *Scotland: James V–James VII*, pp. 193–5.

28 Birch, *Memoirs*, I, pp. 162–3, 178, 181–6, 192, 221, 276, 278, 299, 312, 343, 355, 377, 399, 425, 440, 445, 447, 462; Hammer, *Polarisation of Elizabethan Politics*, pp. 167–70.

29 Murdin, pp. 655–7; Hammer, *Polarisation of Elizabethan Politics*, pp. 344–5.

30 *The Warrender Papers*, ed. A. Cameron, 2 vols. (Edinburgh, 1931–2), II, p. 43.

31 Hammer, *Polarisation of Elizabethan Politics*, p. 346; *Taming of the Shrew*, 4, i, ll. 5–6.

32 *The Tempest*, 4, i, ll. 211–12.

33 SP 15/30, no. 80.

34 *LQEJ*, pp. 100–103.

35 *LQEJ*, pp. 103–5.

36 James would shortly be forced to apologize for his use of the words 'seduced queen' and his quotation from Virgil, see *LQEJ*, pp. 105–8.

37 *LSP, James VI*, pp. 7–8; Birch, *Memoirs*, I, p. 175.

38 *LSP, James VI*, p. 8.

39 Hammer, *Polarisation of Elizabethan Politics*, pp. 170–71. See also A. Courtney, 'The Scottish King and the English Court: The Secret Correspondence of James VI, 1601–1603', in *Doubtful and Dangerous*, ed. Doran and Kewes, pp. 135–6.

40 SP 52/54, no. 5 (corrected draft in English); SP 52/54, no. 4 (fair copy translated into French of the version actually sent); Fowler, *A True Reportarie*, sig. D3. For the phrase 'skrating' or 'scratting hand', see SP 52/69, no. 53.

41 SP 52/54, no. 5.

42 *Memoirs of His Own Life by Sir James Melville of Halhill* (Edinburgh, 1827), pp. 412–13; D. Moysie, *Memoirs of the Affairs of Scotland . . . From Early Manuscripts* (Edinburgh, 1830), pp. 118–19; Birch, *Life of Henry, Prince of Wales*, pp. 9–10; J. Guy, *'My Heart is My Own': The Life of Mary Queen of Scots* (London, 2004), p. 285.

43 SP 52/54, no. 36.

44 SP 52/54, nos. 24, 34. The offending verses were by A. Melville, and were printed by Robert Waldegrave, the king's printer, under the title *Principis Scoti-Britannorum Natalia* (Edinburgh, 1594).

45 SP 52/54, no. 34.

46 Collins, I, p. 357; Birch, *Memoirs*, I, pp. 312–13; R. Doleman [i.e. R. Parsons], *A Conference about the Next Succession to the Crown of England* (Antwerp, 1594), Dedication, sig. ⋆2v–3. Although written in 1593 and printed in 1594, the book was not published and smuggled into England until the summer of 1595. See P. J. Holmes, 'The Authorship

and Early Reception of *A Conference about the Next Succession to the Crown of England*', *HJ*, 23 (1980), pp. 421–2.

47 SP 12/232, nos. 16, 19; SP 12/248, no. 53; Hammer, *Polarisation of Elizabethan Politics*, p. 139.

48 Birch, *Memoirs*, I, pp. 238, 313; HMC, *Hatfield MSS*, V, p. 213; P. E. J. Hammer, 'Sex and the Virgin Queen: Aristocratic Concupiscence and the Court of Elizabeth I', *SCJ*, 31 (2000), pp. 83–4; Hammer, *Polarisation of Elizabethan Politics*, pp. 319–20. Birch mistakenly associates the first of these references with the clandestine relationship of Essex's cousin Elizabeth Vernon, one of the queen's maids of honour, and his friend Henry Wriothesley, Earl of Southampton, which occurred in 1598.

49 Harington, *Tract on the Succession*, ed. Markham, pp. 4, 34, 45.

50 Holmes, 'Authorship and Early Reception', pp. 415–29.

51 Doleman, *A Conference about the Next Succession*, Pt. 1, pp. 12–14, 56–7, 59–63, 129–31. For more general arguments about the significance of the book, see 'Introduction: An Historical Perspective', in *Doubtful and Dangerous*, ed. Doran and Kewes, pp. 3–15.

52 Doleman, *A Conference about the Next Succession*, Pt. 2, pp. 111–20.

53 Arbella, like James VI, was a granddaughter of Henry VIII's niece Lady Margaret Douglas, the daughter of Henry's elder sister Margaret by her second husband, Archibald, Earl of Angus. When the dying Henry made his will, he had not mentioned Douglas. Equally, he had not specifically excluded her. Legally, her descendants were entitled to stake their claim, failing the 'Suffolk line', as 'the next rightful heirs'. *Foedera*, XV, pp. 110–17.

54 *The Letters of Lady Arbella Stuart*, ed. S. J. Steen (Oxford, 1994), pp. 20–21, 161–2; J. Clapham, *Certain Observations Concerning the Life and Reign of Queen Elizabeth*, ed. E. P. Read and C. Read (Philadelphia, 1951), p. 114; Harington, *Tract on the Succession*, ed. Markham, p. 42; *CSPV*, 1592–1601, no. 1143 (for Elizabeth's version of the story); *The true chronicle history of King Leir, and his three daughters, Gonorill, Ragan, and Cordell* (London, 1605), sig. B4v; Doleman, *A Conference about the Next Succession*, Pt. 2, pp. 124–5, 127–9.

55 Doleman, *A Conference about the Next Succession*, Pt. 2, pp. 130–39; C. C. Breight, 'Realpolitik and Elizabethan Ceremony: The Earl of Hertford's Entertainment of Elizabeth at Elvetham, 1591', *RQ*, 45 (1992), pp. 37–8.

56 *CSPSp, 2nd Series*, 1568–1579, nos. 592–3; Doleman, *A Conference about the Next Succession*, Pt. 2, pp. 132–3.

57 Harington, *Tract on the Succession*, ed. Markham, p. 41; Doleman, *A Conference about the Next Succession*, Pt. 2, pp. 141–9.

58 These lines of descent, Parsons claimed, trumped the claims of Elizabeth's grandfather, Henry VII, as the descendant of John Beaufort, Earl of Somerset, Gaunt's eldest (and illegitimate) son from his affair with his long-standing mistress, Katherine Swynford. In addition, Gaunt's legitimate son and heir, Henry Bolingbroke, had become King of England after deposing Richard II in 1399. Doleman, *A Conference about the Next Succession*, Pt. 2, pp. 37–107, 160–93.

59 Doleman, *A Conference about the Next Succession*, Pt. 2, pp. 193–267. In his enthusiasm for this line of argument, Parsons claimed (Pt. 1, pp. 180–81) that bastard sons might more likely become military heroes as rulers than legitimate heirs, since they were conceived in sexual vigour. See also Rodríguez-Salgado, 'The Anglo-Spanish War: The Final Episode in the Wars of the Roses?', in *England, Spain and the Gran Armada, 1585–1604*, ed. M. J. Rodríguez-Salgado and S. Adams (Edinburgh, 1991), pp. 29–30.

60 Doleman, *A Conference about the Next Succession*, Pt. 1, p. 11; Pt. 2, pp. 150–59, 263–4. Such impudent pro-Spanish claims had a familiar ring. While the Armada was preparing to sail, Parsons had helped to improvise something very similar for King Philip and the crockery-throwing Pope Sixtus V. Said to have been 'in the greatest credit' with Philip around this time, Parsons had introduced him to a skilled genealogist, Robert Heighington, a Catholic exile who had fled to Paris in 1569 after the defeat of the Northern Rising. It was Heighington who had first conjured up, for Count Olivares and shortly

afterwards for Philip and the pope, the ingenious 'proof' that, chiefly through his dynastic claim to the throne of Portugal, Philip was the 'true and rightful' heir of John of Gaunt. See *CSPSp, 2nd Series*, 1587–1603, nos. 176–7; Doleman, *A Conference about the Next Succession*, Pt. 1, pp. 6–9.

61 Collins, I, p. 358; *LASPF*, 1595, p. 214. Arguably Parsons' book fell within the scope of the extended 1571 Treason Act passed in response to the Ridolfi Plot. *SR*, IV, i, pp. 526–8. But this would need to have been tested in the courts.

62 SP 59/31, fos. 40–41; P. Lake, 'The King (the Queen) and the Jesuit: James Stuart's *True Law of Free Monarchies* in Context/s', *TRHS*, 6th Series, 14 (2004), pp. 246–7.

63 Hammer, *Polarisation of Elizabethan Politics*, p. 145, n. 179.

64 Collins, I, p. 350.

65 Birch, *Memoirs*, I, pp. 312–14.

66 SP 59/31, fo. 40.

67 SP 59/31, fo. 38.

68 SP 59/31, fo. 40.

69 *A pithie exhortation to her Maiestie*, 'To the Reader', p. [1]. The defence of James is from *A treatise containing M. Wentworth's iudgement*, pp. 7–60 (especially pp. 39–42); Kewes, 'The Puritan, the Jesuit and the Jacobean Succession', in *Doubtful and Dangerous*, ed. Doran and Kewes, pp. 64–5.

70 *A treatise containing M. Wentworth's iudgement*, p. 2.

71 Lake, 'The King (the Queen) and the Jesuit', pp. 244–5.

72 R. Lane, '"The Sequence of Posterity": Shakespeare's *King John* and the Succession Controversy', *Studies in Philology*, 92 (1995), pp. 460–81; M. Axton, *The Queen's Two Bodies: Drama and the Elizabethan Succession* (London, 1977), pp. 107–11; R. Dutton, 'Shakespeare and Lancaster', *Shakespeare Quarterly*, 49 (1998), pp. 1–21.

Chapter 15: A Counter-Armada

1 HMC, *Hatfield MSS*, VI, p. 280; P. E. J. Hammer, *The Polarisation of Elizabethan Politics: The Political Career of Robert Devereux, 2nd Earl of Essex, 1585–1597* (Cambridge, 1999), pp. 318–21.

2 Birch, *Memoirs*, I, pp. 312–14.

3 Collins, I, p. 360.

4 Collins, I, p. 362; Spedding, I, pp. 374–91; *Francis Bacon: A Critical Edition of the Major Works*, ed. B. Vickers (Oxford, 1996), pp. 61–8, 535–7; R. Strong, 'Elizabethan Pageantry as Propaganda', Courtauld Institute Ph.D. (1962), pp. 131–5.

5 This important discovery was made by Brian Vickers. See *Francis Bacon*, ed. Vickers, p. 537.

6 Essex's impatience with Burghley in particular at this time was well understood in Paris. See SP 78/36, fos. 73–4.

7 Collins, I, p. 362; P. E. J. Hammer, 'Upstaging the Queen: The Earl of Essex, Francis Bacon and the Accession Day Celebrations in 1595', in *The Politics of the Stuart Court Masque*, ed. D. Bevington and P. Holbrook (Cambridge, 1998), pp. 41–66; Hammer, *Polarisation of Elizabethan Politics*, pp. 144–6.

8 Collins, I, p. 362.

9 Spedding, I, p. 377.

10 Hammer, *Polarisation of Elizabethan Politics*, pp. 330–31.

11 J. Harington, *A Tract on the Succession to the Crown*, ed. C. R. Markham (London, 1880), pp. 40–41.

12 Hammer, *Polarisation of Elizabethan Politics*, pp. 248, 331.

13 CUL, MS Ee.3.56, nos. 85, 87; BNF, MS FF 15974, fo. 185v.

14 Hammer, *Polarisation of Elizabethan Politics*, p. 330.

15 H. Wotton, *A Parallel between Robert, Late Earl of Essex, and George, Late Duke of Buckingham* (London, 1641), p. 3; S. W. May, 'The Poems of Edward de Vere, Seventeenth Earl of Oxford, and of Robert Devereux, Second Earl of Essex', *Studies in Philology*, 77, special issue 5 (1980), p. 44.

16 Hammer, *Polarisation of Elizabethan Politics*, p. 332.

17 SP 78/36, fos. 115–16, 117–18, 119–26; Hammer, *Polarisation of Elizabethan Politics*, p. 331.

18 SP 78/37, fos. 25–8, 29–30, 36, 37–8; Murdin, pp. 706–16.

19 D. Piper, 'The 1590 Lumley Inventory: Hilliard, Segar and the Earl of Essex II', *Burlington Magazine*, 99 (1957), pp. 298–303; R. Strong, *The Elizabethan Cult* (Berkeley, CA, 1977), pp. 64–5, 156. For a surviving life-sized half-length version copied from the miniature, see R. Strong, *Tudor and Jacobean Portraits*, 2 vols. (London, 1969), I, p. 116.

20 *LASPF*, 1595, pp. 126–7, 128–30, 131–3, 190, 199–200, 205, 214–15, 215–16; R. B. Wernham, *The Return of the Armadas: The Last Years of the Elizabethan War against Spain, 1595–1603* (Oxford, 1994), pp. 32–40.

21 Wernham, *Return of the Armadas*, pp. 25–7, 45–7.

22 HMC, *Hatfield MSS*, V, pp. 127–8; Collins, I, p. 344.

23 Wernham, *Return of the Armadas*, pp. 46–7.

24 My account of the Drake and Hawkins voyage is worked out from Hakluyt, III, pp. 583–90; J. S. Corbett, *Drake and the Tudor Navy*, 2 vols. (New York, 1899), II, pp. 375–400; Wernham, *Return of the Armadas*, pp. 45–54.

25 SP 12/256, no. 111 (I).

26 Hakluyt, III, p. 584.

27 SP 12/259, no. 61.

28 *LASPF*, 1595, pp. 131–4.

29 SP 12/257, no. 32; Camden, p. 516.

30 SP 78/38, fos. 33, 71–6, 77; Collins, I, p. 378.

31 The key clauses are SP 103/8, fos. 79–80. See also SP 103/8, fos. 86–93; *LASPF*, 1596, nos. 181, 183, 186–95, 197–8, 200, 202–204, 207–8, 214, 217, 222, 235; Lodge, II, p. 500.

32 SP 12/252, no. 110.

33 SP 101/81, fos. 156–9

34 Devereux, I, pp. 333–7; Camden, p. 516; Birch, *Memoirs*, I, pp. 459–60, 465.

35 A. L. Rowse, *Ralegh and the Throckmortons* (London, 1962), p. 198.

36 Devereux, I, p. 342; Birch, *Memoirs*, II, pp. 6–7.

37 Hammer, *Polarisation of Elizabethan Politics*, p. 367.

38 HMC, *Bath MSS*, V, pp. 264–5; *Hatfield MSS*, VI, p. 201; SP 12/259, no. 2; Birch, *Memoirs*, II, pp. 11–12, 15–18; Camden, pp. 515–16.

39 Birch, *Memoirs*, II, p. 15; Camden, p. 515.

40 BL, Cotton MS, Otho E.IX, fos. 343–8. See also BL, Cotton MS, Galba D.XII, fo. 48 (for the promises Elizabeth later claimed had been made by the Lords General).

41 My account of the Cádiz expedition is worked out from SP 12/259, nos. 12, 17–18, 31–2, 50, 70–71, 114; SP 94/5, fos. 146–7; SP 84/52, fos. 250–51; HMC, *Hatfield MSS*, VI, pp. 205–6, 226–7, 250–51; *The Letters of Sir Walter Ralegh*, ed. A. Latham and J. Youings (Exeter, 1999), nos. 101–2; Stow, 1605 edn, pp. 1285–93 (a version of Hakluyt's account censored by the Privy Council); Birch, *Memoirs*, II, pp. 45–59; Camden, pp. 518–22; E. Edwards, *The Life of Sir Walter Ralegh*, 2 vols. (London, 1868), II, pp. 139–56; J. S. Corbett, *The Successors of Drake* (London, 1900), pp. 56–115; Wernham, *Return of the Armadas*, pp. 93–113.

42 *Letters of Sir Walter Ralegh*, ed. Latham and Youings, no. 101.

43 SP 12/259, no. 12 (quotation from fo. 31r).

44 SP 12/259, no. 12. *An Apologie of the Earle of Essex against those which jealously and maliciously tax him to be the hinderer of the peace and quiet of his country* (London, 1603), sigs. B2–4; L. W. Henry, 'The Earl of Essex as Strategist and Military Organizer, 1596–7', *EHR*, 68 (1953), pp. 363–93; P. E. J. Hammer, 'Myth-Making: Politics, Propaganda and

the Capture of Cádiz in 1596', *HJ*, 40 (1997), p. 629; Hammer, *Polarisation of Elizabethan Politics*, pp. 255–64.

45 SP 12/259, no. 50; Hammer, *Polarisation of Elizabethan Politics*, pp. 251–2.

46 *APC*, XXVI, p. 7.

47 'Observacions in the Earle of Essex's example, that it is exceeding dangerous to a Favorite to bee long absent from his Prince', BL, Egerton MS 2026, fo. 32; Hammer, *Polarisation of Elizabethan Politics*, pp. 367–8; Hammer, 'Myth-Making', p. 627.

48 Wernham, *Return of the Armadas*, pp. 110–11.

49 *Letters of Sir Walter Ralegh*, ed. Latham and Youings, no. 102; Edwards, *Life of Sir Walter Ralegh*, II, pp. 142–3; Wernham, *Return of the Armadas*, pp. 118–19.

50 Birch, *Memoirs*, II, pp. 59, 93.

51 Birch, *Memoirs*, II, pp. 121–2, 127; Hammer, 'Myth-Making', pp. 627–8.

52 Birch, *Memoirs*, II, p. 94; S. R. Meyrick, 'Report of the Commissioners Appointed to Inquire into the Amount of Booty Taken at Cádiz in 1596', *Archaeologia*, 22 (1829), pp. 172–89; Wernham, *Return of the Armadas*, pp. 115–21.

53 BL, Cotton MS, Galba D.XII, fo. 48.

54 Birch, *Memoirs*, II, p. 131.

55 Wotton, *A Parallel*, pp. 12–13.

56 Birch, *Memoirs*, II, pp. 45, 81–2, 88–9, 95, 97; Hammer, 'Myth-Making', pp. 631–2.

57 Birch, *Memoirs*, II, pp. 95–6; SP 12/259, nos. 109–10, 124; SP 12/260, nos. 16–17, 28–30; BL, Lansdowne MS 82, fo. 178; Hammer, 'Myth-Making', pp. 628, 631–2; Hammer, *Polarisation of Elizabethan Politics*, pp. 252–4.

58 Birch, *Memoirs*, II, p. 137.

59 Hammer, 'Myth-Making', p. 636.

60 The image tallies closely with the description of Essex given by the Venetian ambassador to France a few weeks after the portrait was commissioned: 'fair-skinned, tall, but wiry; on this last voyage he began to wear a beard which he used not to wear'. See *CSPV*, 1592–1601, no. 505.

61 Yale Center for British Art, Paul Mellon Collection, ref. B1974.2.75; R. Strong, *Tudor and Jacobean Portraits*, 2 vols. (London, 1969), I, pp. 116–17.

62 E. Goldring, 'Portraiture, Patronage and the Progresses', in *The Progresses, Pageants and Entertainments of Queen Elizabeth I*, ed. J. E. Archer, E. Goldring and S. Knight (Oxford, 2007), pp. 163–88; R. Strong, *Portraits of Queen Elizabeth I* (London, 1963), pp. 5–8.

63 Bacon's letter is printed in full in Spedding, II, pp. 40–45.

64 Spedding, II, pp. 42–3.

65 Spedding, II, p. 41.

66 Spedding, II, p. 44.

67 J. Dickinson, *Court Politics and the Earl of Essex, 1589–1601* (London, 2012), p. 110.

Chapter 16: One Last Chance

1 *The Letters of Sir Walter Ralegh*, ed. A. Latham and J. Youings (Exeter, 1999), no. 104; Collins, II, p. 18.

2 P. E. J. Hammer, *The Polarisation of Elizabethan Politics: The Political Career of Robert Devereux, 2nd Earl of Essex, 1585–1597* (Cambridge, 1999), pp. 226–9, 321–2.

3 *The Egerton Papers*, ed. J. P. Collier, *Camden Society*, Old Series, 12 (1840), pp. 215–17; Murdin, p. 809.

4 Birch, *Memoirs*, II, p. 163.

5 Chamberlain, pp. 18, 27; A. L. Rowse, *Shakespeare's Southampton* (London, 1965), pp. 120–28.

6 Birch, *Memoirs*, II, pp. 358–9.

7 H. Wotton, *A Parallel between Robert, Late Earl of Essex, and George, Late Duke of Buckingham* (London, 1641), pp. 5–6; Birch, *Memoirs*, II, p. 501; L. L. Peck, *Northampton: Patronage and Policy at the Court of James I* (London, 1982), pp. 13–18; K. McCarthy, 'Byrd's Patrons at Prayer', *Music and Letters*, 89 (2008), pp. 499–509; Hammer, *Polarisation of Elizabethan Politics*, p. 287.

8 E 351/543 (entries for 1596–8); *A Faithful Abridgment of the Works of That Learned and Judicious Divine, Mr. Richard Hooker . . . With an account of His Life*, ed. I. Walton (London, 1705), p. xxi; J. E. Carney, *Fairy-Tale Queens: Representations of Early Modern Queenship* (London, 2012), p. 79.

9 Collins, II, p. 17.

10 Collins, II, pp. 17–19.

11 Birch, *Memoirs*, II, p. 218.

12 *The Letters of Lady Anne Bacon*, ed. G. Allen, *Camden Society*, 5th Series, 44 (2014), pp. 263–4.

13 *Letters of Lady Anne Bacon*, ed. Allen, p. 266; P. E. J. Hammer, 'Sex and the Virgin Queen: Aristocratic Concupiscence and the Court of Elizabeth I', *SCJ*, 31 (2000), pp. 85–8.

14 HMC, *Hatfield MSS*, VII, p. 392; Collins, II, p. 43.

15 Collins, II, p. 38; HMC, *De L'Isle and Dudley MSS*, II, p. 265. Hammer argues convincingly that the man concerned was Essex, see 'Sex and the Virgin Queen', p. 88.

16 R. V. Schnucker, 'Elizabethan Birth Control and Puritan Attitudes', *Journal of Interdisciplinary History*, 5 (1975), pp. 656–7.

17 Birch, *Memoirs*, II, p. 117; *CSPV*, 1592–1601, nos. 469, 473.

18 *CSPV*, 1592–1601, no. 506 (where the dates are New Style).

19 J. C. Thewlis, 'The Peace Policy of Spain', University of Durham Ph.D. (1975), p. 140.

20 *CSPV*, 1592–1601, nos. 507–508; L. W. Henry, 'The Earl of Essex as Strategist and Military Organizer, 1596–7', *EHR*, 68 (1953)–, p. 373; R. B. Wernham, *The Return of the Armadas: The Last Years of the Elizabethan War against Spain, 1595–1603* (Oxford, 1994), pp. 130–40.

21 Collins, II, pp. 36–7 (the correct date is 19 May), 42, 44, 51, 55; Hammer, *Polarisation of Elizabethan Politics*, pp. 381–3.

22 Collins, II, pp. 42, 54–5; BNF, MS FF 15974, fo. 161v (where the amount given is in livres tournois); Hammer, *Polarisation of Elizabethan Politics*, pp. 381–2.

23 SP 12/264, no. 10; *Letters of Sir Walter Ralegh*, ed. Latham and Youings, no. 107.

24 Collins, II, p. 52.

25 Birch, *Memoirs*, II, pp. 327–8; Wernham, *Return of the Armadas*, pp. 151–4.

26 SP 78/39, fo. 283.

27 SP 84/54, fos. 243–4, 245–6, 247, 259–60; *APC*, XXVII, pp. 132–3; HMC, *Hatfield MSS*, VII, pp. 53–4, 222–3.

28 Henry, 'The Earl of Essex as Strategist and Military Organizer, 1596–7', pp. 373–8; Wernham, *Return of the Armadas*, pp. 154–5.

29 C 76/215A; *Egerton Papers*, ed. Collier, pp. 239–44 (containing a crucial misprint at the foot of p. 241); SP 12/263, nos. 102–4; Henry, 'The Earl of Essex as Strategist and Military Organizer, 1596–7', pp. 378–9; Hammer, *Polarisation of Elizabethan Politics*, pp. 264–5.

30 C 76/215A. See also SP 12/263, nos. 102–4.

31 SP 12/263, no. 103.

32 *An Apologie of the Earle of Essex against those which jealously and maliciously tax him to be the hinderer of the peace and quiet of his country* (London, 1603), sig. B3v.; Hammer, *Polarisation of Elizabethan Politics*, p. 265.

33 Devereux, I, p. 414.

34 SP 12/264, nos. 19–20, 25; *Letters of Sir Walter Ralegh*, ed. Latham and Youings, nos. 108–9.

35 SP 12/264, no. 14 (undated, wrongly dated in *CSPD*, 1595–7, p. 452).

36 SP 12/264, no. 57.

37 SP 63/200, no. 61; Hammer, *Polarisation of Elizabethan Politics*, pp. 265–6.

38 SP 12/45, fos. 64–6; SP 12/264, nos. 74, 77; E 351/543 (entries for 1596–7); *Letters of Sir Walter Ralegh*, ed. Latham and Youings, no. III; Collins, II, p. 59; Devereux, I, pp. 441–2; Henry, 'The Earl of Essex as Strategist and Military Organizer, 1596–7', pp. 382–4.

39 Hammer, *Polarisation of Elizabethan Politics*, p. 265.

40 Birch, *Memoirs*, II, p. 360.

41 SP 15/36, no. 94; SP 12/264, no. 110; *Letters of Sir Walter Ralegh*, ed. Latham and Youings, no. 112; Collins, II, p. 68; Henry, 'The Earl of Essex as Strategist and Military Organizer, 1596–7', pp. 386–7.

42 BNF, MS FF 15974, fo. 164v; HMC, *Hatfield MSS*, VII, pp. 438–9; J. S. Corbett, *The Successors of Drake* (London, 1900), pp. 194–207.

43 A. J. Loomie, 'An Armada Pilot's Survey of the English Coastline, October 1597', *Mariner's Mirror*, 49 (1963), pp. 288–300.

44 SP 12/264, no. 148; Corbett, *Successors of Drake*, pp. 212–25.

45 *APC*, XXVIII, pp. 50–53; A. J. Loomie, 'The Armadas and the Catholics of England', *Catholic Historical Review*, 59 (1973), pp. 398–400.

46 Corbett, *Successors of Drake*, pp. 217–24.

47 Birch, Memoirs, II, p. 361; Hammer, *Polarisation of Elizabethan Politics*, p. 268.

48 HMC, *Hatfield MSS*, VII, p. 433.

49 HMC, *Hatfield MSS*, VII, p. 433.

50 BNF, MS FF 15974, fo. 218.

51 Collins, II, pp. 74–5.

52 BNF, MS FF 15974, fo. 161v–2v; Birch, *Memoirs*, II, p. 361.

53 *Troilus and Cressida*, I, iii, ll. 113–14.

54 Collins, II, p. 77; Birch, *Memoirs*, II, p. 365.

55 Collins, II, p. 77.

56 Hammer, *Polarisation of Elizabethan Politics*, pp. 386–7.

57 BNF, MS FF 15974, fo. 162; Birch, *Memoirs*, II, p. 361.

58 Collins, II, p. 75.

59 Hammer, *Polarisation of Elizabethan Politics*, p. 385.

60 BNF, MS FF 15974, fo. 204; Collins, II, p. 77; HMC, *De L'Isle and Dudley MSS*, II, p. 305.

61 Collins, II, p. 77; Hammer, *Polarisation of Elizabethan Politics*, p. 386.

62 BNF, MS FF 15974, fo. 204.

63 BNF, MS FF 15974, fos. 229v, 249v; Birch, *Memoirs*, II, p. 365.

64 *SR*, III, pp. 729–30.

65 HMC, *Hatfield MSS*, VII, pp. 520, 527; Hammer, *Polarisation of Elizabethan Politics*, pp. 386–8.

66 Camden, pp. 555–6; Birch, *Memoirs*, II, p. 384.

67 W. Ralegh, *The Prerogative of Parl[i]aments in England* (Hamburg [i.e. London], 1628), p. 43. A similar account is given by Edward Hyde in 'The Difference and Disparity between the Estates and Conditions of George, Duke of Buckingham and Robert, Earl of Essex', in *Reliquiae Wottonianae* (London, 1654), p. 51.

68 SP 12/45, fos. 60v–61v; Birch, *Memoirs*, II, pp. 384–6 (printed with inaccuracies). Other versions are SP 12/268, nos. 43–4.

69 SP 12/45, fos. 61v–62v; Birch, *Memoirs*, II, pp. 386–8 (printed with inaccuracies). Other versions are SP 12/268, no. 45–6.

Chapter 17: Seeking Détente

1 M. Steele, 'International Financial Crises during the Reign of Philip II, 1556–1598', London School of Economics Ph.D. (1987), p. 345; I. A. A. Thompson, '*L'Audit de la guerre et de la paix*', in *Le Traité de Vervins*, ed. J. F. Labourdette, J. P. Poussou and M. C. Vignal (Paris, 2000), p. 401.

2 J. C. Thewlis, 'The Peace Policy of Spain', University of Durham Ph.D. (1975), pp. 74–6.

3 *Lettres de Henri IV*, IV, pp. 847–8.

4 SP 78/40, fos. 113–16, 128–9; R. B. Wernham, *The Return of the Armadas: The Last Years of the Elizabethan War against Spain, 1595–1603* (Oxford, 1994), pp. 194–6.

5 *Lettres de Henri IV*, IV, pp. 877–8.

6 SP 12/253, no. 37; SP 12/257, no. 105; SP 12/260, no. 27; SP 12/261, no. 60.

7 SP 12/266, no. 3; *Annals of the Reformation*, ed. J. Strype (4 vols., London, 1824), IV, pp. 451–64.

8 The grant of sovereignty was bestowed four days after the signature of the Treaty of Vervins. The grant was for the whole of the Netherlands, but the power of the Arch-dukes (as Albert and Isabella came to be known) lay only in the obedient southern provinces.

9 BNF, MS FF 15974, fo. 236v.

10 BNF, MS FF 15974, fos. 157–268. Paraphrased French extracts may be found in M. Prév-ost-Paradol, *Élisabeth et Henri IV (1595–1598): Ambassade de Hurault de Maisse* (Paris, 1855), pp. 137–89. An English translation is De Maisse, pp. 1–118. Its accuracy was criticized by L. Jardine, '"Why should he call her a whore?" Defamation and Desdemona's Case', in *Addressing Frank Kermode: Essays in Criticism and Interpretation*, ed. M. Trudeau-Clayton and M. Warner (Urbana and Chicago, 1991), pp. 124–53.

11 BNF, MS FF 15974, fo. 192.

12 Harington, II, pp. 139–40, 232–6; J. Arnold, *Queen Elizabeth's Wardrobe Unlock'd* (Leeds, 1988), p. 104.

13 Harington, II, pp. 140–41.

14 BNF, MS FF 15974, fo. 235v.

15 BNF, MS FF 15974, fos. 181v–2; *Queen Elizabeth and Some Foreigners*, ed. V. von Klarwill (London, 1928), pp. 376–7; Arnold, *Queen Elizabeth's Wardrobe Unlock'd*, pp. 7–8, 128–33.

16 De Maisse, p. 25. Among those recently trusting the translation are A. Whitelock, *Elizabeth's Bedfellows: An Intimate History of the Queen's Court* (London, 2013), p. 297.

17 BNF, MS FF 15974, fos. 181v–2. This important point was first made by Lisa Jardine, but on the basis of the paraphrased extracts in Prévost-Paradol's *Élisabeth et Henri IV* and without reference to the French manuscript of de Maisse's diary, leading to unjustified criticism. See Jardine, '"Why should he call her a whore?"', pp. 146–7; S. Mullaney, 'Mourning and Misogyny: *Hamlet, The Revenger's Tragedy* and the Final Progress of Elizabeth I, 1600–1607', *Shakespeare Quarterly*, 45 (1994), pp. 145–8. All meanings of six-teenth-century French words have been verified from R. Cotgrave, *A Dictionarie of the French and English Tongues* (London, 1611).

18 BNF, MS FF 15974, fo. 182.

19 Arnold, *Queen Elizabeth's Wardrobe Unlock'd*, pp. 131–2; for examples of this style of neckline, see the illustrations in C. Vecellio, *Habiti antichi e moderni di tutto il mondo* (Venice, 1598), pp. 97, 98, 101, 102, 104, 105, 106, 111, 112. See also F. Moryson, *An itiner-ary written by Fynes Moryson Gent. First in the Latine tongue, and then translated by him into English* (London, 1617), Pt. III, iv, 1, pp. 172–3.

20 De Maisse, pp. 36–7.

21 BNF, MS FF 15974, fos. 192v–3; Arnold, *Queen Elizabeth's Wardrobe Unlock'd*, pp. 9, 128–9. The costume issues were first fully explained by Arnold, who had access only to

an unreliable transcript of de Maisse's diary among the Baschet transcripts at the NA, but her conclusions are fully justified by the new BNF manuscript.

22 BNF, MS FF 15974, fo. 210v.

23 BNF, MS FF 15974, fo. 210v. I am heavily indebted here to Arnold, *Queen Elizabeth's Wardrobe Unlock'd*, p. 9, who first argued this case on the strength of the Baschet transcripts.

24 BNF, MS FF 15974, fo. 182r–v; De Maisse, pp. 25–6.

25 *Paul Hentzner's Travels in England during the Reign of Queen Elizabeth*, ed. H. Walpole (London, 1797), p. 34.

26 L. E. Tise and S. N. James, 'The Manteo Portrait of Queen Elizabeth I', paper presented at a National Portrait Gallery/ Courtauld Institute conference on *Tudor and Jacobean Painting: Production, Influences and Patronage* (London, 2010). Published at www.npg.org.uk/research/programmes.

27 A. Riehl, *The Face of Queenship: Early Modern Representations of Elizabeth I* (New York, 2010), p. 167.

28 R. Strong, *Gloriana: The Portraits of Queen Elizabeth I* (London, 1987), p. 147; see also Whitelock, *Elizabeth's Bedfellows*, p. 268.

29 PC 2/21, p. 337; *APC*, XXVI, p. 69. The order condemned 'the abuse committed by divers unskilful artisans in unseemly and improperly painting, [en]graving and printing of her Majesty's person and visage, to her Majesty's great offence'. In future, new images were to be vetted by the queen's Serjeant-Painter, George Gower, before they were used.

30 Victoria and Albert Museum, ref P8–1940. See R. Strong, *Artists of the Tudor Court* (London, 1983), p. 124.

31 Strong, *Artists of the Tudor Court*, pp. 124–6.

32 Strong, *Artists of the Tudor Court*, pp. 126–7.

33 HMC, *Hatfield MSS*, XII, pp. 506–7, 560.

34 CP 140/132; *Diary of John Manningham*, ed. J. Bruce, *Camden Society*, Old Series, 99 (1868), pp. 99–100; Chamberlain, pp. 167–8, 169–70; B. Nicholson, 'Manningham's Diary and Sir John Davies', *Notes and Queries*, 7th Series, 4 (1887), pp. 305–306.

35 F. A. Yates, *Astraea: The Imperial Theme in the Sixteenth Century* (London, 1975), pp. 215–22; Strong, *Gloriana*, pp. 158–61; M. C. Erler, 'Sir John Davies and the Rainbow Portrait of Queen Elizabeth', *Modern Philology*, 84 (1987), pp. 359–71; Arnold, *Queen Elizabeth's Wardrobe Unlock'd*, pp. 81–97; K. Sharpe, *Selling the Tudor Monarchy: Authority and Image in Sixteenth-Century England* (London, 2009), pp. 384–6.

36 J. Dickinson, *Court Politics and the Earl of Essex, 1589–1601* (London, 2012), p. 31.

37 BNF, MS FF 15974, fos. 182v, 194v, 214; De Maisse, pp. 26, 38, 59.

38 BNF, MS FF 15974, fo. 264r–v; De Maisse, pp. 113–14.

39 BNF, MS FF 15974, fos. 161, 252; De Maisse, pp. 4, 100.

40 Collins, II, pp. 83, 88–9; Devereux, I, p. 473.

41 Birch, *Memoirs*, II, p. 373.

42 SP 78/41, fos. 177–80.

43 P. Croft, 'Trading with the Enemy, 1585–1604', *HJ*, 32 (1989), pp. 281–302. For wider contexts, see also A. Gajda, 'Debating War and Peace in Late-Elizabethan England', *HJ*, 52 (2009), pp. 851–78.

44 *Mémoires de Bellièvre et de Sillery*, ed. A. Moetjens, 3 vols. (The Hague, 1696), I, pp. 143–54; Birch, *Hist. View*, pp. 99–100.

45 Birch, *Memoirs*, II, p. 374.

46 Birch, *Memoirs*, II, p. 374; Wernham, *Return of the Armadas*, pp. 219–22.

47 SP 77/5, fos. 245–6, 251–2, 262–3, 288, 295–6, 322; BL, Cotton MS, Vespasian C.VIII, fos. 267–70v, 273–4, 276, 281–4, 289–93, 313–14, 315–16v, 217–18, 319–20; Wernham, *Return of the Armadas*, pp. 223–4.

48 SP 77/5, fos. 256–7; SP 12/268, no. 29.

49 *Mémoires de Bellièvre et de Sillery*, ed. Moetjens, p. 208; Wernham, *Return of the Armadas*, p. 222.
50 Phelippes was finally let out of prison by Robert Cecil shortly after Burghley's death. See *CSPD*, 1598–1601, p. 104. Cecil then retained Phelippes as his personal intelligencer for the rest of the reign.
51 SP 78/41, fos. 246–8.
52 Birch, *Memoirs*, II, pp. 374–5; SP 78/42, fos. 51, 54–6, 60–63v; *Mémoires de Bellièvre et de Sillery*, ed. Moetjens, pp. 238–52; *Lettres de Henri IV*, IV, p. 964.
53 Birch, *Memoirs*, II, pp. 375–9; *Mémoires de Bellièvre et de Sillery*, ed. Moetjens, pp. 257–61, 261–2.
54 SP 78/42, fos. 80, 155.
55 *Lettres de Henri IV*, IV, pp. 970–76, 981.
56 SP 78/42, stamped fos. 91–2; *Lettres de Henri IV*, IV, pp. 970–72; HMC, *Hatfield MSS*, VIII, p. 154 (where the dates are New Style).
57 Birch, *Memoirs*, II, pp. 375–80.
58 BL, Cotton MS, Caligula E.IX, Pt. 2, fo. 225; SP 78/42, fos. 129–30, 131–2 (although these are only office copies, the original as sent was in the queen's own handwriting).
59 Camden, p. 548.
60 BL, Cotton MS, Caligula E.IX, Pt. 2, fo. 65; *Lettres de Henri IV*, IV, pp. 1000–1001.
61 BL, Cotton MS, Caligula E.IX, Pt. 2, fo. 226v.
62 *Gedenkstukken van Johan van Oldenbarnevelt*, ed. M. L. van Deventer, 2 vols. (The Hague, 1860–62), II, pp. 257–64; Wernham, *Return of the Armadas*, pp. 235–6.
63 SP 103/35, fos. 192–5v; *Gedenkstukken van Johan van Oldenbarnevelt*, ed. van Deventer, II, pp. 266–8. See also SP 103/35, fos. 203–206v; Wernham, *Return of the Armadas*, pp. 241–2. The numbers of auxiliaries and their costs are given in SP 12/268, nos. 7–8.
64 SP 12/269, no. 71; *Gedenkstukken van Johan van Oldenbarnevelt*, ed. van Deventer, II, p. 268.
65 Camden, p. 559.
66 S. Alford, *Burghley: William Cecil at the Court of Elizabeth I* (London, 2008), pp. 320–31; Wernham, *Return of the Armadas*, pp. 241–3.
67 *CSPV*, 1592–1601, no. 733; Alford, *Burghley*, pp. 330–31.
68 P. E. J. Hammer, '"Absolute and Sovereign Mistress of Her Grace"? Queen Elizabeth I and Her Favourites, 1581–92', in *The World of the Favourite*, ed. J. H. Elliott and L. W. B. Brockliss (London, 1999), p. 50.
69 CUL, MS Ee.3.56, no. 138.

Chapter 18: Opening New Fronts

1 *CSPV*, 1592–1601, nos. 731–2, 734, 737. See also SP 12/270, no. 31 (I).
2 *CSPV*, 1592–1601, no. 737.
3 J. C. Thewlis, 'The Peace Policy of Spain', University of Durham Ph.D. (1975), pp. ii–iii.
4 *Discurso político al Rey Felipe III al comienzo de su reinado*, ed. M. Santos (Madrid, 1990), pp. 78–9; Thewlis, 'The Peace Policy of Spain', p. 139.
5 Thewlis, 'The Peace Policy of Spain', pp. 140–44; B. Bradshaw, 'Sword, Word and Strategy in the Reformation in Ireland', *HJ*, 21 (1978), pp. 475–502; S. J. Connolly, *Contested Island: Ireland 1460–1630* (Oxford, 2007), pp. 90–99, 184–200.
6 F. Moryson, *An itinerary written by Fynes Moryson Gent. First in the Latine tongue, and then translated by him into English* (London, 1617), Pt. II, i, 1, pp. 19–21.
7 Moryson, *Itinerary*, Pt. II, i, 1, pp. 24–5; Chamberlain, p. 17.
8 Collins, II, p. 103; Spedding, II, pp. 122–3; H. Morgan, 'Hugh O'Neill and the Nine

Years' War in Tudor Ireland', *HJ*, 36 (1993), pp. 21–37; H. Morgan, *DIB*, s.v. 'Hugh O'Neill'; T. Clavin and A. McCormack, *DIB*, s.v. 'Thomas, Lord Burgh (Boroughs)'.

9 J. Spottiswoode, *The History of the Church in Scotland*, 3 vols. (Edinburgh, 1850), III, pp. 1–5.

10 BL, Cotton MS, Caligula D.II, fo. 305; *CSPSM*, 1595–7, pp. 346, 524–5, 530–31; *Foedera*, XVI, pp. 312–13 (supplies missing words in Elizabeth's handwriting lost in the Cottonian Library fire of 1731).

11 *LQEJ*, pp. 121–3.

12 *LQEJ*, pp. 123–5.

13 A. J. Loomie, 'King James I's Catholic Consort', *HLQ*, 34 (1971), pp. 303–16.

14 SP 52/59, no. 74.

15 J. D. Mackie, 'The Secret Diplomacy of King James VI in Italy Prior to His Accession to the English Throne', *SHR*, 21 (1924), pp. 274–7; A. O. Meyer, 'Clemens VIII und Jakob I von England', *Quellen und Forschungen aus italienischen Archiven und Bibliotheken, herausgegeben vom Preußischen Historischen Institut in Rom*, VII (1904), pp. 268–83; C. Sáenz-Cambra, 'Scotland and Philip II, 1580–1598', University of Edinburgh Ph.D. (2003), pp. 196–8.

16 *CKJVI*, pp. 38–42; Mackie, 'The Secret Diplomacy of King James VI', pp. 277–82.

17 SP 63/202, Pt. I, stamped fos. 110, 174; R. Rapple, 'Brinkmanship and Bad Luck: Ireland, the Nine Years' War and the Succession', in *Doubtful and Dangerous: The Question of Succession in Late-Elizabethan England*, ed. S. Doran and P. Kewes (Manchester, 2014), pp. 236–52.

18 Chamberlain, p. 15.

19 Birch, *Memoirs*, II, pp. 390–91.

20 Devereux, I, p. 493.

21 SP 12/45, fos. 20v–1 (the printed abstract in *CSPD*, 1598–1603, pp. 88–9 garbles the sense of this passage).

22 *APC*, XXIX, p. 153; Hammer, *ODNB*, s.v. 'Robert Devereux, 2nd Earl of Essex'.

23 Chamberlain, pp. 19–23.

24 Chamberlain, p. 23.

25 SP 63/203, nos. 88, 94–9; SP 63/204, stamped fos. 218–23; SP 12/269, no. 12.

26 SP 63/204, stamped fo. 138r–v.

27 Moryson, *Itinerary*, Pt. II, i, 1, pp. 27–33; Camden, pp. 568–9; Birch, *Memoirs*, II, pp. 396–7.

28 L. W. Henry, 'The Earl of Essex and Ireland', *BIHR*, 32 (1959), pp. 1–23.

29 *APC*, XXIX, pp. 13–34, 73–5, 79–80, 84–7, 90–91, 100–101, 199–201, 274–5, 323–4; Collins, II, p. 155.

30 SP 63/202, Pt. 4, no. 52.

31 Moryson, *Itinerary*, Pt. II, i, 1, p. 26; Henry, 'The Earl of Essex and Ireland', pp. 4–5.

32 Moryson, *Itinerary*, Pt. II, i, 1, pp. 33–7; *CCM*, 1589–1600, no. 304.

33 Hammer, *ODNB*, s.v. 'Robert Devereux, 2nd Earl of Essex'.

34 HMC, *Hatfield MSS*, IX, pp. 188–9; SP 63/205, nos. 52, 67. See also Essex's strident appeals to the Privy Council, SP 63/205, nos. 38, 65.

35 *CCM*, 1589–1600, no. 306.

36 *CCM*, 1589–1600, no. 306; SP 63/205, nos. 79, 85.

37 SP 63/205, nos. 109, 121; SP 63/204, stamped fos. 177v–9v; *CCM*, 1589–1603, no. 307.

38 HMC, *Hatfield MSS*, XI, pp. 47–8, 72–3; R. B. Wernham, *The Return of the Armadas: The Last Years of the Elizabethan War against Spain, 1595–1603* (Oxford, 1994), pp. 312–13.

39 SP 12/273, no. 35. No one ever knew what precisely had been said at the parley, but for a clear summary of Tyrone's mindset and the main issues, see S. J. Connolly, *Contested Island: Ireland 1460–1630* (Oxford, 2007), pp. 242–9.

40 SP 63/205, nos. 164, 172; *CCM*, 1589–1600, no. 321; Birch, *Memoirs*, II, pp. 428–9; *CSPSp, 2nd Series*, 1587–1603, no. 685.

41 Spedding, II, p. 254.

42 HMC, *Bath MSS*, V, p. 271; SP 12/278, nos. 63, 66; Spedding, pp. 254–6; Rapple,

'Brinkmanship and Bad Luck', in *Doubtful and Dangerous*, ed. Doran and Kewes, pp. 236–52.

43 SP 63/204, stamped fo. 201v.

44 *CCM*, 1589–1600, no. 316.

45 SP 12/271, no. 133; Wernham, *Return of the Armadas*, pp. 263–71.

46 HMC, *Hatfield MSS*, IX, pp. 273, 280–82; *APC*, XXIX, pp. 740–41; SP 12/272, nos. 11–12, 25, 35; *CSPD*, 1598–1601, p. 290; Thewlis, 'The Peace Policy of Spain', pp. 144–5.

47 SP 12/272, nos. 21, 49 (I); HMC, *Hatfield MSS*, IX, pp. 282–3; Chamberlain, pp. 56, 58–60, 61–4; Wernham, *Return of the Armadas*, p. 268.

48 SP 12/272, nos. 70, 80, 84; Collins, II, pp. 111, 119; HMC, *Hatfield MSS*, IX, pp. 327–8; Wernham, *Return of the Armadas*, p. 270.

49 E. Pears, 'The Spanish Armada and the Ottoman Porte', *EHR*, 8 (1893), pp. 439–96; A. L. Horniker, 'William Harborne and the Beginning of Anglo-Turkish Diplomatic and Commercial Relations, *JMH*, 14 (1942), pp. 308–13; S. A. Skilliter, 'The Turkish Documents Relating to Sir Edward Barton's Embassy to the Porte, 1588–1598', University of Manchester Ph.D. (1965), pp. 17–19, 120–21; F. Essadek, 'Representations of Ottoman Sultans in Elizabethan Times', University of Durham Ph.D. (2013), pp. 107–9.

50 C. Read, *Mr Secretary Walsingham and the Policy of Queen Elizabeth*, 3 vols. (Oxford, 1925), III, pp. 226–8; Skilliter, 'Turkish Documents', pp. 15–16; L. Jardine, 'Gloriana Rules the Waves, or, The Advantage of Being Excommunicated (and a Woman)', *TRHS*, 14 (2004), pp. 214–17.

51 Moryson, *Itinerary*, Pt. III, iii, 1, pp. 126–8.

52 HMC, *Hatfield MSS*, XIII, pp. 378–80; R. Knolles, *The Generall Historie of the Turkes* (London, 1610), pp. 1006–1007, where the Sultan's reply is misdated to 1589.

53 SP 97/2, fos. 247–50, 261, 263. Don Solomon was Lopez's sister-in-law's brother.

54 SP 97/2, fo. 255. Don Solomon's agent in London, Judasser Fatim, went to great lengths to persuade Burghley to secure an indefinite reprieve for Lopez, oblivious to the fact that Burghley's and Robert Cecil's interests by that time meant that he had to die, whether guilty or not.

55 Skilliter, 'Turkish Documents', pp. 65–83, 146–51.

56 Skilliter, 'Turkish Documents', pp. 157–8.

57 SP 102/61, fos. 82 (original), 80 (Italian translation); Skilliter, 'Turkish Documents', pp. 98–9, 161–2.

58 *CSPV*, 1592–1601, no. 240; S. A. Skilliter, 'Three Letters from the Ottoman "Sultana" Sāfiye to Queen Elizabeth I', in *Documents from Islamic Chanceries*, ed. S. M. Stern, *Oxford Oriental Studies*, III (Oxford, 1965), p. 149; Jardine, 'Gloriana Rules the Waves', pp. 217–20; Essadek, 'Representations of Ottoman Sultans', pp. 118–19.

59 Skilliter, 'Three Letters', pp. 119–57.

60 BL, Cotton MS, Nero B.VIII, fos. 61–2 (original); SP 97/2, fos. 295–6 (Italian translation); Hakluyt, II, i, pp. 311–12; Skilliter, 'Three Letters', pp. 130–33, 147–8; Jardine, 'Gloriana Rules the Waves', p. 219. An inventory and valuation of these gifts prepared under Barton's supervision before they left Istanbul reckoned they were worth £120 (£120,000 in modern values) and also indicates that some items were embezzled before delivery to the queen. See SP 97/2, fo. 230; Skilliter, 'Three Letters', p. 148.

61 SP 102/4, fos. 5, 19; SP 102/61, fo. 74 (Italian translation of SP 102/4, fo. 19); Skilliter, 'Three Letters', pp. 133–40; Jardine, 'Gloriana Rules the Waves', pp. 220–22.

62 SP 97/4, fos. 48–50; Skilliter, 'Three Letters', pp. 150–51.

63 *Early Voyages and Travels in the Levant*, ed. J. T. Bent, *Hakluyt Society*, 1st Series, 87 (1893), p. 63.

64 For a fuller description of the voyage and of Dallam's adventures, see *Early Voyages and Travels in the Levant*, ed. Bent, pp. 4–98. See also J. Carswell, 'The Queen, the Sultan and the Organ', *Asian Affairs*, 25 (1994), pp. 13–23.

65 See *Treasures of the Royal Courts: Tudors, Stuarts and the Russian Tsars* (London, 2013), pp. 159–65.

66 *Early Voyages and Travels in the Levant*, ed. Bent, pp. 61–3; Skilliter, 'Three Letters', p. 150 (where the dates are New Style).

67 *Early Voyages and Travels in the Levant*, ed. Bent, pp. 67–8. The description given by Carswell, 'The Queen, the Sultan and the Organ', pp. 16–18, drawn from an article in the *Illustrated London News* for 20 October 1860, may not conform to the finished version of the instrument, even if the (lost) document from which it purports to be derived is genuine.

68 E 112/26/101. For Schetz's activities, see E 351/543 (entries for 1598–9, 1599–1600); LC 5/31; REQ 2/34/115; REQ 2/136/91; REQ 2/265/25.

69 *Early Voyages and Travels in the Levant*, ed. Bent, pp. 68–70.

70 *Early Voyages and Travels in the Levant*, ed. Bent, pp. 70–73; Carswell, 'The Queen, the Sultan and the Organ', pp. 20–22.

71 *Early Voyages and Travels in the Levant*, ed. Bent, pp. 73–80.

72 SP 97/4, fos. 53–4; *Early Voyages and Travels in the Levant*, ed. Bent, p. 80; Skilliter, 'Three Letters', p. 151 (where the dates are New Style).

73 Skilliter, 'Three Letters', pp. 139, 151.

74 Skilliter, 'Three Letters', pp. 152–3.

75 *Early Voyages and Travels in the Levant*, ed. Bent, p. 98; Collins, II, p. 194.

76 K. N. Chaudhuri, *The English East India Company: The Study of an Early Joint-Stock Company, 1600–1640* (London, 1965), pp. 10–14.

Chapter 19: Defying the Queen

1 Collins, II, p. 114; SP 12/264, no. 77; BNF, MS FF 15974, fo. 174v.

2 Harington, II, p. 291.

3 Harington, II, p. 255.

4 Harington, II, pp. 289–90.

5 SP 63/205, no. 121.

6 SP 63/205, no. 121.

7 P. E. J. Hammer, '"Absolute and Sovereign Mistress of Her Grace"? Queen Elizabeth I and Her Favourites, 1581–92', in *The World of the Favourite*, ed. J. H. Elliott and L. W. B. Brockliss (London, 1999), pp. 49–50.

8 Collins, II, pp. 119–22.

9 Collins, II, p. 128; Devereux, II, p. 77.

10 Collins, II, pp. 127–9; Devereux, II, pp. 77–9.

11 Collins, II, pp. 127–8.

12 Collins, II, p. 129.

13 Collins, II, p. 129.

14 Collins, II, p. 129.

15 Collins, II, p. 129.

16 Collins, II, pp. 131–2.

17 *The Letters and Epigrams of Sir John Harington*, ed. N. E. McClure (Philadelphia, 1930), p. 122.

18 Folger, MS V.a.321, fos. 4v–5; Birch, *Memoirs*, II, pp. 440–41.

19 Folger, MS V.a.321, fos. 4v–5; SP 63/205, no. 246; SP 12/268, no. 45; SP 12/273, nos. 36–7.

20 SP 12/273, no. 38.

21 SP 12/273, no. 38.

22 Collins, II, p. 134; Birch, *Memoirs*, II, p. 436. For the identity of 'Dr Brown', see E 351/543, m. 52.

23 Collins, II, p. 139; Birch, *Memoirs*, II, p. 438.

24 Collins, II, p. 151; Birch, *Memoirs*, II, p. 441.

25 Collins, II, p. 153.
26 Collins, II, p. 159; Birch, *Memoirs*, II, p. 441.
27 Collins, II, p. 167; HMC, *De L'Isle and Dudley MSS*, II, p. 443.
28 Collins, II, pp. 156, 158; Birch, II, *Memoirs*, p. 441.
29 Collins, II, p. 156; Birch, *Memoirs*, II, p. 441.
30 BM, Department of Prints and Drawings, ref O.7.283 (engraving of Essex); Hammer, *ODNB*, s.v. 'Robert Devereux, 2nd Earl of Essex'.
31 Birch, *Memoirs*, II, p. 442.
32 SP 12/274, no. 39.
33 SP 12/274, no. 40.
34 SP 52/52, p. 29 (this entry book is paginated, not foliated).
35 SP 12/274, no. 40 (endorsement).
36 This is the only possible inference from the sequence of events. In any case, Elizabeth had ordered only Windebank's written version of her instructions not to be sent. Her order to him to inform Cecil verbally of her wish to stop the Star Chamber proceedings still stood.
37 SP 12/274, no. 42.
38 Birch, *Memoirs*, II, p. 443.
39 SP 12/274, no. 95.
40 Birch, *Memoirs*, II, pp. 384, 444.
41 Birch, *Memoirs*, II, p. 444. For a highly convincing argument that the printed edition of Essex's *Apologie* would be deliberately disseminated by his secretariat in the context of the peace negotiations at Boulogne in 1601, see A. Gajda, 'Debating War and Peace in Late-Elizabethan England', *HJ*, 52 (2009), pp. 858–62.
42 SP 12/275, no. 13; Birch, *Memoirs*, II, pp. 447–54.
43 Birch, *Memoirs*, II, p. 454.
44 *CKJVI*, p. 105; Birch, *Memoirs*, II, p. 472.
45 Devereux, II, p. 125.
46 *CKJVI*, pp. 105–6.
47 Collins, II, pp. 134, 137, 140, 142, 143–5, 162–4, 165, 177–9, 214; HMC, *De L'Isle and Dudley MSS*, II, pp. 404, 407, 408, 409, 414, 415, 416, 417, 418, 420, 434, 437, 447, 451, 458, 461, 465, 466, 478, 481, 483, 487, 489.
48 F. Moryson, *An itinerary written by Fynes Moryson Gent. First in the Latine tongue, and then translated by him into English* (London, 1617), Pt. II, i, 1, pp. 54–94; S. J. Connolly, *Contested Island: Ireland 1460–1630* (Oxford, 2007), pp. 238–54; R. Hawkins, *DIB*, s.v. 'Charles Blount, Lord Mountjoy'.
49 *CKJVI*, p. 86.
50 *CKJVI*, p. 102.
51 *CKJVI*, p. 103.
52 *CKJVI*, p. 103.
53 *CKJVI*, p. 97.
54 *CKJVI*, pp. 103–4.
55 *CKJVI*, pp. 89, 98, 105–6.
56 *CKJVI*, p. 89.
57 *CKJVI*, pp. 89–90.
58 *CKJVI*, p. 89.
59 *CKJVI*, p. 90.
60 *CKJVI*, pp. 81–5.
61 SP 12/278, no. 92. The timings of these depositions are a little confused. I am following the timings given by Stow, 1631 edn, pp. 792–4.
62 SP 12/278, nos. 49–50, 92.
63 SP 12/278, no. 92.
64 SP 12/278, no. 55.
65 SP 12/278, no. 54; Folger, MS V.a.321, fos. 9v–11.
66 SP 12/278, no. 54.

Chapter 20: 'I am Richard II'

1 It has sometimes been suggested that Essex may at this stage have crossed over into some form of mental illness. If the venereal disease for which Dr Lopez had been treating him shortly before Christmas 1593 were syphilis, then his mind could well have been affected, since the common symptoms of advanced syphilis, and the side effects of the brutal treatment by a medical procedure known as 'salivation of mercury', included disorientation, hallucinations and paranoia. But no proof of this hypothesis can be found.

2 SP 12/278, no. 89.

3 SP 12/278, no. 93.

4 SP 12/278, no. 84.

5 SP 12/278, nos. 84, 87, 89, 93. See also SP 12/278, no. 125.

6 SP 12/278, no. 84.

7 SP 12/279, no. 12.

8 SP 12/278, nos. 62, 72, 78; P. E. J. Hammer, 'Shakespeare's *Richard II*, the Play of 7 February 1601 and the Essex Rising', *Shakespeare Quarterly*, 59 (2008), p. 25.

9 SP 12/279, no. 3.

10 SP 12/278, no. 75. See also SP 12/278, no. 51; Hammer, 'Shakespeare's *Richard II*, the Play of 7 February 1601 and the Essex Rising', p. 15. Hammer argues persuasively that Sir Ferdinando Gorges may have been acting as a spy for Ralegh, and that he told Essex of a plot to kill him in order to push him into some action that would persuade the queen to send him permanently to the Tower.

11 SP 12/278, no. 69.

12 SP 12/278, nos. 71–2.

13 SP 12/278, nos. 47, 51, 75.

14 SP 12/278, nos. 51, 57–60; SP 12/279, nos. 6, 8–9. Sheriff Smyth would later confess that a copy of just such a letter, drafted by Essex in his own handwriting, had been prepared that very morning, because a copy was given to his wife while she was in church. See SP 12/278, no. 59.

15 SP 12/278, nos. 46–7, 97.

16 SP 12/278, no. 97.

17 SP 12/278, no. 97.

18 SP 12/278, no. 56.

19 SP 12/278, no. 46.

20 SP 12/278, no. 44.

21 SP 12/278, nos. 44, 49–50; Stow, 1631 edn, pp. 792–4.

22 SP 12/278, nos. 49–50.

23 Stow, 1631 edn, p. 792; SP 12/278, nos. 45, 91–2.

24 SP 12/278, nos. 44, 49–50; Stow, 1631 edn, p. 793.

25 SP 12/278, nos. 49–50.

26 SP 12/278, no. 84.

27 SP 12/278, no. 44; Stow, 1631 edn, p. 793.

28 SP 12/278, no. 44.

29 SP 12/279, no. 16.

30 SP 12/278, nos. 38–41, 44, 49–50; Folger MS V.b.142; Stow, 1631 edn, p. 793; Camden, p. 610.

31 SP 12/278, no. 44. Interestingly, Cecil first called it 'this tragical accident', but scored out 'tragical' and wrote in 'dangerous'.

32 SP 12/278, no. 61; SP 15/34, no. 34.

33 SP 12/278, nos. 61–2; SP 15/34, no. 34; Hammer, 'Shakespeare's *Richard II*, the Play of 7 February 1601 and the Essex Rising', pp. 8, 16.

34 Haynes, pp. 811–12.

35 SP 12/278, no. 85. See also J. Bate, *Soul of the Age: The Life, Mind and World of William Shakespeare* (London, 2008), pp. 256–7.

36 Bate, *Soul of the Age*, pp. 249–60; Hammer, 'Shakespeare's *Richard II*, the Play of 7 February 1601 and the Essex Rising', pp. 1–35.

37 Bate, *Soul of the Age*, p. 255.

38 *Richard II*, II, iii, ll. 166–7.

39 J. Hayward, *The First Part of the Life and Raigne of King Henrie the IIII, Extending to the End of the First Yeare of his Raigne* (London, 1599), sig. [A2]. After the inflammatory dedication came a 'Preface to the Reader', mysteriously signed 'A.P.', which urged Essex to consider 'the faithful records of histories' to be 'precepts' and 'lively patterns, both for private direction and for affairs of state' (sig. A3). See also Hammer, 'Shakespeare's *Richard II*, the Play of 7 February 1601 and the Essex Rising', p. 9.

40 *The First and Second Parts of John Hayward's 'The Life and Raigne of King Henrie IIII'*, ed. J. J. Manning, *Camden Society*, 4th Series, 42 (1991), pp. 17–25. Asked by the queen if he could find treason in the book, Francis Bacon later claimed to have replied, whimsically, that he was unable to discover treason, merely felony, since Hayward had lifted whole passages and sentences word for word from Tacitus. If true, it is unlikely that she was amused. More likely, the story is *ben trovato*. See *The Works of Francis Bacon*, ed. J. Spedding, R. L. Ellis and D. D. Heath, 14 vols. (Cambridge, 2011), VII, p. 133.

41 SP 12/278, nos. 35, 54–5, 62–3, 66.

42 SP 12/278, nos. 17, 54, 63; Folger MS V.a.321, fos. 9v–11; *The First and Second Parts*, ed. Manning, pp. 32–4; Hammer, 'Shakespeare's *Richard II*, the Play of 7 February 1601 and the Essex Rising', pp. 9–10.

43 *CKJVI*, pp. xxvii–xxviii, and Appendix, Pt. 2, nos. 1–2, pp. 80–81. See also SP 12/278, nos. 69–70.

44 *CKJVI*, Appendix, Pt. 2, no. 6, p. 90; SP 12/279, no. 5.

45 *CKJVI*, Appendix, Pt. 2, no. 1, p. 80.

46 The best contemporary accounts of the trial are SP 12/278, nos. 101–102. The second of these (pencilled fos. 183–98) is, unfortunately, incomplete. Both are superior to the version printed in *State Trials*, I, pp. 197–209. See also BL, Lansdowne MS 94, fos. 127–33.

47 SP 12/278, no. 125.

48 *State Trials*, I, pp. 207–8.

49 BL, Cotton MS, Titus C.VII, fo. 69r–v; SP 12/278, nos. 104, 125; Birch, *Memoirs*, II, pp. 475–81; G. B. Harrison, *The Life and Death of Robert Devereux, Earl of Essex* (London, 1937), pp. 315–18, 321–2, Hammer, *ODNB*, s.v. 'Robert Devereux, 2nd Earl of Essex'.

50 BL, Cotton MS, Titus C.VII, fo. 125v.

51 BL, Cotton MS, Titus C.VII, fo. 68; SP 12/278, nos. 111–12, 114; BL, Lansdowne MS 94, fo. 134.

52 The classic account is L. Strachey, *Elizabeth and Essex* (London, 1928; repr. 1971), p. 166.

53 Camden, p. 622.

54 SP 12/278, no. 111 (pencilled fo. 218).

55 SP 12/278, no. 111 (pencilled fos. 218v–19).

56 Camden, p. 622.

57 BL, Lansdowne MS 59, no. 22; SP 12/279, no. 93; *APC*, XXXI, pp. 55–6, 333–6, 346–8.

58 E 351/543, m. 69; Hammer, 'Shakespeare's *Richard II*, the Play of 7 February 1601 and the Essex Rising', p. 20; Harrison, *Life and Death of Robert Devereux*, pp. 322, 350.

59 BL, Stowe MS 543, fos. 55–8v; Nichols, III, pp. 542–3; J. Scott-Warren, 'Was Elizabeth I Richard II? The Authenticity of William Lambarde's "Conversation"', *Review of English Studies*, New Series, 64 (2012), pp. 208–30. Discussion of this topic has been transformed by the discovery of Kent History and Library Centre, MS U350/C2/15, edited and collated with other versions of the text by Scott-Warren in op. cit., pp. 228–30.

60 Scott-Warren, 'Was Elizabeth I Richard II?', pp. 225–6, 228.

61 Scott-Warren, 'Was Elizabeth I Richard II?', pp. 228–9.
62 For a sceptical view, see Bate, *Soul of the Age*, pp. 282–6. For its refutation, see Scott-Warren, 'Was Elizabeth I Richard II?', pp. 211–14.
63 My interpretation both agrees with, and is informed by, Hammer, 'Shakespeare's *Richard II*, the Play of 7 February 1601 and the Essex Rising', pp. 23–5.
64 *APC*, XXXI, pp. 155, 157.
65 *Richard II*, V, vi, ll. 38–52.

Chapter 21: The Queen's Speech

1 Collins, II, pp. 128, 130.
2 SP 77/6, fo. 46; A. J. Loomie, 'Philip III and the Stuart Succession in England, 1600–1603', *Revue Belge de philologie et d'histoire*, 43 (1965), pp. 492–514; J. C. Grayson, 'From Protectorate to Partnership: Anglo-Dutch Relations, 1598–1625', University of London Ph.D. (1978), pp. 35–9; R. B. Wernham, *The Return of the Armadas: The Last Years of the Elizabethan War against Spain, 1595–1603* (Oxford, 1994), pp. 321–34.
3 SP 77/6, fo. 59; SP 84/59, fos. 164–8; Collins, II, p. 155; Grayson, 'From Protectorate to Partnership', p. 35.
4 J. C. Thewlis, 'The Peace Policy of Spain', University of Durham Ph.D. (1975), pp. 61–2; Grayson, 'From Protectorate to Partnership', pp. 35–41; A. Gajda, 'Debating War and Peace in Late-Elizabethan England', *HJ*, 52 (2009), p. 858.
5 Collins, II, p. 177.
6 Collins, II, pp. 175–6. The play of *Sir John Oldcastle* watched by Verreycken was renamed *Henry IV, Part I* at some time early in the play's maiden run after furious protests from the Cobham family, the descendants of Oldcastle. At the same time, Sir John's name was changed from Oldcastle to Falstaff.
7 L. Duerloo, *Dynasty and Piety: Archduke Albert (1598–1621) and Habsburg Political Culture in an Age of Religious Wars* (Farnham, 2012), pp. 116–17. The English sources, chiefly Collins, II, pp. 175–7, create the impression that Verreycken was sumptuously received as well as treated to a special performance of Shakespeare's *Henry IV, Part I*, but the Flemish sources give a very different impression.
8 SP 12/274, no. 49; SP 77/6, fo. 241; Birch, *Hist. View*, pp. 195–8.
9 SP 77/6, fos. 164, 168–70; Winwood, I, pp. 171–5.
10 BL, Cotton MS, Vespasian C.VIII, fos. 379–83v; SP 77/6, fos. 264–70; Winwood, I, pp. 186–226.
11 Thewlis, 'The Peace Policy of Spain', pp. 144–6 (citing AGS, E2511/3).
12 Thewlis, 'The Peace Policy of Spain', pp. 145–9.
13 SP 63/209, Pt. I, stamped fo. 257; *CSPSp, 2nd Series*, 1587–1603, no. 699; D. Goodman, *Spanish Naval Power, 1589–1665: Reconstruction and Defeat* (Cambridge, 1997), p. 207.
14 *CSPSp, 2nd Series*, 1587–1603, no. 699.
15 SP 63/209, Pt. I, stamped fos. 222–37, 243, 295; SP 63/209, Pt. 2, stamped fos. 43, 50–51, 52–3v; *APC*, XXXII, pp. 222–7, 233–46, 257–8, 260–62, 273–86; Chamberlain, p. 119; Wernham, *Return of the Armadas*, pp. 377–81; S. J. Connolly, *Contested Island: Ireland 1460–1630* (Oxford, 2007), pp. 250–51 (where all dates are New Style).
16 SP 63/209, Pt. II, stamped fo. 257.
17 SP 63/209, Pt. II, stamped fos. 101–2, 366–7; F. Moryson, *An itinerary written by Fynes Moryson Gent. First in the Latine tongue, and then translated by him into English* (London, 1617), Pt. II, ii, 2, pp. 176–8; Connolly, *Contested Island*, pp. 251–2.
18 SP 63/209, Pt. II, stamped fos. 366–7.
19 SP 63/209, Pt. II, stamped fos. 394–5, 404–405; Connolly, *Contested Island*, pp. 251–3.
20 *Secret Corr.*, p. 25.

21 Townshend, pp. 183–5; HMC, *Hatfield MSS*, XV, pp. 1–2; SP 12/273, nos. 35–7; SP
    12/275, nos. 10, 87, 143; SP 12/287, no. 59.

22 J. E. Neale, *Elizabeth I and Her Parliaments*, 2 vols. (London, 1969), II, p. 372.

23 Townshend, pp. 188, 224.

24 D'Ewes, pp. 632–3.

25 D'Ewes, p. 623; Townshend, p. 183.

26 Folger MS V.a.459, fos. 7–27v, 43, 67, 91v–2v; Folger MS V.a.460, fo. 58; E 192/3/1–5;
    HMC, *Hatfield* MSS, III, pp. 311–12, 377; C. Coleman, 'Artifice or Accident? The Reor-
    ganization of the Exchequer of Receipt, *c.*1554–1572', in *Revolution Reassessed: Revisions
    in the History of Tudor Government and Administration*, ed. C. Coleman and D. Starkey
    (Oxford, 1986), pp. 181–91; J. Hurstfield, *The Queen's Wards: Wardship and Marriage under
    Elizabeth I* (London, 1958), pp. 227–8; J. Pennington, *ODNB*, s.v. 'Sir Thomas Sherley';
    P. E. J. Hammer, *The Polarisation of Elizabethan Politics: The Political Career of Robert
    Devereux, 2nd Earl of Essex, 1585–1597* (Cambridge, 1999), pp. 354–5.

27 D'Ewes, pp. 632–3; Hartley, III, p. 338; Townshend, pp. 203–204; F. C. Dietz, *English
    Public Finance, 1485–1641*, 2 vols. (London, 1964), II, pp. 384–8.

28 Hartley, III, p. 338; Townshend, p. 204.

29 D. H. Sacks, 'The Countervailing of Benefits: Monopoly, Liberty and Benevolence in
    Elizabethan England', in *The Tudor Monarchy*, ed. J. Guy (London, 1977), pp. 135–55.

30 D'Ewes, p. 650; Townshend, pp. 238–9, 243–5; Murdin, p. 811; Lodge, III, pp. 6–10;
    APC, XXXI, pp. 55–6; Hartley, III, pp. 387–90; A. Dimock, 'The Conspiracy of Dr
    Lopez', *EHR*, 9 (1894), pp. 440–41.

31 D'Ewes, pp. 158, 554, 555, 558, 567–8, 570, 573, 582, 586; Hartley, III, pp. 203–4, 241,
    242; A. F. Pollard and M. Blatcher, 'Hayward Townshend's Journals', *BIHR*, 12 (1934),
    p. 25; T. B. Nachbar, 'Monopoly, Mercantilism and the Politics of Regulation', *Virginia
    Law Review*, 91 (2005), pp. 1328–30; Neale, *Elizabeth I and Her Parliaments*, II, pp. 352–6,
    365–7; Sacks, 'Countervailing of Benefits', p. 136.

32 SP 12/279, no. 93; SP 12/282, no. 8; *APC*, XXXI, pp. 55–6, 333–6, 346–8; *APC*, XXXII,
    pp. 132–3; Sacks, 'Countervailing of Benefits', pp. 136–7.

33 Townshend, pp. 224, 230–33.

34 Townshend, p. 233.

35 Townshend, p. 234.

36 Townshend, pp. 234–46.

37 Hartley, III, p. 391 (from BL, Stowe MS 359, fo. 285v).

38 Hartley, III, p. 391; Neale, *Elizabeth I and Her Parliaments*, II, p. 383.

39 Townshend, pp. 248–9.

40 Townshend, pp. 249–50.

41 D'Ewes, pp. 652–3; Townshend, pp. 248–52.

42 *The Letters and Epigrams of Sir John Harington*, ed. N. E. McClure (Philadelphia, 1930), p. 90.

43 *TRP*, III, no. 812.

44 Townshend, p. 259.

45 BL, Lansdowne MS 94, fo. 123; *Letters Relating to the Family of Beaumont of Whitley, York-
    shire, from the Fifteenth to the Seventeenth Centuries*, ed. W. D. Macray (London, 1884), p. 10;
    Hartley, III, p. 250; Neale, *Elizabeth I and Her Parliaments*, II, pp. 392–3, 427–8. Next
    day, the queen sent a groom of the Privy Chamber to Savile's house, ordering him to
    allow nobody to see or to copy this version of the speech, though perhaps for no other
    reason than to uphold the royal printer Robert Barker's privileged commercial position.

46 D'Ewes, pp. 658–9.

47 Hartley, III, pp. 288–91, 294–7; *Queene Elizabeth's Speech to Her Last Parliament* (London,
    1628), sigs. A2–[4].

48 Camden, pp. 635–6.

49 This survives as a fair copy in BL, Lansdowne MS 94, fo. 123, where it is endorsed 'Her
    Majesty's speech to the Speaker and knights and burgesses of the Lower House'. See also
    Hartley, III, pp. 292–3.

50 SP 12/282, no. 67 appears to be a proof copy from Cecil's papers. It is not clear whether, as Neale suggested, the printed speech referred to by Sir Dudley Carleton in his letter to John Chamberlain of 29 December refers to the 'Golden Speech' or the speech the queen gave at the close of the session. See SP 12/283, no. 48; Neale, *Elizabeth I and Her Parliaments*, II, p. 392.

51 SP 12/282, no. 67 (title page); Hartley, III, pp. 292–3.

52 Whether all copies, including reprints, had the royal arms is an open question. The proof copy in SP 12/287, no. 67 certainly did.

53 SP 12/282, no. 67 (pp. 2–4); Hartley, pp. 292–3.

54 *The House of Commons, 1558–1603*, ed. P. W. Hasler, 3 vols. (London, 1981), III, pp. 516–17.

55 Townshend, p. 239.

56 Townshend, p. 263.

57 Townshend, p. 264. For commentary on these themes, see Sacks, 'Countervailing of Benefits', pp. 139–41.

58 Townshend, p. 265.

59 Townshend, p. 264–5. For Elizabeth's earlier failure to act on information of abuses of the royal prerogative, see Neale, *Elizabeth I and Her Parliaments*, I, pp. 218–19, 221–2; II, pp. 352–6, 365–7.

60 Townshend, p. 266.

61 Townshend, pp. 271–2.

62 SP 12/264, no. 57 (I); J. M. Green, 'Queen Elizabeth's Latin Reply to the Polish Ambassador', *SCJ*, 31 (2000), pp. 987–1008; R. B. Wernham, *After the Armada: Elizabethan England and the Struggle for Western Europe, 1588–1595* (Oxford, 1984), pp. 199–200.

63 D'Ewes, p. 668; HMC, *Hatfield MSS*, XV, p. 2.

64 D'Ewes, pp. 656–7; R. C. Munden, 'Government and Opposition: Initiative, Reform and Politics in the House of Commons, 1597–1610', University of East Anglia Ph.D. (1985), pp. 128–9.

65 *House of Commons*, ed. Hasler, II, pp. 45–6.

66 SP 12/284, no. 47.

67 SP 12/286, nos. 47–8; *The Reports of Sir Edward Coke, Knight, in English, in Thirteen Parts Complete*, 7 vols. (London, 1777), VI, fos. 84–8v; D. H. Sacks, 'Parliament, Liberty and the Commonweal', in *Parliament and Liberty from Elizabeth I to the Civil War*, ed. J. H. Hexter (Stanford, CA, 1992), pp. 85–121.

68 *TRP*, III, no. 812.

Chapter 22: On a Knife's Edge

1 Chamberlain, p. 99.

2 Harington, II, pp. 256–7. Baynard's Castle was on loan to the Sidneys from Henry Herbert, Earl of Pembroke.

3 J. Clapham, *Certain Observations Concerning the Life and Reign of Queen Elizabeth*, ed. E. P. Read and C. Read (Philadelphia, 1951), p. 86.

4 Clapham, *Certain Observations*, ed. Read and Read, p. 90.

5 Winwood, I, p. 292; M. Wyatt, *The Italian Encounter with Tudor England* (Cambridge, 2005), pp. 130–34.

6 Alnwick Castle, MS 7, fo. 22, facsimile in N. Drumbolis, *The Chamberlain's Notes for Twelfth Night at Whitehall: A Closer Look at the Alnwick Manuscript* (n.p., 2014), p. 56.

7 L. Hotson, *The First Night of Twelfth Night* (London, 1954), *passim*; 'Introduction', *Twelfth Night*, ed. E. S. Donno and P. Gay (Cambridge, 2004; 2nd edn), pp. 1–4.

8 For Hales's presence that day, see Alnwick Castle, MS 7, fo. 22.

9 Wyatt, *Italian Encounter with Tudor England*, pp. 132–3, which is based on the transcript of one of Orsini's letters to his wife by R. Zapperi, *Virginio Orsini: Un paladino nei palazzi incantati* (Palermo, 1993), pp. 60–68. In readiness for Orsini's entertainment, the Earl of Worcester's lodging at Whitehall was refurbished, as were the chapel and closet. See E 351/543 (entries for 1600–1601).

10 De Maisse, p. 95.

11 De Maisse, p. 95; G. Goodman, *The Court of King James I*, ed. J. S. Brewer, 2 vols. (London, 1839), I, pp. 17–18; Wyatt, *Italian Encounter with Tudor England*, p. 133.

12 Chamberlain, pp. 99–100.

13 *CCM*, 1601–1603, no. 315.

14 *The Letters and Epigrams of Sir John Harington*, ed. N. E. McClure (Philadelphia, 1930), pp. 90–91.

15 *Secret Corr.*, p. 26; Hartley, III, pp. 288–9.

16 'The State of England AD 1600 by Thomas Wilson', ed. F. J. Fisher, *Camden Society*, 3rd Series, 52 (1936), pp. 2–6; 'Introduction', in *Doubtful and Dangerous: The Question of Succession in Late-Elizabethan England*, ed. S. Doran and P. Kewes (Manchester, 2014), pp. 4–5.

17 SP 12/273, no. 35; SP 12/278, no. 55.

18 J. Harington, *A Tract on the Succession to the Crown*, ed. C. R. Markham (London, 1880), pp. 38–9.

19 Harington, *Tract on the Succession*, ed. Markham, p. 51.

20 HMC, *Hatfield MSS*, VIII, pp. 77–8, 152–3.

21 A. Courtney, 'The Scottish King and the English Court: The Secret Correspondence of James VI, 1601–1603', in *Doubtful and Dangerous*, ed. Doran and Kewes, p. 136.

22 SP 52/62, nos. 39, 43, 49–51.

23 SP 52/62, no. 44 (endorsed as written in Elizabeth's own hand); HMC, *Hatfield MSS*, XIX, pp. 1–3 (where wrongly dated).

24 HMC, *Hatfield MSS*, XI, pp. 137–8; *LQEJ*, p. 137.

25 *Secret Corr.*, pp. 1–12. That James dictated Mar and Bruce's instructions himself and kept them secret even from his own advisers is clear from SP 52/67, no. 8.

26 *Secret Corr.*, pp. 9–10.

27 *CSPD*, 1601–1603 and Addenda, p. 25; Courtney, 'The Scottish King and the English Court', in *Doubtful and Dangerous*, ed. Doran and Kewes, p. 138.

28 SP 52/67, no. 32, endorsed by the filing clerk 'Copy of her Majesty's letter to the King of Scots written with her own hand'.

29 *CKJVI*, p. xxxv.

30 *LQEJ*, p. 138.

31 *Secret Corr.*, pp. 13–235; *CKJVI*, pp. 38–52. Much of this correspondence was intended for James, to be channelled through third parties, chiefly Edward Bruce.

32 *Secret Corr.*, p. 66. Elsewhere, Howard spoke of the 'diabolical triplicity' of Ralegh, Cobham and Henry Percy, Earl of Northumberland. See *Secret Corr.*, pp. 29, 112.

33 *Secret Corr.*, pp. 27–39.

34 Courtney, 'The Scottish King and the English Court', in *Doubtful and Dangerous*, ed. Doran and Kewes, pp. 143–4.

35 *Letters from Sir Robert Cecil to Sir George Carew*, ed. J. Maclean, *Camden Society*, Old Series, 88 (1864), pp. 84–5, 89, 108, 116; M. Nicholls and P. Williams, *Sir Walter Ralegh in Life and Legend* (London, 2011), pp. 182–5.

36 *The Works of Sir Walter Ralegh, Knight*, 8 vols. (Oxford, 1829), VIII, pp. 756–70.

37 SP 52/67, no. 54; Courtney, 'The Scottish King and the English Court', in *Doubtful and Dangerous*, ed. Doran and Kewes, p. 139.

38 *CKJVI*, p. xxxv.

39 *CKJVI*, pp. xxxv–vi; Courtney, 'The Scottish King and the English Court', in *Doubtful and Dangerous*, ed. Doran and Kewes, pp. 139–41.

40 SP 52/69, no. 65; *Secret Corr.*, pp. 100, 114, 191, 225; *CKJVI*, p. xlii.

41 Courtney, 'The Scottish King and the English Court', in *Doubtful and Dangerous*, ed. Doran and Kewes, pp. 139–40.

42 Collins, II, pp. 326–7; *CKJVI*, pp. xl–xli.

43 Collins, II, pp. 326–7. A report of a narrow squeak in which Cecil's secret correspondence was one day almost intercepted by the queen on its arrival at Greenwich Palace seems to be an invention. See Goodman, *The Court of King James I*, ed. Brewer, I, p. 32.

44 *CKJVI*, p. 13.

45 *CKJVI*, p. 7.

46 'Lethington's Account of Negotiations with Elizabeth in September and October 1561', in *A Letter from Mary Queen of Scots to the Duke of Guise, January 1562*, ed. J. H. Pollen (Edinburgh, 1904), Appendix 1, p. 41.

47 *CKJVI*, pp. 7–8.

48 *CKJVI*, p. 10.

49 *CKJVI*, p. 31; Courtney, 'The Scottish King and the English Court', in *Doubtful and Dangerous*, ed. Doran and Kewes, p. 141.

50 *CKJVI*, p. 35; 'The Journal of Sir Roger Wilbraham for the Years 1593–1616', ed. H. S. Scott, *Camden Society*, 4th Series, 4 (1902), pp. 49–50.

51 J. C. Thewlis, 'The Peace Policy of Spain', University of Durham Ph.D. (1975), p. 165 (citing AGS, E972/sf).

52 Thewlis, 'The Peace Policy of Spain', pp. 154–77; A. J. Loomie, 'King James I's Catholic Consort', *HLQ*, 34 (1971), pp. 305–7; A. J. Loomie, 'Philip III and the Stuart Succession in England, 1600–1603', *Revue Belge de philologie et d'histoire*, 43 (1965), pp. 498–501.

53 J. D. Mackie, 'The Secret Diplomacy of King James VI in Italy Prior to His Accession to the English Throne', *SHR*, 21 (1924), pp. 275–82; A. O. Meyer, 'Clemens VIII und Jakob I von England', *Quellen und Forschungen aus italienischen Archiven und Bibliotheken, herausgegeben vom Preußischen Historischen Institut in Rom*, VII (1904), pp. 277–83; Loomie, 'Philip III and the Stuart Succession in England', pp. 496–8.

54 Thewlis, 'The Peace Policy of Spain', p. 159.

55 Thewlis, 'The Peace Policy of Spain', pp. 160–67.

56 Loomie, 'Philip III and the Stuart Succession in England', pp. 502–3.

57 Winwood, I, p. 26.

58 Loomie, 'Philip III and the Stuart Succession in England', pp. 503–4.

59 Thewlis, 'The Peace Policy of Spain', pp. 167–8; P. C. Allen, *Philip III and the Pax Hispanica, 1598–1621: The Failure of Grand Strategy* (New Haven, CT, 2000), pp. 100–104.

60 SP 52/69, no. 53.

61 Loomie, 'Philip III and the Stuart Succession in England', pp. 507–9, 512–13; Thewlis, 'The Peace Policy of Spain', pp. 170–72.

62 Thewlis, 'The Peace Policy of Spain', pp. 92–128, 172–5; Allen, *Philip III and the Pax Hispanica*, pp. 104–7; G. Parker, *The Army of Flanders and the Spanish Road, 1567–1659* (Cambridge, 1972), pp. 80–86.

63 Although lost, the letter is fully described by F. Moryson, *An itinerary written by Fynes Moryson Gent. First in the Latine tongue, and then translated by him into English* (London, 1617), Pt. II, ii, 2, p. 198.

64 Moryson, *Itinerary*, Pt. II, ii, 2, pp. 184–5; R. B. Wernham, *The Return of the Armadas: The Last Years of the Elizabethan War against Spain, 1595–1603* (Oxford, 1994), pp. 390–91.

65 SP 63/211, Pt. 1, stamped fos. 274–6, 278–83.

66 SP 63/212, stamped fos. 153–6, 161, 213, 271–3.

67 Moryson, *Itinerary*, Pt. II, iii, 1, pp. 267–71.

68 E 351/543, mm. 79v–81; Nichols, III, pp. 577–9, 581–5.

69 Lodge, II, pp. 552–4, 560–3, 568–9; Nichols, III, pp. 577–600; O. Poncet, *Pomponne de Bellièvre (1529–1607): Un homme d'état au temps des Guerres de Religion* (Paris, 1998), pp. 239–40.

70 *Letters from Sir Robert Cecil to Sir George Carew*, ed. Maclean, p. 128.

71 Lodge, II, p. 578.

72 *CSPV*, 1592–1603, nos. 770, 870, 900.

73 *CSPV*, 1592–1603, no. 1135 (where the dates are New Style).
74 *Letters and Epigrams of Sir John Harington*, ed. McClure, pp. 96–8.
75 SP 12/287, no. 50.
76 Adams, *ODNB*, s.v. 'Katherine Howard, née Carey'.
77 *Memoirs of Robert Carey, Earl of Monmouth* (Edinburgh, 1808), p. 116.

Chapter 23: The Final Vigil

1 Bodleian, Tanner MS 76, fo. 167; *ECW*, pp. 404–405. Compare the usual English view of the Gaelic Irish that 'justice without mercy must first tame and command them, without the which . . . they will never be drawn to God or civil good'. See SP 63/145, stamped fo. 178.
2 F. Moryson, *An itinerary written by Fynes Moryson Gent. First in the Latine tongue, and then translated by him into English* (London, 1617), Pt. II, iii, 2, p. 275.
3 Bodleian, Tanner MS 76, fos. 171–2; *ECW*, pp. 405–8; Moryson, *Itinerary*, Pt. II, iii, 2, p. 275.
4 *CCM*, 1601–1603, no. 378.
5 J. Clapham, *Certain Observations Concerning the Life and Reign of Queen Elizabeth*, ed. E. P. Read and C. Read (Philadelphia, 1951), p. 98.
6 SP 14/1, no. 6.
7 BL, Cotton MS, Julius C.III, fo. 64, printed by Ellis, 2nd Series, III, p. 179, where the date is said, wrongly, to be 1596.
8 SP 84/62, fo. 307 (where the date, obligingly, is said to be Old Style). See also *CSPV*, 1592–1603, nos. 1162, 1167, where fanciful gossip about the queen allegedly pining for Essex is interspersed with confirmation of the mouth abscesses.
9 *CKJVI*, pp. xlviii–xlix; HMC, *Hatfield MSS*, XII, p. 667.
10 *Memoirs of Robert Carey, Earl of Monmouth* (Edinburgh, 1808), p. 116.
11 *Memoirs of Robert Carey*, p. 117.
12 SP 14/1, no. 6.
13 'Elizabeth Southwell's Manuscript Account of the Death of Queen Elizabeth', ed. C. Loomis, *English Literary Renaissance*, 26 (1996), p. 485.
14 'Elizabeth Southwell's Manuscript Account', ed. Loomis, pp. 485–6.
15 Southwell's testimony ended up with a large collection of Catholic and Jesuit relics at Stonyhurst College in Lancashire, where it can be found among the papers of Robert Parsons.
16 'Elizabeth Southwell's Manuscript Account', ed. Loomis, pp. 485–6.
17 *Memoirs of Robert Carey*, p. 119.
18 SP 12/287, no. 50.
19 *Diary of John Manningham*, ed. J. Bruce, *Camden Society*, Old Series, 99 (1868), p.146; SP 14/1, no. 6.
20 Birch, *Memoirs*, II, p. 505.
21 BNF, MS FF 3501, fo. 233.
22 *Memoirs of Robert Carey*, p. 120.
23 *Memoirs of Robert Carey*, p. 121.
24 *Memoirs of Robert Carey*, pp. 121–2.
25 SP 12/215, no. 65.
26 *Memoirs of Robert Carey*, p. 122; J. E. Neale, 'The Sayings of Queen Elizabeth', *History*, 10 (1925), pp. 228–32.
27 *Memoirs of Robert Carey*, p. 119
28 *Memoirs of Robert Carey*, p. 120.
29 SP 52/69, no. 53, endorsed by the filing clerk 'Copy of her Majesty's letter to the King of Scots written with her own hand'.

30 *ECW*, p. 97.

31 *Memoirs of Robert Carey*, p. 120.

32 *CSPV*, 1592–1603, no. 1169.

33 *CSPV*, 1603–1607, no. 16.

34 BL, Cotton MS, Titus C.VII, fo. 57r; W. Camden, *Annales rerum anglicarum et hibernicarum Regnante Elizabetha*, ed. T. Hearne, 3 vols. (London, 1747), III, p. 909.

35 BL, Cotton MS, Titus C.VII, fo. 57r–v; Camden, *Annales*, ed. Hearne, III, pp. 911–12; Nichols, III, pp. 607–9. In Cotton's manuscript, the dates given do not match the stated days of the week by a factor of one. I have taken the days to be correct but not the dates, otherwise Elizabeth died one day after she was already dead.

36 Camden, pp. 660–61; Camden, *Annales*, ed. T. Hearne, III, pp. 909–11.

37 The original dispatches are from de Beaumont's letter-book covering the years 1602–1605, now BNF, MS FF 3501 (where all the dates are New Style). Previously, scholars had to rely on the Victorian excerpts by Armand Baschet in the NA.

38 BNF, MS FF 3501, fo. 233v (date given in New Style). See also John Chamberlain's report, SP 14/1, no. 6.

39 *CSPV*, 1603–1607, no. 32 (where the dates are New Style); Neale, 'The Sayings of Queen Elizabeth', p. 229.

40 BNF, MS FF 3501, fos. 275v–7v.

41 BNF, MS FF 3501, fos. 275v–7v; BL, Cotton MS, Titus C.VII, fo. 57r; *Diary of John Manningham*, ed. Bruce, p. 170.

42 Moryson, *Itinerary*, Pt. II, iii, 2, p. 277; R. B. Wernham, *The Return of the Armadas: The Last Years of the Elizabethan War against Spain, 1595–1603* (Oxford, 1994), pp. 405–406.

43 SP 63/215, no. 34; Moryson, *Itinerary*, Pt. II, iii, 2, pp. 278–80. Although the document recording Tyrone's submission to Elizabeth is lost, Fynes Moryson confirms that its terms were identical to those of his later submission to King James, the name only changed. See SP 63/215, no. 13; Moryson, *Itinerary*, Pt. II, iii, 2, p. 281.

44 SP 63/215, nos. 15, 17–18.

45 R. Rapple, 'Brinkmanship and Bad Luck: Ireland, the Nine Years' War and the Succession', in *Doubtful and Dangerous: The Question of Succession in Late-Elizabethan England*, ed. S. Doran and P. Kewes (Manchester, 2014), p. 252.

46 J. C. Thewlis, 'The Peace Policy of Spain', University of Durham Ph.D. (1975), pp. 128, 131.

47 P. C. Allen, *Philip III and the Pax Hispanica, 1598–1621: The Failure of Grand Strategy* (New Haven, CT, 2000), pp. 105–107.

48 Allen, *Philip III and the Pax Hispanica*, pp. 105–107; Thewlis, 'The Peace Policy of Spain', p. 207.

49 A. J. Loomie, 'Philip III and the Stuart Succession in England, 1600–1603', *Revue Belge de philologie et d'histoire*, 43 (1965), pp. 506–14.

50 *CKJVI*, pp. xlix–liv.

51 BNF, MS FF 3501, fos. 227v–9v, 233v–6; *CSPV*, 1592–1603, no. 1162; *APC*, XXXII, pp. 493–4; A. Courtney, 'The Scottish King and the English Court: The Secret Correspondence of James VI, 1601–1603', in *Doubtful and Dangerous*, ed. Doran and Kewes, pp. 144–6.

52 *CSPV*, 1592–1603, no. 1162; *CKJVI*, p. 73.

53 *APC*, XXXII, pp. 491–2; *CKJVI*, p. 73; *CSPV*, 1592–1603, no. 1162.

54 BNF, MS FF 3501, fos. 227v–9v, 233v–6, 239; *CSPV*, 1592–1603, no. 1159.

55 *CKJVI*, pp. li, 47.

56 *CSPV*, 1592–1603, no. 1164.

57 *CSPV*, 1592–1603, no. 1166.

58 *Memoirs of Robert Carey*, pp. 122–4.

59 *Memoirs of Robert Carey*, pp. 124–8. See also SP 14/1, no. 6.

60 HMC, *Hatfield MSS*, XV, pp. 9–10.

61 SP 14/1, nos. 1, 6; Folger MS V.b.142, fos. 65–8; *Stuart Royal Proclamations*, ed. J. F. Larkin and P. L. Hughes, 2 vols. (Oxford, 1973–83), I, pp. 1–4; *Diary of John Manningham*, ed. Bruce, p. 147.

62 *Diary of John Manningham*, ed. Bruce, p. 147.

63 SP 14/1, no. 7.

64 SP 14/1, no. 7.

65 HMC, *Hatfield MSS*, XV, pp. 10–11; J. Richards, 'The English Accession of James VI: "National" Identity, Gender and the Personal Monarchy of England', *EHR*, 117 (2002), p. 519.

66 Richards, 'The English Accession of James VI', pp. 517–18.

67 *CSPV*, 1603–1607, no. 91.

68 *CSPV*, 1603–1607, no. 32; Anon., *England's Welcome to James, by the Grace of God, King of England, Scotland, France and Ireland, Defender of the Faith etc.* (London, 1603), sig. B4. See also I. F[enton], *King James, His Welcome to London* (London, 1603), sig. B3v; Richards, 'The English Accession of James VI', p. 519.

69 *Diary of John Manningham*, ed. Bruce, p. 159. The only dissentient source claiming the queen was embalmed is Clapham, *Certain Observations*, ed. Read and Read, p. 112.

70 *CSPV*, 1603–1607, no. 6; *Diary of John Manningham*, ed. Bruce, p. 159; R. Horrox, 'Purgatory, Prayer and Plague', in *Death in England*, ed. P. C. Jupp and C. Gittings (Manchester, 1999), pp. 99–100.

71 C. Gittings, 'Sacred and Secular, 1558–1660', in *Death in England*, ed. Jupp and Gittings, pp. 156–7.

72 *Diary of John Manningham*, ed. Bruce, p. 159.

73 Clapham, *Certain Observations*, ed. Read and Read, p. 110.

74 Ellis, 1st Series, III, pp. 65–6.

75 *CSPV*, 1603–1607, no. 40; *Memoirs of the Duke of Sully during His Residence at the English Court* (Dublin, 1751), pp. 126–7; Richards, 'The English Accession of James VI', pp. 524–5.

76 *CSPV*, 1603–1607, no. 6.

77 SP 14/1, no. 21.

78 SP 14/1, nos. 51–4; Clapham, *Certain Observations*, ed. Read and Read, pp. 111–15; Nichols, III, pp. 621–7; W. A. Jackson, 'The Funeral Procession of Queen Elizabeth', *The Library*, 4th Series, 26 (1946), pp. 262–71.

79 *CSPV*, 1603–1607, no. 36; Clapham, *Certain Observations*, ed. Read and Read, pp. 111–12.

80 SP 14/1, no. 52; Clapham, *Certain Observations*, ed. Read and Read, p. 112.

81 Clapham, *Certain Observations*, ed. Read and Read, p. 114.

82 Clapham, *Certain Observations*, ed. Read and Read, p. 115.

83 *CSPV*, 1603–1607, no. 36; J. M. Walker, 'Bones of Contention: Posthumous Images of Elizabeth and Stuart Politics', in *Dissing Elizabeth: Negative Representations of Gloriana*, ed. J. M. Walker (Durham, NC, 1998), pp. 252–6, 270–71; J. Guy, *'My Heart is My Own': The Life of Mary Queen of Scots* (London, 2004), pp. 504–5.

84 *The Progresses, Processions and Magnificent Festivities of King James I*, ed. J. Nichols, 4 vols. (London, 1828), I, pp. 98–101.

Epilogue

1 HMC, *Hatfield MSS*, XV, pp. 345–6; Ellis, 1st Series, III, p. 63.

2 SP 14/1, nos. 16, 59.

3 SP 14/1, nos. 18, 21.

4 *Diary of John Manningham*, ed. J. Bruce, *Camden Society*, Old Series, 99 (1868), pp. 168, 171; *The Progresses, Processions and Magnificent Festivities of King James I*, ed. J. Nichols, 4 vols. (London, 1828), I, pp. 52, 98.

5 Neither party would live down the ensuing scandal. Mountjoy died only three months later, in 1606, Penelope following him to the grave within eighteen months.

6 HMC, *Hatfield MSS*, XV, pp. 9–10.

7 M. Lee, *Great Britain's Solomon: James VI and I in His Three Kingdoms* (Urbana and Chicago, 1990), p. 103.

8 *APC*, XXXII, p. 495.

9 *APC*, XXXII, pp. 496–7.

10 HMC, *Hatfield MSS*, XV, pp. 345–6; Ellis, 1st Series, III, p. 63.

11 CUL, MS Ii.5.21, fol. 47v; J. H. Baker, *ODNB*, s.v. 'Sir Thomas Egerton'.

12 *APC*, XXXII, p. 497; Lee, *Great Britain's Solomon*, p. 103.

13 *APC*, XXXII, p. 497.

14 *APC*, XXXII, p. 501.

15 *The Letters of Sir Walter Ralegh*, ed. A. Latham and J. Youings (Exeter, 1999), no. 164; M. Nicholls and P. Williams, *Sir Walter Ralegh in Life and Legend* (London, 2011), pp. 191–2.

16 *APC*, XXXII, p. 498.

17 Lee, *Great Britain's Solomon*, p. 103.

18 *Diary of John Manningham*, ed. Bruce, pp. 160, 171.

19 SP 14/11, no. 44* (stamped fos. 134–5); *Diary of John Manningham*, ed. Bruce, pp. 168, 171.

20 BNF, MS FF 3501, fos. 313v–18v.

21 *CSPV*, 1603–1607, no. 22.

22 *Progresses, Processions and Magnificent Festivities of King James I*, ed. Nichols, I, p. 118.

23 *Progresses, Processions and Magnificent Festivities of King James I*, ed. Nichols, I, p. 152.

24 S. R. Gardiner, *A History of England from the Accession of James I to the Outbreak of the Civil War, 1603–1642*, 10 vols. (London, 1900), I, pp. 108–40; M. Nicholls, 'Treason's Reward: The Punishment of Conspirators in the Bye Plot of 1603', *HJ*, 38 (1995), pp. 821–42; M. Nicholls, 'Sir Walter Ralegh's Treason: A Prosecution Document', *EHR*, 110 (1995), pp. 902–24; M. Nicholls, 'Two Winchester Trials: The Prosecution of Henry, Lord Cobham, and Thomas, Lord Grey of Wilton, 1603', *HR*, 68 (1995), pp. 26–48; P. Lefranc, 'Ralegh in 1596 and 1603: Three Unprinted Letters in the Huntington Library', *HLQ*, 29 (1966), pp. 337–45; Nicholls and Williams, *Sir Walter Ralegh*, pp. 194–222.

25 Nicholls, 'Treason's Reward', pp. 822–3.

26 Gardiner, *History of England*, I, pp. 116–20; Nicholls, 'Sir Walter Ralegh's Treason', pp. 906–10, 912–24.

27 Gardiner, *History of England*, I, p. 117; Nicholls, 'Sir Walter Ralegh's Treason', p. 911.

28 Nicholls, 'Treason's Reward', pp. 907–8.

29 *State Trials*, I, pp. 212–26; SP 12/278, no. 102 (pencilled fos. 199–205, formerly fos. 219–25).

30 SP 12/278, no. 102 (pencilled fos. 204v–5, formerly 224v–5); Nicholls, 'Sir Walter Ralegh's Treason', pp. 907–8.

31 Nicholls and Williams, *Sir Walter Ralegh*, p. 241.

32 *APC*, XXXIV, p. 456.

33 Camden, pp. 659–60.

34 G. Goodman, *The Court of King James I*, ed. J. S. Brewer, 2 vols. (London, 1839), I, pp. 96–8.

35 R. Naunton, *Fragmenta Regalia*, printed in *Memoirs of Robert Carey, Earl of Monmouth* (Edinburgh, 1808), pp. 178–9. For Naunton's career, see Birch, *Memoirs*, II, pp. 198–9, 200–202, 211–13, 237–9, 241–8, 256–66, 286–9, 292–4.

36 Hartley, III, p. 278.

37 Harington, II, p. 292.

38 Harington, II, p. 212.

39 Harington, II, pp. 220–21.

40 *The Works of Sir Walter Ralegh, Knight*, 8 vols. (Oxford, 1829), VIII, p. 246.

41 SP 52/69, no. 53. Elizabeth gave a not dissimilar justification of herself and her foreign policy in her closing speech at the end of the 1601 Parliament. See Hartley, III, pp. 278–81.

42 Hartley, III, p. 278.

43 A. Courtney, 'The Scottish King and the English Court: The Secret Correspondence of James VI, 1601–1603', in *Doubtful and Dangerous: The Question of Succession in Late-Elizabethan England*, ed. S. Doran and P. Kewes (Manchester, 2014), p. 139.

44 *State Trials*, I, p. 217.

Illustration Credits

Equestrian portrait of Henry IV of France before the walls of Paris, 1594, Musée de la Ville de Paris, Musée Carnavalet, Paris/Bridgeman Images

The 'Rainbow Portrait' of Elizabeth, by Marcus Gheeraerts the Younger, Hatfield House, Hertfordshire/Bridgeman Images

British Library

Elizabeth corrects the second version of her reply to Parliament's petition in 1586 urging her to execute Mary Queen of Scots, from Lansdowne MS 94, art. 35, fo. 87, photo © The British Library, 2016

British Museum

Thomas Cockson's engraving of Robert Devereux, Earl of Essex, 1600, ref. O.7.283 © The Trustees of the British Museum

Jan Rutlinger's engraved portrait of Elizabeth *c*.1585, ref. 1905.0414.45 © The Trustees of the British Museum

Clare College, Cambridge

Elizabeth's letter of instructions to Lord Willoughby, concerning the towns of Dordrecht and Geertruidenberg, 30 March 1588 (document on loan from an anonymous benefactor), with the kind permission of the benefactor and by courtesy of the Master, Fellows and Scholars of Clare College

Sir Walter Ralegh captures Don António de Berrío, the governor of the Spanish colony of Trinidad, woodcut by Theodor de Bry, 1602, shelfmark F.3.7, by courtesy of the Master, Fellows and Scholars of Clare College

The meeting on the south bank of the Orinoco between Sir Walter Ralegh and King Topiawari, woodcut by Theodor de Bry, 1602, shelfmark F.3.7, by courtesy of the Master, Fellows and Scholars of Clare College

The Elizabethan Gardens, Manteo, North Carolina

Elizabeth aged sixty-two or sixty-three, studio of Marcus Gheeraerts the Younger, by courtesy of The Elizabethan Gardens. Photographer: Ray Matthews

Lambeth Palace Library

A copy of the warrant for the execution of Mary Queen of Scots, prepared
by Robert Beale for the personal use of the Earl of Kent, one of the officiating commissioners present at Fotheringhay Castle, MS 4769, fo. 1

National Archives, Kew

The cipher used by Elizabeth's peace commissioners at Bourbourg in 1588
to report their negotiations with the Duke of Parma's representatives,
ref. SP 106/1, no. 14, fo. 49

The third draft, heavily corrected by Burghley, of one of Elizabeth's letters
to Essex, recalling him from Rouen, ref. SP 78/25, fo. 388

Private Collection

Robert Vaughan's posthumous portrait of Robert Dudley, Earl of Leicester, 1588, photograph © John Guy, 2016

Elizabeth's tomb in the north aisle of Henry VII's Chapel in Westminster
Abbey, engraved by Magdalena or Willem de Passe

Public Domain

Archduke Albert of the Netherlands and Infanta Isabella Clara Eugenia of
Spain and Archduchess, c.1600, by courtesy of the University of Heidel-
berg/Arolsen Klebeband

Yale Center for British Art, New Haven, Connecticut

An unknown woman, possibly the young Kate Carey, English School

Probably Katherine Carey, Elizabeth's first cousin, wife of Sir Francis
Knollys, by Steven van der Meulen

Anne of Denmark, studio of Nicholas Hilliard, after 1603

Robert Dudley, Earl of Leicester, in his mid-thirties, by Steven van der
Meulen

Sir Francis Walsingham, by John de Critz, c.1585

'The Family of Henry VIII', a copy of a painting Elizabeth gave to Walsingham in *c*.1572, after Lucas de Heere

Robert Devereux, Earl of Essex, depicted with a spade-shaped beard, miniature sketch by Isaac Oliver

James VI of Scotland and I of England, by Nicholas Hilliard, *c*.1610

The ageing Elizabeth, based on Isaac Oliver's face pattern, engraved by Crispijn de Passe, 1596

Index

He just wanted a decent book to read ...

Not too much to ask, is it? It was in 1935 when Allen Lane, Managing Director of Bodley Head Publishers, stood on a platform at Exeter railway station looking for something good to read on his journey back to London. His choice was limited to popular magazines and poor-quality paperbacks – the same choice faced every day by the vast majority of readers, few of whom could afford hardbacks. Lane's disappointment and subsequent anger at the range of books generally available led him to found a company – and change the world.

'We believed in the existence in this country of a vast reading public for intelligent books at a low price, and staked everything on it'
Sir Allen Lane, 1902–1970, founder of Penguin Books

The quality paperback had arrived – and not just in bookshops. Lane was adamant that his Penguins should appear in chain stores and tobacconists, and should cost no more than a packet of cigarettes.

Reading habits (and cigarette prices) have changed since 1935, but Penguin still believes in publishing the best books for everybody to enjoy. We still believe that good design costs no more than bad design, and we still believe that quality books published passionately and responsibly make the world a better place.

So wherever you see the little bird – whether it's on a piece of prize-winning literary fiction or a celebrity autobiography, political tour de force or historical masterpiece, a serial-killer thriller, reference book, world classic or a piece of pure escapism – you can bet that it represents the very best that the genre has to offer.

Whatever you like to read – trust Penguin.